D1034814

JN
3250
E7
C3

PRINCES AND PARLIAMENTS IN GERMANY

PRINCES AND PARLIAMENTS IN GERMANY

*From the Fifteenth
to the Eighteenth Century*

BY

F. L. CARSTEN

OXFORD
AT THE CLARENDON PRESS

Oxford University Press, Amen House, London E.C.4

GLASGOW NEW YORK TORONTO MELBOURNE WELLINGTON
BOMBAY CALCUTTA MADRAS KARACHI LAHORE DACCA
CAPE TOWN SALISBURY NAIROBI IBADAN ACCRA
KUALA LUMPUR HONG KONG

FIRST PUBLISHED 1959
REPRINTED LITHOGRAPHICALLY AT THE UNIVERSITY PRESS, OXFORD
FROM SHEETS OF THE FIRST EDITION
1963

PRINTED IN GREAT BRITAIN

PREFACE

SOME readers will be surprised to find the term 'Parliaments' used in the title of this book, and not the term 'Estates', which seems to be the proper historical term for the representative institutions which came into being everywhere in Germany in the fourteenth and fifteenth centuries. I have deliberately chosen the word 'Parliaments' because the word 'Estates' is too ambiguous; I thus thought it unsuitable for the title of a book which discusses the meetings of the clergy, nobility, and towns in several German principalities, the development of their institutions and, above all, the conflicts between them and their princes. In my opinion the assemblies of the Estates of many German principalities were indeed 'Parliaments' in the proper sense of the term, and their functions in the sixteenth, seventeenth, and eighteenth centuries were very similar to those of the English Parliament—not only in Württemberg, where this comparison has been made before, in the first instance by Charles James Fox.[1] Therefore the use of the term 'Parliaments' seemed to be doubly justified, although on the Continent there is no exact parallel to the House of Commons, whose members were elected and did not sit for the towns alone. Yet the Estates of the German principalities also represented 'the country', and in the sixteenth century their powers were by no means inferior to those of the English Parliament. Why—in contrast with England—these powers did not develop further, but declined, is the subject of the following pages.

The history of the German Estates is a very much neglected subject. Not only is there no general description of their development, and no comparative study of their varying fates in the different principalities, but even *within* individual principalities an attempt has hardly ever been made to write the story of their rise and their decline, using to the full the vast number of documents which have survived. All that exists is monographs

[1] *The Edinburgh Review*, xxix (1818), p. 340.

and papers on a particular reign or dealing with a comparatively short period. There is no history of the Estates of Brandenburg or of the duchy of Prussia, although in both the Estates
played an important part in the making of the Hohenzollern
state. Their selected documents have been published only for
the reign of the Great Elector and, in Brandenburg, for that of
one of his more remote predecessors. The only available histories
of the Estates of Bavaria were published at the beginning of the
nineteenth century. That we now possess for the first time a
history of the most interesting German Estates, those of Württemberg, is entirely due to the accident that in 1957 the
Württemberg Landtag celebrated its quincentenary, so that a
local historian, Dr. Walter Grube, was commissioned to write
the appropriate *Festschrift*.[1] Even in Jülich and Berg, where the
history of the Estates has been studied in great detail by Georg
von Below and his pupils, their researches have been mainly
confined to the medieval period and to the origins of the local
Estates. Equally, the one recent monograph on the Estates of
Saxony, by Professor Helbig, covers only the period to 1485;[2]
while their later history has been studied only for some individual reigns, and their documents still await publication.

In view of these facts it may seem presumptuous to attempt
to write a comparative history of the German Estates. But such
a study seems to be of great importance for an understanding
of the different political traditions in the various parts of Germany, and an attempt ought to be made, which might encourage
others to continue and gradually to complete the picture. As it
would be impossible to cover the whole of Germany within the
limits of one volume, I have deliberately confined my description to the leading lay principalities, both Catholic and Protestant; but I have omitted the ecclesiastical principalities which
present special problems of their own, and the Habsburg territories which, I hope, may become the subject of a separate
volume. I have drawn on Brandenburg and Prussia for purposes
of comparison, but I have decided not to repeat the details of
the history of their Estates, which I have given in *The Origins*

[1] His book, *Der Stuttgarter Landtag, 1457–1957*, was published at the end of 1957
when my manuscript was already completed.
[2] *Der Wettinische Ständestaat*, Münster and Cologne, 1955.

of Prussia. In this somewhat abbreviated form the subject has become more manageable and, I hope, more interesting for the reader: otherwise there would have been too much repetition and overlapping. If this volume is still rather bulky, and if it still contains very many details, the explanation lies in the intricacy of the subject: the history of the Estates of each principality changes so continuously that I have found it impossible to reduce the details any further, for it is only from these details that their different characteristics and their so different fates become clear. It is only from these details that comparisons can be made with the history of representative institutions in other countries.

In many discussions which I have had with German historians it has often been argued that the German Estates never achieved anything positive, that they did not contribute anything to the development of the state, that their history was outside the 'main stream' of German history. I hope to have succeeded in proving the contrary. On the other hand, I am most grateful to those German historians who have helped me with their knowledge of local history during my prolonged work in German archives, especially to Dr. H. R. J. Lieberich and Dr. Hans Rall at Munich and to Dr. Walter Grube at Stuttgart, and equally to the many archivists who have produced for me the numerous documents of the Estates from remote corners of their archives. The librarians of the *Landesbibliothek* at Stuttgart and of Westfield College, London, have been most helpful in obtaining for me the many German books and periodicals which are unfortunately unobtainable in this country. I owe a debt of gratitude to those institutions which have assisted me during long periods of research: the Council of Europe at Strasbourg, the Federal Ministry of the Interior at Bonn, the Ministry of Culture at Stuttgart, and the Central Research Fund of the University of London. Without their generous assistance this work could not have been accomplished. I am also particularly grateful to the *Commission Internationale pour l'Histoire des Assemblées d'État* which has taken great interest in the progress of my work and has accepted it as number 19 in its series of studies of parliamentary institutions. My greatest debt of gratitude is due to my wife, who not only first inspired me to embark on this work, but also, by her interest and advice and her constant help during many years, has enabled me to see it through.

The currency used in most parts of the Empire during the period covered by this study was the guilder or florin, but the thaler was also used in certain areas. In the later seventeenth century the thaler was reckoned as equivalent to $1\frac{1}{2}$ guilders, or 3 French livres, or about 4 English shillings, the pound sterling containing about 5 thalers or $7\frac{1}{2}$ guilders.

F. L. C.

Westfield College
London, June 1958

CONTENTS

x CONTENTS

I

WÜRTTEMBERG

1. *Introduction*

AMONG the multitude of princes, lay and ecclesiastic, counts, noblemen, cities, abbots, and other minor potentates of south-western Germany, since the thirteenth century the counts, later dukes, of Württemberg occupied pride of place.[1] In the whole of southern Germany only the Habsburgs and the Wittelsbachs—to the north in the Palatinate and to the south in Bavaria—had larger possessions and played a more important part in the power politics of central Europe. Starting from comparatively modest beginnings, the counts of Württemberg benefited from the decline of Imperial authority and the dissolution of the Hohenstaufen Empire and gradually extended their sway, but hardly any important acquisitions were made by them after the fifteenth century. At the end of the eighteenth century the duchy of Württemberg by and large still had the same frontiers as three centuries before: so different from its modern size which it owed, together with the royal dignity, to the largess of Napoleon.

Throughout this long period the ducal territories were surrounded and intersected by those of hundreds of minor princes, Free Cities, and Imperial Knights and monasteries, which make an historical map of the area look like an enormously complicated jigsaw-puzzle. Although the princes of Württemberg possessed precedence over them as the foremost princes of the Swabian Circle, they never managed to expand at their cost; the few attempts at such expansion ended in disaster, such as Duke Ulrich's attempt of 1519 against the Free City of Reutlingen.[2] The territorial stability of the area was equally shown by the

---

[1] There is no good modern history of Württemberg. A useful short survey is by Eugen Schneider, *Württembergische Geschichte*, Stuttgart, 1896. Christoph Friedrich von Stälin, *Wirtembergische Geschichte*, 4 vols., Stuttgart and Tübingen, 1841–73, only goes to the end of the sixteenth century. A vast amount of material may be found in Christian Friedrich Sattler, *Geschichte des Herzogthums Würtenberg unter der Regierung der Herzogen*, 13 vols., Ulm and Tübingen, 1769–83.

[2] See below, pp. 14–15.

fact that the territories of the house of Württemberg only under-
went one division, which lasted from 1442 to 1482. In the latter
year the possessions of the two lines of Urach and Stuttgart
were reunited by Count Eberhard the Bearded; Württemberg
was declared indivisible; and this was confirmed in 1495 by the
Emperor Maximilian when he elevated Württemberg to the
rank of a duchy, inheritable by primogeniture in the male line,
and constituted it one Imperial fief. With the death of Eberhard
the Bearded in the following year the Urach line became
extinct.[1] In contrast with many other German principalities,
there were no further partitions of the duchy. The Stuttgart line
ruled uninterruptedly until the revolution of November 1918.

Political stability was matched by social and constitutional
stability. Württemberg was—and is—a country of small towns
and villages, lying along the Neckar and its tributaries, among
the wooded hills and small mountains of the Black Forest and
the Swabian Alb, one of the most pleasant, undulating land-
scapes of Germany, without any natural barriers, and without
any great riches from the soil. Although the woods then covered
a much larger area than they do today and deer and other wild
animals constituted a veritable plague,[2] there was intensive
agriculture, with viticulture steadily gaining ground at the cost
of corn-growing;[3] cattle-breeding and sheep-farming were also
important in the country's economy, the wool being either exported or manufactured into cheap cloth at Calw and other
towns.[4] The position of the peasants was better than in many
other parts of Germany. By the end of the Middle Ages serfdom
had lost its rigours, and the manorial system had disintegrated.

---

[1] Armin Tille, 'Die deutschen Territorien', in *Gebhardt's Handbuch der deutschen Geschichte*, 7th ed., 1931, ii. 295.

[2] Complaints about the *Wildschaden* occurred incessantly during the negotiations with the Estates and indeed formed one of their major grievances.

[3] The conversion of fields, meadows, and woods into vineyards, especially in cold places unsuitable for viticulture, was repeatedly forbidden, apparently with-out much success: A. L. Reyscher, *Vollständige, historisch und kritisch bearbeitete Sammlung der württembergischen Gesetze*, xii. 1, Tübingen, 1841, nos. 56, 77, 214, pp. 285–6, 331, 753 (decrees of 1554, 1565, and 1621); State Archives Stuttgart, *Tomus Actorum*, ii, fos. 593, 598 (1553).

[4] Report of the mayor of Cannstatt of 1599 in *Württembergische Landtagsakten unter Herzog Friedrich I.*, edited by A. E. Adam, ii, Stuttgart, 1911, pp. 106–7; in general ibid., p. 455 (gravamen of 1605), and Arthur Schott, 'Wirtschaftliches Leben', in *Herzog Karl Eugen und seine Zeit*, edited by the Württembergischer Geschichts- und Altertumsverein, Esslingen, 1907, i. 313.

One of the demands raised in the peasant rising of 1514 and incorporated into the famous treaty of Tübingen, the basis of the duchy's constitution, was that every subject must have the right to leave freely, without let or hindrance.[1] All that remained of serfdom were certain public services and certain dues. Thus the serfs were bound to give a number of chickens to the ducal officials every year, and a heriot—the best garment or head of cattle—on their death;[2] while the inhabitants of the small town and district of Liebenzell in the Black Forest had to give a death-duty of 1 per cent., against which custom they petitioned unsuccessfully in 1628.[3]

The decisive fact was that, in contrast with most other parts of Germany and of Europe, the nobility was not the preponderant social group. Although it originally participated in the deliberations of the diets, it soon withdrew because it aimed at gaining the more independent status of Free Imperial Knights.[4] Once this was achieved, early in the sixteenth century, the nobility ceased to play an important part in the affairs of Württemberg, although individual noblemen continued to be employed by the dukes. All the towns, on the other hand, officially numbering about fifty,[5] were small because the more important towns of the area had gained the status of Free Imperial Cities. The two leading towns of the duchy were Stuttgart and Tübingen, the first being the capital and ducal residence, the second the seat of a famous university founded in 1477. As late as 1787 the duchy had only three towns with more than 5,000 inhabitants: Stuttgart then allegedly had 22,000, Tübingen 6,000, and Ludwigsburg, the new ducal residence, 5,300.[6] All the other towns were very small; many were only

[1] See below, p. 12.
[2] Württembergische Landtagsakten unter Herzog Friedrich I., i, 1910, no. 138, p. 286; State Archives Stuttgart, Tomus Actorum, xxxi, fos. 1013–16 (1629).
[3] State Archives Stuttgart, A 34–35, Büschel 44. A similar grievance was raised at the diet of 1651: ibid., Tomus Actorum, xlix, p. 472.
[4] For that reason the nobility no longer attended the famous diet of 1514: von Stälin, op. cit. iv. 104.
[5] Taxation lists of the first half of the sixteenth century usually included 47 or 48 towns: State Archives Stuttgart, A 34–35, Büschel 6b, no. 25; 7, no. i; Tomus Ulrici, fos. 8–10, 53–55; Tomus Actorum, ii, fos. 141–4, 417–19, 734–5. The diet of 1514 was attended by 52 towns.
[6] Schott, loc. cit., p. 314; but in 1727 Stuttgart had only 1,566 burghers and 158 widows (State Archives Stuttgart, Tomus Actorum, cxxxvi, fo. 155) which would indicate a population of about 8,000–9,000.

distinguished from the villages by their administrative and judicial privileges, by the right of direct representation in the diet, and by the fact that the majority formed the centre of an administrative district, the *Amt*, presided over by a ducal official, the *Amtmann*. The urban court was both the court of appeal and the criminal court for the villages of this district:[1] there was no patrimonial jurisdiction. Otherwise the towns had no political or economic privileges in relation to the villages; in particular, the crafts were not limited to the towns, as they were in so many other parts.[2] The strong conflicts between town and country, between burghers and noblemen, hardly existed in Württemberg. The leading urban group, the *Ehrbarkeit*, could not aspire to the wealth and importance of the French *bourgeoisie* or the English middle class; yet in the absence of the nobility it was the 'upper class' of the duchy from which many of the officials were drawn.

As late as 1787 the duchy's exports were almost entirely agricultural, linen being the chief exception and accounting for 20 per cent. of the exports.[3] Württemberg then had well over 500,000 inhabitants; but figures for earlier centuries are much more unreliable. It has often been said that there were as many as 450,000 before the catastrophe of the Thirty Years War, and again before the devastations of Louis XIV, which both caused a severe decline.[4] In 1727, 69,156 burghers (heads of families) and 7,071 widows were counted in the duchy;[5] if multiplied by five, this would give a total population of perhaps 380,000. In 1750 the population amounted to about 467,000, in 1771 to about 484,000, in 1790 to about 620,000: the result of the growing prosperity and the more peaceful conditions of the eighteenth century.[6] The duchy had about 3,600 square

[1] Walter Grube, 'Dorfgemeinde und Amtsversammlung in Altwürttemberg', *Zeitschrift für Württembergische Landesgeschichte*, xiii, 1954, p. 195; Friedrich Wintterlin, *Geschichte der Behördenorganisation in Württemberg*, i, Stuttgart, 1904, pp. 22, 29.

[2] Schott, loc. cit., p. 314.

[3] See the detailed figures, ibid., p. 358.

[4] For different estimates of these losses see Schneider, op. cit., pp. 229, 258, 261, 272, 318; Gebhard Mehring, 'Wirtschaftliche Schäden durch den Dreissigjährigen Krieg im Herzogtum Württemberg', *Württembergische Vierteljahrshefte für Landesgeschichte*, xxx, 1921, p. 72; and 'Schädigungen durch den Dreissigjährigen Krieg in Altwürttemberg', ibid. xix, 1910, pp. 447 ff.

[5] State Archives Stuttgart, *Tomus Actorum*, cxxxvi, fos. 148–57.

[6] Mehring, loc. cit. xxx. 72; Schott, loc. cit., p. 314; Schneider, op. cit., p. 376.

miles, which was only about one-quarter of the size of either Brandenburg or the duchy of Prussia, but it was much more densely populated; for in 1740 Brandenburg with over 15,000 square miles had only about 636,000 inhabitants, and Prussia which reached almost that size only about 604,000.[1] A very dense population, an intensive cultivation of the soil, often with but little reward, the absence of sharp social conflicts, a happy intermingling between towns and countryside and between the social classes, the unimportance of the nobility in political affairs and social life have remained characteristic of Württemberg. Stuttgart has remained the only large town. Although there is a good deal of modern industry, it has not destroyed the basic characteristics of earlier times.

To these basic characteristics also belongs the existence of a strong parliamentary and liberal tradition, distinguishing Württemberg from most other parts of Germany. The constitution of 1819 was based on the ancient constitution, unbroken until 1805 when it was abrogated by the newly-created king.[2] In the later eighteenth century it inspired Charles James Fox to the remark that there were only two constitutions in Europe, the British constitution and that of Württemberg.[3] Yet the Estates of Württemberg came into being comparatively late, about the middle of the fifteenth century. Originally they consisted of the usual three groups, the clergy (i.e. the abbots of the sixteen monasteries which stood under the counts' patronage), the nobility, and the towns. Curiously enough, the latter's representatives were called the *Landschaft* which indicated that they did not only represent the towns, but also the surrounding districts, the *Ämter*. The *Amt* was not only an administrative district, but also a self-governing corporation, a voluntary association.[4] It was, however, dominated by the urban authorities which also represented town and district in the diets, and

---

[1] Otto Behre, *Geschichte der Statistik in Brandenburg-Preussen*, Berlin, 1905, p. 198, gives 636,464 inhabitants for Brandenburg and 603,834 for Prussia according to the census of 1740; but ibid., p. 172, he gives only 469,571 for Brandenburg in 1725. Cf. the figures for the year 1700 given by Erich Keyser, *Bevölkerungsgeschichte Deutschlands*, Leipzig, 1938, p. 301.

[2] Tille, loc. cit., p. 296; Walter Grube, *Der Stuttgarter Landtag, 1457–1957*, Stuttgart, 1957, pp. 505–7.

[3] 'The States of Wirtemberg', *Edinburgh Review*, xxix, 1818, p. 340.

[4] Grube, 'Dorfgemeinde und Amtsversammlung in Altwürttemberg', loc. cit., p. 195.

they were drawn from the ranks of the *Ehrbarkeit*. The assertion of a well-known eighteenth-century writer that the peasants had always sent their deputies to the diets is quite wrong.[1] There were indeed German territories where the peasants were directly represented in the diets. Württemberg, however, was not one of them; the one notable attempt of the peasants to gain direct representation in the diet came to naught in 1514.[2] Nor was there anything in the customary composition, the limited powers, and the modest role of the Estates in the fifteenth century to indicate the peculiar features which were to develop later.

11. *From the Diets of 1457 to the Treaty of Tübingen*

The first definite evidence of a Württemberg diet dates from the year 1457. Under Count Ulrich of the Stuttgart line (1433–80) a conflict developed between his native noble councillors and others, especially foreigners, who wielded influence. Simultaneous conflicts with other rulers, above all the Elector Palatine, Frederick I, forced Ulrich to consult his knights, prelates, and towns. These took the side of the native nobility; grievances were raised; in the end Ulrich had to promise that he would in future govern with the advice of his three Estates, to his benefit and theirs. It does not seem, however, that he kept his promise; for two years later the Estates complained that he was not governing with the help of his councillors from the native nobility.[3] The year 1457 also saw the first diet in Württemberg-Urach. When in November the young Count Louis of the Urach line died and left as his heir his brother Eberhard, then twelve years old, his uncle, Count Ulrich, went to Urach to consult with the noble councillors of his nephew about the country's future and to claim the guardianship; but they closed the gates of Urach against him to allow a rival to

---

[1] L. T. Spittler, 'Entwurff einer Geschichte des engern landschaftlichen Ausschusses', *Zweite Sammlung einiger Urkunden und Aktenstücke zur neuesten Wirtembergischen Geschichte*, Göttingen, 1796, p. 355. For the peasant representation in the diets, see below, pp. 424–5.

[2] See below, pp. 10–11.

[3] *Württembergische Landtagsakten, 1498–1515*, edited by Wilhelm Ohr and Erich Kober, Stuttgart, 1913, p. xviii; Friedrich Wintterlin, 'Die Anfänge der landständischen Verfassung in Württemberg', *Württembergische Vierteljahrshefte für Landesgeschichte*, xxiii, 1914, pp. 329–30.

put forward his claim. A diet was then held at Leonberg to decide the controversial question; it appointed Ulrich the guardian of Eberhard. For him four noble councillors were to govern in ordinary matters; in more important affairs they were to be assisted by ten other councillors and seven representatives of the towns of Urach. These were to have full powers of government and were to decide by a majority of those present; while Ulrich had the right to be present but had no vote. It was the first time that the towns were associated with the government on behalf of a minor ruler.[1]

When two years later Count Eberhard himself assumed the government of Württemberg-Urach, the influence of the Estates sharply declined. He ruled with the help of his noble councillors, as his predecessors had done, and only occasionally consulted the Estates, as in 1462 on the question of war with Bavaria.[2] In the same year they participated in the peace negotiations between Count Ulrich and Frederick, the Elector Palatine, who had won the war and taken Ulrich prisoner. In 1463 a committee was appointed, on which the Estates were represented, to supervise the use of taxation levied to pay the ransom and the debts which the Estates had to guarantee. As in so many other principalities, the princes' growing debts caused them to rely increasingly on the taxes levied by the Estates, out of which developed their power of the purse.[3] There were other reasons for the continuing consultations of the counts of both lines with their Estates: the counts' mutual jealousies, the uncertainty of the succession, the possibility that Count Eberhard would be succeeded by an incapable and irresponsible successor, his aim of gaining the whole of Württemberg and of securing its indivisibility. In the pursuance of these aims treaties were concluded between the counts in 1473, 1482, 1485, 1489, and 1492, always with the participation of the Estates.[4] The treaty of 1489 stipulated that, if Count Eberhard were succeeded by a minor, in both counties each of the three

---

[1] *Württembergische Landtagsakten, 1498–1515*, pp. xix–xxii; von Stälin, op. cit. iii. 505–6; Wintterlin, loc. cit., p. 331; Walter Grube, *Der Leonberger Landtag vom 16. November 1457*, Leonberg, 1957, pp. 10–18.

[2] *Württembergische Landtagsakten, 1498–1515*, p. xxviii.

[3] Wintterlin, loc. cit., pp. 331–3.

[4] The five treaties are printed in Reyscher, op. cit. i. 476–520, and in *Württembergische Landtagsakten, 1498–1515*, pp. xxx–xxxxi.

Estates should elect four representatives who should govern until the prince was eighteen years old. The treaty of Esslingen of 1492 gave to these twelve representatives for the time after Eberhard's death full powers of regency, as if the new count were their ward; they were to consult him in important affairs, but if he declined to give his advice, they were to act without him; while in ordinary, daily affairs they were to act on their own. In this way Count Eberhard entrusted the defence of the country's interests against the caprices of his successor to the Estates whose importance was considerably enhanced.[1]

Count Eberhard died in 1496 without leaving a son and was succeeded by his cousin Eberhard of the Stuttgart line, for the Urach line had become extinct. Henceforth Württemberg remained one duchy under one prince. There was no longer any strife over the succession, which undermined the ruler's position in so many German principalities and strengthened that of the Estates. Duke Eberhard the Younger, however, was one of the most restricted princes ever to assume the government of a country. The terms of the treaty of Esslingen were enforced and the regents assumed their offices, but disagreements among them soon diminished their influence.[2] It was the arbitrary measures and the rash foreign policy of Eberhard the Younger which soon led to his downfall. He wanted to start a war against Bavaria; but his councillors were opposed to it. They pointed out that he first had to consult those who were to risk their lives, honour, and fortunes, as his predecessors had done, and that a war to which the Estates were to contribute, must be just and legitimate:[3] a truly revolutionary doctrine, for clearly the Estates were to decide which wars were just and legitimate, and which were not.

After an initial refusal of Duke Eberhard, his councillors summoned a diet which met in March 1498. The instructions of the deputies called for 'the appointment of a worthy government' in accordance with the terms of the treaty of Esslingen.

---

[1] *Württembergische Landtagsakten, 1498–1515*, pp. xxviii, xxxx, xxxxi; von Stälin, op. cit. iv. 3; Schneider, op. cit., p. 101; Ludwig Friedrich Heyd, *Ulrich, Herzog zu Württemberg*, Tübingen, 1841, i. 6–7. For a detailed discussion of this period see Grube, *Der Stuttgarter Landtag, 1457–1957*, pp. 25–57.

[2] von Stälin, op. cit. iv. 3–4.

[3] Ibid. iv. 9; *Württembergische Landtagsakten, 1498–1515*, p. 7, n. 4 (letter of the councillors of 1496); Grube, op. cit., pp. 58–59.

Eberhard was invited to attend to achieve this purpose; if he
failed to do so, they informed him, they would nevertheless
proceed to that end.[1] The following day, in his absence, the
officials, councillors, prelates, knights, and towns adopted an
'order of government'; the regents' number was completed
through election according to the treaty of Esslingen, and they
promised to aid each other if any danger were to threaten any
of them on account of their action. Two days later Duke Eberhard, with his plate and jewels, left the country and sought
refuge in the Free City of Ulm, from where he appealed to the
Emperor Maximilian. Then the Württemberg officials, regents,
and certain representatives of the Estates renounced their
allegiance and occupied several castles because the duke refused
to accept the new order and hoped to regain power by force of
arms. What began as a movement to revive the terms of the
treaty of Esslingen became a revolution ending in the deposition
of the ruler and the selection of a new prince by the Estates.
The ultimate decision lay with the Emperor. In May 1498
Maximilian decided in favour of the rebels: Eberhard was
deprived of his principality on account of his manifold bad and
disorderly practices. By-passing his mad brother, the succession
was vested in his eleven-year-old nephew, Ulrich; during the
latter's minority the regents were to govern and to exercise
all regalia and rights with which they were enfeoffed by the
Emperor.[2] Thus the Estates successfully asserted their right of
resistance; because the duke disregarded the treaty of Esslingen
they felt entitled to renounce their allegiance.[3] In the end
Eberhard himself had to accept the new order, and recognize
Ulrich as duke. In return he was paid an annuity of 6,000
guilders.[4]

When Duke Ulrich's minority came to an end and he began to rule himself, the Estates lost their influence, and no general diet was summoned; but smaller assemblies granted him

[1] von Stälin, op. cit. iv. 11–12; Wilhelm Ohr, 'Die Absetzung Herzog Eberhards II. von Württemberg', Württembergische Vierteljahrshefte für Landesgeschichte,
xv, 1906, pp. 351–4; Grube, op. cit., pp. 59–61.
[2] Württembergische Landtagsakten, 1498–1515, nos. 5, 11, 19, pp. 23–35, 41–45,
81–84; von Stälin, op. cit. iv. 13–18; Ohr, loc. cit., pp. 356–7; Reyscher, op. cit.
ii, no. 14, pp. 14–21; Grube, op. cit., pp. 61–65.
[3] Ohr, loc. cit., p. 364.
[4] von Stälin, op. cit. iv. 20; Württembergische Landtagsakten, 1498–1515, nos. 24–25,
pp. 94–97 (June 1498).

considerable sums, partly for the war against the Palatinate and partly for purposes of the Empire.[1] Meanwhile Ulrich's expenditure mounted quickly; within a few years his debts increased from 300,000 to 900,000 guilders. Therefore he demanded in 1513 an annual tax on all property for a period of twelve years. The Estates, however, with whom the government had negotiated directly and locally, and who were summoned in small numbers to secure pliancy, would only grant an excise on meat, corn, and wine for three years; it was to be raised through a reduction of weights and measures while maintaining prices at their previous levels. The reduced weights and measures were duly sent out early in 1514; but at Schorndorf they were thrown into the water by an enraged crowd. The consequent uprising—known as 'the Poor Conrad'—quickly spread; it became a veritable precursor of the Peasants' War which broke out in the same area of Germany ten years later. In May 1514 Ulrich had to promise that the new weights and measures would be recalled and that a diet would be summoned. Yet the unrest continued. The rebels demanded free hunting and fishing rights, the right of cutting wood in the forests, and an alleviation of dues and services. Many officials were deposed, or were deprived of the keys to the town gates. New administrators and governors were appointed in many places.[2]

The urban authorities which belonged to the group of the *Ehrbarkeit* were hostile to the rebel demands. But the common burghers, who were excluded from the town governments, made common cause with the peasants and asked for participation. The movement threatened to become a rebellion against the urban *Ehrbarkeit*; many towns were forced to admit deputies or assessors from the Commons. The peasants in their turn demanded the admittance of peasant deputies to the diet where they would be able to voice their own grievances, instead of being represented by the towns as hitherto. When the promised

[1] *Württembergische Landtagsakten, 1498–1515*, pp. 107–8. In 1507 and 1508, for example, the Estates voted 46,000 guilders for a *Römerzug* which had been declared by the Imperial diet; of this sum, 6,500 guilders were paid by the clergy and the rest by the towns and *Ämter*: ibid., p. 115, n. 4; von Stälin, op. cit. iv. 74 and n. 4. Ulrich's minority was terminated by Maximilian in 1503 when he was only sixteen years old.

[2] von Stälin, op. cit. iv. 97–102; Sattler, op. cit. i. 153–4; *Württembergische Landtagsakten, 1498–1515*, p. 270, n. 3; no. 92, p. 278.

diet met in Stuttgart in June, this demand was taken up by some urban deputies: the peasants of each *Amt* should elect two deputies, which would have given them equal representation with the towns. The request was, however, opposed by Stuttgart, Tübingen, and other towns which declared it too difficult 'to treat with such a large crowd from all the villages'. The government in its turn used the split between the *Ehrbarkeit* and the lower orders to get the diet transferred to Tübingen; while the peasant deputies had to remain in Stuttgart and were excluded from the further proceedings.[1]

The diet which assembled at Tübingen at the end of June 1514 was attended by two Estates only: 15 prelates and 52 towns, the latter represented by one each from the urban court and the common burghers—the last time that these were represented throughout. Neither the *Amtleute* nor the nobility attended, the latter because the point to be debated was the ducal debts, to the payment of which the knights were not willing to contribute. They aimed at becoming Free Imperial Knights, a claim which would be prejudiced by attending a diet and thus acknowledging that they were the subjects of the duke.[2] Thus the government to maintain itself against the rebels had to reach an agreement with the urban representatives, which meant the *Ehrbarkeit*, because the lower orders were affected by the revolutionary spirit. The Emperor Maximilian and several neighbouring princes acted as mediators; their councillors brought about an understanding between Ulrich and the Estates. Even before the diet met the towns consulted and formulated their demands as a precondition of a settlement. Some of these were: the foreign councillors and learned *doctores* should be dismissed, and in their place native noblemen and commoners should be employed by the duke; four assessors of the Estates should assist with the repartitioning of taxes; the repayment of the debts should be left to deputies of the Estates who should render annual accounts to the Estates' committee; diets should be held according to old custom when there was

[1] Bernhard Kugler, *Ulrich, Herzog zu Wirtemberg*, Stuttgart, 1865, pp. 29–31; von Stälin, op. cit. iv. 102–4; *Württembergische Landtagsakten, 1498–1515*, no. 41, pp. 127–9; no. 92, p. 278 (letter of Stuttgart to sixteen towns of 1 June 1514, and the peasants' demands as seen by the duke and the Estates); Grube, op. cit., pp. 80–81.

[2] von Stälin, op. cit. iv. 104; Heyd, op. cit. i. 271–2; Grube, op. cit., pp. 81–82.

an important reason, especially when lands were to be sold or
a major war broke out.[1]

The famous treaty of Tübingen, which was concluded on
8 July 1514 and became the main pillar of the country's liberties,
incorporated most of these demands.[2] Natives were to be preferred to foreigners in all important temporal and clerical
appointments; any major war was to be undertaken only 'with
the advice and knowledge' of the Estates; any other war or the
rendering of military assistance for which Ulrich needed the
Estates' help required their advice and good will; no further
taxes or aids were to be levied, but the Estates agreed to take
over the ducal debts amounting to 950,000 guilders and to
become responsible for their administration and repayment;
no part of the duchy was to be sold or pawned without their
consent; every subject was to be free to leave at his will; the
excessive quit-rents were to be scaled down; every duke was to
promise with his letter and seal to preserve these liberties *before*
his subjects rendered homage to him. From that time onwards
a regular tax of 24,213 guilders a year was levied for the service
of the ducal debts. Ulrich had to confirm this treaty which so
severely curtailed his powers.[3]

Yet popular feeling was not assuaged. On the contrary, there
were violent complaints in many parts about the new tax for
the payment of the ducal debts. Renewed riots occurred in
many towns and *Ämter*. Ulrich made military preparations and
secured the aid of neighbouring princes. The rebels, however,
surrendered without offering any resistance; they were punished
severely. Deputies of the Estates functioned as judges; in
August 1514 they sentenced eighteen ringleaders to death, and
many more to perpetual banishment. Those who had escaped

[1] *Württembergische Landtagsakten*, *1498–1515*, nos. 44, 59, 64–65, pp. 139–44, 167–
78, 211–12, 214 (June–July 1514); Fritz Hartung, 'Herrschaftsverträge und
ständischer Dualismus in deutschen Territorien', *Schweizer Beiträge zur Allgemeinen
Geschichte*, x, 1952, p. 171.

[2] The treaty has been printed in ibid., nos. 72–73, pp. 225–40; Sattler, op. cit.
i, nos. 67–68, pp. 145–56; Reyscher, op. cit. ii, nos. 18–19, pp. 40–51. For a similar
treaty in Bavaria six years earlier, see below, p. 358. At the end of the eighteenth
century the treaty was called the *Charta magna* of Württemberg: Grube, op. cit.,
p. 454.

[3] At first the ducal answer to the Estates' demands had been very equivocal:
State Archives Stuttgart, A 34–35, *Büschel 1b*, s.d.: 'Unses Hertzog Ulrichs zu
Wurtemperg etc. Antwurt uff unser Gemeiner Landschafft Furhalten.' For the
taxes levied annually, see ibid., *Tomus Actorum*, xiii, fos. 158–68.

were similarly prosecuted. Duke and Estates agreed that whoever conspired against the government, prelates and clergy, the
urban authorities or the *Ehrbarkeit*, aiming at their oppression,
was to lose his life. A description of these memorable events,
seen through the eyes of the victors, was published in the same
month.[1] It accused the rebels of planning the death of the duke
and his officials, the abolition of all authority, the suppression of
clergy, nobility, and the *Ehrbarkeit*, the division of all property
and making all things common. It was the *Ehrbarkeit* which had
gained its aims, at least for the time being.

III. *The Estates under the Habsburgs and their Eclipse under Duke Ulrich*

After the Estates' victory of 1514 Duke Ulrich was by no
means pliant, for he considered himself not bound by the terms
of the treaty of Tübingen. In April 1515 he declared that he
alone had the right to summon a diet; but he conceded that
Stuttgart and Tübingen should be entitled to petition him to
do so; in future the towns should be represented by one member
each of the urban court and council and by the *Amtmann* of the
district if he was a member of the Estates. Thus the members
of the Commons who had attended the diet of 1514 were
excluded: another victory for the urban *Ehrbarkeit*.[2] As early
as December 1515 Ulrich approached the Estates with new
demands for financial aid. This request they at first rejected,
pointing to the terms of the treaty of Tübingen; but eventually
they agreed to guarantee a new loan of 100,000 guilders and
the interest of another 30,000. Five deputies—one prelate and
four from the towns—were appointed to raise and to receive
this loan, to see to it that it was only used to pay certain burdensome debts, and to render yearly accounts to the Estates; while
the duke promised he would not use the money for any different
purpose. He also wanted to negotiate with a committee of the

---

[1] 'Warhafftig underrichtung der uffrürn unnd handlungen sich im fürstenthumb
Wirtemperg begeben', Tübingen, 1514; also in *Württembergische Landtagsakten,
1498–1515*, no. 92, pp. 268–79, and Sattler, op. cit. i, no. 70, pp. 157–73.

[2] Sattler, op. cit. i, no. 76, pp. 186–7; Reyscher, op. cit. ii, no. 24, p. 56; von
Stälin, op. cit. iv. 115; Grube, 'Dorfgemeinde und Amtsversammlung in Altwürttemberg', loc. cit., p. 198, and op. cit., pp. 89–90.

Estates about the contribution of the clergy, the even distribution of the new aid, and the alleviation of labour services, clearly preferring to treat with a committee rather than with the full diet.[1]

More severe trouble developed during the following years. In 1515 a nobleman, Hans von Hutten, was murdered by Ulrich. For this deed, together with his failure to appear before the appointed court, and the ill-treatment of his wife, Ulrich was put under the ban of the Empire, and the Estates were released from their oath of allegiance by the Emperor Maximilian. Later the sentence was mitigated: the ban was rescinded, but Ulrich had to agree to let a council of regency, on which the Estates were strongly represented, govern in his place for six years, to which further deputies of the three Estates were to be added when important matters were to be discussed. The Estates were to pay a fine of 27,000 guilders to Maximilian, but the nobility made difficulties; many noblemen refused to participate because those present at the negotiations had no powers to bind those absent. They also repudiated the claim that they were one of the Württemberg Estates and vigorously asserted that they had always been treated as free noblemen, and not as the subjects of the dukes.[2] In practice they achieved their aim and became Free Imperial Knights.

Ulrich, however, had not learned his lesson. He continued to rule in an arbitrary fashion, to disregard the treaty of Tübingen and other solemn obligations he had signed, to seek vengeance on his opponents among the Estates, whose leaders were arrested, tried, and executed, to burn villages and castles. Once more he was put under the ban of the Empire; but Maximilian died in January 1519 and so the ban was not executed. Ulrich used this opportunity to attack suddenly the Free City of Reutlingen, which was surrounded by his territories, without any prior consultation with his own Estates. He forced the city to open its gates, made the burghers take the oath of allegiance to him, put a garrison into the city, deprived it of its privileges and treasure, and incorporated it with Württemberg. This time,

---

[1] State Archives Stuttgart, A 34–35, *Büschel* 1c (documents of 1515–16); Heyd, op. cit. i. 421–4; von Stälin, op. cit. iv. 125; Grube, op. cit., p. 96.

[2] Sattler, op. cit. i, no. 95, pp. 242–3; ii, nos. 18–19, pp. 25–29 (correspondence of Feb. 1517 and June 1519); Grube, op. cit., pp. 91–102; von Stälin, op. cit. iv. 134–7.

however, resistance was vigorous and effective. The Swabian League, threatened by this breach of the peace, took immediate counter-measures, and troops under the command of Duke William of Bavaria conquered Württemberg. Ulrich had to flee. A new council of regency was appointed, the majority of its members being drawn from the Estates. In August 1519 Ulrich attempted to reconquer Württemberg. When he reached Stuttgart he made the burghers swear a new oath of allegiance. He declared the treaty of Tübingen null and void: as he came as a conqueror, he did not consider himself bound by it and used the opportunity to free himself from the chains forged by the *Ehrbarkeit*. Yet Ulrich's attempt was foiled by the Swabian League. Its forces reconquered the duchy, and Ulrich had to remain an exile for another fifteen years.[1]

In February 1520 the Swabian League sold Württemberg for 220,000 guilders to the Habsburgs, who thus acquired a valuable territorial link between their possessions in Austria and Tyrol and those on the upper Rhine and in Alsace. The Emperor Charles V, and after him his brother Ferdinand, ruled the country in harmony and close co-operation with the urban *Ehrbarkeit* which was pro-Habsburg and pro-Catholic.[2] It used the opportunity not only to have the stipulations of the treaty of Tübingen confirmed, but to strengthen its position and to extend its privileges. In March 1520 the Imperial ambassador and representative agreed to the demands of the diet: the government should remain inside the country, and no foreign authority should be entitled to interfere with it; the chancery and the high court (*Hofgericht*) should be filled with suitable native noblemen and commoners; the nobility's claim not to be a Württemberg Estate should be disregarded and it should be brought back into the duchy; the *Amtleute*, the ducal officials, should no longer be summoned to the diet as the representatives of the *Ämter*, but from each town and *Amt* only one member of the urban court and one of the urban council, thus giving complete control to the *Ehrbarkeit* whose members sat on both. After these important concessions the Estates granted an annual

[1] Sattler, op. cit. ii, no. 2, pp. 2–4; Heyd, op. cit. i. 525–8, 571–2; von Stälin, op. cit. iv. 140–8, 151–6, 158–95; Kugler, op. cit., pp. 55, 58; Schneider, op. cit., p. 124; Grube, op. cit., pp. 102–11.
[2] von Stälin, op. cit. iv. 198, 211; Ohr, loc. cit., p. 338.

tax of 20,000 guilders for five years.[1] The Estates also used the
negotiations with the Habsburg rulers and the difficulties
caused by the heavy debts to get the financial administration
under their own control. In December 1520 the Emperor
agreed that they should elect one prelate and three burghers,
to whom he added one of his officials: these five were to be
responsible for all revenue and expenditure, for the levying of
all taxes, dues, rents, and regalia, including the income from
the prince's domains. Because the revenues were insufficient to
meet the expenditure, Charles V ceded to them the five-year
tax granted earlier; annual accounts were to be rendered to the
governor, two regents and representatives of the Estates. In this
way an independent, collegiate financial authority, the *Cammer*,
was created after the Austrian example, but in Württemberg
it was controlled by the Estates. The ducal council was similarly
transformed and its competence was exactly defined, to enable
it to govern on behalf of the absent prince. This Austrian
pattern of the administration remained in force after the end of
Habsburg rule.[2]

In 1521 there were formed the two permanent committees
of the Estates which remained in being as long as the Estates
themselves and became their guiding organs: the more important Small Committee, with six burghers, and the Large
Committee with double that number. The diet originally had
the right to replace retiring members through election; but
later new members were co-opted by the Small Committee.
The nobility and the prelates did not participate in the setting
up of the committees, nor in the other negotiations of the
Estates. In 1522 these appointed their first permanent official,
a councillor to give them expert advice. In May 1521 Charles V
acknowledged that they were entitled to maintain their rights
and were not bound to their obedience if he undertook

---

[1] State Archives Stuttgart, A 34–35, *Büschel* 2: 'Der Lanndschafft zu Wirt-
temperg Freyhait', signed by Charles V, Maestricht, 15 Oct. 1520; Reyscher,
op. cit. ii, no. 25, pp. 57–69; Sattler, op. cit. ii. 59; Heyd, op. cit. ii. 55–56; von
Stälin, op. cit. iv. 204–5; Grube, op. cit., pp. 114–15.

[2] von Stälin, op. cit. iv. 209; Heyd, op. cit. ii. 77–78; Grube, op. cit., pp. 117–
23; Irmgard Kothe, *Der fürstliche Rat in Württemberg im 15. und 16. Jahrhundert*
(*Darstellungen aus der Württembergischen Geschichte*, xxix), Stuttgart, 1938, pp. 49–52.
Sattler, op. cit. ii, no. 82, pp. 199–200, prints the powers which the Estates issued
to their three deputies of the *Cammer* (2 June 1522); the original is in State Archives
Stuttgart, A 34–35, *Büschel* 3a.

anything against the established order. Through the policy of the Emperor as well as their own actions the Estates were drawn into closer contacts with other Habsburg territories. In 1521 and 1523 they sent deputies to negotiate with the Habsburg government and the diet of Upper Alsace and of the county of Tyrol respectively, desiring to bring about a closer union and a military alliance, but failed to achieve these aims.[1] Thus the Estates in many ways strengthened their position and developed their machinery during the years of Habsburg rule.

Diets were held almost every year, with a gap only between 1525 and 1529, after the upheaval of the Peasants' War, when only the committees were summoned. Several times two diets were summoned within one year. The diet of 1521 mainly discussed the country's debts; again the Estates tried to induce the nobility to contribute towards the revenue, this time with some success. During the diets of 1523 and 1524 the Estates pressed the Archduke Ferdinand, to whom his brother Charles had meanwhile ceded the duchy, to curtail his expenditure, not to spend more than the annual revenue, to inquire into both and to introduce economies, otherwise the decline and destruction of the country and its inhabitants would follow. The diet of 1525 again discussed the financial situation which was aggravated through the destructions of the Peasants' War. In June the prelates declined any contribution because of the damage they had suffered, while the towns demanded an equal distribution of the burden and a reformation of the monasteries, so that no decisions could be reached. After an adjournment of four months the Estates eventually agreed under protests to pay ducal debts of 50,000 guilders and to collect a reserve of 20,000; in addition to this sum the prelates had to give 36,000 guilders in spite of all their protestations. The Estates elected a committee to discuss their grievances with the government. Ferdinand then confirmed the terms of the treaty of Tübingen and promised he would adjust his expenditure to his income; the three deputies of the *Cammer* and the committee of six were to participate in the work of budgeting revenue and expenditure.[2]

[1] Heyd, op. cit. ii. 85–87, 95; von Stälin, op. cit. iv. 209–11; Grube, op. cit., pp. 123–7, 132–3; State Archives Stuttgart, A 34–35, *Büschel 3a* (letter of Charles V, dated Worms, 22 Mar. 1521; instructions for the Estates' deputies of 1521 and 28 Apr. 1523).

[2] State Archives Stuttgart, A 34–35, *Büschel 1c*, no. xviii; *Büschel 4*, no. D;

In later years the Estates proved even more difficult. In 1530 Ferdinand at first asked them for 80,000, later reduced to 40,000, guilders to finance his impending election as King of the Romans; but they would only promise 20,000; even these were only paid after his election and only as an advance on the ordinary taxes. Again the towns paid the lion's share, 84 per cent., and the prelates the rest.[1] In 1531 Ferdinand asked the Estates to elect a deputation to go to Innsbruck with full powers to decide there, together with similar deputations from the Habsburg territories, upon measures to resist the Turks, a request he had first made in 1529. The Estates, however, again declined to grant such powers: if he desired any aid, he should negotiate with the diet, and not with any committee or with individuals. They equally declined, in view of the country's state, dearth and famine, to maintain 3,000 mercenaries against the Turks for six months and only promised help if the Turks reached Lower Austria. With this reply Ferdinand's envoys had to be content. In the following year the demands were renewed. The Estates finally consented to pay for 1,200 mercenaries (instead of 3,000) for six months, having at first offered money for only 1,000, and this offer was then accepted by the government. In 1533 Ferdinand asked for a loan of 100,000 guilders to pay his debts to his allies for the purchase of Württemberg. The Estates asked to be informed with whom he had concluded an alliance and to what extent the duchy was committed; if they and the government then found that they were protected by such an alliance, they would pay 5,000 guilders every year while the alliance lasted, until they had paid 50,000 and not more. At another diet held two months later to obtain more money the Estates declined to give more and to withdraw all their conditions, but offered to make some concessions.[2] Because of Ferdinand's continuous demands for money the relationship between the government and the Estates deteriorated; their opposition was aroused by attempts

---

Büschel 3b (Recess of 30 Oct. 1525); Büschel 13a (list of diets of about 1565); Sattler, op. cit. ii. 82, 139–42, 146–8; iii, no. 125, pp. 4–8; Heyd, op. cit. ii. 272–6; Grube, op. cit., pp. 131–6, 145–54.

[1] Heyd, op. cit. ii. 297–9, and n. 67; Grube, op. cit., pp. 159–61.

[2] State Archives Stuttgart, A 34–35, Büschel 7, nos. ii, iii, v (4–8 Nov. 1531); nos. E, F, I (20–21 June 1532); nos. 6, 10 (Mar. and May 1533); Grube, op. cit., pp. 158, 162–6, 168–71.

to treat with individual deputies, instead of with the whole diet.[1]

This discontent with the government facilitated the return of Duke Ulrich to his native country. Other factors in his favour were the prevailing political and social unrest and the widespread Protestant feeling, for Ulrich during his exile had become a Lutheran. The possession of Württemberg became an important issue in the growing conflict between Catholics and Protestants, between the German princes and the Habsburgs, whose German position depended on maintaining this link between Austria and the Upper Rhine. In the end it was French money which enabled Landgrave Philip of Hesse, at whose court Ulrich sought refuge, to equip an army and to reconquer Württemberg. In May 1534 the Habsburg forces were defeated. His subjects once more rendered homage to Duke Ulrich, but only after his solemn confirmation of the treaty of Tübingen and of the duchy's liberties.[2] Ulrich, however, owed Philip the costs of the war, amounting to 230,000 guilders. He thus summoned a diet and demanded 60,000 guilders from the towns and half their yearly revenues from the prelates. The latter only granted a quarter and the towns 40,000 guilders; the towns asked that their ancient liberties and the treaty of Tübingen be maintained, while the prelates petitioned for the preservation of the old religion. Yet Ulrich was not satisfied with the grants; the Estates had to concede his demands, and 'everybody was squeezed to the utmost'.[3]

Only eight months later another diet was summoned. Again Ulrich demanded from the prelates half their annual revenues, for 1535 as well as 1536, and from the towns 60,000 guilders each time, to pay the costs of the war. The prelates declared this to be impossible, while the towns offered 80,000 instead of 120,000 guilders. The duke insisted and demanded 20,000 guilders more from the prelates which he would deduct from the towns' share. Thereupon the prelates granted the original

---

[1] Kugler, op. cit., p. 83; Ludwig Thimotheus Freiherr von Spittler, 'Geschichte Wirtembergs unter der Regierung der Grafen und Herzoge', in *Sämtliche Werke*, v, Stuttgart and Tübingen, 1828, p. 316.

[2] von Stälin, op. cit. iv. 366–71.

[3] State Archives Stuttgart, *Tomus Ulrici*, fos. 1–5 (diet of 1534, s.d.); Heyd, op. cit. iii, edited by Karl Pfaff, Tübingen, 1844, pp. 4–5 (report of 11 Dec. 1536); Grube, op. cit., pp. 175–6.

demand, but asked to be spared the additional 20,000 guilders; this Ulrich declined to do, while otherwise accepting the grant. The towns thanked him submissively for the remission of the 20,000 guilders, comparing it to the action of a father towards his children which pleased them immeasurably; they were to pay 40,000 guilders in 1535 and 60,000 in 1536. They petitioned anew for the maintenance of the treaty of Tübingen, or at least for its 'explanation', again indicating the weakness of their position. This 'explanation' accordingly pointed out that Ulrich had ample cause to declare the treaty null and void because the Estates had broken it in many respects and it was consequently invalid. But on account of their humble petition he consented out of grace to negotiate with them and to 'explain and declare' some of its terms. This ambiguous declaration was accepted with expressions of thanks by the Estates; they assured him that they would not seek anything derogatory or damaging to their prince in the treaty. Their position was much weakened on account of Ulrich's conquest and the religious differences between the prelates and the towns; henceforth their privileges were tacitly ignored by the duke.[1]

During 1535 Ulrich introduced the Lutheran Reformation, with some concessions towards the Swiss Reformed faith. No diet was consulted about the religious settlement. Ulrich, always short of money, hastily seized the church property, secularized the monasteries and used their revenues for his own benefit. The abbots received ample pensions of about 250 guilders a year, while the canons and monks had to be satisfied with 40 a year, or a cash payment; those resisting were expelled by force. Some abbots, however, were left in the monasteries and made responsible, together with ducal officials, for the revenues. These enabled Ulrich to pay his debts and even to accumulate a surplus, only a fraction being spent on the maintenance of the clergy.[2] Ulrich thus considerably strengthened his position and became for the time being independent of the Estates' grants. He simultaneously defeated the Catholic party which

[1] State Archives Stuttgart, *Tomus Ulrici*, nos. 1–3, 5–10, fos. 14–23, 30–39, 44–45; A 34–35, *Büschel* 11, nos. 10, x (diet of 8–12 Mar. 1535); Heyd, op. cit. iii. 194–6; Sattler, op. cit. iii. 78–81; Grube, op. cit., pp. 177–81.

[2] Sattler, op. cit. iii. 70–71; no. 33, pp. 149–51; Heyd, op. cit. iii. 79, 120, 124; Kugler, op. cit., p. 104, both stating that Ulrich only spent 24,000 guilders a year on the clergy, while he added 100,000 a year to his treasure.

was still strong among his old enemies, the urban *Ehrbarkeit*. Henceforth he ruled without the Estates, and the country accepted his rule without any further opposition. The Estates' officials became his officials; their committees disappeared; the taxes were paid into the ducal chest. The right of free departure was curtailed, certain dues being imposed on people leaving the duchy. The treaty of Tübingen ceased to be applied although it was not formally abrogated. The Estates were neither consulted about the treaty of Kaaden, in which Ferdinand in 1534 agreed to Ulrich's restitution, nor about the *Landesordnung* of 1536, which regulated the laws and customs of the country.[1]

Hardly any diets were held during the last fifteen years of Ulrich's reign. In 1538 he required new financial aid on account of the dangers threatening the German Protestants and demanded a property tax of $2\frac{1}{2}$ per cent. Special precautions were taken to ensure the acceptance of this demand. Some ducal councillors were sent out to negotiate confidentially with the authorities of the leading towns and to induce them to send deputies with full powers to grant the demand, without any reference back to their principals. The ducal *Amtleute* from the Black Forest were summoned and instructed not to spare any pains to make their districts send deputies with full powers and inclined towards the duke and the *Evangelium*, indicating the persistence of some Catholic opposition. A similar letter was sent to the mayor and court of Tübingen. Most towns duly sent the required full powers. When the diet finally met they elected a committee of twenty-one urban deputies to deliberate the ducal proposition, to whom more deputies and *Amtleute* were added at Ulrich's request. At first they were only willing to grant a property tax of 2 per cent., but after many admonitions they consented to the desired $2\frac{1}{2}$. Every subject had to declare his property to the authorities, and 391,150 guilders were collected during the years 1538–9, a very considerable sum.[2]

In 1540 a different device was used. Only sixteen towns were summoned to send deputies with full powers. They met in Stuttgart in January and deliberated for three days. After

---

[1] Heyd, op. cit. iii. 197, 200; Kugler, op. cit., pp. 98–99; Ohr, loc. cit., p. 338; Kothe, op. cit., pp. 66–67.

[2] State Archives Stuttgart, A 34–35, *Büschel* 9, nos. 3, 4*a*, 6–51 (2–11 May 1538); Heyd, op. cit. iii. 200–1, and n. 88; Grube, op. cit., pp. 183–7.

protestations of poverty they consented to the government's demand to collect five ordinary taxes and to lend the money to the duke, to be kept as a reserve on account of the threatening times—the impending civil war between Protestants and Catholics. Two days later thirteen other towns met at Marbach, and fourteen more at Nagold. To both assemblies the same demands were put and duly accepted after short deliberations. The ducal envoys reported how willingly and obediently the deputies adhered to the decisions taken in Stuttgart, and how submissively they behaved throughout.[1] In 1542 Ulrich borrowed another 65,000 guilders from the Estates, in 1546 116,000, and in 1547 110,000 guilders at an interest rate of 5 per cent.[2] In 1543 he demanded an annual contribution of about 7,000 guilders for the building of fortifications and negotiated about it with individual towns and *Ämter*. Stuttgart at first declined because this might develop into a permanent obligation, but gave way when threatened with Ulrich's disgrace.[3]

During the Schmalcaldic War (1546–7) Ulrich was again expelled from Württemberg by Habsburg forces. After a few months, however, the Emperor Charles V restored him to favour and promised to leave him in the possession of the duchy, against the payment of a fine of 300,000 guilders and the acceptance of the *Interim* which was favourable to Roman Catholicism. In consequence the monasteries were restored; Catholic abbots reappeared, resumed the monastic estates, and once more became one of the Württemberg Estates.[4] Ulrich adhered to his principle of ruling without the Estates and declined to summon a diet to get the treaty with the Emperor ratified. He again sent his officials round the country to secure the consent of the individual towns. Only one small town, Markgröningen, wished the matter referred to a diet, but nevertheless on the following day sent its powers of ratification.

---

[1] State Archives Stuttgart, A 34–35, *Büschel* 10, nos. 1–3, 25–26, 40–42 (10–21 Jan. 1540); the full powers ibid., nos. 9–24, 27–39, 44–57; Grube, op. cit., pp. 188–91.   [2] Ibid., *Tomus Actorum*, ii, fos. 99–104; xiii, fos. 158–68.

[3] Heyd, op. cit. iii. 203, n. 92; Grube, op. cit., p. 191.

[4] Heyd, op. cit. iii. 531–2; 'An die Röm. Kay. auch zu Hungarn unnd Böheimb etc. Königlich May. Aller unterthänigste Anzaig und Bitt: Anwaldts dess Durchleuchtigen, Hochgebornen Fürsten und Herrn, Herrn Eberhardten, Hertzogs zu Würtemberg und Teck . . .', 1641, pp. 15–16. With the revocation of the *Interim*, after the victory of Maurice of Saxony over Charles V, the Catholic abbots once more disappeared and made room for Protestant prelates: see below, pp. 25–26.

All the other towns equally ratified and sealed the treaty; they also agreed to lend Ulrich the required sums, only some excusing themselves with their poverty.[1] In 1548 the nobility and eight towns and *Ämter* were consulted about the introduction of the *Interim*, which had been promulgated by the Emperor and made but few concessions to the Protestants, and about the billeting of Imperial troops in the country: as opposition was out of the question, both had to be accepted.[2] Thus no proper diet was held from 1538 until Ulrich's death in 1550. He was determined to rule without the diet and was largely successful in making himself absolute.

The history of the Württemberg Estates during the first century of their existence was extremely chequered. There were moments of great deployment of power: in 1498 when they deposed the duke and assumed the regency; in 1514 when they forced the duke to accept the treaty of Tübingen; under Charles V when they controlled the finances and developed their permanent organs. These, however, were only short periods. Before as well as after 1514, and again after 1535 there were many years of an eclipse. The secession of the nobility in the early sixteenth century deprived the Estates of much strength, and so did the introduction of the Reformation. An energetic and determined prince, such as Duke Ulrich, could rule without consulting the Estates. The fact that there was no opposition against his strong government indicates that the Estates had not yet acquired a permanent position in the country's constitution, that they did not enjoy popular support, that they were weak and leaderless, that the urban *Ehrbarkeit*, the leading group, could easily be coerced and intimidated. The Estates claimed the right of resistance when their prince violated solemn treaty obligations, but they used it but seldom and only under very exceptional circumstances. All these factors did not augur well for their future. Yet the following

[1] Heyd, op. cit. iii. 475, 480–1; Grube, op. cit., p. 192. On behalf of all the towns the treaty was ratified and sealed on 28 Jan. 1547 by the following towns: Brackenheim, Calw, Göppingen, Kirchheim, Marbach, Schorndorf, Stuttgart, Tübingen, Urach, and Vaihingen: State Archives Stuttgart, *Tomus Actorum*, xxxix, p. 90 (1638).
[2] Sattler, op. cit. iii. 272–3; no. 82, p. 291. This seems to be the assembly referred to as a diet held at Nürtingen on 3 July 1548 in State Archives Stuttgart, A 34–35, *Büschel* 13a; Grube, op. cit., p. 193.

century was to see a much more steady growth of the Württemberg Estates and of their institutions. Although their social base remained as narrow as before, they succeeded in gaining a permanent place in the constitution of the duchy.

IV. *Consolidation of the Estates before the Thirty Years War*

During the reign of Duke Christopher, Ulrich's son (1550–68), the Estates were re-established as an important factor in the constitution of Württemberg. This was partly due to the continuous rise of prices, which made the ducal income quite insufficient and forced many princes to rely on the Estates' votes of credit. The ducal debts grew very considerably because of the Schmalcaldic War; enormous fines had to be paid to the Habsburgs, and Imperial garrisons had to be maintained;[1] the revenues of the monasteries only partially went to the duke on account of the *Interim*. According to Christopher himself, the war had cost 1,300,000 guilders, and his revenues from church lands only amounted to 22,000 guilders a year, while his father had been able to put aside 100,000 annually. In 1551 the ducal councillors estimated the total revenues of the duchy, inclusive of the ordinary taxes of 32,000 guilders, at 124,160 guilders a year, and the total expenditure (mainly on interest) at 123,560; but this allowed nothing for the maintenance of the court or any *accidentalia*, for which a mere 600 guilders was left. The ducal income from land they estimated at only 12,818 guilders a year, a mere 10 per cent. of the revenues, which indicates the inconsiderable size of the domains without the church lands. In January 1552 Christopher invited the Estates to deliberate with him upon the state of revenue and expenditure, but they replied that they were too inexperienced and humble to do so and were leaving the matter to the duke and his expert councillors. Many years later Christopher wrote that he had to spend over 70,000 guilders a year on the maintenance of the clergy, which previously had cost only 24,000, and that the salaries of his servants and officials amounted to nearly 50,000 guilders a year, compared with 12,000 or 15,000 in the past.[2] It is

---

[1] See below, pp. 32–34.
[2] State Archives Stuttgart, *Tomus Actorum*, i, fos. 285–313; i A, fos. 318–44 (proposition of the councillors of 4 May 1551, without any discussion); von Stälin,

difficult to see what advice the Estates could render under these circumstances, except to counsel economy.

In contrast with the practice under Duke Ulrich, six diets were summoned during the first three years of Christopher's reign; but then there was an interval of nearly twelve years, and only two more diets were held at the end of the reign.[1] Thus the diets were not yet regular institutions; they were not held at fairly regular intervals, but rather when pressing needs demanded it. At the very beginning of the first diet of the reign the prelates, who had not attended a diet since the introduction of the Reformation, consulted in a separate room. They then declared that, whenever a diet had been held in the past, prelates and towns had always deliberated together and had returned one answer to the ducal proposition. They requested not to be separated from the towns, but to remain together, to which the urban representatives assented.[2] From that time onwards, until the old order came to its end in the early nineteenth century, the prelates and the towns' representatives formed the Estates of Württemberg, but not as two separate houses, deliberating and voting on their own, but as one house, presenting a united front to the government. The latter therefore had little opportunity of playing off the two Estates against each other, a technique used by so many rulers wanting to strengthen their own power.

As the vote of a prelate had the same value as that of an urban deputy, the fourteen prelates were a small minority in the diet, which might be attended by about fifty towns, each entitled to one vote and represented by one or two deputies.[3] Equally, when the permanent committees of the Estates were reconstituted in 1554, the prelates did not obtain separate committees (as happened elsewhere), but were allotted two

op. cit. iv. 721, n. 1, 727; I. C. Pfister, *Herzog Christoph zu Wirtemberg*, i, Tübingen, 1819, p. 535; Bernhard Kugler, *Christoph, Herzog zu Wirtemberg*, i, Stuttgart, 1868, p. 284; ii, Stuttgart, 1872, pp. 579–80, 589–90 (letters to the ducal councillors of Sept. 1564 and Apr. 1565).

[1] There were two diets in 1551 (5–10 Jan. and 6–15 Apr.), three in 1552 (3–12 Jan., 28 Mar. to 8 Apr., 17–23 Oct.), and one in 1553 (4 Dec. to 8 Jan. 1554); there was one diet in 1565 (14 May to 19 June) and one in 1566 (11–21 Jan.). The following diet was held after an interval of seventeen years, in 1583.

[2] State Archives Stuttgart, *Tomus Actorum*, i, fos. 14–15 (7 Jan. 1551).

[3] The smaller towns did not attend regularly, and usually sent only one deputy each. For the number of towns summoned, cf. above, p. 3, n. 5.

seats, as against six burghers, on the Small Committee, and four seats, as against twelve burghers, on the Large Committee.[1] In contrast with the practice which had obtained under the Habsburgs, they were thus represented on the committees, but only as a minority. This did not prevent individual prelates from playing a leading part in the Estates and their negotiations, for which they were well qualified by their education and experience, often better than the burghers. Between the two groups there seems to have been very little friction or competition, and their relationship was usually quite harmonious; for since the revocation of the *Interim*, after the victory of Maurice of Saxony over Charles V in 1552, the Catholic prelates were gradually replaced by Protestant clergymen, the sons of burghers of the Württemberg towns, who married into the leading burgher families. There was no room for the jealousies and conflicts which existed between the Estates of so many other German principalities. In this respect the Württemberg Estates benefited from the absence of the nobility.

There was another question affecting the composition of the Estates which had to be settled at the beginning of the new reign. In 1515 Duke Ulrich had excluded the representatives of the urban Commons, but had admitted the *Amtleute* of the forty-eight *Ämter* who were members of the Estates to the diet, thus creating an official group which could be used against the urban *Ehrbarkeit*. Five years later, however, the Emperor Charles V conceded the latter's wish and excluded the *Amtleute* from the diet.[2] In April 1551 the Estates petitioned Christopher for a confirmation of this privilege. Although in principle willing to do so, the duke declined to accept the exclusion of the *Amtleute* altogether: at least those should be summoned who had sworn fealty to him, *or* had estates in the duchy—the large majority. This the Estates accepted, apparently without much opposition. They merely asked Christopher to release the *Amtleute* for the duration of a diet from the duties and services they owed to him. They also achieved a small change in their favour in the wording of the ducal declaration, which stipulated that only those *Amtleute* were to be summoned who were

---

[1] State Archives Stuttgart, *Tomus Actorum*, ii, fos. 669, 673; Pfister, op. cit. ii, Tübingen, 1820, no. 1, pp. 136, 140. Cf. above, p. 16, for the composition of the committees in 1521. [2] See above, pp. 13, 15.

members of the Estates *and* owned property in the country.[1]
For the following seventy-eight years the *Amtleute* regularly
attended the diets and supported the ducal policy there; but in
1629 the Estates achieved that they were permanently excluded.[2]

In 1565 Christopher attempted to go beyond the terms of this
agreement and summoned five *Amtleute* who did not fulfil the
stipulated conditions. The Estates immediately insisted that
they must be dismissed and were successful in four cases, while
the fifth could prove that he owned some property in the duchy.[3]
Having obtained the admittance of the *Amtleute* to the diet,
Christopher next attempted to get some of them appointed to
the committee which the Estates habitually elected at the
beginning of each session to discuss the ducal proposition and
to prepare their grievances and other matters which were to
be submitted to the government; it usually consisted of between
five and eight prelates and about twelve to fifteen burghers. In
1552, after the committee had been elected, the *Amtleute* produced a ducal order demanding that they also should sit on it.
The Estates replied that this was against the custom: it should
be left to the committee to co-opt *Amtleute* or others if they
thought this necessary on account of the importance and difficulty of the matter under discussion. Christopher objected to
this prevaricating attitude and repeated his demand for the
future. Yet at the following diets the Estates steadfastly refused
to elect any *Amtleute* to the committee, and in the end they prevailed.[4] This was an important point because all important
matters were prepared by the committee and only submitted
to the plenum for its formal approval which was hardly ever
withheld. The ducal officials were thus excluded from the
confidential deliberations of the committee which they might
have tried to influence in the prince's favour, or might have
divulged to him. There was good precedent for admitting the
officials to the Diet, but none for appointing them to the committee.

[1] State Archives Stuttgart, *Tomus Actorum*, i, fos. 173–4, 180–1, 200, 205; A
34–35, *Büschel* 12a (9–12 Apr. 1551).   [2] See below, pp. 59–60.

[3] Ibid., *Tomus Actorum*, iv, fos. 29–30 (15 May 1565): 'dise seind auch daruff,
bis an unndervogt zu Marpach, der etwas gutter in disem fürstenthumb hat,
abgeschafft worden'.

[4] Ibid. ii, fos. 316–17, 331–2, 455; iv, fo. 29 (17–19 Oct. 1552, 4 Dec. 1553,
15 May 1565).

Quite distinct from this committee, elected at the opening of each diet to expedite business and to negotiate with the government, were the permanent committees of the Estates which were reconstituted at the diet of 1553. It was one of the conditions put forward by the Estates before they took over the ducal debts that the Small Committee should meet at least twice a year without a ducal summons; if anything occurred which they found too difficult to deal with on their own they should have power to summon the Large Committee, but if the matter was so important that the latter could not decide it they would petition the duke to summon a diet. Christopher objected that it would be unfair if either committee met without his prior knowledge: as he was the prince and head, he must bear the care and burden of government and should not be excluded. He equally opposed another proposal of the Estates: that three receivers should be appointed—one by him and two by the Estates—to levy taxes and to pay off the ducal debts, who should take an oath to the Estates and render their annual accounts to the Small Committee which would audit them. Christopher suggested that the accounts should not be rendered solely to the Small Committee and achieved that his own deputies were admitted to the rendering of the yearly accounts. With regard to the summoning of the committees a compromise was reached. The Estates threatened to annul their grant if the Small Committee were not given free access to the financial administration and the business of the Estates; thus Christopher had to consent to its right of meeting freely, as often as was considered necessary or it was summoned by the receivers. The Large Committee, however, was not granted the same privilege, for the duke merely promised to observe the terms of the treaty of Tübingen, which left the right of summons to the prince.[1]

All these points were incorporated into the *Ausschusstaat* of 1554 and repeated in those of 1565 and 1583 and thus became part of the permanent order regulating the functions of the committees. According to them the Small Committee was to consist of two prelates and six burghers, elected in the first instance by the diet; they were to serve until death or incapacity,

[1] State Archives Stuttgart, *Tomus Actorum*, ii, fos. 556–7, 579–80, 599–600, 633–5, 654–6 (13 Dec. 1553 to 8 Jan. 1554); Pfister, op. cit. i. 270–2; Kugler, op. cit. i. 301–3.

whereupon the remaining seven were to elect a successor. To these eight another two prelates and six burghers were added to form the Large Committee, vacancies in which were also to be filled by the Small Committee; in both instances it was to act on its own initiative, without any confirmation by the duke or the diet. The latter indeed was accorded the right of changing the composition of either committee, but in fact this right was hardly ever used.[1] In this way the Small Committee acquired a very strong position and became almost independent of the diet from which it sprang. Only the two leading towns, Stuttgart and Tübingen, were always represented on it. The other towns and the prelates served in rotation: usually a vacancy on the Small Committee was filled by a town or a prelate from the Large Committee, whereupon the town or former monastery which had dropped out of the Small Committee was often appointed to the Large Committee. The Small Committee jealously guarded its right of filling all vacancies itself and strongly refuted attempts made at times by certain towns to influence this right, to claim representation, or to indicate whom they desired to be appointed. Its guiding spirits were the mayors of Stuttgart and Tübingen and some of the prelates, e.g. those of Bebenhausen, Denkendorf, Hirsau, Lorch, or Maulbronn: all famous monastic foundations and, after the Reformation, theological colleges.

In 1563 a conflict occurred between Christopher and the Small Committee over the latter's right of freely electing to vacancies which had been conceded in 1554. The member for Tübingen had died, and the committee as his successor appointed a member of the urban council, Conrad Breuning, the son of a well-known family which had been involved in conflicts with Duke Ulrich more than forty years before. Christopher insisted that the town court had the right of election. He alleged that he could not remember how this right became vested in the Small Committee, because at that time he had been ill and overburdened with work, and he also questioned the loyalty of the Breuning family. Although the law was clearly on the committee's side it gave way and, after a few days' hesitation, elected a member of the town court of Tübingen. Shortly after

---

[1] State Archives Stuttgart, *Tomus Actorum*, ii, fos. 668–74; iv, fos. 396–405; xi, fos. 492–511. The first two are printed in Pfister, op. cit. ii. 135–47.

Christopher's death, however, the Small Committee revived the case. When the member for Tübingen died in 1570, they again elected Conrad Breuning, who meanwhile had been mayor, was a member of the town court and council and was an experienced old man. The ducal councillors once more objected to this choice and suggested a different one. The committee referred to the agreement of 1554, to the *Ausschusstaat* and to the lack of another suitable candidate at Tübingen; in their opinion, children should not be held responsible for the deeds of their fathers. Then, however, they heard that Breuning had had an accident and was so old and ill that he was unable to take up the appointment; twelve months later they eventually elected another in his stead.[1] For the time being the match ended in a draw. The Small Committee's right of freely electing to vacancies was not challenged again until the seventeenth century.

In 1567 two members of the Small Committee, from the towns of Urach and Marbach, died, whereupon both towns, without waiting for an election, sent new members to its next meeting. The Small Committee, however, filled the vacancies by appointing two members of the Large Committee to the Small Committee and relegated Urach and Marbach to the Large Committee; and this was sanctioned by the ducal councillors.[2] In 1578, after the death of the abbot of Denkendorf, Duke Louis appointed as his successor the abbot of Königsbronn, Schropp, and also ordered him to attend the Small Committee in his predecessor's place. The committee pointed to its right of free election. Louis, however, denied any intention of interference. He had thought they were waiting with their election until he had chosen a new abbot and expressed the hope they would accept him now. The committee then duly elected the new abbot of Denkendorf. A few months later he was moved to Maulbronn when a vacancy occurred there through the transfer of its abbot to Stuttgart. Schropp then wrote to the Small Committee referring to the recent prejudicial innovation and put his office at their disposal: his new appoint-

---

[1] State Archives Stuttgart, *Tomus Actorum*, iii, fos. 250, 252–7, 264, 271 (19–24 Apr. 1563); vii, fos. 246, 273–5, 279–80, 284–7, 291, 532 (7 June 1570 to 27 June 1571); Sattler, op. cit. iv. 189. The description by Pfister, op. cit. i. 284–5, and by Kugler, op. cit. i. 308–9, is misleading.

[2] State Archives Stuttgart, *Tomus Actorum*, vi, fos. 3–8 (2–4 June 1567).

ment in no way was to impinge upon their right of free election. The committee, however, confirmed him as a member, while electing another abbot to the Large Committee in place of the former abbot of Maulbronn.[1] In this way the Small Committee tried to safeguard its rights against any interference, be it by the government or by individual towns, and established itself as a permanent organ of the Estates.

An equally important part was played by the Estates' permanent councillors, who attended the meetings of the committees and, as trained lawyers, were able to provide them with expert advice. In January 1552 the Estates petitioned that their secretaries and registrars be reappointed. In March the Large Committee supplicated the duke to order Dr. Caspar Beer to accept the appointment as their adviser and dismiss him from his service. In April the Estates' deputies appointed Dr. Beer their 'Councillor and Orator', with a salary of 50 guilders per annum, and another man to be their secretary with a salary of 40 guilders, pending the ducal approval. Only in October did Christopher confirm both appointments for the period of the diet which was then assembling; but he told the Estates they should look out for other officials because he required both men for his own service. The secretary, however, remained in office until his death in 1579; while after Dr. Beer's death in 1558 a new councillor was found in the person of *Magister* Caspar Wild, who served until his death in 1584.[2] Then the office remained vacant for several years. From 1586 onwards the Small Committee attempted to have the post filled, but Duke Louis prevaricated. In 1590 the committee suggested the name of the son of the abbot of Bebenhausen, *Magister* Johann Bidembach, but Louis refused his consent on the ground that the previous councillors had been his own sworn servants, a practice he wished to continue. In 1591 and 1592 the Small Committee again submitted Bidembach's name for Louis's approval, which was finally obtained. In February 1592 Bidembach was appointed with a salary of 50 guilders, in spite of the considerable rise of prices during the intervening

---

[1] Ibid., ix, fos. 321–2, 328–33, 386–91 (26 Feb. to 1 Mar., 7–26 Nov. 1578).

[2] Ibid., ii, fos. 27, 271; iv, fo. 537; ix, fos. 401, 469; xii, fo. 125; A 34–35, *Büschel* 14, no. 6b; *Büschel* 15, no. 11. Under Duke Ulrich the office had fallen into abeyance.

period.[1] In the later sixteenth century the secretary also received 50 guilders a year, and the two receivers (*Einnehmer*) appointed by the Estates one hundred each. The two prelates who were members of the Small Committee received 50 guilders each, and the six burghers 33 each from the Estates, in addition to what they received from their towns and ecclesiastical positions.[2] These were modest salaries, considering the heavy burden of work which fell on these few men. In Hesse the landgrave's councillors received salaries of at least 100, and rising to 200 guilders, at about this time.[3]

The first diet of Christopher's reign only lasted four days. The Estates elected several committees, one as was the custom at the beginning of a diet; another one to supplicate the Emperor Charles V, begging him to intercede in favour of the duke with his brother Ferdinand, to whom large fines had still to be paid from the Schmalcaldic War; another one to discuss the grievances with the ducal councillors. The Estates petitioned Christopher to confirm the treaty of Tübingen and its declaration and extension by Ferdinand during the years of Habsburg rule. When the diet was resumed three months later the Estates renewed this petition and emphasized that the majority were empowered to treat about other matters only after the confirmation was obtained. They granted Christopher 130,000 guilders on condition that he confirmed the treaty of Tübingen and dismissed his soldiers, although this sum would be difficult to collect from the poor and ruined population. The duke replied that he was not bound by the treaty because they had taken the oath of allegiance to the house of Austria and had sworn never to accept another ruler: yet out of grace he would confirm it, with certain reservations, but his councillors and officials were not to give a similar declaration. In the end, however, Christopher confirmed the treaty of Tübingen and its declaration by Charles V 'word by word'. The only concession he obtained was the readmission of the *Amtleute* to the diet;[4] whereupon the Estates made the promised grant. Again a committee was appointed to discuss their grievances and the ducal

---

[1] State Archives Stuttgart, *Tomus Actorum*, xiii, fo. 209; xiv, fos. 270–1, 607–8, 627; xv, fos. 158, 193, 201, 214.   [2] Ibid. iv, fo. 537; xi, fos. 631–2 (1566 and 1583).
[3] Christoph Rommel, *Geschichte von Hessen*, iv. 1, Cassel, 1835, p. 745.
[4] See above, p. 26.

debts with the government, with full powers to take the necessary measures.[1]

At the following diet the Estates submitted a novel petition with regard to the treaty of Tübingen, indicating the wide interest it aroused in the country: many burghers daily asked to be informed of its contents which were only known to the town courts; therefore it should be read publicly in all towns and large villages, but Christopher would only agree to its being read to those desiring it. The ducal proposition submitted at the beginning of the diet demanded they should devise means for the maintenance of 200 mercenaries to garrison two towns, because of the military preparations made in many parts of the Empire. The Estates opposed this demand, as contrary to the treaty of Tübingen, and pronounced in favour of selecting a number of soldiers from the local militia. Christopher, however, insisted on an affirmative vote; surely, he declared, it was even more against the terms of the treaty when the Estates under the Habsburgs had maintained forces against Duke Ulrich. The Estates, perhaps impressed by his strong words, eventually granted 2 guilders a month for each mercenary, hoping that 100 or 150 would suffice; and finally they consented to the desired 200. They also assented to supply the Imperial garrison on the Asperg with wood if the duke supplied it with other necessities. They further consented to levy a common penny as a reserve for the Empire, which amounted to a sum of 77,714 guilders. After only three months, however, Christopher requested a new grant on account of the worsening political situation, the preparations of Maurice of Saxony against Charles V, and the French armaments in Lorraine. The Estates declined to go beyond an advance of 18,000 guilders from the reserve of the common penny just granted. In the duke's opinion this was so insufficient that the diet was dissolved without any agreement being reached, a very unusual procedure. Six months later the Estates raised similar difficulties, but finally added 20,000 guilders to the 130,000 voted in 1551, emphasizing at the same time the plight of the country, its many burdens,

---

[1] State Archives Stuttgart, *Tomus Actorum*, i, fos. 16, 21, 23, 55–60, 73–74, 169, 179–82, 184, 197–8, 223–68 (7–10 Jan., 9–15 Apr. 1551); A 34–35, *Büschel 12a* (printed confirmation of the treaty of Tübingen); Reyscher, op. cit. ii, no. 33, pp. 91–98; Sattler, op. cit. iv. 14–15; Pfister, op. cit. i. 196–7, 226, 231–2; Grube, op. cit., pp. 197–200.

its poor soil, the lack of industry and mineral wealth, and the many Imperial abbeys, towns, and lordships in its midst, which did not contribute anything to the taxes granted. In addition to these, in 1553 the first 100,000 guilders due to King Ferdinand were collected, 35,000 by the prelates and 65,000 by the towns:[1] no wonder that the Estates made difficulties about higher grants.

Meanwhile Christopher's debts grew steadily, the yearly interest of 86,000 guilders consuming almost the entire revenue exclusive of taxation, and corresponding to a debt of over 1,700,000 guilders.[2] In December 1553 the duke proposed to the Estates they should take over 600,000 guilders of his debts and pay the interest of 30,000 a year, in addition to the 150,000 guilders still due to King Ferdinand. The Estates agreed to the first proposition, but declined the second, and put forward certain conditions: they would pay off the 600,000 guilders within twenty years, but would not pay the interest; they would no longer give the customary taxes (amounting to about 32,000 guilders a year); their permanent committees should have the rights of free assembly and deliberation;[3] and the prelates should not be separated from the towns. Christopher replied that in that case the towns alone should take over debts of 800,000 guilders. To this they agreed, repeating their conditions and adding that the duke should appoint one and the towns two receivers who should render annual accounts to the Small Committee. The prelates in their turn consented to take over 400,000 guilders of the ducal debts: of these, they would pay off 20,000 a year and pay interest of 20,000 guilders on them; while the towns would only pay off 30,000 annually, and not 40,000 as the government desired. The Estates even threatened to revoke their grants if their wishes regarding the rights of the Small Committee were not met.[3] Agreement was only reached after weeks of bargaining. In the end most of the Estates' conditions were accepted: the rights of the Small Committee to assemble freely, to supervise the finances and to audit the receivers' accounts were recognized; the customary taxes were

---

[1] State Archives Stuttgart, *Tomus Actorum*, ii, fos. 16, 25, 32–33, 36, 40, 43, 45–47, 54, 56, 261, 268, 326, 335, 400–1; A 34–35, *Büschel* 14, nos. 1*b*, 13–14, 21; *Büschel* 15, nos. 12, 19; Kugler, op. cit. i. 290 (7–12 Jan., 3–8 Apr., 18 and 21 Oct. 1552, 1 July 1553).

[2] Ibid., *Tomus Actorum*, ii, fo. 441; Reyscher, op. cit. ii, no. 36, p. 113 (4 Dec. 1553). Cf. above, p. 24.   [3] See above, p. 28.

rescinded. They granted 90,000 guilders and took over debts of 1,200,000, on which they paid henceforth 71,097 guilders a year.[1]

From that time onwards the financial administration was dominated by the Estates and their officials. The taxes were repartitioned and levied by them and paid into their chest, the *Landschaftskasse*, out of which the debts they had taken over were paid off. The two receivers (*Einnehmer*) of the Estates controlled revenue and expenditure; they were entirely independent of the ducal *Rentcammer* and its officials, but responsible to the Small Committee.[2] In a different sphere the Estates were much more reluctant to take responsibility. In 1552 a committee of two prelates, four burghers, and four ducal councillors was appointed to discuss the many usages and by-laws in force in town and country and to prepare the draft of a legal code for the duchy. The first task the committee declared futile and impossible: in their opinion it would be better not to take the local usages into consideration, but to deliberate upon an order based on common law and equity. This, however, was an enormous work which required scholars and books; as their members were not qualified to undertake it, the duke should appoint better qualified men who should prepare a report. Christopher replied they should continue their discussions and make a report about the local laws, which they did. After its consideration the Large Committee asked Christopher to entrust trained lawyers with the further work; whereupon four ducal councillors, with the aid of professors from Tübingen, completed the draft of the code. This was discussed by the Estates at the diet of 1553. They suggested several amendments and additions which were taken into account before the code was published in 1555. At the diet of 1565 and on later occasions the Estates complained that it needed emendation and asked for further explanations, with the result that improved editions of the *Landrecht* were published later.[3]

---

[1] State Archives Stuttgart, *Tomus Actorum*, ii, fos. 540, 552–3, 556–7, 565, 579–82, 604, 622, 633–5, 652, 654–6; xiii, fo. 165; Reyscher, op. cit. ii, no. 36, pp. 112–21; von Stälin, op. cit. iv. 728–9; Sattler, op. cit. iv. 62–63; Kugler, op. cit. i. 292–304 (4 Dec. 1553 to 8 Jan. 1554).

[2] Friedrich Wintterlin, *Geschichte der Behördenorganisation in Württemberg*, i, Stuttgart, 1904, p. 40.

[3] Kugler, op. cit. i. 314–18; ii. 602–3; Pfister, op. cit. i. 246, 250; von Stälin, op. cit. iv. 714; Kothe, op. cit., pp. 64–65.

The Estates' permanent committees were similarly consulted by the government before the publication of the Church Ordinance of 1559, which remained the basic law of the duchy in religious and educational matters until 1806, of the Butchers' Ordinance of 1554, of the Building Ordinance of 1568, and of similar regulations. They achieved that the urban authorities were entrusted with the execution of these decrees and that they retained their rights of supervision over the guilds.[1] Thus the government was prevented from encroaching upon the sphere of local government in which the large majority of the members of the Diet were active. The Large Committee entered another important field of activity by buying abroad, during a time of dearth in 1562–3, more than 20,000 *modii* of corn and selling them at a loss of almost 20,000 guilders to alleviate distress in the country. In 1564 the committee bought, with ducal approval, a house in Stuttgart for 2,900 guilders to use it for the meetings, archives, and offices of the Estates.[2] During the eighteen years of Duke Christopher's reign the Estates thus consolidated their position in many ways, especially in the fields of legislation and administration: a surprising recovery compared with their marked decline during the previous reign.

No further diet met after 1553 until 1565. Apparently Duke Christopher was tired of bargaining with the Estates and of making concessions to them; for the time being he could not hope for further financial aid because they had taken over the major part of his debts. Even the Estates' committees met very irregularly: four times in 1554, but not at all in 1555, 1556, and 1558, once only in 1559 and 1560, but six times in 1562. Several times the Small Committee insisted that the matter under consideration was so weighty that a fuller assembly was required and achieved the summoning of the Large Committee—as when an aid against the Turks, a contribution for the Empire, or a reserve for the Swabian Circle was to be levied. Christopher considered such a meeting unnecessary because he was not seeking anything for himself, and because these demands were neither unusual nor controversial, but finally gave way.[3] In 1564, after

---

[1] Karl Weidner, *Die Anfänge einer staatlichen Wirtschaftspolitik in Württemberg* (*Darstellungen aus der Württembergischen Geschichte*, xxi), Stuttgart, 1931, pp. 115–19; Gerhard Oestreich, in *Gebhardt's Handbuch der deutschen Geschichte*, 8th ed., 1955, ii. 347.

[2] State Archives Stuttgart, *Tomus Actorum*, iii, fos. 414–16, 587–8, 591.

[3] Ibid. ii, fos. 836, 841–2, 853 (Mar. 1557); iii, fos. 326–7, 335–41 (Apr. 1564).

ten years without a diet, the committees petitioned anew that it should be summoned, to be told curtly that the duke declined to argue about it and would let the matter rest there.[1]

It does not seem to have been these entreaties, but the continuous rise of prices and expenditure and his pressing financial needs which finally forced Christopher to summon a diet. In 1564 he wrote to his councillors that he was not responsible for the debts: his father had enjoyed much larger revenues from the Church, and his expenditure on the clergy and on his own family had been much smaller—for Christopher had two sons and eight daughters, all still under age at that time. The councillors advised measures of economy, especially on buildings, tapestries, furniture, stud-farms, bears, lions, and other wild animals, swans, peacocks, presents of wine, the hunt, the consumption at court, and in the kitchen. The duke replied that all prices were rising *ad summum*, so were salaries and the cost of maintaining the fortresses, but not his revenues; he knew of no other way out but to petition the Emperor Ferdinand for a declaration and decision between him and the Estates as to the validity of the treaty of Tübingen; if Württemberg was to be a principality they had to maintain him as a prince.[2] The burden of debts was so heavy that it was impossible to manage with the small grants made at the last diet. The ducal councillors were instructed to point to the example of Bavaria, where the Estates at the last diet granted higher customs duties yielding over 200,000 guilders a year and took over the entire debts, and to that of the Palatinate where the Estates had given more than 600,000 guilders; in Baden as well they had granted an excise for fifteen years on top of increased customs and duties, and in Hesse they had assented to levy a penny on drink for sixteen years, a tax yielding more than 50,000 guilders a year, in addition to a large grant. Christopher aimed at much more substantial grants and more permanent duties and taxes than his Estates were willing to concede. This was the time when Duke Albert V of Bavaria was extremely successful in the struggle

---

[1] Ibid. iii, fos. 335–7, 367, 378, 395–6, 400 (26 Apr. to 2 June 1564); Grube, op. cit., pp. 219–21.

[2] Pfister, op. cit. i. 527, 533–4; Kugler, op. cit. ii. 579–80, 584, 588–9 (letters of 21 Sept., 2 and 24 Dec. 1564, and 2 Mar. 1565). For the number and ages of the ducal children, see *Textheft zum Stammbaum des Württembergischen Fürstenhauses*, edited by I. Giefel, T. Schön, and H. Kolb, Stuttgart, 1895, pp. 8–9.

against his Estates which had to make very considerable grants, and Philip of Hesse equally forced his Estates to make far-reaching concessions.[1]

When the diet met in 1565, however, Christopher only obtained a very limited success. Hitherto the Estates had paid just over 70,000 guilders a year in repayment of the ducal debts.[2] After negotiations lasting several weeks they agreed to levy 93,794 guilders a year instead; of this sum the prelates for the time being were to pay over 45 per cent., while the annual payments of the towns and Ämter were increased by about 50 per cent. The Estates were liable not only for the gradual repayment of debts amounting to 1,200,000 guilders, but also for the interest due on them; though that still left Christopher with debts of 900,000 guilders which they had not taken over.[3] Again the duke had to make important concessions to the Estates. Because the nobility was the third Estate of the duchy he promised to think of means to unite it more closely with his principality. He and his successors would for ever maintain the prelates as the second Estate, with their votes and session in the diet and its committees. He would not pawn or alienate any abbey or any ecclesiastical revenues, which were to be paid into a special chest, the Kirchenkasten, and to be used for the benefit of the clergy. The Estates were even allowed a limited right of resistance if anything were demanded from them contrary to their religion—the Confession of Augsburg and Württemberg: in other words, if the duke attempted to modify the Lutheran church settlement.[4]

Christopher thus not only had to renounce many of the financial benefits accruing to other princes from the secularization

---

[1] State Archives Stuttgart, A 34–35, Büschel 16a and 16b; a draft in Büschel 16e (the duke to his councillors on 21 Sept. 1564). See below, pp. 168–9, 381–5 for the events in Hesse and Bavaria.

[2] See above, p. 34.

[3] von Stälin, op. cit. iv. 430; Grube, op. cit., p. 228. According to the Recess of 19 June 1565 the prelates were to pay 40,000 and the towns and Ämter 50,000 guilders a year; but in practice the former paid 44,191 guilders and the latter 49,603 guilders a year: State Archives Stuttgart, Tomus Actorum, iv, fos. 369–71; xiii, fo. 166.

[4] Ibid., iv, fo. 388; A 34–35, Büschel 16d; von Stälin, op. cit. iv. 731; 'Grundtlicher Beweiss, Das die Praelaten und Clöster dess Hertzogthumbs Würtemberg vor 90, 100, 150, 200 und mehr Jahren zu dem Land und Hertzogthumb Würtemberg gehörig gewesen . . .', 2nd ed., 1645, pp. 95–96; Grube, op. cit., pp. 229–30.

of church property, but even the *Jus Reformandi*, which the German princes possessed since the peace of Augsburg of 1555: concessions of great importance for the future history of the country. It is true that the income of the *Kirchenkasten* was used not only to maintain the clergy, the schools, and the poor, but also to subsidize the duke. These contributions, however, remained comparatively small. During the half-century from 1568 to 1618 they amounted only to 1,071,669 guilders, or just over 20,000 guilders a year, a mere fraction of the ducal needs.[1] The richest prize, the abbeys, also remained outside the prince's reach. Thus the authority and the power of the dukes of Württemberg were but little increased in the long run through the introduction of the Reformation; and they were not the only Lutheran princes who benefited so slightly.

A few months later the last diet of Christopher's reign was held. His intention was that his second son, Louis, should inherit nine *Ämter* of the duchy, with all rights and dues, towns and castles; but that the diet should remain undivided and be attended by both dukes with their councillors, and that there should be a single court of appeal and one high court (*Hofgericht*) for the whole duchy. These and other provisions of Christopher's will were read to the assembled Estates. They strongly opposed any formulations which could be interpreted as stipulating a division of Württemberg or of the *corpus* of the Estates, which had been declared indivisible and inseparable. The will was nevertheless incorporated into the *Recess* ending the diet and thus became law. But it was repeated that neither the principality nor the Estates' *corpus* were to be divided, and the treaty of Tübingen and all agreements reached at previous diets were once more confirmed.[2] Christopher's elder son, however, died a few months before his father, so that Louis in 1568 succeeded to the whole duchy.

During Louis's reign, which lasted twenty-five years, only one diet was held, in 1583. If it had not been for the financial situation, the institution might have disappeared entirely. The Small Committee, on the other hand, met several times every

---

[1] *Württembergische Landtagsakten unter Herzog Johann Friedrich, 1608–1620*, edited by A. E. Adam, Stuttgart, 1919, pp. 175, 558, n. 2.

[2] State Archives Stuttgart, *Tomus Actorum*, v, fos. 11–20, 33–35, 68–83; va, fos. 12–24, 40–44, 87–109 (11–19 Jan. 1566); von Stälin, op. cit. iv. 733; Grube, op. cit., pp. 231–2.

year, and the Large Committee usually once. In 1573 the
committees petitioned Louis, who was then nearly twenty years
old, to marry, a matter in which they were highly interested.[1]
However, it was another two years before their wish was fulfilled and Louis was married to a suitable lady of the Augsburg
Confession, and even so the desired successor was not born.
The Small Committee also took the initiative when corn prices
rose quickly during the winter of 1579–80 after a bad harvest.
They worked out a scale of maximum prices and petitioned for
its publication. The government sent it to the *Ämter*, but asked
for further information before publishing it. Finally the decision
was left to the local authorities whether to accept it or not
because prices were beginning to fall. Two years later, however, the suggestion was carried out because of renewed dearth,
and the scale of maximum prices was published, imposing the
penalty of confiscation on those disregarding them.[2]

Louis inherited from his father considerable debts and was
as little inclined as he had been to curtail his expenditure: the
court continued to cost very large sums, and the building of one
new château alone devoured 300,000 guilders.[3] In the end he
had to propose to the Large Committee that they should take
over a further 600,000 guilders of the ducal debts. In Louis's
opinion the Estates were *ratione naturali* obliged to come to his
aid in such an emergency. His expenditure was much larger
than the revenues of the ducal chamber, although the incomes
of the former nunneries were used for the benefit of the ducal
kitchen; while those of the monasteries and other church lands
were used to pay the parsons and schoolmasters, to assist the
poor and sick, and for pious purposes in general. The Large
Committee, however, replied curtly that they had no power to
grant a tax or imposition.[4] Thus a diet had to be called. The
Estates' committee elected at the beginning deliberated the
ducal proposition for many hours, and several votes were taken,

---

[1] State Archives Stuttgart, *Tomus Actorum*, viii, fos. 529–40 (5–6 Oct. 1573). A
similar petition was submitted in 1584 after the death of Louis's first wife without
issue: Grube, op. cit., p. 248.

[2] State Archives Stuttgart, *Tomus Actorum*, x, fos. 30, 61–62, 84, 147, 794 (3
Mar. to 10 May 1580, 30 Nov. 1582).

[3] Sattler, op. cit. v. 81–82; Schneider, op. cit., p. 192.

[4] State Archives Stuttgart, *Tomus Actorum*, x, fos. 752–4, 771–3, 779 (19–20
Nov. 1582).

but unanimity could not be reached. In the end the majority decided in favour of taking over debts amounting to 600,000 guilders with the interest, half of the burden falling on the towns and *Ämter*, and the other half on the monasteries and church lands. The Estates once more petitioned Louis to bring the nobility closer to the duchy as its third Estate, so that they would participate in the burdens. Louis, however, could see no way of achieving this because the nobility had acquired their liberty through prescription in the course of more than a hundred years.[1]

This grant was not large enough to solve Louis's financial difficulties. In the following year the Small Committee complained that several former monasteries had had their schools closed, the pupils being sent elsewhere and all the income confiscated. At a time when the Papacy was endowing the obnoxious, bad Jesuits with so many stately colleges and houses, members were sorely grieved to see useful Evangelical foundations ruined and laid waste. Yet the same committee, which had intended to remind the duke to restrain his household expenditure, on being informed that Louis objected to such a course and was himself planning measures of economy, gave up this plan and decided to await further developments.[2] Nor was there any opposition when in 1591 he demanded from the Large Committee a further increase of taxation by one-third for the duration of four years so that a reserve could be collected because of the dangerous times, during which period the redemption of old debts should cease. The duke explained to the committee that he had intended to submit the project to a diet for approval, but had not done so because it was confidential and meant to save the country, so that the Estates would in any case be obliged to contribute.[3]

On one occasion only did the Large Committee enter a protest, when in 1588 the government submitted a Bill against

[1] Ibid. xi, fos. 248–50, 328–9, 463–4 (3–17 Mar. 1583). In practice the prelates henceforth paid 67,191, and the towns and *Ämter* 74,485 guilders a year: ibid. xiii, fo. 167. Compared with 1565 the increase for both amounted to about 50 per cent.: see above, p. 38, n. 3.

[2] Ibid. xii, fos. 154, 190–1, 289 (12 and 18 Nov. 1584).

[3] Ibid. xv, fos. 107–8 (21 June 1591). Henceforth the prelates and church lands paid 93,318, and the towns and *Ämter* 99,333 guilders a year: ibid., fos. 111–21. Cf. below, p. 53, the Estates' reference to this grant thirty years later.

poaching which stipulated much heavier penalties than hitherto. These they considered too heavy. They also declared that
they had no mandate and no powers to discuss the Bill and asked
that a diet be summoned to debate the matter. Yet a few months
later the ordinance was published without any further consultation with the Estates. At their next meeting the Large
Committee complained about this procedure and asked to be
informed of the opinion expressed by the legal faculty of
Tübingen which had been consulted by the government, so that
they could formulate their own views. Louis replied sharply
that the promulgation of such mandates and decrees, as well
as the amending of old ones, belonged to his princely prerogative, without anybody's participation. He declared that he had
no intention of further arguments with the committee on this
score, and that it was not necessary to communicate to them
the legal faculty's opinion. He expected them to obey the new
ordinance, to spare him further petitions and entreaties, especially from persons in holy orders, not to waste their time in
such ways and to behave more dutifully towards their prince
who was ordained by God. The ducal councillors also told the
committee that they had submitted such petitions on previous
occasions and had claimed a right of participating in legislation,
which in truth came within the duke's regalia and jurisdiction
alone. In future they should spare him such demands. It was
a long time since the Estates had been treated to such language.
Clearly Louis was determined not to allow them any share in
legislation other than money bills, while in his father's reign
they had often been consulted about new laws and decrees
before publication.[1]

Duke Louis summoned but one diet during a long reign and
tried to curtail the influence of the Estates. Yet he did abide by
the terms of the constitution and unlike his successor did not
aim at absolute power. As he had no children he even attempted
to tie his successor—from the Montbéliard line of the ducal
house—by the provisions of a will which expressly confirmed
the constitution and granted to the Estates a limited right of resistance. The treaty of Tübingen and all liberties and privileges

---

[1] State Archives Stuttgart, *Tomus Actorum*, xiii, fos. 514–47, 576 (23–27 Jan.
1588); xiv, fos. 225–32, 250–3 (27 Feb. to 2 Mar. 1589); Sattler, op. cit. v. 109–
10. Cf. above, pp. 35–36, for the practice under Duke Christopher.

were to remain in force. If his successor declined to confirm them, the Estates should not be obliged to render homage to him. If the will were disregarded by his successor, the Estates should be entitled to withhold all dues and taxes, which should be allocated to their chest, and to pay themselves *per modum retentionis*. The duchy should be neither divided, nor pawned, nor burdened, but its liberties and customs should be protected and maintained.[1] A few months before his death Louis even suggested that his heir should sign a solemn assurance that he would leave the Estates in the full enjoyment of all their customs, rights, and privileges granted under the treaty of Tübingen and its later declarations. Two weeks later Count Frederick accordingly confirmed the treaty of Tübingen, its declarations of 1535 and 1551, all later *Recesse* and agreements, and promised that he would not burden the Estates and the country in any way contrary to the old custom.[2]

After his accession in 1593, however, Frederick did not, as he had promised, renew this confirmation before homage was rendered to him. It was only in 1595 that he agreed to confirm the treaty of Tübingen under his great seal, after protracted negotiations with the Small and the Large Committees. These committees refused any money grant until a diet was called, complained about the delay in the confirmation and raised many other grievances. Only after the confirmation had been obtained did the Estates grant Frederick a loan of 80,000 guilders and another 120,000 for the purchase of two small districts.[3] Among the grievances raised at the diet was a complaint that the ducal foresters contrary to the old custom at times demanded chickens (*Leibhennen*) from former serfs who had moved into town and thus gained their freedom. Frederick, however, replied that it was news to him that serfs became free by moving into towns. But the diet insisted that this was so. Three years later a decree was promulgated to the *Amtleute* that a subject leaving the duchy was to give a departure due of a tenth penny and a suitable redemption due for his manumission.

---

[1] Reyscher, op. cit. ii, no. 42, pp. 208, 221, 229–30; Sattler, op. cit. v. 147; von Stälin, op. cit. iv. 814–15 (6 Mar. 1587).

[2] State Archives Stuttgart, *Tomus Actorum*, xv, fos. 406, 489–90 (27 Feb., 14 Mar. 1593).

[3] Sattler, op. cit. v. 191; Freiherr von Spittler, op. cit. v. 397; Grube, op. cit., pp. 251–6.

In the Small Committee there were complaints against this violation of the right of free departure which had been recognized by the treaty of Tübingen and other laws. The committee then informed Frederick of this position and referred him to his own confirmation of the treaty and their liberties. Even the ducal councillors took the side of the Estates. But Frederick only gave way some months later, after further unfavourable reports, and only because a diet had to be summoned to grant large sums due to the house of Habsburg. He then asserted rather feebly that the whole affair was due to an error and misunderstanding, the order applying only to recently purchased and not yet incorporated districts.[1]

With the purpose of strengthening the side of his supporters Frederick summoned to the diet of 1599 not only the *Amtleute*, who were members of the Estates and owned property in the duchy, but also others who did not fulfil these conditions. Strangely enough, the Estates consented to let them attend on this occasion, on condition that no precedent would be created. They insisted, however, that Frederick should confirm anew the treaty of Tübingen. Otherwise they would not be bound by the agreements hitherto reached at the diet because their instructions forbade them to grant anything contrary to their liberties. Their achievement was that the treaty was once more expressly mentioned in the *Recess* at the conclusion of the diet, which was against Frederick's intentions. He severely reprimanded his councillors because they had conceded this point and had accepted the grievances of the Estates. Yet he was unable to dispense with their co-operation. For in the treaty of Prague the house of Habsburg had just renounced its rights of mesne fief over Württemberg, according it the status of a free fief of the Empire, for which privilege 400,000 guilders had to be paid, and this was impossible without a grant by the Estates which also had to confirm the treaty.[2] At the same time Frederick removed obnoxious prelates and officials of the Estates and replaced them by his tools; he tried to strengthen

---

[1] *Württembergische Landtagsakten unter Herzog Friedrich I.*, i, nos. 138, 149, 154, 270, 279, 287, 295, pp. 286, 312, 332, 523-4, 532-3, 542-4, 549-55, and n. 2; ii. 9-10 (28 Apr. to 7 May 1595, 23 June 1598 to 2 Feb. 1599).

[2] Ibid. ii, nos. 10, 57, 68, pp. 20-21, 118 and n. 2, 138 (6 Feb. to 15 Mar. 1599); Sattler, op. cit. v. 220-3. For the summoning of the *Amtleute*, see above, pp. 13, 15, 26-27.

his own resources and to become more independent of the Estates. In 1598 he introduced a monopoly in favour of his ironworks, which stipulated that all iron must be bought from them and met with strong opposition on the side of the Estates.[1]

The relations between Frederick and the Estates were thus strained for several reasons. From the outset he objected to the restrictions imposed on him by the treaty of Tübingen and confirmed its terms only with great reluctance. He aimed increasingly at introducing far-reaching changes that would allow him to replace the old-fashioned militia system by a small professional army and to gain more financial independence. In 1606, at his request, one of his councillors, Dr. Matthias Enzlin, drew up a memorandum on the treaty of Tübingen. He pointed out, as interpretations had differed, that the duke as the sole ruler was entitled to lay down the standards and the system for the future. With regard to a major war, he envisaged an agreement by which the Estates undertook to levy in advance the necessary amount, because it would be much too late if they started collecting money only at the beginning of hostilities: a not unreasonable proposal considering how imminent the outbreak of war appeared at that time. However, when this was submitted to the diet early in 1607, the Estates declared the treaty of Tübingen to be so clear, plain, and easy to understand that no further interpretation was required. As to war, in their opinion they were bound merely by the treaty and old custom to serve with their bodies and to provide transport, and to nothing else. When this reply was handed to the ducal *commissarii* they insisted that everybody should sign it with his name. Hereupon the *Amtleute*, who as usual attended the diet and at the outset had been reminded of their duties, refused to sign, and four *Amtleute* who had already signed withdrew their signatures 'so as to preserve unanimity among them'. In other ways too the presence of the *Amtleute* weakened the Estates. As one of the prelates wrote, they informed the duke of everything that went on and how everybody voted. Frederick was above all irate that the prelates, his appointed servants, voted against him. A few days after the negative reply of the Estates he dissolved the diet. His wrath was especially directed against the committees which he believed to be responsible for all opposition.

[1] Weidner, op. cit., p. 122; Grube, op. cit., pp. 259–60, 262–3.

They were usurping much more power than was their due and dared to claim something like a co-regency. After their customary resignation at the beginning of the diet, he continued, his consent and confirmation was not obtained for the new committees. For all these reasons he declared them dissolved. In future there was to be neither a Small nor a Large Committee, and their former members were not to act on their behalf. The Estates' permanent councillor was dismissed, and many threats were uttered against their leaders.[1]

A fortnight after the dissolution Frederick instructed some of his officials to travel round the country and to visit the towns and *Ämter*. These were to send their deputies to the next diet with full powers to agree to the necessary 'interpretation' of the treaty of Tübingen. They were further instructed to prevent the election of obnoxious deputies by certain towns, while only four out of fourteen prelates were summoned. The mission was largely successful. Most towns and *Ämter* issued the desired full powers, some of them expressly referring to the written declarations given to the ducal officials, and only a minority demanded in their instructions the redress of grievances. When this 'packed' diet assembled in March 1607, it proved extremely pliant. The Estates agreed to an 'interpretation' of the treaty of Tübingen: in case of a major war, instead of personal service a sufficient aid in money was to be granted to pay professional soldiers, but such a war was to be started only with the consent of the Estates. Having obtained this point, Frederick next proposed that the Estates should pay three-quarters of the costs of such a war, and he himself the remaining quarter, while many were willing only to concede two-thirds. Eventually a vote was taken, and for once the result of the vote was written down. Two prelates and thirty-five towns accepted unconditionally, the other two prelates and twenty-five towns accepted *conditionaliter* if the duke was not satisfied with two-thirds, and only three towns were against.[2]

---

[1] *Württembergische Landtagsakten unter Herzog Friedrich I.*, ii, nos. 291, 324, 327, 329, 332, pp. 511–14, 562, 572–6, 587–8, 594 (27 Nov. 1606, 27 Jan. to 3 Feb. 1607); Sattler, op. cit. v. 271–4; Grube, op. cit., pp. 266–9.

[2] *Württembergische Landtagsakten unter Herzog Friedrich I.*, ii, nos. 337, 338–41, 343, 348–9, pp. 604–6, 608–15, 627–33, and n. 2 (16 Feb. to 17 Mar. 1607). In 1608 the Estates called the meeting a *Zwangstag* in distinction to a *Landtag*: ibid., no. 332, p. 594.

Then Frederick proposed the payment of a tax on capital of 16 per cent. spread over twelve years, a considerable increase over current taxation, which met with opposition. The Estates declined such a semi-permanent tax, but were willing to take over another 600,000 guilders of the ducal debts. Frederick demanded more than twice that amount, and the Estates gradually increased their grant to almost that figure, 1,100,000, on condition that their grievances were redressed and, in particular, their committees were restored. This Frederick finally accepted, but with the reservation that two committees were unnecessary and that only the Small Committee was to be re-appointed. Yet when three members of the old committee were re-elected, he refused to accept them because they were head-strong and obstinate, and other names had to be submitted for his approval—a clear violation of the right of free election vested in the diet. If a vacancy occurred a name was likewise to be submitted for the ducal consent. New and inexperienced councillors were given to the Estates in place of their dismissed *advocatus*. That was not all. Frederick decreed that in future his subjects first had to take the oath of allegiance, and then only would the treaties and privileges be confirmed, while the treaty of Tübingen stipulated the opposite. Taxes were to be levied only with the consent of the diet; but in case of need the diet was to adopt a positive attitude, and privileges granted by the Emperor to increase customs and duties were to be valid without its assent—another departure from precedent which threatened to deprive the Estates of the power of the purse. These and other points were incorporated in a ducal 'inter-pretation' of the treaty of Tübingen which did not meet with any opposition.[1] Frederick seemed to be supreme. He proved, as Duke Ulrich had proved sixty years earlier, that a deter-mined ruler aiming at absolute government found it compara-tively easy to break the resistance of the Estates and to disregard their privileges.

Power was restored to the Estates by an accident, the death of Frederick in January 1608, only nine months after his

[1] Ibid. ii, nos. 353, 362, 365, 377, 382, 385, pp. 648, 660, 687–9, 690, 706, 745, 751, 760; no. 332, p. 594; p. 636, n. 1; p. 638 (20 Mar. to 13 Apr. 1607). The interpretation of 17 Mar. 1607 is printed in Reyscher, op. cit. ii, no. 49, pp. 272–84. Cf. above, p. 12, for the terms of the treaty of Tübingen.

triumph over them. His successor, John Frederick, needed the
Estates' support to be able to join the Union of Protestant princes
formed under the leadership of the Elector Palatine, for many
church lands and monasteries would have to be restored to the
Catholic Church if the Catholic interpretation of the clauses of
the religious peace were accepted. A few weeks after Frederick's
death the members of the old and the new Small Committee
met and discussed in what form the new duke should be asked
to confirm the privileges, 'because the treaty of Tübingen
stipulated that the Estates were not obliged to render homage
unless this treaty and their other liberties were first . . . confirmed'. They considered the 'interpretation' of 1607 to be null
and void. Yet their plan miscarried. A few days later homage
was rendered, first in Stuttgart, and then throughout the
country.[1] In April 1608 a diet was summoned in the course
of which the Estates granted 141,000 guilders and took over
another 300,000 guilders of the ducal debts. John Frederick in
his turn rescinded the 'interpretation' of 1607 which incorporated his father's gains, and promised to observe the terms of
the treaty of Tübingen with regard to the summoning of a diet,
the undertaking of a major war, the costs it would necessitate,
the confirmation of the liberties prior to the rendering of the
oath of allegiance, &c. The dismissed officials were reappointed;
the Large Committee was restored, as was the right of free
election to the committees, without the confirmation of the
duke, which was held to be an innovation.[2] The constitutional
revolution was undone. In the following month Württemberg
joined the Protestant Union, as John Frederick desired it.

The Estates then proceeded to take vengeance on the evil
councillors of the late duke whom they considered the chief
culprits. At the end of April they dismissed their secretary and
their receiver Johann Enzlin, ordered him to vacate his office
in their house and to hand over to a successor. The main tar-
get of their wrath was Enzlin's brother, the privy councillor Dr. Matthias Enzlin, against whom many complaints were
brought forward. At first he was retired with full salary. In May

---

[1] *Württembergische Landtagsakten unter Herzog Johann Friedrich, 1608–1620*, pp. 17 and
n. 3, 20, n. 1 (end of Feb. to early Mar. 1608).
[2] Ibid., nos. 20, 34, 37, pp. 57–59, 94–95, 108, and n. 2; Reyscher, op. cit.
ii, no. 51, pp. 291–7; Schneider, op. cit., p. 215; Grube, op. cit., pp. 274–6 (13–25
Apr. 1608).

a committee of inquiry was appointed to interrogate him. In August he was arrested and his property confiscated. He was then sentenced to be eternally imprisoned, to pay damages of 100,000 guilders and a fine of 11,000 guilders, and had to swear that he would abstain from any hostilities and intrigues. Because he did not keep this oath, a new inquiry was instituted in 1612, and a new court sentenced Enzlin to death for breaking his oath and on four other counts. The sentence was carried out in November 1613.[1] Above all, the growing dangers of the political situation and the deteriorating finances of the duke restored the Estates' influence. In 1610 his councillors informed John Frederick that, in view of the ever-increasing expenditure, it was inevitable to consult with the Estates about the diplomatic negotiations; otherwise they might refuse a contribution because, according to the treaty of Tübingen, they were not bound by alliances concluded without their knowledge. Agreement with the diet was indeed promoted when John Frederick justified to the Estates his membership of the Protestant Union, informed them of the causes that had induced him to join it, and explained the present condition of the league.[2]

Meanwhile the ducal debts continued to mount. Between 1608 and 1617 John Frederick sold or pawned lands to the value of 323,000 guilders and contracted debts to the tune of 1,541,000. For many of these the Small Committee acted as a guarantor, at a rate of interest of 5 or 6 per cent. In one instance the committee was not even in session, and the agreement of the members was obtained through messengers sent out at night and during the bad weather of December, as they put it. The credit of the Estates stood much higher than that of the prince and enabled him to borrow at low rates of interest. Their own debts, i.e. those they had taken over from the dukes, in 1616 amounted to 2,612,760 guilders of funded obligations, on which 153,650 guilders of interest were paid, and 460,356 guilders of current debts.[3] During the following years matters went from bad to worse through the debasement of the coinage to which John Frederick resorted as a way out of his financial difficulties.

[1] *Württembergische Landtagsakten unter Herzog Johann Friedrich*, pp. 22, n. 2, 111, 142–5.
[2] Ibid., p. 230; Sattler, op. cit. vi. 51–52; Grube, op. cit., p. 278.
[3] *Württembergische Landtagsakten unter Herzog Johann Friedrich*, pp. 174–5, 322, n. 4, 325–6, 333, n. 3, 558, n. 2.

In 1608 the thaler was still reckoned, as it had always been, at
1⅓ guilders; in 1614 and 1615 it was put at 1½, and in 1620 at
over 2 guilders; but in 1622 it rose to 8 and even 10 guilders.
The neighbouring districts were flooded with bad coins, but in
due course these ceased to be accepted and were driven back
into the duchy. Commerce was gravely impeded; goods were
bought up with the bad coins, and eventually exchanged only
in kind. It was not until 1623 that the price of the bad guilders
was officially fixed at one-sixth of their face value, and that of
the smaller coins at one-third or one-half.[1] The Estates indeed
used the occasion to pay back debts in debased coins, but they
reckoned that their losses through the stabilization of the currency amounted to about 250,000 guilders. As they took over
more and more ducal debts—1,100,000 guilders in 1618 and
200,000 in 1620—their expenditure on payment of interest rose
to 288,575 guilders by the end of 1621. At the diet of 1618 they
further agreed to raise a reserve of 200,000 guilders for the
defence of the country in case of foreign aggression, on the condition that it would not be spent without their approval, and
accordingly mercenaries were recruited in 1619.[2]

Thus Württemberg entered the Thirty Years War with a
constitution which was more than a hundred years old; the
Estates' influence had been restored after temporary defeats
under Duke Ulrich and Duke Frederick. It remained to be seen
how this constitution would work under the great stresses caused
by the war. Indeed, one important concession the Small Committee made almost unwittingly to John Frederick even before
these stresses became felt. In 1616 one of its members, the abbot
of Maulbronn, died. The ducal chancellor summoned the
committee and informed them that the duke wished his place
to be filled by the abbot of Bebenhausen: not that he wanted to
interfere in any way with their right of nomination, but merely
to ensure that the vacancy would be filled by a qualified man.
This the committee discussed and decided in favour of accepting

    [1] *Württembergische Landtagsakten unter Herzog Johann Friedrich*, pp. 412, n. 1, 472,
514, 515, n. 1; State Archives Stuttgart, *Tomus Actorum*, xxvi, p. 169; Sattler,
op. cit. vi. 193-4.
    [2] State Archives Stuttgart, *Tomus Actorum*, xxvi, pp. 394-402, 746; A 34-35,
Büschel 39 (list of 14 Dec. 1621); *Württembergische Landtagsakten unter Herzog Johann
Friedrich*, nos. 301, 323, 330-1, pp. 690-1, 740, 746, 748 (17 Aug. 1618 to 20 Apr.
1619).

the ducal nominee; but so as not to create the impression that they were forsaking their right of free election and carrying out princely orders, they nominated him *quasi proprio motu* and asked John Frederick to confirm the appointment! They thus not only gave way to their prince's wish, but gave up an important right by asking for the ducal confirmation: a fatal step which may have been due to the inexperience of their young secretary.[1]

In 1619 John Frederick returned to the point and demanded that in future they should request his formal confirmation in case of appointments to vacancies. A few months later the issue was decided in his favour. A councillor of Nürtingen, who was also a member of the Small Committee, was suspended from his offices because of an alleged slander of the duke. John Frederick then ordered the committee to appoint in his place a representative of the town of Leonberg. The committee, however, while accepting the suspension, elected the mayor of Kirchheim, 'because they were not tied to one place', and did not ask for the ducal confirmation of the election. John Frederick rebuked them for this omission, for 'nobody could be imposed upon him against his will'. He asserted that, if nothing was said in the *Ausschusstaat* of 1554 about his right of confirmation, this in no way diminished his prerogative, because whatever was not expressly mentioned remained a *jus* of the prince. The following day the Small Committee implicitly accepted this strange interpretation and expressed the hope that their election would find favour in his eyes and that he would not hesitate to approve it. They apparently hoped to save something by avoiding the obnoxious word 'confirmation'; yet by asking for the ducal 'approbation' they gave away the substance without a real fight. Later in the same year the Small Committee several times referred to the ducal 'approbation' as an old custom when notifying the prince of elections to either committee.[2] John Frederick had gained a point of great importance. If he was entitled to withhold his 'approbation', he might easily go one step further and press his candidates upon the committee. About the same time he also claimed the right of appointing all

---

[1] *Württembergische Landtagsakten unter Herzog Johann Friedrich*, pp. 498–9, and n. 1 (9 June 1616).

[2] Ibid., nos. 328, 349, 351, 354, 356, pp. 744, 746, n. 2, 778–80, 782, 783, and n. 1 (16 Apr. 1619, 19 Jan. to 4 Feb. 1620); State Archives Stuttgart, *Tomus Actorum*, xxiv, fos. 214–15, 510–1 (14 June and 4 Nov. 1620).

parsons and deacons: a new system was beginning. Probably
for similar reasons he preferred foreigners and noblemen as his
officials—a policy which was contrary to the treaty of Tübingen
—while hitherto most of the ducal councillors and officials had
been drawn from the ranks of the urban *Ehrbarkeit* which also
dominated the Estates.[1] If the duke wanted to gain greater
independence, he had to try and find his officials outside this
narrow group; but such a policy was bound to lead to new
conflicts with the Estates. For the time being, however, these
issues were overshadowed by the approaching perils of the
Thirty Years War.

v. *The Thirty Years War; Exile and Restoration*

Between the Schmalcaldic War and the Thirty Years War
Württemberg experienced more than seventy years of peace
and relative prosperity. These were followed by an even longer
period during which the duchy was frequently invaded and
occupied by foreign troops, first those of the Catholic League
and the Habsburgs, later those of Sweden and France. During
the Thirty Years War, and again during the wars of Louis XIV,
Württemberg suffered badly from heavy taxation, forcible
billeting and requisitioning, looting and burning by an ill-
disciplined soldiery or at the express orders of the king of France.
It is quite impossible to give precise figures for the war damages
or the losses of population or livestock. In 1652 the government
ordered a survey of all ruined houses and deserted lands throughout the duchy. In eleven *Ämter* the number of destroyed and
uninhabited houses exceeded that of the inhabited ones; in the
whole country there were still over 41,000 destroyed houses and
barns; about 310,000 *Morgen*, or about one-third of the total
area farmed, was still deserted four years after the end of the
war. According to a survey of 1655, there had been 3,004 houses
and barns in twelve small towns in 1629, while in 1655 their
number amounted to 1,874.[2]

In 1654 Württemberg claimed it had suffered damages of

[1] *Württembergische Landtagsakten unter Herzog Johann Friedrich*, nos. 112, 114, 264,
pp. 279, 285, 578, 609, n. 1, 783, n. 1.
[2] G. Mehring, 'Schädigungen durch den Dreissigjährigen Krieg in Altwürttemberg', *Württembergische Vierteljahrshefte für Landesgeschichte*, xix, 1910, pp. 449–
52; and ibid. xxx, 1921, p. 72; State Archives Stuttgart, *Tomus Actorum*, liv (detailed
report of 15 Dec. 1655).

118,742,864 guilders between 1628 and 1650; this figure included 60,000,000 caused by looting and burning, which clearly was nothing but a vague estimate. Probably the Estates' estimate of 6,797,537 guilders for the years 1638–50 came nearer to the truth; but this included only billeting and similar war costs and excluded looting, burning, and other exactions. The worst four years of the war were also excluded, from the autumn of 1634 to the autumn of 1638 when, after the battle of Nördlingen, the duke and government fled the country and it was occupied by Spanish and Bavarian troops, who levied contributions without consulting the Estates and squeezed many millions out of the duchy. In the Württemberg claim of 1654 these four years indeed accounted for six to seven times the damages inflicted during the preceding six or the succeeding twelve years (without taking into account the 60,000,000 guilders damages caused by looting and burning).[1] In 1652 the large majority of the *Ämter* reported that they had 58,865 burghers before 1634 and that only 19,071 remained—a loss of over two-thirds; while the remaining *Ämter* merely reported a loss of 18,546 burghers during the same period.[2] Even allowing for all possible errors and exaggerations the picture would seem very dark.

While only three diets were held during the first twelve years of John Frederick's reign, after 1620 almost annual diets became necessary on account of the growing political and military dangers. In June 1620—five months before the battle of the White Mountain—he proposed to the Estates that they should collect a reserve fund for an emergency, as they had done in 1591, and take over 300,000 guilders of his debts. They replied that it was impossible to grant these demands: the previous reserve had been granted by the Large Committee alone, which had caused much annoyance among the Estates, and it would hardly have been conceded by a whole diet. They assented, however, to levy 100,000 guilders for the maintenance of

---

[1] The figures are: 1628–34: 6,354,326 guilders; 1634–8: 45,007,000 guilders; 1639–50: 7,381,538 guilders: see Sattler, op. cit. ix. 134; State Archives Stuttgart, *Tomus Actorum*, I, pp. 2075–95; cf. von Stälin, 'Württembergische Kriegsschäden im dreissigjährigen Krieg', *Württembergische Vierteljahrshefte für Landesgeschichte*, viii, 1899, pp. 54 ff.

[2] Mehring, loc. cit. xix. 448. Ibid. xxx. 72, he assumes that by 1652 the population recovered to almost 40 per cent. of the pre-war figure from the lowest point which was reached in 1639.

mercenaries for ten months. If this proved insufficient, they would give powers to their committees, reinforced by two prelates and fourteen towns, to reach agreement with the duke, so that the whole diet need not be recalled. John Frederick replied that his army of 1,000 horsemen and 2,000 infantry cost him 30,000 guilders every month and that their pay was already two months in arrears. Therefore the grant was too small, and he needed a monthly aid of 20 or 25,000 guilders which should be raised by *extraordinaria media*, a general and equal tax on wine, corn, salt, meat, timber, and enterprises, excluding domestic needs. He was willing to let the troops be paid by deputies of the Estates, and he promised that he would not intervene in Bohemia, much less undertake anything against the Emperor Ferdinand II, the highest authority of the Reich. Thereupon the Estates increased their grant to 150,000 guilders and took over debts of 200,000, but again declined the excise on drink and corn, which would above all hit the poor. As this was a matter of the defence of the country, in their opinion the nobility ought to bear a share of the contribution: at least the noble estates and property inside the duchy which were not fiefs ought to be assessed.[1]

After further entreaties the Estates consented to pay the sum granted within eight, and eventually within seven months, whereupon John Frederick abandoned his plan of an excise for the time being. If the defence measures should continue for longer, the committees together with the duke should decide upon what was necessary. The duke declined, however, to give the undertaking desired by the Estates that he would not come back to the *extraordinaria media*, because it was impossible to know what extreme necessity might demand. He also sharply rebuked the Estates because of a complaint that the monasteries had been ordered to hand over their stocks to the *Kirchenkasten*, and not to pay them into the Estates' chest, thus separating the prelates from the towns and increasing the latter's share. He disclaimed any such intention and emphasized that the prelates belonged to the Estates only on grounds of their ecclesiastical positions, and not with regard to the administration of their

---

[1] State Archives Stuttgart, *Tomus Actorum*, xxiv, fos. 235–8, 240, 245, 252–3, 262–3, 269–70, 281, 287, 290, 299, 411 (17–30 June, 8 July 1620). Cf. above, p. 41, for the events of 1591.

estates. Such unnecessary complaints should cease, for this was none of their business. Four months later the committees duly extended the grant by 120,000 guilders payable within six months. John Frederick again insisted on the need to adopt *extraordinaria media* because the money was coming in very slowly. Meanwhile the Estates declared that they would not pay anything if he introduced this new tax on his own initiative. Before the grant expired, however, the crushing defeat of the Elector Palatine in Bohemia and the Palatinate induced the Protestant Union to dissolve itself and to pay off its troops. For this purpose the Estates paid another 80,000 guilders and made a loan of 118,000 guilders.[1] Württemberg was to enjoy another spell of peace.

Before the next diet met at the end of 1621, the old conflict about the ducal right of confirmation of elections to the Estates' committees flared up once more. The Small Committee filled a vacancy by electing the abbot of Maulbronn, a member of the Large Committee, in whose place they elected the abbot of Hirsau, and asked John Frederick that both should be summoned to future meetings. He thereupon reminded them sharply of his right of approbation and confirmation which they had to seek first, instead of adhering to their vain delusions. As the abbot of Bebenhausen wrote, the Small Committee had got into their prince's bad books, a feeling which they were in vain trying to assuage. When the diet met the Estates took the matter up, referred to the old custom of free election and the ducal promises of 1608, and begged for their retention. John Frederick sharply denied any intention of interfering with old customs. But he refused to let himself be degraded by his own subjects to the extent that he merely had to say 'yes' to an election, as if he were their inferior, without being able to say anything against a man nominated, or against one of the members if he were opposed to him and he wanted to change the composition of the committee. He urged that they should stop molesting him and turn to a discussion of the main business,[2] and thus implicitly claimed not only a right of confirmation, but the right of removing obnoxious members of the committees.

[1] Ibid. xxiv, fos. 329–30, 406, 414, 417, 419, 428, 459–61, 572–4, 582; xxv, fo. 160; A 34–35, *Büschel* 38a (3–20 July, 14–18 Nov. 1620, 19 May 1621).
[2] Ibid., *Tomus Actorum*, xxv, fos. 214, 222, 322–4, 370–2, 378–80 (1 Oct. to 1 Dec. 1621).

The Estates asked once more to be maintained in their rights, as conceded in 1608, and declined to start debating the main proposition. For this attitude they were sharply reprimanded. According to John Frederick, there was no example to be found in the whole of the Empire or any higher assemblies where the *praeposterus ordo* was observed of taking grievances before supply and of declining to discuss the main business before redress was obtained. But he did confirm those elected in their offices, with the reservation that this was not to be a precedent. A few days later a conference was held between some ducal representatives and the two committees to discuss the matter. Its result was that the Estates finally gave way. As a sign of respect towards their prince they would in future petition for his confirmation of those appointed to the committees, without any prejudice of their right of free election. John Frederick came back later to the underlying issue and once more refuted the idea of taking grievances before supply which could have but one meaning: that the prince would have to fulfil their wishes, and only thereafter would the Estates say 'yes' or 'no' to his proposals—a principle which he refused to accept. From that time onwards the Small Committee regularly submitted the names of those appointed to vacancies for confirmation, which was granted with equal regularity. The duke, having gained his point, made no attempt to withhold his assent or to press his candidates upon the committee. Likewise, when the latter notified him that they had chosen the young Johann Adam Dapp as their secretary, he merely reaffirmed his right of confirmation and did not make any difficulties about the appointment.[1]

At the opening of the diet of 1621 John Frederick asked for a grant of 200,000 guilders for the maintenance of 1,400 mercenaries. When the Estates eventually discussed this proposition they consented to pay 170,000 within ten months. The duke, however, insisted on his demand, of which 30,000 guilders were to be paid forthwith, and on powers which should enable the Large Committee to make further grants if need be. Otherwise he would have to introduce the *extraordinaria media*. There-

[1] State Archives Stuttgart, *Tomus Actorum*, xxv, fos. 384, 392–3, 398–402, 409, 461; xxvi, pp. 87, 175 (3–20 Dec. 1621, 11–15 Sept. 1623). Examples of ducal confirmations of elections may be found in ibid. xxv, fos. 593–4, 838–9; xxviii, fos. 19, 306–7; xxxi, fos. 939–40; xxxia, fos. 2–3; xxxiv, fo. 85 (from the years 1622–3, 1626–7, 1629, and 1631).

upon the Estates granted under protest the 200,000 guilders.
Yet John Frederick was not satisfied. He wanted to supplement
the antiquated militia with professional soldiers and professional officers, for whose pay he demanded 12,000 guilders a
month. This new request was rejected by the Estates' deputies
on the grounds that they were too few and had no powers of
consent. Thus the diet was recalled in May 1622. In addition
to the officers' pay John Frederick requested a considerable aid
to recruit 600 horsemen and 4,000 foot-soldiers; and the Estates
granted 180,000 guilders, payable within six months. When the
duke demanded a further 80,000 for the contingent of 2,000
men he had to furnish to the Swabian Circle, the Estates increased the grant to 210,000 guilders, and this was accepted by
John Frederick. He complained, however, that the committee
dominated the proceedings to such an extent that the decisions
were not even debated in the plenum, but merely formally
approved, the vote not even being recorded by the secretary,
so that there was no time for reflection. The Estates denied that
the committee's decisions were merely reported to the plenum
in the form of unanimous conclusions and asserted that there
were some days for thinking matters over and that the committee did not vote first, but that the votes were collected
according to their proper order of sitting.[1]

When the grant expired in November 1622, the Small Committee declined to extend it because it had no powers to consent
to any tax, or to concede anything that was against the Estates'
liberties. A diet had to be summoned from which John
Frederick demanded 60,000 guilders a month for an army of
5,000 foot-soldiers and 500 horsemen, which came to less than
half its total cost. The Estates would only grant 40,000 guilders
for ten months, which they subsequently increased to 45,000.
The ducal councillors advised the acceptance of this offer
because it would be well-nigh impossible to obtain more, and
also recommended permission for them to pay half in debased
coins because they would be unable to collect more good coins.
This necessitated another diet early in 1624, which consented to
levy 300,000 guilders, more than one-third of which fell on the

---

[1] Ibid. xxv, fos. 356, 447, 482–3, 522–4, 545, 550, 577–8, 589, 609, 613, 646,
652, 655; Sattler, op. cit. vi. 164, 178–9; Grube, op. cit., pp. 287–90 (26 Nov. 1621
to 6 June 1622).

Church and the monasteries. Again John Frederick threatened
to introduce a general and equal tax by virtue of his prerogative
as soon as he saw fit and denied that this would be contrary
to the terms of the treaty of Tübingen.[1] How unpopular this
continuous burden of taxation became was shown in 1625 when
another diet was summoned. So many towns petitioned to be
allowed to give full powers to a neighbouring town and to be
spared personal attendance that the summonses were withdrawn. No further diet was held until after John Frederick's
death in July 1628. By that time the war had definitely reached
Württemberg; for Imperial troops were quartered in the duchy
and over 195,000 guilders were levied for their maintenance in
the spring of 1628, the first indication of things to come.[2]

The subsequent five years of a ducal minority and the administration of the duchy by different guardians were used once
again by the Estates to reassert their influence. They complained
repeatedly about the large numbers of officials, councillors,
secretaries, musicians, alchemists, alleged artists, and servants
at the court and urged measures of economy. Another of their
grievances was that the subjects had to render the oath of
allegiance to the new duke before their privileges were solemnly
confirmed in writing—a procedure adopted because of the
dangerous times, but contrary to the treaty of Tübingen. By
1629 the ducal debts which the Estates had not taken over
amounted to nearly 4,000,000 guilders, including arrears of
interest of 428,000, so that a diet had to be summoned. Already
before it met the Small Committee petitioned the government
not to summon the *Amtleute*, with the purpose of saving costs,
and this request was granted. As recently as 1624 these ducal
officials had numbered over one-quarter of the urban deputies
present, providing the duke with an official group on which he
could rely.[3]

---

[1] State Archives Stuttgart, *Tomus Actorum*, xxv, fos. 724–5, 795–6, 812–15, 846,
858; xxvi, pp. 1122–4, 1165–73; A 34–35, *Büschel* 40, nos. 14, 18 (8 Nov. 1622 to
3 Mar. 1624). The cost of 5,000 foot-soldiers was 105,372 guilders a month, and of
500 horsemen 22,981 a month, together 128,353 guilders: ibid. xxv, fos. 799–803.

[2] Ibid. xxixa, fos. 534–56 (the figure includes deliveries in kind). Ibid. A 34–35,
Büschel 42, eleven petitions of towns to be spared attendance at the diet (27 July to
2 Aug. 1625). Cf. Grube, op. cit., pp. 293–4, putting forward a different argument
for the postponement of the diet.

[3] State Archives Stuttgart, *Tomus Actorum*, xxx, fos. 40–41, 93–94; xxxi, fos. 9–14,
61–66, 79; xxxia, fo. 6 (25 Aug. 1628 to 14 Mar. 1629). In 1624 there were 20

The diet soon took up this point. The Estates referred to the promise of 1514 that the *Amtleute* were no longer to be summoned, and declared that they did not belong to the Estates, could not vote in their name, only attended the diet *pro forma*, at great cost to the towns, and could therefore bring no advantage to the government. They urged that the *Amtleute* should not be summoned any longer, and that the ducal War Council (*Kriegsrat*) should be abolished. The duke's guardian declared himself willing to fulfil these wishes if the Estates took over the entire debts. During the period of guardianship he would conclude no alliance and enter into no agreement without the advice of the Estates, or at least of the Small Committee. He was not unfavourably inclined towards their wish that the *Amtleute* should no longer be summoned, but could not see how he could bind his ward and future dukes. Most of the expenditure on the War Council had already ceased, and he hoped it would come to its end in due course. The Estates in their reply offered to take over 2,000,000 guilders of the debts, but more they considered impossible; they insisted on their point regarding the *Amtleute*. This was taken *ad referendum* by the chancellor and conceded after a few days for the period of the minority, and thus accepted by the Estates. They also declared their willingness to pay the interest of 25,000 guilders a year on another half-million of ducal debts, while the government wished them to take over 3,000,000 in all.[1]

The proceedings were interrupted for seven months. When they were resumed at the end of 1629, the Estates somewhat increased their offer. Under certain conditions they would pay the interest on 600,000 (instead of 500,000) guilders, and this was accepted by the government, together with the earlier offer of taking over debts of 2,000,000 guilders. In their turn the government promised not to burden the domains or the Estates with any more debts, not to pawn or to sell any revenues, castles, towns or villages. Whoever contravened this could be impeached by the Estates for violating the *leges fundamentales* of the duchy. To the promises regarding the conclusion of alliances

---

Amtleute among 75 deputies, in 1621 25 *Amtleute* among 118 deputies: ibid. xxv, fos. 350–6; xxvi, pp. 683–94. For the issue in general, see above, pp. 13, 15, 26–27.
[1] Ibid., xxxi, fos. 88–89, 91, 139, 146, 151–2, 223, 226, 233, 250, 257, 291, 294; A 34–35, *Büschel* 45a (14 Mar. to 9 May 1629); Grube, op. cit., pp. 297–9.

and the summoning of the *Amtleute* was added an undertaking that no major alteration in general ordinances would be made without the knowledge of the Small Committee, thus allowing this body a definite share in legislation. Another important wish of the Estates was met: the privy council of the duke was brought into the framework of the constitution by the *Recess* at the conclusion of the diet of 1629, and its members had to swear to observe this *Recess*.[1] In this way the Württemberg privy council attained a character quite different from that of other principalities, and the Estates' influence over it was permanently guaranteed. The *Amtleute*, although only excluded from the diet for the duration of the ducal minority, never again attended a diet, and thus another old demand of the Estates was fulfilled.

In this way the Estates used the time of the duke's minority and a period of political uncertainty to strengthen their position. In particular the Small Committee became increasingly associated with the machinery of government. In the summer of 1631 they were asked by the regent to decide upon the issue of war or peace. In December 1631 they were consulted by the government as to whether the protection offered by Gustavus Adolphus should be accepted, how the Imperial troops could be removed as the king of Sweden demanded, and regarding the answer to his letter. In their reply the Small Committee emphasized their inexperience in affairs of the Empire, but pronounced in favour of accepting the proffered protection and asked for the summoning of the Large Committee, which adopted the same attitude. Further meetings urged the regent to conclude an alliance with Sweden. In the following year the Small Committee were consulted by the Duchess Barbara Sophia as the guardian of her son, the young Duke Eberhard, and asked whether it was advisable to let him participate in the business of government. To this the committee agreed because the same had been done under the previous guardian and in earlier instances, as they pointed out in a detailed memorandum. A few months later, when Eberhard reached the age to take over the government, the duchess again asked the Small Committee to advise how this could best be done. The Large

[1] State Archives Stuttgart, *Tomus Actorum*, xxxi, fos. 814, 816–18; A 34–35, *Büschel* 45*a*; Reyscher, op. cit. ii, no. 56, pp. 328–39; Sattler, op. cit. vii. 17–18; Schneider, op. cit., p. 233; Wintterlin, op. cit. i. 63–64; Grube, op. cit., pp. 299, 303–4.

Committee suggested that he should be proclaimed and presented as the prince and asked for the confirmation of their privileges according to the treaty of Tübingen, for the oath of allegiance had already been taken. When the Small Committee received the draft of the confirmation, they objected that Eberhard had not yet assumed the government because there had been no public proclamation and the privileges had not yet been confirmed. The ducal councillors agreed that the confirmation should precede the assumption of government, and the draft was accordingly altered and signed on 2 May 1633. All this was carefully noted for the information of future generations.[1]

Meanwhile the duchy had to pay larger and larger sums to the Imperial troops billeted in the country. In the spring of 1630 they received nearly 73,400 guilders a month, not counting deliveries in kind, while units which had been transferred elsewhere received arrears of 38,800 guilders monthly, making a total of about 125,000 guilders a month inclusive of corn deliveries. From May 1631 onwards 52,400 guilders a month were levied. In July 1631 an Imperial army invaded the duchy and demanded 270,000 guilders monthly. After some weeks, however, its commander was induced to remove his troops, excepting twelve companies, for whose maintenance 28,000 guilders a month were to be levied, in addition to 10,000 for the Emperor and a present of 15,000 for the commander. In spite of all entreaties, the Estates' councillor, Dr. Joachim Faber, was unable to obtain better conditions: these were the Emperor's orders, otherwise the army would remain. During that one month they consumed 286,000 guilders. The last Imperial troops did not leave before January 1632 when Gustavus Adolphus stood near the Rhine. The arrears of unpaid taxes amounted to over 1,300,000 guilders, compared with 76,000 two years previously. In spite of these burdens the Estates, at Duke Eberhard's first diet, not only adhered to their grant of 2,600,000 made in 1629, but agreed to take over another 400,000 guilders of ducal debts with interest and capital.[2]

[1] State Archives Stuttgart, *Tomus Actorum*, xxxiv, fos. 800–1, 813–18, 822, 834–43; xxxvi, fos. 6–7, 44–46, 280–1, 283–4, 289–90; *Landtags-Protokolle*, i, 3 Nov. 1632; Grube, op. cit., pp. 305–6; Sattler, op. cit. vii, no. 19, pp. 86–88 (13–24 Dec. 1631, 4 Mar. to 2 May 1633).

[2] State Archives Stuttgart, *Tomus Actorum*, xxxii, fos. 23–25, 177–80; xxxiii, fos. 151–3, 409–12, 548; xxxiv, fos. 190–6, 418, 454–61, 672–729; xxxv, fos. 55–70;

This, however, was not sufficient for the needs of the government which had to pay contributions to the Swedish army and to maintain two regiments of mercenaries. Early in 1634 Eberhard informed the Large Committee that, unless larger grants were forthcoming, it would become inevitable to levy taxes by the military, with the consequent excesses and great dangers to the liberties. Alternatively he would have to take resolutions for the country's benefit on the basis of his princely authority. The Swedish contribution was like a tax for the Empire which the Estates were obliged to pay, and he therefore hoped that they would assent to the *extraordinaria media*. When the diet assembled in June, the Estates' councillor, Dr. Joachim Faber, supported this idea on the grounds that the money would flow into their own chest, and that they could rescind the tax whenever they pleased. If they did not consent to it, Eberhard would introduce it *ex officio*, which would sow the seed of distrust in the subjects' hearts and lead to the ruin of the country. Two weeks later the Estates, with similar arguments, sent a circular to all towns and *Ämter*, asking them to send within ten days full powers to the Small Committee, so that the *extraordinaria media* could be introduced without delay. The powers were duly sent, and the Estates then granted the new tax, on condition that it should be paid into their chest, that it should be regulated and controlled by their organs, and that they should be spared any further grants.[1]

When matters had proceeded thus far, however, the diet was interrupted by the approach of the Imperial and Bavarian army which had conquered Ratisbon. The deputies were permitted to return home. The diet was adjourned, to be resumed only after a lapse of more than four years; for the great Imperial victory at Nördlingen in August 1634 shattered the Swedish power in Germany and forced Eberhard and his government into exile. Imperial troops once more occupied Württemberg and showed scant respect for the Estates and their privileges. Neither the diet nor the committees met until the restoration of the duke by the Emperor Ferdinand III in October 1638.

xxxvii, fo. 142. On 5 Jan. 1630 the tax arrears amounted to 76,416 guilders, on 27 Apr. 1632 to 1,301,749 guilders.

[1] State Archives Stuttgart, *Tomus Actorum*, xxxvii, fos. 298–9, 403, 613–24, 664–6, 694–5, 722, 773, 798–802; Sattler, op. cit. vii. 102–3; Grube, op. cit., pp. 308–9 (30 Jan. to 19 July 1634).

For four years the country's constitution was in abeyance. Yet this was not entirely the case, for Eberhard was followed into his exile at Strasbourg by deputies of the Estates. In September 1634 three members of the Small Committee—the mayor of Tübingen and the prelates of Bebenhausen and Lorch—and another prelate from the Large Committee left the country, and with them the Estates' councillor, their secretary, and the two receivers. They took with them their most important documents and charters as well as their ready cash. They reached Strasbourg after a perilous journey during which many insults were heaped upon them and members of their own escort threatened to pay themselves from their treasure.[1] While at Strasbourg, they continued to advise Eberhard on matters of high policy. They counselled him to join the peace of Prague which the Emperor was concluding with some German Protestant princes, and they advocated not too close an understanding with Sweden, which was continuing the war against the wishes of many German Protestants. Later, however, these functions of the deputies were curtailed by the death of their most prominent members. The mayor of Tübingen died early in 1635 and was followed by the Estates' councillor, Dr. Faber, and the two prelates from the Small Committee in 1637. The cash in their chest dwindled quickly, and the remainder was handed to Eberhard after the death of the two prelates.[2]

The Estates' secretary, Dapp, remained in exile some time longer and, before his return home, deposited the documents and records in safe custody, from which he collected them again after the end of the war.[3] In this way continuity was preserved, and so was the dual character of the Württemberg constitution during the worst period of military rule in the country. The good understanding between the duke and the Estates was not broken; both shared the bitter experience of exile and the last pennies they had been able to save. This was also shown in Eberhard's later attitude. After his restoration one of his privy councillors expressed the surprise of certain people that the duke so warmly took the side of the Estates who had lost all

[1] State Archives Stuttgart, *Tomus Actorum*, xxxviii, fos. 2–3, 27, 49–73, 139–40.
[2] Ibid. xxxviii, fos. 35–49, 73, 96–97, 108–28, 317, 321, 334 (31 Dec. 1634 to 23 July 1637). For the peace of Prague, cf. below, pp. 231–2.
[3] Ibid. lviii, pp. 293–4 (testimonial for Dapp of Oct. 1658).

their privileges through the battle of Nördlingen, and warned him that the Emperor was trying to negotiate separately with the Estates. This attitude Eberhard did not share, for in his opinion prince and Estates were *correlativa*, so that the ruin of the Estates would bring about that of the prince.[1] This truly was an exceptional attitude for a German ruler of the seventeenth century, even if allowance is made for the possibility that through this explanation the duke wanted to influence the Estates against the Emperor.

Meanwhile Württemberg suffered terribly under the occupation. Shortly before his restoration Eberhard in moving words begged Ferdinand III to remedy the plight of his country. Both the General Commissariat and the Imperial government in Stuttgart were endeavouring to ruin it, to make it completely deserted, and to impoverish the few remaining inhabitants of the principal towns, with the consequence that they were starving and perishing, or else running away into bitter misery. That these complaints were not unjustified was shown by the resulting Imperial order to the government to treat the inhabitants more leniently so that they should not be utterly ruined, because it was evident that they could not pay anything more.[2] Two months later Ferdinand III issued another order, this time to his commanding general. He protested in strong terms that, because of the soldiery's unparalleled methods of looting and tyranny, the countryside was deserted, all people seeking refuge in the towns and perishing miserably there. He complained also that the poor burghers of the towns were not secure either, but were sucked to the marrow of their bones by the commandants and officers, who exacted higher maintenance than their entitlement, imposed a toll on everything going into or coming out of the towns, and, by letting the indiscipline of the soldiers go unpunished, encouraged them to still further licence. In this way, he pointed out, the Empire was becoming virtually depopulated, and the towns and villages were no longer in a position to contribute to the preservation of the Imperial army, garrisons, and fortresses. He considered that all

---

[1] State Archives Stuttgart, *Tomus Actorum*, xxxix, pp. 350–1 (3 Nov. 1638).

[2] Sattler, op. cit. vii, nos. 57, 59, pp. 212–15 (25 June, 7 Aug. 1638). Cf. ibid., no. 41, pp. 151–2, a report of 1636 about the state of the duchy, and no. 69, pp. 232–4, a list of the ruined and damaged towns and districts of 1640.

the excesses had been left unpunished for too long. The general, therefore, was ordered to have these matters remedied, to depose and punish the commandants of towns according to their deserts, to dismiss superfluous officers, and to insist on the restitution of what they had taken illegally, or obtained by blackmail. A similar Imperial order was sent to the quarter-master-general because he levied simultaneously the costs of quartering during winter and summer in the district of Cannstatt, arrested the mayor and other burghers, and closed the town gates for some time. No wonder that at his restoration about that time Duke Eberhard found the duchy 'not only totally deserted of people and cattle, but so emptied of all food and sustenance that his ducal chamber was as it were deprived of every piece of bread . . . while he was unable to see how his few remaining subjects . . . could bear the burden any longer. . .'.[1]

In the autumn of 1638 emissaries of the Emperor Ferdinand III summoned a diet to prepare the restoration of Duke Eberhard. It was the Emperor's express wish that the restoration and the conditions attached to it should be ratified and agreed to by the Estates. These, however, were once more limited to the towns only: for during the occupation the monasteries had been restored to the Catholic Church, and the religious orders were reinstalled, a state of affairs which Eberhard had to recognize before his restoration. It was only at the peace of Westphalia that these conditions were cancelled and that the monasteries reverted to the Protestant prelates who had occupied them since the mid-sixteenth century. Not until 1651 were the fourteen Protestant prelates again summoned to the diet.[2]

Only thirty-six towns appeared at the diet of 1638. One of the first steps they took was to confirm the returned Johann Adam Dapp as their secretary, their councillor having died at Strasbourg. They then ratified and sealed the treaty with the Emperor regarding the restoration of Eberhard. The Estates' committees had shrunk sadly during the preceding four years:

[1] State Archives Stuttgart, *Tomus Actorum*, xxxix, pp. 243-4, 591-6 (instruction for the ducal embassy to the Elector of Bavaria of 25 Oct., and Imperial orders of 17 Oct. and 18 Nov. 1638).

[2] Ibid. xxxix, pp. 8-14, 80, 621; xliv, fo. 419; xlix, pp. 5-7. The Emperor expressly referred to the precedent of 1547 when Charles V had insisted on the ratification of the restoration terms by the towns: ibid., xxxix, p. 87, and above, pp. 22-23.

only one member of the Small Committee was present and two
of the Large Committee. These three met and, in a very irregular fashion, filled the vacancies by electing the two remaining
members of the Large Committee and the mayors of Stuttgart
and Tübingen on to the Small Committee, leaving the remaining seat to the mayor of Urach who had not been summoned
to the diet. The three survivors also elected the mayors of six
towns to the Large Committee and asked Eberhard to confirm
all these appointments. The Estates' machinery having been
restored, Eberhard proposed the adoption of the *extraordinaria
media*, which had been granted by the diet of 1634, but not been
introduced because of the government's flight and the occupation. The Estates had the relevant documents and arguments
of their former councillor read to them whereupon long discussions and *rationes pro et contra* ensued. It was then decided
to consult an outside expert. Only after some weeks did the
Estates consent to the proposed indirect tax on corn, meat, fats,
cattle, salt, wine, timber, merchandise, and sales of land and
securities, provided that their privileges were continued, that
they retained the administration of the tax and the right to
rescind it, that the money collected would be spent on their own
as well as the duke's expenditure, and that the tax officials would
take an oath to the prince and to the Estates. When these vital
conditions had been accepted the towns granted full powers to
the Large Committee to act on their behalf in all excise matters.[1]

During the last ten years of the war the Estates' committees
further strengthened their position. In spite of the lapse of their
privileges during the preceding four years, their influence was
not seriously impaired, as was the case in other German principalities. Duke Eberhard needed their support and co-operation
to enable him to pay the remaining Imperial garrisons, to carry
the burdens of the administration, to regain possession of the
monasteries, and strengthen his hand at the Imperial diet and
at the peace negotiations at Osnabrück. In 1644 he himself told
the representatives of the Estates through the mouth of the
governor that he did not consider them as a party, but as

---

[1] State Archives Stuttgart, *Tomus Actorum*, xxxix, pp. 17–28, 106, 125, 129–31,
151, 166–7, 170, 175–83, 188, 259–86, 405–12, 422–7, 532–41; A 34–35, *Büschel* 49;
Reyscher, op. cit. xvii, no. 74, pp. 162–5; Grube, op. cit., pp. 315–16 (8 Oct. to
19 Dec. 1638).

councillors, that what was discussed between their representatives and his advisers should be referred back to the plenum and debated there until a decision was reached, and that this should then be sent back to him for ratification—a relationship entirely different from that existing at that time in Bavaria, or Brandenburg, or Jülich and Berg. In May 1639 the post of Councillor of the Estates, vacant since 1637, was filled again by the election of Professor Rimmelin, Vice-Chancellor of the University of Tübingen. In 1641 the Small Committee appointed two of its members as assessors to the High Court (*Hofgericht*) at Tübingen. A few months later it filled the two ecclesiastical vacancies among its own ranks by the election of two dispossessed prelates; and in 1644 two more Protestant clergymen were elected to the Large Committee.[1]

When in 1641 the town of Stuttgart elected its present mayor instead of its former mayor to the Small Committee, the committee pointed out to the town that this was contrary to the old custom because the town had no right of election. Nevertheless, they accepted the new mayor as a member because they had no objections against him. In the following year another member of the Small Committee, the mayor of Urach, died. In his place they then elected the mayor of Kirchheim, and when he died soon afterwards, the mayor of Nürtingen. Urach petitioned to be left in possession of the seat on the Small Committee, claiming that it had occupied it *immemoriali tempore*, but had to be content with a seat on the Large Committee. In 1649, when another vacancy on the Small Committee occurred, Urach renewed its request for a seat, claiming that it had been represented on the committee for more than a century before 1642, that it was the third principal town of the duchy and a former princely residence; but it acknowledged that the committee were entirely free in their choice. The committee, however, did not reply and elected the mayor of Göppingen to the vacancy.[2] The Small Committee in 1641 were also granted the right to assemble in Stuttgart on the death of the ruler and to arrange that the treaty of Tübingen and the other liberties and funda-

[1] State Archives Stuttgart, *Tomus Actorum*, xxxix, pp. 696–7; xl, pp. 238–9, 636, 651; xli, pp. 2536–8 (May 1639 to Mar. 1644).

[2] Ibid. xl, pp. 569–72; xli, pp. 5–7, 15–16, 21, 134–5; xlv, fos. 742–5; xlvi, fos. 27–29 (Dec. 1641, Nov. 1642, Mar. to June 1649).

mental laws were confirmed before the oath of allegiance was rendered.[1]

Meanwhile Imperial and Bavarian troops continued to be billeted on the inhabitants, their strength varying from a few hundred men to three or four regiments; but the burden was alleviated by the fact that the ordinary civil authorities were now responsible for the repartition and collection of the taxes. In the summer of 1640 only 11,000 guilders a month were levied, but during the following winter the figure rose to 38,000. In the winter of 1641-2 over 5,000 guilders a month were levied for the garrisons of seven fortresses, and more for other units; in addition, 110,000 guilders were paid to the Empire as 'Roman months', and half that sum was granted to Eberhard. Even such sums proved a heavy burden for the devastated country, especially because the yield of the excise remained far below expectations. In 1640 the Small Committee resolved to put an additional half-guilder on each pail of wine, for which purpose all cellars had to be visited and all stores of wine listed in town and country, although the majority of the towns were rather doubtful about new taxation.[2] Twelve months later they expressed themselves much more forcefully in favour of lower taxes, and especially against a continuation of the excise which prevented people from coming into the duchy. The Large Committee had to allot to the arguments against the excise a prominent place among the grievances. It was unbearable, they declared, that bread and even the food of the youngest was liable to be taxed; the hard-working poor often did not own the penny demanded by the mills; all imports were made more expensive, and all commerce was impeded; and to escape the excise many had their corn ground outside the towns in the mills of noblemen. The ducal reply made no attempt to deny these assertions. It admitted that the excise had not achieved its object and that nothing would have been obtained if military force had not been used; but it advised careful reflection before the excise was revoked. In the end,

[1] State Archives Stuttgart, *Tomus Actorum*, xl, pp. 620-3 (*Ausschusstaat* of 16 Dec. 1641).
[2] Ibid. xxxix, p. 1307; xl, pp. 112-19, 172-8, 731-2, 1712-19; xliii, fos. 402-3 (June 1640 to July 1645): all this without the church lands and the monasteries. For the strength of the occupying forces, see ibid. xxxix, pp. 721-2, 1171-5, 1289-90; xl, pp. 183-6, 1718-19.

however, Eberhard had to give way. Early in 1642 the excise was rescinded, after the Estates had granted him 55,000 guilders.[1]

In the following year the towns, as it seems forced by pressure from below, again asserted their influence over the committees. A ducal circular instructed all the towns and *Ämter* to give full powers to the Large Committee to discuss and to decide, without any reference back, what would be propounded to them for the needs of the country. Several towns, however, which were not represented on the committee, declined to do so and sent their own deputies to hear the ducal proposition, referring to their previous complaints about oppressive taxes. They thus compelled the government to convert the meeting of the Large Committee into a diet, but it was attended by only thirty-one towns. To these the government proposed, to avoid the ruin and division of the duchy and the destruction of its liberties, the reintroduction of the *extraordinaria media* out of sheer necessity. Other rulers also had been forced to resort to unusual means because laws and treaties became invalid in an emergency. The Estates, after careful deliberation, pronounced against the excise because it would inhibit whatever little trade remained and cause total ruin. Eberhard, however, insisted that an indirect tax did not only hit the poor, but also the wealthy and the foreigners, that extraordinary times demanded exceptional remedies, that with a general improvement the excise would be rescinded, and that a precedent would not be created. Some further concessions were made: the excise was introduced for one year only, levied only on wine and corn, imported goods, and goods sold to foreigners, on foreign merchants and travellers, and on sales of real property, and it was to be paid into the chest of the Estates. A few months later, however, it was extended by decree to beer bought in taverns, after an attempt by correspondence to obtain the agreement of the Small Committee to this step had failed: thus proving how justified were the fears of the Estates.[2]

[1] Ibid., *Landtags-Protokolle*, ii, 15 Dec. 1640 (instead of 1641); *Tomus Actorum*, xl, pp. 719-22, 770-1, 791, 1070-1; Sattler, op. cit. viii. 32; no. 13, pp. 57-58 (23 Dec. 1641 to 18 Feb. 1642).

[2] State Archives Stuttgart, *Tomus Actorum*, xli, pp. 1337, 1349-61, 1369, 1377, 1401-10, 1449-52, 1673-5, 2044, 2108-10, 2364, 2466-74, 2508-15, 2936-45; Grube, op. cit., pp. 318-19; Sattler, op. cit. viii. 70 (24 Oct. 1643 to 11 July 1644). Beer was taxed at 15 *kreuzer* a pail, compared with 48 *kreuzer* on wine.

Meanwhile, owing to the movements of the Bavarian and other armies, Württemberg suffered once more the billeting of troops, and their looting and indiscipline. For the six summer months of 1644 the cost was put at 456,787 guilders, and for the following six winter months at 250,835. In 1645 the situation improved, but 1646 brought much heavier burdens. In 1645 the government approached the members of the Small Committee with the proposal to continue the excise and to obtain powers to do so from the Large Committee; but as the Large Committee were legally unable to grant such powers, the proposal was addressed instead to all towns and *Ämter*. When the Small Committee met in November these powers had not yet arrived. Eventually, however, the majority did grant the requested powers on account of the prevailing extreme calamity, although the project was universally hated. On the following day the Small Committee accepted the excise once more, which was to last thirteen months and to cease automatically at the end of 1646. When this term approached, however, it was prolonged until further notice.[1] Again it was proved how easily the excise could become a semi-permanent tax, in spite of all the initial precautions taken by the Small Committee.

To the salaries of the two receivers of the Estates were added 50 guilders each for their labours in connexion with the excise; for their other work they each received 250 guilders. Their salaries had trebled since the late sixteenth century, corresponding to the general rise of prices, and equalled that of the colonel who commanded the garrison of Stuttgart. The secretary then received 175 guilders a year, compared with 50 at the earlier date; but as Dapp was also one of the receivers, his salary amounted to 375 guilders, and to 475 guilders from 1646 onwards, because of the 'daily growing amount of business' for which he was responsible. An excise inspector, appointed in 1645, received only 100 guilders a year. This was the same as the salary of a second councillor, engaged by the Small Committee in 1648 because of the growing burden of work; but he also received one guilder for every day he attended its meetings. The members of the Small Committee themselves received only

[1] State Archives Stuttgart, *Tomus Actorum*, xlii, pp. 1543–5; xliii, fos. 69–70, 73, 75–76, 97–101, 158–62, 402–4; Reyscher, op. cit. xvii, no. 87, p. 178, and n. 113 (8 Aug. 1645 to 24 July 1646).

50 guilders a year, hardly more than in the sixteenth century; while the members of the Large Committee had no salaries, but were granted travelling expenses of up to 3 guilders a day and a *per diem* allowance of 0·4 guilders while attending meetings of the committee. If the meeting was held in place of a diet with powers to act in its place, another half guilder *per diem* was added to this sum.[1]

At the end of 1647 the government attempted to induce the Small Committee to make a further grant, only to meet with a new refusal. Thus the Large Committee had to be called, and, as in 1643, the towns and *Ämter* were ordered to empower the committee to reach a decision without any reference back. This time, however, a proviso was added that, if the towns desired to attend themselves, they could send their deputies at their own expense. Nineteen towns made use of this permission, five of them empowering the mayor of another town to act on their behalf. Four of them were already represented by a member of the Small or the Large Committee, but sent a second deputy; and ten sent their own representatives, so that the meeting was attended by the deputies of twenty-two towns in all. Clearly, there was a certain distrust of the committees and their actions in the country, and their attitude was considered too pliant by some towns. This feeling had to be taken into account by the members of the committees if they did not want to lose the confidence of the towns, and their back was to some extent stiffened by this pressure from below. For the time being the excise was continued, but the yield remained small, amounting to only 93,200 guilders in the course of nearly six years.[2]

The conclusion of peace in 1648 did not bring an immediate improvement of the country's situation. The foreign armies remained until 1650. A war indemnity of 7,500,000 guilders had to be paid to Sweden, over 230,000 of which had to be furnished by Württemberg. The Small Committee declared it virtually impossible to raise one-third of this sum immediately, as the officials attending to the forcible levying of taxes would testify. They deemed it better to borrow at high rates of interest

[1] State Archives Stuttgart, *Tomus Actorum*, xliii, fos. 130–3, 364, 641; xliv, fos. 287, 329; xlix, pp. 712–13 (Nov. 1645 to May 1651). For the salaries in the sixteenth century, see above, pp. 31–32.

[2] Ibid. xliv, fos. 154–5, 177, 362 (Dec. 1647 to Mar. 1648). The six years are: 11 Nov. 1638 to 23 Apr. 1642 and 1 Dec. 1645 to Mar. 1648.

than to force people to sell their draught-animals and cattle. Yet the Estates were still able to borrow large sums at a mere 6 per cent. rate of interest. Their total debts of 4,822,000 guilders only demanded 241,100 guilders in annual interest. Their credit still stood high, although the payment of interest on many debts had been suspended since 1626. At the end of 1646 the Small Committee pointed out to the duke that all the grants, including the excise, had expired twelve months ago, that they strongly objected to further extensions and could not grant any for constitutional reasons. They indicated that there were murmurs in the country that they were exceeding their powers, and begged to be spared any further prolongation of the taxes, which should be proposed to a full diet, or at least to a meeting of the Large Committee with full powers to act. A few months earlier the Small Committee had protested that taxes were levied by the receivers without their prior knowledge and consent, in consultation with only those members who were present in Stuttgart. They had objected that this was against the country's constitution, and affirmed that such practices ought to cease.[1]

In this way the Small Committee vigorously asserted its rights and insisted that the constitutional proprieties should be observed as soon as the emergency reached an end. The Estates' privileges had weathered the storm of the Thirty Years War, although they had been temporarily in abeyance. It remained to be seen how they would develop during the period of peace which followed, which was interrupted by new wars and invasions and marked by continuous attempts of the princes to create a small standing army.

VI. *The Attempts to establish a Standing Army; the Wars of Louis XIV*

The relationship between the German princes and the Estates was influenced in many ways by the military and economic disasters of the Thirty Years War and the subsequent French

---

[1] State Archives Stuttgart, *Tomus Actorum*, xliv, fos. 504–5, 530–1; xlv, fos. 289–91, 296, 842–4; xlvi, fos. 193–5, 446–7, 487 (15 Aug. 1648 to 19 Dec. 1649). On 18 Aug. 1649 the Estates' debts amounted to 4,821,938 guilders, and the annual interest they had to pay to 241,096 guilders.

wars. On the side of the princes there developed the tendency to make themselves more independent, to disregard out-of-date privileges and liberties, to copy the occupying powers and their methods of levying taxes by the military, to raise a standing army which would enable them to play a more conspicuous part at home and abroad, and if need be to intimidate their own subjects. The Estates, on the other hand, were bound to doubt the usefulness of such an army against the might of France or of Spain, especially in the frontier regions of Germany which lay open to any invader. They were equally bound to fear that such an army, once agreed to, might easily grow and their own liberties diminish in proportion. In the eighteenth century a Württemberg historian wrote: 'When finally the Estates consented to pay taxes for the maintenance of a few hundred guardsmen, this was as good as if they assented to 6,000 men; and as the guards grew in numbers, so, on the analogy of the history of nearly all German provinces, the memory of the Estates' liberties was bound to disappear. . . .'[1] He might have added that the same lesson could have been learned from the events of the Puritan Revolution or of the reign of James II.

If the Estates were anxious to preserve their liberties and their power of the purse, their physical ability to meet the growing tax demands of their ruler was very seriously affected by the devastations and the economic decline of the seventeenth century, which equally diminished their power of resistance. They were indeed in an unenviable position: unable to deny that many princely claims were justified, unwilling to risk an open conflict in which they were unlikely to be victorious, fully aware of the difficulties and often the impossibility of raising large sums, and having to listen to the groans of the people. On the one hand they were blamed by their prince for insufficient grants, and on the other by the population for too liberal grants. One cannot help pitying them and sympathizing with their helplessness in the face of grave dangers. Perhaps their counsels and their methods were becoming outdated in the age of rising military monarchies. Yet their opposition to petty despotism and the selfishness of numerous princes served the interests of their country. What is more, the policy also

[1] Ludwig Thimotheus Freiherr von Spittler, *Sämtliche Werke*, v, Stuttgart and Tübingen, 1828, p. 405 (written in 1783).

served the future interests of their country by keeping alive the
spirit of constitutional government during a period when constitutional government was fading away or being destroyed in
so many countries of Europe. In a more mundane way, the
Estates not only prevented the worst extravagances of some
princes, and saved the country many useless expenses, but they
also achieved one result which was much more important. If
the princes had had their way, many a German state would
have acquired an army much too large for its size, a constant
menace to its neighbours, and imposing a well-nigh insupport-
able burden on its inhabitants. Against the might of Louis XIV
such armies, however large, would have been insufficient,
especially in view of the permanent hostility between the princes
of the Empire, but they would have been extremely useful in
their mutual quarrels. That most German states did not acquire
such large forces was, above all, due to the fact that the Estates
succeeded in preserving some of their influence and in frustrat-
ing the more ambitious schemes of their princes. In doing
so, they also preserved much of Germany. If more princes
had followed the Hohenzollerns' example, eighteenth-century
Germany would have become a permanent battlefield, and the
Thirty Years War might have been followed by a Hundred Years
War. That this did not happen was largely due to the negative
attitude adopted by the Estates of Württemberg and many
other German states towards their rulers' military ambitions.

Two issues dominated the relations between the duke and the
Estates during the decades after 1650: his attempts to recruit
and to retain a small standing army instead of the antiquated
militia were strenuously opposed by the Estates; they also
opposed the connected attempts to induce them to vote more
money over a longer period and to adopt a more permanent
system of taxes, such as the excise. In May 1650 Duke Eberhard
proposed to the Large Committee that the excise should be
continued until God brought about the hoped-for improvement; but the committee would only extend it by twelve
months, when it was to cease automatically. They also granted
small sums for specific purposes: 1,500 guilders for the ducal
court; 1,300 guilders a month for mercenaries until the end of
the year, or until the conclusion of the negotiations concerning
the details of the peace settlement; 9,000 guilders for the ducal

servants, and 8,800 guilders for the infeudation of Eberhard by
the Emperor. Three months later when the negotiations for
the peace had been concluded, the Small Committee reminded
Eberhard that the grant for the mercenaries had expired and
petitioned that the terms of the earlier agreement should be
kept. The privy councillors, however, hesitated to pass on this
reminder, for Eberhard would be so offended that it would
become more difficult to expedite more important matters.
Thereupon the committee did not insist, but omitted the reminder and granted the 1,300 guilders until the end of the year.[1]

Early in 1651 the Small Committee again emphasized that
the grant had expired and should be terminated. Eberhard
replied that they had given a verbal promise to the chancellor
to continue it until an agreement had been reached between
him and them, and that he hoped they would make no
further difficulties. The Small Committee then excused itself,
pleading lack of powers to alter the previous agreement, while
Eberhard stressed his lack of money and ordered the amount
due for January to be collected. The committee emphasized
that this was contrary to the treaty of Tübingen and the other
compactata and maintained that according to their constitution
they had no power to concede further supply. Eventually they
offered a loan of 3,000 guilders, but firmly refused to convert
it into a definite grant. Thus a diet had to be summoned, the
first after an interval of seven years. With two interruptions of
about four weeks each it lasted from May 1651 to January 1652
and was once more fully attended by fourteen prelates and sixty-
three towns and *Ämter*, the Catholic abbots having finally
disappeared as a result of the conclusion of peace. The government proposed that they should continue the excise, take over
ducal debts amounting to 3,300,000 guilders (including the
3,000,000 agreed to in 1633) and vote money for the maintenance of the ducal forces and the repair of the fortresses. The
Estates first dismissed four deputies who were in their opinion
inadmissible: one because he was a 'Papist', two because they
belonged neither to the urban court nor the council of the town
which had sent them, and one because he was a ducal official

[1] State Archives Stuttgart, *Tomus Actorum*, xlvii, fos. 14, 101, 213, 226–9, 421,
428–9; Reyscher, op. cit. xvii, no. 91, p. 181, and n. 117 (3 May to 15 June, 16–19
Sept. 1650).

in charge of an *Amt*.[1] They thus vindicated their right to deter-
mine their own composition, to exclude the *Amtleute* who had
not attended a diet since 1629, and to preserve the virtual
monopoly of the urban *Ehrbarkeit* which controlled the town
courts and councils.

The Estates then examined the powers granted to them by
their principals and established that these did not embrace the
reintroduction of the *extraordinaria media*. They resolved to demand such powers from the towns and *Ämter*; and then the
excise was duly granted, to be levied on all foreign merchandise,
wool imports and exports, hides, cattle, horses, timber, salt,
wine, beer, and sales of real property, to be administered solely
by the Estates, and to be used only for the redemption of their
debts. In reply to the ducal proposition they pointed to the
thousands of deserted fields and vineyards and the depopulation
of the country. In their opinion hardly one-quarter of the men
was left and new impositions could not be borne. Four months
later, however, they consented to take over the debts amounting
to 3,000,000 guilders agreed on in 1633 under the conditions
then stipulated, and granted 40,000 guilders to the duke to
make good the deficit of his chamber. But they declared that
they were not obliged to maintain the fortresses and their
garrisons and refused to pay for them. The only other concession which the government could wring from them was that
they empowered the Large Committee to make another 'voluntary contribution' to Eberhard for twelve months if need be.
But they insisted that he should not contract any new debts
without the prior knowledge of the Small Committee. He
promised further that the grievances would be redressed. These
were debated at great length, but without much result. Instead
of a standing force, there remained only the militia, consisting
of thirty-two companies of infantry and seventeen of cavalry,
which were mustered a few times every year.[2]

[1] State Archives Stuttgart, *Tomus Actorum*, xlviii, fos. 91, 98, 102, 129, 175–6,
394–6, 419; xlix, pp. 74–93, 106–7, 129, 131, 159–60 (23 Jan. to 5 May 1651).
There seems to be no precedent for the exclusion of a 'Papist'. For the exclusion
of the *Amtleute*, see above, pp. 59–60.

[2] Ibid. xlix, pp. 649, 666–9, 1035–6, 1043, 1048–9, 1066, 1199–1207, 1594–5,
1617–18, 1658–62, 2364–7, 2373, 2387, 2398–9; A 34–35, *Büschel* 50, nos. 37, 49;
Büschel 51, nos. 26, 55, 97; Sattler, op. cit. ix. 108–9; Reyscher, op. cit. xvii, no.
92, p. 181; Grube, op. cit., pp. 320–4; Schneider, op. cit., pp. 282–4 (30 May 1651
to 8 Jan. 1652).

It was against these musters and the costs of the equipment of this force that complaints arose in the country. In 1653 the Small Committee declared that these expensive measures, especially the cost of horses for the cavalry, were contrary to the treaty of Tübingen and the uninterrupted custom of the country. They were also considered unnecessary because no danger was threatening, and because no neighbour or other member of the Swabian Circle was taking similar measures. Their demand for redress only resulted in a ducal order to General von Holz that all excesses were to cease, that if possible the clothes and horses were to be spared, and that unnecessary expenses for food and equipment were to stop, so that the Estates would have no further cause for complaint. Eberhard also demanded from the Large Committee after the expiration of the previous grant a contribution for his court of 34,000 guilders for twelve months: if they did not agree he would issue an order to the towns and *Ämter* to grant them the required powers. The Large Committee excused themselves on the ground that there were many rumours in the country that they granted much more than the subjects were able to bear, in view of the notorious shortage of money and the heavy taxation, and that people were blaming the committee for this state of affairs. Eberhard accordingly ordered the towns and *Ämter* to grant within four or five days full powers to the Large Committee, who then granted a 'voluntary contribution' of 16,000 guilders for one year. The privy councillors considered this sum insufficient. As the committee had full powers, they suggested a grant of 25,000; but the committee would consent only to 20,000 guilders, and this offer was finally accepted.[1]

Twelve months later the procedure was repeated. Eberhard then desired an annual grant of 30,000, or at least 25,000 guilders, for three or a minimum of two years, from the Large Committee. The towns and *Ämter* were instructed to empower either the whole committee or one of their members, although the Small Committee wished to give them an opportunity to send a deputy of their own if they so desired. When the powers had been received, the Large Committee offered a sum of 10,000 guilders for one year only, a sum which was gradually

[1] State Archives Stuttgart, *Tomus Actorum*, li, pp. 285–6, 291–2, 511–12, 875–6, 933–4, 945–6, 951–3, 1191, 1351–2, 1392, 1415–16 (6 June to 22 Dec. 1653).

increased to 20,000, in addition to the cost of an embassy to attend the Imperial diet at Frankfurt. But a grant for a longer period was refused, as was the redemption of the crown jewels which the duke had pawned twenty years earlier. As the grant expired in November 1655, a diet was summoned early in 1656. Eberhard proposed the continuation of the grant of 20,000 guilders for two years, to which 8,000 guilders a year were to be added for the officers of the militia, which then contained four regiments of infantry and eighteen companies of horse. The Estates complained that clergymen and schoolmasters were not paid punctually, that the monastic schools and the theological seminary at Tübingen had too few pupils, that pious alms and subsidies were not given according to instructions, that no prelates had been appointed to certain monasteries after their restoration, and that the whole administration of the *Kirchenkasten* was not conducted in accordance with the constitution. Only after weeks of bargaining did the Estates consent to pay 30,000 guilders for two years, on condition that they were spared the officers' pay, a grant which they eventually increased to 33,000. This Eberhard accepted, but without the attached condition. The Estates emphasized that the inhabitants of neighbouring principalities and Free Imperial Cities and those under the nobility fared better than those of Württemberg, while previously the reverse had been the case. Consequently people were longing to emigrate because of the heavy impositions which would continue for so many years that they could not hope for any alleviation. Eberhard therefore had to be satisfied, and the diet was dissolved.[1]

In September 1658 Duke Eberhard approached the Small Committee with more important matters of state. With the electors of Cologne, Mainz, and Trier, the bishop of Münster, the count of Palatinate-Neuburg, and other German princes, the kings of France and Sweden had just concluded the Rhenish Alliance which was to constitute a counter-weight to the Habsburg power and to the new Emperor Leopold. An army of 10,000, to be furnished by the contracting powers, was to give the alliance the necessary strength and to defend its members if

---

[1] State Archives Stuttgart, *Tomus Actorum*, liii, pp. 18–19, 44, 213, 356, 1279–82; lv, pp. 52, 109–11, 172–3, 730–3, 983–6, 1046, 1246, 1260, 1291–2, 1338–40; Grube, op. cit., pp. 326–7; Sattler, op. cit. ix. 143–4 (16 Nov. 1654 to 10 June 1656).

any were attacked. Eberhard suggested the committee should deliberate this important issue and think of means by which some mercenaries could be recruited and maintained. The committee replied that they had no powers to do this and asked for reconsideration of the matter by the ducal councillors. These pointed out that in 1631 the committee had consented to a similar alliance; and that the present one was in their opinion different from the Union of 1608, which later had been declared rebellious, because it included Catholic members. Yet the committee insisted that then they had been empowered by the Estates, whereas now such powers were lacking, and that the Estates should be summoned because they alone were competent, which meant that the committee had to be dismissed. Yet Eberhard did not desist. The members of the Alliance pressed him to declare himself. France and Sweden resented his reluctance and wished to know the strength of the Württemberg contingent, while the Imperial ambassador pronounced the Alliance detrimental to the Empire and contrary to its constitution. This resistance undoubtedly increased the opposition of the Estates who doubted whether the Alliance would help to preserve the duchy and feared to incur the displeasure of the Emperor, which they had good reason to remember.[1]

Early in 1659 Eberhard submitted the matter to a diet, and the Estates debated it, first in the Small Committee, then in the Large Committee, and finally in the plenum. They decided to compose a memorandum setting out their arguments against the Alliance, which was read and approved in the same order of procedure and signed by all present. Thereupon Eberhard declared it sufficient if the old fortresses were repaired and one more place were fortified. The Estates granted him 50,000 guilders for the following three years, in return for his promise not to take amiss their memoranda and neither to join the Alliance nor build a fortress. He believed it was not contrary to the treaty of Tübingen if he joined the Alliance without asking for a grant, and he apologized to France and Sweden, referring to the Estates' opposition. Early in 1660, however, he declared his adherence, in contrast with his recent promise, and without having the means of paying for the required contingent

[1] State Archives Stuttgart, *Tomus Actorum*, lviii, pp. 18–19, 122–3, 129–30, 268–9, 284 (20 Sept. to 8 Oct. 1658); Sattler, op. cit. ix. 224–31.

of 300 soldiers. He therefore notified the Estates of these facts and asked them to double the excise, to levy 5 per cent. on stores of wine and corn, and 10 per cent. on income from interest, so that at least a hundred horsemen and their officers could be maintained. The Estates declared this to be contrary to the old custom and their liberties and restated their opposition to the Alliance. Eberhard refused to disband his troops and repudiated the idea that the Estates' assent was required to join the Alliance, because the treaty of Tübingen and the other *compactata* spoke only of their 'advice and knowledge', and not of their consent. The Alliance was destined for the defencé and protection of the country, which entitled him to disregard their opinions. He pointed to the examples of the Emperor, Brandenburg, Hesse, and Mainz, who had not paid off their armies, so that it was difficult for him not to do the same. The Estates, however, were willing only to grant a 'voluntary contribution' of 32,000 guilders for 1660–2, provided that the other demands were dropped and their grievances were redressed. Eberhard desired a grant of 60,000 guilders, but in the end had to be satisfied with 50,000, while the Estates again emphasized that this did not include the 'unnecessary military undertaking'.[1]

Thus Eberhard gained his objective. He joined the Rhenish Alliance against the opposition of the Estates. He 'interpreted' the treaty of Tübingen in a sense favourable to him. The Estates declined to pay for his troops, but granted money to be spent at his discretion and did not insist that their grievances should be redressed first. They merely saved appearances and tacitly agreed to both the Alliance and the maintenance of the troops. Eberhard told them that 'nearly all temporal and ecclesiastical Electors and princes, for similar considerations and reasons, had established such life-guards, their maintenance being furnished by their Estates and subjects';[2] and reminded them that in 1654 the Imperial diet had decreed that it was the duty of all subjects to pay for the defence of the principality.[3] The prosperity of the country was sapped by the ravages of the war, and the Estates were conscious of the weakness of their position.

[1] State Archives Stuttgart, *Tomus Actorum*, lviii, pp. 562–81, 679–704, 880–918, 1168, 1311–12, 1417; lx, fos. 235–8, 241, 406–7, 515–19, 553–4, 579, 614, 648, 670–1, 722–3; Sattler, op. cit. ix. 234, 251–2; no. 65, pp. 158–71; Grube, op. cit., pp. 327–30 (5 Jan. 1659 to 28 July 1660).

[2] Ibid., *Tomus Actorum*, lx, fo. 236 (3 May 1660).   [3] See below, pp. 438–9.

On the whole the tactics of the Estates were limited to whittling down the ducal demands for money and to attempts to make their grants dependent on certain conditions, which attempts were usually unsuccessful. At the diet of 1662 Eberhard demanded 35,000 guilders for each of the following three years, but eventually accepted 25,000 for two years, to which 13,000 guilders were added for the costs caused by the Imperial diet. In 1663–4 the Large Committee agreed to levy the Württemberg share of the Turkish aid which had been voted by the Imperial diet. A contingent of two companies of horse and two of infantry was recruited and fought in the battle of St. Gotthard on the Raab in 1664. A special committee was formed to supervise the recruiting, paying, equipping, and victualling of this force, consisting of two officials of the Estates and two ducal councillors. The Estates would not assent to the establishment of a special war chest in the ducal chancery, which would have curtailed their control of expenditure; but for the payment of small items an iron chest was put into the office of the War Council, with two separate locks and an amount of 1,000 guilders in it, the keys being handed to the members of the committee. This mixed committee worked harmoniously for more than two years, even after the return of the forces from abroad, and thus the Estates preserved their financial powers intact.[1]

The Large Committee also pressed for the summoning of another diet, while Eberhard held that the Estates were obliged to carry out decisions of the Imperial diet or of a meeting of the Swabian Circle, so that such questions could be settled without reference to a diet between him and the Large Committee. The Estates, however, were neither willing to accept such Imperial decisions as automatically binding, nor to bear the cost of such meetings. When a diet was summoned early in 1665, they would grant only 30,000 guilders for two years and another 3,000 to pay off the troops returning from Hungary. Eberhard demanded 50,000 and 6,000 respectively, assuring them that he did not intend to keep a *miles perpetuus*, nor to make the fruits of peace sour to his loyal subjects, but that he only

[1] Ibid. lxii, fos. 499, 551, 614, 638, 691–8; lxiii, fos. 781–2; lxiv, fos. 52, 55–58 (10 Nov. 1662 to 24 Dec. 1663); ibid. lxiv, fos. 571–7, a report about the battle of St. Gotthard, dated 8/18 Aug. 1664; ibid. lxiv contains the correspondence of the committee to Jan. 1666; Grube, op. cit., pp. 330–1.

wanted to keep 170 horsemen for a few months, until it was
possible to see more clearly what was likely to happen. The
Estates again compromised and slowly increased their two-year
grant to 48,000 guilders, and the sum for paying off the troops
to 4,500 guilders, but refused to pay for their maintenance; and
this decision was finally accepted. Yet the cavalry was not paid
off. Later in the same year the Small Committee complained
that soldiers of the horse-guards who received their food and
fodder in kind nevertheless extorted money from the peasants
and burghers, contrary to the earlier agreement. They asked
for the removal of this burden, for they had never consented to
maintain these guards and it was equivalent to a silent contribution.[1]

Another military issue caused friction between Eberhard and
the Estates. About ten years previously he had started to fortify
the small town of Freudenstadt in the Black Forest, although it
was surrounded by mountains and therefore unsuitable to block
the route an invader might take from the west. The Estates
urged repeatedly that such works would cost millions, were
militarily useless and beyond the resources of a poor country.
Yet the fortification was continued and was fairly well advanced by 1666. Then Eberhard summoned a diet and requested a considerable sum for the fortress and an extraordinary
aid for four to five years, to be raised by the ordinary taxes as
well as by *extraordinaria media*. Later he demanded a grant of at
least 30,000 guilders a year for three years. The Estates agreed
to give him 15,000 for two years, but declined the extraordinary aids which they had no powers to grant. After protracted negotiations they agreed to pay 25,000 guilders for two
years, making this sum an almost regular grant, and to empower
the Large Committee to grant 20,000 for the third year, with
which Eberhard had to be content. The agreement was almost
wrecked at the last moment because he desired a clause to be
inserted expressing his concurrence: 'in so far as this was not
prejudicial to his princely state'. The Estates were informed
that this was done at his express order, whereupon they
requested the addition of the words 'and to the privileges of

---

[1] State Archives Stuttgart, *Tomus Actorum*, lxv, fos. 177–8, 712, 812, 818, 865,
966, 1011, 1034; lxvi, fos. 146–7, 212–14, 698–9; Sattler, op. cit. x. 82; Grube,
op. cit., p. 332 (19 Apr. 1664 to 10 Nov. 1665; repeated on 22 Aug. 1666).

the Estates'. Eberhard finally agreed that the clause should be dropped, but with bad grace, and ordered them not to bother him with such trifles in future.[1] The work at Freudenstadt continued despite the wishes and misgivings of the Estates. How justified these were was shown in 1674 when the fortification was inspected by an expert who found the place entirely unsuitable, with the result that it was abandoned.[2]

The main expenditure to be met out of the Estates' chest was the payment of interest on the ducal debts which they had taken over. In 1667 this amounted to 150,400 guilders a year, considerably less than the 241,100 of 1649; but there were arrears of interest amounting to 123,000 guilders. The Estates' receivers now considered 25,000 guilders to be the ordinary annual grant and estimated that another 20,000 were required for the payment of embassies and other expenditure, so that the total expenditure came to almost 200,000 guilders a year. Tax arrears amounted to only 33,000 guilders, excluding those of the previous year. These figures are indicative of the soundness of the Estates' financial position; but this was not the opinion of the Small Committee, which complained vigorously about the bad state of the finances and the plight of the country.[3] The Estates gave to the duke in addition an annual birthday present of 100 or 200 gold ducats and a New Year present of 200 ducats, as well as smaller presents to all the members of the ducal family, including the numerous children and their governesses.[4] Furthermore, when the Estates were invited to become godparents to one of Eberhard's children, they presented the infant with 500 ducats, and the duchess with 100 which were given to her likewise when they did not act as godparents.[5] When Eberhard married for the second time he suggested a wedding present of 4,500 guilders which was duly

---

[1] State Archives Stuttgart, *Tomus Actorum*, lxvii, fos. 46, 50, 135, 159–62, 172, 182–5, 190–201, 313, 389, 440–2, 446; Sattler, op. cit. ix. 231; x. 10, 123–4; Grube, op. cit., pp. 334–5 (30 Oct. to 21 Dec. 1666).

[2] Sattler, op. cit. x. 124; Grube, op. cit., p. 334.

[3] State Archives Stuttgart, *Tomus Actorum*, lxviii, fos. 3–6, 27–28 (14 May to 8 June 1667). For the figures of 1649, see above, p. 72.

[4] Ibid. liv, fos. 272–3; lvii, pp. 694–5; lviii, pp. 505–8; lxii, fos. 124, 140–1; lxvii, fo. 329; lxx, fo. 88; lxxi, fo. 127; lxxv, fo. 543 (from the years 1656–73). The sum of the New Year presents was usually well over 1,000 guilders. A ducat was worth 3 guilders. Eberhard had 18 sons and 7 daughters from two marriages.

[5] Ibid. l, pp. 1472–87; lvi, pp. 1489–1505; lxi, fo. 953; lxii, fos. 314–34; lxiii,

granted. The Estates presented him further with sets of plate engraved with the coats of arms of bride and bridegroom, and table-linen for eighteen people, for the sum of 4,756 guilders[1]— a considerable expenditure less than ten years after the end of the Thirty Years War.

These facts show a fairly close relationship between the ducal family and the Estates, especially the Small Committee, and the absence of sharp conflicts and rigid class distinctions. When daughters of the duke found themselves in financial difficulties they did not hesitate to inform the Small Committee that a present of 100 ducats would be welcome: whereupon the committee, always careful, presented them with half that sum. When the two eldest princes entered the University of Tübingen, the committee wished them luck, and an *oratio congratulatoria* was held by the secretary of the Estates. When the same two princes returned from their grand tour of France, England, and Holland in 1671, and were to proceed to Denmark and Sweden, Eberhard asked the Small Committee for a contribution of 6,000 guilders. It alleged lack of powers, but offered a loan of 4,000, though Eberhard insisted on 6,000. The committee replied that this could be granted only by a diet, but consented to make a loan of the same amount, which was accepted. Four months later on his return home the Estates presented the heir to the throne with a silver stag gilded and adorned with a Diana and Cupid costing 333 guilders, and 60 ducats, while his brother received 150 guilders.[2] When the same prince married a princess of the house of Hesse, the Estates' wedding present was a silver table-service and table-linen, costing almost 4,000 guilders. When a princess of the house of Württemberg married, the Estates, according to an ancient custom, had to provide a dowry of 32,000 guilders: a duty on which Eberhard

fo. 472; lxviii, fo. 269; lxix, fos. 708–28; lxxi, fos. 335–41; lxxii, fos. 426, 485–6, 501, 520; lxxvii, fos. 357–9 (from the years 1652–74). The total expenditure in these ten cases came to 3,833¼ ducats or 11,500 guilders. Similar examples from the following reign may be found ibid. lxxvii, fos. 153–9; lxxviii, fos. 289, 646 (from the years 1674–5).

[1] State Archives Stuttgart, *Tomus Actorum*, lvi, pp. 143, 149, 197–8 (July 1656). When Duke Louis got married in 1579 the Estates' present of plate had cost 10,000 guilders, but those had been far more prosperous times: von Stälin, op. cit. iv. 793.

[2] State Archives Stuttgart, *Tomus Actorum*, lviii, pp. 1061–3; lxvi, fos. 474–9; lxxi, fos. 444–6, 465–9, 525, 528–9, 539–542, 692 (from the years 1659, 1666, 1671–2).

insisted.[1] The Estates thus had manifold financial obligations towards the ducal house, which they always fulfilled willingly, in spite of difficult times and burdensome taxation.

From 1668 onwards the times indeed became more difficult and taxation more burdensome. The War of Devolution had started in the previous year, and Louis XIV made military preparations in Alsace and on the Rhine. Early in 1668 Eberhard summoned a diet and declared that no time was to be lost. He required that the Estates should make a voluntary contribution to enable him to recruit troops, but that if they preferred they should give powers to the Large Committee and return home. Eberhard intended to raise five infantry companies of 307 men each and five of cavalry of 100 each, at a cost of 6,000 guilders a month. The Estates complained bitterly that after only twenty years of peace they had once more to consider war and expensive armaments. Eventually, they voted a 'voluntary contribution' of 35,000 guilders, which did not imply that they assented to the recruiting and maintenance of mercenaries, and petitioned against the increase of the *extraordinaria media*. Some days later they increased the grant to 50,000 and again declined an excise on meat and wine, for they were instructed on the contrary to obtain the decrease of the existing excise, but not to impose further duties, and it was hardly possible to wring even this from the people. Eberhard promised to leave things as they were and accepted the grant. As the Estates pointed out, Württemberg was incapable of raising an army able to withstand a great power, and the militia was sufficient to prevent raiding and foraging by small parties. The thirty-two companies of infantry and eighteen of horse which made up its strength were accordingly mustered.[2]

The conclusion of the peace of Aix-la-Chapelle made further military measures unnecessary. Early in 1669, however, Eberhard demanded from the Large Committee the 20,000 guilders

---

[1] Ibid. lxxi, fos. 113–17; lxxvi, fos. 21–22 (Nov. 1670, Feb. 1674). The silver cost 3,832 guilders, the linen 118, and incidental expenses 15, a total of 3,965 guilders: about 800 less than the wedding present of Eberhard in 1656. For the custom of providing a dowry of 32,000 guilders for a princess, see ibid. xiii, fos. 167–8; von Stälin, op. cit. iv. 732.

[2] State Archives Stuttgart, *Tomus Actorum*, lxviii, fos. 390–400, 416, 419, 428, 493–5, 523–4, 528, 580–1, 586–93, 659, 665–6, 758; Sattler, op. cit. x. 149–50; Grube, op. cit., p. 335.

promised in 1666 and a loan of 5,000 for repairs to the fortress on the Hoher Asperg, so that he and his family as well as the Estates and the archives would have a place of refuge in case of danger. When the committee emphasized their devotion to their prince, but also the difficulties of the times, he expressed his satisfaction with the Estates' past attitude and loyalty and invited the deputies to dinner. A privy councillor made a speech in which he stressed how heavily Bavaria, Brandenburg, and the bishop of Strasbourg were burdening their subjects. On the following day the Large Committee granted all demands.[1]

Twelve months later Eberhard requested from the diet an annual contribution of 50,000 guilders for three to four years because his ordinary revenues were utterly insufficient. The Estates at first would grant only 25,000 guilders for the first and 20,000 for the second year, if their grievances were redressed. Some days later they debated whether they should increase this grant, or first insist on redress, or comprise both matters into one reply. They decided to adopt the first course because, if they stopped meanwhile with the main issue, Eberhard would think of resistance or unbecoming importunity, as if they wanted to bring pressure to bear upon him. They therefore increased the grant to 30,000 guilders for the first year, 25,000 for the second, and 20,000 for the third year. Eberhard, however, insisted on grants of 45,000, so that the Estates finally increased each sum by 10,000 guilders, which he accepted. On the following day all the deputies were entertained to dinner, the banquet lasting from 11 a.m. until 7 p.m. The prelates, the mayors of Stuttgart and Tübingen, the councillor and the secretary of the Estates ate at the ducal table, sitting between his noble councillors, and the other deputies sat at other tables.[2] Again the Estates had proved pliant. They chose not to use their one effective weapon, that of grievances before supply, hoping that their grievances would be redressed if they met the ducal demands. But was that hope really justified? Would their pliancy not result in yet greater demands, demands which again they would have to meet more than half-way?

[1] State Archives Stuttgart, *Tomus Actorum*, lxix, fos. 437–8, 442–3, 474–6 (24–26 Jan. 1669). The next diet decided that the loan of 5,000 guilders need not be repaid: ibid. lxx, fo. 373 (10 Feb. 1670).

[2] Ibid. lxx, fos. 137, 141, 172, 203, 214–15, 229, 260, 373–4, 383–4 (12 Jan. to 11 Feb. 1670); Grube, op. cit., pp. 336–7.

Again it was Louis XIV who decisively influenced the development during the following years. This was the time when the king tried to gain allies among the German princes for his intended invasion of the Low Countries and went out of his way to create a favourable impression. When the two Württemberg princes on their grand tour arrived in Paris, not only were they visited in their lodgings by the leading grandees of France and royally entertained in their palaces, but presently Marshal Turenne appeared and conducted them in his carriage to an audience in the Louvre. There they were received by the king in the friendliest fashion. He discoursed with them for half an hour in his private closet, without putting on his hat, which was considered quite unusual, and he later congratulated their tutor on the good qualities of his pupils.[1] Yet when the war broke out in 1672 Württemberg loyally fulfilled its obligations towards the Empire and furnished the Imperial army with the required contingent. A few days before Louis's invasion of Holland Eberhard proposed to the diet a grant of 40,000 guilders a year for three to four years and the increase of the *extraordinaria media* to pay 150 horse and 300 foot-soldiers, which formed his contribution to the Imperial army of 30,000 (about one-seventh of the contingent of the Swabian Circle). In Eberhard's opinion it was the duty of the Estates to pay for this force; but they suggested that the men should be selected from the militia and only offered 25,000 guilders for each of the following three years. A few days later they empowered the Large Committee to act on their behalf and were dismissed. The committee then increased the grant to 30,000 guilders a year, and offered 400 a month as a contribution towards the military contingent, and this was accepted. Only 200 foot-soldiers were recruited and the other 100 were selected from the militia, but left at their places of work for the time being. After an adjournment the Estates eventually agreed to pay 500 guilders monthly for six months for a company of 86 horse, which was just sufficient for their maintenance.[2]

In 1673 the war came closer. In January the Estates sent presents of red and white wine to the Great Elector of Branden-

[1] State Archives Stuttgart, *Tomus Actorum*, lxxi, fos. 269–70 (report to the Small Committee of 13 Feb. 1671).

[2] Ibid. lxxii, fos. 18, 179–82, 193–5, 203, 240–1, 252–71, 300–1, 390, 433–4, 901–2, 906; Sattler, op. cit. x. 207, 212; Grube, op. cit., pp. 342–3 (31 May to 28 Sept. 1672).

burg, to the Imperial commander, Count Montecuccoli, and
their generals into their camp at Rüsselsheim on the Main.
Some weeks later Eberhard summoned another diet and informed the Estates that they were obliged to contribute to the
defence of the Empire, its fortresses and garrisons, that he intended to recruit 600 cavalry and 2,000 infantry, and that they
should decide how to raise the money. The Estates pointed out
how doubtful it was whether such a force would be able to
prevent the danger of war and the marches and quartering of
troops. They nevertheless granted 28,000 guilders to recruit
200 horse and 400 foot-soldiers: if this were insufficient, a further
400 or 500 men could be selected from the militia. They also
declared that they had no powers to increase the *extraordinaria
media*, but were instructed, on the contrary, to ask for the
abolition of the existing ones. Eberhard, however, insisted on
increasing these, for they did not weigh down the poor and he
would contribute like any subject. He affirmed that he needed
a force of 400 horse and 1,500 foot-soldiers of his own, at an
annual cost of over 172,000 guilders, so that these taxes were
necessary. Thereupon the Estates sent a circular to all towns
and *Ämter*, requesting them to grant the necessary powers to
their deputies, and the majority duly sent them. In their turn
the Estates empowered the Large Committee, and then a
considerable increase of the excise was agreed to, but only for
twelve months. The military requirements were progressively
scaled down: only 200 horse and 1,000 foot-soldiers (later reduced to 800) were to be newly recruited, while 100 horse and
300 foot-soldiers were to be selected from the militia and combined with them.[1]

In 1674 the Estates prolonged the increased excise by nine
months. They could find no other means to pay for the soldiers'
maintenance, although the majority of the towns and *Ämter*
instructed their deputies that the excise should be reduced to
its former level. The Estates complained that all burdens were
devolved upon them, as if it were their duty to bear them, while

---

[1] State Archives Stuttgart, *Tomus Actorum*, lxxiii, fos. 137, 207-9, 226, 232-3,
318, 326, 340, 412, 415, 547; lxxiv, fos. 23, 27, 306-10, 455 (7 Jan. to 3 May
1673); ibid. lxxiii, fos. 365-8, the detailed estimates of the cost of 400 horse and
1,500 foot-soldiers; Grube, op. cit., p. 344; Reyscher, op. cit. xvii, no. 120, p. 236
(decree of 3 May 1673). The increase of the excise in most instances amounted
to between 50 and 100 per cent.

in the past the dukes had always contributed to such *onera regiminis* from their ordinary revenues, their subjects giving them for that reason customs, rents, tithes, and other dues. At first the ducal share had been about two-fifths, and even during the Thirty Years War it had amounted to one-quarter, and that proportion Eberhard should again contribute himself. Yet they did not persist, and in the end they paid this quarter in addition to the three-quarters they offered initially.[1] A few months later Eberhard III died after a long and eventful reign of more than forty years. He was succeeded by his son, William Louis, whose reign lasted only three years. When he died in 1677 the heir to the throne, Eberhard Louis, was nine months old, and there followed sixteen years of ducal minority and guardianship, the regency being in the hands of an uncle of the infant duke.

At the beginning of William Louis's reign the Small Committee listed the main grievances which had not yet been settled. A list of the twelve most important *gravamina* was compiled, four of which were concerned with the hunt, various services demanded for it, and the severe damage caused by game. The other eight were of small importance, most of them being concerned with minor economic grievances. It was only the diet of 1675 which added to this list the great cost of the defence measures and the interference of the government with free trade and with the right of free departure. Apart from these, the Württemberg Estates seem to have had no major complaints. They consented to maintain for the time being not only the Württemberg contingent with the Imperial army, but also the five companies conceded in 1673 which formed the nucleus of a standing force. When the diet was resumed at the end of the year the Estates petitioned for the reduction of these companies and for their payment in part by the ducal chamber, but granted their maintenance for another six months. The duke not only declined to contribute anything from his own revenues, but also asked for a voluntary contribution of 30,000 guilders a year for three years because the previous grant was due to expire. This the Estates declared to be impossible and likely to bring them into severe disrepute if they agreed to it; yet they granted *semel pro semper* 25,000 guilders and prolonged the increased excise,

---

[1] State Archives Stuttgart, *Tomus Actorum*, lxxvi, fos. 80, 87–90, 145, 261–2 (6–30 Mar. 1674).

first until the end of 1675, and then by a further twelve months.[1]
Once more they had conceded most of the ducal wishes, above
all the maintenance of a small Württemberg army, distinct from
the contingent for the defence of the Swabian Circle.

A few months later a new contribution was imposed upon
the duchy for the first time. The French commandant of
Philippsburg on the Rhine produced an express command from
Louis XIV that he was to put the duchy to fire and sword
unless it paid him a monthly contribution of 22,500 guilders.
For the time being this sum was paid only once, for the Imperial
army presently laid siege to this outpost of French power, and
the immediate danger passed. Even so the Estates estimated the
damage caused by the French and other troops since 1672 at
nearly 950,000 guilders. In spite of this, they not only continued
to maintain the Württemberg contingent with the Imperial
army, but in 1676 again extended the increased excise by
twelve months and granted the duke 24,000 guilders for his
personal use, having at first asked to be spared this contribution.
With regard to his own forces, the Estates again asked that
they should be reduced; but they only achieved that the
three infantry companies were combined into two, while the
horse-guards remained at one company of 100 men.[2]

The long reign of Eberhard Louis, which nominally began in
1677 and lasted until 1733, saw renewed devastations of the
country by foreign armies and new heavy burdens imposed
upon the luckless inhabitants. The disputes between the prince
and the Estates revolved more and more around the question
whether they had to bear the cost of a small standing army in
addition to that of the Württemberg contingent for the Swabian
Circle. In peace-time this numbered 391 infantry and 190
horsemen according to the Imperial repartition of 1681, which
envisaged an army of 28,000 infantry and 12,000 cavalry, to
be provided by the ten circles of the Empire, and within the
Swabian Circle by as many as ninety-one different Estates.[3]

---

[1] State Archives Stuttgart, *Tomus Actorum*, lxxvii, fos. 557–9, 675, 865–6; lxxviii,
fos. 377–8, 430–6, 476, 522–3, 528, 633–4, 886–91 (28 Jan. to 22 Dec. 1675).

[2] Ibid. lxxix, fos. 113, 246, 287–8, 470–8; lxxx, fos. 418–20, 425–6, 430–4
(9 Feb. to 18 Sept. 1676); Grube, op. cit., pp. 348–9.

[3] State Archives Stuttgart, *Tomus Actorum*, lxxxix, fos. 331–2, 348–52, giving the
complete list of the 91 *Kreisstände* and their contingents. Friedrich Wintterlin,
'Wehrverfassung und Landesverfassung im Herzogtum Württemberg', *Württem-*

This contribution was always willingly furnished by the Württemberg Estates, although it became much larger in war-time, and although the military value of this army for the protection of the duchy was not very great. But they were much less willing to pay also for the private army of the duke, especially in peace-time. Yet in the course of this reign it came slowly to be recognized that the duke was entitled to maintain a *miles perpetuus*, and eventually a fixed sum for this purpose was levied every year.

Only a few months after the appointment of Duke Frederick Charles as the regent and administrator of the duchy, the Small Committee tried to reassert its influence in military affairs. The privy councillors begged their members to remain in Stuttgart and to share with them the responsibility caused by the country's dangerous situation. On the following day, however, the privy councillors deliberated and decided on their own, and only informed the committee of the decisions reached and the action taken, so that the members of the committee did not know why they had been asked to stay; while during previous wars the Estates' deputies had actually sat in the War Council the whole day, all plans had been communicated to them, and military matters had been treated as a matter of common interest. The Large Committee again, in 1677 as well as in 1678, extended the excise and granted the maintenance of the four Württemberg companies, which were not serving with the Imperial army, for the time being. Early in 1678, however, the Small Committee declined to pay for the ducal garrison on the Hoher Twiel and for the repair of the fortress, as this was a *regale* of the prince, and such expenditure fell on his shoulders alone. For this purpose the government demanded labour services of three to four weeks from about 150 peasants; but the committee insisted that they should be given two pounds of bread and a measure of wine as well as 4 kreuzers a day, and declared it could not assent to such unusual services without informing the Estates. Frederick Charles, on the other hand, denied that this demand was contrary to their privileges: when the work was started the armies of Louis XIV were moving towards Alsace and the Rhine, and some troops had already crossed the river. In such a situation unusual means had to be employed to avert

bergische Vierteljahrshefte für Landesgeschichte, xxxiv, 1928, pp. 244–5, gives quite different figures; so does Grube, op. cit., p. 352.

the danger, and these means must be prescribed to suit the
nature of the illness. He was aggrieved that the Estates made
difficulties over so small a matter. He bore in mind that the
people should not be burdened with excessive services; but that
objection could not apply to this work, undertaken during an
emergency and lasting such a short time. This argument proved
decisive, at least for the time being.[1]

Early in 1679, however, France and the Empire concluded
peace at Nymegen, and a diet was summoned a few months
later. The Estates declared that during the war they and the
hard-pressed towns had to contract debts upon debts, that they
themselves had sunk into a morass of arrears of interest amounting to 561,000 guilders, and that now they foresaw the on-
slaught of impatient creditors; they wanted to be freed from the
onerous burden of the mercenaries and to enjoy the fruits of
peace. They offered a present of 15,000 guilders to the young
duke, but they were persuaded only with difficulty to extend
the increased excise by two months. Thereafter the increase of
1673 was to be rescinded, and the reduced excise was to be used
solely for the redemption of their debts, as had been agreed
upon in 1652. Then the diet was adjourned for four months.
When it was resumed in the autumn the Large Committee
begged the duke to consider the miserable state of the country
and of the Estates' chest and to pay off his own troops for whose
maintenance he was asking. The Estates repeated this plea: if
the duke desired to keep this force, they should not be burdened
with its maintenance, especially in view of the rising corn prices
and the food shortage. Frederick Charles replied that he would
have to keep the troops for some time, until the political dangers
had lessened somewhat, and that, as he had no intention of
burdening them with a *miles perpetuus* or the garrisons of the
fortresses, he would pay them off soon. The Estates, however,
remained firm because they had no powers to alter the previous
decision, and demanded that the infantry should be reduced to
200 men. In fact 223 were kept on, and 190 were discharged
with one month's pay, while the company of horse also remained: a total of only 300. In addition, there was the militia

[1] State Archives Stuttgart, *Tomus Actorum*, lxxxii, fos. 504, 555, 736; lxxxiii,
fos. 152-3, 155, 181, 188, 580, 613-14, 663-6; lxxxv, fos. 83, 86, 122 (13 July 1677
to 11 Sept. 1678).

with 4,000 infantry and 1,000 cavalry, to which another 3,300 men could be added in case of an emergency.[1]

Then the diet was once more adjourned, to meet again in the spring of 1680. The Large Committee renewed its humble petition for the complete disbanding of the army. The duchy would consider itself unhappy if it alone of all the Estates of the Swabian Circle had to retain a *perpetuum militem*, contrary to its privileges and constitution; though in the event of a hostile attack or incursion this force would be far too weak *contra vim majorem*. Frederick Charles replied that total dismissal was inopportune and suggested that the decision should be deferred until the autumn. The Large Committee consented and granted in addition 34,000 guilders, provided that the church lands contributed their share of one-third and the ducal chamber one-quarter; for Louis XIV had to be paid 127,000 guilders for the fortress of Philippsburg, a claim based on his interpretation of the peace of Nymegen. To this sum the church lands indeed contributed 15,000, and to the other levies 40,000 guilders; but there is no record of a contribution from the ducal chamber. A few months later another diet was summoned 'to consider carefully how this duchy could be preserved in security and quietness, for which purpose it was necessary . . . that a *nervus* and means to recruit and keep a considerable force should be collected . . . in addition to the maintenance of the existing body of mercenaries. . . '. The towns and *Ämter* were instructed to send deputies with full powers to discuss these issues, on account of the unusual military preparations inside and outside the Empire. After some hesitation the Estates granted about 50,000 guilders for defence and 36,000 for various purposes, apart from the regular levy of about 200,000 guilders a year for the payment of the debts which the Estates had taken over. Thus two more companies of infantry or 400 men could be recruited.[2]

[1] Ibid. lxxxvi, fos. 71, 83, 278, 594, 727, 771, 773, 881-8; Grube, op. cit., pp. 350-1; Sattler, op. cit. xi. 55-56, 69 (28 May to 30 Dec. 1679). In Nov. 1680 the Small Committee put the arrears of interest at 521,924 guilders: State Archives Stuttgart, *Tomus Actorum*, lxxxviii, fo. 64. The detailed excise instructions of 20 Dec. 1679 are printed in Reyscher, op. cit. xvii, no. 126, pp. 241-64. Schneider, op. cit., p. 298, wrongly asserts that 600 infantry were kept on: this refers to 1681. See above, p. 76, for the agreement of 1652.

[2] State Archives Stuttgart, *Tomus Actorum*, lxxxvii, fos. 225-8, 270-1, 276, 287-8, 365, 492, 502-4, 602; lxxxviii, fos. 250-2, 286-7, 511, 520, 642-9, 714-17 (27 Apr. 1680 to 4 Apr. 1681); Grube, op. cit., p. 351.

A few weeks later Frederick Charles informed the Large Committee that it was necessary to increase the infantry to 800 and the cavalry to 100 men because the Imperial diet at Ratisbon had decided to raise an army of 40,000 on account of the dangerous times. No diet and no grant were required for this purpose because the Estates were obliged to undertake this duty towards the Empire. They had to provide the fodder of the cavalry company which hitherto was furnished by the ducal chamber. They had also to pay 7,900 guilders for recruiting and equipping one company of dragoons—a course which they preferred to the alternative of recruiting them themselves, which would 'inevitably cause many great inconveniences'. These were still very small forces; yet arrears of the taxes destined for their use had to be paid quickly, otherwise the soldiers themselves would be sent to collect them by force, which would only add to the cost, as the government pointed out in 1682 and 1683. Frederick Charles further demanded 30,000 guilders a year for three years as a contribution to the cost of government, but the Large Committee would grant only 20,000. Three years later, however, the grant was increased to 24,000 a year, while the regent himself was offered a present of 10,000 guilders a year for five years, another one of 10,750 guilders, and a wedding present of plate to the value of 4,130 guilders.[1]

In 1686 Frederick Charles proposed the recruiting of another two companies of infantry with 300 men, referring to the admonition of the Emperor to undertake 'mutual measures of defence . . . at the present very threatening junctures'. The Large Committee replied that such anticipated measures had done little good in the past and had caused only great cost and damage; but that as soon as the Swabian Circle took any decision, they were willing to furnish their quota. The privy councillors expressed surprise that the deputies were criticizing what the duke—who was absent—considered necessary after mature deliberation in the privy council. The ducal orders were that one company of 200 should be recruited whether they liked it or not. After his return it would be decided where to take the money from, and the committee's presence was no longer

---

[1] State Archives Stuttgart, *Tomus Actorum*, lxxxix, fos. 82–83, 328, 531–6, 568; xc; fos. 269, 416, 541, 564, 697, 731, 737; xci, fos. 569, 579, 675; xcii, fos. 808, 823, 829, 837, 852, 902; xciii, fo. 55 (14 May 1681 to 23 Mar. 1686); Grube, op. cit., pp. 352–3.

required if they adhered to their negative attitude. The committee denied any intention of opposing measures which the duke considered necessary after deliberation in the privy council; but pointed out that the orders to the officers had already been issued, while, according to the treaty of Tübingen, they should be consulted about all military preparations and that all recruiting had always been discussed with them, in proof of which they quoted precedents from five previous diets. The members of the committee could not understand what use these 200 men could be to the duchy with its open frontiers. Nevertheless they consented in the end, especially because matters were so arranged by the duke that they could not easily be rescinded. Again the committee gave way without any protest or show of resistance, although at first they resolved not to remain quiet and expressed their resentment of the unconstitutional procedure adopted. A sharp speech by the president of the privy council sufficed to bring them to heel. He told the members curtly that the duke had taken this *conclusum*, therefore they must not resist, for they were only subjects, yet wanted to be the equals of the prince. When the Estates' secretary suggested limiting the size of the proposed company to 150 men—the same strength as that of the other companies— he was informed that these were the ducal orders, and that the privy councillors had no authority to depart from them.[1]

These were the years of the seizure of Strasbourg, of the *Réunions*, of renewed war along the Rhine and in the east, of the siege of Vienna by the Turks and their repulse; but only faint echoes of these great events penetrated to the Estates. When they received the 'sad news that the Emperor's residence, Vienna, was really besieged by 200,000 Turks and Tartars', the Small Committee interrupted its proceedings for one afternoon because of 'the great consternation this caused';[2] but no further action was taken. It was only in October 1688, after the second French invasion and devastation of the Palatinate had begun, a few weeks before William of Orange sailed for England, that the war once more reached Württemberg. It was the second of these events which provided Louis XIV with the pretext. Frederick Charles, the regent, had recruited troops to serve

---

[1] State Archives Stuttgart, *Tomus Actorum*, xciii, fos. 21–23, 36–39, 42–47, 76–81 84–85 (12–20 Mar. 1686).   [2] Ibid. xci, fo. 7 (12 July 1683).

under the Prince of Orange. Therefore the French *Intendant* in Alsace ordered the Estates to pay within eight days the sum of 150,000 guilders, otherwise some of the regiments of dragoons would devastate the duchy with fire and sword. In vain did they protest that they could not possibly raise such an amount, and that they had nothing to do with the recruiting for the prince, which had been done privately by the regent. The deputies debated whether the militia should be raised, but desisted because there were no trained officers to command it and the result would be utter ruin. There was nothing to do but to pay not only this contribution, but also a second one, in instalments, and to suffer the depredations of the French forces until the country was relieved by the arrival of Imperial troops at the end of the year.[1]

In 1689 the war continued. After the terrible devastation of the Palatinate during the preceding winter the Empire declared war on France. The Emperor Leopold repeatedly commanded the Württemberg Estates to cease their opposition to the plans of the government for the defence of the country and the provisioning and garrisoning of the fortresses: otherwise he would hold them responsible. Thus reinforced, Frederick Charles proposed to the Large Committee that one cavalry and three infantry regiments, and five companies of dragoons and chasseurs should be recruited, a force of 4,564 men, and that a poll-tax should be introduced, graduated according to property, as well as the continuance of the voluntary contribution; for it was impossible to summon a diet because of the war. All the committee were willing to grant, however, was a defence tax of 8,000 guilders because of the exhaustion of the country and the chest through the exactions of the past months. Thus a diet was summoned in the autumn. The Estates declared that it was quite impossible to maintain a force of 5,200 mercenaries and 5,000 to 7,000 chosen from the militia because the majority of the people were starving. Thereupon the government suggested an army of 2,500 mercenaries and 8,000 from the militia. The Estates, however, were willing to grant only 20,000 guilders for each of the following three years, 15,000 for the militia, and 20,000 to indemnify the regent for the retention of six

[1] State Archives Stuttgart, *Tomus Actorum*, xciv, fos. 239–40, 244, 283–4, 547 (Oct.–Dec. 1688). The sum demanded was 300,000 livres, equivalent to 100,000 thalers or 150,000 guilders.

companies of cavalry which he had recruited for the Prince of Orange.[1]

Early in 1690 the excise was again increased to the level of 1673, and another 20,000 guilders were granted by the Large Committee. Yet this proved a boomerang. Even the five members of the ducal chamber (*Rentcammer*) pointed out nine years later that the main result of this increase was to drive away trade from Württemberg, and thus very considerably to decrease the revenue from tolls and customs, to the benefit of the duchy's neighbours.[2] The yield was so insufficient that Frederick Charles decreed the levy of an extraordinary tax of 7,000 guilders a month, which would enable him to garrison some frontier places with the militia. For October and November this levy was trebled, again without obtaining the consent of the Estates. But it proved very difficult to collect the money and most places did not heed the ducal decrees, so that the militia could not be kept together for lack of maintenance and the government had to threaten that soldiers would be used to collect the money. During the winter of 1689–90 alone troops quartered on the duchy consumed 1,374,000 guilders.[3]

Duke Frederick Charles intended to create an army independent of the contingents of the Swabian Circle, which would enable him to cut a better figure on the allied side. Early in 1691 he proposed to the Small Committee that they should reflect how to transform the inadequate militia into a regular army and thus demonstrate to the allies that the duchy was able to maintain a considerable force. The committee replied that they had no powers to discuss this proposal and asked that it should be dropped and the militia be left *in statu quo*. These and similar declarations made no impression upon the duke. He merely promised that nobody would be retained against his will in the 'transformed' militia and that those wishing to leave would be replaced by others. Rumours that the army would be sent to Savoy were contradicted by the government which declared

[1] Ibid. xcv, fos. 7–10, 59, 66–68, 75–76, 219, 222, 257, 449, 462, 513, 637, 641, 916; xcvi, fos. 104–5, 378–80; Grube, op. cit., pp. 357–9 (29 Apr. 1689 to 21 Mar. 1690).

[2] State Archives Stuttgart, *Tomus Actorum*, xcvi, fos. 266, 535; cviii, fo. 5; Reyscher, op. cit. xvii, no. 140, p. 280 (8 Mar. and 6 June 1690, 12 May 1699).

[3] State Archives Stuttgart, *Tomus Actorum*, xcvi, fos. 409, 603–6, 698–704; xcvii, fo. 21 (13 May to 27 Oct. 1690).

it would be employed only in the defence of the country. Yet the number of people willing to serve remained very small. As the Estates pointed out, many burghers and burgher sons were taken along simply because they belonged to the militia, and many were forced to sign on by 'blows, dire threats and other practices', so that the majority could not possibly be classified as volunteers. Thanks to the support of the Emperor the plan was nevertheless carried out and a regular Württemberg army of about 6,000 men was formed, taxes on wine and corn being levied for its maintenance.[1]

The Estates were not satisfied with protests against these measures which they considered contrary to the constitution. Early in 1690 they took steps to safeguard their rights by proceeding against the duke at the Aulic Council, the *Reichshofrat*, and appointed an agent there with a salary of 150 guilders a year. In the following year he submitted a memorandum in which he emphasized that the longer Frederick Charles's policy prevailed, the more dangerous it was because, under the specious pretext of the defence of the country, he was preparing the basis of a *perpetuus conscriptus miles*, in time of peace as well as of war, which would lead eventually to the annihilation of the Estates' privileges, and even of their *corpus* itself, as was shown by the sad examples of Bavaria, Brandenburg, Lüneburg, &c. In 1692 the Estates submitted to the Emperor Leopold complaints against the transformation of the militia into a regular force, and against a ducal order to all officials that, on pain of dismissal, the extraordinary taxes were not to be paid into the Estates' chest, but into the privy chancellery. They accused the duke's councillors of being the cause of all the trouble which had arisen during the regency, and of aiming at a *perpetuus miles*, and they reserved their right of proving their innocence to the young heir to the throne. Their achievement was that the Emperor ordered an inquiry and sent the vice-president of the Aulic Council to investigate on the spot their complaints against the regent and to promote the redress of their grievances.[2] As the revenue was insufficient to maintain

[1] State Archives Stuttgart, *Tomus Actorum*, xcvii, fos. 348–9, 445, 509–15, 518–19, 521–32, 543–4c, 618b; xcviii, fos. 33, 53; Grube, op. cit., p. 361; Schneider, op. cit., p. 308 (14 Jan. to 29 May 1691).

[2] State Archives Stuttgart, *Tomus Actorum*, xcvi, fo. 209; xcviii, fos. 68–69, 662–82, 818–19; xcix, fos. 163, 543 (23 Feb. 1690 to 10 Sept. 1692).

the army, Frederick Charles intended to hire out troops to the Emperor Leopold or to William of Orange; but the Estates succeeded in preventing the use of the 'transformed' militia outside the duchy. When in 1692 the duke became a prisoner of war in French hands, the Estates at first denied any obligation to pay his ransom and his subsistence, because he was not the reigning duke and had started an offensive war against their will and against so powerful an enemy. Only after some months could the Small Committee be persuaded to lend 12,000 guilders for this purpose.[1] A further exacerbation of the conflict was only avoided by an Imperial declaration that the sixteen-year-old Eberhard Louis had attained his majority, so that he could assume the government at the beginning of 1693.

The years following were dominated by the actions of Louis XIV. In June 1693 a French contribution of 149,000 guilders was levied on twelve Württemberg towns. Two months later the French army advanced and occupied a large part of the duchy. Many towns and villages were looted and burnt. The towns of Backnang, Calw, Marbach, Vaihingen, Winnenden, and Zavelstein were totally destroyed, as was the beautiful abbey and castle of Hirsau in the Black Forest. A contribution of 600,000 guilders, payable within twelve months, was levied, and a further 150,000 for every year that the war continued. The mayors of Stuttgart and Tübingen, two prelates, the Estates' councillor, Dr. Sturm, and nine others were taken as hostages to Strasbourg, and then to Metz where they remained in custody for over three years. At the end of 1693 the Estates estimated the damage caused through looting and burning during the past months at over 1,400,000 guilders, although an agreement was signed about the contribution and hostages were taken as a security for its payment. After the peace of Ryswick the total damage was estimated at more than 8,000,000 guilders. The misery and suffering rivalled that caused by the Thirty Years War, and the population once more declined sharply.[2]

[1] Ibid. xcix, fos. 668–9; c, fos. 94–95, 218; Sattler, op. cit. xi. 228 (20 Oct. 1692 to 25 Feb. 1693).

[2] State Archives Stuttgart, *Tomus Actorum*, c, fos. 366, 585, 593–4, 606; ci, fos. 352–64; ciii, fos. 15–18; cv, fo. 213; Grube, op. cit., pp. 364–6. Schneider, op. cit., p. 318, states that the population declined from 450,000 to 300,000, but these are only estimates.

VII. *The Issue of the Army in the Reign of Eberhard Louis*

The reign of Eberhard Louis started in very troubled circumstances. Because of the country's plight the Estates were more than ever determined to curtail expenditure and, above all, to get rid of the burden of the small ducal army, then numbering three regiments. There were, moreover, two other issues which caused friction between the prince and the Estates, although neither was to lead to such bitter and long-drawn-out conflicts as that of the army. The one was brought forth by ducal attempts to gain some control over the Estates' financial administration; the other concerned the prelacies, many of which were kept vacant for reasons of economy.

In 1694 Eberhard Louis proposed to the Small Committee that measures should be taken to improve the administration of the Estates' chest, but the committee did not react. The duke then pointed out that he was unwilling to leave the control of revenue and expenditure to their *arbitrium*. He was determined to supervise closely how *his* revenues and the country's income were dispensed and not to leave the direction any longer in other hands. The Estates repudiated the idea of a joint direction of their chest, which would be contrary to the *leges fundamentales* and the ancient custom. They could not understand why the duke called their contributions *his* revenues, a phrase no previous ruler had ever used, and which was in their opinion prejudicial to their rights. Eberhard Louis replied he would soon nominate a qualified man to share the administration of the revenues with the two receivers of the Estates. The fact that the receivers' administration was supervised by the Small Committee did not preclude the presence of his deputies if he found that convenient. Nor did it mean that the Estates could claim the sole direction of the chest and its administration, so that they allowed the prince at most a condominium, and even this they now dared to deny him with disrespectful expressions. For such words he strongly reprimanded especially the prelates who were appointed merely by his grace, for the abbeys had been restored in the peace of Westphalia to the house of Württemberg, and not to the Estates. He wished to know who had granted them powers to deny to their prince his greatest regale; he quoted the authority of Seneca's *De Beneficiis*, according to which everything within the realm belonged to the prince, including all private property. The Estates in their turn strongly denied that the duke could deprive the prelates and leave the monasteries vacant and quoted as proof the *Recess* of 1565, and there the controversy ended for the time being.[1]

Only three months later the Small Committee begged Eberhard Louis to relieve the country from the burden of his three regiments, so that the unity between himself and his obedient Estates might be restored and maintained, to the benefit of the public weal. Again they were severely reprimanded for submitting such an absurd petition on a matter that was not at all under discussion, and for implying in an odious and unbecoming fashion that their prince and his councillors were not solicitous for the public weal. Such repeated misbehaviour would be punished, for it was for the duke alone to consider and to decide what was necessary for the public weal, and he must insist that the committee would respect this in future.[2] For many years the Estates had not been treated to such language. It was the language of the age of princely despotism, an age in which diets and Estates' privileges seemed antiquated institutions. Accordingly, only one diet was held during Eberhard Louis's long reign of forty years; but there were numerous meetings of the Small as well as the Large Committee, the latter usually being empowered to act on behalf of all the Estates.[3]

In 1695 Eberhard Louis came back to his demand that a third receiver should be appointed by him to the Estates' chest and its status revised; he also demanded a contribution of 400,000 guilders payable within three years. This the Estates declined on account of the war and the French contribution; in their opinion the appointment of a third receiver was neither necessary nor useful, for the duke had no cause to distrust them and hold them in disgrace. Eberhard Louis, however, insisted on his demands. Otherwise he would have to take other measures during the emergency on grounds of his princely authority. If

---

[1] State Archives Stuttgart, *Tomus Actorum*, cii, fos. 56–57, 108–9, 227–31, 290 (10 July to 18 Aug. 1694). The quotation from *De Beneficiis*, lib. 1, cap. 6, was: 'Caesar omnia habet, fiscus ejus privata tantum ac sua, et universa in imperio ejus sunt, in patrimonio propria.' For the *Recess* of 1565, see above, p. 38.

[2] State Archives Stuttgart, *Tomus Actorum*, ciii, fos. 161, 184 (14–20 Nov. 1694).

[3] This was called a *Bevollmächtigter Grosser Ausschuss*. It met every year and in practice took over the functions of the diet.

they considered three receivers too many, they should dismiss
one of theirs. The appointment of eight prelates was sufficient,
for the six vacancies served to alleviate the finances of the
Church. The Estates then granted 20,000 guilders, but Eberhard Louis demanded 200,000. The Estates gradually increased
their grant to 117,000 guilders, payable within four years, on
condition that no third receiver would be appointed and that
they were not burdened with the maintenance of the ducal life-
guards. In their opinion a prince's best life-guard was the love
of his loyal subjects, as shown by the example of Eberhard the
Bearded who, two centuries earlier, deemed it his greatest treasure
that he could sleep quietly in the lap of every one of his subjects.
Appointments to prelacies had never been refused, at least *ad
designationem*, which did not cause any expense. According to
the treaty of Tübingen and their privileges, no tax was to be
levied without the Estates' consent, and that remained valid
during an emergency. Their predecessors had always esteemed
this treaty the duchy's most precious jewel, and its spirit and
its letter must be preserved. Eberhard Louis's reply again showed
deep irritation. The *exercitium collectationis* was absurd and against
evident reason, against the real meaning of the duchy's constitution and the customs of the Holy Roman Empire and of the
whole world. It was due to an almost ridiculous, nonsensical
observance. The appointment of a third receiver was a right he
refused to forgo; but the other conditions were accepted, with
the difference that the money granted should be paid within a
shorter time.[1] Yet no third receiver was ever appointed.

In the following year four of the six vacant prelacies were duly
filled by appointments *ad designationem*, as the Estates had suggested.[2] Eberhard Louis then demanded from the Large Committee their assent to an increased excise on meat and wine and
to an excise on the mills for the grinding of corn. This the committee declined because it was an innovation which the common
man would not understand. Yet the decree introducing the new
tax was published and the committee was told to ask for new
instructions, while the ducal officials were ordered to supervise

---

[1] State Archives Stuttgart, *Tomus Actorum*, ciii, fos. 545, 585–9, 593–5, 626, 631–2,
641, 649, 664–6, 669, 671–2, 675, 689–92, 714 (20 Apr. to 10 June 1695).
[2] Ibid. civ, fo. 657 (24 Mar. 1696). The prelacies filled were those of Alpirsbach,
Hirsau, Königsbronn, and Maulbronn.

the local deliberations and to see to it that the instructions were given in the desired form. The aim, however, was not attained. When the new powers arrived, they varied greatly, and there was no majority in favour of the new excise. Some were against, some in favour, but on conditions. Some desired a diet to decide the issue, with the result that the Large Committee voted against the mill-excise, but consented to other increases which were then introduced. Yet the defeat rankled: two years later Eberhard Louis refused to confirm the election of the prelate of St. Georgen to the Large Committee because he had voted against the mill-excise, had not shown due respect to his prince, and therefore did not enjoy his confidence. In spite of several petitions in favour of the prelate, the duke declined to change his resolution so that in the end another prelate was elected to the committee.[1]

In September 1697 peace was concluded at Ryswick between Louis XIV and his enemies, according to which he gave up his bridge-heads on the right bank of the Rhine and some of his other conquests. The threat from France was diminishing. Six months after the conclusion of peace the Small Committee renewed the petition for the total disbanding of the three ducal regiments, numbering 1,600 infantrymen and 1,200 cavalry, whose pay alone came to about 173,000 guilders a year. The Estates' debts stood at the record figure of 5,400,000 guilders, including arrears of interest of 300,000, which made them more anxious than ever to effect economies. Their opposition to the maintenance of the three regiments was stiffened by their knowledge that the privy councillors were also opposed to it, the matter being in the hands of the cabinet councillors only. Some privy councillors wanted to arraign these as traitors before the Aulic Council. The Small Committee alleged that the lives of the members would be in danger if they made the slightest concession on this point and insisted that the matter should be submitted to a diet. Eberhard Louis agreed to reduce his 2,800 men to 1,800, not counting the Württemberg contingent of 1,040 men serving with the army of the Swabian Circle, which cost 110,000 guilders a year. The Small Committee once more

[1] Ibid. civ, fos. 713*b*, 755; cvi, fo. 316; cvii, fos. 281-2, 470; Reyscher, op. cit. xvii, nos. 150, 152, pp. 306-12 (7 Apr. to 6 May 1696, 25 May 1698 to 17 Jan. 1699).

suggested that a diet should be summoned; but the duke called only the Large Committee. This repeated the demands for the total disbanding of the army and the summoning of a diet; otherwise the question should be decided by the Emperor; yet after some hesitation it granted the taxes required until the end of the year, pending the decision of a diet which was to meet in the autumn of 1698.[1]

This diet—the only one of the reign—met in September 1698 and lasted, with an interruption of three weeks at Christmas, four months, without leading to an agreement between the prince and the Estates: clearly the reason why the experiment was not repeated.[2] The bone of contention was the three ducal regiments, which Eberhard Louis offered to reduce by another 100, and later 200, men, but on whose maintenance he insisted, while the Estates were willing only to pay for the contingent with the Swabian Circle. They felt they were the *procuratores publici* of more than 280,000 inhabitants of the duchy, and in their opinion the ducal plans were contrary to its constitution. All the towns and *Ämter* voted against the maintenance of these troops, which they considered unnecessary, useless, and an unbearable burden. The prelates, however, always more inclined to compromise and more dependent on the duke, were less united. Some were in favour of accepting a further reduction of the regiments and of discharging the Württembergers on condition of re-enlistment in case of an emergency, while keeping on the officers and employing them if possible in a civil capacity, and these suggestions were adopted by a majority. The Estates even appealed to Eberhard Louis's mother who took their side, but counselled moderation. They blamed everything on the young duke's evil councillors whose machinations they were determined to prevent, and whom they wanted to remove from their positions of influence, even if that necessitated an appeal to the Emperor. This declaration was considered to be so disrespectful by the councillors that they returned it to its authors, informing them that the Emperor Leopold had

[1] State Archives Stuttgart, *Tomus Actorum*, cvi, fos. 107, 110, 114–15, 133–4, 174–6, 179, 181–2, 206b, 235, 247–65, 279–92, 312–15, 493–5, 667 (19 Mar. to 29 July 1698); Grube, op. cit., pp. 367–8.

[2] A diet was concluded by a *Recess* or *Abschied* which embodied the agreements reached during its duration. This time there was no *Recess*, which meant a rupture.

instructed the Circles to take further defence measures against the Turks and others.[1]

When the diet was resumed in January 1699 the Estates repeated their demand for the disbandment of the three regiments and rejected a mere reduction. Until this main grievance was redressed they would not vote any money, a decision which was approved unanimously. Eberhard Louis refused to give up his intention, which in his opinion was the best for the country, but offered to pay off another 200 men. He pointed out that Württemberg was now a frontier province of the Empire and surrounded by powerful neighbours. The bastions of Alsace and Burgundy had gone, and this created entirely new conditions. The Estates' councillor, Dr. Sturm, submitted a memorandum in which he said that in the Estates' opinion *salus publica suprema lex esto* was the foundation of a Christian state, while now many advocated the godless principle that a prince need not respect the welfare of his subjects, but should aim at splendour, pomp and ambition; the privy council no longer spoke for the country, but only for the duke. The Estates then granted powers to appeal to the Emperor, but this step was opposed by three of the prelates. Dr. Sturm was dismissed from his post as ducal councillor, whereupon the Small Committee resolved to support him energetically and to indemnify him and any others who might have to suffer, a resolution which they decided to keep secret. Eberhard Louis in his turn instructed the *Amtleute* to examine the mayors and urban courts and councils and inquire whether they had given powers to their deputies to arraign him before the Emperor, and whether they wanted this suit to continue.[2]

Thus the diet ended in an open rupture. In the following century a Württemberg historian commented: 'the most ignorant knew and remembered that the country was not obliged to maintain a standing army'. He praised the Estates for their perseverance and their courage which made them willing to risk the utmost.[3] As the Estates had not made a grant,

[1] State Archives Stuttgart, *Tomus Actorum*, cvii, fos. 52, 94-100, 145, 233, 244, 251-6 (6 Oct. to 15 Dec. 1698).
[2] Ibid., fos. 491-2, 513, 515-21, 528-9, 562-73, 576-80, 583, 599 (20 Jan. to 3 Feb. 1699); Grube, op. cit., pp. 369-72.
[3] L. T. Spittler, 'Entwurff einer Geschichte des engern landschaftlichen Ausschusses', op. cit., pp. 481-2.

Eberhard Louis resorted to levying taxes without their consent,
against which the Small Committee protested in vain. The
army was reduced, but only to about 1,800 men whose maintenance still cost 130,000 guilders a year. The ducal officials were
ordered to levy the taxes decreed and to use the money to pay
the soldiers billeted in the district in question. If there was a
surplus they should pay it into the Estates' chest—orders which
caused renewed protests.[1]

Meanwhile the Small Committee proceeded with drafting
the complaint to the Emperor. In June 1699 the majority pronounced in favour of sending it to their agent in Vienna with
instructions to submit it; but the two clerical members advocated waiting until the autumn because Eberhard Louis had
not yet been invested by the Emperor. Some weeks later the
privy councillors summoned the Estates' councillor, Hörner,
and strongly pressed him to withdraw the complaint. This after
a long and acrimonious discussion he promised to do and
accordingly sent instructions to Vienna to hold back the suppli-
cation until further orders. Then the privy councillors began
to work on the prelates, trying to persuade them to sign a revocation of the petition, and through intimidation they succeeded
in obtaining five signatures. They then called before them the
two prelates who sat on the Small Committee, reprimanded
them for signing the original petition and enjoined them to sign
the revocation. This the two prelates declined to do and suggested calling a meeting of the Large Committee. Eberhard
Louis, however, threatened all prelates who would not sign with
dismissal. Thereupon five prelates declared that if they signed
as ordered this would mean the separation of the two Estates
which, according to the *Recess* of 1565, were to decide everything together: for reasons of conscience they found it impossible
to do as commanded. Thus the prelates were deeply disunited,
five opposing the duke and siding with the towns, five giving
way to pressure, and three whose attitude is not recorded. Yet
Eberhard Louis did not make good his threat of dismissal,
perhaps fearing the intervention of the Emperor. Only one
prelate, the abbot of Denkendorf, had his salary stopped by,
as he expressed it, a *decretum horribile* which took him twenty-

---

[1] State Archives Stuttgart, *Tomus Actorum*, cviii, fos. 183, 198, 200–203, 206,
288; cix, fos. 283–94 (17 June to 6 July 1700).

four hours to digest; and even this measure was rescinded in the following year.[1]

For three years, between 1699 and the spring of 1702, not even the Large Committee was summoned, and only the Small Committee met several times each year. As it did not proceed with the complaint to Vienna, there was no open conflict. Indeed, the committee found itself in the unenviable position of being blamed by Eberhard Louis for its opposition, and by the Estates for conceding more than they had powers to do and for not knowing how to act. This argument the committee put forward when faced with a ducal demand for a voluntary contribution, emphasizing rightly that it was not empowered to make a grant and that it was expressly instructed not to grant anything until the army was disbanded. Yet only two weeks later it granted 30,000 guilders, without, as it expressed it, consenting to the upkeep of the troops. Naturally, there was nothing to prevent Eberhard Louis from using the money for that purpose. During 1701, however, financial stringency forced him to discharge more and more men: one of the three regiments was to be disbanded, the cavalry regiment was to be reduced to 300 men, and the infantry regiment to 800, decreasing the military budget to 92,573 guilders. When the Estates refused to accept this, he further promised that half the infantry would be transferred to the regiment serving with the Swabian Circle, thus reducing his own troops to 700 men. By May 1702 their number had shrunk to a total of 660, a negligible size; while the Württemberg forces serving with the Swabian Circle were increased from less than 1,000 to 2,000 men through new recruiting caused by the imminent struggle for the Spanish succession.[2]

At this stage Louis XIV once again lent his indirect support to Eberhard Louis. At the outbreak of the War of the Spanish Succession he summoned the Large Committee and proposed an increase of his own forces to 1,000 cavalry and 1,600 infantry because of the advance of the Bavarian army and the threatening situation. The committee, however, replied that it was impossible to raise so many in addition to their contributions

[1] Ibid. cviii, fos. 216–48, 400, 421, 467–8, 491–4, 497–9, 502–4, 508–10; cix, fo. 672 (2 June to 3 Oct. 1699); Grube, op. cit., pp. 372–4.

[2] State Archives Stuttgart, *Tomus Actorum*, cix, fos. 403–4, 430; cx, fos. 5–6, 9, 33–36, 44, 47–48; cxi, fos. 52–54 (25 Nov. 1700 to 8 June 1701, 24 May 1702).

to the Swabian Circle, that its forces, seconded by the militia, would suffice, and that in any case the duchy could not be defended by two regiments. When Eberhard Louis insisted, they consented to the recruiting of 1,000 infantry and 450 horse; whereupon he came back to the old project of a regulated militia, which was to consist of three infantry regiments with 1,500 men each and two of cavalry with 500 each, under officers to be selected by the Estates. This force, with the existing ducal troops and the contingent for the Swabian Circle, would cost the sum of 776,339 guilders a year. No wonder that the Estates protested solemnly and declared that such an amount could not be squeezed out of the country by methods however harsh. They opposed the plan of a regulated militia and even declined to participate in a deputation to discuss the project of an army reduced to 3,000 infantry and 600 horse. Again the Estates' unanimity was marred by the dissent of the prelates of Hirsau and Blaubeuren, who were in favour of a compromise. Tempers became more frayed when it became known that Eberhard Louis was proceeding with his plan without awaiting the Estates' consent, which caused renewed protests. After months of protracted negotiations they eventually assented, on condition that they would no longer have to pay for the duke's own troops and that the regulated militia would not be employed outside the country—conditions which Eberhard Louis refused to accept. The privy councillors informed the Estates that he would not wait for their consent, but would do what was necessary for the duchy's welfare. They were ordered to abstain from all interference with state business and not to stir up any trouble, otherwise the duke would take measures to guarantee the respect due to his princely state.[1]

During the following years military affairs became more and more prominent in the negotiations between Eberhard Louis and the Estates. At the end of 1703 the regulated militia was increased by one regiment of 1,500 men, for which the unmarried over eighteen years of age, with the exception of certain groups, were to be conscripted. Four months later two new regiments with 1,200 men each were recruited and the

---

[1] State Archives Stuttgart, *Tomus Actorum*, cxi, fos. 259, 266, 271, 299, 301–3, 408–9, 452–5, 459, 462–6, 472–3, 592–4; cxiii, fos. 60, 96–99 (20 Sept. 1702 to 21 Mar. 1703).

existing two ducal regiments brought up to strength. By the end of 1704 these forces (without the militia) amounted to four regiments and two companies of horse-guards, whose maintenance (including the payments to the Swabian Circle) cost nearly 1,200,000 guilders a year. Twelve months later the figure had risen to almost 1,300,000 guilders. These amounts the duchy could not have raised if Eberhard Louis in 1704 had not concluded a subsidy treaty with the United Provinces by which they agreed to pay Württemberg 300,000 guilders a year for the duration of the war. As this was only a proportion of the total cost, the Large Committee granted for the army a new tax, the *tricesimae*, a levy in kind of one-thirtieth on corn and wine. This tax was extended year after year, in addition to the customary taxes and special voluntary contributions amounting to hundreds of thousands of guilders. Yet the committee attached certain conditions to the grant: the treaty with Holland was to be communicated to them; the subsidies were to be paid into the Estates' chest, as were also the *tricesimae*; natives of Württemberg were not to be forced to serve outside the duchy and were to be replaced in due course by mercenaries. The treaty with Holland was duly inspected by the Estates' deputies, and Eberhard Louis agreed that the subsidies and the *tricesimae* should be paid into their chest, though reserving to himself the right of disposing of the money by decree.[1]

Thus the Estates strove to preserve their influence in matters of finance and foreign policy in spite of the war. In 1706 the Large Committee declared that they would vote a contribution to the ducal chamber only if their grievances were redressed: in particular, the military burdens and the court expenditure should be reduced, and the existing 'absolute government' should be abolished and the constitution be observed. A fortnight later, however, they made a substantial grant—although less than the government desired—while repeating their demands for a more constitutional government and for the disbanding of the ducal army after the end of the war. Eberhard Louis, however, replied that he could not tie his hands as far

[1] Ibid. cxiv, fos. 38–39, 332–3, 340, 344–5, 368–78, 390, 400–3; cxv, fos. 14–16; cxvi. 1, fos. 5–14 (18 Dec. 1703 to 19 Nov. 1705). For the grants of 1705–6, see ibid. cxv, fos. 395, 398, 400, 417; cxvi. 1, fos. 34, 39–43, 46–55, 395–404; cxvi. 2, fos. 150, 162, 173, 177–85.

ahead as that, for this would depend on the general situation, and he had to protect his subjects against foreign aggression. Again the Estates had been too weak to carry through the policy of grievances before supply and had to be content with such vague and ambiguous declarations. All that was left to them was to whittle down the ducal demands for more money, to renew their *gravamina* about the court and the army, and to maintain that they were not obliged to pay for the horse-guards—tactics which left the initiative entirely in the hands of the government.[1]

Once again the negotiations were interrupted by the approach of the French army. In May 1707 Marshal de Villars invaded Baden. A few weeks later a contribution of 1,500,000 guilders was demanded from Württemberg, with the intention, according to the French *Intendant*, of making the duchy incapable of rendering any assistance to the Emperor Joseph. Through negotiations the demand was reduced to 1,100,000, but that sum was duly paid within five months. Then the three hostages which the country had to furnish were released, and Louis XIV took it and its inhabitants under his royal protection. At the beginning of 1708 a new French demand for the payment of the same amount within five weeks was received;[2] but the change in the fortunes of war henceforth allowed Württemberg to escape further payments. Thanks to the victories of Marlborough and Prince Eugene, the French were now on the defensive, and western Germany was safe from invasion. Yet the ducal demands continued to grow, amounting to 1,500,000 guilders between May 1708 and April 1709 for an army of only 4,350 men. A graduated poll-tax was introduced, rising from half a guilder for servants, &c., to 24 guilders, only beggars of great age and infirmity and children under the age of fourteen being exempt.[3] This enormous burden brought forth rumblings of revolt. Somebody wrote on the door of the Estates' house in Stuttgart: 'if you consent to the Duke's demands, we shall revolt'. The Large Committee feared that they would lose their heads if they granted what *Serenissimus* demanded. A privy councillor admitted that, if a rising broke out, the government

---

[1] State Archives Stuttgart, *Tomus Actorum*, cxvi. 1, fos. 379–80, 395–6, 408–10, 425–9; cxvi. 2, fos. 19, 160–1, 422–3 (15 Apr. 1706 to 7 Apr. 1707).

[2] Ibid. cxvii, fos. 32, 112–13, 122–5, 295; cxviii, fos. 117, 326 (5 June 1707 to 20 Jan. 1708). The figures in livres are twice those in guilders.

[3] Ibid. cxviii, fos. 565, 593–604; cxix, fos. 259–74 (Mar. to Nov. 1708).

would be unable to put up any resistance. The commander-in-chief, General von Phul, suggested changing the name of the guards to 'life-regiment' because their name was so hated. Even he had to acknowledge that things could not go on like that, and that but for the Estates the whole state would long since have collapsed. Matters only improved when the United Provinces in 1709 took four ducal regiments into their pay, the whole army excluding only about 300 horse-guards, and the regiments marched into the Netherlands.[1]

By that time a new conflict had arisen between the prince and the Estates in which they found unexpected allies. Eberhard Louis lived in separation from his wife and had contracted a morganatic marriage with the Countess Wilhelmina von Grävenitz. This aroused much adverse comment in the country, which also feared he might become a convert to Roman Catholicism to achieve the annulment of his first marriage, and the native Lutheranism began to assert itself. The privy councillors felt slighted because the duke surrounded himself with foreign advisers and did not consult them any longer. The duchess informed the Estates that it was Eberhard Louis's intention to usurp the *jus collectandi*, and to take over the debts and the financial administration of the Estates, under the pretence that their privileges only existed because they had taken over the prince's debts. She suggested they should appoint an agent at the Aulic Council, whose expenses her father, the margrave of Baden-Durlach, was willing to share. Eberhard Louis's attitude was simple: if anybody wanted to see the 'Countess' removed, they should give him money for the purpose, and he suggested to the Small Committee that they should pay 150,000 guilders for this to be achieved. This they declined to do, in spite of all his entreaties, and instead brought forward their grievances. Thereupon they were told that they should address him in future in more modest and respectful terms, otherwise he would proceed against the authors. He expressed strong annoyance that they spoke of the 'Countess' (whose title he had bought with good money) as 'the von Grävenitz' and returned their letter. He further told them that they had no business to intrude into his cabinet where they had nothing to seek, nor to meddle

[1] Ibid. cxviii, fos. 55, 89 (reports of the Prelate Johann Osiander of 9–23 Dec. 1707); cxx, fo. 3 (20 Mar. 1709).

with the affairs of his princely family—an audaciousness to
which he took exception. The committee conceded her the title
of 'Countess', but refused to grant her any money. Its members
feared arrest and contemplated meeting at Göppingen, instead
of Stuttgart, if need be, under the pretence of inspecting the
Estates' original privileges, which for reasons of safety were kept
in the Free City of Ulm. They reported matters to their agent
in Vienna, instructing him to ask for the protection of the
Emperor.[1] Yet the feared arrests did not take place. In the end
Eberhard Louis gave way and removed the 'Countess' from his
entourage for the time being, without obtaining a grant for
this purpose and without effecting a reconciliation with his
wife. Perhaps he feared complications with Baden-Durlach or
with the Emperor; perhaps he wanted to reconcile public
opinion; perhaps the 'Countess' had lost some of her charms,
which Eberhard Louis seems to have been quite ready to trade
for a mess of pottage.

When in 1709 the four ducal regiments departed for the
Netherlands, there remained only two companies of horse-
guards which the Estates agreed to maintain, in addition to their
contribution to the defence of the Swabian Circle. Eberhard
Louis, however, immediately ordered the recruitment of two
companies of life-guards with 240 men, later increased to 450.
Thus the total military budget still came to almost 400,000
guilders a year. Although this was a much lower sum than
before, the Estates declined to pay for the two new companies,
but made the usual grants of ordinary taxes and the *tricesimae*
on a reduced level. They also objected to the extortion of taxes
militari manu by unheard-of methods (if certain districts could
not pay punctually), to the repartition of taxes by the War
Council through decree, instead of through an agreement with
the Estates, and to the fortification of Ludwigsburg, for which
demands had been put forward during the past five years.[2]

In 1710 the Large Committee went further and declared they
had no powers to consent to the heavy burden of maintaining

---

[1] State Archives Stuttgart, *Tomus Actorum*, cxviii, fos. 843–4; cxix, fos. 24, 27–36,
129, 135–6, 191, 211–12, 224 (15 June to 1 Sept. 1708); Grube, op. cit., pp. 380–2.
[2] State Archives Stuttgart, *Tomus Actorum*, cxx, fos. 5–6, 17, 25, 32–39, 66,
70–71, 75–81, 532–6; cxxi, fos. 297–9; cxxii, fos. 10–14; cxxiii, fos. 12–14; cxxiv,
fos. 8–9; cxxv, fos. 17, 111, 184–6 (9 Apr. to 23 May 1709, and detailed figures
of military expenditure until 1714).

the guards: these should be reduced to the strength they had had in the previous reign. Eberhard Louis promised a reduction to about 500 men, but this they considered insufficient. In the end they voted certain taxes, but declined to pay for the guards, for which they had no mandate, and which was beyond the country's power. Eberhard Louis believed that the Estates were incited against him by certain people and uttered threats against these alleged ringleaders who prevented the restoration of harmony. The Estates on the other hand sent a deputation to the privy councillors to inform them that if there were no change of policy, they would in the end be obliged to seek in all modesty the decision of the Emperor; for the country was gradually sinking into a state of slavery for which their successors would hold them responsible, and they considered it their duty to prevent this. One of the duke's confidants, the prince of Hohenzollern-Hechingen (to the south of Württemberg), offered to mediate between him and the Estates. In his opinion, 120 guardsmen were sufficient for the duke's protection; but he admitted that the government's order that all muskets were to be handed over was due to the fear of an uprising.[1]

During the following years the Estates continued to make substantial grants, though always less than Eberhard Louis demanded, and not for the maintenance of the guards. For these the government used the *tricesimae* which were administered by the War Council and withdrawn from the Estates' control. They repeatedly protested against this practice, but nevertheless continued to grant the tax. Occasionally they threatened to withhold their consent, but did not carry out their threat, on one occasion with the curious argument that they had already given their assent and therefore did not wish to impede the levy of the tax. Naturally, the government did not heed their complaints. The same applied to the repeated complaints about the levying of tax arrears by the military who even took away the beds of the poor, about the labour and carrying services and the quit-rents demanded for the building of the new ducal residence at Ludwigsburg, about the tobacco monopoly, and about the burdens imposed upon the church lands, &c. Even when

[1] Ibid. cxxi, fos. 12–13, 122–3, 125, 127, 300–1, 303–4, 309, 403, 409, 425, 435 (25 Jan. to 14 May 1710).

Eberhard Louis refused to confirm the election of the prelate
of Maulbronn to the Large Committee, the Small Committee
acquiesced and elected another prelate. During the war the
Estates thought it was their duty to support their prince, but
equally that they would have to appeal to a higher judge if
the restoration of peace did not bring an alleviation of their
burdens and the redress of their grievances.[1] This declaration
was made a few days before the treaties of Utrecht were signed
between France and her enemies. The wars of Louis XIV,
which time and again so strongly influenced the relations
between the prince and the Estates, finally came to an end.

The crucial question was how these relations would shape in
the ensuing long period of peace. Would the Estates be able to
make good their claim that they were not obliged to maintain
a standing army, or would the duke succeed in preserving and
increasing its strength? Would the Estates' privileges remain
unscathed, or would they have to give way to *raison d'état* in the
age of absolute government? Bitter conflicts about these issues
were to fill the following half-century; but the weakness of the
Estates in resisting the demands of their prince, their habit of
making concessions, their failure to insist on the redress of their
grievances, did not augur well for the outcome of these conflicts.

After the restoration of peace Eberhard Louis reigned for
twenty more years during which no diet was summoned. The
main issue between him and the Estates continued to be that
of the army, of his own regiments which were released from
service with the United Provinces. For the moment, however,
the problem was solved because Prince Eugene took these four
Württemberg regiments into the pay of the Empire for twelve
months. Thus their cost was to be borne by the Swabian Circle
to which the duchy had to contribute its customary share. In
1713–14 this contribution and the cost of the guards amounted
to nearly 700,000 guilders. The four regiments then numbered
4,040 men and the ducal forces at home 633, a total of only
4,673, of whom 823 were cavalry.[2] In the same year the new
king of Prussia, Frederick William I, decided to keep a standing
army of 8,250 cavalry and 39,000 infantry, about ten times the

---

[1] State Archives Stuttgart, *Tomus Actorum*, cxxii, fos. 479, 502–3, 511; cxxiii, fos.
16–17, 25, 363; cxxiv, fos. 20, 46–47, 195, 466, 491, 541–2 (25 Apr. 1711 to 27
Mar. 1713).

[2] Ibid. cxxv, fos. 16–17, 110–14, 184–6 (17 June to 29 Nov. 1713).

figure of Württemberg, although Prussia then had at most four times the population of Württemberg.[1]

The Estates adhered to their policy of granting the contributions to the Swabian Circle, but refusing those for the ducal guards. They declared that the *tricesimae* had been consented to only because of the war and unanimously declined to prolong them. Their councillor told the privy councillors that *Serenissimus* was not absolute, but that the duchy possessed beautiful privileges which included the participation of the Estates in the levying of taxes and in military affairs. In the end the Estates agreed to the levy of the *tricesimae*, but insisted it was the last time, a clause which had to be inserted into the decree, and protested that this did not imply a tacit consent to the maintenance of the duke's own troops. The prelate of Hirsau, Johann Osiander, even tried to sow fear into the hearts of obnoxious privy councillors by reminding them of the fate of those who in the past attempted to suppress the Estates, especially the Chancellor Enzlin who was executed in the early seventeenth century.[2]

At the end of 1714 Eberhard Louis informed the Estates once more that he could not disband his own troops because the terms of the peace of Baden had not yet been carried out, nor had the security of the Empire been established, and already there were new rumours of war. Even if the peace were carried out, in his opinion it would not last long. A small army would let money circulate more quickly and help the improvement of manufactures, and the total military budget would only require just over 500,000 guilders, including the contribution to the Swabian Circle. The Estates, however, remained steadfast and demanded at least an assurance that after six months the troops would either be paid off or taken into the pay of another power —an assurance which Eberhard Louis declined to give. Early in 1715 they eventually voted about 150,000 guilders for six months and at first unanimously declined a larger grant. But when Eberhard Louis insisted on more they again gave way and increased the sum to about 195,000 guilders, most of this being

---

[1] Carl Hinrichs, 'Der Regierungsantritt Friedrich Wilhelms I.', *Jahrbuch für die Geschichte Mittel- und Ostdeutschlands*, v, Tübingen, 1957, p. 194.

[2] State Archives Stuttgart, *Tomus Actorum*, cxxv, fos. 476, 482–4, 504, 507, 524–7, 551–2 (20 Apr. to 7 June 1714). For the fate of Dr. Enzlin, see above, p. 49.

destined *ad militaria*, and this arrangement was accepted for the time being. In other words, in spite of all their protestations to the contrary, the Estates had in practice conceded the maintenance of a small standing army in peace-time. Yet the grant was insufficient for the need of the government. When the *tricesimae*, which had been granted 'for the last time' in 1714, expired they were prolonged for another year, without the Estates' consent, by simple decree in July 1715. A few weeks later the Large Committee declared that they would permit the collection *passive* 'for the last time'. They pointed out that this tax was introduced only during the French wars and rescinded immediately after the peace of Ryswick, that the treaty of Tübingen stipulated that the *jus collectandi* depended on their consent, and that most towns and *Ämter* had negatived the *tricesimae*. They further asserted that the treaty of Tübingen, the famous *palladium hujus ducatus*, regulated the *jus belli* in this way that, if the duke wanted to begin a war and desired the Estates' help, his subjects had to serve with their bodies, whereas he was obliged to pay the mercenaries. If the duke held different opinions, a diet should be summoned. Yet again the Estates agreed not only 'passively' to the levy of the *tricesimae*, but they also granted 138,000 guilders, and then declined to increase this sum and dispersed without waiting for a formal dismissal. For this they were sharply reprimanded by Eberhard Louis, and likewise for the disrespectful terms of their last declaration, which he ordered to be returned to them and to be removed from their files, where it nevertheless survived the centuries.[1]

During the following year these moves were repeated. The Estates insisted that they were not bound to maintain a standing army in peace-time, pressed Eberhard Louis to transfer his regiments to a foreign power, asked to be relieved from the burden of the *tricesimae*, and begged that a diet should be summoned. Yet in the end they consented once more to the levy of the *tricesimae*, 'only for the current year', and made considerable grants. Eberhard Louis in his turn pointed to the examples of Bavaria and Poland (by which in the Estates' opinion he meant Saxony) where the Estates granted millions to their rulers; but

[1] State Archives Stuttgart, *Tomus Actorum*, cxxvi, fos. 7–8, 10–11, 19, 29–30, 161–2, 170, 174, 176–85, 192–3, 199–201, 204, 439–42, 448–56, 464, 468–73, 708–9 (28 Nov. 1714 to 21 Aug. 1715).

he did promise that the *tricesimae* would cease and that the repartition of the taxes for the army would be transferred from the War Council to the receivers of the Estates. These were very important points, for thus the financial administration of the Estates would be restored to its former strength and the independent ducal administration of taxes would cease. In spite of his promise, however, the *tricesimae* were continued by decree during the following years against the Estates' protests. It is true that the obnoxious War Council was dissolved in 1719; but the same decree established, after the model of Prussia, the *Generalkriegskommissariat* and appointed as its head the vice-president of the dissolved council; the new authority also became responsible for military administration and finances and the *tricesimae*, as its predecessor had been.[1] In other words, this was the dissolved War Council under a new name.

Another ducal promise, that all troops except the horse-guards and a small number of infantry would be transferred to the service of the Emperor, was fulfilled only to a limited degree. One infantry regiment was indeed transferred. Military expenditure, however, only declined from 514,000 guilders in 1714–15 to about 455,000 in 1717–18 and about 395,000 in 1719–20; but then it increased again to 439,000 in 1720–1 and to 737,000 in 1721–2 (including arrears of 305,000); in 1722–3 it amounted to 553,000, and in 1723–4 to 506,000 guilders, inclusive of substantial arrears. Thus the military burden was alleviated only for a few years, and the army's strength remained at the level of two squadrons of cavalry and three infantry regiments; while its numbers were gradually reduced from about 3,100 after the peace of Baden to 1,800 in 1722, excluding the contingent serving with the Swabian Circle.[2] The continuing high level of military expenditure was no doubt due

[1] Ibid. cxxvii, fos. 477–84, 488, 490–8, 508, 522, 532–6, 539, 542–3, 547, 550, 566, 583, 591–8; cxxviii, fos. 452–3, 468, 869; cxxix, fos. 36–37, 859, 864; cxxxi, fos. 72, 286; cxxxii, fos. 43–44, 122–5, 598; cxxxiii, fo. 448 (11 June 1716 to 19 May 1723).

[2] Schneider, op. cit., p. 332; L. I. von Stadlinger, *Geschichte des Württembergischen Kriegswesens*, Stuttgart, 1856, p. 386. Details of military expenditure from 1714 to 1724, separately for each regiment, the general staff, the contingent for the Swabian Circle, &c., may be found in State Archives Stuttgart, *Tomus Actorum*, cxxvi, fos. 10–11, 391–2; cxxviii, fos. 430–3, 822–4; cxxix, fos. 12–14; cxxx, fos. 9–11, 268–73; cxxxi, fos. 9–13, 365–8; cxxxii, fos. 7–10, 235–9, 573–7; cxxxiii, fos. 36–41, 284–9, 474–8.

partly to the many arrears, and partly to the fact that the reduction in numbers did not cause corresponding economies
because the units were not dissolved and the number of higher
ranks increased proportionately. It was in vain that the Estates
declared they were not empowered to consent to a ducal
army, that they referred to the treaty of Tübingen and their
privileges, that they desired a diet to be summoned, and pointed
out that during the minority of Louis XV it was unlikely that
France would break the peace. It was equally in vain that the
prelate of Hirsau, Johann Osiander, journeyed to London to
try to negotiate the transfer of the ducal regiments into British
pay, for during his stay there peace was concluded between
Britain and Spain.[1]

Eberhard Louis, to obtain more money from the Estates,
threatened that he would introduce *media extraordinaria*, in
particular a stamp duty or a salt monopoly. In 1720 the stamp
duty was indeed introduced by decree; but it was rescinded
again eight months later, for the Estates insisted on this as the
condition of making a somewhat larger grant. In the following year the *Generalkriegskommissariat*, without consulting the
Estates, ordered the towns and *Ämter* to collect a tax from the
communes for the construction of barracks. The new excise
regulations stipulated that all reports and queries were no
longer to be sent to the Estates but to the committee appointed
by the duke. In 1718 he informed the Large Committee that he
would never accept their careless advice and disrespectful demand that he should transfer into Imperial service his old, war-
experienced infantry. The committee were not to question and
dispute further his right of maintaining in the country as many
troops as he considered necessary and were to stop insisting that
the matter should be referred to a diet. They should consent
obediently to what was implicit in his princely authority and
done continuously by other princes of the Empire. He hoped
that they would finally learn and understand what was the duty
of loyal subjects in this respect. For some time, he continued,
he had noticed to his utmost displeasure and annoyance that
the Estates had no qualms in trying to force him to redress their

---

[1] State Archives Stuttgart, *Tomus Actorum*, cxxviii, fos. 855–6; cxxix, fos. 64–65,
70, 74–79, 506–7, 516; cxxxi, fos. 17–19, 571–2; cxxxii, fos. 16–19, 230–1 (16 Dec.
1717 to 1 Oct. 1721).

grievances, even in inventing them in an irresponsible fashion, outside their competence, and invading his princely prerogative. The use of most disrespectful expressions made their last declaration look like a malicious pasquil rather than a reasonable representation.[1]

Some years later Eberhard Louis went much further and simply announced to the Estates' deputies: 'I am a great prince and have adopted the forms of government which befit a great prince, like others of my kind. These forms are now utterly different from what they used to be thirty, fifty, and sixty years ago: other great princes who are my equals, even those owning smaller territories than I possess, maintain more troops, six, eight, even twelve thousand men . . .'. As the privy councillor von Schütz told the mayor of Stuttgart, the army was the dominant passion of *Serenissimus*. Whereupon the mayor replied modestly: great princes truly had different passions, one the army, another the hunt, another a splendid court, or new buildings; 'but with us so many dominant passions come together, and they all cause great expenditure'.[2] For the construction of Ludwigsburg as the new ducal residence and capital and that of other buildings and châteaux went on side by side with the expansion of the army and necessitated untold labour and carrying services, causing incessant complaints from the over-burdened subjects. Eberhard Louis infringed another right of the Estates by nominating the mayor of Ludwigsburg as a member of the Small Committee, a place which in his opinion was due to the town as the duchy's third capital. Yet the Small Committee acquiesced although realizing that this appointment was an innovation prejudicial to their privileges. In 1729 the duke similarly refused to confirm the appointment of the mayor of Tübingen as councillor of the Estates and suggested instead the name of a professor of law from Tübingen University. The Estates petitioned that their right of free election should be respected; but he insisted on his candidate, and the Estates once more gave way, although the law was undoubtedly on their side.[3]

In 1720 the Estates again deliberated whether they should

---

[1] Ibid. cxxviii, fo. 505; cxxix, fos. 41–42, 59–60, 719–20; cxxx, fo. 443; cxxxi, fos. 297, 355, 570, 580, 667; cxxxii, fo. 21 (21 Aug. 1717 to 28 May 1721).

[2] Ibid. cxxxii, fo. 263; cxxxiii, fo. 598 (20 Nov. 1721, 10 Dec. 1723).

[3] Ibid. cxxxi, fos. 396–7, 401; cxxxviii, fos. 25–26, 30, 33, 133–7 (3 June to 14 Nov. 1720; 17 Dec. 1729 to 24 Jan. 1730).

complain to the Emperor against their prince. But Osiander, the prelate of Hirsau, voted against this plan. He pointed to the example of 1698 when some of the prelates were intimidated and revoked the powers they had granted, showing how little they would stick to their colours when it came to the point. Since then the newly appointed prelates had to promise and to swear that they would never consent to such a step. Thus either they would have to violate their oath, or the *corpus provinciale* would be split. It is understandable that under these circumstances the Estates did not proceed with the complaint, thus giving up a very important weapon and encouraging their prince to continue his policy. In 1726 the Estates' councillor reported how indignant Eberhard Louis was with their last declaration because it did not show the respect due to him, especially with regard to the army—which was known to be his passion. He wanted to tear up their declaration and throw it at the feet of their deputies. In the end the offending document was merely returned to them.[1] The language of princely despotism asserted itself more and more, in spite of many expressions of devout obedience used by the Estates when addressing *Serenissimus* and in spite of all the gracious titles they employed.

During the first ten years after the end of the French wars the Estates steadfastly refused to consent to the payment of the standing army and to make a grant for several years, thus preserving their power of the purse. In 1724, however, Eberhard Louis, to achieve his 'great passion', took measures which were to serve as a precedent for many later ventures to put pressure on the Estates and gain their assent to unpopular demands. A circular was sent to each *Amt* of the duchy ordering the summoning of a local assembly (*Amtsversammlung*), attended by deputies from each town and village of the district. To these the question was to be submitted whether they would empower the Large Committee to grant the money for a regulated and well-trained *miles* for several years as well as higher taxes, against the abolition of the *tricesimae* and the suspension of the conscription for the militia. The point of this clearly was to induce the deputies to vote in the affirmative, and the presence of the ducal *Amtmann*

---

[1] State Archives Stuttgart, *Tomus Actorum*, cxxxi, fos. 23–45; cxxxv, fos. 241–2 (22–26 Apr. 1720, 12–14 Dec. 1726). For the precedent of 1699 (not 1698) see above, pp. 106–7.

would further serve to bring about the desired result; for the
majority of the deputies were humble village mayors, not likely
to resist pressure and cajolery. Such attempts to coerce the local
assemblies which issued the powers instructing the committees
were bound to undermine their opposition, for their members
were delegates, not representatives. When the powers given by
the towns and *Ämter* were examined by the Large Committee a
few weeks later, it was found that some districts complained
about the unusual way of collecting the votes 'across country',
because a matter of such importance ought to be discussed by
a diet and because they did not know what had been transacted
previously. Others pronounced in favour of the army, provided
it required neither the continuation of the *tricesimae*, nor increased taxation. Still others assented to the ducal proposals,
or left the decision to the Large Committee. The latter then
agreed to levy about 367,500 guilders a year for two to three
years, provided that the *tricesimae* were entirely rescinded and
the money paid into the Estates' chest. The amount was
accepted by Eberhard Louis; but he wished the grant to extend
over six years and the money to be paid to, and administered
by, his own officials. These demands were rejected by the committee, which declared that it was empowered only to grant
money for three years, and that the administration was to be
left *in statu quo*, otherwise the grant would not stand. Eberhard
Louis then gave way on this and other disputed points, and the
tricesimae were finally rescinded.[1]

The Estates had accepted the principle of a standing army,
numbering at that time only 1,800 men, and of regular grants
for its maintenance. From that time onwards they always
granted about 368,000 guilders for the troops and another
40,000 for the ducal chamber.[2] This does not take into account
the excise and the so-called 'ordinary' tax which were levied by
the Estates for the payment of interest on, and the repayment
of, the debts which they had taken over and together yielded
about 300,000 guilders a year, nor many small payments to

[1] Ibid. cxxxiii, fos. 694–5, 735–7, 740–2, 754–6, 766–9, 775, 777 (18 Jan. to 16
Mar. 1724). For the composition of the *Amtsversammlung*, see Grube, loc. cit. xiii.
206 ff.
[2] State Archives Stuttgart, *Tomus Actorum*, cxxxiv, fos. 127–32, 203, 207–12,
450–4, 548, 575–81; cxxxv, fos. 104–9, 249–54, 243, 508–13; cxxxvi, fos. 296,
302–10, 620–4; cxxxvii, fos. 229–34, 287, 509 (from the years 1724–9).

different members of the ducal family, contributions to the
Imperial High Court, against the Turks, &c. Thus the total
amount of taxation came to well over 700,000 guilders a year.
These concessions undoubtedly constituted a victory for Eberhard Louis. Yet, in contrast with Brandenburg and Bavaria,
no permanent tax was accepted by the Estates; they continued
to meet regularly, and their financial administration remained
intact. Absolute government could be established only if these
rights disappeared. Only then could the size of the army be
increased at the pleasure of the prince.

The agreement of 1724 did not terminate the conflicts between Eberhard Louis and the Estates. In 1727, when the three
years' grant expired, he demanded an extension by four years
and the payment of substantial arrears, but in the end had to be
content with two years. A year later he again took up this point,
but without any more success. Then the meeting of the Large
Committee was adjourned, and during the adjournment he once
more sent his officials round the country. They hurriedly con-
voked the deputies of each *Amt*, and in the presence of local
officials pressed them to assent to the ducal demands. They also
requested copies of the decisions taken so that they could forward them to Stuttgart. All this intimidated the deputies who—
in the words of the Large Committee—'could neither vote
freely, nor speak their minds openly'. This time, however, the
committee themselves were not browbeaten and adhered to their
original decision of granting money for two years only. A few
months later Eberhard Louis again demanded an extension
to four years, but once more in vain.[1]

In 1730 Field-Marshal von Phul himself, as the *Oberamtmann*
of three local districts, addressed their assemblies, explained
how important it was that the deputies should agree to the
payment of arrears demanded by the duke, and requested a
protocol of their decisions. These were then sent to the other
Oberamtleute in the country, with orders to proceed in the same
way, which they not only did, but some of them remained
present even when the vote was taken. Others demanded a
record of the individual votes cast, or that the powers already

[1] State Archives Stuttgart, *Tomus Actorum*, cxxxvi, fos. 281–2, 288–90, 444–5,
461–2; cxxxvii, fos. 86–87, 212–14, 285–6, 304–6, 313, 482–3, 489–90, 509, 522;
cxxxviii, fos. 3, 10, 12 (25 Nov. 1727 to 10 Dec. 1729).

granted should be revoked and new instructions sent in. The Large Committee demanded that these new powers should be declared null and void, but in vain. The majority of its members felt that they could not escape the payment of the arrears and voted for this purpose 10,000 guilders *semel pro semper*. In spite of threats from the duke that he would repartition the tax himself, they repeatedly refused to increase this sum. All they were eventually willing to concede was another 10,000 guilders, a sum which Eberhard Louis declared to be quite insufficient because the powers had been given in his favour. He announced that he would not let the matter rest there and indeed came back to it at every meeting during the following years. At one point the privy councillors even threatened the members of the committee that they would not be allowed to depart until they had fulfilled the princely wishes. All that was achieved in the end was a further grant of 15,000 guilders towards the arrears, while all further requests met with a determined refusal, as did all the attempts to have the duration of the main grant extended beyond two years.[1] Thus the conflicts of the reign of Eberhard Louis prepared the way for the great struggles which were to follow. So did the methods employed by him against the Estates. His victory of 1724 did not decide the issue; nor did the attempts to cajole the local assemblies behind the backs of the Large Committee bring about the hoped-for results. The last years of Eberhard Louis's reign again produced a stalemate in his relations with the Estates.

VIII. *The Great Conflicts of the Eighteenth Century*

The duke who ascended the throne in 1733, Charles Alexander, was a convert to Roman Catholicism, from a different branch of the reigning house. This fact alone was to complicate his relations with his Lutheran subjects who insisted on having

---

[1] Ibid. cxxxviii, fos. 300, 303–4, 308–9, 319, 353, 357, 364, 367, 386, 389–94, 397–8, 401–11, 533–4, 543–63, 580–1; cxxxix, fos. 8–10, 36, 45–47, 60–62, 79–80, 97–99, 122–3, 349–50, 370, 413, 525–6, 528–34, 540, 544–8; cxl, fos. 4, 8–10, 13–14, 25, 27, 268–9, 276–8, 289–90, 293, 300, 503–4, 520–5, 553–5 (17 June 1730 to 17 Dec. 1732). I think it goes too far if Grube, op. cit., p. 388, asserts that the whole constitution was in a state of dissolution during the last years of Eberhard Louis's reign and that he had largely succeeded in transforming the Estates into a tool of the absolute state.

their religious rights safeguarded. He had to consent that his episcopal prerogative should be exercised by the privy councillors, including economic and police matters relating to the Church, and they were instructed to consult the Estates in such matters.[1] Yet he remained determined to gain an equal legal status for Catholicism and to destroy Protestantism as the established religion of the duchy, and simultaneously the influence of the Estates which was so closely connected with it. Exactly as in Saxony,[2] their resistance to absolute government was strengthened by the religious issue and the unpopularity of the duke's non-Lutheran favourites, advisers and officers, which provided the Estates with a popular backing of a strength hitherto unknown. Outstanding among these confidants were General von Remchingen, the army's new commander and a Roman Catholic, and the Jew Süss Oppenheimer, who in 1734 was charged with the supervision of the coinage and the mint and became responsible for finding the means required to increase the army and to destroy the financial power of the Estates.[3] Both men, for obvious reasons, were strongly opposed to the privileges of the Estates which they considered completely out-of-date, for they made it impossible to raise the money for the army and to follow the example of Prussia and other absolute monarchies. Following their example, taxes on salaries and appointments, on property and families, on the church and inns, on stamped paper, &c., were introduced by virtue of the ducal prerogative, disregarding the privileges of the Estates and their financial administration. Titles and offices were sold, and heavy fines imposed on alleged offenders, so that the duke received substantial revenues of his own.[4]

The inspiration for this absolutist policy came from another Catholic, Frederick Charles, bishop of Würzburg and Bamberg, a protagonist of princely power. He corrected with his own hand the draft of a ducal decree which sharply reprimanded the

[1] Reyscher, op. cit. ii, nos. 76–77, pp. 460–70; Eugen Schneider, 'Regierung', in *Herzog Karl Eugen von Württemberg und seine Zeit*, Esslingen, 1907, i. 147; Friedrich Wintterlin, 'Landeshoheit', ibid. i. 170; Grube, op. cit., pp. 389–90.

[2] See below, pp. 244–5, 248–9.

[3] State Archives Stuttgart, *Tomus Actorum*, cxlii, fos. 621–4 (protest of the Large Committee against his appointment of 30 June 1734). About his financial plans in general, see Ismar Elbogen, *Geschichte der Juden in Deutschland*, Berlin, 1935, pp. 138–9, and Selma Stern, *The Court Jew*, Philadelphia, 1950, pp. 121–6.

[4] Selma Stern, *Jud Süss*, Berlin, 1929, pp. 86–103.

Large Committee for its opposition to some of the planned fiscal measures, making the words more emphatic and more threatening. He visited Charles Alexander and advised him in political and religious affairs, on the drafting of his will and the education of his successor. A privy councillor of the prince bishop served as the go-between and the recipient of confidential messages. He was charged by Charles Alexander with the task of drafting a memorandum on the duties of the duke and the Estates towards each other. This assigned to the Estates purely advisory functions and made them mere executors of the ducal orders.[1] No diet was summoned during Charles Alexander's reign. The privy council was deprived of its importance and replaced by confidential advisers who were entirely independent of the Estates.[2]

At the end of 1735 Charles Alexander informed the Large Committee of the necessity of increasing the army to 10,000 infantry and 2,100 cavalry and of keeping it permanently on that footing. This was a large force, approximating to the size of the Prussian army twenty years earlier, if the much smaller population of Württemberg is taken into account. The cost of an army of only 10,000 men and of the contributions to the Swabian Circle and the fortresses was estimated at over 700,000 guilders a year, equivalent to the total amount of taxation. The Estates were ordered to ask the towns and Ämter for the necessary powers; but these were deprived of the libertas votandi. Promises and threats were used freely to make them assent, and often a prepared formula was put before them which they were pressed to accept. In this way the Large Committee was made to consent to an army of 12,100, to the payment of 372,000 guilders yearly and the continued levy of the tricesimae, which had been reintroduced on account of the War of the Polish Succession: a total of about 480,000 guilders, not counting the excise, the 'ordinary' tax, contributions to the ducal chamber (usually about 40,000 guilders a year), and extraordinary contributions to the Swabian Circle (about 45,000 guilders). The grant was clearly insufficient to maintain an army of 12,000, but was much larger than ever made previously in

[1] State Archives Stuttgart, Tomus Actorum, cxlvi, fos. 276–7, 279; cxlviii, fos. 553–7, 569; Schneider, op. cit., pp. 348–9; Grube, op. cit., pp. 392–6.
[2] Stern, The Court Jew, pp. 120–1.

peace-time.[1] As a precedent it was to prove very important in later negotiations.

From the point of view of Charles Alexander and his advisers, however, this was only a first step. During the negotiations about the grant General von Remchingen developed his ideas to the deputies of the Estates: subjects could not prescribe conditions to their master who had the right to command; the Estates called themselves loyal and obedient, but in reality were contrary; the duke as a high and mighty prince knew what was best for his subjects. A clever prince did not need any Estates, as the general emphasized by knocking with his fist on his chest. In France the *Parlement* was so exalted and yet, when it was disobedient, the king ordered 10,000 men to march,[2] and the same could happen to the Estates. *Serenissimus* was informed that there were differences among the Estates, that during their last discussion a majority had been mustered only after four, five, or six votes, and that one member had said he would vote thirty times 'No', even if the question were put thirty times. Therefore His Princely Highness intended to visit the Estates in person and to inspect the votes.[3] It seems that the government was only too well informed about the discussions of the committee, and even about individual votes. The Estates strongly suspected that one of their permanent councillors and the prelate of Hirsau, Weissensee, were the culprits. Both were removed from their posts after Charles Alexander's death.[4]

General von Remchingen proceeded to put his ideas into practice. He instructed the *Generalkriegskommissariat* not to render in future any accounts of military expenditure to the Estates. He also pushed aside the Protestant war councillors and seemed determined to command *despotice in militaribus*. Lists of all young men over the age of ten were drawn up. They were to be enrolled with a regiment, to receive a kind of uniform, and

[1] State Archives Stuttgart, *Tomus Actorum*, cxliv, fos. 4, 77–82, 325–6, 343–8, 517, 523–9; cxlv, fo. 194 (31 Dec. 1735 to 27 Nov. 1736); Grube, op. cit., pp. 391–2. Wintterlin, 'Wehrverfassung und Landesverfassung im Herzogtum Württemberg', loc. cit. xxxiv. 252, states that the grant of 1724 of 360,000 guilders was increased to 460,000 in 1736, but the increase seems to have been larger.

[2] This seems to refer to the exile and arrest of many members of the *Parlement de Paris* by Louis XV in 1732: see H. Carré, *Le Règne de Louis XV* (E. Lavisse, *Histoire de France*, viii. 2), Paris, 1909, pp. 113–14.

[3] State Archives Stuttgart, *Tomus Actorum*, cxliv, fos. 292–3 (13 May 1736).

[4] Ibid. cxlv, fos. 139, 322–3, 373; cxlvii, fos. 193–5.

to be drilled on Sundays and holidays by officers.[1] The example of the Prussian army clearly served as a model for these plans. The general further planned the division of the duchy into twelve military districts, the commanders of which were to be responsible for the general administration, so that the privy councillors and the other officials would lose their power—a plan reminiscent of Oliver Cromwell's major-generals. At the beginning of 1737 he wrote to the Würzburg privy councillor, who acted as a go-between and confidant, that it was advisable to arrest with the leaders of the Estates also 'the godless ministers': that would enable them to stand more firmly still on the heads of the hydra. The recipient in his turn remarked, after reading the Estates' declaration against the newly-founded Office of Wards (*Pupillenamt*), that its author deserved to lose his head. Charles Alexander also objected violently to this remonstrance and reprimanded the privy councillors for accepting it. For some time there had been rumours of arbitrary measures planned against the leaders and councillors of the Estates, and these now increased.[2]

Charles Alexander deeply resented the fact that the Estates tried to play the part of co-regents and always referred to their ancient privileges. In his opinion the time when these privileges had been granted had to be taken into consideration. What had been justified many years ago was no longer satisfactory. The privileges should not serve as a pretext for some people to further their own interests. If any laws or customs stood in his way, it was for him alone to change them or to make new ones.[3] It is not clear whether the Estates only suspected the far-reaching plans of Charles Alexander and his advisers, or whether they had precise information. Most of the details were not revealed until after his death. What is clear is that the Estates were in no position to offer any effective opposition to these plans. There can be little doubt that they would have been carried out if Charles Alexander had lived longer. While he lived the Estates

[1] Thus the Estates' declaration of 28 Mar. 1737 against the late duke's 'evil counsellors': ibid. cxlv, fos. 183–5.

[2] Ibid. cxliv, fo. 319; cxlviii, fos. 553, 557–9 (25 May 1736 to 3 Jan. 1737). For the *Pupillenamt* and its functions, see Selma Stern, *Jud Süss*, pp. 92–93, and ibid., pp. 152–5, for the plans of General von Remchingen.

[3] State Archives Stuttgart, *Tomus Actorum*, cxliv, fo. 460; cxlv, fo. 189; cxlviii, fos. 555–6 (16 Oct. 1736, 1 Feb. 1737); Grube, op. cit., pp. 394, 396.

made verbal protests, but did not even revive their old plan of complaining to the Aulic Council. Much less did they contemplate any resistance against these unconstitutional schemes. Once more the weakness of their position stood clearly revealed.

It was the death of Charles Alexander (as many believed through foul play) on 12 March 1737 which caused the whole project of absolute government to collapse like a house of cards, exactly as the death of Duke Frederick in 1608 ruined his plans;[1] for the successor, the future Duke Charles Eugene, was then only nine years old. At the time of his death rumours arose that Würzburg troops were marching on Stuttgart, and some burghers were preparing to defend their religion and their liberties by force of arms. The closest agnates, who administered the duchy on behalf of the infant duke during the following seven years, could not halt the tide of reaction that set in immediately. Charles Alexander's will, which appointed the bishop of Würzburg one of the young duke's guardians, was declared invalid. On the day after Charles Alexander's death the hated Süss Oppenheimer, some other Jews, and two ducal councillors were arrested, followed a few days after by the arrests of General von Remchingen and others, because of the 'traitorous and pernicious counsels they had given and the irresponsible violence they had perpetrated under the previous government'. Most of them were expelled from the country. General von Remchingen succeeded in escaping. Süss Oppenheimer alone was sentenced to death by a specially appointed criminal court after a lengthy trial, because he had 'fomented distrust against ministers, councillors and Estates, had violated all the laws of the country, and had thrown overboard all orders and constitutions'. At the trial a witness declared that Süss Oppenheimer had said that Charles Alexander ought to imitate Louis XIV and have the representatives of the Estates beheaded, another that in the opinion of Süss the Estates would cease to exist if the duke lived for two more years and that everything his subjects owned belonged to the prince. The death sentence was carried out early in 1738 under the eyes of many thousands of spectators.[2]

[1] See above, pp. 47–49.
[2] State Archives Stuttgart, *Tomus Actorum*, cxlv, fos. 128, 143, 252; cxlvi, fos. 19–20 (13 Mar. 1737 to 4 Feb. 1738); Schneider, op. cit., pp. 351–2; Stern, *Jud Süss*, pp. 148–9, 155–75, 339, and *The Court Jew*, pp. 131–2, 135–6, 259–66; Grube, op. cit., p. 423.

At the end of March 1737 the Large Committee asked that a diet should be summoned and published a declaration 'against the evil counsellors' of the late duke, and above all against General von Remchingen and Süss Oppenheimer.[1]

The diet met in July 1737, after an interval of nearly forty years. Several small towns demanded to be represented by a deputy of their own, as did the *Amt* Stuttgart (as distinct from the town), but these demands were refused. One *Amt* sent three deputies, but was told that only large towns and *Ämter* had the right to send two, but never three, and that even those two deputies had only one vote. In the plenum the prelate of Lorch attempted to make the procedure less oligarchical by suggesting that fuller discussion should take place *in pleno* and that the Estates' councillors should vote there. He complained that the Small and Large Committees arranged their votes in advance and formed their conclusions separately and thus curtailed the freedom of voting. Nothing, however, came of these attempts to widen the basis of representative government because the regent and the privy council sided with the committees. The majority of the committees' members, with only three exceptions, were confirmed in office by a majority of the deputies. Of the prelate of Hirsau, Weissensee, it was expressly stated that the whole country had lost confidence in him, and the mayors of Sulz and Waiblingen were apparently also compromised on account of their actions during the previous reign.[2]

The Estates then demanded that the army should be reduced 'to a convenient footing', that their burdens should be alleviated and the *tricesimae* abolished, adding that they were not disinclined to revive the militia on a selective basis *in omnes eventus*. The subsequent negotiations, which lasted—with short interruptions—for nearly two years, were mainly concerned with the reduction of the army, the taxes required for its maintenance, and the question whether the *Recess* of 1736, which obliged the Estates to greatly increased payments, was still valid. The Estates were of the opinion that it had been extorted by General von Remchingen and should be declared null and void. The

[1] State Archives Stuttgart, *Tomus Actorum*, cxlv, fos. 161–7, 180–95 (26–28 Mar. 1737).

[2] Ibid., fos. 347–8, 350, 353–4, 373, 427 (26 June to 1 Aug. 1737); Grube, op. cit., p. 414, 419–22.

privy councillors insisted on its validity and demanded payments according to its stipulations, partly to be used for the war against the Turks. The army, however, was quickly reduced. The regiment of dragoons, two infantry regiments, and units of two other infantry regiments were transferred to the service of the Emperor, the Garde du Corps and the Cuirassiers were considerably reduced, and the Hussars disbanded. What remained was a very small army of about 500 men, mainly cavalry, to which might be added the contingents serving with the Swabian Circle and the two infantry regiments at Breisach and Freiburg in the pay of the Empire, altogether only about 3,000 men. After the outbreak of the War of the Austrian Succession one infantry and one cavalry regiment entered the service of Prussia, while another infantry regiment was withdrawn from the Imperial service to strengthen the Württemberg army; but the total strength remained at about 3,000, including the units serving with the Swabian Circle.[1]

The very considerable reduction of the army was, however, not sufficient in the eyes of certain deputies, who declared that whoever advocated the maintenance of a small standing army acted against the interests of the country and sharply opposed the policy followed by the Estates' councillors. One councillor, Sturm, protested in the name of his colleagues against these insinuations, since this was not the moment to abolish the army, and such a demand was tantamount to dashing one's head against a wall. Finally a majority consented to continue a moderate

[1] State Archives Stuttgart, *Tomus Actorum*, cxlv, fos. 543–7; cxlvi, fos. 22, 49, 61, 66, 132–4, 675–7, 682–3, 706–8; cxlviii, fos. 354–61; cxlix, fos. 304–10, 335; cli, fos. 227–31, 375–9 (11 Sept. 1737 to 20 Oct. 1743). The figures were as follows:

	Winter 1740–1	Winter 1741–2	Summer 1743	Winter 1743–4
General Staff . . .	6	..	..	..
Squadron Garde du Corps .	89	95	95	94
Cuirassiers (later Dragoons) .	301	320	Into Prussian service	
Artillery company . . .	58	60	60	56
Infantry regiment . . .	..	..	1,200	1,200
Contingents with the Circle .	1,069	1,717	1,739	1,728
Two regiments in pay of Empire	1,589	677	Into Prussian and Württemberg service	
Total	3,112	2,869	3,094	3,078

force for another two to three years. Some weeks later the three councillors again protested against the slanders spread about them by some deputies who accused them of being court advocates and procurators, of acting in favour of the government, protracting the meetings of the diet, accepting presents of a thousand and more guilders, and of collusion with the privy councillors.[1]

The internal differences among the Estates again became apparent when a few months later a plot came to light which involved the prelate of Hirsau, who was removed from the committee after Charles Alexander's death. It revealed such detailed knowledge of the affairs of the Estates that information must have been furnished by a deputy to the diet.[2] The plot's author, Professor Hobhahn, had planned to win the support of the army, especially that of certain staff officers and the new commander, General von Gaisberg, against the privy council and the Small Committee, who allegedly arranged everything between them and formed a narrow clique, dominated by the Estates' councillors and the mayor of Stuttgart. This faction, as the author knew, aroused the jealousy of the Large Committee which was supported by the majority of the deputies. The aim of the plot was to make Charles Alexander's widow a co-regent and guardian side by side with the duke of Württemberg-Oels, which was desired by many officers. News was to be spread abroad how greatly she regretted the reduction of the army and how much she had its plight at heart. The faction strife among the committees was to be fostered and exploited, with the ultimate aim of altering the government during the duke's minority and changing the constitution. This project, so revealing in its information about the factions among the Estates, took shape in the autumn of 1737, but was not discovered until eighteen months later when a note of the prelate of Hirsau was found in the street. It does not seem to have developed very far. Probably the speedy reduction of the army deprived it of support, and of a chance of success.

Perhaps because of their disunity, perhaps because of the moderating influence of the councillors and their understanding

---

[1] Ibid. cxlvi, fos. 941–3, 1186 (8 Nov. to 20 Dec. 1738).
[2] Ibid. cxlvii, fos. 193–5, 354–85 (21 Mar. 1739); Grube, op. cit., p. 416. It was the Estates' opinion that the information was furnished by a deputy to the diet.

with the government, the wishes of the Estates were only partially fulfilled. The monopolies established by Süss Oppenheimer and the *tricesimae* were abolished, but in their place an annual levy of 100,000 guilders was introduced. The *Recess* of 1736 was not revoked. The Estates had to be satisfied with an undertaking of the regent that during his regency he would use the *Recess* only to maintain his princely state, while they had aimed at obtaining a similar promise for the future and the suspension of the *Recess*. The grievances regarding the sending out of ducal officials to obtain the powers of the local assemblies, regarding their presence at the meetings, the forcible recruiting for the army, and the transfer of the ducal residence from Stuttgart to Ludwigsburg were not redressed. Taxation remained at a high level because the Estates, after much bargaining, took over more than 2,000,000 guilders of ducal debts.[1]

At that time the Estates began to participate more actively in the general administration. As early as 1710 a commercial *deputation* was founded by Eberhard Louis, consisting of six ducal councillors and two representatives of the Estates. This was an isolated case, but during the minority of Charles Eugene the examples multiplied. A member of the Small Committee took his seat on the *deputation* for accounts. Three deputies were appointed by the Small Committee to the *deputation* responsible for the building of barracks. One prelate was nominated by the government to the workhouse *deputation*, a procedure which was criticized by the Small Committee. A few years later the Estates were also represented on the medical *deputation*, the tax revision *deputation*, the excise *deputation*, the wine *deputation* (formed to revive the wine trade), &c., usually by the mayor of Stuttgart and one of the Estates' councillors.[2] At the end of the century there were twenty-four permanent deputations, on seventeen of

---

[1] State Archives Stuttgart, *Tomus Actorum*, cxlvii, fos. 20–22, 46–47, 124, 131–2, 136–7, 251, 350, 430–1 (27 Jan. to 18 Apr. 1739). Annual taxation, without the excise and the 'ordinary' tax, amounted to about 468,000 guilders, hardly less than previously: ibid., fos. 485–93, 710–19. But this was not the military budget as asserted by von Pfister, 'Militärwesen', in *Herzog Karl Eugen von Württemberg und seine Zeit*, i. 120, although this figure later became the standard figure of military expenditure; Grube, op. cit., p. 424.

[2] Sattler, op. cit. xiii. 139; Wintterlin, op. cit. i. 91–92; State Archives Stuttgart, *Tomus Actorum*, cxlvii, fos. 561–2; cxlviii, fo. 26; cliii, fos. 43–44; cliv, fo. 16; clv, fo. 53; clvi, fo. 47; clvii, fos. 116, 127, 232; clix, fos. 137, 183–4; clxi, fos. 62, 88–90; clxii, fos. 153, 197 (from the years 1738 to 1754).

which the Estates were represented.[1] In this way their distrust of new authorities was overcome, and they were drawn more closely into the framework of the state and the new bureaucracy.

No other diet was held during the years of the minority of Charles Eugene. Higher taxes were granted to the regent, but no friction arose; for the army remained very small, and the country's prosperity was increasing during a long period of peace. This continued during the reign of Charles Eugene. Within sixty years the population increased by about 200,000, or nearly 50 per cent., and its density from 125 to 174 per square mile. Cattle and sheep, linen, wool, wine, corn, and timber were exported in growing quantities, and the development of agriculture made Württemberg one of the more advanced German territories.[2] There was no threat from abroad, and none from the duchy's neighbours, during the major part of the eighteenth century. Yet internally this was the most troubled period in the history of the Estates, though the troubles were not caused by the need to defend the country or dangers threatening from outside, as had so often been the case in the sixteenth and seventeenth centuries. Charles Eugene, who assumed the government in 1744 at the age of sixteen, fully shared the great 'passion' of his two predecessors and intended to build up the army from the few thousand men to which it had been reduced during the regency. Such a policy was bound to meet with strong opposition, especially at a time when the country was so little threatened and after the experiences made under Eberhard Louis and Charles Alexander. Furthermore, Charles Eugene, like his father, was a Roman Catholic, and the Estates feared a revival of the Catholicizing policy of the previous reign. As early as the beginning of 1744 they addressed themselves to the leading Protestant rulers of Europe, George II of England and Frederick the Great of Prussia, and asked them for a declaration in favour of their religion which they had guaranteed in 1733. Both kings assured them in rather vague terms that they had the interests of Protestantism at heart and would promote them to the best of their ability.[3]

[1] L. T. Spittler, op. cit., pp. 499–500; Wintterlin, op. cit. i. 77, 83, 96, 101–2.
[2] Arthur Schott, 'Wirtschaftliches Leben', in *Herzog Karl Eugen von Württemberg und seine Zeit*, i. 313–14, 358.
[3] State Archives Stuttgart, *Tomus Actorum*, clii, fos. 53–54, 61 (royal declarations dated St. James's, 9/20 Mar., and Berlin, 7 Apr. 1744).

During the first years of Charles Eugene's reign there was no indication that Protestantism was threatened in Württemberg, nor was there any conflict between the young duke and the Estates. They granted him increased taxes, amounting to well over 500,000 guilders a year, and an additional 30,000 guilders a year for the building of a palace in Stuttgart, so that he would be able to reside in the capital, instead of at Ludwigsburg, the new residence which the Estates strongly disliked.[1] These growing amounts were granted by the Large Committee without much difficulty, although no diet was summoned, and the army was slowly increased by the addition of one infantry regiment and some cavalry squadrons. The military expenditure furnished by the Estates amounted to over 300,000 guilders a year, inclusive of sums for the barracks and fortresses and for the contingent serving with the Swabian Circle.[2] This was less, however, than the Estates had conceded to Charles Eugene's predecessors, and less than 40 per cent. of the revenue from taxation. These factors and the increasing prosperity of the eighteenth century assuaged any criticism or opposition for the time being. For Charles Eugene's marriage the Large Committee in 1748 granted the large sum of 56,700 guilders, far more than had been given to any other duke.[3]

As during previous reigns, complaints from the Estates arose over the issue of the army and the conduct of the soldiers. In 1746 the Large Committee stated that the country was not obliged to maintain the army perpetually, that the costs were much too heavy, and that the young men were being enrolled by force. In 1750 and 1751 they again complained that the fundamental laws and precious liberties were violated by the taking away of the burghers' sons and their enrolment into

[1] The taxes, excluding the excise and the 'ordinary' tax (which together yielded over 300,000 guilders), amounted to 510,774 guilders in 1744–5, 557,673 in 1745–6, 557,799 in 1746–7, 557,843 in 1747–8, 573,219 in 1748–9; thereafter they declined to just under 500,000 guilders: State Archives Stuttgart, *Tomus Actorum*, clii, fos. 119–25, 292–9; cliii, fos. 188–93, 271–8; cliv, fos. 137–43, 245; clv, fos. 103–10, 237–43; clvi, fos. 128–34, 245–52; clvii, fos. 139–49, 271–82; clviii, fos. 222–30; clix, fos. 121–8, 263–70, 426–34; clx, fos. 230–42, 372–82; clxi, fos. 226–33; clxii, fos. 133–41.

[2] Ibid. clvii, fo. 71; clviii, fo. 381; clix, fo. 45; clx, fo. 387 (from the years 1748 to 1752): military expenditure remained constant at 272,000 guilders, excluding 4,000 for the general staff, 30,000 for barracks, 3,000 for fortresses, &c.

[3] Ibid. clvi, fos. 121, 127 (22–28 May 1748).

the army; military expenditure was growing from year to year, and so were the debts of the military chest (*Kriegscasse*). In 1752 the committee once more raised the issue of those pressed into the army against their will. These young men were locked into the town halls to be forced to sign on, and though summoned with the promise that only volunteers would be enrolled, were intimidated and made drunk, had recruiting money pushed into their pockets against their wish, and were finally led away by the hundred as 'volunteers', without any opportunity to consult with their parents. Charles Eugene's opinion, however, was that the Estates had no business to oppose the increase of the army, nor to pry into his motives and intentions, so long as he did not demand more money than stipulated in the *Recess* of 1736, i.e. 460,000 guilders a year. He assured them that volunteers only were enrolled and those sons only who could be spared by their parents. A few months later he promised that no force or stealth would be used in recruiting, that nobody would be pressed into the army, except in a case of emergency, and even then strictly within the framework of the country's liberties, that nobody would be retained in the army against his will, and that drafts from the militia would take place solely as an emergency measure.[1]

Charles Eugene thus admitted the irregularity of the methods used; but he continued to consider recruiting a *regale*, the aim and limit of which it was for him alone to prescribe, and objected to the grievances raised on this score. He also alleged that not a single man was enlisted without his own and his father's consent. In their reply the Small Committee did not find it difficult to list numerous examples of forcible enrolment, in spite of the ducal promise made only eight months before. To quote but one example: twelve young men were taken to the barracks at Ludwigsburg, where they were threatened with starvation unless they enlisted, and their parents were forbidden to bring them any food. Then they were put on a wooden donkey and heavy stones were laid on their feet which they had to raise, and if any stone dropped, they were so severely beaten on their shins that some fainted. Timber was put into their hands which they had to hold with outstretched arms, and if they let one arm

[1] Ibid. cliv, fos. 213, 216–18; clviii, fo. 214; clix, fos. 17, 114; clx, fo. 401; clxi, fos. 22–23, 164 (29 Nov. 1746 to 25 June 1753); Reyscher, op. cit. ii, no. 86, pp. 544–9 (*Recess* of 22 Sept. 1753); A. E. Adam, 'Herzog Karl und die Landschaft', in *Herzog Karl Eugen von Württemberg und seine Zeit*, i. 198–203.

sink they were so beaten on the elbow that their wounds were still unhealed. This torture continued until they promised to enlist; but five escaped, whereupon their fathers were arrested and only released on payment of 100 guilders.[1]

The Large Committee began to urge that these and other grievances should be redressed before they granted further contributions to the ducal chamber, but continued to vote the usual taxes. Charles Eugene, on the other hand, reverted to the tactics of his predecessors and by-passed the committees, addressing his demands directly to the towns and *Ämter*. Without any prior deliberation in the privy council, which he considered useless for his plans, some officers and officials were sent round the country to make promises locally about an impending redress of certain grievances. Simultaneously they demanded large grants for a period of six years, the money not to be paid into the Estates' chest. They did not allow the assemblies sufficient time for deliberation, nor did they ask that the necessary powers should be sent to the committee. Instead they demanded immediate written consent to their proposals, which were to be kept secret. Thus, in the words of the Small Committee, they deprived the subjects of their constitutional right of recourse to the Estates as the only *collegium patriae repraesentativum* before which such matters belonged. The committee protested and declared that they would take counsel as to what attitude to adopt, but nevertheless granted the customary taxes, thus enabling Charles Eugene to ignore the protest.[2] All the willingness of the Large Committee to grant taxes had been of little avail and had not put the young duke into a more conciliatory mood. As his arbitrary methods and his ambitions grew, a conflict could no longer be avoided.

Meanwhile Charles Eugene found another way of achieving his military ambitions, a way which made it essential to continue forcible recruiting, in spite of his promises to the contrary. In September 1752 he concluded a treaty with Louis XV which obliged him to recruit 6,000 infantrymen. For these France undertook to pay 290,000 guilders, and for their maintenance

---

[1] State Archives Stuttgart, *Tomus Actorum*, clxii, fos. 152, 216–17, 257, 272–5 (4 Mar. to 7 June 1754).

[2] Ibid., fos. 213–14, 217–18, 220–7 (18–24 May 1754); Adam, loc. cit., pp. 205–6. The grant amounted to 257,211 guilders, somewhat *more* than those of previous years.

in peace-time 387,000 a year, and in war-time 479,000 a year, for the period of six years. These French subsidies made Charles Eugene financially much more independent. He began to see himself as a great military leader and would not shrink from any violence to achieve this ambition. He was greatly attracted by the Prussian military system, and Prussian methods were introduced from 1754 onwards with the arrival of Prussian officers and instructors. Recruiting, however, did not become easier, and force and stealth had to be used to fill the ranks, causing new protests from the Estates. The outbreak of the Seven Years War in 1756 brought matters to a head. After Frederick the Great's invasion of Saxony the Imperial diet declared war on Prussia, and Württemberg had to double the size of its contingents serving with the Swabian Circle through a transfer from the ducal army. It then became known, however, that most of the army was in French pay and would have to serve France. In March 1757 each *Amtmann* was informed how many recruits he had to furnish and to send to Stuttgart within a fortnight. France ordered the Württemberg regiments to take the field immediately, but they were considerably under strength and short of all equipment, so that Charles Eugene could not fulfil his treaty obligations. The Small Committee reminded him of his duty to consult them about all treaties, including subsidy treaties, and not to go to war without asking their advice.[1]

During the spring and summer of 1757 thousands of young men were conscripted by force and pressed into the army. The contingent for the Swabian Circle was drafted into the corps destined for French service, but the troops mutinied when they were mustered. The churches were surrounded during services and the young men led away; and those abducted were left without food and drink until they gave in. The soldiers were brutally treated and deserted *en masse*. Badly trained and armed and without any discipline, they were beaten, with the Austrian army, by Frederick the Great at Leuthen on 5 December 1757: out of about 6,000 only 1,900 returned some months later to Württemberg. Desertion increased, and men-hunts for deserters were organized throughout the duchy.[2] The articles of

[1] Adam, loc. cit., pp. 209–10; von Pfister, ibid., pp. 121–2, 124–5; Schneider, ibid., p. 149; Grube, op. cit., p. 429.

[2] Adam, loc. cit., pp. 211–12; von Pfister, ibid., pp. 126–30; A. E. Adam,

war published early in 1758 stipulated that all soldiers who left
their posts or duties in front of the enemy or fled were to be
executed without mercy. If not in front of the enemy, those
leaving their posts before being relieved were to run the gauntlet
thirty-six times. Apprehended deserters were to be hanged and
all their property was to be confiscated; and a similar fate was
to overtake those found at a distance of a quarter of an hour
from their units during a march without just cause.[1]

The Estates did not receive any reply to their many petitions
on behalf of the suffering inhabitants and against the growing
burden of taxation. In March 1758 Charles Eugene curtly informed them that, if the 10,000 guilders he demanded were not
paid within twenty-four hours, he would borrow the money in
their name and at their expense. He declared this was an
'absolute order' and declined to listen to further remonstrations.
The Large Committee, however, steadfastly refused to make
any more advances and increased grants until their grievances
were redressed and only granted the customary sums, while the
duke commanded 'unconditional obedience' to his orders.
When the committee hesitated to exceed their powers, the
government decreed that the sums they had not consented to
were to be levied in their name. Yet the money came in very
slowly, and the ducal debts mounted. Domains were pawned,
forced loans raised from the officials, debased coins minted.
A tobacco and a salt monopoly were introduced, and every in-
habitant was forced to buy fifteen pounds of salt. In January
1759 troops surrounded the Estates' house in Stuttgart; their
receivers were compelled to empty their chest in the presence
of ducal councillors and to pay them 30,000 guilders. Six
months later the procedure was repeated, and more taxes were
levied without the committee's consent. One of the Estates'
councillors, Johann Jacob Moser, whom Charles Eugene
considered the leader of the opposition, was arrested and kept
in solitary confinement for five years without ever being interrogated. The committee members were threatened with
trials for *lèse majesté* unless they agreed to levy another 200,000
guilders. This the Large Committee unanimously declined to

Johann Jakob Moser als Württembergischer Landschaftskonsulent, Stuttgart, 1887,
pp. 34–35; Schneider, *Württembergische Geschichte*, pp. 357–8.
[1] Reyscher, op. cit. xix, no. 450, p. 667.

do; but then the towns and *Ämter* were instructed to send the necessary powers, and when these had arrived the sum was granted. This, however, was insufficient, for the army now cost more than 1,634,000 guilders a year and was gradually increased to about 12,000 men. A forced loan of 265,000 guilders was raised, allegedly to provide capital for the administration of the salt monopoly, and this was farmed out for twenty years. Charles Eugene refused to recognize the right of the Small Committee to assemble without his permission and prohibited such meetings. He insisted that he was entitled to abolish laws, treaties and privileges if it was for the good of the country.[1]

In spite of all these breaches of the constitution the attitude of the Small Committee continued to be hesitant and weak. Its members were disunited and helpless. They were not accustomed to seek support from the people and became unpopular on account of their prevaricating policy. As on previous occasions they were suspected and disliked by both sides. During the following years the arbitrary régime continued, and so did the deficit in the ducal budget, in spite of considerable French and Imperial subsidies. Taxes were collected by military force, the corn reserves of the communes were confiscated, new monopolies and new offices were created and sold, a lottery was organized, the lots being allocated compulsorily like a tax, and heavy labour services were imposed upon the hapless inhabitants. Although, in practice, Württemberg took no part in the later stages of the Seven Years War, the military expenditure continued to mount. At the end of 1762 a new military plan was published which required the levy of 1,622,000 guilders a year in peace-time, about $3\frac{1}{2}$ guilders per head of the population, an imposition approximating to the burdens imposed upon the inhabitants of Prussia. A more than doubled monthly contribution was introduced by decree, but very little was collected in spite of ruthless military measures. By that time the Seven Years War was drawing to its end, but the peace concluded in February 1763 did not bring an alleviation of the burdens.[2]

[1] Adam, loc. cit., pp. 213–19, 221–7, and *Johann Jakob Moser*, pp. 52–54; Schneider, op. cit., pp. 358–60; L. T. Spittler, op. cit., no. 1, pp. 16, 23; Grube, op. cit., pp. 430–1.

[2] Adam, loc. cit., pp. 228–35, and *Johann Jakob Moser*, pp. 45–51; von Pfister, loc. cit., pp. 132–4; Spittler, op. cit., p. 23; Schneider, op. cit., pp. 361–3. The

Yet the coming of peace enabled the Estates to seek protection outside the duchy and to petition the kings of Britain,
Prussia, and Denmark as the guarantors of the Württemberg
religion and constitution, a function they had assumed when a
Catholic duke ascended the throne. In June 1763 the Estates
petitioned the Emperor Francis and the three Protestant kings
and asked for their protection. There was no response from
Vienna, but the three kings wrote to Charles Eugene asking him
to preserve the fundamental laws of the duchy. A diet was
summoned to meet in September; but the ducal proposition did
not even mention the redress of grievances and simply asked for
suggestions how the increased needs of the army could be satisfied. The Estates remonstrated against the levying of taxes by
military force and asked for the release of their arrested councillor. They declared the country was neither able nor obliged
to maintain so large an army. They raised their grievances
and declined to consent to any advances. After seven weeks
the diet was dissolved without any result, and the régime of
forcible recruiting and levying of taxes and vexatious labour
services continued unabated. During the seven years from 1758
to 1764 nearly 10,000,000 guilders were squeezed out of the
country, only 3,117,000 of which had been granted by the
Estates.[1]

As the diet had not produced any means to balance the
budget, Charles Eugene in March 1764 resolved on the introduction of a graduated poll-tax. The population was to be
divided into twelve classes: the lowest group, labourers, appren-
tices, servants, &c., were to pay a quarter of a guilder, and the
highest group 25 guilders a year. In this way 1,621,000 guilders
were to be collected and paid into the military chest. The
Estates would lose the power of the purse and the control of the
financial administration. The duke would be absolute at last.
The project was directly submitted to the local assemblies, the
Amtsversammlungen. These stood, under new regulations promulgated in November 1762, entirely under the control of the
Amtleute and other local officials of the duke, with whom the

burden imposed in Prussia came to about 2½ thalers a head, only slightly more
than 3½ guilders.
    [1] Adam, loc. cit., pp. 236–41, and *Johann Jakob Moser*, pp. 72–73; Schott,
'Wirtschaftliches Leben', loc. cit., p. 357; Grube, op. cit., pp. 389, 431–6.

village mayors had to consult before voting.[1] Yet some assemblies, although instructed to accept 'without demur', declined the poll-tax, others accepted only with reservations, and many revoked their consent during the following weeks. Charles Eugene tried to overcome this opposition by summoning the leaders into his presence and by billeting dragoons on the recalcitrants, but in vain. In the end the poll-tax was not introduced. Instead an annual tax of 920,000 guilders—twice the usual amount—was decreed and levied by soldiers together with the salt-tax, those refusing to pay being arrested or fined. These methods at last overcame the hesitations of the Small Committee. In June 1764 they resolved to send a complaint to the Aulic Council, and this was delivered at the end of July. After only five weeks the court issued an injunction ordering Charles Eugene to summon a diet and to discuss all grievances with it, to release Moser, to abstain from all unconstitutional demands and the levying of unusual taxes through soldiers.[2]

The success of the injunction was immediate. The diet was summoned to meet again in October of the same year. Moser, who had been kept a close prisoner for five years, was at last interrogated and released a few days later. Yet the diet again ended in a deadlock because Charles Eugene insisted on his exorbitant demands, while the Estates would only grant the customary 460,000 guilders for the army and once more instructed the towns and *Ämter* that they should not pay the double amount which was illegal. They also declined all demands for higher taxes and insisted that the country's liberties should be respected in future and the *status quo* restored—entreaties to which they received no reply. The diet dragged on without producing any result. Meanwhile Charles Eugene not only continued his arbitrary methods of government, but claimed in a report to the Aulic Council that he was entitled to keep as many soldiers as he pleased and that his subjects were obliged to provide the necessary means. The court, however, found against him. In May 1765 it decided that he had to be satisfied with 460,000 guilders for the army according to the

[1] Reyscher, op. cit. xiv, p. 801; xvii, no. 219, pp. 597–627; Adam, loc. cit., p. 241; Grube, 'Dorfgemeinde und Amtsversammlung in Altwürttemberg', loc. cit., pp. 211–12, and op. cit., pp. 436–7.

[2] Adam, loc. cit., pp. 241–6, and *Johann Jakob Moser*, pp. 74–76; Schneider, op. cit., p. 364; Grube, op. cit., pp. 437–9.

Recess of 1736, but it instructed the Estates to pay up to 200,000 guilders to meet arrears and to pay off the redundant officers. Some regiments were indeed disbanded, but the grievances were not redressed, and new taxes were demanded in 1766. This proved the stumbling-block, for the Estates became less and less inclined to grant more money before their grievances were redressed.[1] Through bitter experience they had learnt not to trust their ruler's promises, and their opposition was stiffened by popular resistance, which had been called forth by the heavy burdens and the brutal behaviour of the soldiers.

At the Aulic Council in Vienna the case dragged on for years. The Estates were strongly supported by Frederick the Great, and the new Emperor Joseph II was his ardent admirer. Charles Eugene's financial difficulties grew apace, but that did not stop him from spending vast sums on his court and new buildings. By the end of 1765 his debts amounted to over 13,000,000 guilders.[2] These factors strengthened the case of the Estates. In 1770 the Aulic Council proposed a compromise, the terms of which were then accepted by both sides.[3] They fulfilled most of the wishes of the Estates, while foreign pressure and urgent financial needs induced Charles Eugene to accept an agreement which would alleviate his financial distress, and which could be 'interpreted' in his favour if an opportunity arose later. After many years of struggle he had exhausted his means and yet not succeeded in crushing the opposition. He was not a Richelieu, nor a Great Elector, and times had changed since the seventeenth century. Thus he gave way, at least on paper, with the object of obtaining large sums of money. This giving way of their prince saved the Estates from the fate of those of Bavaria, Brandenburg, and Prussia, and of many other countries.

The treaty of 1770 restored the principle of the Württemberg constitution as it had developed during the past three centuries. Charles Eugene had to resign his plans of absolute government and of making himself independent of the Estates and their

---

[1] Adam, loc. cit., pp. 247–65, and *Johann Jakob Moser*, pp. 78–79, 82; Grube, op. cit., pp. 439–42; Schneider, op. cit., p. 364.

[2] Adam, loc. cit., pp. 267–72; Schneider, 'Regierung', ibid., p. 158; Spittler, op. cit., no. 1, pp. 1 ff.; Grube, op. cit., pp. 443–4.

[3] The *Erbvergleich* of 27 Feb./2 Mar. 1770 is printed in Reyscher, op. cit. ii, no. 88, pp. 550–609.

privileges. He promised that all grievances would be redressed, especially that the illegal labour services would cease, that nobody would be compelled to enlist against his will, and that those entitled to be discharged would be released without having to pay anything for their discharge. With regard to military expenditure, the Estates' contribution was to remain fixed at 460,000 guilders a year, even in war-time, including the payments to the Swabian Circle, and 70,000 guilders of this grant were to be used to pay off the old debts of the ducal chamber, thus leaving less than 300,000 guilders for the ducal army itself. This sum would only allow for the retention of an army of about 3,000 men, inclusive of the contingents serving with the Swabian Circle. The plans of military expenditure were to be communicated to the Estates not merely in a general form, but the annual accounts were to be scrutinized in detail by a mixed committee and approved by the Estates' officials. Then they were to be submitted to a *deputation* on which the Estates were again represented, thus giving them effective control over the details of military expenditure. The levying of taxes and dues to which the Estates had not consented was to cease and not to be resumed under any pretence whatsoever. The Military Commissariat was to be satisfied with the assignments of money it received from the Estates, and not to issue any on its own initiative: if it did so, the towns and *Ämter* were not obliged to honour them. Charles Eugene was to address his financial demands to the Small Committee, and not to the Estates' receivers who were their subordinates. He was not to take any money out of the Estates' chest against the will of the Small Committee, and to rescind all monopolies.[1]

All matters which, according to the duchy's constitution, required the Estates' consent, or in which their advice was to be heard, were to be communicated to them and not to be settled without their assent. The stipulations of the treaty of Tübingen and of later treaties were to be observed with respect to the participation of the Estates in the conclusion of alliances, justifying their attitude with regard to the subsidy treaty with France. The right of free assembly which the Small Committee

[1] Reyscher, op. cit. ii, no. 88, pp. 560–1, 563–4, 579–82; Adam, loc. cit., p. 271; Schneider, ibid., pp. 159, 163; Wintterlin, ibid., p. 177, and *Geschichte der Behördenorganisation in Württemberg*, i. 94–95; Grube, op. cit., p. 444.

possessed was not to be curtailed, but they were to notify the privy council of their meetings. Their right of freely electing the Estates' receivers was to continue, but they were to be confirmed in office by the duke. The privy council was to be restored to its constitutional position as the highest authority under the duke; all other officials were to be responsible to it, with the only exceptions of the war council and the military commissariat. They had to send their reports to the privy council, which would then submit them to the duke for his decision. The right of free election of mayors and local officials and the right of free voting in the *Amtsversammlungen* were to be restored to the towns and *Ämter*—rights of which they were deprived by the regulations of 1762 which were rescinded— and the ducal officials were again excluded from these assemblies. This guaranteed the independence of local government and provided the diet with a stronger basis, for during the constitutional struggle it became customary to elect the deputies in enlarged *Amtsversammlungen* in which the peasants were strongly represented. If new grievances of a major character arose and the Estates could obtain no redress, they should not be tied to their grants and should be entitled to recover what they had paid. The oath of allegiance was to be rendered to the duke only if he accepted this treaty, and the Emperor was to have the decision if there was any difference about its interpretation.[1]

The great constitutional struggle was over. The Estates had succeeded in preserving their liberties; yet the ducal promises of 1770 were not entirely fulfilled, and complaints continued for a long time. As early as October 1770 the Small Committee compiled a long list of infringements of the treaty and refused to pay the desired advance. Labour services were still being exacted, those pressed into the army were not released, the army was still larger than stipulated, and the vast expenditure was continuing. During the following years the conflict went on, although on a minor scale. The Estates again complained to the Aulic Council because the free trade in salt was inhibited, and obtained its restoration. In 1772 the Large

---

[1] Reyscher, op. cit. ii, no. 88, pp. 557–9, 584, 598–600, 604; Adam, loc. cit., p. 271; Schneider, ibid., p. 159; Wintterlin, ibid., p. 171, and op. cit. i. 73; Grube, loc. cit. xiii. 212.

Committee made new grants after a reduction of the army and other concessions had been obtained; yet many were still retained against their will, and the petitions for their release never ceased. The sum of 460,000 guilders did not cover the military expenditure, and new debts accumulated. Therefore after 1775 the Estates declined to make further grants to the ducal chamber and threatened with a new complaint to Vienna. A new grievance arose when Charles Eugene recruited troops for the Dutch East India Company and many were pressed into the army and shipped abroad against their wishes. A monopoly of iron was created, new labour services were demanded, and offices were again sold. Thus there remained grave dissatisfaction, and the relations between the prince and the Estates remained strained, for Charles Eugene continued to promise redress with little result, so that the Estates once more refused their contribution to his chamber. Yet during the remaining years of his reign (1770–93) they paid off 4,684,000 guilders of ducal debts, while their own debts remained stationary.[1]

In one respect, however, the Estates achieved their object: at the end of the reign the ducal army numbered hardly 1,200 men, not counting the 2,000 serving under the Dutch East India Company and the 1,400 serving with the army of the Swabian Circle against that of the French Revolution. By then the Württemberg army was in a very bad condition and no longer a threat to the country's liberties.[2] These liberties, however, did not mean that the Estates were a broadly based institution. On the contrary, in the course of the eighteenth century the position of the Small Committee became stronger and stronger. In practice they alone exercised the powers of the Estates. They filled all appointments and became almost co-regents by the side of the duke. After 1770 no diet was held for more than twenty years, and even before the importance of the diet had declined sharply. As Johann Jacob Moser pointed out in a memorandum to the diet, it was 'indeed an empty name and a mere shadow of what Diets meant elsewhere and had once meant in Württemberg'. He attributed this decline to the ignorance of most deputies concerning their rights and duties, to the fact

---

[1] For details see Adam, loc. cit., pp. 278–304; Schneider, op. cit., pp. 366–8.
[2] von Pfister, 'Militärwesen', loc. cit., p. 142; Schneider, 'Regierung', loc. cit., p. 152; Adam, loc. cit., pp. 298–9, 301.

that much was now kept secret from the diet which previously had been communicated to it and ratified by it, and to the slowness and dilatoriness of the proceedings. Previously much more time had been spent on discussion, and sessions had got through far more business, but now they were concluded because of an alleged lack of material, while in reality much was left undecided.[1] Thus the Small Committee were no longer interested that a diet should be held. They also combated the claims of certain towns, such as Stuttgart and Tübingen, that they had a right to be represented on the committee, although they had in fact occupied such a seat since the sixteenth century.[2]

The Small Committee were a narrow oligarchy drawn from a few leading families. The members and the Estates' councillors and other officials usually had legal training and considerable administrative experience. Although their functions were very different from those of modern representative government, they stood much closer to them than the absolute military monarchies of the time. Through their active participation in the work of the state the members of the Small Committee proved that the machinery of the Estates could be adapted to the needs of a more modern state, that this machinery worked efficiently and cheaply, that the creation of a large bureaucracy was not the only possible way of advance towards the modern state, that absolute monarchy was not the only form in which this transition could be accomplished. Württemberg was and remained a constitutional monarchy, a fact of permanent importance for its history. The Estates' position was so strong that after the outbreak of the French Revolution they pursued an independent pro-French foreign policy and repeatedly negotiated with the French government through their own envoys.[3]

For what reasons were the Württemberg Estates able to prevent their princes from creating a large standing army and making themselves absolute? They were socially homogeneous and consisted of one house only; but even so they were far from

[1] Adam, loc. cit., p. 307; Schneider, op. cit., p. 366; Adam, *Johann Jakob Moser*, pp. 123–4 (memorandum of 17 May 1770); Grube, op. cit., pp. 445–7.

[2] Adam, loc. cit., p. 307; Spittler, op. cit., no. 14, pp. 138 ff. (letter of the Small Committee to the town council of Stuttgart of 9 July 1793).

[3] Hermann Christern, *Deutscher Ständestaat und englischer Parlamentarismus am Ende des 18. Jahrhunderts*, Munich, 1939, p. 31; Grube, op. cit., pp. 463–6, 471–6.

united, and the prelates in particular were easily intimidated. Pressure could equally be brought to bear on the local assemblies which instructed the deputies and the committees of the Estates. The large majority of the towns was much too small and weak to render any effective opposition, and no active resistance was ever attempted. Those dukes who knew what they wanted and energetically carried through their policy of ruling without the Estates—Duke Ulrich in the sixteenth, Duke Frederick in the seventeenth, Dukes Eberhard Louis and Charles Alexander in the eighteenth century—were surprisingly successful. Time and again the Estates were saved only by the death of the duke and a consequent change of policy. Time and again they contented themselves with promises that their grievances would be redressed, granted money without sufficient guarantees, sought a compromise or gave way under mere verbal protests. They never effectively wielded the weapon of 'grievances before supply'. Even their complaints to the Aulic Council were not pushed energetically and were soon dropped under pressure. The great issue of the seventeenth century—whether the duke was entitled to maintain a standing army in peace-time—was decided against the Estates in the eighteenth century.

Under these circumstances it is really surprising that Charles Eugene was not much more successful in continuing his father's policy. He might have been in the seventeenth century when ancient liberties were falling to the ground all over Germany. By the later eighteenth century, however, the climate had changed to a certain extent. In Württemberg there existed then a marked pride in the ancient constitution and a well-established tradition of opposition to the army, to its methods of recruiting and levying taxes, a strong dislike of anything military,[1] and this strengthened the Estates. They were strengthened likewise by the Roman Catholic policy of the dukes, which was highly unpopular in the country, by their profligacy and extravagance, by their petty despotism, and by the ill-success of the foreign policy on which they embarked at such cost to the country. By this ill-success the Estates' policy of passive resistance to a standing army was vindicated. Last but not least, the support finally extended to the Estates from Vienna and from Berlin provided them with effective backing. Charles Eugene would not, or

[1] Thus von Pfister, loc. cit., p. 133.

could not, entirely disregard the decisions of the Aulic Council, as a stronger ruler might have done, for that would have entailed the risk of a popular uprising. Apart from this, the Estates of Württemberg owed their survival and ultimate victory to their own efforts and to the more favourable circumstances of the eighteenth century. They stubbornly clung to their ancient liberties and retained their control of the financial administration, proving how well they understood the issues which were at stake.

II

HESSE

1. *Introduction*

To the north of Württemberg, in central Germany, there lay the scattered possessions of the landgraves of Hesse, bordering upon Saxony in the east and upon Brunswick and Lüneburg in the north, and stretching southwards to the Rhine and across the Main to the frontiers of the Palatinate. The landgraves of Hesse were descendants of the dukes of Brabant. They established themselves in this region in the thirteenth century and chose the town of Cassel as their capital. In long-drawn-out struggles against the local nobility and towns, and especially against the archbishops of Mainz, the landgraves slowly extended their territories through conquest, purchase, hereditary treaties, and marriage alliances. The steady growth of their possessions was, however, interrupted in the fifteenth century by conflicts within the ruling family and the division of its domains between hostile brothers, so characteristic of many German principalities of the time. These conflicts and the rule of minor landgraves favoured the development of the Estates, which came into being in the later fourteenth century and were summoned to a diet for the first time in 1387.[1] In contrast with Württemberg, but in conformity with the large majority of the German principalities, the nobility remained throughout the leading group among the Hessian Estates; while the towns, led by Cassel and Marburg, were too weak to counterbalance its power, and the clergy ceased to be of importance with the introduction of the Lutheran Reformation. The leading towns of the area, Frankfurt and Wetzlar, were Free Imperial Cities, and their absence from the diet tipped the scales in favour of the nobility. The fifty or more towns usually represented in the diet of Hesse were small and unimportant, and many were nothing else but little market towns.[2]

[1] Armin Tille, 'Die deutschen Territorien', in *Gebhardt's Handbuch der deutschen Geschichte*, 7th ed., 1931, ii. 235–6.

[2] In the sixteenth century between 50 and 70 towns were usually summoned:

II. *The Estates in the Sixteenth Century*

When Landgrave Hermann the Learned died in 1413, his heir, Louis I, was only eleven years old. During Louis's minority members of the nobility formed the government. On his death Louis divided his territories between his sons, Louis II and Henry. On account of this division long feuds occurred between the hostile brothers, the Estates had to act as arbiters between them, and the treaty which terminated the war was submitted to a diet in 1470 for its approval. When Louis II died Henry became the guardian of his two nephews, who were minors, and the nobility was again predominant in the regency government. Moreover, the elder nephew, William I, was mad and unable to rule. After Henry's death in 1483 the second nephew, William II, assumed the government of Lower Hesse with Cassel as the capital, while Henry's son, William III, succeeded to Upper Hesse with Marburg. Soon new conflicts occurred between the two cousins, and the Estates again had to arbitrate between the hostile members of the ruling house, the continuous division of Hesse strengthening their position. It was only with William III's death in 1500 that his cousin William II succeeded in reuniting all the Hessian territories, which had been divided for more than forty years, and in consolidating his possessions and his government. In 1500 he married Anna, a princess of Mecklenburg, who after four years gave birth to a son, Philip. As William II suffered from venereal disease, which eventually caused his death in 1509, the succession of another landgrave who was still a minor seemed likely. William II's elder brother, William I, was still alive, but excluded from the succession through his madness.[1]

During his long-drawn-out illness in 1506 William II drew up a will in which he appointed five members of the nobility as guardians and regents on behalf of his son Philip, who was then less than two years old. The regents were to be responsible to a committee of the Estates, the twelve members of which were to

Hans Siebeck, 'Die landständische Verfassung Hessens im 16. Jahrhundert', *Zeitschrift des Vereins für hessische Geschichte und Landeskunde, Neue Folge*, xvii, 1914, pp. 11, n. 1, 21, 72, n. 1.

[1] For details see Hans Glagau, *Eine Vorkämpferin landesherrlicher Macht: Anna von Hessen, die Mutter Philipps des Grossmütigen*, Marburg, 1899, pp. 3-4, 12, 16; Tille, loc. cit. ii. 235-6.

be chosen in equal numbers from each of the three Estates. If any grievances arose the regents were to inform the Estates and ask for their advice. The regents were to rank above William I and his wife as well as above the widow of William II who was to retire to her estates. In practice the five regents, all members of the native nobility, assumed the direction of affairs already during William II's severe illness which completely incapacitated him. They were advised by a council of twenty-four native noblemen, while the two other Estates did not participate in the work of government. It was in vain that William II forbade the summoning of diets without his knowledge and threatened that he would take them to account. These threats were disregarded by the powerful nobility who saw themselves as the rulers of the country during the expected long minority. This situation was used by the Landgravine Anna who persuaded William in 1508 to alter his will and to appoint her Philip's guardian, with his uncle, Archbishop Hermann of Cologne, as the co-regent. The archbishop, however, died a few months later, ten months before William II himself. Already, before his death in 1509, his noble opponents publicly prepared to dispute this will, to exclude Anna from the government and to take it over themselves.[1]

A few days before William's death the Estates assembled on their own initiative, complained bitterly about oppression and abuses of the government, and elected a deputation to demand redress from the landgrave whom they found no longer alive. The Estates were supported by the Elector Frederick the Wise of Saxony, who was jealous of Anna's influence and hoped to acquire Hesse for himself if the boy Philip died; for there was no male heir, and Saxony had claims upon Hesse on the basis of a fourteenth-century hereditary alliance in case the ruling family died out. Frederick's cousin of the Albertine line, on the other hand, Duke George the Bearded, took Anna's side because, according to William's will, he was to succeed her as regent in case she remarried. The deep rift between the Ernestine and the Albertine lines of the house of Wettin, which was to cause civil war thirty-six years later, strongly influenced the events in Hesse during the following years. This dissension was, above all,

[1] Glagau, op. cit., pp. 5–6, 12–14, 17, and in *Hessische Landtagsakten*, i (1508–21), Marburg, 1901, p. 21.

due to the division of Saxony which had been effected in 1485,
and created permanent hostility between the two lines.[1] Some
days after William's death Anna asked George the Bearded to
come to her aid with a hundred well-equipped horsemen against
the enemies of the principality, which he promised to do. Anna
had been surprised by William's death and was unprepared.
To make his will public she summoned the Estates of Upper and
Lower Hesse to two separate places; but the plan thus to weaken
the opposition miscarried, for it was reinforced through the appearance of an envoy of Frederick the Wise. The Estates of
Lower Hesse declined to hear the will in the absence of those
from Upper Hesse, and the diet had to be adjourned pending
their arrival. The Estates then declared that they would not
suffer Anna and her followers as the regents and appealed for
support to Frederick the Wise, thus hoping to strengthen their
own influence. The envoys of the princes of Saxony effected a
compromise which in practice set aside the will of William II.
A preliminary government of eight was appointed, only three
of whom belonged to Anna's side, the other five to that of the
Estates; and in important matters they were to be advised by a
committee chosen from the Estates.[2]

This compromise did not last long. Only four days later the
Estates concluded a union which was openly hostile to Anna.
They complained that wars and feuds had been started without
their consent, contrary to old custom, and that it was intended
to pawn lands without consulting them. They promised protection to every signatory of the union, even against the prince,
and arranged that complaints should be addressed to a committee of three drawn from the three Estates. If these three
supported a complaint, it was to be submitted to a diet, and
the Estates would help those wronged with advice and deeds.
Adherence to this union was sworn to throughout the country.
Officials who were disliked by the Estates were removed and
others appointed in their place. The Estates then on their own
initiative summoned another diet to meet in October 1509 and
to elect a regency government from their own ranks, 'according
to the old usage and custom of the principality of Hesse'.

[1] See below, pp. 200–1, 212–13.
[2] *Hessische Landtagsakten*, i, nos. 4, 6, 7, pp. 24–30; Glagau, op. cit., pp. 17, 19,
21–22, 24–28, and in *Hessische Landtagsakten*, i. 22–23 (16–25 July 1509).

Against this the Saxon envoys protested, but the election took place nevertheless. The Estates, assembled in large numbers, refused to wait and elected a government of nine: one prelate, six noblemen, and the mayors of Cassel and Marburg. They claimed that they had the right of electing the regents during the minority of the landgrave. In important matters the regents were to consult with the Estates, and in less important ones with the Estates' committee, to which they were to render annual accounts of their administration and of the revenue and expenditure.[1]

In November 1509 deputies of the Estates met the four dukes of Saxony, the Landgravine Anna and her brothers, the dukes of Mecklenburg, at Mühlhausen in Thuringia in an attempt to bring about an agreed settlement. Anna, however, would not acknowledge that the Estates were entitled to dispute William's will and to conclude a union; while they were opposed to any woman's rule, doubted the validity of the second will, and asserted that the right of resistance was their 'indisputable and unadulterated right'. For each side three long speeches were made; and then the negotiations began, but did not lead to any result. Duke George of the Albertine line took Anna's side. She demanded the deposition of the regency government elected by the Estates and for herself the guardianship of Philip until he reached his fourteenth year. This the Estates declined and appointed the three other Saxon dukes the guardians of Philip. Thereupon the dukes promised their support of the regency government and refused to recognize William's will. Early in 1510 negotiations were resumed at Cassel, but again with no result. Anna protested and left the town to petition the Emperor Maximilian for help. The Emperor feared the growing power of Frederick the Wise and the Ernestine line, while Anna was trying to exploit this rivalry and the friction between the Ernestine and Albertine lines. In March 1510 she claimed the Hessian seat in the Imperial diet as the guardian of the infant Philip. Maximilian, however, supported Frederick the Wise and gave the seat to the regents. He then appointed commissars under whose chairmanship negotiations were resumed at Marburg in July 1510. These ended with another victory for the

[1] *Hessische Landtagsakten*, i, nos. 8, 14, pp. 31–34, 42–46; Glagau, op. cit., pp. 29–30, 37–43 (29 July, 2 Oct. 1509).

Estates, who were left in charge of Philip while he was a minor, and only one representative of Anna was admitted to the annual rendering of accounts and to discussions of important affairs.[1]

A few months later a new party appeared in the many-sided conflict: Anna of Brunswick, the wife of the mad William I, Philip's uncle and only male relative. She claimed that William's health had improved and demanded for him a share in the government and recognition as a regent. The Estates, however, suspected her of aiming at a partition of the country and refuted her claims several times. Soon after the Ernestine dukes of Saxony ordered the country to swear allegiance to them to provide for the eventuality of Philip dying without leaving a male heir, and this oath was duly rendered by the regents and in the country. But some noblemen hesitated and certain towns, instigated by Anna of Brunswick, refused because they feared that the dukes aimed at the incorporation of Hesse with Saxony. The towns of Homberg and Treysa had to be reduced by force. They were compelled to surrender the leaders of the resistance, their urban privileges and the keys to the town gates, and had to take the oath of allegiance and to pay heavy fines. These incidents caused considerable opposition and led to a renewed intervention by the Emperor Maximilian. The parties were cited to appear before him at Worms and new negotiations took place there. The claims of William I were rejected by the Emperor, but the regents were ordered to pay his debts before he returned to Hesse. The disputes over this point continued until 1513, for William's stay at Worms cost nearly 20,000 guilders, or two-thirds of the annual revenues of Hesse; and the Emperor again had to adjudicate between rival claims and counter-claims.[2]

Meanwhile Anna of Mecklenburg's chances were improving for several reasons. The regents elected in 1509 were no longer united; and the two urban representatives retired, leaving the

---

[1] *Hessische Landtagsakten*, i, nos. 16, 19, 24, 28–30, pp. 49–79, 85–92, 102, 106–17 (protocols of the negotiations of Nov. 1509 and Jan. 1510, 22 Mar., 13–26 July 1510); Glagau, op. cit., pp. 45–67.

[2] *Hessische Landtagsakten*, i, nos. 34, 37, 40–41, 46, 49, 50, 52, 59, pp. 125–7, 130, and n. 1, 134–9, 144, 146–9, 151–2, 158–64, 164–5, notes; Glagau, op. cit., pp. 74–86; Friedrich Münscher, *Geschichte von Hessen*, Marburg, 1894, p. 146. In 1513 the total revenue of Hesse amounted to only 28,588 guilders.

field entirely to the nobility. Among these several groups appeared. Some of the regents resented the overbearing attitude of their leader, Ludwig von Boyneburg, who decided most questions himself; they complained about him to Frederick the Wise, and even approached Anna in an attempt to gain her support. In addition, there was much dissatisfaction with the regents because they relied too much on support from Saxony. The Saxon dukes looked upon the regents as mere officials: if a vacancy occurred they were to submit names to the dukes who would then select one of these to fill the post. The dukes also forbade the regents to render accounts to the Estates' committee as it had been stipulated. They maintained that its claims to participate in the financial administration were quite improper, and that a diet could be summoned only with their assent. The dukes' claims were not opposed by the regents who thus came into conflict with the Estates from which they had sprung.[1]

Anna of Mecklenburg in her turn eagerly seized this chance of exploiting the rifts among her enemies. With the agreement and in the name of fifty-four noblemen she summoned a diet to meet at the beginning of 1514 and to decide upon the question of Philip's guardianship. At the diet she sharply attacked Ludwig von Boyneburg who 'ruled as if he were himself a prince' and decreed the levying of taxes without rendering an account; but she appeared to recognize the claims of the Estates whom she needed to overthrow the power of the Saxon dukes. The Estates complained about the curtailment of their rights and sent a list of their grievances to Frederick the Wise. Another diet was summoned to meet four weeks later. In vain did Frederick the Wise forbid its attendance: 6 prelates, 235 noblemen, and 37 towns appeared, but Cassel and 17 other towns did not. They sided with the regents and with Saxony, but were threatened from inside by a rebellion of the guilds, to whom Anna's party appealed over the heads of the municipal authorities. This time Anna reached an agreement with the majority of the Estates. The union of 1509 was revoked and a new one concluded which severely limited her power. The Estates were granted the power of the purse; they were to be

---

[1] *Hessische Landtagsakten*, i, no. 61, pp. 168–9; Glagau, op. cit., p. 42, n. 1; pp. 86–87, 91–94 (reports of Aug. and Sept. 1513).

consulted before a war or feud was begun and in other important affairs. If they found fault with the government, this was to
be remedied with their 'advice and will'. A diet was to be summoned every year, and if this proved impossible for weighty
reasons, at least every other year. The guardians of the minor
landgrave were to render annual accounts to the Estates' committee. The Estates were entitled to assemble on their own initiative and to resist any infringement of this treaty, which was
signed and sealed by Anna and those present.[1]

During the following months the struggle continued. Both
sides armed and prepared for civil war. Ludwig von Boyneburg
told the Saxon dukes that the new union was directed against
all authority, and that it would result in everybody wanting to
be free, like the Swiss cantons. Another diet met in March 1514
and led to an open breach with the Ernestine dukes. The large
majority stood on Anna's side and sharply attacked von Boyneburg. They demanded that the regency government should
resign and that Philip and William I should be handed over to
them. Suggestions for a compromise were rejected by Anna and
the Estates as well as by the councillors of George the Bearded
who took their side. The Estates then declared that the guardianship of the Ernestine dukes was terminated and that the regents
were deposed. They took possession of the castles, but there was
no serious resistance. In Cassel, where the urban council sided
with the regents, a rising broke out which forced it to come over
to Anna's side. The Ernestine dukes and the regents had to
leave the capital. They then tried to win over Marburg, but had
no more success there. Anna's enemies were imprisoned or
fined and their estates seized. She was successful in winning over
the burghers against the nobility that had risen against her five
years previously. In April 1514 another diet met without the
participation of the pro-Saxon and pro-regent group. It elected
a new government consisting of Anna and five noble councillors. If there was disagreement between them Anna was to
decide. It also elected two committees: a smaller one with 13
knights and 8 burghers, without whose consent the government
was not to take any important decision, and a larger one with

[1] *Hessische Landtagsakten*, i, nos. 64–65, 67, 71, 74, 78, pp. 172, n. 1, 172–6, 181,
186, 189, 192–8, and n. 1; Glagau, op. cit., pp. 97–109; Christoph Rommel,
Geschichte von Hessen, iii. 1, Cassel, 1827, p. 221 (9 Jan. to 10 Feb. 1514).

27 knights and 26 burghers (representing 13 towns) which was to wield plenary powers. The prelates and the pro-Saxon part of the nobility were not represented.[1]

Frederick the Wise, whose hold on Hesse was thus irretrievably destroyed, then appealed to his own Estates and to the Emperor. In October 1514 representatives of the Estates of Saxony—one count, three abbots, two knights, and four burghers —met those of Hesse, but these refused to make any concessions. Maximilian simultaneously ordered Anna not to interfere with the rights of the Saxon dukes as the guardians of her son, or to appear before him to give an account of her actions. In the following month Anna and representatives of the Estates duly appeared at Innsbruck to report to the Emperor. Six months later new negotiations about the guardianship took place before him at Augsburg. He proposed that the case be referred to the Imperial High Court, the *Reichskammergericht*, alleging that he had not sufficient time for a decision, and there the case was effectively buried. Soon after Anna concluded an alliance with George the Bearded, which was also signed by representatives of the Estates—one prelate, two knights, and two leading towns of each side. The Ernestine dukes expressed their disapproval and invited the Hessian Estates to a diet so that an agreement about the guardianship could be reached. Anna, however, prohibited the attendance and recruited horsemen to watch the roads and apprehend those purposing to attend, so that the diet could not take place.[2]

As long as Anna was afraid of interference from Saxony she had to co-operate with the Estates. Their committee was consulted about the conclusion of alliances and even in many less important matters; but no further diet was summoned. As Anna's position grew stronger the importance of the committee declined, and gradually it fell into abeyance—so much so that in 1518 her councillors could inform the Imperial envoys that they knew little about the committee and its functions. When the envoys invited the committee to hear the Emperor's message

[1] *Hessische Landtagsakten*, i, nos. 99, 114, 118, 121, 123–6, 129–31, pp. 215, 242–320, 324–5, 327, 329–39, 342–9; p. 332, n. 2; Glagau, op. cit., pp. 115, 119–41 (21 Feb. to 27 Apr. 1514).

[2] *Hessische Landtagsakten*, i, nos. 160, 166–8, 176–8, 181, 184, 196–8, 200, pp. 393, 412–24, 440–56, 461, 464–6, 488–94; Glagau, op. cit., pp. 149–56, 159–61 (Oct. 1514 to Oct. 1516).

Anna used force to prevent this.[1] During these years she
became in effect the regent on behalf of her infant son. Owing
to the specially favourable circumstances after 1509, the power
of the Estates had suddenly developed and reached great heights,
but after a brief space it declined equally suddenly. It relied on
foreign support, and when this became unpopular, it collapsed.
It rested almost entirely on the nobility, and this proved too
narrow a base. The burghers and the lower orders had little to
hope from the rule of a self-seeking aristocracy and were therefore willing to support the prince against the nobility and
foreign interference. From 1513 onwards the nobility itself was
split into factions, and one of these began to look towards the
young landgrave and his mother for support against the other
group. It proved of great importance that in 1518 the Emperor
Maximilian pronounced the thirteen-year-old Philip to be of
age and thus made him the crystallizing point of his mother's
party. For he was now the ruler, if only in name, and the
Saxon dukes were deprived of all pretexts for interfering.

   Philip's coming of age, however, did not terminate the party
struggles. In the same year they flared up once more, partly
because Anna proved irreconcilable towards her enemies and
refused to relinquish their confiscated estates, and partly because
she ruled with the help of two favourite councillors and without
consulting the Estates. The followers of Ludwig von Boyneburg
proposed that a diet should be held to effect a change of the
government and tried to win over the towns. Anna again forbade the attendance of the diet on pain of escheat and appealed
to the Emperor for a mandate prohibiting such unauthorized
meetings on pain of incurring the ban of the Empire. Yet the
opposition assembled in October 1518 at Homberg, and Anna
and the young Philip had to flee to the castle of Spangenberg
where they collected the loyal members of the nobility. She
declined to listen to the grievances of the opposition and
ordered that they should be submitted to the landgrave who
would summon a diet if necessary. The opposition refused to
obey, recalled the union of 1509, and sought the arbitration of
the dukes of Saxony. Anna in her turn summoned the nobility
and the towns in small groups and let the young Philip negotiate

---

[1] *Hessische Landtagsakten*, i, nos. 144–5, 147–8, 210, pp. 353, 367–78, 498, 521–2;
Glagau, op. cit., pp. 167–9 (July 1514 to Apr. 1518).

with each separately. He admonished them to obedience and forbade any meetings on their own initiative. When the deputies of the nobility petitioned him for the summoning of a diet, he replied that this was too difficult, but promised a small meeting to discuss their grievances. This was accepted by the deputies who then submitted the names of twenty-four noblemen. From this list Philip was to select ten who should discuss his and their grievances with four of his councillors and two each from Cassel and Marburg. To this Philip assented, although he declared it obnoxious to accept names proposed by his subjects. The meeting duly took place early in 1519 and was attended by the envisaged eighteen members, in addition to one prelate—the Commander of the Teutonic Knights' Commandery at Marburg—and the councillors of the Saxon dukes.[1]

The tactics of the government were entirely successful. The Estates were split into rival factions and were without a leader. The instigators of the last revolt were removed from the council and replaced by Anna's willing tools. They continued to form the government when in the following year Anna resigned the regency and Philip began to rule himself. No diet was held until 1527 when the Reformation was introduced, and the Estates ceased to play any part in state affairs. Anna had defeated the political ambitions of the nobility; and these were checked again when Landgrave Philip in 1523 destroyed the castles and the power of the Imperial Knights who had risen under Franz von Sickingen and Ulrich von Hutten. This victory also strengthened Philip's internal position and enabled him to rule without the Estates, and especially without the nobility. Only the towns were summoned when he needed money during the following years, and they duly granted it. In 1527 Ludwig von Boyneburg was reinstated in his offices and estates. By then Philip was strong enough to forgive the leader of the noble fronde which had troubled him during his early youth. He was also strong enough to play a leading part in the struggles which broke out in Germany during the Reformation period.[2]

---

[1] *Hessische Landtagsakten*, i, nos. 212, 214, 216, 221, pp. 523, 526–34, 538; Glagau, op. cit., pp. 171–2, 176–8, 185–93 (Oct. 1518 to Feb. 1519).

[2] *Hessische Landtagsakten*, i, no. 221, pp. 538, 560, n. 1; Glagau, op. cit., pp. 193–4, 196; Siebeck, loc. cit., pp. 1–2, 9, 178.

In the religious question Philip acted entirely on his own and introduced what changes he considered necessary on his own authority. But he found it expedient to associate the Estates with his new policy and to hear their advice with regard to the disposal of monastic property. In October 1526 he called a synod, attended not only by the clergy, but also by representatives of the nobility and the towns. To this assembly he submitted the *Reformatio Ecclesiarum Hassiae*. This was above all the work of Lambert of Avignon, a former Franciscan trained at Wittenberg, and envisaged a church with a far-reaching autonomy of the congregations and the election of bishops and synods. Luther, however, was opposed to such experiments and his influence prevailed over the more democratic ideas. Philip became the supreme head of the new church. The system developed in Saxony by Frederick the Wise was introduced, and the Church became effectively controlled by the secular authorities.[1]

Twelve months after the synod, to which the new religious order had been submitted, Philip—after an interval of nine years—summoned a diet to hear the Estates' opinion upon what should be done with the dissolved monasteries and nunneries. An outright appropriation by himself would have alienated the nobility whose support he needed on the religious issue. For the noblemen were accustomed to use the religious houses as places which provided for their younger sons and unmarried daughters. The questions were discussed at the diet of 1527 and it was decided that the monastic revenues were to be paid into a separate chest, controlled by the princely councillors and four noble commissioners; that the revenues of two former nunneries were to provide dowries for poor noble ladies; that four hospitals were to be established, as well as the University of Marburg to train future clergymen and officials; that two deputies of the landgrave, two of the nobility and two of the towns were to supervise the spending of the monastic revenues on pious, educational, and ecclesiastical purposes, to which 59 per cent. of them were allocated; and that the remaining 41 per cent. were to be used for the prince and the state. Yet the envisaged committee to supervise the expenditure never came

[1] Gustav Wolf, 'Reformationszeit', in *Gebhardt's Handbuch der deutschen Geschichte*, 7th ed., 1931, i. 586–7; Walther Peter Fuchs, 'Das Zeitalter der Reformation', ibid., 8th ed., 1955, ii. 70–71.

into being, and the Estates did not acquire any control over the secularized monasteries, nor over the donations made from their revenues—in contrast with the developments in Saxony and in Württemberg.[1] By these arrangements Philip's power was not curtailed, and his financial gains were very considerable, in spite of liberal allocations to the new university and to pious and charitable institutions. The Estates had not been consulted before the introduction of the Reformation. The Regulations for the Church of 1532 and those for the Visitation and Order of the Church of 1537 were published without their participation; but the latter were based on discussions with a committee of the Estates, formed to deliberate upon measures against the Anabaptists and other questions of the Church regiment, and acting in an advisory capacity. The Estates of Hesse did not acquire any right of taking part in legislation; but occasionally the nobility or the towns or their deputies were consulted by Philip before the promulgation of decrees.[2]

As a result of the Reformation the prelates disappeared as an Estate. The only survivor was the Commander of the Teutonic Knights at Marburg whose possessions were legally beyond Philip's reach, as the Order was an Estate of the Empire. The commander therefore steadfastly refused to obey a summons to the diet because he did not consider himself a member of the Hessian Estates nor a subject of the landgrave. It was only much later, in 1584, that a treaty was concluded between the landgrave and the Grand Master of the Teutonic Order, according to which the commander had to attend diets and to pay taxes like members of the nobility. By that time a separate house of prelates had again come into being, beginning in the later sixteenth century with the representatives of Marburg University. To these were added the presidents of the two noble foundations created at the diet of 1527, one of whom also represented the four hospitals founded at the same time. These five 'Estates' until the end of the eighteenth century formed a truncated house of prelates: as in Württemberg, most of its members were Protestants, but they were not clergymen, and

---

[1] Siebeck, loc. cit., pp. 27–28, 142–3, 177; Rommel, op. cit. iii. 1, pp. 348–9; G. F. Teuthon, *Ausführliche Geschichte der Hessen*, viii, Biedenkopf, 1777, pp. 54–55, 74.

[2] Siebeck, loc. cit., pp. 150–1, 161, 166, and n. 3, with several examples of such consultations from the 1530's.

their influence among the Estates was very small. Although the Commander of the Teutonic Knights was also a member of the house of the nobility, the 'prelates' continued to sit separately from that house:[1] in contrast with Württemberg where the existence of but one house gave to the Estates their unity and coherence. Distinct from many other Protestant principalities, in this curious form the classical order of three separate Estates was preserved in Hesse. But it seems doubtful whether this was to the advantage of the Estates.

The two other houses represented the whole country. Only with their consent was it possible to levy a general tax. A separate house of the high nobility, the counts, did not come into being, although Philip repeatedly attempted to treat them as his subjects and to make them participate in taxation; but they insisted on paying their inconsiderable contributions to the Empire so as to escape paying the Hessian taxes. As they were backed by the Emperor, Philip had to desist. Occasionally, however, the counts did attend a diet, for example the very important one of 1547 after the Schmalcaldic War. The lower nobility attended in large numbers, usually from 120 to 200 being present, for every member of a noble family who held a fief had the right to be summoned. Well over a hundred noble families were domiciled in Hesse, so that 230 noblemen were summoned in 1547, and as many as 430 in 1566. In 1583 there was an attempt to limit representation to one member of each family, who was to receive powers from the others, but this caused sharp complaints at the following diet. In 1594 and in 1603 it was left to every family to decide whether they would grant powers to one of their number or whether they wished to appear in full strength. But in 1598 the landgrave selected one nobleman from each family who was summoned and commanded to appear without fail with the powers of the other members of his family, if he wanted to avoid his prince's severe displeasure.[2]

---

[1] Siebeck, loc. cit., pp. 28–36; Rommel, op. cit. iv. 1, pp. 227–8; C. W. Ledderhose, 'Von der landschaftlichen Verfassung der Hessen-Casselischen Lande', *Kleine Schriften*, i, Marburg, 1787, p. 20. In the terminology of the time each member of the Estates was called 'an Estate'; and the same applied to the members of the Imperial diet, the difference being that between a *Landstand* and a *Reichsstand*.

[2] Siebeck, loc. cit., pp. 11 and n. 1, 13–15, 38–48, 70, n. 2, 71, n. 1, 74, 76–77, 122, 124.

The number of towns summoned varied also. In 1542 as many as 75 were summoned, in 1547 only 31, and in 1563 only 25; though usually the number was between 50 and 70. As in Württemberg, the towns also represented the surrounding districts, the *Ämter*; but in Hesse this excluded the peasants under the nobility, who were considered to be represented by their masters. As a rule the urban representatives were the mayors, councillors, or secretaries of the towns in question. But the urban Commons often sent their own representatives to the diet:[1] which was rather exceptional in sixteenth-century Germany, when the municipal authorities monopolized all offices and strongly opposed any challenge to their power. Perhaps this difference was due to the struggles during Philip's minority when Anna had appealed to the Commons of Cassel, Homberg, and other towns against the pro-Saxon urban aristocracies.[2] Only a few towns, Cassel, Marburg, Homberg, Treysa, were of any importance, and in one of these the diet usually met, while the large majority of the towns summoned were unimportant little country towns. Probably for this reason the towns among the Estates had much less influence than the nobility and were often willing to support the prince against the latter.

Among the higher officials and the councillors of the landgraves there was a marked preponderance of the native nobility, exactly as had been the case in the various councils of the regency during Philip's minority. This fact also strengthened the nobility's weight among the Estates and decreased that of the towns. While the noble officials had strong personal and family ties, the officials who were commoners usually had no connexions whatever with the towns.[3] An official of the Estates themselves was the *Erbmarschall*, their spokesman and the intermediary between them and the landgrave during the sessions of the diet. He was not elected, but the office was hereditary in the noble family von Riedesel who held it as a fief from the landgrave.[4] In contrast with the Estates of Württemberg, Bavaria, Cleves and Jülich, and of many other principalities, the Estates

---

[1] Ibid., pp. 11, n. 1, 21, 72, n. 1, 121.
[2] *Hessische Landtagsakten*, i, 198, n. 1, and above, pp. 155–6.
[3] This against the remarks made by Siebeck, loc. cit., pp. 146–7.
[4] Teuthorn, op. cit. ix. 285, 297; Ledderhose, op. cit. i. 33.

of Hesse did not have their own salaried officials. Nor did they develop the permanent committees which played such a vital part in Württemberg, Bavaria, and elsewhere. Without this machinery the functioning of the Estates depended on the summoning of a diet, and this was a prerogative of the prince since the Estates had failed to wrest this right from him during the struggles of the regency period. For Philip was determined not to let the Estates assemble on their own initiative. The experiences of his youth had made him determined to keep the Estates down and to deprive them of political power.[1] All these points indicate how weak the Estates of Hesse were in comparison with those of Württemberg, Saxony, Brandenburg, and Prussia, whose princes had not made any real gains from the introduction of the Lutheran Reformation.

After the Reformation diet of 1527 no diet was summoned for five years because Philip's financial problems had been solved for the time being. From 1532 onwards, however, diets were held at fairly regular intervals every few years: eleven more during Philip's reign which lasted until 1567, excluding negotiations with one of the Estates only.[2] The continuous rise of prices and Philip's ambitious foreign policy in the interest of Protestantism defeated all his attempts to manage without the diet which had the right to grant general taxes; for the entire burden could no longer devolve upon the towns which had borne it so far. Thus for the first time in 1532 the nobility were asked to grant a tax on their own and their peasants' property. They assented to this proposal and agreed also to bear a share of a tax for the Empire. As both were innovations, Philip had to promise that in future the nobility would not be taxed, but that their ancient privileges would be maintained. A more important concession was that the administration of the new property tax was left to the Estates. They elected twelve receivers from their own ranks, six each from the nobility and the towns, who were to render their accounts to an elected committee of four noblemen and four burghers, which had the right of co-opting new members. The levying of the tax in town and country, on the

[1] Siebeck, loc. cit., pp. 62–63, 178; H. Glagau, 'Landgraf Philipp von Hessen im Ausgang des Schmalkaldischen Krieges', *Historische Vierteljahrschrift*, viii, 1905, pp. 27, 34–36.

[2] There is a list of the sixteenth-century diets in Rommel, op. cit. iv. 1, p. 67, n. 15, p. 223, n. 31.

other hand, was left to the officials of the landgrave, for the Estates possessed no machinery for this purpose: only the members of the nobility levied it directly from their own peasants.[1] This did not amount to the full financial control which the Estates of Bavaria, Württemberg, Brandenburg, and other territories exercised, but it was an important step in that direction. The next steps would have been the establishment of a separate chest of the Estates and the appointment of officials of their own; but neither was achieved.

Perhaps it was because Philip was disappointed with the results of the diet, perhaps because he feared such demands, that in the following year he reverted to the earlier practice and only summoned the towns. He proposed to them the introduction of an excise on drink, a measure which would have put his finances on a sounder and more permanent basis, but the towns demanded that the nobility should participate. Philip, however, did not want to submit the proposal to a diet. He thus summoned the majority to Cassel, and the others a week later to Ziegenhain; but the meetings were cancelled because Philip had to go abroad. The towns declined the proposed excise and instead granted a direct tax. As early as 1536 Philip acted against his promise of 1532 that the nobility would not be taxed. He called a diet and submitted a new demand for a tax: partly to form a reserve in case Hesse was attacked, and partly for the Empire to be used against the Turks. For the Schmalcaldic League had been formed in 1531 under Philip's leadership to protect Protestantism, and the Turks were battering at the gates of Vienna and Hessian contingents were fighting against them. The nobility granted a tax for the war against the Turks and a tax on the sheep of their tenants, but declined to make a contribution of their own.[2] In spite of the dissolution of the monasteries Philip's income was quite insufficient to enable him to pursue the active Protestant policy which he favoured. It was only French help which allowed him in 1534 to recruit an army against the Habsburgs and to conquer from

[1] Ledderhose, op. cit. iii, 1789, pp. 268–70; Siebeck, loc. cit., pp. 78, 102–3, 131–4; Rommel, op. cit. iii. 2, p. 165, notes; p. 197; B. W. Pfeiffer, *Geschichte der landständischen Verfassung in Kurhessen*, Cassel, 1834, p. 45.

[2] Siebeck, loc. cit., pp. 80–81, 106; Ledderhose, op. cit. iii. 270–1; Rommel, op. cit. iii. 2, p. 197. Another tax for the war against the Turks was granted by the nobility in 1542: Siebeck, loc. cit., p. 103.

them the duchy of Württemberg in the name of the exiled Duke
Ulrich; Ulrich was reinstated and then introduced the Lutheran
Reformation, a victory over the Habsburg policy of unification and aggrandizement.[1] Before Philip left for the campaign
in Württemberg he called the Estates together. He handed them
his will, by which he appointed six noble regents and entrusted
them, in the event of his being killed, with the government and
the guardianship of his children who were minors, and this will
was solemnly signed and sealed by twenty-eight knights and
eight towns. At the diet of 1536 the Estates again undertook
to execute Philip's will and not to act against it in any way.[2]
Thus Philip was forced through his foreign policy to win the
support and co-operation of the Estates.

During the following years the foreign dangers grew. Hesse
and Saxony armed. In 1546 the two princes with considerable
forces advanced to the Danube, while the Emperor Charles V
was busy trying to detach other Protestant princes from the
alliance and winning Maurice of Saxony over to his side,[3]
concluding treaties with the Pope and the duke of Bavaria, and
having Hesse and Saxony put under the ban of the Empire.
The campaign on the Danube went against the Protestants on
account of their disunity and indecision. In the spring of 1547
Maurice of Saxony invaded the lands of the Elector John
Frederick of Saxony who was then defeated by Charles V at
Mühlberg and taken prisoner. Already before, Maurice had
tried to detach Philip from the Saxon alliance and to induce him
to conclude a separate peace with the Emperor. Charles V in
his turn attempted to win over members of the Hessian nobility
who disliked Philip's strong rule. He pictured to them Philip's
hopeless position and encouraged them to desert their master
and to sue for peace, but without much success. Only a few
disaffected noblemen met without Philip's consent and in vain
sought to gain the support of the towns. Philip himself was
spurred into action by these intrigues. In March 1547, six
weeks before the fateful battle of Mühlberg, he called a meeting
of notables to Cassel, put before them the articles he had received from Maurice as the basis of a peace with the Emperor,

---

[1] See above, pp. 19–20.
[2] Rommel, op. cit. iii. 2, p. 140; iv. 1, pp. 11, 13.
[3] See below, p. 211.

and asked them for their advice. One of the conditions was that Philip was to join in the war against John Frederick; but the meeting pronounced against any undertaking which they could not answer for to 'God, their honour and good conscience', and in favour of peace only on condition that the Protestant religion suffered no harm.[1]

These tactics deprived Philip's opponents of any opportunity to stir up trouble. The nobility were once more forbidden to meet without his permission, but two such meetings were held nevertheless. His councillors, however, found only nine noblemen present who were anxious to declare that they had not met with any evil intention, but that they would observe their oaths and duties and not separate from their prince. The attempt to play off the nobility against Philip failed.[2] After the defeat and subjugation of Saxony Charles V called upon Philip to surrender, promising that his life would be spared and that he would not suffer perpetual imprisonment, and demanding the payment of a large fine. As resistance was out of the question, it was necessary to summon a diet and hear its advice. The Estates pronounced in favour of accepting the Emperor's conditions and of paying the fine of 150,000 guilders. They granted a property tax of 2 per cent., in which the nobility was to participate, so as to bring the war to a speedy end, and the towns expressed their special thanks to Philip for his readiness to make peace. Both Estates emphasized their loyalty. The nobility declared not one of their members had any intention of deserting, for whoever did so would be a knave and traitor, and they asked for the due punishment of such people if any were found. The towns denied any knowledge of such plans. When the Imperial army reached Hesse there was no disaffection. Two weeks after the diet Philip gave himself up to Charles V, surrendered his cannon and fortresses, and was taken prisoner by the Emperor. The Estates were summoned by the fifteen-year-old Prince William and promised that they would pay the fine and carry out the conditions of the capitulation as the Emperor commanded them to do. When Philip was freed from

[1] Glagau, loc. cit. viii. 27–33, quoting a letter of Philip of 9 Mar. 1547; in general see Gustav Wolf, 'Reformationszeit', loc. cit. i. 617–19, and Walther Peter Fuchs, 'Das Zeitalter der Reformation', loc. cit. ii. 96–97, and the literature quoted by them.

[2] Glagau, loc. cit. viii. 33–36 (Mar. 1547).

captivity five years later he as well as the Estates had to acknowledge these conditions once more.[1]

The years of Philip's absence in captivity did not cause any
new political instability. It was only a question of time until he
regained his liberty. Meanwhile his eldest son, William, held
the reins of government, and the nobility did not attempt to
recover their influence. At the diet of 1551 the majority of them
refused to participate in a tax for the Empire and departed
without waiting to be dismissed, whereupon the remainder
declined to take a decision; but the towns granted a tax on their
own property and that of the peasants not under the nobility
and petitioned for the negotiations with the nobility to be resumed.[2] This separation of the Hessian Estates proved to be
their greatest weakness. In most other German principalities
taxes were granted by the diet, and not by the towns alone. In
Hesse, however, the towns frequently made separate grants, and
often the nobility were not even summoned.[3] A short time after
his return from captivity Philip again summoned the towns
only. This time he succeeded in persuading them to grant the
excise on drink, which they had refused him twenty years
before, for a period of eight years, to pay off his debts and to
redeem the pawned domains: an aftermath of his defeat in the
Schmalcaldic War. The towns merely asked him to negotiate
with the nobility about the same tax. This was done, but only
in the form of negotiations with individual noblemen. Some of
them accepted, others declined. It was only in 1555 that the
whole nobility agreed to pay the excise on drink, which was
simultaneously extended to 1569. When this grant expired it
was renewed to 1581, and then by another ten years to 1591,
by twelve years to 1603, &c. The excise thus became a semi-
permanent tax, always extended by fairly long periods, and
always by the nobility and the towns separately. In 1591, indeed, the Estates demanded to deliberate the matter together,
but Landgrave William declined this request, and they did not
persist.[4] That the lesson was not lost on the rulers of other

[1] Glagau, loc. cit. viii, pp. 53–54; Siebeck, loc. cit., p. 107; Münscher, op. cit.,
pp. 224–5, 230, 240 (June 1547 to Aug. 1552).   [2] Siebeck, loc. cit., p. 104.
[3] See above, pp. 159, 165. Cf. the opinion of Siebeck, loc. cit., p. 179, that
the diet was lacking in unity and in reality consisted of two separate corporations.
[4] Ibid., pp. 81, and n. 3, 99, 108, 115–17; Rommel, op. cit. iv. 1, p. 240; iv.
2, pp. 70–71.

principalities was shown by the fact that in 1564 Duke Christopher of Württemberg instructed his councillors to point out to his Estates how those of Hesse had granted an excise for sixteen years which yielded over 50,000 guilders a year, not counting their previous large grant to the landgrave.[1]

The new tax completely transformed the landgrave's financial situation and made him almost independent of further grants. For many years the towns were requested only to contribute to the dowries of princesses and the building of fortresses, apart from taxes collected for purposes of the Empire. Only in 1566 was another general property tax levied, to which the towns and *Ämter* contributed 81 per cent., the nobility and their peasants 14 per cent., and the clergy and pious foundations 5 per cent. It yielded just under 62,000 guilders.[2] It was thus much less important than the excise. This tax provided the landgraves with a regular income and fundamentally influenced the relationship between them and the Estates. Philip himself recognized the importance of this. In his will of 1562 he recommended to his sons that they should continue the excise until all the debts had been paid off and the domains had been redeemed, and pointed to the warning example of other princes who had sunk into such debts that they had to hand over their principalities to their Estates or had to sell them otherwise.[3] The fact that the excise was levied in the towns by officials of the landgrave was equally important. It is true that for the rendering of accounts some burghers were associated with them, so that they would not only see 'what came in, but also to what useful purposes the money was put'. For that reason in 1567 two officials and two burghers were entrusted with the supervision of the levying and of the financial administration. But they had no say in the allocation of the money which was a princely prerogative.[4] What the Hessian Estates lost by

---

[1] State Archives Stuttgart, A 34–35, *Büschel* 16a, 16b, 16e (draft).

[2] Siebeck, loc. cit., p. 115; Rommel, op. cit. iv. 1, p. 284: the total yield was 61,978 guilders, to which the nobility contributed 8,704, and the towns 49,920 guilders.

[3] Teuthorn, op. cit. ix. 37; Pfeiffer, op. cit., p. 55; Rommel, op. cit. iii. 2, p. 373, note. In 1544 Duke Ottheinrich of Palatinate-Neuburg sold his country to his Estates, his debts amounting to 1,050,000 guilders: State Archives Munich, 'Altbayerische Landschaft', no. 431, fos. 58, 103; see below, p. 372.

[4] Siebeck, loc. cit., pp. 56, 140; Pfeiffer, op. cit., p. 61; Rommel, op. cit. iv. 1, p. 240, quoting from the *Recess* of 26 Apr. 1569.

granting a semi-permanent tax for long years, they did not regain through a control of revenue and expenditure and of the whole tax administration, which at this time in Bavaria, Brandenburg, Württemberg, and elsewhere passed into the hands of the Estates.

That the influence of the Hessian Estates had declined sharply became clear in the years after 1555. In 1557 the nobility asked to be spared a tax for the Empire; thereupon Philip ordered eight of the most vociferous noblemen and eight from the towns to appear before him, and on the following day the nobility gave way; only their own houses and cattle and the produce needed for their own consumption remained exempt.[1] Shortly before his death Philip by his last will of 1567 divided Hesse among his four sons, without any consultation with the Estates, and without asking them to guarantee his will, as he had done in 1534 and 1536. The only concession made to meet their wishes was that the Estates of the four new principalities should be summoned to common diets. Seven common diets were indeed held in the course of the later sixteenth century; but they did not assume great importance and petered out in the course of the seventeenth century.[2] Only the death without issue of two of these four sons prevented a permanent fragmentation of Hesse.[3] The division between the other two sons, however, was permanent. Hesse-Cassel and Hesse-Darmstadt became separate states, which were engaged in long-drawn-out conflicts over the partition of the other two principalities, conflicts which were exacerbated by the different religions adopted by their rulers in the early seventeenth century.

After Philip's death all the towns and 'some of the most prominent noblemen' were summoned to a diet and asked to grant 25,000 guilders to relieve the debts of the princely chamber, and for another sum to enable Philip's younger sons to establish separate residences. Apparently the Estates did not protest against the irregular procedure of not summoning the whole nobility, nor against the division of the country which had been

[1] Siebeck, loc. cit., pp. 105–6; Rommel, op. cit. iv. 1, p. 231.
[2] Siebeck, loc. cit., pp. 10, 77; Rommel, op. cit. iv. 1, p. 66; ibid., p. 223, n. 31, a list of the common diets to 1603.
[3] Philip II died in 1583, Louis III in 1604: their territories were then divided between the other two sons, William IV and George who were the founders of the lines of Hesse-Cassel and Hesse-Darmstadt.

carried out without their knowledge. They only asked for an assurance that the landgraves would maintain their privileges and redress their grievances and made a grant of 18,000 guilders. The landgraves, however, refused to confirm the privileges unless a bigger grant was forthcoming. They then increased the sum to 20,000 guilders and voted another 12,000 for the new residence, whereupon the confirmation took place. The Estates further asked for a confirmation of the main points of Philip's will, and this was also conceded, but only in very general terms and without enumerating specific points for the confirmation of which they had asked: the maintenance of the Augsburg Confession, the preservation of unity between the brothers, the avoidance of war, the minting of good coins, &c. There is moreover, no evidence that the grievances were in fact redressed.[1] Two years later the towns of Hesse extended the excise on drink by as many as twelve years. In 1572 only 'some' of the Estates were summoned, but granted a tax for the war against the Turks without making any difficulties.[2]

At the diet of 1576 the Estates again enumerated their grievances, but did not receive a reply until the following diet seven years later. At the diet of 1594 the princely councillors went further and declared that they were not instructed to discuss grievances, but that the Estates should put them in writing, and that they would pass them on to the landgraves. At these diets Landgrave William IV seized the initiative by moving 'counter-grievances' against the nobility on behalf of their peasants. In 1576 he emphasized that it was his duty as a prince to preserve equal rights for rich and poor and chided those noblemen who treated their peasants as if they were Wends or slaves and as if they possessed power over their lives and limbs, who threw old men for trifling reasons into dungeons and put them into the stocks, who poured water over them in mid-winter so that their toes and feet froze. In 1583 he once more took the side of those burdened with new services and dues, attacked the extraction of promises from tenants that they should vacate their holdings at the bidding of their noble masters, and strongly criticized the appropriations of church

[1] Siebeck, loc. cit., pp. 77, 94, n. 1, 98, n. 2; Rommel, op. cit. iv. 1, pp. 79–81 (Aug. 1567).

[2] Siebeck, loc. cit., pp. 55, 77; Rommel, op. cit. iv. 1, pp. 239–40.

lands by the nobility and their neglect of his spiritual jurisdiction.[1] The quickly rising corn prices of the sixteenth century tempted many noblemen—not only in eastern Germany—to exploit their peasants and to increase their demesnes at the expense of the peasants and the Church, and this provided an opportunity for an energetic prince to take their side against the nobility.

To the diet of 1598 only 'some' towns were summoned, and only one member of each noble family, and even these were selected by the government; while those not summoned were instructed to give full powers to those selected. The landgraves wished to obtain the grant of a tax to save the country from the Spanish danger, and this purpose was achieved in spite of much opposition against this extraordinary levy.[2] All the diets lasted only a few days because the grievances were either presented after the main negotiations were concluded and were discussed in committee, or their discussion was postponed, or they were settled by resolutions of the prince. The Hessian Estates never learnt to wield the weapon of grievances before supply.[3] All these events confirmed the continuous decline of the Estates' power, which began in the earlier sixteenth century under Landgrave Philip and continued under his sons. Would the Estates be able to survive in the divided principality under the unpropitious circumstances of the seventeenth and eighteenth centuries? Would the nobility and the towns be able to overcome the deep rift which separated them?

III. *The Estates' Decline in the Seventeenth and Eighteenth Centuries*

William IV, the eldest son of Philip, inherited the most important part of his father's domains, Lower Hesse with Cassel as his capital, a share that was considerably increased at the death of his two brothers Philip II and Louis. The division of Hesse, however, brought to its end the leading part which the principality had played in German politics during the Reformation period, and the never-ending quarrels between the divided and

---

[1] Siebeck, loc. cit., p. 94, n. 2; Rommel, op. cit. iv. 1, pp. 256–7, 259–60. Cf. the quotations from William IV's will of 1586, ibid., pp. 658, 843, n. 346.

[2] Siebeck, loc. cit., pp. 70, n. 2, 71, n. 1, 110, 137.

[3] Rommel, op. cit. iv. 1, p. 238; Siebeck, loc. cit., p. 94, and n. 1.

further subdivided principalities in the seventeenth century
made their princes powerless, the victims of the great powers
which were to fight out their conflicts on German soil. An important new element was added to these internecine quarrels
when William's son and successor, Maurice (1592–1627), in
1605 carried out a long-contemplated plan. He adopted the
Calvinist faith—as John Sigismund of Brandenburg was to do a
few years later—and introduced it in all his lands. He thereby
violated his grandfather's will, which stipulated the preservation of the Augsburg Confession, and equally that of his uncle
Louis, which forbade any change of religion in the lands
Maurice had inherited from him. As Louis V, the landgrave of
Hesse-Darmstadt, remained a Lutheran and tended to a more
cautious foreign policy than his cousin Maurice of Hesse-Cassel,
the conflict between the two princes was not merely a quarrel
over their uncle's inheritance and a family conflict. It also
mirrored the deep division and mutual hatred among the German Protestants, especially when Maurice in 1608 joined the
Protestant Union under Palatine leadership and therewith the
forward Protestant party in the Empire, while his cousin Louis
refused to join.

The imposition of Calvinism on the Hesse-Cassel territories
was not only opposed by Louis V of Hesse-Darmstadt who
claimed some of Maurice's lands; it also called forth widespread opposition inside his principality, above all in Upper
Hesse and at Marburg. The new catechism, the abolition of
ceremonies, and the altered communion service-proved very
unpopular in the strongly Lutheran country. Maurice's arbitrary
measures antagonized many noblemen who exercised the *jus
patronatus* on their estates. This resistance made it impossible to
uproot Lutheranism. In Upper Hesse especially it remained
stronger than the Calvinist faith.[1] Exactly as the Calvinist
Hohenzollerns, and later the Catholic rulers of Saxony and
Württemberg, Maurice found the Lutheran opposition so strong
that he was unable to use the *jus reformandi* which the German
princes had acquired by the terms of the peace of Augsburg of
1555. He was too weak to enforce his new religion upon the
country, and he needed the support of his Estates in the quarrels
with Hesse-Darmstadt and Waldeck, for his foreign policy and

[1] Teuthorn, op. cit. ix. 733–40; Münscher, op. cit., pp. 292–6, 320.

alliances, for the taxes to be paid to the Protestant Union, and for the measures of defence necessitated by the darkening political situation; for, with the exception of about 4,000 guilders a year for the maintenance of the fortresses, the Estates did not pay any military contribution. For these reasons more than twenty diets were summoned during a reign of thirty-five years, and during the first decade of the Thirty Years War there was one nearly every year. Each diet, however, lasted only a few days.[1] As during the previous century, the grievances were not redressed, but redress was only promised in very general terms at the dissolution of the diet. To avoid the rather cumbersome machinery of the diet and the opposition which might crystallize there Maurice attempted to use committees, which were to prepare and continue the discussions, to carry out uncompleted measures, to consent to the payment of taxes within a shorter time than originally stipulated. Yet the plan to create a permanent committee with powers to act on the Estates' behalf had to be abandoned because of strong opposition which Maurice was unable to overcome, in spite of many attempts at the persuasion of the deputies, the summoning of officials, threats and pressure, and his personal presence at sessions of the diet. This opposition, fanned by the religious controversy and the war, eventually induced Maurice to adopt a policy directed against the Estates and led to a complete rupture.[2]

There were few signs of this final rupture before the actual outbreak of the Thirty Years War. The diet of 1609 granted Maurice 150,000 guilders payable within five years on account of the dangerous situation in the Empire and the dispute over the Cleves-Jülich inheritance in which he was strongly interested.[3] Two years later the towns extended the excise on drink by ten years, Maurice desiring a prolongation by twenty; but they demanded the summoning of the other Estates, 'so that their *corpus* would remain united in matters of taxation', the first sign of a less pliant spirit. The diet of 1614 granted another 150,000 guilders for defence purposes payable within five years. Maurice, however, soon requested payment within a shorter time, and this was conceded under certain conditions. A few

---

[1] Thus the diet of 1609 lasted five, that of 1615 eleven, that of 1620 six days.
[2] Rommel, op. cit. iv. 2, p. 705; iv. 3, pp. 4, 6, 19–21; Pfeiffer, op. cit., pp. 96–98.   [3] For this dispute, see below, pp. 289 ff.

months later the grant was again anticipated and a further
50,000 guilders was added by another diet. At the diet of 1617
Maurice demanded the establishment of a militia and more
money; but the Estates declined on account of poverty and left
the meeting without waiting for the dissolution. After the outbreak of the revolt in Bohemia, on the other hand, the diet of
1619 granted Maurice 300,000 guilders for the Protestant Union,
100,000 in cash and the rest as a credit. In the following year
Maurice again summoned the Estates and inquired whether
they wanted to impede his recruiting, whether the noblemen
were willing to serve in person, and whether the Estates would
make regular contributions for defence purposes. This they
declined to do, but granted 'once and for all' 200,000 guilders,
a sum which Maurice declared to be insufficient.[1]

Before the next diet met the Elector Palatine was defeated and
lost Bohemia, while the forces of the Union in vain tried to hold
the Rhenish Palatinate against the Spanish army under Spinola.
Discord and fear reigned in the Protestant camp which lacked
an army and a leader. In this situation Maurice was forced to
rely on the help of his Estates. At the beginning of 1621 he
summoned a diet to hear their opinion and advice: should he
negotiate with Spinola and send envoys to Bingen as the general
demanded, or should he defend himself to the last against the
troops and demands of the Emperor? Should he send envoys
to the assembly of the Protestant Union at Heilbronn, and
should a deputy of the Estates be among them? He then declared
that he wished to be present when the vote was taken, but this
innovation was repudiated by the deputies, who pronounced in
favour of neutrality and negotiations with Spinola because it
was impossible to resist the power of the Catholic League.
Maurice retorted that the Estates should 'be men, not women
and children', but their appreciation of the situation was clearly
much more realistic than his own. Only five weeks later they
were again summoned to a meeting in the open air. Without
any written proposition being submitted to them according to
custom, they were asked for a contribution to the recruitment
of mercenaries and the garrisoning of the fortresses. The Estates
complained about the place of the meeting and the lack of a

[1] Rommel, op. cit. iv. 3, pp. 23, 27, 29, 32, n. 22, 43–44, 50–51, 55–57, 101–6,
112, 119–20; Pfeiffer, op. cit., p. 76.

written proposition, but nevertheless granted 75,000 guilders
on condition that Maurice left the Union and negotiated with
Spinola. These conditions he rejected as an invasion of his
prerogative. Yet only four days later he recalled the Estates and
agreed to the resumption of the negotiations. In the same month
a treaty was concluded with Spinola by which Hesse undertook
to leave the Union and not to aid the Elector Palatine and his
allies in any way. The Estates had prevailed over their indignant
prince, and Hesse-Cassel became neutral. At the end of 1621
they granted him 60,000 guilders and an extension of the excise
by eight years, but half of it was to be paid in debased coins,
and only against the opposition of the nobility, who did not
want to share in the war burdens and desired to leave the
meeting, but were prevented from doing so.[1]

At the following diets the opposition increased. In February
1622 Maurice again requested to be present at the voting; but
the deputies declined, fearing they would be confounded by
his presence and unable to speak their minds openly. They
petitioned Maurice to preserve the neutrality of Hesse. The
towns granted another 140,000 guilders and consented to an
increase of the army to 800 horse and 3,400 foot-soldiers for
three months; but the nobility left the diet in protest against
these decisions. They were summoned to another meeting but
refused to acknowledge their fault, and it took a considerable
time before the majority accepted the *Recess* and the grant. A
few months later Tilly, the general of the Catholic League,
decisively defeated the allies of the Elector Palatine in southern
Germany; their troops were disbanded, so that Hesse and
northern Germany lay open to the advancing Catholic forces.
In this situation Maurice in August 1622 demanded from the
Estates more money to garrison his fortresses; but they would
only allow 50,000 guilders and advised him to seek peace from
the Emperor and Tilly, whom the country could not possibly
oppose. Maurice tried to resist the paying-off of his army, but
had to give way. In September selected members of the Estates
were again called together, but insisted that a diet should be
summoned. This met in December and granted only 60,000
guilders. Maurice wanted to make Hesse a bulwark against the
rising tide of Catholicism; he emphasized that neutrality could

[1] Rommel, op. cit. iv. 3, pp. 59–66, 69–77, 143–7 (Jan. to Dec. 1621).

be maintained only if backed by a strong force. The Estates, on the other hand, early in 1623 declared that the more soldiers were recruited, the more likely was it that Hesse would become a theatre of war, and the more hostile the Emperor would become. They declined also to pay the arrears due to the cavalry for ten months.[1]

The worst fears of the Estates were justified when a few weeks later Tilly advanced into Hesse and occupied several towns. The militia dispersed without any attempt at resistance, and no help came from outside. In July 1623 Maurice consulted the Estates' committee as to whether he should ask Christian of Brunswick and the Lower Saxon Circle to help him reconquer the occupied towns, and as to what attitude he should adopt towards Tilly. Most towns favoured an alliance with Christian, but the nobility feared the consequences and the power of the Emperor. Maurice had two of their leaders arrested and accused the others of being rebels, suspecting a secret understanding with Tilly. But they protested, insisted that they were entitled to vote freely, and asked to be dismissed, so that Maurice had to give way. Only a few weeks later Christian of Brunswick was heavily defeated by Tilly at Stadtlohn near the Dutch frontier. Again the assessment of the situation by the Estates had proved much more realistic than that of the landgrave. In October 1623 Hesse was occupied by the victors, who remained only until the spring of 1625, but during that time levied nearly 5,000,000 guilders from the towns and *Ämter* alone. Maurice escaped abroad, leaving his son William behind as a governor. The nobility advised their exiled prince to make his peace with the Emperor, to re-establish confidence between himself and the Estates, and to take to heart the old maxim *salus populi suprema lex esto*: advice which Maurice in his reply called 'a totally unjustified and improper pressure'.[2]

Tilly, on the other hand, tried to win the support of the Hessian Estates. He several times summoned them and played on the dissatisfaction of the nobility with Maurice's arbitrary policy. In March 1625 the Emperor Ferdinand II took them under his protection in exchange for a promise that they would

---

[1] Ibid., iv. 3, pp. 77–78, and n. 65, 80–85, 89–100, 539 (Feb. 1622 to Apr. 1623).

[2] Ibid., pp. 543, 551–8, 566–70, 576, 580, 600, 682–91 (May 1623 to Aug. 1624).

render assistance to his and his allies' armies. The noblemen
held their own local assemblies and levied taxes for their own
purposes. The Estates summoned by Tilly declared that they
would not allow any foreign armies into the country. If Maurice
insisted on it, they would declare their oaths and obligations
towards him invalid. They promised free passage to the Imperial forces and prohibited foreign recruiting: steps which
were repudiated by Maurice. His councillors informed him that
the nobility had misled the towns into accepting the promises
and guarantees of the Emperor. After many months of occupation the towns desired to buy relief with these concessions to the
Emperor and undertook that they would disregard their prince's
orders to the contrary. Then Tilly's army left. Maurice returned
and declared the Estates' promises to be contrary to the constitution and null and void. He only summoned the towns and
obtained from them a grant and a declaration of loyalty. In
April 1626 he recalled them and obtained another grant, the
money to be levied also from the estates of the nobility, which
was entirely outside their powers to concede.[1]

Soon after Hesse was once more invaded by Tilly's forces. He
summoned the Estates and demanded that certain ill-intentioned councillors of Maurice should be dismissed and the
government taken over by William, Maurice's son, threatening
that otherwise the whole country would be reoccupied by his
army. The Estates, fearing the results of such an occupation,
sent deputies to Maurice and petitioned him to comply and thus
to avoid the siege of Cassel. They did not desire his abdication,
but had to seek a better and quieter status out of necessity so
as to bring the never-ending tribulations to an end. Even his
councillors advised Maurice to resign for the time being or on
conditions, while Tilly demanded that he should sign a declaration of obedience towards the Emperor. This he did in July 1626.
Simultaneously he promised that he would effect an agreement
and reconciliation with the nobility and the Estates, and treat
them in accordance with the Imperial mandates and letters of
protection, so that they would not incur any dangers and inconveniences in future and Tilly would be completely satisfied.
Eight months later Maurice finally abdicated in favour of his
son in the presence of a deputation of the Estates, from which

[1] Münscher, op. cit., pp. 313–15; Rommel, op. cit. iv. 3, pp. 596–8.

the disaffected nobility were excluded. He then pointed out that the main reason for this step was the declaration of the preceding July, which he had been compelled to sign by Tilly and the nobility, and the scant respect shown to him by the Estates and his own servants.[1]

William V thus came to the throne in very troubled circumstances, in the midst of war, faced with a hostile army in the country, a mutinous nobility, and never-ending impositions. Yet the worst years of the war were still to come. The opposition of the nobility continued. At the diet of 1627 they declined to contribute anything from their own estates or for the garrisons of Cassel and Ziegenhain. In 1629 only the towns granted an extension of the excise on drink by twelve years and 26,000 guilders. In the summer of 1631 the noblemen again assembled on their own initiative and asked Tilly for letters of protection, after he had called upon them to deflect their ruler from his evil ways. But then Tilly marched eastwards to meet the army of Gustavus Adolphus and Hesse was relieved for the time being. In 1634 William demanded from the Estates a tithe from all fields; but only certain noblemen obeyed his summons, and they asked to be excused from this imposition, while the towns consented but complained about the separation of the nobility and neither signed nor sealed the *Recess*. In the following year William communicated to the Estates the terms of the peace of Prague between the Emperor and the Elector of Saxony and asked them to advise whether he should join the peace, and what conditions he should try to obtain: questions which the exiled Duke Eberhard of Württemberg also submitted to his advisers from the Estates. The Estates, as might be expected, strongly pronounced in favour of peace, provided that certain concessions were made. In 1637 William V died after a reign of only ten years. His successor, William VI, a boy of four, came to the throne in a year when Hesse was frightfully devastated by the warring armies and lost a large part of her population.[2]

According to the will of William V, his widow Amalia Elisabeth became the guardian of the young William VI, with

---

[1] Rommel, op. cit., iv. 3, pp. 633–6, 641–3, 646, n. 609, 674, n. 636; Münscher, op. cit., pp. 315–17; *Zeitschrift des Vereins für hessische Geschichte und Landeskunde*, iv, 1847, pp. 320–2 (June 1626 to Mar. 1627).

[2] Rommel, op. cit. iv. 4, pp. 25, 62, 292, n. 370, 465; Münscher, op. cit., pp. 333, 344; Pfeiffer, op. cit., pp. 128–9.

five privy councillors—two of whom were noblemen—as the co-regents. They were to be assisted by a council of sixteen: six noblemen, six burghers, and four learned officials. At the diet of 1638, however, the nobility demanded the appointment of a noble council of regency, or at least the majority on the council. Several noblemen declined to serve on the council of sixteen. They referred to the precedents of the union of 1509 and the agreements of 1514, and thus prevented the appointment of the sixteen.[1] At the diet of 1640 the conflict broke out anew. The nobility again insisted that the co-regents should be elected by the diet and quoted the agreements of 1514, the validity of which was denied by the privy councillors. Some even proposed to replace the expensive official receivers of taxes by deputies of the Estates, as they functioned elsewhere; but on this point as on others the towns dissented, and this helped the regent to maintain some of her influence.[2] During the same year Hesse once more became a theatre of war; friend and foe alike were quartered in the country and levied contributions, although an armistice had been concluded with the Emperor in 1638. At the end of 1647 the war again engulfed Hesse. In addition, there was war between Hesse-Cassel and Hesse-Darmstadt over the possession of Upper Hesse, in which Sweden and France sided with Hesse-Cassel, and the Emperor with Hesse-Darmstadt. When peace finally came in 1648 Hesse-Darmstadt retained the larger part of Upper Hesse, and in the remaining part—around Marburg—the Lutherans were granted religious toleration, although Calvinism remained the official religion of Hesse-Cassel.[3] That was the outcome of the long struggle in the course of which Hesse had suffered so much.

In 1648 Hesse-Cassel possessed a regular army of six regiments of cavalry and fourteen of infantry: a very considerable force considering the state of the country. All these were paid off in the course of the year, with the exception of only 600 foot-soldiers and 40 horse-guards. Otherwise there was only the militia with about 12,000 men.[4] This quick reduction was

[1] See above, pp. 152, 156–7.
[2] Rommel, op. cit. iv. 4, pp. 474–6, 523–4, and n. 24, 564–5, and n. 66; Pfeiffer, op. cit., pp. 125–6.
[3] Münscher, op. cit., pp. 348, 357, 360, 363; Teuthorn, op. cit. ix. 740; x. 235, 476–7.
[4] 'Die hessen-kasselsche Kriegsmacht unter dem Landgrafen Karl bis zum

achieved by the united pressure of the Estates which aimed at
the abolition of the monthly contributions introduced during
the war. Their disunity, however, quickly reappeared over the
questions of defence and the maintenance of the fortresses, in
which the nobility refused to participate. In 1647 it complained
to the Imperial Court, the *Reichskammergericht*, because its members were assessed for taxation and forbidden to meet on their
own initiative. Two years later the nobility tried to win over the
town of Cassel by communicating its complaints to the town
council. Soon after its leader, the *Erbmarschall* Otto von der
Malsburg, was arrested because he had called meetings of the
nobility without the landgrave's knowledge. About this arrest
the nobility strongly complained at the diet of 1650, at which
Amalia Elisabeth resigned the regency and the young William
VI assumed the government. They denied that they were rebels
and asked that their ancient privilege of free meeting be maintained. They appealed to the Emperor and the Imperial Court
and demanded the restitution of the fines imposed on von der
Malsburg. William replied sharply and refused to fulfil their
demands. As the grievances of the nobility were not redressed,
they withdrew their offer of a grant of 50,000 guilders, and no
Recess was promulgated. At the orders of the Imperial Court at
Speyer his confiscated cattle and corn had to be returned to
von der Malsburg, and he himself had to be released later.[1]

In spite of these gains the opposition of the nobility continued,
and so did their conflicts with the towns. At the following diet,
in 1653, the nobility again left the meeting, so that the *Recess*
could be concluded only with the towns. This continuous
disunity between the Estates provided William with an opportunity to restore his authority and to render the Estates powerless. As a contemporary chronicler put it: 'but after the Estates'
corpus was separated we have been made slaves and must do as
we are bidden'.[2] A decisive step in that direction was taken by

Frieden von Ryswick 1697', *Zeitschrift des Vereins für hessische Geschichte und Landeskunde*, viii, 1860, pp. 118–20; Münscher, op. cit., p. 377; Rommel, op. cit. iv. 3,
p. 787.

[1] Rommel, op. cit., iv. 4, pp. 783, 786–7; Münscher, op. cit., p. 368; Pfeiffer,
op. cit., pp. 135, 138–40.

[2] Pfeiffer, op. cit., pp. 135–6, 140; cf. the comment of Rommel, op. cit. iv.
4, p. 787, who attributes the decline of the Estates to the impoverishment of the
nobility and to the development of a military despotism during the war.

an agreement reached in 1655 which became the basis of the Hessian constitution for the following century and a half. In this the nobility renounced their claim of being entitled to meet without the landgrave's permission. If they considered a meeting necessary, they were to petition him that a diet should be summoned, and he was to take the necessary steps. William reaffirmed his willingness to consult with his Estates and to hear their advice in matters concerning the country's interest when this was necessary, but it was left to him to define this necessity. Full diets were to decide on the levy of taxes for the country and the army, while taxes for the Empire and the Upper Rhenish Circle (to which Hesse belonged) were to be voted by smaller diets or by a committee empowered to do so. In case of an emergency the landgrave was entitled to decree a tax for the army, but afterwards he should seek the approval of a diet which was to be summoned 'as soon as convenient'. These stipulations weakened the Estates' power of the purse and could be used to weaken it still further. That the Estates were aware of this danger was shown in 1655 when they extended the excise on drink by eight years and pronounced that the tax was not to become permanent, but was to depend on their grants and to be used solely to pay off the country's debts. Taxes for the army, moreover, they always granted for very short periods only.[1]

The standing army slowly grew. Its expansion had begun already under William VI, who ruled until 1663. It was continued by Landgrave Charles who came to the throne in 1670. In 1673 the army consisted of three companies of cavalry and eleven of infantry, not counting the life-guards, the garrisons and the artillery. Five more infantry companies were recruited in 1676, bringing the total number to twenty-three. The diets of 1682 and 1687 granted an increased monthly contribution of 24,000 guilders; while the nobility in 1682 consented to a special contribution of 36,000 guilders a year for two years, a total of 324,000 guilders a year being levied. Thus the army in 1683 could be increased to sixteen companies of cavalry and thirty-one of infantry. Five years later, during the war against Louis XIV, it consisted of forty-one cavalry and seventy-five

[1] Ledderhose, op. cit. i. 72; Pfeiffer, op. cit., pp. 77, 142–4; Adolf Lichtner, *Landesherr und Stände in Hessen-Cassel, 1797–1821*, Göttingen, 1913, pp. 1–2, and n. 1.

infantry companies, and its strength amounted to over 10,000 men, and with the militia to over 13,000. This large force could not possibly be maintained by such a small country. As the Estates firmly declined to make higher contributions, Landgrave Charles, as so many other German princes of the time, concluded subsidy treaties with foreign powers, especially with Venice and the United Provinces, whose place was taken by Britain in the eighteenth century.[1] A special military chest was established into which the taxes granted by the Estates were paid; but this *Kriegskasse* was entirely removed from their supervision and control.[2]

As the military expenditure continued to be much larger than the revenue from taxation, foreign subsidies remained essential for the maintenance of the army. In 1727 King George II took the whole Hessian army of 12,000 men into British service; but under Charles's successor, Frederick I, its numbers were very considerably reduced. In the Seven Years War Hesse fought again on the British side and received millions of thalers as subsidies in consequence. In 1776 Landgrave Frederick II concluded a new treaty of alliance with Britain by which he undertook to supply 12,000 men for the war in America. Between 1776 and 1784 Hesse received subsidies amounting to 19,056,778 thalers, sums which enabled Frederick to rescind contributions and arrears, so that the treaty met with the approval of the Estates. 13,000 Hessian soldiers were sent to North America, but only half their number returned.[3] In this way the landgrave became solvent and the country was relieved of the military burdens, in contrast with Prussia which in the eighteenth century received no subsidies, so that the weight of the army crippled the country's economic and social progress in peacetime. In this way also an open conflict between the prince and the Estates could be avoided; the survival of the Estates—in a restricted form and with limited powers—was not incompatible with the existence of a large standing army.

Diets continued to be held frequently until the very end of the

---

[1] 'Die hessen-kasselsche Kriegsmacht unter dem Landgrafen Karl . . .', loc. cit., pp. 120, 122, 124–5, 129–34, 139, 155–7, 162; Münscher, op. cit., p. 405.

[2] The *Kriegskasse* was mentioned for the first time in 1674: Lichtner, op. cit., p. 5; cf. below, pp. 184–6.

[3] Münscher, op. cit., pp. 405, 428–30; Heinrich Schnee, *Die Hoffinanz und der moderne Staat*, iii, Berlin, 1955, p. 201.

eighteenth century. Between 1754 and 1786 at least fifteen were
summoned, or one nearly every other year, showing the vitality
of the institution. These were, however, no longer full diets as
they had been called in the sixteenth and seventeenth centuries,
but deputation diets. The nobility and the towns were divided
into five groups each, according to the rivers flowing through
the country. On receiving the summons each group assembled
separately and elected a deputy. In addition to these ten the
towns of Cassel and Marburg and St. Goar (on the Rhine) were
each represented by one deputy. The preliminary assemblies
also discussed the agenda of the diet and instructed their
deputies. In this way the number of deputies was kept very
small, and the duration of the diet remained short. Even with
the so-called prelates, there were never more than fifteen or
sixteen deputies at the diet. Nominally, it still consisted of three
houses, for there were three Estates. But the prelates and the
nobility deliberated together. Within each house decisions were
taken by a majority; but all three houses had to consent to a
proposal, especially in matters of taxation, and in case of
a disagreement between the houses the landgrave only had a
limited right of decision. The noble *Erbmarschall* was the director
of the two upper houses and of the whole diet. As in the past, he
was not elected, and the Estates had no officials of their own.
Only the *Erbmarschall* was assisted by a permanent councillor.
Nor did the Estates possess a chest of their own. The monthly
contributions, first introduced during the Thirty Years War,
were paid into the military chest, the *Kriegskasse*, and had more
or less assumed the character of an ordinary, permanent tax.[1]
In all these matters the Estates had not been able to overcome
the weaknesses which characterized their development as early
as the sixteenth century. Hence their power—apart from short
exceptional periods—remained very weak.

Under these circumstances the Estates' power of the purse in
practice was limited to granting taxes in extraordinary cases,
above all in war-time. While the estates of the nobility were
exempt from the monthly contributions, the noblemen participated in such extraordinary taxes, but only at half the rate paid
by the towns from each hundred guilders of taxable capital.

[1] Pfeiffer, op. cit., p. 188; Ledderhose, op. cit. i. 38, 43–46, 77–79; Lichtner,
op. cit., pp. 2–5.

Furthermore, as there was no up-to-date register of taxable property, there were many cases of concealment, of property not declared, and exemption claimed without justification. From 1767 onwards, indeed, preparations were begun for compiling a new land register, and local investigations revealed many cases of such malpractices. In the face of strong noble opposition, however, the work progressed very slowly. At the diet of 1798 the towns urged that it be speeded up; but Landgrave William IX decided that it should be stopped and the discussion postponed to the following diet—a decision which the towns in vain tried to get reversed.[1] The nobility from its own ranks elected four receivers of taxes, whose names were incorporated into the *Recess* at the dissolution of the diet. Each receiver was assisted by a tax councillor, who was appointed by the landgrave, and a secretary. The taxes collected in the towns and *Ämter*, on the other hand, were levied by receivers nominated by the landgrave.[2] Thus the nobility, as in Brandenburg and Prussia, enjoyed greater rights of self-government than the rest of the country.

The diet of 1764 was summoned to devise means to pay off the enormous debts caused by the Seven Years War and the expensive tastes of Landgrave Frederick II, which even the British subsidies could not cover. In contrast with their earlier practice the Estates granted taxes for a long period, until the beginning of the nineteenth century, including an extension of the excise on drink until 1802, which indicates how restricted their power of the purse had become. They stipulated, however, that no further extraordinary taxes were to be demanded from them before that time, with the exception of taxes for the Empire, the Upper Rhenish Circle, and the dowries of princesses of the ruling house. The Estates also appointed a committee of thirteen, which was to meet but once in six years, to supervise the levying of taxes and the local accounting. They suggested that a separate chest should be established into which these taxes should be paid, but without success; and even the excise was paid henceforth into the military chest and used for paying off the debts.[3] Thus the Estates failed to gain any influence in the

---

[1] Lichtner, op. cit., pp. 4–5, 35–38.

[2] Ibid., p. 7; Ledderhose, op. cit. i. 54–57.

[3] Lichtner, op. cit., pp. 7–8; Pfeiffer, op. cit., pp. 172, 191; Ledderhose, op. cit. i. 114.

fields of financial administration and expenditure which remained a prerogative of the prince. The committee of thirteen only lasted until 1798, and no system of permanent committees developed. At the following diet, in 1772, the amount of the monthly contribution was fixed at 24,750 thalers, or 445,500 guilders a year, and thus became a regular tax. The diet of 1774 only was called to approve the appointment of ten *Landräte*, an institution taken over from Prussia. These new officials were to be responsible for all taxation outside the towns, recruiting and billeting, the control of local budgets, and the exercise of police authority in the countryside. The landgrave was to select them from a list drawn up by the Estates and thus had a right of confirmation. As they were in practice officials exercising state authority, the Estates did not consider them their representatives and insisted that they were not to have a vote at the diet.[1]

Frederick II was satisfied with the liberal grant of 1764, and his finances further benefited from the British subsidy treaty of 1776. Under his successor William IX, however, who ascended the throne in 1785, new heavy demands were submitted to the Estates. A diet was summoned in 1786, and the Estates were asked to refund very considerable sums which had been allegedly advanced by the military chest for the garrisons, transport, visitations, &c. This they declined to do, for the military chest received its money from the country, and what had been paid once could in their opinion not be demanded again. They also argued that the landgrave's income had increased considerably as a result of the British treaty, and that their duty to pay only started if he had no other means. The Estates realized that this was a 'new kind of contribution', which would make their power of the purse a mere formality and finally enable the landgrave to dispense with it. On account of this opposition, William postponed the introduction of the new system.[2] No further diet was summoned for eleven years, until the autumn of 1797, a longer interval than had occurred during the whole of the eighteenth century.

To the diet of 1797 another list of alleged advances from the military chest was submitted, totalling almost 2,534,000 guilders, nearly six times the amount of the annual contribution, and

---

[1] Lichtner, op. cit., pp. 4, 41–42; Pfeiffer, op. cit., p. 191.
[2] Lichtner, op. cit., pp. 9–11.

including such demands as the dowries of princesses in sixteen retrospective cases. This one item was put at 400,000 guilders, while the Estates would only acknowledge twelve cases at half that figure. While they had granted about 136,000 guilders for road construction, over 300,000 had been spent up to 1796, the difference figuring as an advance from the military chest. The only demands which the Estates did not dispute were payments to the Empire and the Circle which had been specifically excluded from the agreement of 1764. As to the others, they declared that they were contrary to that agreement and that some of them had long been paid. The towns offered 225,000 guilders in settlement of all demands, a sum they later increased to 300,000, together with an extension of the excise on drink by a further eight years, and the prelates concurred. The deputies of the nobility, however, prevaricated. They desired the redress of their grievances and wished to obtain the consent of their principals. They did not enter into a discussion of the different demands as the towns did and avoided a binding declaration by suggesting that the questions should be postponed to the next diet. This attitude made any united opposition impossible. William then demanded 600,000 guilders and an extension of the excise by another eighteen years. To this the prelates and the towns assented, while the deputies of the nobility offered 450,000 guilders. Agreement was only reached when William indicated that as an act of grace he would be content with that sum, on condition that 600,000 were granted. This promise was accepted without any checking of the individual items, so that the landgrave was free to repeat the procedure, the 'advances' being treated like debts which the Estates had to pay.[1]

In the demands put forward by the Estates there were a few signs of the revolutionary events which had occurred across the Rhine. They wished the size of the army to be reduced because every tenth man was conscripted, but William ordered all petitions concerning the army to be rejected. They asked for the abolition of the regulation limiting admission to the University of Marburg to the sons of the seven top groups of the official table of ranks. This regulation created a monopoly of these groups to state appointments, but in the Estates' opinion talent

[1] Ibid., pp. 13–32 (Oct. 1797 to Jan. 1798).

was not a monopoly of one group or rank, and it limited the freedom of parents to educate their children as they wished. It was even more revolutionary when the diet took up a suggestion of the towns and petitioned that labour services should be commuted, for 'the subjects' dizzy ideas have grown everywhere and make them rebel against their masters'. The towns went even further and proposed that the peasants should be represented in the diet, but this was negatived by the other Estates and not even submitted to the landgrave. The towns also complained that the institution of the *Landräte*, imported from abroad twenty-four years ago, had not fulfilled its object and was redundant. In spite of noble opposition, this motion was accepted by William and the *Landräte* were abolished. The town of Ziegenhain complained about the work the burghers had to do on the fortifications without any participation of the soldiers, about fines the commandant had imposed when they refused, and about his petty tyrannies. It claimed that the work was ordered only to prevent the desertion of criminals, like the recruits for the war in America whom they had had to guard in years gone by. While the nobility were above all anxious to defend their privileges, the towns had become the defenders of the rights of the Estates and the promoters of a new spirit aiming at greater independence.[1]

The picture presented by the last diet of Hesse under the *ancien régime* was that of weak and divided Estates, retreating under the pressure of a government which was almost absolute. It had no need to summon another diet until the new grant expired, i.e. for twenty-two years, and could then present another list of 'advances' made by the military chest during the intervening years. The Prussian example had been only too influential in the development of the state. It has been maintained that the diet of 1797-8 provided evidence of a strong and vital institution, and that it showed the Third Estate appearing with loud demands in front of the princely throne.[2] This, however, only seems true to a very limited extent and in comparison with Prussia where the Estates had in practice disappeared. The demands of the Third Estate were raised only in a very submissive form which never questioned the existence of

[1] Lichtner, op. cit., pp. 43, 47-48, 61-64, 68, 70-74 (Jan. 1798).
[2] Ibid., pp. 71-72, 75.

absolute government. In Württemberg and Cleves, in Mecklenburg and Saxony, the Estates were much stronger, and the
diets showed much more vitality. Nor can it truly be held that
the rights of the Hessian Estates survived uncurtailed.[1] Their
power of the purse was progressively whittled away, and they
had lost their influence in the fields of legislation and administration, and the right of meeting on their own initiative which they
had exercised successfully at times.

The Estates of Hesse only wielded political power at two
points of their history, during the minority of Landgrave Philip
in the early sixteenth century and during the Thirty Years
War. In both instances this was due to very exceptional conditions and support from abroad, in the first case from the dukes of
Saxony, in the second from the Emperor Ferdinand and the
Catholic forces. One is almost tempted to say that it was the
Thirty Years War which saved the Estates from extinction, for
already in the later sixteenth century their power was very
weak. The conversion of Landgrave Maurice to Calvinism and
the events of the war strengthened their opposition and provided them with support inside and outside the country, so that
in the end Maurice was forced to abdicate. By 1655, however,
the Estates' power had again declined from the previous height
owing to their lack of unity, and by the end of the eighteenth
century it had almost disappeared. The nobility and the towns
always remained separate and antagonistic orders. This permitted the quick recovery of princely power which took place
even during two periods of regency, under Anna of Mecklenburg and Amalia Elisabeth, and even more so when the minority
came to an end and capable landgraves, Philip and William VI
respectively, ascended the throne. The existence of a large
standing army, on the other hand, did not prove incompatible
with that of the Estates. They survived into the nineteenth
century, and at the end of their history they began to show the
first signs of a new spirit. This new spirit emanated from the
towns, which in the past had sided with the prince and against
the nobility and thus had made possible the growth of princely

[1] This is the opinion of Pfeiffer, op. cit., p. 8, quoting Karl Friedrich Eichhorn,
Deutsche Staats- und Rechtsgeschichte, according to whom the Estates of Saxony,
Mecklenburg, Württemberg and Hesse survived in full strength to the end of the
eighteenth century.

power. The new spirit, however, was too weak to effect any change in the distribution of power. At the last diet of the *ancien régime*, ten years after the outbreak of the French Revolution, not the demands of the burghers, but the decisions of the landgrave carried the day, and the system of quasi-absolute government prevailed.

III

SAXONY

1. *Introduction*

To the east of Hesse, stretching as far as Bohemia in the south and as far as Silesia in the east, were situated the possessions of the house of Wettin. This family established itself in the region of the middle Elbe in the eleventh century, after the Germans had begun their penetration eastwards across the Saale river. From the tenth century onwards the triangle formed by the rivers Saale and Elbe became part of the Holy Roman Empire. The Slavonic inhabitants were subjugated and baptized; soon the Elbe was crossed in an easterly direction, and later the Germans advanced into Silesia. In the conquered lands frontier marches were founded, bishoprics and towns were established and granted important possessions and privileges. German noblemen, burghers, and peasants settled among the Slavs and gradually transformed very backward areas into flourishing territories. By the thirteenth century the districts of the middle Elbe had reached, if not surpassed, the cultural level of the mother country, as was shown in the architecture and the sculptures of Naumburg, Magdeburg, Meissen, and Freiberg. From this as well as the economic point of view the region of the middle Elbe became much more important than the Brandenburg Mark to the north, which was conquered and developed at about the same time. Around Freiberg rich silver mines were discovered which greatly contributed to the economic prosperity of the area. Most of the towns remained small; but the episcopal cities of Naumburg, Merseburg, and Meissen became important centres of urban activity. Originally founded to promote the mission among the heathen Slavs, the bishoprics entered into close relations with the house of Wettin, long before the Reformation which eventually put an end to their independent existence and transformed them into dependencies of the ruling house. Farther to the north, the great archbishopric of Magdeburg was even more prominent in its missionary and colonizing enterprises, its princes becoming rulers in their own right. The urban law of Magdeburg was adopted by hundreds of towns not only in eastern Germany, but far into Poland, Bohemia, and Hungary, establishing everywhere trial by jury and the right of appeal to Magdeburg. Leipzig and Freiberg, founded in the later twelfth century, rose to importance through their trade and industrial activities.[1]

Among the frontier marches established by the Germans on the middle Elbe the margraviate of Meissen rose to prominence in the twelfth century. Extending their sway from the Saale river eastwards to Lusatia the margraves of the house of Wettin, at a time of growing weakness of the Imperial power, extended their possessions at the cost of many small territories and created a large, compact principality; they reached the height of their influence in the thirteenth century. Their financial power rested on the great mineral wealth of the mountain region in the south of their lands. It contrasted strongly with the increasing poverty of so many German rulers who were forced to sell lands and prerogatives, tolls and revenues, thus diminishing their income further and further. In the fourteenth century, however, this favourable position of the house of Wettin began to change for the worse, for the most easily accessible silver seams became exhausted, attempts to open up new ones failed, and the yield declined because mining technique was not far enough advanced to permit a more rational exploitation. Furthermore, the many wars of the period caused great expenditure; the many subdivisions of the territory resulted in conflicts between hostile brothers and further wars which weakened the Wettin family and its influence. From the mid-fourteenth century onwards the margraves frequently had to ask their subjects for aids, especially the wealthy towns whose contributions soon became fixed. The bishoprics and monasteries as well as the nobility were equally approached, and the country districts were taxed even before them.[2] While these payments were

---

[1] Rudolf Kötzschke and Wolfgang Ebert, *Geschichte der ostdeutschen Kolonisation*, Leipzig, 1937, pp. 67–71; Walter Schlesinger, 'Die mittelelbischen Lande', in *Gebhardt's Handbuch der deutschen Geschichte*, 8th ed., 1955, ii. 570–4. The best modern history of Saxony is by Rudolf Kötzschke and Hellmut Kretzschmar, 2 vols., Dresden, 1935.

[2] Herbert Helbig, *Der Wettinische Ständestaat* (*Mitteldeutsche Forschungen*, iv), Münster and Cologne, 1955, pp. 3–4, 396–400; Schlesinger, loc. cit., pp. 572–4; Armin Tille, 'Die deutschen Territorien', loc. cit. ii. 259.

made by separate groups or districts, the increasing need of money later induced the margraves to approach the clergy, the nobility and the towns together. This happened for the first time in 1376, but only in the district of Meissen, and in 1385 in the whole territory belonging to Margrave William I. The three Estates consented to the required tax, but only against a promise of the margrave that he would not repeat his request except in case of defeat or damages caused by war. Clearly, it was easier for him to negotiate with each Estate separately, for general assemblies would create a feeling of common interests, of belonging together, and would prepare the way towards constituting the Estates into one corporation.[1]

Yet, perhaps because of the much greater wealth of their possessions, perhaps because of the continuity of the ruling house in spite of all divisions, the position of the margraves of the house of Wettin remained much stronger than that of the margraves of Brandenburg, where the ruling family changed no less than four times within one century. There, the lands and prerogatives of the prince were sold or pawned during the semi-anarchy of the fourteenth century to such an extent that only remnants were left when the Emperor Charles IV in 1375 conducted his famous survey to ascertain his remaining rights. There, whole districts were alienated to foreign princes, for example the whole New Mark to the Teutonic Order and parts of the Old Mark to Magdeburg and Brunswick. There, the towns and the nobility gradually acquired all the prerogatives on their lands, including the tax of the *Bede*, the public services, the tolls, and the entire jurisdiction, which made them immune from their prince's interference; this development made him almost powerless because the rights of public administration disappeared, and the *advocatiae* through which his rights were exercised disintegrated.[2] The territories of the house of Wettin were 'colonial' lands like those of the margraves of Brandenburg; but the privileges they granted to the nobility and the towns remained much more limited, and the prerogatives to a large extent remained in their hands. This fact was to

[1] Helbig, op. cit., pp. 400–2; C. W. Böttiger, *Geschichte des Kurstaates und König- reiches Sachsen*, i, Hamburg, 1830, p. 280, putting the first general *Bede* into the year 1350.

[2] For details see F. L. Carsten, *The Origins of Prussia*, Oxford, 1954, especially chap. vii.

be of fundamental importance for the later history of these districts, in the political as well as in the social and economic fields.

The vassals of the margraves of Meissen were exempt from the *Bede* for their demesne lands because they were obliged to render feudal services; but the tax was not sold to them as the normal practice. A privilege of 1428 confirmed to them that they were entitled to exercise the lower jurisdiction on their estates; but the margraves retained the jurisdiction over crimes, and this was repeated several times during the following century. The large majority of the nobility remained subject to the jurisdiction of the *Ämter* into which the country was divided for purposes of administration, and were accordingly called *Amtssassen*, to distinguish them from those noblemen and others who paid their contributions directly to the prince—the higher clergy, the towns, families of dynastic status, and the high nobility. Even the towns did not exercise the higher jurisdiction themselves, as they did in many other principalities. The leading town, Leipzig, only in 1423, and again in 1434, bought the higher jurisdiction, but redeemably; equally the town of Meissen in 1423, Freiberg in 1479, Dresden in 1484, Pirna in 1491. But as a property without the right of redemption Leipzig only acquired it in 1508, Pirna in 1619, and Dresden in 1660.[1] Even the three bishops of Meissen, Naumburg, and Merseburg were taxed like the nobility; they had to render vassal services to the margraves and lost to them important judicial privileges. The margraves also exercised the right of appointing to canonries in the cathedral chapters. The bishops were dependent on the house of Wettin, if only for the reason that most of them had been in the margraves' service before their elevation and often continued in it afterwards, or came from noble families of the margraviate. By the end of the fifteenth century they in practice belonged to its Estates and stood no longer directly under the Emperor, thus adding considerably to the margraves' influence.[2] Their strength was and remained much greater than that of the princes of Brandenburg, Pomerania, or Prussia before the great

---

[1] Helbig, op. cit., pp. 353–4, and n. 21, 412; Martin Luther, *Die Entwicklung der landständischen Verfassung in den Wettinischen Landen bis zum Jahre 1485*, Leipzig, 1895, pp. 36–45, and nn. 20, 21.

[2] Helbig, op. cit., pp. 364–7, with many details.

changes of the seventeenth century, and in consequence the power of the Estates remained much weaker.

The nobility did not increase their demesnes to the extent they did in the more northern and eastern territories at the cost of the peasantry, nor was there any general tendency to impose heavier and heavier labour services. In the sixteenth century these were even frequently commuted into money rents because the landlords wanted to increase their revenues, and the rulers saw to it that the peasants were not forced to sell out. Peasant farming remained the preponderant form of agriculture, and the peasants' position remained much better than in the territories to the north and east.[1] There, the weakness of the princes and the decline of the towns paved the way for the rule of the nobility: its members wielded all the prerogatives on their estates, and the peasants became their helpless victims. At a time when the towns of Brandenburg were sinking to the level of little market towns, when even the towns on the Baltic coast were declining owing to the rise of the nobility, Leipzig assumed its central position in the economic life of central eastern Europe. At the end of the fifteenth century the Emperor Maximilian granted the first privileges for its fairs; a university, founded early in the century, contributed to its rise; its trade, fostered by the dukes, grew throughout the sixteenth century. New silver and tin mines were developed at Annaberg and Schneeberg in the mountains to the south and this led to a more intensive settlement of the mountain regions, the foundation of new towns and the growth of the old ones, the adoption of more advanced capitalist methods in mining and the trade in metals. Leipzig, Freiberg, and other towns became wealthy. In Chemnitz and its neighbourhood the linen industry flourished; at Zwickau and elsewhere the cloth industry developed. Characteristically enough, it was not so much the nobility which bought up peasant land and added it to their demesnes, but wealthy burghers of Leipzig, Freiberg, and other towns who bought noble estates, became landlords and drove up the price of land: as the noblemen claimed, this damaged their livelihood,

[1] Woldemar Goerlitz, *Staat und Stände unter den Herzögen Albrecht und Georg, 1485–1539*, Leipzig and Berlin, 1928, pp. 125–8; Schlesinger, loc. cit. ii. 574; Friedrich Lütge, *Die mitteldeutsche Grundherrschaft*, Jena, 1934, pp. 110–11, 129–30, 198–9.

caused the decline of the feudal services and ought to have been prohibited.[1] Thus Saxony was much more highly developed than its northern and eastern neighbours.

II. *The Estates in the Fifteenth Century*

During the late fourteenth and the fifteenth centuries the power of the house of Wettin declined sharply, partly for economic reasons, especially the growing debts and the diminishing yield of the silver mines, partly because of the many partitions of its possessions and the resulting fratricidal wars. These would have caused the fragmentation of the territory if many of the younger lines had not died out after a short time. The sons of Margrave Frederick II and of Margrave Frederick III in 1379 and in 1382 divided their fathers' lands without consulting the Estates, or even their own councillors; in the different parts the nobility and the towns were simply ordered to swear fealty to their new master. Further divisions in the early fifteenth century brought about conflicts between the different parties. After preliminary negotiations between the princes and the Estates these were invited to act as arbiters at a meeting held at Naumburg in 1410, which resulted in a new partition. During the following years there were more conflicts and further subdivisions. In 1415 four noble vassals were appointed to arbitrate, and the towns of Leipzig and Altenburg guaranteed the execution of the new treaty. Three years later the settlement of new strife that had arisen was entrusted to four knights and four burghers; in 1423 they pronounced their verdict in a new quarrel in the presence of the bishop of Naumburg. In this way the Estates extended their influence into new spheres and their cohesion developed. Only the fact that his brothers died without issue enabled Frederick IV in 1425 to reunite the different parts in his own hands. In the same year he was enfeoffed with the Electorate of Saxony, to the north of Meissen, by the

---

[1] Schlesinger, loc. cit. ii. 574; Goerlitz, op. cit., pp. 131, 211; no. 21, p. 521; Böttiger, op. cit. ii. 52; Robert Wuttke, *Die Einführung der Land-Accise und der Generalkonsumtionsaccise in Kursachsen*, Leipzig-Reudnitz, 1890, pp. 2–3; Karl Steinmüller, 'Die Gesellschaft der Kaufleute in Leipzig im 15. und 16. Jahrhundert', *Forschungen aus mitteldeutschen Archiven, Festschrift für Hellmut Kretzschmar*, Berlin, 1953, pp. 129, 132, 139–42.

Emperor Sigismund as a reward for the services he had rendered him against the Hussites.[1]

Frederick IV only ruled for another three years over his reunited and enlarged territories. When he died in 1428 he left four minor sons who came to the throne at a time when the country was threatened by the invasions of the Hussites; a large part of the nobility had been killed in the battle of Aussig (Usti) and the country was practically defenceless. The Estates were summoned to take the oath of allegiance to the young princes who promised that they would maintain all their subjects in their rights and old customs and guaranteed the exercise of the lower jurisdiction to the clergy and nobility, after complaints had been raised about the interference of princely officials with their rights. The three Estates deliberated together and put forward their grievances and desires. The devastations of the country by the Hussites during the following years and the debts caused by the war forced the princes to make further concessions. In 1437 the two remaining brothers, Frederick and William, reached an agreement about the future administration of the country, which was to be revised three years later, with the participation of their counts, lords, knights, and towns: evidence that such matters came within their competence.[2]

In the following year the margraves were forced by their desperate financial situation, the decline of trade and industry and of their revenues on account of the continuous disturbances, to summon to Leipzig the first diet in the proper sense of the term from all their territories; it was attended by counts, knights, and towns, but again not by the clergy. To this assembly the margraves explained that they had to pawn towns and castles, rents and revenues, and had incurred heavy debts on which they had to pay much interest; to provide for defence and to prevent the ruin of the country they needed its support, either in the form of a property and cattle tax, or in that of an excise of 5 per cent. on all sales, for four years; but they were willing to leave to the Estates the control over the money raised. These favoured the second project; two of the clergy, two of the nobility, and three from the towns were appointed to work out the details. A few weeks later the Estates reassembled and

---

[1] Helbig, op. cit., pp. 403–6; Tille, loc. cit. ii. 259–60.
[2] Helbig, op. cit., pp. 353, 411–14; Kötzschke and Kretzschmar, op. cit. i. 165.

agreed to levy the excise, but only for two years, and only at the rate of 3⅓ per cent.; clergy and nobility were to be exempt for sales of their own produce, and burghers for the corn they grew within the town boundaries. For each of the four territories belonging to the margraves one nobleman and one urban mayor were appointed to act as 'excise masters'; these eight were to assemble at Leipzig every three months and, together with four princely councillors, to account for the sums collected and to decide how they should be used to pay the princes' debts. The Estates concluded a union to prevent a continuation of the excise after the two years stipulated, while the margraves gave an undertaking not to extend it any further and not to introduce any other tax: if they acted contrary to this promise, 'their lands' should be entitled to combine and to take measures for their protection. These events signified the development from separate Estates into a corporation, bound by a solemn treaty and recognized by the princes, who handed over the administration of the new tax to their representatives, much earlier than this was done in other principalities.[1]

When the Thuringian branch of the house of Wettin died out in 1440 the brothers Frederick and William intended to effect a new partition of their possessions which caused renewed conflict. To prevent the threatening civil war the Estates in 1445 assembled on their own initiative and concluded an alliance to preserve peace and to intervene in the proposed partition. Their aim, however, was not achieved: the fratricidal war which broke out soon after lasted for six years. Frederick tried to win the support of the Estates and in 1446 he summoned a diet and requested a new tax to pay off his debts. To this the Estates agreed, but they demanded to be informed how he had incurred such debts and clamoured for the dismissal of the foreign, Thuringian, advisers so that he could be advised by native councillors—demands to which Frederick had to consent. In the following year he consulted his Estates about the guardianship of his son if the latter should succeed to the throne as a minor. In that case the government should be exercised by his mother

---

[1] Helbig, op. cit., pp. 415-25; Johannes Falke, 'Die Steuerbewilligungen der Landstände im Kurfürstenthum Sachsen', *Zeitschrift für die gesamte Staatswissenschaft*, xxx, 1874, pp. 401-2; Böttiger, op. cit. i. 346; Kötzschke and Kretzschmar, op. cit. i. 165-6; Hans Spangenberg, *Vom Lehnstaat zum Ständestaat*, Munich and Berlin, 1912, p. 152 and n. 3.

and sixteen members of the Estates, eight of the nobility, four of the clergy, and four burghers; they should appoint all officials and receive and audit the accounts; if a war or feud threatened and in other important affairs they should summon all the Estates and leave the decision to them. As Frederick lived for another seventeen years, these provisions never came into force.[1] In 1451, after the end of the fratricidal war, Frederick summoned another diet to obtain relief from his pressing debts, largely caused by the employment of foreign mercenaries. Again the Estates granted a tax and appointed a committee of eighteen (ten of the nobility, two of the clergy, and six mayors) to levy and administer the tax; nothing was to be paid out without their assent, and the town council of Leipzig was to act as their banker. In 1454, 1458, and 1481 new grants were made under similar conditions; in 1454 all the members of the committee came from the nobility which also predominated in that of 1481.[2]

During the reign of Frederick's sons, Ernest and Albert, who came to the throne in 1464, more peaceful conditions obtained, internally as well as externally. There was no civil strife, but both were engaged in feuds with neighbouring princes. The Estates met only seldom and were above all concerned with financial questions, for many rents and revenues pawned previously had to be redeemed. In exchange for a substantial grant the young princes had to promise in 1466 that they would hear the Estates' advice in case of a war for which they required their aid. If there were a conflict between them and members of the Estates, the latter should appeal to the ducal councillors or to their own representatives. In 1470 their debts compelled the two brothers to summon another diet and to propose the levy of an excise on wine, beer, mead, meat, and bread for six years. The Estates accepted the period, but declined the duty on meat and bread; instead of an excise on drink only one on beer was introduced, in the yield of which the Estates participated with one-quarter, so that they became interested in its regular

[1] Helbig, op. cit., pp. 430–43, 446; Böttiger, op. cit. i. 347, n. 1; Falke, loc. cit., p. 403; Kötzschke and Kretzschmar, op. cit. i. 166.

[2] Helbig, op. cit., pp. 451–3, 458–60; Böttiger, op. cit. i. 346; Wuttke, op. cit., pp. 5–6; Falke, loc. cit., p. 404; Christian Ernst Weisse, *Geschichte der Chursächsischen Staaten*, ii, Leipzig, 1803, pp. 368–9. The exact composition of the committees of 1458 and 1481 is not known.

levy. This fact probably also explains why the Estates never refused its continuation when this was requested later. When the original grant expired after six years the princes did not even make this request and only a few towns refused to go on paying the excise. Nor did the Estates protest when the ducal brothers disregarded their promise of 1466 that they would hear their advice in case of a war. The more settled conditions, economic recovery, and the income which accrued to them from the excise permitted the princes to forgo new demands for their own purposes; only for those of the Empire, for wars against the Turks and Bohemia were further taxes levied by the Estates.[1]

These factors strengthened the dukes and weakened the Estates. Nor did the Estates take an active part in the final partition of the country between Ernest and Albert in 1485. Only the counts and knights were invited to attend, and they declined to advise the younger duke when he consulted them. Forty years earlier the Estates' part had been far more active and constructive.[2] After the many short-lived divisions and subdivisions of the preceding century the partition of 1485 proved permanent. The margraviate of Meissen itself was divided, and its name was superseded by that of Saxony; but there were now two Saxonies, ruled by the Ernestine and Albertine lines respectively. The elder brother, Ernest, and his heirs remained the Electors of Saxony, residing at Wittenberg in the north and ruling over the Electorate itself and parts of Meissen, Thuringia, Franconia, &c. The younger brother, Albert, received the major part of Meissen with Dresden and Leipzig and scattered lands in Thuringia and elsewhere. The possessions of the two lines were so intermingled and so dependent on each other that it was thought some unity would be preserved between them; yet this partition, as the preceding ones, was bound to create friction and conflicts. As we have seen, during those concerning Hesse in the early sixteenth century the hostile cousins always took exactly opposite sides, and the same occurred at every other opportunity.[3] When the Ernestine dukes became the defenders of Luther and the leaders of the Schmalcaldic League, Duke

---

[1] Helbig, op. cit., pp. 453–9, 458, nn. 168–9, 462; Kötzschke and Kretzschmar, op. cit. i. 166.   [2] Helbig, op. cit., pp. 461–2.

[3] For the conflicts in Hesse, see above, pp. 151 ff. In general, Tille, loc. cit. ii. 260, 277; Schlesinger, loc. cit. ii. 575; Gustav Wolf, 'Reformationszeit', in Gebhardt's Handbuch der deutschen Geschichte, 7th ed., i. 619.

George the Bearded remained a protagonist of Catholicism. Thus new fuel was added to old flames by the religious issue. The famous attack of Duke Maurice on the Elector John Frederick in 1546 was merely the culmination of much older rivalries and feuds. It resulted in a catastrophe for German Protestantism, but had nothing to do with religion, for by that time both lines of the house of Wettin were Protestant.

During the first half of the fifteenth century the Estates had gained considerable political power on account of the never-ending internal conflicts between the members of the ruling house. With the return of more settled conditions their political influence declined sharply, and the partition of 1485 further weakened it, because it was carried out without their participation, and presumably against their wishes. By 1485 their organization into a corporation had not been completed. They had no permanent committees, the clergy were not regularly summoned, and in 1485 not even the towns attended the all-important meeting about the partition. It was left to the dukes to decide which abbots, noblemen, and towns they wanted to summon, or not to summon, to the diet. Even the Estates' right of voting taxes, the corner-stone of their privileges, was set aside when their grant of the beer excise expired in 1476—not to mention other ducal promises which were disregarded in the later fifteenth century; and at that time no more far-reaching demands were put forward by the Estates.[1] This was not exceptional, however, for in many other German principalities—in Hesse, in Württemberg, in Prussia—the Estates developed comparatively late, and their rights and privileges were by no means clearly defined by the end of the fifteenth century.

III. *Albertine Saxony and the Issues of the Reformation*

The late fifteenth and the early sixteenth centuries were a time of economic recovery and prosperity, facilitated by the return of internal peace. In foreign affairs Duke Albert and his successor, George the Bearded, were involved in struggles over Frisia; but in 1515 it was sold to the Habsburgs and peace was

---

[1] Helbig, op. cit., pp. 462–3, 472–3. The Estates' power of the purse had been disregarded in 1476–7: ibid., p. 458, n. 168, so that it cannot be maintained that they had gained the right of voting taxes, as Dr. Helbig does on p. 462.

restored. As in the past, the wealth of the duchy and the financial strength of the duke depended largely on its mineral resources. In the late fifteenth century Duke Albert received less than 10,000 guilders a year from the mines, but in the sixteenth century the mining industry prospered to such an extent that in two years Duke George derived an income of 146,000 guilders from the same source, the income from mining amounting to over two-thirds of his revenue exclusive of taxation.[1] In the early years of his reign, which lasted from 1500 to 1539, he had to cope with grave financial difficulties, mainly caused by the fighting over Frisia. In the 1530's, however, Duke George was able to lend large sums to other princes and came to be called 'George the Rich'. Yet he also borrowed freely at low rates of interest. When he died he left debts of about 500,000 guilders and a treasure of only 128,393, and the interest payable on his debts amounted to over 26,000 guilders a year.[2]

Duke George's relations with the Estates were very harmonious. They granted him large sums without making any difficulties, which enabled him to conduct an ambitious foreign policy. In 1502 they extended the beer excise by ten years, while George promised that he did not consider the granting of such an aid his right and their duty.[3] The diet of 1506 granted another substantial aid. Two years later George simply ordered his local officials, the *Amtleute*, to levy a quarter of the same tax anew in their districts. When the nobility protested against this arbitrary taxation George negotiated separately with each Estate rather than with the diet. In November 1508 the towns consented to levy the tax of 1506 once more, and the prelates followed suit. Six months later the nobility also assented, but insisted on a promise that in future taxes would not be raised

[1] Goerlitz, op. cit., p. 387, gives the following figures:

Year	Annual revenue from mining	Total 'ordinary' revenue
	guilders	guilders
1488–97 (average)	9,645	?
1536–7	58,061	90,930
1537–8	87,722	121,015

[2] Ibid., p. 403; Falke, 'Die landständischen Verhandlungen unter dem Herzog Heinrich von Sachsen, 1539–41', *Archiv für die Sächsische Geschichte*, x, 1872, p. 41.
[3] Falke, in *Zeitschrift für die gesamte Staatswissenschaft*, xxx. 410.

without the common counsel and consent of the Estates of the duchy. This, however, did not prevent George from again ordering his *Amtleute*, in 1510 and in 1511, to levy another quarter of the tax levied previously. The taxes were duly paid. The Estates were satisfied with stating their legal objections, and no conflict occurred. George, on the other hand, after the end of the war in Frisia, did not demand any further direct taxes, but was content with the excise on beer and wine. This duty was extended by four years by the diet of 1513 and by eight by the diet of 1516. It expired in 1525, but was again prolonged by eight years in November 1526 and by six years in 1534, and finally granted to the duke for his life-time in 1537. In peace-time this tax and the growing 'ordinary' revenues proved sufficient for the ducal needs.[1]

As in Brandenburg and in other principalities, the nobility and clergy were exempt from the excise for the wine they grew and the beer they brewed for their own use. This privilege naturally led to many conflicts with the towns because the noblemen did not only brew for their own consumption, but sold beer to the country inns and taverns and forced their tenants to buy it from them, so that neither the nobility nor the inns paid the excise which fell mainly on the urban breweries and inns. Noblemen also bought and sold wool and other rural produce and established many artisans and weavers in the villages. It was in vain that the towns complained at the diets and committee meetings about these and similar practices. As the duke declined to intervene, and as no valid decree regulating these matters was ever promulgated, in spite of all the towns' efforts, nothing was achieved and the towns continued without much success to defend their privileges and monopolies against the encroachments of the countryside. With regard to the complaints of peasants against their noble masters, George strictly saw to it that they were not punished for complaining to the courts, in contrast with the practice which existed in Brandenburg at that time. The ducal suggestions for a settlement often were so

[1] Goerlitz, op. cit., pp. 360-2, 380-1, 478; Falke, loc. cit. xxx. 412, 421. The average annual yield of the excise on drink was 16,350 guilders for the years 1513-17, and rose to 25,815 for the years 1535-9: see the detailed figures in Goerlitz, op. cit., p. 381, n. 5. In addition the town of Leipzig paid a fixed sum of 4,000 guilders which took no account of its rapidly increasing wealth. For figures of the 'ordinary' revenues, see above, p. 202, n. 1.

favourable to the peasants that the noblemen repudiated them
more often than the peasants. If both sides accepted his decision,
but the nobleman later broke the terms or wronged the peasant,
George intervened: the nobleman might be fined, his revenues
might be seized, or his right be transferred to a ducal *Amtmann*.[1]
In this way the excesses of noble power, so common in the sixteenth century, were avoided. The ducal administration was
strengthened and remained a reality for the lower classes which
enjoyed the protection of the prince.

Sixteen diets were summoned in the course of a long reign of
nearly forty years. The longest interval between two diets was
5½ years and significantly occurred after the diet of 1516 which
prolonged the excise by eight years.[2] Yet the importance of the
diet declined because the more weighty issues were submitted
to small assemblies of the Estates which were attended by many
ducal councillors and *Amtleute*. Through these George exercised
a strong influence on the decisions of such assemblies, especially
on those of the Estate of the nobility, because the large majority
of his councillors and *Amtleute* came from this class. At the diet
of 1526 his influence was even more pronounced. Out of a
committee of twenty-nine as many as fourteen were officials;
twenty were noblemen, four abbots and five burghers, and all
the members were selected by the duke. The committee was
empowered to deal with the grievances of the Estates and with
questions relating to the war against the Turks, and such an
arrangement was clearly advantageous to the government.
Three years later the diet empowered a different committee
to deal with matters concerning the war with the Turks; it also
appointed four commissioners for each of the four districts of
the duchy to supervise the levy of the tax and to receive and
keep the money collected. In this tax the nobility participated
with about 8 per cent. of the total, the towns with about 30,
the peasants with about 45, the bishops with less than 2, and the
clergy with about 16 per cent.[3] As in other German principalities, the nobility, while in principle exempt from taxation,
contributed nevertheless in cases of emergency and to taxes for

---

[1] Goerlitz, op. cit., pp. 133, 171, 211, 221, 226-8; no. 8, p. 498; no. 21, p. 528;
no. 24, p. 533; no. 29, p. 541 (from the years 1506-37).
[2] See the list of diets, ibid., pp. 433-63.
[3] Ibid., pp. 370, 372, 376, 448-9, 479-81; Falke, loc. cit. xxx. 414-15.

purposes of the Empire, above all against the Turks; but even then it only paid a small part of the total.

Thus the power of the Estates declined during George's reign, partly because there was peace and prosperity, partly because their money grants were no longer essential, partly because the excise on beer and wine became a semi-permanent tax, partly because small assemblies and committees took the place of the diet. Yet it became clear in 1537 that the Estates were not entirely pliant. George then did not want to hold a diet, but summoned the Estates to four separate places and asked them for money to fortify several towns and castles, to extend the excise (due to expire in 1540) for his life-time, and to levy again the tax granted in 1529 against the Turks. If he hoped that the opposition against these projects would be lessened by holding four separate meetings, his hopes were disappointed. In contrast with Württemberg, where the same tactics applied in 1540 were entirely successful,[1] all four assemblies raised difficulties. Two meetings in Thuringia protested, demanded that a diet should be summoned, and declined to reply to the ducal proposition. The third assembly similarly protested and refused to make a specific grant, but in principle accepted the proposed taxation. The fourth consented to the tax against the Turks, but the nobility demanded it should be taxed less, to which the towns refused to agree, so that no decision could be taken. The nobility also made the grant dependent on the participation of the bishops, who had paid a small sum in 1529, but hesitated to do so again.[2]

As the device had failed, a diet was summoned two months later to meet at Leipzig in May 1537. There George repeated his proposition emphasizing that he had no intention of dividing the Estates and that these matters concerned them as much as him: they should elect some men to collect the money and to take charge of it, to inspect the places which were to be fortified, to advise how and where the work should be done, and to render their accounts to the Estates. He also announced that he would appoint a committee of twenty-four from the Estates— eighteen noblemen, two prelates, two mayors, and two non-noble

---

[1] See above, pp. 21–22.
[2] Goerlitz, op. cit., pp. 255–6, 462; nos. 30–31, pp. 543–7; Falke, loc. cit. xxx. 418–20 (Feb. 1537).

officials—to form a council of regency after his death and to
govern on behalf of his feeble-minded son Frederick; three
or four of them were always to be present at the court, so that
the decisions taken by the Estates could be carried out the more
easily. These propositions were accepted by the diet without
much difficulty. The cathedral chapters were to participate in
the taxes granted for the Turkish war and for the building of
fortifications, but the general issue of the participation of the
bishops was shelved, for only the cathedral chapters were
members of the Estate of the clergy.[1] The bishops themselves,
on the other hand, did not belong to the Estates and were not
bound by the decisions of the diet, and this aroused the hostility
of the Estates. The bishops held their own diets and levied their
own taxes from their bishoprics until the introduction of the
Reformation. The Estates acceded to the ducal requests, but
they had successfully asserted their claim that only a diet could
grant taxes, and they exercised a strong influence over the
collection and the use of the sums granted: rights which they
were to retain under future rulers. Their consent was also
considered necessary for changes in the law, in the privileges
of individuals and corporations, such as their own, and in the
organization of the law courts.[2]

Duke George died in 1539 and was succeeded by his brother
Henry, and not by the mad Frederick. Henry, strongly influenced by his wife, Catherine of Mecklenburg, immediately
introduced the Lutheran Reformation, which had been done in
the Ernestine territories many years before. He did so without
consulting the Estates which were not united on the religious
issue. But the considerable debts which George had left and his
own pressing need of more money made it necessary to summon a
diet at the end of the year. In his proposition to the diet Henry
recognized that it was an old custom to hear the advice and
criticisms of the Estates when the country's welfare, advantage,
or ruin was at stake. Therefore he did not want to undertake
anything without consulting them, nor let the monastic lands
pass into other hands or become deserted, but see to it that they

---

[1] Goerlitz, op. cit., no. 32, pp. 547 ff.; Friedrich Karl Hausmann, *Beiträge zur
Kenntnis der Kursächsischen Landesversammlungen*, ii, Leipzig, 1798, p. 125, n. 4;
Christian Ernst Weisse, *Zusätze und Berichtigungen zu Schrebers ausführlicher Nachricht
von den Churfürstl. sächsischen Land- und Ausschusstägen*, Leipzig, 1799, pp. 97–106.

[2] Goerlitz, op. cit., pp. 248–9, 255–7, 476–7; Falke, loc. cit. xxx. 421.

were used for the country's needs according to their counsel.[1]
These were important concessions, allowing the Estates influence over the disposal of monastic property. Apparently
Henry was in a weak position on account of opposition to his
Protestant policy and the dangers threatening from abroad a
few years before the outbreak of the Schmalcaldic War; for
many noblemen were still Catholics, and others were deeply concerned about their rights of patronage and the threatening loss of
religious sinecures, as it became clear from the Estates' reply.

As might be expected, the prelates protested against the
religious innovations. The lay Estates declared that it would
have been more fruitful if their advice had been heard earlier,
but that they would show obedience to the new order as much
as possible. That they only accepted it with reservations emerged
from their further demands. Everybody should be free so to
conduct himself in religion as he could answer to God; no force
and compulsion should be used because they frightened many
away; the duke should not make any change in the bishoprics
and monasteries without the Estates' knowledge, because they—
especially the nobility—were strongly interested in them; the
monasteries and ecclesiastical foundations under the nobility
should be left undisturbed under their authority; those leaving
the monasteries voluntarily should be financially secured; the
church lands should be used to maintain the clergy, the church
servants, and the schools. Henry should also promise he would
not levy any tax except in a case of emergency and with the
Estates' consent, would not conclude an alliance for which he
needed their aid, nor start anything that affected the country's
ruin and welfare, without obtaining their agreement. These
latter demands were accepted by Henry. With regard to religion
he asserted that he was entitled to create a Christian order in
his principality, but promised he would not use force against
anyone. The Estates, however, repeated their religious requests
and asked that a committee be appointed to discuss the future
of the religious foundations and the church lands. If they
received a favourable reply, they would extend the expiring

[1] Böttiger, op. cit. i. 491, 530; Weisse, *Geschichte der Chursächsischen Staaten*, iii,
Leipzig, 1805, pp. 270, 298 and n. 2; Falke, 'Die landständischen Verhandlungen
unter dem Herzog Heinrich von Sachsen', loc. cit. x. 40–42 (12 Nov. 1539). For
Duke George's debts, see above, p. 202, and Goerlitz, op. cit., p. 403.

excise on wine and beer by ten years, but this should remain
their only contribution. Henry then accepted the grant and
promised he would never seek any aid without the Estates'
consent, and they would be entitled to withhold it.[1]

A committee of fourteen was appointed to deal with the
monasteries and their lands. It met in August 1540 to discuss
these issues with the ducal councillors. It proposed that in
Meissen as well as in Thuringia two noblemen and one commoner should be appointed as sequestrators of monastic property. The members of religious orders should be provided for,
the surplus should be administered by the Estates, and yearly
accounts should be rendered in the presence of ducal councillors.
Again Henry conceded most of these wishes. The ecclesiastical
foundations were to be maintained undiminished and only to
be used to relieve the poor and to support the Estates, the
Church, the schools, and the university. The Estates were entrusted with the administration of these foundations through
sequestrators and other qualified people, who were to render
annual accounts to the Estates and the princely councillors
jointly. A corresponding instruction was issued. In August 1541,
shortly before Henry's death, the committee met again. It
suggested an investigation into the leasing out or disposal of the
monastic lands, in so far as this had taken place, and a decision
to be taken as to the future of the remaining ones; but further
measures were prevented by Henry's death. In Saxony, as in
several other Lutheran principalities, the duke derived but
little benefit from the introduction of the Reformation. Only
a few monastic estates became his domains to compensate him
for the heavy expenditure religion had caused him in the past.[2]
The main benefit, however, accrued to the Estates, especially
the nobility, for their influence increased as a result of their
acquisition of many abbey lands and of the supervision they
exercised over the property of the former monasteries. Gradually
more than fifty monasteries and nearly thirty nunneries were
dissolved, to the detriment of learning and education, but to
the benefit of the landed classes.[3]

---

[1] Falke, loc. cit. x. 45–46, 49, 51, 53–57; Böttiger, op. cit. i. 491; Weisse, op. cit.
iii. 270–1 (Nov. 1539).
[2] Falke, loc. cit. x. 61–70; Böttiger, op. cit. i. 492, 540; Weisse, op. cit. iii. 272.
[3] Böttiger, op. cit. i. 538.

Three months after Henry's death his successor Maurice summoned the Estates' committee and proposed that for the war against the Turks 1,000 horsemen and 5,000 foot-soldiers should join the Imperial army at a cost of 500,000 guilders a year, and if need be these figures might be doubled. This obligation the committee did not deny, but considered it necessary to summon a diet, which in their opinion would not refuse a grant. Maurice should appoint some from their ranks to receive the money, to disburse it, and to render their accounts to the Estates, and the nobility should contribute 1 per cent. of the value of their productive lands, burghers and peasants 1½ per cent., the clergy and the bishops with their subjects one-third of their revenues and incomes. Maurice replied that a diet need not be summoned because everybody knew this was a matter of urgency which could brook no delay; but in the end he had to give way, and a diet was summoned to meet the following month. The second point at issue was the disposal of the monastic lands. On his accession Maurice found great disorder prevailing. Administrators appointed by the Estates had got rid of the monastic landlords and clergy under the pretence that they were acting for the Estates, had put their friends into their places and disposed of the properties in a way that brought little credit to either prince or Estates. Maurice suggested that the monks and nuns still living in their houses should be left undisturbed, and where only a few inmates were left they should be concentrated in another house until they died, and the vacated lands should be sold. In that way 50,000 guilders a year could be saved, and with that sum the clergy and preachers could be maintained and education be provided for the children of the poor. The committee declared a detailed investigation necessary before it was decided whether to sell or lease the abbey lands. In contrast with Maurice it favoured a lease for some years, so as to keep them together, and proposed that seven noblemen and two burghers should carry out a thorough investigation and visitation. This point Maurice accepted, but he insisted that selling would bring more lasting profit than leasing; the revenues should only be used for pious purposes and for the benefit of the country. Yet the committee rightly pointed out how difficult it would be to find buyers who would give the full value, and the matter was left to the diet for further discussion.[1] While the committee desired a permanent settlement, Maurice only saw the short-term advantage of getting ready cash and neglected the opportunity of bringing about such a settlement, from which not only the prince but the country would have benefited. Maurice's attitude was not dissimilar from that adopted by Henry VIII at about the same time.

The diet assembled a few weeks later and, following the committee's suggestions, granted the tax for the war with the Turks. It was to be levied by members of the Estates, to be kept and disbursed by a large committee of twenty-seven noblemen and four burghers, who were entitled to take decisions in matters arising and to be responsible to the Estates; in case of need the committee was empowered to levy more money. A small committee of six was to receive and keep the accounts and revenues of the monastic lands, to make suggestions as to their use, and to report back to the large committee which was to have power of decision. Maurice assented, but proposed that the large committee should have fewer members and that the tax receivers should send their reports to him. He promised he would delegate his councillors into the small committee to co-operate in its work. This committee, composed of five noblemen and two urban mayors, met early in 1542 and decided to lease the monastic lands for six years, although Maurice now favoured only three years; their administration should be controlled by the committee. The *Amtmann* and the mayor of Leipzig were entrusted with the keeping of the accounts of revenue and expenditure, but there was little improvement. Therefore the large committee was summoned twelve months later. Maurice declared that, to avoid a deficit, he would have to take over the administration himself, and that he had issued instructions to his *Amtleute* to supervise the monasteries so that the accounts would not be tampered with. He intended to sell some small houses to redeem pawned revenues and to pay off his debts, and to found three schools for 230 boys, one-third of whom should be of noble birth. The committee agreed to these propositions, and Maurice appointed a deputation to see to the

[1] Johannes Falke, 'Zur Geschichte der sächsischen Landstände: Die Regierungszeit des Herzogs Moritz, 1541-46', *Mittheilungen des Königlich Sächsischen Alterthumsvereins*, xxi, 1871, pp. 61-68; and in *Zeitschrift für die gesamte Staatswissenschaft*, xxx. 426-9 (Nov. 1541).

sales. Twelve months later it made a report to the large committee: only two schools for 120 boys had been founded, but donations had been máde to the University of Leipzig and to other schools for scholarships and the maintenance of chaplains and teachers, as well as for pious purposes.[1]

Although the bulk of the monastic spoils did not pass into Maurice's hands, but was used for educational and pious purposes, or for the benefit of the nobility, he did not require new grants until the dangers threatening from abroad and his own ambitions made them necessary. In 1545 the Estates' committee agreed to the levy of a small tax for eight years for the building of fortifications; in each district two noblemen and two burghers were to be responsible for receiving and disbursing the money and for rendering their accounts to the Estates, and the money was not to be used for any other purpose but that stipulated.[2] That this grant was made by the committee, and not by the diet, caused such dissatisfaction that it was discontinued after a few years. Maurice intended to use the opportunity of the civil war threatening between the Emperor Charles V and the Protestant princes to deprive his cousin of the Ernestine line, the Elector John Frederick of Saxony, of territory and the electoral dignity, and equally of the rich secularized sees of Magdeburg and Halberstadt. In June 1546 Maurice concluded a treaty with the Emperor in which Charles promised him those Ernestine territories he would conquer and the protectorate over the two sees, while Maurice undertook to remain loyal to Charles and recognize the decisions of the Council of Trent. Only thereafter did he summon a diet and request, without giving any information about the treaty or his intentions, the election of a committee of six to advise him, a young prince, during the time that the dangerous situation in the Empire continued. The Estates were willing to do so, but not to empower the committee to grant any money, or to take any decisions, as Maurice desired it. They then elected five noblemen and the mayor of Leipzig, and advised him to remain neutral and to avoid an unnecessary war, but to arm himself for any

[1] Falke, in *Mittheilungen des Königlich Sächsischen Alterthumsvereins*, xxi. 72–92; in *Zeitschrift für die gesamte Staatswissenschaft*, xxx. 429–35; Weisse, op. cit. iii. 288–9 (Dec. 1541 to Jan. 1544).

[2] Falke, in *Mittheilungen des Königlich Sächsischen Alterthumsvereins*, xxii, 1872, pp. 91–93, and in *Zeitschrift für die gesamte Staatswissenschaft*, xxx. 444–5.

eventuality. They were prepared to pay for 400 horsemen and 4,000 foot-soldiers for three or four months, and this offer was accepted by Maurice.[1]

Two weeks later Charles V commanded Maurice to execute the Imperial ban which had been pronounced against the Elector John Frederick, on pain of incurring the same penalty himself. Maurice reported this to the Estates' committee of six, but they considered the matter so weighty that they asked for the diet to be summoned. Maurice for the time being only summoned a deputation of the Estates and asked for their advice. They counselled him to spare no effort to preserve peace: he should support the Imperial army according to the Emperor's orders and thus preserve the ruling house and the country, for it was neither possible nor permitted to resist his forces. Six weeks later, however, a diet was summoned and the same question was submitted to it. The Estates declared it impossible to resist the Emperor if he occupied electoral Saxony by force of arms, but were opposed to Maurice executing the Imperial mandate. If, however, John Frederick was unable to protect his country, then Maurice should occupy and protect it. They granted a considerably increased excise on beer and wine for twelve months for the army, to be levied by their own receivers and responsible to them, and appointed six of their members to muster the mercenaries and to give advice whether to recruit any more. Maurice clearly hoped the Estates would support his aggressive designs on the Electorate; he is reported to have been deeply annoyed when they advised him not to execute the Imperial ban against John Frederick and he declined to accept a compromise proposal which they made.[2] But he had got the grant for the mercenaries and decided to act. Early in 1547 he invaded the Electorate and, after John Frederick's defeat and capture at Mühlberg, he received as a reward the major part of his cousin's territories and the electoral dignity; the Ernestine line was confined to Thuringia. Maurice now ruled over the whole of Meissen and Saxony from the Bohemian mountains in the south to the Brandenburg frontier in the

[1] Falke, in *Mittheilungen des Königlich Sächsischen Alterthumsvereins*, xxi. 94–99, and in *Zeitschrift für die gesamte Staatswissenschaft*, xxx. 436–7; Hausmann, op. cit. ii. 135, n. 13 (July 1546).

[2] Falke, in *Mittheilungen des Königlich Sächsischen Alterthumsvereins*, xxi. 101–5, 109–13; Weisse, op. cit. iii. 164–5; Böttiger, op. cit. i. 531–2 (Aug. to Oct. 1546).

north, to which were added the secularized bishoprics of Meissen, Merseburg, and Naumburg, but not the coveted Magdeburg and Halberstadt. The new Electorate of Saxony was, after the Habsburg territories, the most important and the most developed German principality. In the course of the sixteenth century further lands were added to it, especially the valuable county of Mansfeld and other possessions in Thuringia. Its population has been estimated at more than 1,200,000.[1]

The Estates had become deeply suspicious of Maurice's policy because he did not consult them when his financial situation allowed him to do without their grants, because he preferred to negotiate with a committee and not with the diet, and because he acted against their advice during the crisis of the Schmalcaldic War and embarked on a policy of aggression against other Protestants. While they wanted to curtail his power, the new Elector aimed at making himself more independent and at vesting the right of granting taxes in a small committee, which would govern together with his councillors and make the summoning of diets unnecessary. Yet he failed to achieve these aims because the difficulties of the political situation and the cost of his wars forced him to rely on the support of the Estates. Their influence increased rather than diminished in spite of all his gains.[2] These issues emerged clearly when the diet met in 1547 after the defeat and imprisonment of John Frederick. The towns wanted to admonish Maurice that in future he should respect the old privilege that he was not to start a war without the Estates' assent; if the matter had been debated by the diet, a war might have been avoided. The Estates, however, went no further than to request Maurice that he should not conclude an alliance nor begin to arm himself without their knowledge and advice and should pay off his mercenaries because they were prepared to defend the country with their lives. Maurice was in principle willing to hear their advice on foreign policy, but pointed to the dangers of the time and desired that a small committee be appointed for this purpose and a reserve of money be collected. The Estates declined to elect such a committee because the previous one had been a failure. They offered to extend the increased excise by two years

---

[1] Böttiger, op. cit. ii. 47; Tille, loc. cit. ii. 277; Schlesinger, loc. cit. ii. 575.
[2] Weisse, op. cit. iii. 299; Kötzschke and Kretzschmar, op. cit. i. 239; ii. 6, 10.

on condition that the tax for the building of fortifications—
which had been granted by the committee two years ago—was
rescinded: they obviously still resented this tax because it was
not granted by the diet. Maurice insisted on more money and
on the election of the committee, but was only able to obtain the
continuation of the excise and of the fortification tax for the
time being. The Estates gained another concession which he
had at first refused. Five from the Estates and four ducal
councillors were to check the accounts of the former monastic
lands which were allocated to educational purposes, and they
elected four noblemen and the mayor of Leipzig as auditors.[1]

At the end of 1548 another diet was summoned to discuss the
Interim, which Charles V promulgated after his victory in the
Schmalcaldic War and which made only very limited concessions to the Protestants, and to vote a tax for the Empire. The
Estates asked Philip Melanchthon and other Protestant theologians for their opinion, and under their guidance a compromise
was adopted, which made certain concessions to the Catholics
in ritual and doctrine; this so-called Leipzig *Interim* was severely
attacked by the orthodox Lutherans. The *Interim* promulgated
by the Emperor only conceded to the Protestants communion in
both kinds and the marriage of priests; on the other hand it
made them dependent on papal dispensation and restored the
Catholic ritual. But even these unfavourable conditions were
accepted by the diet following Melanchthon's advice. With regard to taxation, the Estates offered to extend the increased
excise on beer and wine by two years, on condition that the
fortification tax and the small tithes were rescinded. The towns
pronounced in favour of a direct and more equal tax and
demanded the participation of the nobility in the excise, which
in their opinion mainly burdened the towns. Maurice insisted
on an extension by four years as a precondition of his discon-
tinuing the other taxes; the Estates at first offered three, but
eventually agreed to four years. Again Maurice demanded the
election of a permanent committee to deal with urgent business,
but was unable to obtain this point. He also had to promise he
would not conclude an alliance nor start a war without the

---

[1] Falke, in *Mittheilungen des Königlich Sächsischen Alterthumsvereins*, xxii. 78–91;
Weisse, op. cit. iii. 299; iv. 6–7; Hausmann, op. cit. ii. 72–74, 138, n. 16; Böttiger, op. cit. i. 502–3 (July 1547).

Estates' consent, and this was incorporated into the *Reversales* issued at the end of the diet, in contrast with the preceding year.[1] Thus Maurice had to make important concessions and to allow the Estates considerable influence in foreign and religious affairs because he needed their support against Charles V.

When the next diet met in 1550 Maurice revived the proposal that a committee be elected, this time to promote a final settlement with his Ernestine cousins, but the Estates again declined. He further proposed the continuation of the excise by four years, until 1556, but the Estates replied that this would involve those consenting in grave dangers and cause much irritation among the people. The nobility offered half the amount, and only for two years; more they declared to be impossible because they had not yet recovered from the war and the taxes were too heavy. When Maurice insisted on a longer period, the Estates eventually granted a property tax of about 120,000 guilders, and this was accepted by Maurice. After the dissolution of the diet, however, he declined to sign the undertaking about alliances and wars because it tied his hands too much, and he claimed that the nobility was exercising pressure upon him and was placed too high. He summoned only sixteen noblemen and two towns to a meeting which was to negotiate with Magdeburg; but those summoned appeared without any powers, were therefore unable to negotiate, and departed again without accomplishing anything.[2]

Fifteen months later issues of foreign policy induced Maurice to summon another diet. He reported to the Estates that he had dispatched some of his councillors and some theologians to attend the session of the Council of Trent then in progress; there the councillors had demanded a safe-conduct for the theologians who had already reached Augsburg, but not gone any farther. The Estates should advise him whether they should do so or not. The Estates were strongly in favour of the attendance of the

[1] Falke, in *Mittheilungen des Königlich Sächsischen Alterthumsvereins*, xxii. 96–99, 103, and in *Zeitschrift für die gesamte Staatswissenschaft*, xxx. 447–8; Weisse, op. cit. iii. 300; iv. 7, 13; Hausmann, op. cit. ii. 76; Böttiger, op. cit. i. 531 (21 Dec. 1548 to 1 Jan. 1549).

[2] Weisse, 'Chursächsische Landtagsverhandlungen von 1550, 1552, 1557 und 1561', *Diplomatische Beyträge zur Sächsischen Geschichte und Staatskunde*, Leipzig, 1799, pp. 212–24; Falke, in *Mittheilungen des Königlich Sächsischen Alterthumsvereins*, xxii. 103–8, and in *Zeitschrift für die gesamte Staatswissenschaft*, xxxi, 1875, pp. 114–15; Hausmann, op. cit. ii. 76–78, 140, n. 20 (Oct. to Nov. 1550).

theologians at Trent and replied that they should proceed on their journey. Before the diet was dissolved, however, a letter arrived from them that it was too late because the last session of the council would be held on 19 March 1552. It was then decided to instruct them they should send their confession, composed by Melanchthon, to the council and apologize for their absence. The other point concerned the negotiations with Maurice's Ernestine cousins, the sons of the imprisoned John Frederick, who declined to accept the new conditions and to sign a treaty. The Estates advised that the negotiations should be continued because they thought there was hope of reaching a settlement, and this was accepted by Maurice. The third, even more important point concerned the continuing imprisonment by the Emperor Charles V of Maurice's father-in-law, Philip of Hesse, whose liberation he had guaranteed. Maurice felt his honour was at stake; he made military preparations, ostensibly against the Protestant city of Magdeburg, which had been put under the ban of the Empire, and negotiated with other Protestant princes and with Henry II of France who was willing to protect the 'liberties' of the German Protestants in exchange for territorial gains. After these preparations and determined to act on Philip's behalf, Maurice asked his Estates for advice. As might be expected, they were opposed to any use of force and any alliances with foreign rulers and counselled him not to take up arms against the Emperor, who was ordained by God as His highest authority. Maurice replied that he had no objections against the Estates sending a deputation to Charles V to obtain the release of Philip. The Estates' opposition, however, did not deter him from breaking with the Emperor and from making himself the leader of the anti-Habsburg forces. As the Estates were in favour of peace and compromise and suspected their prince of the opposite intentions, it is not surprising that they declined to pay the tax of the common penny he demanded. In their opinion it was his duty to pay it to the Empire and to garrison the fortresses, for that had been a condition of their granting the increased excise to him.[1] The diet showed that the

---

[1] Weisse, in *Diplomatische Beyträge zur Sächsischen Geschichte und Staatskunde*, pp. 228–44, and *Geschichte der Chursächsischen Staaten*, iv. 27–28; Falke, in *Mittheilungen des Königlich Sächsischen Alterthumsvereins*, xxii. 110–14; Böttiger, op. cit. i. 512 (28 Feb. to 8 Mar. 1552).

policy of Maurice and that of the Estates were irreconcilably opposed to each other, and that he could not reckon on their support in his adventurous foreign policy.

When the following diet met a few months later, the situation had completely changed. Maurice had carried out his successful coup against Charles V, Philip had been freed, and the treaty of Passau had established a perpetual religious peace in the Empire, for King Ferdinand, Charles's brother, needed Protestant support against the Turks. These events Maurice in August 1552 reported to the diet and once more demanded the payment of the common penny to save Christendom from the Turks who were conquering Hungary. This time the Estates were more pliant: the points at issue were only how much money they would vote, and on what conditions. The towns demanded that the noble estates should not be exempt, for if they were the towns had to pay two-thirds of each tax, and their burghers also had to render military services at their own expense. But all the nobility was willing to concede was a tax of one-thirtieth of the value of their property and lands, against one-twentieth of those of the burghers and peasants, which altogether would have yielded less than 50,000 guilders. Maurice, on the other hand, demanded 200,000 and the taking over of considerable ducal debts, which at that time amounted to about 700,000 guilders,[1] by the Estates. The latter then consented to give 150,000 for the war against the Turks and to take over debts of 400,000 guilders, on condition that the excise on wine and beer was ceded to them and reduced by half and that their grievances were redressed, above all that the mercenaries were paid off. Maurice insisted on 200,000 guilders for the war and debts of 600,000 to be taken over, and the Estates eventually agreed to both demands. The excise was ceded to them, and it was agreed that it was only to be used for the payment of the ducal debts; it was to be continued for another three years at the old level, then to be reduced to half, and to terminate when the debts were paid. Maurice further promised that the grievances would be redressed and the mercenaries be dismissed. The Estates then appointed seven noblemen and the mayors of four towns as receivers of the excise, who were instructed to use it only for the

[1] Wuttke, op. cit., p. 6; Walther Däbritz, *Die Staatsschulden Sachsens in der Zeit von 1763 bis 1837*, Leipzig, 1906, p. 41.

stipulated purpose and no other.[1] The army, however, was not
disbanded. Maurice, instead of using it against the Turks, in
1553 attacked Margrave Albert Alcibiades of Brandenburg-
Bayreuth, and levied 120,000 guilders without a grant by the
Estates for this war. This naturally caused great embitterment,
for it showed how little the Estates could rely on Maurice's
promises. But an open conflict was avoided because in July he
was fatally wounded in battle and died soon after.[2]

The dangerous situation abroad and the threats of Margrave
Albert Alcibiades that he would seek revenge from Saxony induced Maurice's brother and successor, Augustus, to summon
a diet to meet six weeks after Maurice's death; for the existing
forces were in his opinion quite insufficient to defend the country
and should be increased to at least 2,000 horse and 3,000 foot-
soldiers. As his brother had left him large debts, he had to seek
the aid of the country. He also proposed that the Estates should
nominate a committee to advise him and promised he would
maintain the Augsburg Confession and preserve peace and law
and order. He did not share Maurice's ambitions, nor did he
possess his brother's bellicose and adventurous temperament;
he desired to bring about a settlement with the Ernestine line,
which might attempt to regain its lost position and to deprive Augustus of the electoral dignity. His peaceful tendencies naturally
met with the approval of the Estates. They suggested retaining
the mercenaries for another month or two, without increasing
their number, until it was possible to see how matters stood with
Margrave Albert Alcibiades. They protested against the levy
for the war against him by Maurice without their assent and
demanded a refund of the money advanced by the towns and
the appointment of auditors from their ranks; no alliance or
military expedition should be attempted without their approval.
They also put forward several demands with regard to the religious settlement. The revenues of the church lands should be
used for the stipulated purposes, especially the payment of the
clergy and schoolmasters; clergymen with insufficient stipends
should receive supplements, poor noble maidens should be

---

[1] Weisse, in *Diplomatische Beyträge zur Sächsischen Geschichte und Staatskunde*,
pp. 246–57; Falke, in *Mittheilungen des Königlich Sächsischen Alterthumsvereins*, xxii.
122–32, and in *Zeitschrift für die gesamte Staatswissenschaft*, xxxi. 123–4 (23 Aug. to
2 Sept. 1552).

[2] Hausmann, op. cit. i. 76; Wolf, loc. cit. i. 629–30.

educated in two former nunneries which should be properly endowed, the former monasteries should be visited and their accounts be checked every year by special deputies. These demands were accepted by Augustus, who promised that the tax levied without their consent would not constitute a precedent and that he would make inquiries about the advances made by the towns. But he insisted on the appointment of a committee and the increase of the army, to which he would contribute. The Estates considered an army of 1,000 horse and 2,500 foot sufficient and declared that more was impossible to bear. Augustus then requested they should pay for 1,500 horse and 2,000 foot in addition to the garrisons of the fortresses, and the bishops and counts for another 500 horse, and renewed his demand for the nomination of a committee. This the Estates again firmly rejected, but granted the money required for the mercenaries for three months, which Augustus accepted. They elected twelve of their members to discuss the grievances with the electoral councillors, and Augustus promised solemnly that no tax or aid would ever be levied without their free and voluntary consent, which they were entitled to withhold—a clause which from then onwards was incorporated into every agreement marking the conclusion of a diet.[1]

Only seven months later Augustus summoned another diet because the threat of war had not receded and the previous grant had expired. He also desired to hear the advice of the Estates about the circulation of foreign debased coins, the presence of suspicious vagrants and other police matters, as well as about the treaty negotiations with the Ernestine line. The Estates agreed to sign and seal this treaty as was stipulated, and a settlement was thus brought about between the two houses. The Estates further tendered their advice about the coinage and the vagrants and renewed their demands for the maintenance of the existing and the promised church schools, the revenues of which were alienated according to their assertion. The towns sharply opposed the exemption of the noble fiefs from the previous tax, for it was levied in an emergency and

[1] Falke, 'Zur Geschichte der sächsischen Landstände: Die Regierungszeit des Kurfürsten August, 1553–61', *Mittheilungen des Königlich Sächsischen Alterthumsvereins*, xxiii, 1873, pp. 59–72, and in *Zeitschrift für die gesamte Staatswissenschaft*, xxxi. 125–7; Hausmann, op. cit. ii. 80 and n. 12; Böttiger, op. cit. ii. 38; Weisse, op. cit. iv. 171 (20–29 Aug. 1553).

should be treated like one for the war against the Turks to which the nobility had always contributed. They offered proof that previously the prelates and the nobility had contributed to the payment of the ducal debts and to other emergencies. Augustus once more agreed to the demands concerning the religious houses. He requested the appointment of a committee—which the Estates again declined—and the payment of about 360,000 guilders from all property, exclusive of the noble fiefs, but not of other noble property. The Estates granted about 240,000 guilders, payable within two years, a sum which they later increased by another 40,000, payable two years after, and this was eventually accepted. The towns' demand that the noble fiefs should also be taxed was declined. A committee was appointed to discuss the grievances, especially the claim of the counts and high nobility that they were not an Estate, and consequently did not have to pay any taxes. The towns complained about the brewing and selling of beer by noblemen and about their trading in corn and woad; and the committee pronounced in favour of the closing of the new taverns and the cessation of trade by noblemen, unless it were done for their own needs. The nobility countered these attacks by complaining about the damage they had suffered through the abolition of the canonries and the dissolution of the nunneries and by demanding that commoners should be forbidden to buy noble estates and that the Elector should preserve the nobility and its privileges[1]—evidence of the continuing conflicts, but also of the social equilibrium, between the nobility and the towns, in contrast with the state of affairs in Brandenburg and Prussia. Indeed, the reign of Augustus was a period of peace and good government, of growing trade and prosperity, especially in Leipzig, whose fairs and rights were protected by the government and flourished at the cost of those of other towns.[2]

At the beginning of 1555 the committee was recalled and a new demand for taxation was submitted to it by Augustus. He

---

[1] Falke, in *Mittheilungen des Königlich Sächsischen Alterthumsvereins*, xxiii. 74–86, 89–92, and in *Zeitschrift für die gesamte Staatswissenschaft*, xxxi. 134; Hausmann, op. cit. i. 91; iii. 124; Weisse, op. cit. iv. 160 (29 Mar. to 1 June 1554). In 1570 the nobility renewed its complaint about the buying out of noble estates by the Elector as well as the towns: Falke, loc. cit. xxiv. 115–18.

[2] Böttiger, op. cit. ii. 46–47, 52.

accepted the Estates' wishes with regard to the visitation and the income of livings and schools and promised he would secure the endowments of the two schools at Pforta and Grimma, founded out of monastic spoils. With regard to the noble estates he pointed out that poor noblemen often moved into the towns and became burghers and that he could not prevent this from happening: in Saxony clearly the class-barriers were less rigid than elsewhere in Germany. The committee in its turn declined to vote any money because the Estates had always refused to appoint one precisely for this reason, and suggested a diet should be summoned to grant an extension of the increased excise on beer and wine. This was accordingly done. The diet consented to extend it for another six years, although they had hoped the ordinary excise would suffice in peace-time; but when Augustus desired a larger grant, they prolonged the excise by eight years. The Estates demanded the fulfilment of the promise that three schools would be founded in former nunneries, but without success. Augustus also declined to reserve all posts in the court called the *Hofrat* to members of the nobility, asserting that not enough suitable candidates were available so that he had to employ commoners as well, thus again preserving his freedom of action and a social equilibrium.[1]

The following diet met in 1557 because in the previous year the Imperial diet had voted a tax for the war against the Turks. This time the towns were successful in securing the participation of the nobility. Even noble fiefs were assessed at 40 per cent. of the amount given from other people's property, although the noblemen emphasized that they were liable to render feudal services. But this was the last time that noble fiefs were taxed; only other noble property remained taxable, contrary to the custom in Brandenburg and Pomerania where all noble property became exempt. Augustus renewed his promise that he would not conclude any alliance or start any war without the Estates' consent, and would not undertake anything else which might endanger the country.[2] During the first four years of the reign, which lasted until 1586, the diet met very frequently;

[1] Falke, in *Mittheilungen des Königlich Sächsischen Alterthumsvereins*, xxiii. 93–99; Böttiger, op. cit. i. 538 (Feb. to Apr. 1555).

[2] Falke, loc. cit. xxiii. 100–4; Hausmann, op. cit. i. 91–92; ii. 54–55, 144, n. 27; Weisse, in *Diplomatische Beyträge zur Sächsischen Geschichte und Staatskunde*, pp. 261–70 (29–31 Mar. 1557).

during the remainder the Estates were only summoned every four to six years. The longer intervals were due to the more peaceful conditions obtaining in Germany after the religious peace of 1555 and to the prosperity of Saxony. These made the Estates willing to vote taxes for six or eight years at a time and made it unneccessary to consult them on foreign or religious affairs. The relations between them and their prince remained harmonious; there was no reason to distrust Augustus as they had distrusted Maurice and his ambitions. Augustus did not attempt to curtail their privileges or to make himself independent of their votes of credit, and the country benefited from this absence of sharp conflicts.[1]

As the excise was due to expire in 1563 and the princely debts were growing, a diet was summoned in 1561. It agreed without much difficulty to extend the ordinary excise on drink by eight years. This grant was later modified to embrace the increased excise, on condition that it would solely be used to pay off the princely debts and the interest due, that the accounts would be rendered to the diet and that the grievances would be redressed, but without actually pressing this point. In addition, the Estates consented to levy nearly 150,000 guilders by way of a property tax, but shortened the duration of the excise by two years, and this was finally accepted. The towns renewed their complaints about the brewing and selling of beer by noblemen, about their trading in salt, woad and other goods, about their malting and buying up of barley before it reached the towns, and continued to do so at subsequent diets with equal lack of success. As on previous occasions, the Estates departed without awaiting the princely decisions regarding their grievances.[2]

After an interval of four years another diet was summoned. Again the Estates were willing to make large grants in return for a general promise that the grievances would be redressed, that Augustus would rescind the newly imposed tax on coal, and would not ask them for any contribution for the Empire. They at first offered to pay about 240,000 guilders. When Augustus declared this was insufficient, they offered twice, or

[1] Kötzschke and Kretzschmar, op. cit. ii. 21.
[2] Weisse, loc. cit., pp. 272–9; Falke, loc. cit. xxiii. 106–11; xxiv. 88, 94, 120–1, 127 (3–8 June 1561).

even thrice, that amount, payable within six years. This Augustus desired to be shortened to four years and agreed to the conditions stipulated, but the Estates would not go beyond six, which he then accepted—a grant amounting to about 120,000 guilders a year. Augustus gained another important success when the Estates for the first time agreed to the often-repeated request for the appointment of a committee and elected a small committee consisting of thirty noblemen and a large one of twice that size. Later diets followed this example. To these committees were added in 1592 two similar committees of the towns, with eight and thirteen members respectively. But their committees were never amalgamated with those of the nobility which retained precedence.[1]

Augustus soon made use of the existence of the committee. In 1567 he summoned it, and not a diet, to obtain its consent to an earlier payment of the taxes granted in 1565 because of the dangers allegedly threatening from the Ernestine line. Duke John Frederick, the son of the last Elector with the same name, had been put under the ban of the Empire for supporting William of Grumbach, an Imperial Knight engaged in a long-lasting feud with the bishop of Würzburg. Augustus had been entrusted with the execution of the ban and was besieging his cousin's capital, the town of Gotha in Thuringia. He informed the committee that John Frederick was planning to invade Saxony and that it was impossible to summon a diet because war was so near and the matter so urgent. These arguments were, however, not accepted by the committee which urged that all the Estates should be summoned, for they had always declined to nominate a committee and had always been assured that no tax would be levied without their express consent. Although they declared it impossible to anticipate the levy because of crop failure and dearth, this was nevertheless done by the government.[2]

A diet was only summoned three years later, and new demands for more taxes were submitted to it, partly on account of

[1] Falke, loc. cit. xxiv. 88–91; Hausmann, op. cit. i. 48–52; Böttiger, op. cit. ii. 135; Weisse, *Geschichte der Chursächsischen Staaten*, iii. 296, n. 6, 298; Oskar Hüttig, *Der kursächsische Landtag von 1766*, Leipzig, 1902, pp. 45–46 (23 Sept. to 1 Oct. 1565).

[2] Falke, loc. cit. xxiv. 97–101; Wolf, loc. cit. i. 648; the committee met in Apr. 1567, and Gotha capitulated in the same month.

the siege of Gotha of 1567, partly on account of the marriage of Augustus's daughter, and partly because of his growing debts. Augustus demanded an extension of the increased excise on beer and wine, an annual tax on property of about 120,000 guilders, and a special contribution for his daughter's dowry. In return he was willing to leave the levy and receipt of all taxes and the paying off of his debts entirely to the Estates. Four of their members and four of his councillors should be responsible for these matters and report to him every year. The Estates in their reply complained that their grievances had not been redressed but had increased, that they had granted him an unheard-of tax to pay his debts as recently as 1565, that in Saxony it was not customary to pay a tax on the marriage of princesses—in contrast with the custom prevailing in other principalities. They asked to be excused from new impositions on account of the country's poverty and begged him to take pity on them. After some further exchanges the Estates nevertheless consented to the increased excise and the property tax for a period of six years, but not to the aid for the princess; in future no loans or debts should be contracted without their approval. The grant and the attached conditions were then accepted by Augustus, and all his debts were taken over by the Estates.[1] Four noble receivers of taxes and four princely councillors henceforth administered the country's taxes and formed the so-called *Obersteuercollegium*, but without any participation of the towns. In each district or 'circle' there existed a committee of the Estates which was responsible for the repartition and collection of taxes, with a nobleman at its head who acted as a receiver. Only for the rendering of accounts were some urban deputies admitted. Thus the electoral chamber, which administered the ruler's considerable revenues from domains, mines, and tolls, became separated from the administration of taxes which was taken over by the Estates.[2] In contrast with Bavaria, Brandenburg, Württemberg, and other principalities,

[1] Falke, loc. cit. xxiv. 105–13, and in *Zeitschrift für die gesamte Staatswissenschaft*, xxxi. 149 (26 Sept. to 6 Oct. 1570).

[2] Weisse, op. cit. iv. 181–2; Böttiger, op. cit. i. 529; ii. 39; Wuttke, op. cit., p. 6; Hüttig, op. cit., pp. 40–41; Fritz Kaphahn, 'Kurfürst und kursächsische Stände im 17. und beginnenden 18. Jahrhundert', *Neues Archiv für Sächsische Geschichte und Altertumskunde*, xliii, 1922, p. 66. For the later developments in this field, see below, pp. 237–8, 256, and n. 1.

however, the *Obersteuercollegium* was a mixed commission, only
partially controlled by the Estates, and the accounts were not
submitted to them, so that the Elector did not lose all influence
in the field of taxation. In this mixed form the *Obersteuercollegium*
survived for more than two centuries. In Brandenburg, on the
other hand, the Great Elector reassumed the financial powers
which his ancestors had lost and thus broke the influence of the
Estates, not only in financial affairs.

Two more diets were held during the remaining years of
Augustus's reign, at intervals of six years, because the grants
were made for periods of six years at a time. At the diet of 1576
the Estates prolonged the increased excise on drink by six years,
and in 1582 by five years. The property tax was reduced to
about 80,000 guilders a year in 1576 and only conceded for
three years; in 1582 it was maintained at that level and granted
for six years. In both instances the Estates affirmed that larger
grants were impossible on account of the country's poverty,
plague and dearth. The excise in practice became a regular tax
which was extended almost automatically as the Estates participated in its yield, but the property tax was still granted at
different rates and for varying periods. At both diets the Estates
demanded that their grievances be redressed, but were content
with a general promise that this would be done and that if need
be a special commission would be appointed to discuss them.
They insisted, on the other hand, that an excise on corn, which
Augustus had imposed by virtue of his prerogative, should be
abolished and they won this point against him as a condition of
making a grant.[1] If they had permitted the prince to invade
their power of the purse, a main pillar of their power would have
fallen to the ground. The general peace and prosperity Saxony
enjoyed permitted the Estates to make substantial grants and
helped both sides to avoid a conflict.

Augustus's successor, Christian I, only ruled for five years,
and only one diet was held during that time, in 1587. The
Estates protested anew against the imposition of taxes without
their consent contrary to ancient custom, but Christian denied
any knowledge of such a step. The Estates again extended the

---

[1] Falke, in *Mittheilungen des Königlich Sächsischen Alterthumsvereins*, xxiv. 124–6,
129–34, and in *Zeitschrift für die gesamte Staatswissenschaft*, xxxi. 150–3 (Sept. 1576
and Sept. 1582).

excise on drink as well as the property tax of about 80,000 guilders a year by six years, and this was accepted.[1] Christian's main adviser and mentor was Dr. Nicolaus Crell who was promoted chancellor in 1589 and governed almost alone, without the privy council which Augustus had established. Crell's autocratic rule, his methods of administration, and especially his leanings towards Calvinism, aroused strong opposition among the Estates, the clergy and the officials, the adherents of the rigid orthodox Lutheranism that had been established under Augustus. Clergymen and officials had to accept, solemnly and under oath, on pain of dismissal the formulas of Lutheran orthodoxy drawn up to eradicate any clandestine Calvinist influences and any tendencies towards a religious compromise. This obligation Crell removed, and equally the Consistory and the church regiment introduced in 1580. Christian further tended towards co-operation with the forward Protestant party in the Empire, which was led by the Elector Palatine and Landgrave William IV of Hesse, and with Henry IV of France.[2] Indeed, it would have been of fundamental importance for the future of German and European Protestantism if Saxony had joined that party and had not played the part she was to play in the Thirty Years War: that of siding with the Habsburgs and against the Elector Palatine when he was elected to the crown of Bohemia. This whole policy was, however, very unpopular in Saxony. When Christian I died in 1591 and a strict Lutheran, the Ernestine Duke Frederick William of Saxe-Weimar, became the administrator and guardian of the minor Christian II, Crell fell from power. A committee of the nobility immediately demanded his arrest which was carried out a few weeks after Christian's death. At the diet of 1592 Frederick William urged the Estates to act as Crell's accusers in a formal trial. Some, however, rejected such procedures, adopted by men 'seeking vengeance in the Estates' name'. Gradually Crell's enemies gained the upper hand, and in 1594 he was put on trial for having used force in religious affairs and having conducted dangerous negotiations with Henry IV. After a protracted trial he was finally sentenced to death by the court of appeal at

---

[1] Falke, in *Zeitschrift für die gesamte Staatswissenschaft*, xxxi. 154–5.
[2] Weisse, op. cit. iv. 215, 243; Böttiger, op. cit. ii. 62–65; Wolf, loc. cit. i. 653–4, 661.

Prague, to which the case had been referred, and which was strongly anti-Calvinist; he was executed in 1601. In 1606 the old forms of administration, the Consistory and the strict Lutheran church government were restored at the request of the Estates.[1]

Five diets were summoned during the twenty years of Christian II's reign, at regular intervals depending on the length of the grant made. In 1592 the administrator and guardian demanded the prolongation of the excise on drink until Christian should reach his majority, but this the Estates declared contrary to custom and only extended it by three years. In 1595, 1601, and 1605, however, they prolonged it by six years on each occasion without much difficulty. In the last instance they went further and offered to increase the rates by 50 per cent., and when Christian declared this to be insufficient, they doubled them. With regard to the property tax, they granted it to the amount of about 80,000 guilders a year in 1595, increased it to about 120,000 a year in 1601 and to about 160,000 in 1605, in exchange for a promise that no further taxes would be levied during the period of the grant and that grievances would be redressed. In spite of this promise Christian as early as 1609 submitted new demands to the Estates against the advice of his councillors and requested the election of a committee to facilitate the deliberation. This the Estates declined to do, as they had done on previous occasions. Instead they enumerated their grievances and demanded to see the accounts of the last taxes. Christian then promised the redress of grievances and the nomination of a deputation to discuss questions of defence and police. The Estates consented to the prolongation of the excise by six years and to a further increase of the property tax by about 40,000 guilders a year. Christian, however, requested twice that amount for eight years as well as the participation of the noble fiefs in the tax, and this the Estates would not concede. Eventually he accepted their offer and promised not to incur any new debts and to use the money solely for paying his old ones, while the Estates' receivers were absolved from their duty of obedience if they should be ordered to raise money without the Estates' consent.[2]

[1] Weisse, op. cit. iv. 215–27, 243; Böttiger, op. cit. ii. 68–70; Wolf, loc. cit. i. 661.
[2] Falke, in *Zeitschrift für die gesamte Staatswissenschaft*, xxxi. 156–60, 165–71, 173–80; Kaphahn, loc. cit., p. 67.

Thus the Estates granted the Elector increasing sums, in spite of all their protestations that the country was poor and unable to bear any more taxes. Partly no doubt these larger grants can be explained by the rising prices and the inflationary tendencies of the period, but they also indicate that the country's prosperity continued until the outbreak of the Thirty Years War, and that the Estates were willing to meet the legitimate demands of the government. Under these circumstances, there was no cause for a sharp conflict and no issue on which the interests of the prince and the Estates diverged strongly. In the course of the sixteenth century the Estates' rights and privileges became clearly defined. They became a corporation with a well-defined membership and definite rules of procedure. The diets met at regular intervals and wielded the power of the purse. They exercised a certain influence in foreign affairs and a considerable one in the fields of financial administration and religion. They strongly favoured a policy of peace and orthodox Lutheranism. There is no evidence that the position of the prince improved to any great extent as a result of the introduction of the Reformation. The Estates saw to it—as they did in Württemberg and to some extent in Hesse—that the wealth of the monasteries was not entirely dissipated and did not entirely accrue to their prince. The continuous rise of all prices forced him to rely on their grants, a contingency which they used to increase and reaffirm their privileges. Thus the equilibrium between the prince and the Estates, and within them between the nobility and the towns, was preserved. The Elector did not become the prisoner of a ruling nobility, as happened in Brandenburg and Prussia at that time because there the towns sank into insignificance. Even the Thirty Years War did not destroy this equilibrium.

iv. *Electors and Estates in the Seventeenth Century*

The peace and prosperity which Saxony enjoyed in the later sixteenth century were shattered by the outbreak of the Thirty Years War. During the first twelve years of the war Saxony was not directly touched by the fighting. It was hostility towards the Calvinists, which was fanned by the court chaplain, and jealousy of the Elector Palatine—whose election to the crown of Bohemia threatened to make him the strongest prince of the Empire—which induced the Elector John George I (1611–56) to accept the overtures of the Emperor Ferdinand II and to conclude an alliance with him at the beginning of 1620. John George was promised the repayment of all his expenses and the possession of Lusatia, to the east of Saxony, as a reward for rendering aid against the Bohemians. When the troops of the Emperor and the Catholic League invaded Bohemia, John George marched into Lusatia, and a month before the battle of the White Mountain, conquered its capital, Bautzen. The Estates of Saxony, however, did not approve of this close co-operation with the Emperor against their Protestant brethren. When the Estates of Bohemia appealed to them for help, the Saxon nobility expressed their disinclination to fight against 'their dear neighbours, their friends through blood and other ties, and also their co-religionists', and declared they were not obliged to serve outside the country. Yet the Estates continued to grant considerable sums to pay off their prince's debts, which in 1622 amounted to no less than 3,300,000 guilders; and even the nobility made a voluntary contribution from their noble estates.[1]

At the diet of 1628 it was announced that the electoral debts had more than doubled within six years and stood at the formidable figure of 7,100,000 guilders, on which an average of 6 per cent. of interest had to be paid. The Estates asked how this unheard-of increase had occurred, and how the taxes granted in 1622 had been used to pay the electoral debts. John George, however, refused to supply this information, for he was not obliged to render accounts to the Estates, and such a request did not show the respect that was due to him and infringed his princely authority. The Estates did not dispute his claim, but showed their dissatisfaction with John George's policy by demanding that the director of his chamber, Dr. David Döring, be dismissed and arrested. In their eyes Döring was the main culprit; he was put on trial, but the investigation did not reveal anything incriminating and was concluded two years later through a settlement. The Estates nevertheless took over 2,000,000 of the debts and granted an entirely new tax of one

---

[1] Weisse, op. cit. iv. 271–2, and n. 1, 352, 356, n. 5; Böttiger, op. cit. ii. 88; Wuttke, op. cit., p. 14; Wolf, 'Der Dreißigjährige Krieg', loc. cit. i. 684–6.

pfennig on each pound of meat for six years. While this new tax was proposed by the nobility, the towns favoured a tax on the grinding of corn, but John George accepted the suggestion of the nobility. The meat tax was doubled in 1641 and became a permanent tax, always prolonged for periods of six years at a time. Usually it was farmed out to the butchers' guilds.[1]

Meanwhile the war approached Saxony. The Imperial and Catholic forces advanced into northern Germany. Gustavus Adolphus landed on the coast of the Baltic and tried to win over to his side the two leading Protestant principalities, Brandenburg and Saxony, but both hesitated to commit themselves. John George still preferred the alliance with the Emperor Ferdinand. In 1631, however, Tilly laid siege to the great city of Magdeburg, where John George wished to install his second son as the administrator of the secularized archbishopric, while Ferdinand desired it for one of his own sons. In May 1631 Magdeburg fell, and John George had to take defensive measures against Tilly which provoked counter-measures on his side. Thus John George, very much contrary to his inclinations, finally became involved in the war on the Protestant side and began to negotiate with Gustavus Adolphus whose army was advancing southwards.[2] In this situation he was forced to seek the support of his Estates and their backing for his new policy. He summoned them and inquired whether he should ally with Sweden, in view of the sufferings of the Protestants and the violence of Tilly, partly directed against his own close relatives. The Estates, however, would not commit themselves to a pro-Swedish policy, but facilitated a more active foreign policy by making large grants.[3] Thus Saxony entered the war and became a battlefield. The Swedish army occupied the country and retained possession of it after severe fighting with the armies of Tilly and Wallenstein, in which Gustavus Adolphus met his death at Lützen. A Saxon army made its appearance, directed by a new War Chancery (*Kriegskanzlei*).[4] John George, however, like the Elector George William of Brandenburg, was unable to influence the outcome of the war or to bring its end

---

[1] Weisse, op. cit. iv. 356, n. 5, 358–61; Böttiger, op. cit. ii. 134; Wuttke, op. cit., pp. 15–17.
[2] Wolf, loc. cit. i. 703–7, and the literature quoted there.
[3] Böttiger, op. cit. ii. 100.   [4] Weisse, op. cit. v. 305.

nearer. Saxony became the helpless victim of the warring parties, plundered by friend and foe alike. It is therefore not surprising that John George became more and more inclined to conclude a separate peace with the Emperor if a general peace was unobtainable.

This tendency was reinforced after the severe defeat of the Swedes at Nördlingen in August 1634, which forced them to abandon southern Germany and drove the duke of Württemberg into exile.[1] Ten weeks later John George concluded a preliminary peace with the Emperor which guaranteed Lusatia and Magdeburg to his son during the latter's life; it also envisaged that Saxony should combine with Ferdinand to force the other belligerents to make peace and to drive the Swedes from German soil.[2] These terms John George then submitted to his Estates and requested their opinion whether he should accept or decline the offer of commanding one-quarter of the Imperial forces: they should appoint deputies to discuss the peace terms with him. This the Estates refused to do, as they had on previous occasions, in spite of the Elector's repeated entreaties. Eventually they advised him to inform the other Protestant princes in detail of the peace terms and consult with them. He should obtain a satisfactory compensation for Sweden, a firm assurance with respect to the secularized church lands, if possible settle the question of the Palatinate by a compromise, and not refuse the high command offered to him; for it was better to bear arms oneself than to entrust them to others, especially foreigners—a first sign of national feeling aroused by foreign depredations. John George replied that better terms were unobtainable and requested an opinion whether he should ratify the peace, to which the Estates replied in the affirmative. With regard to the higher taxes demanded, they declared that even the most ruthless form of levying by military force, which employed whole companies as if it were against the enemy, was not able to squeeze more out of the country which was totally impoverished. They only voted money for two—instead of six—years, and only half of the desired property tax. After lengthy negotiations, however, they conceded about 82 per cent. of the demand, while John George promised that he would

[1] See above, p. 62.
[2] Wolf, loc. cit. i. 718–19.

not burden them with any other tax or imposition, that he
would not contract any new debts, nor conclude an alliance,
nor negotiate in religious or other important questions, without
their consent. This did not prevent him from imposing a few
months later an excise on all merchandise as an extraordinary
aid on his own authority. The peace of Prague was signed in
May 1635; Saxony obtained peace with the Emperor, but the
sufferings continued, and many taxes and duties were imposed
and levied without the assent of the Estates.[1]

No diet was summoned before 1640, although the grant of
1635 had expired much earlier. The Estates then granted a
property tax for six years and consented to the reintroduction
of the excise of 1635, allocating one-quarter of the yield of both
to the army.[2] Further and increased levies for military purposes
were made during the later years of the war. Thus in 1639 John
George without the Estates' consent levied 34 guilders from
each knight's service. In 1646 the Estates' committees not only
extended the property tax and the excise on drink and meat, but
also introduced a new tax for the army, a combination of a poll-
tax with one on trade and enterprise. After the war this became
a regular tax which was levied every quarter, hence called a
'quarter-tax'; its amount gradually increased until in the early
eighteenth century it reached about ten times the original
figure. In 1653, when the war was over, it was again only the
committees which were summoned and extended the existing
taxes by four years. They proposed that instead of the militia
a defence force of 4,000 mercenaries should be retained, and
this was accepted by John George. How dangerous this trend
was emerged two years later when not even the committee was
called, but only fourteen noblemen and six towns, and even this
irregular assembly, which had no legitimate powers, consented
to certain extraordinary contributions. No diet was summoned
between 1640 and 1657 because since 1628 the Estates' committees were a permanent institution and served the prince's
purpose much better than the diet, as the Estates had always
feared. Exactly as in Württemberg, the small committees of the

[1] Weisse, op. cit. iv. 331–6, 363–6, 378–82; v. 73; Böttiger, op. cit. ii. 111;
Wuttke, op. cit., pp. 15, 22. The diet of 1635 lasted much longer than usual, from
6 Jan. to 13 Mar.
[2] Weisse, op. cit. v. 71–73; Hüttig, op. cit., p. 28; Wuttke, op. cit., pp. 21–23.

nobility and the towns co-opted their own new members and those of the large committees. The main difference was that in Saxony the nobility and the towns retained their separate committees, the membership of which was much larger.[1]

In view of the grant of new and heavier taxes by the Estates' committees, and not by the diet which did not meet for many years, and in view also of the economic decline caused by the war, one might expect a serious weakening of the Estates' power as a result of the Thirty Years War, and this indeed was the case in Bavaria, Brandenburg, and elsewhere. Curiously enough, in Saxony this did not occur, partly no doubt because John George I was a weak ruler and during his long reign did not follow a concerted policy directed against the Estates. His successor, on account of the enormously increased debts and the poverty of his domains and other revenues, relied not less, but more, on the support of the Estates. During the war they had repeatedly advised the Elector in questions of high policy. Events after the end of the war further strengthened their influence[2]—at a time when such influence was sharply declining in many German principalities and practically disappeared in Brandenburg and Prussia. Thus the Elector did not use the opportunity of depriving the Estates of their political influence, which survived into the eighteenth century.

When John George I's long reign reached its end in 1656, he left certain territories, acquired in the sixteenth century, mainly secularized bishoprics, to his younger sons, stipulating at the same time that these territories had to carry a proportion of the large debts accumulated and that the Elector should retain certain rights and prerogatives within them. The separate territories thus created—Weissenfels, Merseburg, and Naumburg—were only reunited with Saxony ninety years later. These provisions of John George's will made it necessary to summon a diet and to ask the opinion of the Estates, who were

---

[1] Weisse, op. cit. v. 76–77; Hausmann, op. cit. ii. 56; Böttiger, op. cit. ii. 135–7; Georg Wagner, *Die Beziehungen Augusts des Starken zu seinen Ständen während der ersten Jahre seiner Regierung*, Leipzig, 1903, p. 35. Cf. below, pp. 255–6.

[2] Kötzschke and Kretzschmar, op. cit. ii. 68–69; Kaphahn, loc. cit., pp. 69–70; Paul Haake, *August der Starke*, Berlin and Leipzig, 1927, p. 29. In 1657 the debts of the electoral *Rentkammer* amounted to 11,867,720 guilders, including arrears of interest of 4,358,047; while the Estates were responsible for debts of 13,288,085 guilders, including arrears of interest of 7,269,046: Wuttke, op. cit., pp. 47, and n. 2, 108; Däbritz, op. cit., p. 43.

also requested to extend their grants by six years and to consent to further extraordinary aids. They replied they were unable to debate an unknown matter as the will had not been fully communicated to them, nor to discuss the other points of the proposition unless this were done. When their request had been fulfilled, they expressed disapproval that their rights had been disposed of in this unheard-of way without any prior consultation with them. They applauded the provision that the prerogatives were to remain in the Elector's hands, together with the fortresses and matters of defence, and declined to apportion the debts between the new territories. Exactly as in Bavaria and Württemberg, the Estates were strongly opposed to any division of the principality, which would weaken them and split their corporation. These sentiments were naturally shared by the Elector John George II, who stood to lose most through the partition and welcomed the support he thus received. The Estates then demanded to see extracts of the accounts of taxation and of the debts with capital and interest; they claimed that in 1653 they had granted the quarter-tax to the amount of 64,000 guilders a year for the army, but that about 420,000 had been levied during the past four years, or 165,000 too much. This and the continuous levying by military force were burdens they could no longer bear; they did not exist elsewhere and many people were emigrating. The country was putting its last hope in the diet to obtain relief.[1]

Three weeks later, however, the Estates extended the doubled excise on drink, granted a property tax of about 150,000 guilders a year for four years, and prolonged the quarter-tax for the army by two years at the previous level, indicating that they did not consider the army a permanent institution. The towns complained that their own authorities were deprived of the right of tax collection in favour of state officials in spite of all remonstrances. The Estates suggested economies at court and the cessation of the excise on merchandise, repeating a demand made in 1653 and in 1655, because it resulted in trade by-passing Saxony and a decline of the yield of tolls and customs;

---

[1] Weisse, op. cit. v. 185; Böttiger, op. cit. ii. 167–8; Haake, op. cit., p. 29; Kaphahn, loc. cit., p. 70; Falke, 'Die Steuerverhandlungen des Kurfürsten Johann Georgs II. mit den Landständen, 1656–60', *Mittheilungen des Königlich Sächsischen Alterthumsvereins*, xxv, 1875, pp. 79–87.

furthermore, a tax on meat was not levied elsewhere, and at most a duty should be imposed on foreign goods. John George, on the other hand, considered the grants insufficient. He desired one for six years and a contribution to his expenses as Imperial Vicar after the death of the Emperor Ferdinand III— a position occupied by the Elector of Saxony until the new Emperor was elected.[1] But this the Estates declined because it had not been demanded on previous occasions, and they were equally reluctant to vote money for six years. They consented, however, that the excise on meat should be continued for four years and granted 32,000 guilders for the garrisons, 10,000 for embassies and about 20,000 a year for fortifications for four years, thus bringing the total military budget to about 115,000 guilders a year. These were very considerable grants less than ten years after the end of the Thirty Years War and met most of their ruler's wishes. In return John George promised that tax arrears would no longer be collected by military force, that taxes would be levied in the towns according to old custom, that arrears from the war years would be remitted, that the accounts of taxation would be scrutinized and audited, that home-grown corn and food would be exempted from the excise, that the garrisons would be reduced and the remaining grievances be decided by a committee appointed for the purpose. The Estates remonstrated in vain against the continuation of the excise, which stifled trade and enterprise and favoured Saxony's neighbours, and of other taxes they had not consented to. In vain did the Hanseatic and the south-German towns remonstrate that their trade with Leipzig was bound to suffer as long as the excise lasted and that it would seek new channels. The merchants of Leipzig went further and for many years refused to pay the excise. But in 1658 they gave 13,700 guilders in lieu of all arrears.[2]

Nine months after the dissolution of the diet of 1657 the privy councillors summoned eleven noblemen and five urban mayors because John George was opposed to the calling of another diet.

[1] Ferdinand III died on 2 Apr. 1657, and Leopold was not elected Emperor until 18 July 1658. In 1612 and in 1619 John George II's father had been the Imperial Vicar.

[2] Falke, loc. cit. xxv. 90–100; Weisse, op. cit. v. 187–8; Wuttke, op. cit., pp. 29, 32–34, 41–42, and n. 2. The diet lasted longer than four months, from 8 Feb. to 15 June 1657.

They requested a grant of 60,000 guilders as a contribution to the costs of his journey to Frankfurt to attend the election of the new Emperor. Those summoned, however, declared they were not empowered to discuss the matter or to vote money, a power which was vested in the diet, but they pointed to the assemblies held in each of the six 'circles' into which Saxony was divided. These were accordingly convened and granted amounts varying from 1 to 1½ quarter-tax, which yielded together about 31,300 guilders, or just over half the desired sum.[1] In 1659 different tactics were adopted. Each circle was instructed to send deputies with full powers because a diet would only cost money. To these deputies the privy councillors explained that the previous grants were insufficient and that the yield of the excise was falling, so that the losses had to be made good. The deputies replied that their grievances had not been redressed, that the excise had not been rescinded and that it was used entirely for the benefit of the electoral chamber, while according to the agreement of 1640 half of it should go to the *Obersteuercollegium*, i.e. be used to repay the debts. They also complained that the excise officials were interfering with the urban jurisdiction and requested to be informed of the details of expenditure, otherwise they were not able to discuss the proposition. John George replied that war was threatening—alluding to the War of the North then in progress—and that he had to prepare measures of defence, so that an army could be raised without delay in case of need. But the deputies considered the situation less dangerous and the defensive preparations of the Upper Saxon Circle sufficient, while John George insisted that a more reliable force was necessary. The towns asked that its size be limited to 4,000 men, and the nobility agreed to give 11½ guilders from each knights' service so that 300 horsemen could be recruited. The deputies consented to the continuation of the excise duties, on condition that half their yield went to the *Obersteuercollegium*; but later they dropped the condition and allocated the entire yield to the Elector until the following diet met, and then the duties should terminate. They declared it impossible to vote more for the army, but granted 10,000 guilders towards the cost of embassies (16,000 having been demanded) and about 16,000 guilders for the funeral of the widow of John George I. Although in John

[1] Falke, loc. cit. xxv. 101–4 (21 Mar. to 23 Apr. 1658).

George's opinion these sums were insufficient for the purposes intended, he accepted them.[1]

The grants were indeed quite insufficient to meet the deteriorating financial situation, caused by heavy government expenditure independent of the state of the revenues, disorder in the electoral chamber, and malpractices in taxation, which brought the state to the verge of bankruptcy. At the end of 1660 a diet had to be summoned, which resulted in more concessions to the Estates in exchange for large money grants. The electoral debts reached a figure of well over 5,000,000 guilders, so that the existing taxes on property, merchandise, meat, beer, and wine had to continue and the introduction of new taxes on drink, luxuries, stamped paper, &c., was proposed. The government further suggested that measures of defence should be taken because there was danger in delay and the taxes for the army of 128,000 guilders a year should be continued, like the other taxes, not for four but for six years. Moreover the mines were decaying because it proved necessary to sink much deeper shafts and many old ones were no longer being worked; a committee should be appointed to discuss these points, so that the rest of the Estates could be dismissed. These consented to a new method of defence: six companies of 500 men each were to be chosen from the militia and to be used in case of need, but not outside Saxony. They demanded that the excise duties and the new tolls be rescinded, and the free trade in salt and corn be restored, and strongly complained about the financial malpractices; taxation should be completely separated from the electoral chamber which should stop issuing so many assignments on the taxes. They emphasized that the diet was protracted month after month because of John George's evil councillors who destroyed all confidence between him and them and barred their free access to their prince. The towns again demanded that their right of levying their own taxes should be restored and the officials appointed for that purpose dismissed, and also that one urban representative be admitted to the *Obersteuercollegium*, whose members should be nominated by the nobility and the towns jointly, and not by the nobility alone as the custom was. The Estates declined to continue the excise on home-grown food and to vote the new taxes on drink, luxuries

[1] Ibid. xxv. 104–17 (12 Feb. to 11 May 1659).

and stamped paper, but assented to most of the other demands. They voted the usual quarter-tax for the army for four years, an increased property tax, the excise on beer, wine, and meat, and special contributions to the electoral chamber for six years, and certain sums for the embassies, fortresses, and mines for four years: all this on certain conditions which were embodied into the *Reversales* at the dissolution of the diet and repeated at every subsequent diet.[1]

In these John George had to promise that he would fulfil his undertaking of 1657 and abolish the excise on home-produced food, that he would not partition the country without consulting the Estates and that he would seek their advice in all important matters. Further, he would impose no new taxes on the country and would separate matters of taxation entirely from those of his chamber, which should not be entitled to issue orders to the local and central tax collectors, and would leave the latter a free hand in the appointment of all tax officials. The Estates further acquired important new privileges: if the prince attempted any changes in the established religion, their votes of credit were to be null and void; three deputies from each of the six 'circles'—two of the nobility and one burgher—were granted the right of free assembly on their own initiative to discuss matters connected with the diet and other important affairs; they were to be summoned every year or as often as necessary by the *Erbmarschall* who presided over the meetings of the nobility, provided he notified the government in advance and sent it a written report afterwards. The wish of the towns to be represented on the *Obersteuercollegium* was not fulfilled. It continued to be composed of four representatives each of the Elector and the nobility, to whom were now added one each from the three separate territories ruled by his brothers,[2] making a total of eleven, only four of whom came from the Estates. Thus their influence on this highly important organ did not increase, although its separation from the electoral chamber was more strictly observed. It stood directly under the privy council and remained responsible for all matters of taxation,

---

[1] Falke, loc. cit. xxv. 117–28; Weisse, op. cit. v. 175–8, 186–8; Böttiger, op. cit. ii. 167–8 (12 Nov. 1660 to 9 Apr. 1661), the diet lasting nearly five months.

[2] i.e. Merseburg, Naumburg, and Weissenfels: see above, p. 233. The reason was that these territories had to participate in taxes voted by the diet.

more an organ of the state than of the Estates. The latter also
appointed a deputation to work out a new order of defence
which concluded its work in 1663.[1] Thus the Estates preserved
and even strengthened their influence and prevented the partition of Saxony into minute principalities, a policy which destroyed the power of the Ernestine line. While an absolute form
of government was founded by the Great Elector of Brandenburg, in Saxony the equilibrium between the prince and the
Estates remained, to the advantage of the country. The burdens
which the people had to bear increased, but not out of all proportion to the country's strength.

As the Estates always limited their grants to a few years at a
time, diets continued to be summoned at fairly regular intervals.
In the later seventeenth century the grants of direct taxation
slowly increased, until they stood in the last decade at about five
to six times the figures of the sixth and seventh decades: proof
of the country's quick recovery from the ravages of the Thirty
Years War.[2] As this increase also applied to the 'quarter-taxes'
destined for the army, John George was able to create a small
standing army: it comprised 8,260 men in 1675 and grew
during the remaining years of his reign, but was considerably
reduced at his death in 1680. His successor, John George III,
increased it to about 10,000 men, consisting of four regiments
of cavalry, four of infantry, and one of dragoons; during the
Turkish war, at the end of the century, it numbered nearly
20,000 men.[3] This was a sizeable force, weaker indeed than the
army of the Great Elector of Brandenburg, but stronger than
that of any other German prince. It enabled the Elector of
Saxony to participate in the wars of the Empire against Louis
XIV and against the Turks, but it did not destroy the influence

[1] Weisse, op. cit. v. 175, 190–1; Hausmann, op. cit. ii. 10, 14–15, 81; Böttiger,
op. cit. ii. 195–6; Falke, loc. cit. xxv. 129; Kaphahn, loc. cit., pp. 67, 70–73;
Haake, op. cit., pp. 29–31.

[2] Between 1653 and 1660 an annual average of 3 'penny-taxes' and 4 'quarter-
taxes' was granted, and between 1661 and 1670 of 5 and 4½ respectively; but
between 1690 and 1699 every year 20½ 'penny-taxes' and 24 'quarter-taxes' were
granted: see the detailed figures in Weisse, *Zusätze und Berichtigungen zu Schrebers
ausführlicher Nachricht von den Churfürstl. Sächsischen Land- und Ausschusstägen*, Leipzig,
1799, pp. 47–48, 52–53. This did not mean that the yield of these taxes increased
equally quickly, but it also improved very considerably: see the figures in Wuttke,
op. cit., pp. 52–53, nn.

[3] Weisse, *Geschichte der Chursächsischen Staaten*, v. 178–80; Böttiger, op. cit. ii. 198;
Haake, op. cit., pp. 41, 48; Kötzschke and Kretzschmar, op. cit. ii. 70.

of the Estates. On the contrary, as the wars increased the electoral debts, they made him rely not less, but more, on the financial support of the Estates.[1] In Brandenburg and Prussia, on the other hand, the growth of the *miles perpetuus* caused the withering away of the power of the Estates, and the new military bureaucracy became independent of their votes of credit, using if need be military force to collect the taxes.

At the diet of 1666 the Estates revived an old complaint with regard to the secularized church lands. They protested that they were used to make up the shortages of the electoral chamber and that their revenues were alienated by officials and others. A committee on which the Estates were represented was appointed to investigate and to report to the following diet, which it did four years later. The diet of 1670 also revived the old grievance about the excise: costly merchandise from Italy was now sent northwards through Thuringia, linen from Bohemia and Silesia took the route through Brandenburg (this was prior to the introduction of the excise there): in short, the excise caused the country's ruin, especially that of the cloth and linen industries. But the Estates only achieved the abolition of the excise on home-produced goods and only by voting an equivalent in direct taxes and considerably increasing the allocation to the army; in spite of this the excise was reintroduced by the diet of 1681. Taxes destined for the army grew from a mere 112,000 guilders in 1660 to 228,000 in 1670 and 343,000 in 1673. In 1676 571,000 guilders were demanded and 457,000 were granted; in 1681 the figures were 1,143,000 and 800,000 respectively: a sevenfold increase within twenty years.[2] In 1684 a special War Council was set up to deal with all military affairs, and the Estates were instructed that such matters henceforth had to be negotiated with the new authority. The nobility consented to raise two cavalry companies with a complement of 172 men instead of the out-of-date knights' services.[3] Otherwise its fiefs remained exempt. Noblemen were preferred to fill the leading posts in state and army, and commoners received much slower promotion. In this way the sons of the nobility,

[1] Heinrich Gössel, *Die kursächsische Landtagsordnung von 1728*, Weida, 1911, p. 43.
[2] Weisse, op. cit. v. 178–80, 204–5, 224–6, 298; Wagner, op. cit., p. 25; Wuttke, op. cit., pp. 36, 100; Böttiger, op. cit. ii. 194, 198–9.
[3] Weisse, *Zusätze und Berichtigungen zu Schrebers ausführlicher Nachricht von den Churfürstl. Sächsischen Land- und Ausschusstägen*, p. 29.

who had lost their positions in the Church owing to the Reformation, were provided for; and this no doubt partly explains why the Estates so willingly increased their grants to the army. Yet, as in Bavaria and even in Prussia, the nobility showed little military inclinations and remained more interested in brewing and other commercial activities, as the continuing complaints of the towns prove.[1] The nobility also tried to prevent the purchase of noble estates by commoners. In 1681 it presented a list of 195 estates which had passed into burgher hands, and a committee was appointed to look into the matter, but without result.[2] In contrast with Brandenburg and Prussia, commoners were not excluded from possessing a noble estate, and the towns did not become subservient to the nobility.

In 1680 instead of the diet only twenty noblemen and seven towns were summoned and ordered to appear with full powers to vote money. These powers, however, were only granted with much reluctance and on condition that such *extraordinari conventus* would not be held again. The deputies did make grants as requested, but they insisted that the constitution should be preserved and that the usual *Reversales* be issued which absolved the Estates from their duty of paying the money voted if the Elector acted contrary to his promises.[3] Thirteen years later under John George IV the experiment was repeated; but meanwhile three ordinary diets were summoned, in 1681, 1687, and 1692, and the Estates' committees met even more frequently.[4] In 1694 John George IV proposed to the committees the introduction of a general excise on consumption as it existed in Brandenburg. This proposal, however, aroused the opposition of the nobility which would have lost its privilege of exemption. The indignant Elector replied that he would disregard their 'worthless reasoning and ideas', introduce the new *modi* by decree by virtue of his prerogative, and have them levied through the military if there was opposition. But his death in

---

[1] Daniel Gottfried Schreber, *Ausführliche Nachricht von den Churfürstlich-Sächsischen Land- und Ausschusstägen*, Halle, 1754, pp. 67, 124, listing urban complaints of 1673, 1676, and 1687; Weisse, *Geschichte der Chursächsischen Staaten*, v. 66, 311–13; Haake, op. cit., p. 34; Kötzschke and Kretzschmar, op. cit. ii. 70–71.

[2] Weisse, op. cit. v. 307, n. 2; Wagner, op. cit., p. 23; Curt Thümmler, *Zur Geschichte des sächsischen Landtags*, Leipzig-Reudnitz, 1896, p. 11 and n. 2.

[3] Hausmann, op. cit. i. 64–65, 112–13; Böttiger, op. cit. ii. 195, n. 1.

[4] See the lists in Hausmann, op. cit. ii. 156–60, and Böttiger, op. cit. ii. 195, n. 1.

the same year spared the Estates from this contingency.[1] It was likely, however, that the conflict about the excise would be renewed under his successor.

v. *The Estates in the Eighteenth Century*

John George IV's successor, Frederick Augustus I, soon revived the project of the general excise and equally his father's policy against the Estates. In Brandenburg the Great Elector had created a large standing army—an example which was bound to influence her neighbour to the south, not only because of the potential threat to the security of Saxony, but also because the army enabled Brandenburg to play a more prominent part in the power politics of Europe. From the time of his accession Frederick Augustus tried to regain the ground lost in the competition for power and status by attempting to gain for himself the crown of Poland, at which the Great Elector had aimed thirty years previously. This policy Frederick Augustus pursued with great energy and cost, especially after the death of John Sobieski in 1696. It was crowned with success in the following year, due above all to the large sums of money spent on the election campaign. He thus required vast sums not only for this purpose, but even more so later for his requirements as king of Poland and for the forces he had to maintain there, for the Polish Diet was more than reluctant to grant him the necessary means. Frederick Augustus's indebtedness increased by leaps and bounds: it forced him to rely to some extent on the support of the Estates, to consider their wishes so as to induce them to vote money, but also to conceive plans to curtail their influence and to make himself independent of their votes of credit, as the Great Elector had done.[2] In contrast with this prototype, however, Frederick Augustus never clearly chose between the one course and the other. Very likely it was preoccupation with Poland which prevented him from adopting a more consistent course towards his Estates.

As early as 1694, shortly after his accession, a pupil of the Great Elector and previously one of the foremost generals in

---

[1] Wagner, op. cit., pp. 16–17; Kaphahn, loc. cit., p. 75.

[2] Gössel, op. cit., p. 24; Wagner, op. cit., pp. 75, 144; Kötzschke and Kretzschmar, op. cit. ii. 81.

Brandenburg, Field-Marshal Hans Adam von Schöning, urgently entreated Frederick Augustus to increase the standing army to a minimum of 20,000 and to transform it according to the Brandenburg pattern. He strongly adhered to an anti-Estates and anti-Habsburg policy and had done everything to fan his master's distrust of the Emperor while commanding the Brandenburg contingent fighting in Hungary against the Turks.[1] Following his advice, a proposal was submitted to the diet to introduce a general excise on consumption on the Brandenburg model. This was supported by the towns, exactly as in Brandenburg thirty years before, because it would do away with the exemptions of the nobility, but it naturally met with its opposition. A committee appointed by the Estates to consider the question pronounced in favour of the old modus, against the vote of some towns. As the Brandenburg envoy reported later, the Estates quite correctly believed that, if the modus of levying were left to the War Council, the quantum would become permanent and the freedom of voting taxes would disappear. In conformity with their previous practice the Estates granted most of the electoral demands, but declined the general excise and suggested a reduction of the army to the size of 1683. Only after considerable efforts and lengthy negotiations did they consent to a 'quarter-tax' of 612,500 guilders a year for the army, plus another 195,000 for military needs: they were not even maintaining their military contributions at the existing level and certainly not allowing for any increase of the army. Frederick Augustus eventually accepted their grants, gave the customary promises to maintain their privileges and the constitution, and decided to make further inquiries about the Brandenburg excise.[2]

A few months later, however, the army was quickly increased to nearly 20,000 men for the war against the Turks. The Estates strongly protested against recruiting by force and other excesses of the military, and demanded the release of those pressed into the army and the promulgation of a decree prohibiting such practices. The nobility also protested against the general excise

[1] Haake, op. cit., pp. 41, 50; Hans Prutz, *Aus des Grossen Kurfürsten letzten Jahren*, Berlin, 1897, pp. 140–1, 319.
[2] Wagner, op. cit., pp. 47, 53–56, 59; Haake, op. cit., pp. 42–44; Wuttke, op. cit., no. 19, p. 111; Weisse, op. cit. v. 302–3 (18 Nov. 1694 to 1 Apr. 1695).

suggested by the towns. As this was a condition of their granting additional supply, Frederick Augustus once more had to
acquiesce.[1] As he urgently needed more money, especially in
view of the impending Polish election, he then initiated an
investigation of administrative methods and a stricter control
of taxation, so as to curtail the influence of the nobility and to
limit corruption and court expenditure. A 'great commission'
was appointed to achieve these objects, and a 'council of revision' began to inquire into the state of the general and the
urban administration. But the financial gains were inconsiderable, and the most important towns were left alone because
they were too powerful and the Elector's creditors. The Saxon
revenues were quite insufficient to meet the needs of the new
king, many domains and *regalia* had to be sold or pawned, and
a *banco de depositi* was founded, in reality a form of concealed
borrowing, against which the Estates protested strongly.
Although they increased their contributions to the army by
about 30 per cent., the soldiers' pay was many months in arrears
and recruiting became more and more difficult.[2]

In 1698 the Estates' representatives began to press for the
redress of their grievances and for the summoning of an assembly
because their grants had been anticipated four times. When
they received no reply they demanded that a diet be summoned
because in their opinion it alone was competent according to
the country's constitution; but meanwhile they extended their
grants and thus showed their readiness to compromise.[3] A new
element of friction appeared in 1697 when the Elector became
a Roman Catholic, hoping to gain the support of Vienna and of
Rome for his policy in Poland. The Estates feared the growth
of foreign influences at court which would diminish their own
power. They complained about the saying of mass, especially
in Dresden, about the holding of forbidden Popish services,
about the buying of property by Catholics contrary to the law.
Exactly as in Württemberg thirty-five years later,[4] their opposition was strengthened by religious zeal and by a popular movement in defence of the threatened Protestant religion, which

---

[1] Wagner, op. cit., pp. 65, 68; Haake, op. cit., pp. 48–49 (Mar. 1696).
[2] Wagner, op. cit., pp. 75–76, 85, 93, 102, 108, 111–13, 121–2, 144, 147, 150–1.
[3] Ibid., pp. 155–6, 159 (Feb. to Dec. 1698).
[4] See above, pp. 123 ff.

found its expression in pamphlets and lampoons and led to local disturbances. It was the first time that the Estates received such popular backing, and their religious complaints irritated Frederick Augustus very considerably. In 1717, when it became known that his son also had become a convert to Catholicism, the opposition received a strong new impetus.[1]

In 1699 Frederick Augustus for financial reasons acceded to the wish of the Estates and summoned a diet to meet in August. He submitted to it his demands for new taxation and again proposed the adoption of the general excise, at least—following the Brandenburg example—in the towns. The Estates made a number of partial grants and demanded the reduction of the army, to which food and fodder should no longer be supplied in kind; above all, they sharply attacked the 'council of revision', which arrogated to itself unlimited powers and carried on illegal procedures, and they promised to show their gratitude if it were dissolved before the dissolution of the diet. No reply was vouchsafed to their demands, but in November a royal resolution was received which rejected the reduction of the forces and the abolition of supplies in kind. In February 1700 much higher demands were put forward; the Estates countered this by granting the customary taxes on property, drink, and meat for six years and only 700,000 guilders a year for the army, still demanding that it should be reduced and the 'council of revision' be dissolved, and that they should be permitted to assemble on their own initiative. Frederick Augustus, however, desired 1,143,000 guilders a year for the army and the introduction of the general excise. The Estates then offered 1,000,000 on condition that the 'council of revision' was liquidated, a condition which their prince was extremely reluctant to accept. They went further and consented to the 1,143,000 guilders for the army and even to later additional demands. They thus achieved their main aims: the investigations of the 'council of revision' were to terminate, or to be continued by a committee of the Estates, which was entitled to release those arrested on bail and to obtain a legal verdict for them; if innocent, the deposed urban authorities were to be restored; the excesses committed were to be investigated, and no similar revision was to be undertaken

[1] Gössel, op. cit., p. 34; Haake, op. cit., p. 163; Kötzschke and Kretzschmar, op. cit. ii. 77, 81.

in the future. A 'permanent deputation' was appointed which could make representations to the government in matters affecting the country's welfare and the Estates' privileges. It could meet without a summons, as could the Estates' committees, but had no powers to vote money. The Estates desired this deputation to have four noble and four urban members, but this the government would not concede, and membership remained limited to the directors of the seven 'circles' into which Saxony was divided, all of whom were noblemen. The general excise was not introduced; but this proved to be a short-lived success of the Estates, for it was done two years later.[1]

As in Brandenburg, the towns hoped that the introduction of the general excise would bring them relief from the mounting burdens and the forcible levying of taxes because the nobility would share in it. Zwickau and some other towns petitioned for the adoption of the new modus, and Frederick Augustus was able to use this to further his aims. As one of his advisers pointed out to him, he would thus acquire complete financial control and the diet need no longer be summoned. In 1702 an 'excise inspection' was established and charged with the transformation of the existing taxes into a general excise on consumption in those towns which desired this. By the end of 1703 this had been done in 112 towns, most of them small: as in the Hohenzollern dominions, the excise was levied at the gates of each town, separating them by customs barriers from the surrounding country and damaging their trade and enterprise. Early in 1704 the Estates protested and refused to vote any money and even to pay the instalments of the taxes granted in 1700. They were dismissed unceremoniously and a kind of rupture ensued. Frederick Augustus announced he would not be deflected from his 'rights and just intentions by obstinacy and pressure', and the Estates gave way. In 1705 the excise was extended by decree to the countryside. In 1707 a comprehensive regulation of the general excise was promulgated, according to which the surplus over the yield of the taxes then levied was to accrue to the towns, a measure calculated to assuage their opposition. Later, however, only one-third of the surplus was ceded to the towns, and

---

[1] Weisse, op. cit. v. 347–50; Hausmann, op. cit. ii. 22–24; Wuttke, op. cit., pp. 60–61, 73; Wagner, op. cit., pp. 162–94; Haake, op. cit., pp. 76, 88–90 (29 Aug. 1699 to 17 Mar. 1700), the diet lasting nearly seven months.

new direct taxes, granted above the level of 1707, were also imposed upon them.[1]

As a result the income from taxation grew very considerably.[2] But if Frederick Augustus hoped he would be able to make himself independent of the Estates, his hopes were disappointed. Meanwhile the Great War of the North had broken out, in which he was a most active member of the coalition formed against Charles XII of Sweden. Because of the war the Saxon army had to be increased to 30,000 men and taxes had to be levied without the Estates' consent. The war, however, went very badly for Frederick Augustus. Charles XII quickly drove him out of Poland and had him deposed from his throne. He then invaded Saxony, and in September 1706 forced him to make peace and to resign the Polish crown. From the Estates meanwhile Charles XII demanded enormous contributions: 570,000 guilders a month and large deliveries in kind. This they declared to be impossible and offered 365,000 a month, whereupon they were dismissed. The Swedish army then proceeded to levy within five months 2,170,000 guilders, confiscating all the revenues and incoming taxes and using military force on a large scale to obtain its ends. Leipzig alone had to pay 80,000 a month and the nobility 285,000 guilders in all.[3] The Swedes did not evacuate Saxony until the autumn of 1707, when Charles XII began to prepare his Russian campaign.

Saxony had suffered very badly from the Swedish occupation, but the burdens continued. After the battle of Pultava and the shattering defeat of Charles XII in Russia the hopes of Frederick Augustus revived. In 1709 a new poll and property tax was levied without any consultation with the Estates. In 1710 he demanded 1,028,000 guilders for the army, which with the help of foreign subsidies was eventually increased to 36,000 men. In 1711 he increased his demand to 1,143,000 guilders for the army and the same sums for other war requirements and for advances made by the chamber to the war treasury; furthermore,

[1] Weisse, op. cit. v. 350–4; Böttiger, op. cit. ii. 230–1; Hüttig, op. cit., p. 25; Wuttke, op. cit., pp. 78–85, 121–3; Haake, op. cit., pp. 91–92, 112.

[2] See the detailed figures for the years 1708–55 in Wuttke, op. cit., no. 28, p. 124.

[3] Weisse, op. cit. v. 357–8; Böttiger, op. cit. ii. 231, 246–7; Arno Günther, 'Das Schwedische Heer in Sachsen', *Neues Archiv für Sächsische Geschichte und Altertumskunde*, xxv, 1904, pp. 245–6.

the Estates were to take over debts of 3,500,000 guilders, and the surplus yield of the general excise was no longer to benefit them, but to accrue to the electoral chamber. The Estates granted 1,037,500 guilders for the army for two years, but not the second million requested for the war. To what extent their influence was weakened by the events of the past years was proved by a unilateral change in the princely *Reversales* at the dissolution of the diet. Frederick Augustus omitted, in spite of all protests, the promises of his predecessors that he would not start any recruiting or a war, nor conclude an alliance, nor make any change in matters of religion and taxation, nor pawn any lands, nor incur any debts, nor levy any tax without the assent of the Estates, and he did not promise that he would uphold the separation between matters of taxation and those of his chamber. It was in vain that the Estates tried, at this and at subsequent diets, to get the customary form of the *Reversales* restored. They were equally unsuccessful in obtaining the restitution of the 'permanent deputation', established in 1700 with the right of making representations to the government. Frederick Augustus dissolved it in 1709 on the ground that he did not wish to countenance any further their remonstrances against royal orders emanating from the privy council. He was also determined not to suffer the right of the Estates' committees to assemble on their own initiative, for this amounted to a *condominium* and to their prescribing laws to him. This no prince would allow and it would not be permitted any longer; he was determined to shake off the tutelage which they had imposed on his predecessors.[1]

Thus the Estates' power was declining sharply, but it did not disappear. It was partly the religious issue, partly the continuing need of money and more money, partly the government's lack of enthusiasm for Frederick Augustus's absolutist policy, partly the distraction provided by Poland and other foreign issues, which prevented him from following the Hohenzollern example more consistently. At the diet of 1718 the Estates, because of the recent conversion of the crown prince to Catholicism, thought all their religious fears justified and solemnly undertook to remain faithful to the Augsburg Confession, to admit

[1] Weisse, op. cit. v. 347; vi. 7–8, 24–25; Böttiger, op. cit. ii. 266; Kaphahn, loc. cit., pp. 75–77; Haake, op. cit., pp. 117–19.

only its members to their assemblies, and to sell property only to fellow Lutherans: whoever became a convert was to lose his membership of the Estates.[1] At the following diet, in 1722, they demanded the abolition of the general excise, but without success. Frederick Augustus warned them that he would be extremely displeased if they repeated this request; and its yield continued to flow into the electoral chamber over which they had no control. They were also informed that he considered their grievances in religious questions unnecessary and wished them to stop.[2] When the War of the North was over the army was reduced to 15,000 men. But as early as 1725 the government declared a grant of 893,570 guilders insufficient for the army's needs and demanded an increase to 1,143,000 as during the war. The Estates' committee was willing to concede 940,000 guilders which was accepted. The army was then increased to more than 26,000, so that this sum was clearly insufficient.[3] In this situation Frederick Augustus revived his earlier plans of levying taxes without the Estates' consent. He consulted his privy councillors on whether the expiring grants should be prolonged by a diet, or by a committee, or 'by other means', namely by virtue of his prerogative. The majority, however, themselves members of the Estates, came out strongly against government without the Estates and against a transfer of the power of the purse to a committee; they were well informed about the developments in Brandenburg and Prussia and did not favour a similar one in Saxony. Frederick Augustus desisted, and a diet was summoned to meet at the beginning of 1728.[4]

The diet granted another 1,430,000 guilders for military purposes, to be paid within three years. When this grant expired, the diet of 1731 increased it to 742,000 guilders a year for the following three years, on condition that it should not be anticipated. The army was once more increased to over 30,000 men, only 11 per cent. of whom were non-Saxons. Recruiting, however, proved very difficult; there was general opposition,

[1] Weisse, op. cit. v. 413, n. 2; Haake, op. cit., p. 150; Gössel, op. cit., p. 51.
[2] Weisse, op. cit. vi. 18–19, 264; Gössel, op. cit., p. 34.
[3] Weisse, op. cit. vi. 16, 31; Böttiger, op. cit. ii. 268; Haake, op. cit., p. 179. In 1726 the army counted 7,047 cavalry and 19,415 infantry.
[4] Kaphahn, loc. cit., pp. 77–78; Haake, op. cit., pp. 162–3; Kötzschke and Kretzschmar, op. cit. ii. 81.

and desertion was rife. The church bells were rung on the arrival of the recruiting sergeants, and riots were frequent. The young men escaped or married to gain exemption; many clergymen lent their help, and even the courts supplied false information. In 1729 recruiting was abolished in favour of drawing by lot. But matters did not improve, and the army remained inferior to that of Frederick William I. His magnificent army was the envy of all his neighbours, and Frederick Augustus remained determined to follow in his footsteps; but he lacked one quality of his Prussian counterpart, his extreme parsimoniousness. Frederick Augustus's love of outward splendour, his enormous building activities, especially in Dresden, his art collections, and his lavish entertainments cost vast sums which could not entirely be raised by taxation. The entertainment of Frederick William I at the camp near Mühlberg in 1730 alone cost as much as 1,140,000 guilders. By the middle of the century debts to the tune of 35,000,000 guilders burdened the administration of taxes, excluding those of the electoral chamber; and the payment of interest consumed a large proportion of the revenues.[1] These ever-growing financial needs of the government made it fall back, time and again, on the votes of credit of the Estates.

After a reign of almost forty years Frederick Augustus died in 1733. During its second half Saxony recovered from the War of the North and the Swedish occupation, but her population remained stationary. It has been estimated that at the beginning of the eighteenth century it amounted to about 2,000,000, but then declined on account of the wars.[2] This was much more than all the Hohenzollern dominions together had at that time, for their estimated population was only 1,600,000 in 1713. Reckoned per square mile, the population of Saxony at the beginning of the eighteenth century was more than three times as dense as that of Brandenburg, more than four times as dense as that of the New Mark and of Pomerania.[3] During the reign of Frederick William I, however, the population of Prussia

---

[1] Weisse, op. cit. vi. 17; Haake, op. cit., pp. 180–1, 184; Böttiger, op. cit. ii. 268–9, 314.

[2] Kötzschke and Kretzschmar, op. cit. ii. 79.

[3] Günther Franz, *Der Dreissigjährige Krieg und das deutsche Volk*, 2nd ed., Jena, 1943, p. 100, n. 135, with figures of population density for different parts of Germany. Cf. Keyser, op. cit., p. 301, with slightly differing figures for 1700.

increased to about 2,250,000 although his only important
territorial acquisition was part of Swedish Pomerania with
perhaps 100,000 inhabitants. The population of Saxony, on the
other hand, was about 1,660,000 in 1722 and 1,695,000 in 1755,
and declined by 90,000 during the Seven Years War.[1] Even
without taking into account the acquisition of Silesia by Prussia,
the position had been reversed. The reason is not far to seek:
during the thirty years of the reign of Frederick Augustus II
Saxony was involved in three major wars, the Polish Succession
War, the Austrian Succession War, and the Seven Years War.
Especially during the latter the country was occupied for long
years by the Prussian army and very badly mulcted by Frederick
the Great. He levied contributions of 55,000,000 guilders in
Saxony and issued many millions of debased coins; in the end
these contained only 28 per cent. of the prescribed amount of
silver and became a veritable plague. The Imperial army equally
levied large quantities of corn and fodder accompanied by much
violence and looting.[2] In addition, Frederick Augustus II, a weak
ruler, was dominated by Count Brühl whose management of the
finances was disastrous and almost led to the state's bankruptcy.
Poland continued to cost vast sums, and so did the court and
the grandiose embellishment of Dresden. As a result of all this
the total debts of the state amounted to 35,000,000 guilders in
1749 and to 56,000,000 at the end of the Seven Years War when
more peaceful times began. In 1745 the army was 37,000 men
strong; but during the consequent years of peace after the end
of the War of the Austrian Succession it was reduced to 16,000.[3]

[1] Böttiger, op. cit. ii. 353; Däbritz, op. cit., pp. 33, 63; Hellmuth Schmidt-
Breitung, 'Der Wiederaufbau der Volkswirtschaft in Sachsen nach dem Siebenjährigen Kriege', *Neues Archiv für Sächsische Geschichte und Altertumskunde*, xxxviii, 1917,
p. 126. The figures for Prussia are taken from Otto Behre, *Geschichte der Statistik in
Brandenburg-Preussen*, Berlin, 1905, p. 198.

[2] Schmidt-Breitung, loc. cit., p. 111, n. 3; Carl Görler, 'Studien zur Bedeutung
des Siebenjährigen Krieges für Sachsen,' *Neues Archiv für Sächsische Geschichte und
Altertumskunde*, xxix, 1908, pp. 123 and n. 1, 125–6, 135–6; Däbritz, op. cit., p. 63.

[3] Böttiger, op. cit. ii. 313, 317; Weisse, op. cit. vi. 163–4, 182: between 1734
and 1755 the grants to the army increased from about 950,000 guilders a year to
over 1,500,000 a year. Böttiger gives a figure of 100,000,000 as that of the debts at
the end of the Seven Years War; but Horst Schlechte, 'Zur Vorgeschichte des
"Retablissement" in Kursachsen', *Forschungen aus mitteldeutschen Archiven*, Berlin,
1953, p. 346, gives a figure of about 45,000,000 thalers or 51,400,000 guilders; and
Schmidt-Breitung, loc. cit., pp. 111–12, a figure of 49,000,000 thalers or 56,000,000
guilders. Cf. Görler, loc. cit., pp. 137–8, and Däbritz, op. cit., pp. 48, 60, 63–64, 74.

Saxony, however, benefited little from the large military expenditure, for at the outbreak of the Seven Years War the army proved quite unable to defend the country against Frederick the Great.

Diets continued to be held at fairly regular intervals, for the Estates always limited their grants to between four and six years at a time. When it was impossible to summon them on account of the Seven Years War, Frederick Augustus specifically guaranteed their rights when he decreed the continuation of the existing levies in 1761 and in 1763.[1] When the war was over the government found it necessary to restore the co-operation with the Estates in view of the country's plight. In August 1763 a diet was summoned, and the Estates undertook to pay a reduced rate of 3 per cent. interest on the 33,640,000 guilders of debts to which the *Obersteuercollegium* was liable. For this purpose a special sinking fund was established into which every year 1,257,000 guilders were to be paid, leaving a certain margin for the gradual repayment of the capital. The government promised that the debts would not be increased any further and that an account of revenue and expenditure would be submitted to every diet; seven noble and seven urban deputies were to administer the sinking fund and the drawing of the bonds issued by the Estates—the first time that the towns achieved equality of representation with the nobility. A poll-tax was introduced from which the noblemen were not exempt. Other steps were taken to restore harmony with the Estates. The vast court expenditure was severely curtailed, and the military budget was reduced from over 1,900,000 guilders a year to 1,143,000 guilders, 171,000 of which the new Elector, Frederick Christian, promised to contribute himself. His father on the contrary until his death had always insisted on a minimum of 1,143,000 a year and on a gradual increase of the army from 19,000 to over 35,000 men, which would have imposed enormous burdens on the ruined country. The Estates raised strong objections against these demands, but did not insist on a large-scale reduction of the army which would have promoted the economic recovery of Saxony. They petitioned that the sons of the nobility should be admitted, in preference to foreigners, to the *Corps de Cadets* and that qualified noblemen, adherents of the Augsburg Con-

[1] Hausmann, op. cit. i. 78–79.

fession, should be appointed officers before others, thus proving
the strong interest of the native nobility in military appointments.[1]

In later years, however, the Estates strenuously opposed
demands for an increase of the army and of their military contributions. As early as 1766 Prince Xavier, regent and guardian
of the minor Frederick Augustus III, declared that the contributions were utterly insufficient and demanded that they be
increased by 90 per cent. so that a further 8,500 men could be
recruited. Until then the Estates had benefited from Frederick
Christian's offer of paying himself 171,000 guilders of the
military budget of 1,143,000, so that they only paid 972,000
guilders a year; they now offered to restore their contributions to the level of 1,143,000 for three years, but Prince
Xavier insisted on a minimum of 1,543,000. The *Erbmarschall*
as the leader of the nobility was summoned before the privy
council, which expressed to him Xavier's strong displeasure and
threatened him with dismissal. He was instructed that the small
committee of the nobility must discuss the demand immediately; each member was to sign his vote, and the protocol was
to be sent to the privy council. To this unconstitutional procedure the committee consented. Only eight of thirty-one
members present opposed the demanded increase of the direct
taxes; but only seven were in favour of the proposed new tax
on the grinding of corn, and nineteen voted against. The whole
Estate of the nobility repeated this negative vote, but consented
to the increase in direct taxation; while the towns assented to
the tax on grinding, but only agreed to 60 per cent. of the desired increase in direct taxes. This offer Xavier accepted and
thus forced the nobility to pay the tax on grinding, from which
they only remained exempt for their personal consumption. In
contrast with the excise, which was largely paid by the towns,
the new tax fell mainly on the countryside; its yield was added
to the general excise and thus removed from the control of the
Estates. These then retracted their earlier offer of increasing the

---

[1] Weisse, op. cit. vi. 257–60; Böttiger, op. cit. ii. 377–8; Görler, loc. cit. xxix.
137–8, 144–6; Schmidt-Breitung, loc. cit., pp. 112–14; Däbritz, op. cit., pp. 67–68;
Otto Rudert, *Die Reorganisation der Kursächsischen Armee, 1763–69*, Leipzig, 1911,
pp. 35, 39–43; Oskar Hüttig, 'Die Segnungen des Siebenjährigen Krieges für
Kursachsen', *Neues Archiv für Sächsische Geschichte und Altertumskunde*, xxv, 1904, p. 89,
and *Der kursächsische Landtag von 1766*, pp. 11–12, 31.

military grant to 1,143,000 guilders, and it remained for the time being at the figure of 972,000 a year.[1]

When Frederick Augustus III reached his majority the military grant was raised to the level of 1,143,000 guilders in peace-time. For the War of the Bavarian Succession the Estates made an extraordinary grant which came to an end with the conclusion of peace in 1779. Grants were made for six years at a time, so that—from 1769 until the early nineteenth century—a diet was summoned every six years. The standing army was increased from 19,000 to 28,000 and remained at that strength.[2] It thus remained comparatively small and did not prove too heavy a burden for a country which was recovering from the wars of the mid-eighteenth century, and whose trade and industries were quickly developing. The level of taxation during the reign of Frederick Augustus III was higher, but not very much higher, than it had been during that of Frederick Augustus I at the beginning of the century.[3] Within thirty-five years after the end of the Seven Years War the debts burdening the Estates were reduced from 33,640,000 to 20,528,000 guilders, and the price of their 3 per cent. bonds rose from 58 to 105 per cent., showing how sound were their finances and their credit.[4]

To the diet of 1728, 234 noblemen and 128 towns were summoned, each of the latter being represented by two or three members of the urban council. The number of towns summoned did not vary much in the course of the century, and about 100 always attended a diet; but the numbers of the nobility entitled to a summons declined steeply because more and more noble estates passed into the hands of commoners. As only the owners of a noble fief received a summons, only 81 noblemen attended the diet of 1787, only 75 that of 1799, and only 78 that of 1805.[5] These figures reflect the progressive

[1] Weisse, op. cit. vii. 13–16; Böttiger, op. cit. ii. 390; Hüttig, op. cit., pp. 51, 54–62; Rudert, op. cit., pp. 77–80.

[2] Weisse, op. cit. vii. 78–79, 93; Böttiger, op. cit. ii. 377, 390, 460, 477; Rudert, op. cit., p. 116. In 1803 the army mustered 27,859 men (6,203 cavalry, 21,048 infantry, and 608 in companies of invalids).

[3] See the detailed figures in Weisse, *Zusätze und Berichtigungen zu Schrebers ausführlicher Nachricht von den Churfürstl. Sächsischen Land- und Ausschusstägen*, pp. 49–56.

[4] See the detailed figures in Däbritz, op. cit., p. 93.

[5] Weisse, *Geschichte der Chursächsischen Staaten*, vii. 90, n. 31; Böttiger, op. cit. ii. 459; Thümmler, op. cit., pp. 17, 20; Schreber, op. cit., pp. 17, 27–28, 86–90; Hüttig, op. cit., p. 17.

economic development of Saxony, a country in which no arti-
ficial legal barriers protected the nobility as they did in Prussia.
The equilibrium existing between the nobility and the towns
was also shown in the fact that only those noblemen who were
exempted from the jurisdiction of the *Amt* and themselves
possessed all rights of jurisdiction on their estates—the so-called
Schriftsassen—had an automatic right of attending and voting.
The majority of the nobility—the so-called *Amtssassen*—merely
attended the preliminary meetings in each *Amt*, each of which
elected one or two deputies to the diet; and these meetings were
also attended by the commoners who possessed noble estates
within the *Amt* in question. In addition to these two Estates
there was an upper house, composed of six deputies of the
cathedral chapters of Meissen, Merseburg, and Naumburg,
nine deputies of the high nobility, and six of the universities of
Leipzig and Wittenberg, twenty-one in all. In this way the
formal division into three Estates was preserved. In contrast
with the former bishopric of Meissen, which was completely
incorporated with the Electorate, the former bishoprics of
Merseburg and Naumburg retained their separate governments
and Estates, as did Lusatia and the Thuringian principalities of
Querfurt and Henneberg.[1]

The towns of Leipzig, Dresden, Wittenberg, and Zwickau
formed the directorate of the towns and were responsible for the
preparation and drafting of all documents for the diet. Eight
towns, under the chairmanship of Leipzig, formed the 'small
committee' and twenty other towns, under the chairmanship
of Annaberg, the 'large committee' of the Estate of the towns.
The 'small committee' of the nobility had forty members, and
the 'large committee' sixty, who were appointed by the former.
Three Protestant prelates sat on the 'small committee' of the
nobility, as they sat on the committees of the Württemberg
Estates. But in contrast with Württemberg, the Elector did not
possess a right of confirmation of the members of the committees: they merely informed him of appointments they had
made.[2] As in Württemberg, these permanent and self-governing

[1] Gössel, op. cit., pp. 47, 50; Thümmler, op. cit., p. 9; Böttiger, op. cit. ii. 353,
457; Hausmann, op. cit. i. 36, n. 4; Schreber, op. cit., pp. 18–19; Hüttig, op. cit.,
pp. 16–18.
[2] Schreber, op. cit., pp. 11–12, 17, 86–87; Böttiger, op. cit. ii. 353; Gössel, op.
cit., pp. 56, 59; Thümmler, op. cit., pp. 10, 18–20; Hüttig, op. cit., pp. 45–46.

committees preserved the influence of the Estates; had they been amalgamated, the growing weight of the towns and the decline of the nobility would have become more evident within them. The Estates of Saxony had lost their influence in religious and in foreign affairs; but they retained their privileges, their power of the purse, and some influence in the field of financial administration, although this had diminished owing to the introduction of the general excise.[1] Their history was fairly uneventful, a history of steady development and not of violent conflicts with their prince.

In this form, virtually unchanged since the sixteenth century, the Estates of Saxony survived into the nineteenth century. The rules of procedure which were adopted by the diet of 1728 remained in force until the old constitution came to its end in 1831.[2] Only after the revolutions of 1830 was this constitution superseded by a more liberal written constitution, which was the result of deliberations between the king and the Estates, exactly as the Württemberg constitution of 1819 was the result of a treaty between the king and the Estates—a very exceptional development in Germany. Thus the old constitution of Saxony successfully weathered the storms of the French Revolution and the Napoleonic period: an example of unparalleled continuity in rapidly changing times. In spite of the efforts of Frederick Augustus I, the Electors of Saxony were not successful in emulating the example of Prussia. They lacked the single-mindedness and the ruthlessness of Frederick William I and Frederick the Great.[3] Their preoccupation with Poland between 1697 and 1763 prevented the Electors from concentrating on the internal affairs of Saxony and forced them to seek the aid of their Estates. When the Polish connexion came to an end in 1763, there was a period of minority government. This again had to rely on the Estates' help in remedying the disasters of the war years. In this way the one-sided political and military

[1] At the end of the seventeenth century the *Obersteuercollegium*, which was partly controlled by the Estates, furnished nearly 60 per cent. of the total budget, but this declined to 30 per cent. owing to the introduction of the excise: Görler, loc. cit., p. 147; Wuttke, op. cit., p. 53, nn. 1–2.

[2] Böttiger, op. cit. ii. 461; Gössel, op. cit., p. 39; Kaphahn, loc. cit. p. 78.

[3] Thus Kötzschke and Kretzschmar, op. cit. ii. 78, 81, with regard to Frederick Augustus I. This applied even more strongly to his successors, Frederick Augustus II, Frederick Christian, and Frederick Augustus III.

development of Prussia was avoided, to the benefit of the country and of its inhabitants. In the social field also the nobility never became as powerful as the Junkers did in Brandenburg, Pomerania, and Prussia. Leipzig and the other towns wielded much greater influence than Berlin or Königsberg and successfully balanced that of the nobility, even surpassing it in the course of the eighteenth century. Thus the survival of the Estates could not be equated with the rule of the nobility, as was the case in Mecklenburg and in Poland, and might even have been the case in the Hohenzollern territories. In the constitutional field also there resulted an equilibrium between the prince, the nobility, and the towns. Even the lower classes benefited from this equilibrium in the social and constitutional fields, for serfdom never assumed the rigours which it did in the principalities farther to the north and east. Thus Saxony resembled much more the territories in the south and in the west of Germany than those in the east, in spite of her geographical position and her 'colonial' character.

IV

THE DUCHIES ON THE RHINE

1. *Introduction*

IF Bavaria and Brandenburg, Saxony and Württemberg, in spite of temporary divisions, provide examples of historical continuity which in the end made them the leading principalities of Germany, there was little such continuity on the lower Rhine. Perhaps because this was an area of much older traditions, going back to Roman days, perhaps because its general level of development was much higher than that of southern or eastern Germany, it proved very difficult for one princely family to establish itself on the lower Rhine and to create a large and compact principality. In the south and east the towns, especially those inside the principalities, were small and unimportant; even Leipzig rose to importance comparatively late and did not play an important political part. The political resistance of certain towns, especially those connected with the Hanseatic League, was broken in the fifteenth century by the margraves of Brandenburg and other princes who made their towns obedient and dependent on the ruler; their economic decline and the rise of the nobility sapped their strength.[1] On the lower Rhine, on the other hand, there were many important towns, mainly situated close to the river and its tributaries and benefiting from this great artery of trade. In addition to trade, there were well-established linen, woollen, mining, and metal industries, especially in Westphalia. Situated on vital crossroads of European trade and traffic, the towns early enjoyed great prosperity and maintained close connexions with those of Brabant and Guelders which were their neighbours. The density of urban civilization on the lower Rhine can be illustrated by the fact that in the early eighteenth century more than half the population of Cleves lived in towns.[2]

---

[1] For details see F. L. Carsten, *The Origins of Prussia*, chaps. ix and x.

[2] 44,005 out of 85,988 in 1722 and 38,261 out of 76,255 in 1734: *Acta Borussica, Behördenorganisation*, ii. 2, Berlin, 1922, p. 32; Max Lehmann, *Freiherr vom Stein*, i,

Only a few towns of the area, such as Cologne and Aachen, became Free Imperial Cities. The large majority remained the subjects of a territorial prince, a factor of great importance for the history of the Estates. Within them the towns were able to balance the weight of the nobility whose importance was declining, as it was in the neighbouring Netherlands. The noble estates were comparatively small and scattered, and the income derived from peasant dues and rents was shrinking owing to the rise of prices and the depreciation of the currency. Demesne farming was of small importance, and manorial jurisdiction was unknown. The princes retained the prerogatives and public rights in their own hands and did not sell them to the landlords, as happened in Brandenburg, and to a lesser extent in Bavaria and Saxony. The peasants were participating in the growing prosperity of the area. They were obliged to give dues to their landlords from whom they usually held their farms in the form of a hereditary leasehold, but they were not dependent on them in any other way, because the rights of public authority had not disintegrated. Taxes were levied by the officials of the prince, and not by the landlords. On account of the greater wealth of their small territories the princes also retained other revenues, especially the general tax, the *Schatz*; if this was pawned in certain districts, it was later redeemed, in contrast with Brandenburg where nearly all rights and revenues were sold in course of time, and where as a result the powers of the prince almost disappeared. Yet in the Rhineland too the princely domains were severely reduced through gifts, infeudations, and sales, and their revenues depreciated through the decline in the value of money.[1] This was one of the factors which caused the development of the Estates, for the princes had to rely increasingly on their votes of credit, especially in case of war or internal conflict.

If the lands on the lower Rhine were much favoured by nature, they were also involved in endless political conflicts,

Leipzig, 1902, p. 106, n. 1. In general see: August von Haeften, 'Die landständischen Verhältnisse in Cleve und Mark bis zum Jahre 1641', *Urkunden und Actenstücke zur Geschichte des Kurfürsten Friedrich Wilhelm von Brandenburg*, v, Berlin, 1869, p. 7; Otto Hötzsch, *Stände und Verwaltung von Cleve und Mark in der Zeit von 1666 bis 1697*, Leipzig, 1908, pp. 329–31; Gustav Schmoller, *Preussische Verfassungs-, Verwaltungs- und Finanzgeschichte*, Berlin, 1921, p. 49.

[1] Georg von Below, *Die landständische Verfassung in Jülich und Berg bis zum Jahre 1511*, part ii, Düsseldorf, 1886, pp. 57–58; part iii. 1, Düsseldorf, 1890, pp. 54–55; part iii. 2, 1891, pp. 101–2.

partly resulting from struggles within the ruling families, partly
from the rivalries between different princely houses and their
striving for more power, partly from the great struggles in the
Low Countries. The lower Rhine was more exposed to the
conflicts of the great powers than almost any other region of
Europe—except only Italy. In the fifteenth century these
struggles were connected with the rise and expansion of the
dukes of Burgundy, in the sixteenth with the wars between
Habsburg and Valois, the Counter-Reformation and the Revolt
of the Netherlands, in the seventeenth with the ascendancy of
France and her wars with Spain and the United Provinces: for
all these powers coveted the rich territories on the lower Rhine
for strategical and other reasons. They thus suffered terribly
from war, pillage, and occupation, especially in the later sixteenth
and seventeenth centuries, and their prosperity was sapped. It
proved impossible to defend these open lands which could be
invaded with impunity. The small local princes were quite
unable to defend them, and occupation or garrisoning by a
stronger neighbour only provoked counter-measures by others.
Nor were Cleves and Mark any better protected when they
became part of the Hohenzollern state, for many new burdens
were imposed upon them from Berlin, and in the event of war
the Prussian army could not protect them. The principalities
on the lower Rhine would have been far happier if they had
succeeded in joining the United Provinces with which they had
so much in common, but that they were not permitted to do.

During the high Middle Ages the most important principality
of the area was the archbishopric of Cologne. It occupied a long
stretch of the left bank of the Rhine. Later it expanded to the
right bank and acquired large possessions in Westphalia, and
played a very important part in the affairs of the Empire. The
power of the archbishops was, however, weakened by the rise
of the city of Cologne to the status of a Free Imperial City and
the most important commercial town on the Rhine, and equally
by the rise of several territorial princes who originally were the
liegemen and dependants of the archbishops. On both counts
the archbishops were involved in long-lasting wars and feuds,
in the course of which they had to renounce their claims of
feudal overlordship and lost much territory. In the thirteenth
and fourteenth centuries four counties rose to importance at the

cost of the archbishopric. These were in the north, close to Guelders and connected with it, the county (later duchy) of Cleves on both banks of the Rhine; on the left bank, the county (later duchy) of Jülich dominating the routes between the Rhine and the Meuse; on the right bank opposite Cologne, the county (later duchy) of Berg, and farther to the east the county of Mark. All four were much smaller than many other German principalities, but their dense population, their geographical position, and their wealth enhanced their importance. Their rulers engaged in endless wars with each other, with the archbishops of Cologne, the bishops of Münster, and other princes, and their lands were often divided and subdivided.[1] In 1368, however, the counts of Mark succeeded to Cleves through a marriage with the last count's daughter, and in 1423 Duke Adolf of Berg acquired Jülich, though he was unable to make good his claim to Guelders. Thus Cleves became united with Mark, and Berg with Jülich, a union destined to last for centuries. In 1496 Duke William IV of Jülich and Berg and Duke John II of Cleves and Mark signed a treaty according to which William's daughter was to marry John's son and Jülich and Berg were to be her dowry; a formal hereditary union was concluded between the four principalities. The marriage was celebrated in 1510. When Duke William died in the following year, he was succeeded by Duke John III of Cleves, who also inherited Cleves and Mark on his father's death ten years later. Thus the four principalities were united in one hand and remained so until the death of the last native duke without a male heir in 1609, when they were divided between different claimants.

Even during this period of union the principalities retained their separate administrations, governments, diets, and other institutions. They never became one state, but there was a much closer union between Jülich and Berg on the one hand, and Cleves and Mark on the other. The diets of Jülich and Berg, like those of Cleves and Mark, were usually held in common, although they deliberated separately or were preceded by

[1] Tille, loc. cit. ii. 210, 239–45, 256; Schlesinger, 'Die Territorien am Niederrhein', loc. cit. ii. 467–9, and the literature quoted there. Berg was the largest of the four principalities, with about 2,040 square miles; Jülich had about 1,628, Mark about 911, and Cleves about 868 square miles: a total of less than 5,500 compared with the 15,000 of Brandenburg. There is no general history of the four principalities, nor one of Cleves nor of Jülich.

separate assemblies; in the sixteenth century a common diet of the four principalities was held frequently.[1] Had the union between them lasted longer, they might have grown more closely together, but differences of religion and the permanent partition of 1609 drove them apart, in spite of their common political and economic interests. Thus, what had been the promising beginning of a large and wealthy principality in the most advanced part of Germany came to naught, although the Estates tried to maintain their union and their common interests under the new rulers. Cleves and Mark became a province ruled in the interests of Berlin and remained outsiders in the Prussian state with which they had nothing in common. Jülich and Berg fared no better under the Counts Palatine of Neuburg whose capital was on the Danube, and who later also acquired the Palatinate. Both ruling houses looked at their Rhenish provinces as the providers of revenues and soldiers, but did little to further their development. In spite of this, modern industry began to grow on the lower Rhine, which in the course of the nineteenth century reassumed its great political and economic importance. But that was after the whole region, owing to the decisions of the Congress of Vienna, had become a province of the Prussian state.

II. *The Estates before the Union of 1521*

Estates made their appearance in each of the four principalities in the second half of the fourteenth century. As no documents from that time have survived, we know little about their origin, their constitution, and procedure, although Georg von Below and others have done much painstaking research to unravel this early history.[2] Clearly, the Estates were not yet a well-defined institution with firmly stipulated privileges, nor did they meet regularly. As in other German principalities,

[1] Georg von Below, in *Landtagsakten von Jülich und Berg, 1400–1610*, i, Düsseldorf, 1895, pp. 2–3, 48, 50 and n. 124, 81; von Haeften, loc. cit., pp. 12–13; Tille, loc. cit. ii. 239–42. Two small principalities, Ravensberg and Ravenstein, were linked with the four major ones through personal union, but remained quite separate and did not play an important part in the history of the other four.

[2] See especially von Below, *Die landständische Verfassung in Jülich und Berg bis zum Jahre 1511*, Düsseldorf, 1885–91; Rudolf Schulze, *Die Landstände der Grafschaft Mark bis zum Jahre 1510*, Heidelberg, 1907; von Haeften, loc. cit.; von Below, *Territorium und Stadt*, Munich and Leipzig, 1900.

they were opposed to partitions of the principality, to sales of land and domains, even if they were sold to subjects of the prince, because his impoverishment was bound to lead to demands for taxation which the Estates disliked. In cases of sales of territory and of the conclusion of alliances they began to insist that their consent was required; the second demand was incorporated into a collection of laws made in Berg in the later fourteenth century. At the end of that century a conflict between Duke William III of Berg and his sons, in which he sought the Estates' support, brought them new privileges and a recognition of their right of consenting to transfers of lands, even if they were only pawned. In contrast with most other German principalities, apparently only two Estates, the nobility and the towns, participated regularly in the meetings, but not the clergy. The latter were summoned separately if the prince desired financial aid from them. The same applied to the high nobility, the so-called *Unterherren*, dynastic families which had put themselves under his protection, but whose territories in fact remained outside the principality in question.[1]

As in Bavaria, Hesse, and Saxony, the fifteenth century was the period of many new conflicts and clashes between hostile brothers and other members of the ruling families, for the principle of primogeniture was not recognized until much later. Thus Gerhard, the younger brother of Count Adolf II of Cleves, claimed from him the county of Mark and was supported by its Estates and by the archbishop of Cologne. In 1413 the two brothers concluded an armistice and undertook to summon the Estates of Cleves and Mark to decide their quarrel by arbitration, the first time that the Estates of both principalities took common action against the prince. Three months later peace was concluded. Gerhard only received some small districts, and not the whole county of Mark. As Adolf II had no sons, but only daughters, the Estates of Cleves in 1418 consented that his daughters should succeed him. In Mark, however, only eight knights and the towns assented, the latter after considerable hesitation. In the following year a son was born to Adolf, and a few weeks later Gerhard renewed the war

---

[1] von Below, *Die landständische Verfassung*, ii. 53–54, 69–70, and in *Landtagsakten von Jülich und Berg*, i. 15–17, 95; Schulze, op. cit., pp. 18, 30; Bernhard Schönneshöfer, *Geschichte des Bergischen Landes*, 2nd ed., Elberfeld, 1908, p. 174.

against his brother, supported by the nobility of Mark and the town of Hamm. Six months later the nobility and four towns of Mark concluded a union in favour of armed neutrality and mediation. At the end of 1420 another peace treaty was signed, according to which Gerhard was to have the towns of Duisburg and Hamm for his lifetime, but Adolf's son was to inherit both Cleves and Mark undivided. In 1423, however, the hostilities were renewed. Gerhard was supported by the Estates of Mark and by Cologne and succeeded in conquering Mark. In 1426 the nobility and seven towns of Mark concluded a new union with him and undertook to defend his rights against Adolf. In 1429 they demanded from him that he should reach an agreement with his brother within one month, or they would accept the archbishop of Cologne as their prince. An armistice for six years was concluded in 1430, and a definite peace in 1437. Gerhard received Mark for his lifetime, but before the Estates swore fealty to him he had to recognize their union. Their influence grew very considerably owing to the long-lasting feud in which both brothers needed their help; they met without being summoned and for the first time exercised real political power.[1]

Another factor strengthened the Estates in the fifteenth century: the increasing impecuniousness of the princes, caused above all by the many wars and feuds which they engaged in. In 1446 the clergy, nobility, towns, and freemen of Cleves granted Duke Adolf a general poll-tax for the war against Cologne which began because the town of Soest seceded from the archbishopric and put itself under the protection of Adolf's son John. John, who ruled from 1448 to 1481, was engaged in further wars with Cologne over Soest and over a disputed election to the see of Münster, and supported Charles the Bold of Burgundy against Guelders. Because of his many wars John frequently had to ask his Estates for grants, to make new concessions to them, and to accept their nominees as his councillors. In 1470 the Estates of Mark refused to pay him the general tax he requested. Under his successor, John II, matters became worse. He was educated at the Burgundian court, was knighted by Charles the Bold, his cousin, and took an active part in Charles's many wars and the long struggles over his

[1] Schulze, op. cit., pp. 16–17, 32–44, 98; nos. 2–3, pp. 132–5; von Haeften, loc. cit., p. 5.

inheritance after his death in battle in 1477, especially against Guelders. The Estates of Cleves and Mark were strongly opposed to these many wars which were not in the country's interest, to the lavish court expenditure, the pawning of so many lands, domains, and tolls, and the never-ending demands for money, including sums for the many illegitimate children who earned John the nickname of 'the child-maker'. The towns bitterly complained about 'the incapable government' and declined to pay anything more. In 1484 the towns of Mark on this account refused to obey the summons to the diet. At the diet of 1489 John asked the Estates' advice on how good government could be restored, while the towns of Cleves concluded a new union for the defence of their rights and privileges. The Estates forced him to reorganize the administration, to introduce a strict control of the expenditure and accounts, and to nominate a proper council. As the condition of a grant made in 1486 John had to promise he would rule according to the decisions of his four principal councillors. If he violated his promise, they should retire from the court and government. This promise was repeated at the diet of 1489.[1]

In Jülich and Berg also the duke became more and more dependent on the money grants of the Estates which, from 1440 onwards, voted simultaneously in both duchies. There also the Estates assembled on their own initiative on account of the precarious position of the government, declaring in 1445 that they only did so in the best interests of prince and country. In 1447 the first general tax was levied in Jülich, while Berg made a contribution to the redemption of pawned domains. In 1464. the first common diet of the two duchies met, but the Estates continued to deliberate separately, each in two houses, that of the nobility and that of the towns. All the towns were still represented; as in other principalities, their deputies appeared with instructions which they were not allowed to modify without a reference back to their principals. Further grants were voted in both duchies in 1469, 1478, 1483, and 1496, usually for the redemption of pawned lands. In 1451 Duke Gerhard II

[1] von Haeften, loc. cit., pp. 5–8; Schulze, op. cit., pp. 63–66; no. 15, p. 147; Kurt Schottmüller, *Die Organisation der Centralverwaltung in Kleve-Mark vor der brandenburgischen Besitzergreifung im Jahre 1609*, Leipzig, 1897, pp. 7–8; nos. 1–2, pp. 84–91; Johann Diederich von Steinen, *Westphälische Geschichte*, i, Lemgo, 1797, pp. 407–8; Tille, loc. cit. ii. 241–2.

conceded to the Estates the right of being the guardians of minor dukes, but this remained theoretical. They frequently participated in the conclusion of alliances and of unions with other principalities. In 1475 they only took the oath of allegiance to William IV several days after he had confirmed their privileges and had promised he would not employ any foreigners: if he did so, they need not obey them, and if he did not redress the grievances, they need not serve him until the wrong was righted. Three years later the Estates were granted a passive right of resistance against unjustified tax demands. They also began to exercise influence in the field of foreign policy. When the Emperor Frederick III in 1487 summoned Duke William to render him assistance against the Hungarians, the Estates not only declined to participate, but insisted that William should not do so either. In the endless wars with Guelders he proposed in 1499 to accept the arbitration of Louis XII of France, while John II of Cleves desired William's help against the bishop of Utrecht. Both issues were then submitted to a diet of Jülich and Berg to which the Estates of Cleves also appealed. The diet consented to the proposed measures which were then carried out by Duke William. Thus the Estates of Jülich and Berg in the course of the fifteenth century acquired important privileges and consolidated their position.[1]

In Cleves and Mark John II neglected his promises of 1486 and 1489 and aroused new opposition by his arbitrary and belligerent policy. In 1499 the Estates refused to pay the second instalment of the tax which they had granted to redeem the prisoners taken in the war with Guelders, because it was used for other purposes. Two years later they succeeded in extending their influence into the field of administration, a success which was not paralleled in Jülich and Berg. Eight members of the Estates from Cleves and four from Mark were to be appointed ducal councillors; four of them were always to be present at court and to approve all documents before his signature, and six of them had to consent to all sales and pawnings of lands and

---

[1] von Below, op. cit. ii. 60; iii. 1, pp. 60–64, and in *Landtagsakten von Jülich und Berg*, i. 18, 22, 36–37, 45–48, 58, 65–66, 69, 91, 96, 98–99, 103, 160; J. J. Scotti, *Sammlung der Gesetze und Verordnungen, welche in den ehemaligen Herzogthümern Jülich, Cleve und Berg und in dem vormaligen Grossherzogthum Berg über Gegenstände der Landeshoheit, Verfassung, Verwaltung und Rechtspflege ergangen sind*, Düsseldorf, 1821, i, no. 1, pp. 1–3.

revenues, all appointments and dismissals of officials, and all innovations in matters of taxation. They were to nominate a treasurer (*Generalrentmeister*) who was to receive all the revenues, to be responsible for all expenditure, and to render annual accounts to the prince and his twelve councillors, and the domains were not to be mortgaged any further. In 1505 a committee of the Estates was entrusted with the putting in order of the ducal finances and the supervision of the levying of taxes. They thus acquired strong influence over the administration of taxes granted by them. In 1507 the towns of Mark joined the union which those of Cleves had concluded in 1489. In the following year the towns renewed their union, again sharply criticized the incapable ducal government, and demanded a change as the precondition of further aids. They refused a grant for the never-ending war with Guelders and pledged themselves to establish 'a good government'. As John's son needed the Estates' support to bring about his desired marriage with the daughter of Duke William of Jülich and Berg, he took their side against his father whose finances were in a chaotic state.[1]

Early in 1510 the Estates of Cleves and Mark concluded a new union which Duke John and his son had to confirm solemnly. After negotiations lasting many months the dukes had to consent to a whole list of demands and to issue the demanded *Reversales*, and only then was the desired marriage between John of Cleves and Mary of Jülich and Berg celebrated. In the following year John succeeded his father-in-law as the duke of Jülich and Berg. From 1521 onwards he also ruled as John III over Cleves and Mark. In 1511 he had to promise the Estates of Jülich and Berg that he would not start any war or feud without asking their advice. The Estates equally participated in the marriage treaties between Anne of Cleves and the duke of Guelders and those between Sibyl of Cleves and the electoral prince of Saxony. John was successful, however, in warding off

---

[1] von Haeften, loc. cit., pp. 9–10; Emil Niepmann, *Die ordentlichen direkten Staatssteuern in Cleve und Mark bis zum Ausgang des Mittelalters*, Düsseldorf, 1891, pp. 60–61; Schulze, op. cit., pp. 66, 90, 118–21, 127; no. 30, pp. 165–9: union of the towns of March 1508. The privilege of 1501 is printed in J. J. Scotti, *Sammlung der Gesetze und Verordnungen, welche in dem Herzogthum Cleve und in der Grafschaft Mark über Gegenstände der Landeshoheit, Verfassung, Verwaltung und Rechtspflege ergangen sind*, Düsseldorf, 1826, i, n. 11, pp. 30–33.

the claim of the Jülich nobility that deputies of the Estates should control the financial administration and the expenditure, as their counterparts did in Cleves and Mark. He seems to have conceded this demand in 1513, but ignored it later.[1] He no longer summoned twenty-one towns from Jülich and fourteen from Berg to the diet, as William IV had done, but only four from each duchy, thus making it easier to impose his wishes.[2] In 1517 these deputies requested that the smaller towns should participate, but apparently the small towns themselves did not insist on receiving a summons and gave up their right of being represented without making difficulties.[3] In Cleves about the same time representation became limited to seven towns, and in Mark to six: these 'principal towns' henceforth formed the second Estate.[4] The first Estate was formed by all members of the nobility who fulfilled certain qualifications with regard to their property and their ancestry, which were made more stringent in course of time, so that the number of noblemen entitled to attend gradually declined.[5]

In the early sixteenth century members of the nobility took part in the levying of taxes by ducal officials, but they were appointed and instructed by the government and not by the Estates. There were no standing committees of the Estates, but committees were formed as occasion demanded, and they only met when summoned by the government. The duke retained some influence in the field of financial administration; there was no sharp difference between his chest and that of the Estates, and both were in the hands of the same official. The Estates were disinclined to allow the duke too much say in financial affairs and were animated by a strong distrust of his management of revenue and expenditure. The Estates'

---

[1] von Haeften, loc. cit., pp. 10–12; von Below, in *Landtagsakten von Jülich und Berg*, i. 76–84, 87–90, 128–30; Scotti, Jülich-Berg (1821), i, no. 156, p. 91.

[2] Cf. the summons of 1505 and 1509 with those of 1514 and 1516 in Hans Goldschmidt, 'Landtagsakten von Jülich-Berg, 1400–1610', *Zeitschrift des Bergischen Geschichtsvereins*, xlvi, 1913, nos. 6, 24, 28, pp. 61–62, 78, 83–84. The four towns were: Jülich, Düren, Euskirchen, and Münstereifel in Jülich, and Düsseldorf, Lennep, Ratingen, and Wipperfürth in Berg.

[3] von Below, op. cit. iii. 1, p. 84, and in *Landtagsakten von Jülich und Berg*, i. 21.

[4] These towns were Wesel, Cleves, Calcar, Duisburg, Emmerich, Rees, and Xanten in Cleves; Camen, Hamm, Iserlohn, Lünen, Schwerte, and Unna in Mark.

[5] von Below, 'Zur Entstehung der Rittergüter', *Territorium und Stadt*, pp. 106–7; Hötzsch, op. cit., p. 255, n. 1; cf. below, p. 339.

committees tried to supervise the repartition and collection of taxes as well as the use to which the money was put, and the ducal officials had to render accounts to them of their administration. But it is difficult to say how effective this supervision was. The nobility was exempt from taxation, and the clergy were taxed separately, so that the taxes fell on the burghers and the peasants. In 1513 the towns of Jülich demanded the nobility should participate, but they declined, claiming it was unfair and contrary to custom, and the ducal councillors took their side.[1] This issue was to lead to bitter conflicts in the future, but at that time it seems to have been an isolated instance. The Estates were—and remained—stronger in Cleves and Mark than in Jülich and Berg; but they were not particularly strong, and their influence was to decline during the following period.

III. *The Duchies under one Ruler; the Religious Struggle*

When Duke John II of Cleves died in 1521, he left debts of only 46,700 thalers, in spite of his many wars and the constant complaints of the Estates about his bad administration.[2] Under his successor, John III, matters greatly improved. As he ruled over all four principalities, he possessed much greater resources. Through good government, economies, and a policy of neutrality, his finances recovered. He became less dependent on the Estates and their grants and was able to disregard their unions and the concessions made to them. According to the union of 1496, within each principality only people born in it were to be employed; but John employed officials of Jülich and Berg in Cleves and thus gained greater freedom of movement, although the Estates tried to insist on the observation of their *jus indigenatus*. He moved his court to Jülich and thus diminished the importance of the council which remained in Cleves. Taxes he only requested for the marriages of his daughters and for purposes of the Empire, above all for the wars against the Turks and for the expedition of 1535 against the Anabaptists of Münster, and these the Estates could not refuse. In Jülich and

[1] von Below, *Die landständische Verfassung in Jülich und Berg*, iii. 2, pp. 11, 101, 133–7, 140; Schottmüller, op. cit., p. 73; Schulze, op. cit., pp. 96 and n. 68, 121–3.

[2] Schulze, op. cit., p. 67. At that time there was hardly any difference between the thaler and the guilder; but in later centuries the thaler was equal to 1½ guilders.

Berg this last tax was granted by a committee of eight noblemen and the principal towns, but it was empowered to do so by the diet of the previous year. The towns of Cleves and Mark several times renewed their union of 1508 and decided to meet every year and not to grant any aid to John unless he followed their advice. But the opposition was impotent, because he no longer relied on their grants.[1]

During the long reign of John III's son, William, who ruled from 1539 to 1592, this trend was reversed for several reasons. The long period of peace which the country had enjoyed under John came to an abrupt end. In 1538 William inherited Guelders and occupied the duchy. The Emperor Charles V, however, was determined not to let this part of the Netherlands fall into William's hands and achieved his object in the War of the Guelders' Succession of 1542–3. Düren, Jülich, and other towns were taken by the Imperial troops, and William had to re-nounce all claims to Guelders which became part of the Habs-burg possessions. The debts resulting from the war amounted to 633,000 thalers,[2] and William's position was much weakened. He had to promise to the Emperor that he would not permit the introduction of the Reformation to which he had previously inclined, and this caused friction with the Estates, many of whom were Protestants. Henceforth the religious issue became very important in William's relations with the Estates, especially after the outbreak of the Revolt of the Netherlands and the spread of Calvinism into Cleves. The outbreak of the revolt transformed the whole region into a battleground, and the principalities suffered from violations of their neutrality and the growth of Spanish influence—another issue which strongly affected the relations between the prince and the Estates.

For the War of the Guelders' Succession the Estates of Cleves and Mark in 1542 only granted enough money to maintain some mercenaries for a few months, hoping that peace would be restored soon, and in 1543 another 60,000 guilders. But the nobility refused to contribute anything, although the towns had made this a condition of their grant. The towns renewed their

---

[1] von Haeften, loc. cit. pp. 13–16; von Below, op. cit. iii. 1, pp. 65, 78, 83; Schottmüller, op. cit., p. 12.

[2] von Haeften, loc. cit., pp. 17–19; Schönneshöfer, op. cit., p. 207. In general see Walther Peter Fuchs, loc. cit. ii. 95; Tille, loc. cit. ii. 228.

union of 1508 and decided to meet every year. The nobility
followed suit, elected a permanent committee of four to assert
their privileges, and demanded the exclusion of the ducal
councillors from their discussions and the summoning of all the
signatories of the union to the diet.[1] The nobility of Cleves and
Mark also refused to participate in a tax for the war against the
Turks. After lengthy negotiations they agreed, in 1542 and
1543, to pay a small amount, but not from their own estates,
only from those of their tenants. In 1544 the towns strongly
protested against this, maintaining that under these circumstances their burghers would not contribute. The ducal councillors, however, sided with the nobility so that there was no
change. In 1546 and 1548 the nobility contributed nothing at
all. In Jülich and Berg each Estate appointed two members to
receive this tax, to whom the duke added two appointees of his
own and the clergy two, making a committee of eight in each
duchy. Their duty was to keep the money and to make certain
that it was not spent on a different object.[2]

In 1552 the Estates of Cleves and Mark declined to vote a tax
for defence and asked William to maintain neutrality in case of
a new war in the Empire. The towns granted a tax for the
building of fortifications, but again demanded that the nobility
should participate. William suggested an excise, but the towns
declined because that would deprive them of the revenues from
their own excise duties. William nevertheless began to introduce
the excise, but the opposition was too strong. The Estates
decided that no taxes were to be levied without their common
consent and that accounts were always to be rendered to their
deputies.[3] The Estates of Jülich and Berg refused to elect a
committee, which was to deliberate together with the ducal
councillors and to take decisions without the Estates if anything
urgent or dangerous should occur. They left it to the government to nominate the committee, which then appointed four
noblemen and two urban mayors from each of the two principalities. The committee thus lost all representative character
and its decisions did not bind the Estates. Five years later they

---

[1] von Haeften, loc. cit., pp. 17–18.
[2] Schulze, op. cit., pp. 76–79; *Landtagsakten von Jülich und Berg*, i, nos. 92, 103,
pp. 408–9, 424 (July to Aug. 1542).
[3] von Haeften, loc. cit., pp. 20–21.

again declined to elect new members, whereupon William appointed six noblemen and two mayors from each duchy, while five noblemen and two mayors from each were to repartition the tax to be levied for the war against the Turks. Whereas in Cleves and Mark the attempt to introduce an excise failed, William was more successful in Jülich and Berg. In 1554 their Estates consented to an excise for twelve years on beer and wine, flax, wool and cloth, coal and metals, sheep and horses, corn and seed, which was to be used for the building of fortifications. It seems, however, that the results were unsatisfactory, for as early as 1560 the Estates of Berg granted 5,000 guilders annually for six years on condition that the excise be abolished.[1]

Meanwhile in Cleves and Mark the conflict between the nobility and the towns over the former's contributions continued. In 1554 the nobility again declined to give anything from their own estates, but in 1557 the towns' opposition became so strong that William decided in favour of a noble participation in taxes levied for defence and for the wars against the Turks.[2] The towns began to make their grants for these purposes dependent on the fulfilment of certain conditions. Among these there figured, for the first time in 1558 and again in 1560, the demand for the introduction of the Reformation which had gained a firm foothold in most towns. After the end of the diet of 1563 the Estates of Cleves and Mark petitioned William to establish a 'good Christian order through pious men' with the advice and consent of the Estates, to abolish the prevailing abuses in religion, and to reform the existing order 'which did not accord with God's word'. William, however, replied that he did not intend to separate himself from the general Christian Church.[3] No similar demands were put forward in Jülich and Berg, where Protestantism was not equally strong, but the Estates of Jülich demanded that a diet be summoned regularly every two or three years to redress their grievances. This was rejected by William on the grounds that diets were only held for special and important causes, and that the recent ones had been too lengthy and argumentative and had cost too

---

[1] *Landtagsakten von Jülich und Berg*, i, nos. 213, 234, 249, 254, 271, pp. 660-1, and n. 3, 697-9, 740-1, 750-1, 783 (July 1552 to June 1560).
[2] Schulze, op. cit., pp. 77-78; von Haeften, loc. cit., p. 21.
[3] Ludwig Keller, *Die Gegenreformation in Westfalen und am Niederrhein*, i, Leipzig, 1881, nos. 6, 12, 18-19, pp. 85, 92, 98-99 (Nov. 1558 to Nov. 1563).

much—an opinion he declined to modify when the Estates offered to bear the cost themselves.[1]

About the same time the Estates began to take part in the work of legislation and to wield greater influence in foreign policy. In 1554 William submitted to those of Jülich new regulations for the conduct of lawsuits, which they discussed and accepted. Those of Cleves and Mark followed suit 'to achieve equality'; but the nobility of Berg opposed the proposals, wished their privileges to be safeguarded, and only gave way under pressure.[2] In foreign affairs the Estates strongly favoured a policy of strict neutrality and opposed the joining of any league or alliance. When William in 1569 was invited by Duke Albert V of Bavaria to join the League of Landsberg which had a Catholic flavour, he submitted this to a committee selected from the Estates, but they asked for a diet to discuss the question. William gave way and summoned all the Estates of the four principalities. These voiced their criticisms. The maintenance of peace was a task for the Emperor and the Imperial diet, they argued, and the expense was too great: as their assent was necessary for financial reasons, William accepted their advice.[3] When William's daughters, Mary Eleanora and Anne, were married in 1574—the one to Duke Albert Frederick of Prussia, the other to Philip Louis, Count Palatine of Neuburg, both Protestants—the marriage treaties were read to the Estates because the marriages were also concluded in their interests, so that they would in case of need receive support from the two princely houses. Thereupon the Estates of the four principalities granted the required aids for the two princesses. The town of Jülich expressly instructed its deputies that the nobility should participate in these aids which were not connected with defence and concerned all the Estates.[4] Forty years later the heirs of the two princesses were to divide the principalities between them. For the building of fortifications the

[1] *Landtagsakten von Jülich und Berg*, ii (1907), nos. 8, 11, 14, 25, pp. 27–28, 39–40, 43, 60 (Dec. 1563 to May 1564).

[2] Schönneshöfer, op. cit., pp. 215–16; Schulze, op. cit., pp. 109–10.

[3] *Beiträge zur Geschichte Herzog Albrechts V. und des Landsberger Bundes, 1556–98*, edited by Walter Goetz, Munich, 1898, nos. 456, 562, pp. 560, 700 (Nov. 1569 to May 1570); Keller, op. cit. i, nos. 81, 84–85, 88, pp. 149–53 (Apr. to July 1570); von Haeften, loc. cit., p. 22.

[4] *Landtagsakten von Jülich und Berg*, ii, no. 91, pp. 223–5; von Below, op. cit. iii. 2, no 67, pp. 293–4.

Estates of Jülich and Berg in 1570 granted an excise for eight years, on condition that no further demands would be submitted to them during that time. But the yield was disappointing, amounting on average to no more than about 10,000 guilders a year.[1]

It was not the issue of taxation, however, but that of religion which became more and more prominent in the relations between the prince and the Estates in the later sixteenth century. The dukes were and remained Catholics, although they at times tried to mediate between the hostile groups, and although their foreign policy and their matrimonial alliances had a Protestant flavour. For many years Protestantism could spread in the principalities almost unhindered and win over the majority of the inhabitants. It did not rely on government support, but on its own resources, the congregations electing their preachers and administering their own affairs, and the government did not intervene, showing an amount of toleration virtually unknown elsewhere. From abroad new influences penetrated the principalities and created new problems. Religious refugees from the Netherlands, especially from Liège and Antwerp, introduced Calvinism and its organization. In 1569 Wesel, the leading town of Cleves, forsook Lutheranism and adopted the Calvinist creed, and this example was quickly followed by other towns of the duchy. A synod met as early as 1572 and accepted a Presbyterian system; from that time meetings of the *classis* were held regularly, always at Wesel. The towns eagerly welcomed refugees from the Netherlands. They also benefited commercially from the new-comers, and their cloth industry flourished. William demanded that the refugees be expelled, but the towns ignored his orders. At an assembly of the Cleves towns held in 1570 the mayor of Wesel emphasized that expulsion would be a disadvantage to the towns, and twenty out of twenty-four voted that the orders should be revoked. Two years later an attempt was made to enforce them in one of the four towns which had pronounced in their favour, but even there the attempt had to be abandoned.[2]

---

[1] *Landtagsakten von Jülich und Berg*, ii, nos. 67, 105, pp. 151, 253–5 (June 1570 to Nov. 1577).

[2] Keller, op. cit. ii. 7; iii. 37; Walther Tuckermann, 'Die Lage der Weseler Lutheraner und Katholiken im 17. und 18. Jahrhundert', *Veröffentlichungen des Historischen Vereins für den Niederrhein*, ii, Cologne, 1909, p. 388; Heinrich Kessel,

In opposition to the extreme Protestants, who co-operated with the rebels in the Netherlands, Wesel soon earning the name of 'the mother of the *Gueux*', a Catholic party was formed which looked towards Spain and was inspired by the policy of the Duke of Alva in the Netherlands. To this party belonged leading noblemen and officials, who hoped that William, gravely ill and mentally debile since 1566, would make his son John William co-regent: until the death of his elder brother he had been destined to become a bishop and was a much more devout Catholic than his father. This party secured the appointment of more Catholic officials and began to negotiate only with the Catholics among the Estates, who were strong in Jülich, but weak in the other principalities. Bitter complaints about these methods were raised at the diet of Cleves and Mark in 1573, and repeated in 1574; for in some towns Protestant clergymen were deprived, and the towns asked for succour and redress. The government then promised a 'Christian Reformation', but all that happened were more deprivations and visitations ordered by the ducal councillors. Early in 1575 the Elector Palatine, Frederick III, was informed from Cleves that most towns had to reintroduce the mass fearing that otherwise force would be used. In Cleves only the towns of Wesel and Duisburg were still faithful. The principalities of Mark and Ravensberg were equally steadfast in their opposition to Popery, and many burghers refused to attend mass, so his informant told him.[1]

In 1577 the conflict became sharper. In August the Cleves towns met and demanded that the visitations by ducal commissions should cease. Officially they were directed against forbidden sects, but in reality they had an anti-Protestant character, and in the towns' opinion were 'a kind of Spanish Inquisition'. A few weeks later the diet of Cleves and Mark met at Essen to discuss the levy of a tax for the war against the Turks. To this the nobility and the towns consented, but insisted that their grievances about the visitations and other religious issues be redressed first. If some could not be redressed immediately, a

'Reformation und Gegenreformation im Herzogtum Cleve', *Jahrbuch des Düsseldorfer Geschichtsvereins*, xxx, 1920, pp. 35–42.

[1] von Haeften, loc. cit., pp. 23–26; Kessel, loc. cit., pp. 53–54; Schottmüller, op. cit., p. 24; I. G. Sardemann, 'Der Landtag zu Essen 1577 und die Inquisition', *Zeitschrift des Bergischen Geschichtsvereins*, i, 1863, p. 212; Keller, op. cit. i, no. 188, p. 224.

committee should be appointed and take action within six months, and meanwhile the later instalments of the tax should be withheld. The free exercise of the Augsburg Confession, which was permitted in the Empire, should not be impeded. The Estates decided to remain together until William agreed to the holding of another diet for this purpose, for previous experience showed how many promises were made at the diets and how few were kept, as was shown by the promise of 1573 of 'a Christian Reformation', which had resulted in a 'deformation'. The Estates bound themselves to uphold the Augsburg Confession and solemnly promised to stand by each other, *defensive et non offensive*, to risk their lives if need be and to preserve their union loyally.[1] The Estates of Berg some weeks later also complained about the deprivations of non-Catholics, about the prohibition of German hymns and godly services under severe penalties, and about the refusal of communion in both kinds contrary to previous ducal orders. William, however, replied that the free *exercitium religionis* was only permitted to the Estates of the Empire. Because many of his subjects desired to receive the sacrament *sub utraque*, he had published an edict permitting this and would repeat it, although he preferred a uniform order in the church. He had also permitted the singing of the Lord's Prayer, the Creed, and other Christian hymns in German, but he could not permit different ceremonies to each priest and other irregularities, and those not obeying would be dismissed.[2]

Similar complaints were raised by the Estates of Berg two years later. For the first time they were joined by the nobility of Jülich who criticized the persecutions and expulsions of those desiring communion in both kinds: this, and equally 'the tyrannical and almost Spanish Inquisition', should cease.[3] In 1580 the Estates of Cleves and Mark repeated their religious grievances, but did not make good their threat to withhold supply if they were not redressed. William merely replied that he could not grant the free exercise of religion, while claiming at the same time that he had no intention of aggravating those who adhered to the Augsburg Confession. At the following diet,

[1] Sardemann, loc. cit., pp. 208–13 (report of the mayor of Wesel of Sept. 1577); Kessel, loc. cit., p. 78; von Haeften, loc. cit., pp. 25–26; Keller, op. cit. i, nos. 226–8, pp. 249–52.
[2] *Landtagsakten von Jülich und Berg*, ii, nos. 118–19, pp. 275–6, 281–2 (Nov. 1577).
[3] Ibid., nos. 153–4, pp. 335–6, 346–7 (Nov. 1579).

in 1583, the Estates repeated their demand for the free exercise
of religion, while William's policy remained unchanged. The
Estates were satisfied with a promise that he would in due
course deal with the grievances not yet redressed, and made a
grant of 53,000 thalers, later increased to 60,000, in spite of the
fact that meanwhile the Protestant councillors of the town of
Rees had been removed from office and banished. The Estates,
however, declined to appoint the committee, which William
desired, and declared they were confident that he would not
issue any orders in important affairs without previous consultation with them.[1] Exactly as the Estates of Saxony, they did not
want to leave such decisions to a committee which could be
influenced more easily.

In Jülich, however, William was more successful. At first the
Estates adopted the same attitude: such a committee was contrary to custom, and nobody would be willing to serve on it.
Only four days later they elected nine noblemen and two urban
deputies and empowered them to deliberate and to take action
for the protection and defence of the duchy during the troubles
connected with the archbishopric of Cologne, and to discuss
and settle their grievances, but not to vote any money. They
also granted 33,000 thalers, and even the nobility decided to
participate in this grant. They complained that in religious
matters the promises of 1577 were not kept, but did not insist
on this point. Three months later the Estates of Berg, which had
to be summoned several times before they appeared in sufficient
numbers, again complained that in some places German hymns
and communion in both kinds were still forbidden, that for
some time only Catholics had been appointed to offices, while
in the Empire nobody was allowed to harm the adherents of the
Augsburg Confession in their honour, lives, or possessions. But
they also raised the required sum of 22,000 thalers without
making any difficulties.[2]

This willingness to contribute was no doubt due to the dangers

[1] Keller, op. cit. i, nos. 233, 235–7, 241, 245–6, pp. 255–8, 261–6; *Landtagsakten
von Jülich und Berg*, ii, no. 225a, p. 479; Sardemann, loc. cit., p. 214 (Aug. 1580 to
Sept. 1583).

[2] *Landtagsakten von Jülich und Berg*, ii, nos. 213, 215, 219, 221–2, 239, 258,
pp. 451–3, 464, 469–70, 474–5, 495–6, 532–6; Goldschmidt, loc. cit. xlvi. 51; no. 61,
p. 114 (Aug. 1583 to May 1584). In Jan. 1586 the Estates of Berg renewed their
religious complaints: *Landtagsakten von Jülich und Berg*, ii, no. 284a, p. 568.

threatening the principalities on account of the outbreak of war in their immediate neighbourhood. The warring parties in the Netherlands took scant notice of the duchies' neutrality and used them for provisioning and billeting purposes. Furthermore, at the end of 1582 the archbishop of Cologne, Gebhard Truchsess von Waldburg, adopted the Calvinist faith, declined to give up his see, and tried to introduce Calvinism in the archbishopric. Had Cologne become Protestant, the whole Catholic position on the lower Rhine would be jeopardized. No wonder that determined opposition was rendered, not only by the Pope, Gregory XIII, and the cathedral chapter, but also by Alexander of Parma, the Spanish commander in the Netherlands, and the house of Wittelsbach. Duke Ernest of Bavaria had been the unsuccessful candidate at the election to the archiepiscopal see in 1577 and had to be content with the see of Liège. In 1583 the Pope deposed Gebhard Truchsess, and the chapter which was purged of his adherents elected Duke Ernest as his successor. Bavarian and Spanish troops then invaded the principality and defeated the forces of the deposed archbishop who received little help from the Protestant side, although the war lasted several years. Troops of both sides ravaged Jülich and Berg, which were so close to the archbishopric, and this happened again in 1588 when Bonn was besieged by Spanish forces.[1] At the same time the pro-Spanish and pro-Catholic party was gaining ground at the ducal court, partly on account of Duke William's prolonged mental illness. His son, John William, a staunch Catholic, began to participate in government affairs. The Catholic party obtained another success when in 1585 he got married, despite William's opposition, to the Margravine Jacoba of Baden, a cousin of the Bavarian dukes and a pupil of the Jesuits. Soon John William was engaged in a confidential correspondence with Duke William V of Bavaria and with Alexander of Parma about the affairs of the principalities, especially religion and foreign policy. The ducal government often acceded to Spanish demands and wishes, but was itself deeply split on religious and political grounds.[2]

[1] Friedrich Küch, 'Die Lande Jülich und Berg während der Belagerung von Bonn 1588', *Zeitschrift des Bergischen Geschichtsvereins*, xxx, 1894, pp. 214, 222, 243–52; von Haeften, loc. cit., p. 26; Gustav Wolf, loc. cit. i. 658–9.
[2] Keller, op. cit. ii. 7–8; Schottmüller, op. cit., p. 24; Küch, loc. cit., p. 239.

Against this darkening background the Estates began to press for more effective measures for the defence of the principalities against foreign intervention. In 1586 the Estates of Berg emphasized that alone they were unable to resist this evil and that all the principalities would have to combine; a committee should be elected by each and joint deliberations be held on how the defence could best be organized. These suggestions soon bore fruit. Early in 1587 deputies of the four principalities met at Essen and drafted a 'defence constitution' in the form of a union of the Estates who promised each other mutual help. Deputies of the Estates were to be responsible for musters and recruiting, the selection of officers, the direction of the troops, and the levying and administration of the funds raised. In each principality a director was to be appointed to conduct the current business and to call for help in case of need; the director was entitled to summon the deputies who were to have the right of free assembly. The deputies were to be confirmed in office by the duke, but the committee's composition could only be changed by the Estates who also were to fill the vacancies which might occur. The taxes granted, however, proved insufficient for the maintenance of the mercenaries who were very ill-disciplined and held the country to ransom. The deputies pointed out to the duke that neutrality could only be preserved if his son abstained from all interference and foreign commitments and promised he would always remain neutral. The deputies appointed by the towns of Jülich and Berg strongly criticized the ducal government, the foreign councillors and their partisan advice, the non-recognition of the Augsburg Confession, and the expulsions on religious grounds, while Cleves and Mark enjoyed much greater independence of the government in Düsseldorf. As John William wrote to his Bavarian cousin William V, the Estates, much influenced by sectarian errors, knew that he would live and die a Catholic and stand by the Pope, the Emperor, and the king of Spain. Therefore they petitioned him to maintain neutrality, to dismiss two of his councillors, and not to employ any foreigners. It was obvious, he claimed, that they wanted to remove all Catholics from the court and equally his Jesuit court preacher, and to stop the expulsions of their co-religionists; but he had refused to sign and asked the Pope for support. Two months later John

William reported that the Pope, Sixtus V, had actually written on his behalf to the dukes of Parma and Lorraine, and that the archbishops of Mainz and Trier had promised to assist him if he were attacked, while the duke of Lorraine had expressed his good will.[1]

During the following months the cleavage deepened. According to John William, the Protestant councillors no longer discussed important questions in his presence. His father took his councillors, few of whom were Catholics, with him to the hunt and discussed business there. John William appealed to the Emperor Rudolf to intervene on his behalf. In December 1587 the deputies of the four principalities met again in Düsseldorf and submitted their demands to the government. The duke should maintain neutrality with regard to the struggle in the Netherlands and forgo all alliances, nobody should suffer for his religion, to expedite affairs directors should be elected who would be entitled to summon the Estates in case of need, the committee should be elected at the beginning of the year, and the measures taken for defence should be approved by the government. William, against the wishes of his son, accepted most of these demands, but he rejected that for religious toleration, although it was repeated five times. While he insisted several times that it was his prerogative to summon the Estates, he gave way in the end and permitted their directors to summon them in case of urgency. Cleves and Mark each appointed one director, and Jülich and Berg three each. The committee itself consisted of twelve noblemen and eight urban deputies drawn in equal numbers from each principality. It had the right to recruit soldiers and to take other military measures while the war lasted. Within each principality its members were entitled to meet freely with their directors, but only the duke had the right to summon the full committee. John William protested against all these steps. He suspected the Estates of aiming at becoming masters themselves because they voted and levied their own taxes, of being in league with the Protestant princes and intending to

---

[1] *Landtagsakten von Jülich und Berg*, ii, nos. 321, 361, 363, 405, 410, pp. 608, 661, 666, 731, 736–7; Keller, op. cit. ii, no. 7, pp. 81–82; von Haeften, loc. cit., pp. 28–29; Küch, loc. cit., p. 215; Goldschmidt, loc. cit., no. 67, p. 119 (May 1586 to Sept. 1587).

appeal for their protection, contrary to the constitution of the Empire.[1]

At the beginning of 1588 the Estates of Jülich asked that a diet should be summoned so that counter-measures against the approaching Spanish army could be discussed, and the ducal councillors agreed to the request. The committee of Berg recruited mercenaries and mustered the men of military age, and they wrote to the committee of Mark that they should hold themselves in readiness—all this without informing the duke. John William again protested and asked for the intervention of Imperial ambassadors. In his opinion the Estates were following the example of those in the Netherlands and levying taxes at their pleasure. They intended to resist Spain, but not the Dutch; but because they knew of his good contacts with Alexander of Parma, they were adopting a more cautious attitude; their fortunes, he hoped, would decline with those of their associates in France and the Netherlands.[2] The Estates were certainly strong enough to flout his orders. In 1586 he ordered the town of Wesel to dismiss its Calvinist preachers and to replace them by Catholics, but resistance was so vigorous that the order could not be enforced. The great weakness of the Estates, however, was their own disunity. A minority, especially the nobility of Jülich, was Catholic and pro-Habsburg. The majority were Protestants, but divided between Calvinists who were strong in Cleves and outspokenly pro-Dutch, and the more cautious Lutherans who were fairly numerous in Berg and Mark.[3]

In Jülich, moreover, the old conflict between the nobility and the towns over the former's participation in taxes broke out anew in 1587. The towns strongly objected to the exemption of the noble sees and houses from the tax levied by the Estates for defence, as the public weal had priority over all privileges, but they were unable to obtain their point. Against this decision

[1] Keller, op. cit. ii, nos. 14, 17, pp. 86–90; *Landtagsakten von Jülich und Berg*, ii, nos. 446, 455, pp. 785–9, 797–802; Scotti, *Cleve-Mark* (1826), i, no. 98, pp. 194–5 (Oct. to Dec. 1587).

[2] Keller, op. cit. ii, no. 20, p. 91; *Landtagsakten von Jülich und Berg*, ii, nos. 460, 480, pp. 810, 834 (Feb. to Mar. 1588).

[3] *Zeitschrift des Bergischen Geschichtsvereins*, ii, 1865, pp. 178–9 (letter to Wesel of 14 Aug. 1586); K. W. Bouterwek, 'Drei Huldigungstage der Stadt Wesel', ibid. ii. 154; Sardemann, loc. cit., p. 214; Johannes Krudewig, 'Der "Lange Landtag" zu Düsseldorf 1591', *Jahrbuch des Düsseldorfer Geschichtsvereins*, xvi, 1902, pp. 10–11.

they appealed to the Imperial High Court, the *Reichskammergericht*, maintaining that the noblemen should at least contribute to taxes raised for defence and in times of emergency. Their case dragged on for centuries and was never decided. Meanwhile most towns of Jülich refused to pay their share of the tax granted, and most country districts followed suit, while the government decided to use force against the recalcitrants. In 1588 the towns of Jülich again insisted that in times of emergency no privileges were valid; while the nobility, emphasizing that they were not obliged to contribute, granted the same tax as the towns from their lands and revenues, but excepted the noble sees with their pertinences. As the towns and clergy strongly protested against the exception, it was eventually limited to one noble see with its pertinences for each family. John William in his turn considered the holding of so many diets disadvantageous and advocated the levying of taxes without a grant of the Estates, which would save much cost, time, and effort and prevent many inconveniences and irregularities, as well as the decline of his father's authority.[1]

In 1588 John William went temporarily mad and at the beginning of 1590 his illness became permanent. Duke William was equally incapable of ruling and died two years later. The government thus was in the hands of the ducal councillors, the majority of whom were pro-Catholic and pro-Spanish. They were supported by the Emperor Rudolf who wanted to gain a foothold on the lower Rhine, so close to the Netherlands. It was clear that John William would not leave a direct heir, and in that case a dispute over the succession to the rich duchies was practically inevitable, especially as the Revolt of the Netherlands had not been suppressed. Duke William had been granted an Imperial privilege that, in the absence of a son, his daughters and their male heirs were entitled to the inheritance. Of his four daughters, however, only the second, Anne, married to the Protestant Count Palatine of Neuburg, had a son, while the husbands of two other daughters were also Protestants. In 1590 three Protestant princes with claims to the inheritance, the Elector of Brandenburg and the Counts Palatine of Neuburg

---

[1] *Landtagsakten von Jülich und Berg*, ii, nos. 381, 383, 387, 407, 434–5, 466–7, 473, 483, 507, 523, 550, pp. 689, 692–3, 704, 734, 767–9, 819–22, 828, 839, 870–2, 891, 919, 945–6 (June 1587 to Apr. 1589).

and Zweibrücken, claimed the guardianship of the mad John William. But their claim was opposed by the Emperor, while the majority of the Estates and the councillors with Protestant sympathies supported it. The others appealed to the Emperor who sent an envoy to collect information and to assist the councillors during the duke's illness. The claimants feared that the Emperor wanted to occupy the principalities and themselves also sent envoys to Düsseldorf. The Estates feared that the councillors might act independently in affairs which concerned them all and requested a diet to be summoned. They then discovered an unexpected ally in the person of John William's wife, the Margravine Jacoba. She hoped to gain for herself the power of which he had been deprived and hated the ruling councillors who excluded her from all influence. In April 1591 she wrote to the Emperor supporting the demand for a diet and thus openly joined his adversaries.[1]

The pressure of the Protestant claimants and of the Estates finally overcame the opposition of the ducal councillors, and in September 1591 a common diet of the four principalities met in Düsseldorf. The Estates desired the confirmation of their privileges and participation in the government. This was opposed by the councillors who wanted to perpetuate their own power, and they were supported by the Catholic Estates of Jülich and the envoys of the Emperor. The Estates demanded that only natives of the principalities be appointed to offices, independent of their religious creed. They blamed the councillors for the dangerous situation that had arisen and the bad financial position, accused them of filling all posts with their favourites and of hindering the spreading of the Gospel. They requested that four representatives of the Estates be associated with the government of Jülich and Berg and with that of Cleves and Mark. The councillors opposed any innovation in religion and the introduction of Protestantism where it had not yet been adopted, but promised they would give official appointments to adherents of both creeds. They were clearly pursuing a defensive policy in the face of the offensive tactics of the Estates who

[1] Schönneshöfer, op. cit., pp. 244–6; von Haeften, loc. cit., pp. 30–33; Krudewig, loc. cit., pp. 9–26; Wolf, loc. cit. i. 669. The Brandenburg claim was at best a very indirect one, for Mary Eleanora of Cleves and Jülich was married to Duke Albert Frederick of Prussia who had no son and therefore would be succeeded by his distant Brandenburg cousins, one of whom his only daughter married later.

were against anything that hindered the progress of Protestantism. Finally the Estates informed the councillors that their
consciences did not allow them to carry on the negotiations and
departed. Then the Imperial envoys issued an order of government which safeguarded the power of the councillors and of the
Emperor and confirmed them in their offices and rights. They
were to decide important matters in conjunction with some
leading members of the Estates and report to the Emperor in
case of disagreement; his assent was required for the filling of
high offices and the summoning of the diet. The Estates protested, as did the Count Palatine of Zweibrücken and the envoys
from Neuburg. In spite of this, the order of government was
promulgated as a provisional guidance for the government under
the signatures of Duke William and the Imperial envoys. The
government remained in Catholic hands; the Estates' attack
had been defeated.[1]

Three weeks later Duke William died and the mad John
William became the reigning duke. His wife, Jacoba, summoned the Estates' committees to Düsseldorf where they declared that the order of government had expired through
William's death and asked her to take over. Jacoba, however,
had to share the government with the ducal councillors who
continued in office, and most of whom were Catholics. She
promised the Emperor and the archbishop of Cologne, Ernest
of Wittelsbach, that the Catholic religion would be maintained,
and instructed the councillors of Cleves to appoint only Catholics
to offices and not to suggest the names of any Protestants. In
Prague, the Imperial capital, however, it was believed that John
William's madness was used to the disadvantage of the Catholics
because Jacoba was supported by the Protestant Estates, so that
her applications did not find a ready ear. Another Imperial
embassy was sent to Düsseldorf and issued a new order of
government which was accepted by both sides.[2] Yet the struggle,
in which so many outside powers were interested for their
own reasons, continued, as did the frequent incursions of the

---

[1] Krudewig, loc. cit., pp. 27–28, 32–33, 37–43, 59–64, 102–3, 112–16, 122–30;
P. Hassel, 'Ein Bericht über den "langen Landtag" zu Düsseldorf 1591', *Zeitschrift
des Bergischen Geschichtsvereins*, v, 1868, pp. 243–5, and n. 2; Schönneshöfer, op. cit.,
pp. 246–7 (Sept. to Dec. 1591).

[2] Schönneshöfer, op. cit., pp. 249–51; Bouterwek, loc. cit., pp. 161, 189; Keller,
op. cit. ii, no. 103, p. 145.

Spanish and Dutch forces. In 1593 the Protestant claimants in lengthy negotiations persuaded the Estates to send a deputation to Prague to petition the Emperor to transfer the guardianship of John William to the claimants. The ducal councillors and the Estates of Jülich declined, but those of Cleves, Berg, and Mark consented, and the claimants promised support for their petition for assistance against the foreign invasions. The councillors and Jacoba protested against the plan, but the Estates proceeded in spite of their opposition. The deputation had no success because the Emperor Rudolf had no intention of strengthening the position of the Protestant claimants and of forgoing the advantages resulting from the unstable conditions in the duchies.[1]

Jacoba, however, found it difficult to manœuvre between the party of the Protestant Estates and that of the Catholics, for both distrusted her. The Catholics planned to dissolve the marriage of the mad John William, to remarry him, and to free him from his virtual imprisonment. At the diet of Jülich and Berg held early in 1595 the Estates demanded his personal appearance, the Protestant leaders siding with Jacoba's enemies. One of them, Schenkern von Waldenberg, whose attitude was pro-Spanish, organized a coup, occupied the town and castle of Jülich, seized Jacoba's papers, and put her under strict surveillance. This was confirmed by the Emperor who revoked the order of government of 1592 and promulgated a new one which excluded Jacoba from the government, removed her adherents, and declared her actions null and void. The power of the ducal councillors was restored. In Cleves the Estates assembled contrary to Imperial orders and protested against the new order of government. They dismissed their director of defence, who was an Imperial councillor, and elected a new one. But the ducal councillors took legal proceedings against him and the Estates' deputies. He had to flee to escape arrest, and the castles were occupied by ducal troops. The Estates were disunited and intimidated. Only in Cleves and Mark did their influence remain strong, for the government in Düsseldorf was too weak to make its will felt throughout the duchies and was short of

---

[1] Hans Goldschmidt, 'Reise der ständischen Gesandten von Kleve, Berg und Mark an den kaiserlichen Hof nach Prag im Jahr 1593', *Zeitschrift des Bergischen Geschichtsvereins*, xlii, 1909, pp. 95–96; von Haeften, loc. cit., pp. 35–36.

money.[1] In 1596 it published a decree forbidding the *conventicula* of the Estates and their meetings behind the government's back, which they used for secret discussions and to its disadvantage. The towns of Cleves replied that they were entitled to meet to discuss their grievances and asked that their privileges be respected, for the distress was so great that they had to meet. The towns of Mark reacted even more sharply and asked to be spared such mandates which they would not obey. In Cleves and Mark, in contrast with Jülich and Berg, there was no pro-government group and very few Catholic officials on whom the government might rely.[2] The towns were in practice small republics, regulating their own affairs and looking abroad for protection and support.

During the following years matters went from bad to worse. The Margravine Jacoba was put on trial for alleged adultery and sorcery, mainly owing to the efforts of her sister-in-law, Sibyl, but she died before the trial was concluded—as it was believed through foul play. Jacoba's enemies also fell from power some years later, for in 1599 the mad John William married again. His second wife, the Duchess Antoinette of Lorraine, resented the power of the councillors who ruled in his name, and succeeded in ousting them and in becoming herself the regent. Schenkern von Waldenberg fled abroad. Meanwhile Cleves was occupied by large Spanish forces which looted the country and committed many atrocities against the Protestant inhabitants. The government was powerless and hampered by intrigues and corruption. The finances were in a chaotic state. The country was exhausted and at the mercy of the foreign armies which continued to march at will through the principalities.[3] At the diet of 1598 the nobility of Cleves and Mark declined to consider the government's proposition until the free exercise of religion was conceded, as it allegedly existed in all the principalities of the Empire. The ducal councillors believed that, if this were conceded, the towns next year would think that everything was permitted and would always claim that their

[1] Schönneshöfer, op. cit., pp. 251–3; von Haeften, loc. cit., pp. 37–38.

[2] Scotti, Cleve-Mark (1826), i, no. 106, pp. 207–8; Keller, op. cit. ii, nos. 168–9, pp. 190–1; Kessel, loc. cit., p. 79 (June to Aug. 1596).

[3] Schönneshöfer, op. cit., pp. 253–7, 259; von Haeften, loc. cit., pp. 39–40. When John William died in 1609, he left debts amounting to 836,665 thalers: Schottmüller, op. cit., p. 66, n. 1. Cf. above, p. 269, for the small debts of 1521.

consciences urged them to do things, and in the end the duke would be without any power: as Duke William had never promised the free exercise of religion, they should not demand it now. The Estates, however, pressed for a reply on the religious issue and complained about the edict against their *conventicula*. But the government insisted that they were not entitled to meet without a summons and persevered.[1]

At their following meeting, in 1601, the Estates' deputies once more raised both points and declared they could not rest content with the declaration of 1598, because they possessed freedom of religion and conscience according to the constitution of the Empire, and because Duke William had 'never molested anyone in his conscience'. At the diet of 1603 they again requested that the *status quo* be preserved and declined to forgo the right of exercising their religion in public. In 1605 the government tried to prevent a meeting of the Estates' deputies summoned without its knowledge, which in its opinion was contrary to the Emperor's decrees. But the towns insisted that they were entitled to meet freely and protested against this interference with an old privilege. In the following year the government informed the Estates' deputies that it would not disturb people in their Christian consciences, nor the adherents of the Augsburg Confession as long as they remained quiet and gave no offence, but that the innovations recently introduced in many towns of Cleves and Mark had to be abolished forthwith. As this was clearly aimed at the Calvinists, the deputies refused to obey and departed without waiting for a discussion of their grievances.[2] By 1600 Wesel, the leading town of Cleves, and most places in its neighbourhood were almost entirely Calvinist. At Wesel there were only a few Lutheran families, and their members were treated as citizens with minor rights, having to pay a special due and being excluded from offices and the right of voting. In 1610 the first General Synod of the Reformed Churches of Jülich, Cleves, and Berg was held and attended by thirty-four deputies of the Provincial Synods from each principality. The General Synod was to meet every

[1] Keller, op. cit. ii, nos. 182–3, pp. 203–6; Scotti, Cleve-Mark (1826), i. 209 (Aug. 1598).

[2] Keller, op. cit. ii, nos. 215–18, 224–6, 235–7, 242–5, pp. 232–5, 242–4, 252–3, 257–8, and n. 1; Scotti, Cleve-Mark (1826), i. 209.

three years; all lower organs were obliged to execute its decisions, and a standing committee was set up which was entitled
to investigate the state of each congregation. In the following
year the Synod of Mark decided to join the General Synod of
Cleves and Jülich. Thus a new authority, independent of the
power of the state, was established for wide regions of the lower
Rhine across the existing political frontiers.[1]

When John William finally died in May 1609, the principalities were in a state of semi-anarchy, their prosperity was
gravely impaired, and the problem of the succession was
entirely unsolved. A stronger ruling house might have created
a powerful state on the lower Rhine, a focus of stability in the
direct neighbourhood of the United Provinces, whose *de facto*
independence was recognized by Spain in the same year that
saw the end of political unity among the principalities. A
struggle for the succession was bound to occur, in the outcome
of which not only the claimants, but the Habsburgs, Spain,
France, and the Dutch would be deeply interested. The period
of uncertainty, strife, and weak government had strengthened
the power of the Estates, especially in Cleves and Mark. Their
deputies were responsible for measures of defence and for the
levy of taxes. These were paid into the Estates' chest, the
Pfennigmeistereikasse, which was in the charge of the *Pfennigmeister*, one of whom was appointed by the Estates of each
principality. Another official of the Estates was the *Syndicus*,
a councillor and secretary, also one to each of the principalities.[2] The Estates were, however, deeply divided by religion
and different foreign sympathies, and to a lesser extent by the
cleavage between the nobility and the towns. The economic
prosperity of the region was jeopardized by political instability
and the long-drawn-out wars which affected the area many
years before the outbreak of the Thirty Years War. It remained
to be seen how the Estates would fare under new and foreign
princes and during continuing wars and conflicts.

[1] Tuckermann, loc. cit., pp. 388–90, 393; Kessel, loc. cit., p. 158; Keller, op. cit.
iii. 39–41; nos. 105–6, pp. 172–81; p. 185, n. 1.
[2] Ernst Baumgarten, 'Der Kampf des Pfalzgrafen Philipp Wilhelm mit den
jülich-bergischen Ständen von 1669 bis 1672', *Jahrbuch des Düsseldorfer Geschichtsvereins*, xviii, 1903, pp. 32–33.

IV. *The Great Conflicts between the Estates and their new Rulers*

Already before the death of John William, the last native duke, the Estates of the four principalities took steps to preserve their old unions and their other privileges under his successors. They feared an open breach between the chief claimants, the Elector John Sigismund of Brandenburg, the husband of Anne of Prussia (the daughter of Mary Eleanora of Cleves), and the Count Palatine Wolfgang William of Neuburg, the son of Anne of Cleves (Duke William's second daughter). Both claimants were Protestants, but both wanted the whole inheritance. Their mutual jealousies played into the hands of the Emperor Rudolf who wanted to sequester the duchies and to appoint meanwhile a Habsburg administrator. The Estates met in April 1609, decided not to opt for either prince, nor to let the duchies pass into anyone's hands without the consent of all the Estates, and advocated a speedy agreement between the claimants. The Estates renewed their old union and bound themselves to resist jointly any attempt to use force and any foreign intervention, although many noblemen did not assent and left the diet. The Estates of Jülich and Berg decided to recruit troops so as to preserve the country for the legitimate ruler. In Mark all but a minority of Catholics were in favour of Brandenburg, and so apparently was the town of Wesel in Cleves. Everywhere the burghers were on their guard against a sudden coup. The ducal councillors negotiated with the Count Palatine of Neuburg, but the Estates declined to treat with them unless they undertook to stand by the Estates, which they eventually promised.[1]

After John William's death in May 1609 an agreement was concluded between the two Protestant claimants through the good services of Landgrave Maurice of Hesse-Cassel, and a provisional common government was formed. Margrave Ernest of Brandenburg (John Sigismund's brother) and Wolfgang William together confirmed all the privileges of the Estates, promised to redress their grievances and to maintain their unions and the free exercise of religion; if a conflict should arise between the two princes, the Estates were to be absolved from their promise of fealty. This promise was rendered by the Estates

[1] von Haeften, loc. cit., p. 41; Keller, op. cit. iii, nos. 5, 6, 14, 19, pp. 96–98, 103–4, 110 (reports to Landgrave Maurice of Hesse, Apr. and May 1609).

of Cleves and Mark, only six noblemen refusing. In Berg the towns were in favour, but the nobility was evenly divided, and the princes then declared this to be a majority decision. In Jülich, however, only twenty-two noblemen were in favour and rendered the required promise against the opposition of the majority. The Emperor Rudolf intervened and forbade the establishment of the provisional government. The Estates began to waver and declined to obey a new summons by the claimants. In spite of Imperial mandates, which were posted throughout the country, the towns of Jülich joined the other Estates. But the fortress of Jülich was occupied by Catholics acting in the name of the Emperor, and a counter-government was formed there under an administrator sent by him, the Archduke Leopold of Habsburg, who appealed for help to the three ecclesiastical electors and to the governor of the Netherlands, the Archduke Albert. On the opposite side, the Protestant Union, including the Palatinate and Württemberg, made military preparations, and so did Henry IV of France. Troops of France and the Union marched into Jülich and defeated the forces of the Imperial administrator, the Archduke Leopold. The outbreak of a general war was only avoided because Henry IV was murdered in May 1610, and because the Twelve Years' Truce had just been concluded in the Netherlands, resulting in the partition between the north and the south. The troops recruited by the Estates proved quite insufficient and very ill-disciplined; they used force to extract their maintenance from the inhabitants, and Jülich in particular suffered from their extortions.[1]

Thus Brandenburg and Palatinate-Neuburg were left in the possession of the duchies, hence called the *possidentes*. In 1610 the Estates of Jülich and Berg granted them an excise for six years and a considerable direct tax. Those of Cleves and Mark, however, proved much more difficult, mainly because the princes, terribly short of funds, imposed a duty on all goods passing through the principalities or imported into them, whether by land or water, which severely damaged the trade

---

[1] Keller, op. cit. iii. 22; nos. 56–59, 64, 66, 70, pp. 140–4, 148–9, 151 (reports to Landgrave Maurice of July and Aug. 1609); von Haeften, loc. cit., pp. 42–43; Schönneshöfer, op. cit., pp. 266–8; Gustav Wolf, loc. cit. i. 670; Hans Goldschmidt, 'Kriegsleiden am Niederrhein im Jahre 1610', *Zeitschrift des Bergischen Geschichtsvereins*, xlv, 1912, pp. 143 ff., with many details of the war damages.

on the Rhine. Soldiers supervised the levy from boats anchored in the river. The Estates demanded that a common diet of all the principalities be summoned, the princes that they should furnish the means for an army of 3,800 men. The diet met, but produced no result; for the Estates of Cleves, the principal sufferers from the new duty, demanded its control by a committee of the Estates, while those of Jülich were more conciliatory. When their demand was not granted, the Estates of Cleves and Mark left the diet, followed by others, in spite of the prohibition of the princes. Those of Jülich and Berg returned later and voted some money to pay off the troops, but its levy proved very difficult on account of the war damages. The Estates of Cleves and Mark, on the other hand, raised their grievances and claimed that the princes had no right to issue orders to their two *Pfennigmeister*, to assume control of taxation, and to introduce new duties. In 1612 they granted some money and consented to the continuation of the new duty on goods transported by water, but under the control of a mixed committee on which they were represented. The princes had to agree to the discontinuation of the duty on goods transported over land and to dismiss the officials in charge. In spite of this concession, the towns of Cleves refused to obey the summons to the diet. A few months later the new duty on goods shipped on the Rhine also had to be rescinded, because of protests of the Rhenish Electors. The princes' attempt to by-pass the Estates had come to naught.[1]

Meanwhile in Cleves the old conflict between the nobility and the towns over the repartition of taxes broke out anew. The towns considered their quota too high and protested, with the result that it was reduced from one-fifth to one-sixth of the total, a very small part considering their wealth and their population. The nobility did not oppose the new duty, but declined to contribute anything itself, which caused new protests by the towns. The Estates of Cleves and Mark were strongly in favour of the Protestant claimants and intervened on their behalf with the Emperor. But the friction between the *possidentes* was continually growing, and the Estates tried in vain

[1] Wilhelm Cürten, 'Die Organisation der jülich-klevischen Landesverwaltung vom Beginne des Erbfolgestreites bis zur Abdankung des Markgrafen Ernst (1609–13)', *Jahrbuch des Düsseldorfer Geschichtsvereins*, xxiv, 1912, pp. 254–61; Friedrich Küch, introduction to *Landtagsakten von Jülich-Berg, 1624–53*, i, Düsseldorf, 1925, pp. ii–ix; von Haeften, loc. cit., p. 45.

to mediate between them. Their antagonism grew considerably when at the end of 1613 John Sigismund of Brandenburg became a Calvinist, while some months later Wolfgang William married the sister of Duke Maximilian of Bavaria, the leader of the Catholic League, and himself became a Catholic. When war seemed imminent, the Estates intervened and threatened to renounce their allegiance. Yet both sides continued to arm. In May 1614 the United Provinces occupied the town of Jülich, and Wolfgang William the town of Düsseldorf. In his name Spanish forces seized many fortified places, while John Sigismund appealed for aid to the Dutch who furnished him with troops and money. The conversion of the two princes dramatically changed the situation and drove the Dutch and many of the Estates onto the side of Brandenburg whose ruler had become their co-religionist, while the Habsburgs now supported Wolfgang William. Once more a general war was narrowly avoided through negotiations in which the Estates actively participated. In November 1614 the two princes concluded the treaty of Xanten, by which they provisionally partitioned the principalities, Brandenburg receiving Cleves and Mark, and Neuburg the much larger Jülich and Berg. The treaty was also signed by the Estates and guaranteed by the United Provinces; it confirmed the privileges of the Estates and promised them that their grievances would be redressed and that neither Catholics nor Protestants would suffer for their religion.[1]

In spite of this promise, Protestant officials were soon dismissed in Jülich and Berg, and Catholic ones in Cleves and Mark. The power of the Estates was weakened by the partition. Although they tried to uphold their unions and privileges, they were less able to play off one prince against the other. They had been almost co-regents and courted by all sides, but now both princes tried to curtail their influence and to rule without them. No proper diet was summoned for several years. The Brandenburg government of Cleves and Mark attempted to prevent the unauthorized meetings of the Estates and to insist that it be

---

[1] von Haeften, loc. cit., pp. 45–49; Küch, loc. cit., pp. xiii–xviii; Keller, op. cit. iii. 63; Baumgarten, loc. cit. xviii. 37. Jülich and Berg were more than twice the size of Cleves and Mark, about 3,668 compared with 1,780 square miles, but Cleves was the most developed and most prosperous part.

notified of the agenda and its consent be obtained first. But the government was weak and without funds, for the Estates made no grants. In 1616 the revenues and domains were pawned to the Dutch for a loan of 100,000 thalers, the repayment of which was to cause enormous difficulties, and the remaining soldiers were taken into Dutch pay. In spite of the prohibition of the government the Estates of Cleves planned to send envoys to Brussels, The Hague, &c., to obtain the execution of the treaty of Xanten, a matter which the government considered to be outside their competence. The diet of 1620, however, only voted money on condition that the envoys were sent and that Spain and the United Provinces agreed to evacuate the towns and to recognize the country's neutrality. The Estates of Jülich and Berg tried to achieve the same end through envoys of their own, but the towns nevertheless remained occupied by foreign garrisons.[1]

Meanwhile the Thirty Years War had broken out, which on the lower Rhine turned into a continuation of the struggle between Spain and the United Provinces, during which both sides were vitally interested in the possession of the duchies. Against the military might of the two great powers the distant rulers in Berlin and Neuburg had little chance of asserting their rights. In 1621 the Spaniards took Jülich, invaded Cleves and Mark and devastated the country. The Elector George William of Brandenburg had no choice but to accept the conditions of the United Provinces whose troops then occupied most of Cleves. They were the real masters, levied heavy contributions for many years, imposed new duties and an excise on trade, declined to summon a diet, and forbade all meetings of the Estates. As these refused to pay the sums demanded from them, they were collected by military force. With the progress of the war matters became even worse. The princes' own forces, maintained at great cost, were incapable of protecting the inhabitants and only added to the heavy burdens which they had to bear. The contributions decreed by the foreign powers were levied by brute force; their soldiers squeezed the population, organized looting expeditions, and got involved in fighting

[1] von Haeften, loc. cit., pp. 49–52; Küch, loc. cit., pp. xxi–xxiv; Scotti, Cleve-Mark (1826), i, nos. 162, 166, pp. 237–9 (decrees of 1615 and 1618); similarly no. 173, pp. 244–5 (1623).

with the desperate inhabitants. These methods were soon copied by the two rulers. They also levied taxes without any consultation with the Estates and used military force to collect the money if it was not forthcoming. They insisted that they were entitled in cases of emergency to decree taxes and to increase existing ones by virtue of their prerogative. They negotiated with committees summoned *ad hoc*, and not with the diet. They violated one of the Estates' most cherished privileges, the *jus indigenatus* (confining official appointments to natives of the principality in question), by using officials from Brandenburg and Neuburg respectively, who took no account of the desires of the Estates and had no links with them. They forbade the Estates to busy themselves with matters of high policy and to correspond with foreign powers.[1]

At the diet of Jülich and Berg of 1624 Wolfgang William suggested the appointment of a small and a large committee composed of councillors, officials, and members of the Estates, so that he would be able to negotiate with the committees, but the Estates insisted that this was contrary to custom. He instructed the Estates not to accept any letter from the Elector of Brandenburg in future, but to hand to him any that might reach them. The Estates, instead of replying to his proposition, demanded the redress of their grievances, especially that concerning the employment of foreign officials, and the confirmation of their privileges. They also objected to voting in their ruler's presence, while in his opinion it was shameful that nothing had been settled within a fortnight. The Estates then granted an aid of 60,000 thalers, and the nobility also an excise, but the towns opposed it on the grounds that goods would by-pass the country and the revenue from customs would decline. In spite of this, the excise was introduced for twelve months, to be levied on wine, beer, cattle, and goods, whether exported or passing through, or merely sent from one principality into the other. If the yield were satisfactory, it was to be continued, but the produce of the nobility was exempted. Early in 1625,

---

[1] von Haeften, loc. cit., pp. 53–56; Küch, loc. cit., pp. 2–4; Hans Fahrmbacher, 'Vorgeschichte und Anfänge der kurpfälzischen Armee in Jülich-Berg, 1609–85', *Zeitschrift des Bergischen Geschichtsvereins*, xlii, 1909, pp. 41–42; K. Spannagel, 'Die Grafschaft Mark als Teil des brandenburgisch-preussischen Staates', *Die Grafschaft Mark*, edited by A. Meister, Dortmund, 1909, i. 32; Schönneshöfer, op. cit., pp. 278–81.

moreover, the government decreed a tax to be levied, claiming that it was impossible to convene all the Estates at that time. The towns protested against this procedure and refused to repartition the tax, which was levied nevertheless.[1]

More protests were raised at the following diet. But the unity between the Estates was broken, for the towns insisted that the noble estates should contribute, whereupon the nobility declined to have any further communication with the towns. Wolfgang William reproached the Estates for accepting and opening a letter from the Elector of Brandenburg, in spite of his earlier prohibition, and dismissed their two *directores* and *syndici* from their offices. The Estates petitioned that they be reappointed, and this was conceded, after they and the Estates had kissed the hands of their prince and vowed obedience to him. Shortly after, however, the director of the Jülich nobility was again dismissed because he declined to recognize the version of the last *Recess*, which differed from the protocol and the agreement reached at the end of the diet. The nobility then refused to appear without their director, and Wolfgang William had to give way. The towns of Berg offered 30,000 thalers if the excise were rescinded, but he insisted on its continuation. At the end of the diet the Estates protested against the version of the *Recess*, which was merely read to them and was contrary to the decisions reached and the protocol, and equally against the voting in Wolfgang William's presence. The *Recess* stipulated a grant of 70,000 thalers, and another of 40,000 as an equivalent for the excise which he promised to rescind. The Estates decided to appeal to the Emperor Ferdinand II and to the Aulic Council. The nobility of Jülich and Berg and the towns of Jülich did so in 1626, petitioning for a *poenale mandatum inhibitorium* against the levying of taxes by decree; for Wolfgang William decreed the levy of another 120,000 thalers and planned to reintroduce the excise.[2]

At the beginning of 1627 the Emperor issued the desired mandate of inhibition, but revoked it two months later, on condition that Wolfgang William would promise to maintain

---

[1] *Landtagsakten von Jülich-Berg 1624–53*, edited by F. Küch, i, Düsseldorf, 1925, nos. 2, 3, 33, 40, 47, 66, 68, pp. 13–33, 36, 69–70, 75–76, 82–95, 113–14 (Mar. 1624 to May 1625).

[2] Ibid., nos. 76, 133–6, 141–4, 152–5, pp. 122–30, 144, 148–52, 162, n. 1, 218–26, 236–8 (Aug. 1625 to Nov. 1626).

the Estates' privileges. The Estates several times renewed their applications to the Emperor and declined to make any grants, whereupon the government continued to levy taxes by decree. The Estates then sent envoys to Prague, and in 1628 were successful in obtaining a letter of protection from Ferdinand which forbade the government to impose any burdens contrary to the terms of the letter or to punish the Estates for appealing to the Aulic Council. They formulated their complaint in detail, but the towns of Berg and the town of Jülich (but not the other towns of the duchy) dissociated themselves from it, claiming they knew nothing about it, so that it lost much of its efficacy. The Estates no longer trusted Wolfgang William and relied on the protection of the Emperor, for their prince was unable to coerce them; and Tilly, the general of the Catholic League, who was charged with the execution of the Imperial orders, took no notice of him. At the opening of the diet of 1628 the Estates renewed their old union of 1451 and 1452. The towns of Berg at first hesitated to sign, but finally did so. The Estates undertook to stand by each other and not to separate, nor to make any grant before their grievances were redressed *realiter et effective*; whatever was consented to contrary to the terms of the union was to be null and void. Wolfgang William demanded that his proposition and their grievances be discussed and settled simultaneously, but they declined and threatened him with another appeal to the Emperor. They strongly protested when weeks passed and their grievances remained undecided, and again announced they would proceed with their appeal to the Aulic Council.[1]

Early in 1629 Wolfgang William declared that the Estates' union had to be repealed, otherwise everything that had been settled would be null and void. They declined to obey, however, and asked for their dismissal, whereupon he desisted. The Estates demanded the restoration of their right of free meeting and of their power of the purse, the refunding of the money levied without their consent, the use of the taxes for the purposes they were voted for, the acknowledgement of their right of

[1] *Landtagsakten von Jülich Berg 1624–53*, i, nos. 158, 162–3, 185, 200, 214–15, 224, 233, 236, 244–5, 262–3, 267, 283, 286, 309, 325, 327, 345, 367, pp. 239, 241–2, 252–3, 259, 268–75, 280–4, 290, 303–11, 321–5, 345, 360–76, 426–8, 451, 473–4; Baumgarten, loc. cit. xviii. 38–39; Schönneshöfer, op. cit., pp. 281–2 (Jan. 1627 to Nov. 1628).

refusing supply without incurring the prince's displeasure, the annulment of the *Recesse* of 1624 and 1625 which they could not recognize as valid, an assurance that in future the draft of a *Recess* would be submitted to them before promulgation for their approval, and the dismissal of all foreign councillors and officials. Orders for the dismissal of these were indeed issued, and some further assurances were given. After six months the Estates of Jülich eventually voted 150,000 thalers, and those of Berg 90,000, sums which were to include the costs of their appeal to the Aulic Council. But Wolfgang William declared this to be insufficient, for it would not even last for six months. The Estates instructed their two *Pfennigmeister* not to pay out any money without their written orders, except for certain military purposes in case of urgency. They also protested that everything which had been agreed on required the Emperor's confirmation, a stipulation omitted from the *Recess*: a point which they repeated in October 1629. In the opinion of the governor of Jülich and Berg, their leaders aimed at the sequestration of the principalities by the Emperor and at assuming the leadership of the government which would then be formed; in his opinion, they opposed any measures of defence so that they could complain in Vienna if the United Provinces or Brandenburg made any move. Despite the government's opposition the Estates again decided in 1630 to send envoys to the Emperor, to his generalissimo Wallenstein, and to the assembly of the Electors at Ratisbon to voice their wishes and complaints.[1]

The Estates of Cleves and Mark in 1629 also concluded a new union, simultaneously with those of Jülich and Berg. Their wrath was aroused by the governor appointed from Berlin, Count Schwartzenberg, the favourite of the Elector George William, for he disregarded their privileges, vigorously resisted their attempts at independence, and was obnoxious to them as a foreigner and a Catholic. In the eyes of the Estates Schwartzenberg was responsible for all the taxes levied by force and for all the military violence from which the country suffered. In June 1630 the Estates informed the Elector that they also would have to appeal to the Emperor unless there was a change of policy.

[1] *Landtagsakten von Jülich-Berg 1624–53*, i, nos. 325, 330, 407–8, 414–16, 418, 434, 443, 449, 451, 463–4, 479, pp. 398–9, 432–9, 530–4, 548–50, 552, 556–7, 571–2, 582, 599, 602, n. 1, 603, 629–30, 633, n. 2, 641–2 (Oct. 1628 to July 1630).

At the diet of 1631 they declined to debate the proposition before their grievances were redressed and refused to negotiate further with Schwartzenberg; they then left the diet and held their own free convention at Xanten. There they undertook to stand by these conditions, and they decided to exclude those holding different opinions from future diets and from participation in their privileges. Yet in the following year the diet granted 100,000 thalers, on condition that the Estates' deputies would take part in the levy and administration of the tax, but less than half the grant was collected. In 1633 the Estates were permitted to send envoys to The Hague to negotiate with the United Provinces the levy of a duty on trade and a guarantee of the neutrality of Cleves on the right bank of the Rhine. The government, however, refused to recognize their right of free assembly: if this was one of their privileges, they should prove it and should notify the government of the purpose of the intended meeting.[1]

When the Swedes and their allies advanced victoriously through Germany, Wolfgang William in 1633 demanded money from the Estates of Jülich and Berg so as to be able to oppose them; but they declined and advised him to conclude an alliance with the Emperor Ferdinand. Three regiments were recruited without their consent, and the sums required for their maintenance levied by decree. The Estates thereupon assembled at Cologne, outside the duchies, countermanded the levy, and renewed their appeal to the Emperor. They claimed that they were entitled to consent to recruiting, to allocate billets to the Imperial troops, and to levy taxes themselves; while Wolfgang William insisted that their privileges were safeguarded because he had summoned them before he started recruiting. The Emperor nevertheless instructed the Count of Mansfeld to prevent the levy of the tax to which the Estates had not assented. In 1635 their complaints were investigated, and Wolfgang William received orders to redress their grievances and to transfer his troops, with the exception of only 900 men, to the Imperial army, according to the terms of the peace of Prague. In spite of his countermands, the colonels with their men marched into the camp of Count Piccolomini, the Imperial

[1] von Haeften, loc. cit., pp. 57–60, 66–70; Spannagel, loc. cit., p. 32; Scotti, Cleve-Mark (1826), i, no. 173, p. 245.

general, the soldiers threatening those officers who intended to remain loyal to Wolfgang William. Ten companies was all that he retained, a negligible force. It remained on the same footing until 1647 when it was increased to 1,773 men; but after the conclusion of peace in 1648 it was again reduced to 900.[1]

In 1636 the Estates of Jülich and Berg renewed their union of 1629, while Wolfgang William in vain petitioned the Emperor to annul their unions. Equally in vain were his efforts to prevent the Estates from meeting and levying their own taxes, rights which the Emperor conceded to them. The Estates in their turn for years refused to obey the summons to the diet, held their own meetings at Cologne, where their documents and reserves were deposited outside their prince's reach, countermanded his orders to pay taxes, negotiated with the commanding officers of the occupying forces and allocated billets to them, in spite of all the penalties which Wolfgang William threatened to inflict upon them. They refused to vote any money before their grievances were redressed, and were backed by the Emperor Ferdinand III, who in October 1638 gave a verdict in their favour. Six months later Wolfgang William summoned a 'Peasants' Diet' of officials and village mayors, who granted all his demands; but its decisions were declared null and void by the Emperor. The local officials, the *Amtleute*, who were members of the nobility, refused to levy taxes to which the Estates had not consented and were dismissed from their offices; but in 1640 the Emperor ordered them to be reinstated. Wolfgang William instructed the *Vögte*, officials who were not members of the Estates, to repartition the taxes directly if the *Amtleute* refused to do so. But the inhabitants would not pay the taxes, and the officials charged with the compulsory levy were driven out of many villages by members of the local militia led by noblemen. In 1641 two Imperial envoys, sent to investigate locally, published a verdict which once more supported the Estates: their privileges were to be observed, taxes were only to be levied with their consent, money levied without it was to be refunded, and princely orders to the contrary need not be obeyed. Philip William, Wolfgang William's son and heir, promised that he

[1] Baumgarten, loc. cit. xviii. 40–41; Fahrmbacher, loc. cit., pp. 42–44; Hegert, 'Einige Actenstücke zur Geschichte des Pfalzgrafen Wolfgang Wilhelm', *Zeitschrift des Bergischen Geschichtsvereins*, v, 1868, pp. 290–2.

would abide loyally by these decisions and would rescind all decrees conflicting with them. But his father pursued a different policy, and the struggle continued unabated during the following years. The Estates held their own meetings as previously and did not appear when summoned.[1] As long as the Emperor supported the Estates, Wolfgang William was powerless.

If Imperial influence was strong in Jülich and Berg, that of the United Provinces, whose troops occupied the country, was paramount in Cleves and Mark. More and more revenues were pawned to Dutch financiers; even the interest on the old debt of 1616 could not be paid regularly, in spite of some grants for that purpose, so that the load grew continuously. Within twenty-five years the Dutch troops levied over 1,500,000 thalers in Cleves.[2] At the diet of 1637 the Estates of Cleves and Mark solemnly protested against the treaty between the Elector and the United Provinces and renewed their union of 1629. They bound themselves to meet at the summons of their own directors or of a principal town as if summoned to a diet, to accept the decisions of the majority, and not to grant anything until all their demands had been met. The towns refused to recognize the tax exemption of the nobility and to pay more than one-sixth of a tax. At the diet of 1639 the towns on the right bank of the Rhine—Wesel, Emmerich, and Rees—declined to pay their share of a levy intended for the creditors of the old debt of 1616. They publicly countermanded the government's orders to pay and forced it to withdraw them, and then concluded a separate union, according to which every town had the right of voting and refusing taxes. A group among the nobility aimed at the appointment of a council of regency which was to be responsible to the Estates and to render accounts to them; they should be entitled to suggest two candidates for each office, one of whom the Elector was to appoint within four weeks for his lifetime. The opposition of the towns and of some noblemen, however, wrecked this proposal which would have given the

---

[1] Scotti, Jülich-Berg (1821), i, nos. 293, 299, 300, 305, 319, 321–3, 326, 335–6, 339, 341, 346, 348, 357–8, 362, 366–8, pp. 96–108; Hegert, loc. cit., pp. 292–4; no. 5, pp. 301–8; no. 7, p. 311; no. 11, pp. 316–18; Baumgarten, loc. cit. xviii. 41–43, 51 (Apr. 1636 to May 1643).

[2] *Urkunden und Actenstücke zur Geschichte des Kurfürsten Friedrich Wilhelm von Brandenburg*, v, Berlin, 1869, p. 137. Cf. *Kort Begrip Waerom Haer Ho. Mo. recht hebben de Cleefsche Steden beset te houden*, 1647, with details of the financial agreements.

nobility complete control of the government.[1] It was only their own disunity which prevented the Estates of Cleves from virtually ousting the weak Brandenburg government, for simultaneously it lost its hold on Brandenburg itself which was occupied by the Swedish army.

The young Elector, Frederick William, who succeeded to the throne at the end of 1640, was unable to remedy this state of affairs for the time being. He had neither time nor money to spare for his far-away Rhenish territories which were controlled by the United Provinces. Only after 1645, when conditions somewhat improved in Brandenburg, was he able to play a more conspicuous part. In 1644 seventeen companies were recruited in Cleves, although all recruiting required the consent of the Estates. In the following year, instead of ordering them to move elsewhere, another five companies of cavalry were brought into Cleves from Brandenburg. The Estates were threatened that, unless they voted money for their maintenance, the troops would be billeted on the burghers and peasants and taxes would be levied by military force. In 1646 these threats were carried out, but the Estates took vigorous countermeasures. They met and decided to countermand these orders and to exhort the inhabitants not to pay the taxes. When army officers attempted to collect them by force and to seize cattle and goods they met with the resistance of the Dutch garrisons which supported the Estates. These appealed to the United Provinces which took their side and instructed their commandants to prevent the forcible levying by Brandenburg soldiers.[2] Nor was Frederick William more successful when, on account of continuing friction with Wolfgang William of Neuburg, he used his troops for an attack on the duchy of Berg. The venture found no support. At the beginning of 1647 the Estates of the four principalities—Jülich, Cleves, Berg, and Mark—met at Cologne, renewed their hereditary union of 1496 and undertook to defend their privileges, to help each other,

[1] von Haeften, loc. cit., pp. 70, 76–77, 80–81.
[2] The States General to Frederick William on 12 Sept. 1646: in *Refutatie in name ende van wegen de Land-Stenden uyt Ridderschap ende Steden des Hertogdoms Cleve*, The Hague, 1647, pp. 11–13; *Urkunden und Actenstücke*, v. 219, 283, 285, 287, 291, 299, 303–4 (July 1644 to Oct. 1646). The States General claimed the right of intervention in the principalities as the guarantors of the treaty of Xanten of 1614 (printed in the same pamphlet, pp. 22–24).

and to act jointly in the common interests of the duchies. If a prince oppressed any of them, they would resist together; if any of their own members acted contrary to this union, he should be excluded from their assemblies, and so should be whoever refused to sign it. The Estates also appealed to the United Provinces for help against their warring rulers.[1]

Frederick William in his turn accused the leaders of the Estates of seeking not the maintenance of their freedom and privileges but their own profit, and of trying to stir up muddy waters. According to him, it was the duty of a loyal subject to obey, and not to examine the motives and decisions of his prince. He claimed that some of the ringleaders had recently proclaimed that they would treat him as the English Parliament treated their king, and that some of the Estates' party did not object when they were hailed publicly as Parliamentarians in The Hague.[2] There is no evidence, however, that the Estates themselves made such comparisons or were in any way influenced by the contemporary struggle in England and by the victory of Parliament over the Crown. They always claimed that they were defending their ancient privileges and liberties; they were not innovators or revolutionaries, and only seldom ventured into the field of political theory. Their concerns were practical, related to the war and the plight of the country, the military occupation, taxation, appointments to offices, and other problems of administration. They must have known about the events in other countries, but they did not refer to them in their documents.[3]

[1] *Erf-Vereeninge der Landt Stenden uyt Ridderschap ende Steeden der Hartogdommen Gulick, Cleve, Berge, ende der Graefschappen Marck ende Ravensperg,* 15 Feb. 1647; Baumgarten, loc. cit. xviii. 44; Lieuwe van Aitzema, *Saken van Staet en Oorlogh in, ende omtrent de Vereenigde Nederlanden,* The Hague, 1669, iii. 191–2; Scotti, Jülich-Berg (1821), i, nos. 386, 389, pp. 114–15. In 1654 the union of the Estates was confirmed by the Emperor.

[2] *Cleefsche Patriot. Verthoonende de intentie van de Missive, gesonden aen hare Ho. Mogende Heeren Staten Generael der Vereenighde Nederlanden, van wegens de Cleefsche Landt-Stenden, gepresenteert den 20. May deses Jaers 1647,* Wesel, 1647, pp. 3, 7, 23. The same comparison with the English Parliament was made in 1684: Justus Hashagen, 'Die preussische Herrschaft und die Stände am Niederrhein', *Westdeutsche Zeitschrift für Geschichte und Kunst,* xxviii, 1909, p. 20; Hötzsch, op. cit., p. 730.

[3] It is incorrect if Gerhard Schilfert, 'Zur Geschichte der Auswirkungen der englischen bürgerlichen Revolution auf Nordwestdeutschland', *Beiträge zum neuen Geschichtsbild,* Berlin, 1956, p. 127, asserts that the Estates of Cleves and Mark worked with arguments drawn from the English Revolution: only the opposite side accused them of such tendencies, probably with the intention of blackening them in the eyes of the States General.

When the long war was over both rulers had to reach an agreement with their Estates which had been considerably strengthened by the events of the past years and by the fact that the principalities were still only 'provisionally' divided between Brandenburg and Neuburg, so that neither prince could risk a permanent estrangement from his Estates. In September 1649 Wolfgang William confirmed all the privileges of his Estates, their right of consenting to all taxes (which should not be construed as a duty of doing so), the use of the money voted *ad destinatos usus*, and their right of negotiating with the creditors and the officials. Their power of the purse was strengthened by a promise that he would not introduce an excise or increase the existing duties and customs; he also promised that he would neither recruit troops nor start a war or feud without their assent, that he would redress their grievances, respect their *jus indigenatus*, and have a majority of native noblemen among his councillors. The Estates, on the other hand, renounced the right of levying taxes without their prince's consent, but made no other concessions.[1] A fortnight later Frederick William of Brandenburg made even more sweeping concessions to his Estates. He had to confirm their rights of free assembly on their own initiative and of freely negotiating with foreign powers; no fortresses were to be built, and no troops to be recruited without their consent, and none to be brought in from outside; all foreign officials were to be dismissed, and the *jus indigenatus* was to be upheld. A few weeks later Frederick William further promised that in the *collegia* of the government of Cleves and Mark the nobility would always occupy two-thirds of all posts; annual accounts of revenue and expenditure were to be submitted to the Estates; all officials were to swear that they would abide by these agreements; if these stipulations or the Estates' privileges were violated by the Elector, they were entitled to refuse the payment of the taxes they had granted.[2] It seemed that in all four principalities the Estates had emerged victoriously from the long struggle with their new rulers.

Yet the conflict was by no means over. Neither Frederick William nor Wolfgang William was willing to accept the

[1] Baumgarten, loc. cit. xviii. 45–48; Helmuth Croon, *Stände und Steuern in Jülich-Berg im 17. und vornehmlich im 18. Jahrhundert*, Bonn, 1929, p. 7 (25 Sept. 1649).
[2] *Urkunden und Actenstücke*, v. 390–5, 397–8 (9 Oct. and 15 Nov. 1649).

agreements of 1649 as final. Nor had their mutual antagonism
come to an end. A bitter quarrel ensued over the question of
whether the year 1612 or 1624 was to be accepted as the *annus
normalis* for regulating the religious state of the principalities. If
Wolfgang William oppressed the Protestants of Berg, Frederick
William took repressive measures against the Catholics in Cleves
and Mark. In June 1651 he decided on another *coup de main*
and, aiming at territorial gains, invaded Jülich and Berg. He
announced to their Estates his intention of taking possession
of the two principalities and asked them to support and obey
him, claiming he was defending their rights and freeing them
from oppression. If Frederick William reckoned with their support on religious or other grounds, he was bitterly disappointed.
Not only the Estates of Jülich and Berg, but equally those of
Cleves and Mark, put the maintenance of peace above any
religious issue and strongly opposed his act of aggression. The
Estates of the four principalities met in July 1651, renewed
their hereditary union, and placarded an admonition to all the
inhabitants of the duchies that they should not enter military
service on either side and, if they had done so, should quit it
at the earliest opportunity. They warned the officials against
burdening the people, and the people not to pay any contributions to which the Estates had not consented, and not to supply
the troops with food and maintenance. Frederick William had
these mandates torn down and the leaders of the opposition
arrested. He was supported by fourteen noblemen of Cleves,
the majority of whom stood in his service, and who protested
against the mandates to which they had not agreed. The towns
of Mark also declared that they were prepared to retract the
mandates, which their deputies had not even read, and to ask
his pardon. The Estates of Cleves and Mark were deeply split,
but the opposition continued, above all in Cleves. The Emperor
Ferdinand III sharply intervened against Frederick William
and forbade support for him in any form; other powers threatened to intervene against him. In the end Frederick William
had to accept the decision of the Emperor and to withdraw his
forces. The *status quo* was restored.[1]

---

[1] *Urkunden und Actenstücke*, v. 509–10, 512, 514, 534 (July to Aug. 1651); *Kort
Bericht Waerom Sijn Cheurfurstelijcke Doorluchticheyt van Brandenburgh is bewogen ende
veroorsaeckt worden, eenighe Plaetsen inde Vorstendommen Gulick ende Bergh in te nemen,*

If Frederick William had not gained any advantage from the military enterprise against Palatinate-Neuburg, he now had troops in Cleves and Mark, contrary to the stipulations of the *Recess* of 1649, and these could be used against the inhabitants and the opposition. In spite of the mandates of the Emperor the regiments remained in the country, contributions were levied by military force, the cows and horses of the burghers and peasants were seized and driven away. The Estates in vain appealed to the Emperor and to the United Provinces for protection, for the removal of the troops, for the restitution of what had been carried away by force, for the termination of the harsh methods employed by the soldiery, of the forcible levying of taxes, and of the services demanded for the army. As the Estates refused to vote any money, these measures were continued after the conclusion of peace between Brandenburg and Neuburg. The towns on the right bank of the Rhine were protected by the Dutch garrisons, but those on the left bank were not. Therefore they were in favour of making a grant so that the troops could be paid off, while the towns on the right bank and the nobility found it impossible to raise the money on account of the inhabitants' plight. The government tried to exploit these and other differences among the Estates. A more determined and radical group among them was led by the deputies of Wesel and Rees, while the other towns of Cleves and those of Mark were inclined towards a compromise. The nobility was equally disunited, for many of its members had entered the electoral service or were receiving new privileges and other favours from Frederick William.[1]

As their complaints did not achieve any result, the Estates of Cleves and Mark in November 1652 decided to send envoys to the Emperor to petition him to intervene on their behalf. Some towns of Cleves and those of Mark, however, were opposed to such a step; and twelve members of the nobility, the majority of whom were government servants, protested because they had

1651; *Placeaet Gepubliceert By ende van wegen d'Erf-vereenigde Landtstanden Uyt de Ridderschap ende Steden der Lantschappen Cleve, Gulick, Berge, ende Marck tot Conservatie van haer Privilegien*, 1651; *Mandaet van syne Keyserl: Maiesteyt van avocatie ende inhibitie aende Chur-Brandenburghsche Soldatesque*, 1651; Hans Prutz, *Preussische Geschichte*, i, Stuttgart, 1900, pp. 448–9.

[1] *Urkunden und Actenstücke*, v. 541, 544–5, 548, 550–3, 561, 565–6, 574, 577, 579, 583, 618 (Sept. 1651 to Nov. 1652).

not been admitted to the deliberations of the Estates. These demanded at the beginning of 1653 that their grievances be redressed entirely before they granted any supply, above all that the troops be removed and the towns of Hamm and Lippstadt be evacuated. The government of Cleves was inclined to accept these conditions. The Estates' disunity, however, continued in spite of the exhortations of Wesel to the other towns that they should preserve their old union. In August 1653 the Estates met in two separate assemblies, Wesel being the leader of the opposition, and the town of Cleves leader of the loyalists. The latter decided to revoke the mandate of the envoys sent to the Emperor, while the opposition instructed them to proceed. When the envoys returned from their mission, Frederick William ordered them to be arrested, and one of them was actually apprehended, while the others escaped. Wesel was in favour of another appeal to the Emperor to obtain a penal mandate against their prince, but the Estates merely protested against the arrest. Again some towns of Cleves and the towns of Mark dissociated themselves from this protest so that it lost force. The Estates of Jülich and Berg proposed to ask the Elector of Saxony and other princes to intercede on behalf of the arrested nobleman; but the towns of Mark energetically repudiated the idea of agreeing to the deputation to the Emperor, which they had opposed from the outset.[1] It was this lack of unity among the Estates which proved the most effective weapon in the hands of Frederick William.

In Jülich and Berg the struggle between the prince and the Estates continued along similar lines, but Wolfgang William was in a much weaker position than his rival. At the end of 1648 his forces were reduced to a bare 900 men, and only in 1651 were they increased again for the war with Brandenburg. At the end of that year they numbered 2,845 men; but early in the following year the majority were paid off, and only five companies and some guards were retained.[2] This was a negligible force, insufficient to coerce the country. As early as 1651 the Estates reverted to their old tactics of disobeying the summons to the diet and of holding their own meetings at Cologne

---

[1] *Urkunden und Actenstücke*, v. 622, 624–5, 638, 649–51, 655, 662–3, 665, 667–9, 733–4, 740, 745–6, 764 (Nov. 1652 to Nov. 1654).

[2] Fahrmbacher, loc. cit., pp. 44, 49.

outside their prince's reach. This was repeated several times in the course of 1652. The Estates were strengthened by a secret agreement with Wolfgang William's son, Philip William, who wanted to gain their support against Brandenburg. The Estates of Jülich accused Wolfgang William of plotting their suppression. This he pronounced to be a term suitable for use against a tyrant, but not against a just and Christian ruler; in his opinion, those accusing him of such intentions were knaves devoid of honour—an opinion he upheld even when the Estates' *Syndicus* informed him that he had written it on the instructions of all the Estates. They were ordered to reappear at the diet and to discuss the proposition, otherwise he would have to issue the necessary orders without their assent. Thereupon the Estates reappeared, but insisted that their honour must be vindicated because it had been harmed by the expressions he had used against them. As no such vindication was forthcoming, they again departed, and so did the Estates of Berg from their diet. Wolfgang William in vain tried to induce them to obey his summons during the months which preceded his death in 1653. Under his successor Philip William the relations improved. But the Estates steadfastly refused to grant him money for the army with which he wanted to conquer Cleves and Mark, so that it remained quite insufficient for this purpose.[1]

During the very years that Philip William was forced to remain inactive for lack of means and could not make any headway against his Estates, a decisive change occurred in Cleves and Mark. This was above all due not to any developments inside the two principalities, but to a completely extraneous event, the outbreak of the War of the North in 1655. It proved to be of vital importance that Frederick William was also the Elector of Brandenburg and the duke of Prussia and therefore able to draw on the resources of his different territories. As duke of Prussia he soon became involved in this war for predominance in the north between Sweden and Poland which was largely fought out on Prussian territory. During the war Frederick William used his Rhenish possessions, which were much wealthier than any of his others, as recruiting grounds and entrepôts for the equipment of soldiers, and equally as suppliers

---

[1] Scotti, Jülich-Berg (1821), i, nos. 399, 401, 406–8, 412, 415, 417, pp. 117–22 (Jan. 1651 to Jan. 1653); Baumgarten, loc. cit. xviii. 51–52, 55–56.

of money for the war. During the five years that the war lasted
the colossal sum of 1,500,000 thalers was levied in Cleves and
Mark, exclusive of deliveries in kind and the waste and destruction due to the levying by the military.[1] As the Estates
would not, and could not, grant such sums, the régime of
military force continued unabated. Soldiers were billeted on
the burghers and peasants, their cattle and horses were seized.
Even the burghers themselves were arrested if they ventured
outside the towns, and the troops behaved as if they were in
enemy territory. As the Dutch garrisons no longer protected the
towns for political reasons, no effective resistance was possible.
But many people refused to pay, and the government feared
an uprising of desperate subjects and armed resistance to the
levying by soldiers. Yet the forces maintained in the country
throughout the war years proved an effective deterrent, and the
Estates were no more united than before. The towns insisted
that the taxes were levied for purposes of defence, and that
therefore the nobility should participate; but the noblemen
refused, and this rift played into the hands of the government.[2]

After the end of the war in 1660 Frederick William felt strong
enough to annul the *Recess* of 1649 unilaterally and to send
to Cleves from Berlin a new *Recess*, already signed and sealed,
which was not to be debated as was the custom, but to be
accepted unconditionally by the Estates. When they hesitated
they were threatened that their prince would come with a large
army if they did not accept, and the majority gave way. Some
noblemen and some urban deputies did indeed leave the diet,
but later on they also accepted. Their resistance was broken.
The Estates retained the rights of voting and auditing the taxes
and of free assembly, but only after notification of the meeting-
place and of the agenda to the government; as previously, all
official appointments were to go to natives of Cleves and Mark.
In other respects, however, there were very important changes.
The Estates lost their rights of negotiating with foreign powers,
of consenting to the recruiting and bringing in of troops, of
being absolved from the duty of paying taxes if the prince did

---

[1] It had taken the Dutch twenty-five years to collect that sum during the Thirty
Years War: see above, p. 300.

[2] *Urkunden und Actenstücke*, v. 768–9, 773, 777, 783, 793, 807–8, 811, 816–18, 853,
860, 874, 881, 884–5, 895, 907–9, 915, 932–3, 970; Aitzema, op. cit. iii. 1204–5
(Dec. 1654 to Apr. 1660).

not observe their privileges or the stipulations of the *Recess*. His officials no longer had to swear that they would abide by these stipulations, and their appointment and dismissal were recognized as part of his prerogative, as were foreign policy and military affairs.[1] Throughout the seventeenth and eighteenth centuries this *Recess* remained the basis of the relations between the ruler and the Estates. Only eleven years separated it from that of 1649, but a fundamental change had occurred during these years. There was no longer a *condominium*; the Estates ceased to be an independent power which not only their prince, but also other princes, the Emperor, and the United Provinces had to consider and to conciliate. Instead, the Estates became an organ of the nascent Brandenburg state, functioning under the supervision of its officials and voting regular supplies to its army. The existence of the standing army was the best guarantee that the independent power of the Estates would not revive. A few years later the towns of Cleves were forced to assent to an increase in their share of each tax from one-sixth to one-fifth and to the exemption of the noble estates from all taxes, including those levied for defence and for purposes of the Empire: a claim which the towns had contested strenuously for many years.[2]

Whereas in Cleves and Mark the issue was decided against the Estates, and especially against the towns, this was not the case in Jülich and Berg. There the conflicts between the prince and the Estates continued into the eighteenth century, and the Estates' power remained much stronger, although it had been weaker in the past. The first fifteen years of Philip William's reign saw few clashes between him and the Estates. They voted him comparatively large sums, nearly 500,000 thalers for the army in 1666, for instance, and 373,333 thalers in 1668 to enable him to compete for the crown of Poland after the abdication of King John Casimir. This sum was to be levied within eight years and only to be used for the redemption of pawned domains. Diets were to be summoned every year to

---

[1] *Urkunden und Actenstücke*, v. 958–61, 964–9, 972–4; Scotti, Cleve-Mark (1826), i. 337–8, 340–3, 346–7, 350–1, 374–5, 382 (Aug. 1660 to Mar. 1661); von Haeften, loc. cit., p. 959, nn. 1 and 3; p. 960, n. 4; Schmoller, *Preussische Verfassungs-, Verwaltungs- und Finanzgeschichte*, pp. 60–61.

[2] *Urkunden und Actenstücke*, v. 1024; Scotti, Cleve-Mark (1826), i, no. 295, pp. 478–9 (Oct. 1666).

redress the grievances, and no war was to be started and no troops were to be recruited without the consent of the Estates. These conditions were not observed, in fact, and the Estates' deputies were neither admitted to the rendering of the accounts nor to the paying out of the money. But the Estates again assembled at Cologne without a summons and against the orders of the government and asked that the further instalments of the tax granted be suspended. This request they repeated at the diet of 1669. They demanded that the promises of the previous year be kept and the accounts be communicated to them, that the army should be reduced from 900 to 200 men, the general officers be discharged and the general staff be dissolved. Philip William declared a reduction to be impossible because the soldiers were needed to garrison the fortresses, but the Estates insisted and asked for an adjournment, before entering on a discussion of the princely proposition, until his answer to their requests was received from Neuburg: otherwise they would take their leave without being dismissed. The councillors tried to retain them, but they departed without waiting for a reply, the diet having lasted only three weeks.[1]

Two months later a new diet was opened, and again the Estates insisted on the redress of grievances prior to a discussion of the proposition, on the observance of the conditions stipulated in 1668, and on a reduction of the army; Berg was against any concession, and Jülich more conciliatory. Any compromise, however, was made impossible by a sharp reply from Philip William, which arrived three weeks later, refusing all their requests. It also accused them of burdening the country with heavy payments to their creditors and officials and with their wages and expenses (which amounted to a *per diem* of $1\frac{1}{2}$ thalers for each deputy): in future diets should be short, and the numbers of their servants and horses be curtailed. The Estates again pressed for the redress of their grievances, and the ducal councillors proposed they should be discussed by a committee. To this the Estates eventually assented and granted 37,500 thalers, although the army alone required 49,000. The money was quickly spent, and the soldiers went unpaid. Thus another diet was summoned in May 1670. In June the Estates, without

[1] Scotti, Jülich-Berg (1821), i, nos. 544, 552, pp. 152–3; Baumgarten, loc. cit. xviii. 56, 66–76, 79, 81–84 (July 1668 to Sept. 1669).

reviving their previous tactics, granted 39,000 thalers, in spite of the prevailing economic distress. This sum they increased to 48,000, on condition that there would be no further demands during the next twelve months; this was accepted by the councillors and later ratified by Philip William. Yet already in the following month new demands were made for the fortresses, and a stop of the Estates' chest was decreed until they would hand over lists of their creditors and of their officials with their salaries. The Estates' deputies declined these new demands and left Düsseldorf. Thereupon the government forbade the *Pfennigmeister* to make payments to the Estates' creditors and officials. The standing army was increased to 1,600 men, while the Estates continued to insist that it should be reduced.[1]

At the end of 1670 two decrees were promulgated which caused a complete breach between Philip William and the Estates, especially the nobility. One was directed against noble encroachments on the princely hunting rights, the other aimed at the elimination of inequality and muddle in the levy of taxes by means of a land-survey and the compilation of a new land-register, which would have brought to light the many tax evasions of the nobility. Early in 1671 the Estates' deputies met and discussed the possibility of appealing to the Emperor against the second decree, but did not reach a decision. Hence the deputies summoned a diet to Cologne, while the government demanded the summons to be withdrawn. One ducal councillor went to Cologne to prohibit the meeting and to threaten punishments to those attending, but without success. The Estates decided to appeal to the Emperor Leopold and to ask him for his protection, as Ferdinand II had protected them during the Thirty Years War. The nobility further decided to appeal to the Aulic Council against the second decree, claiming that it infringed their privileges and that they should have been consulted before its publication; but the towns objected and thought that Philip William was entitled to order a land-survey to be undertaken. He instructed his councillors to prevent the appeal, to suggest punishments for its authors, and to break all opposition against the survey. He annulled the decisions of the

[1] Baumgarten, loc. cit. xviii. 85–99, 102–5, 109–15, 120–4, 129–33; Fahrm-bacher, loc. cit., p. 54 (Nov. 1669 to Aug. 1670). The Estates' *Syndici* received 2½ thalers *per diem* and the members of their committees 2 and 4 respectively.

diet which had met at Cologne and forbade all *conventicula* and
unauthorized meetings. The city of Cologne was threatened
with counter-measures if it permitted these meetings to continue. Inquiries were made in Cleves about the penalties which
were imposed there for unauthorized meetings. The land-
survey proceeded, but very slowly; and so did the Estates' case
pending at the Aulic Council.[1]

In June 1671 another diet was opened at Düsseldorf. The
Estates were informed that Philip William had concluded a
defensive alliance with the Elector of Brandenburg and the
bishop of Münster against Louis XIV and that large sums were
required for recruiting and the repair of the fortresses. The
nobility was accused of aiming at a share in the government and
of being inclined to rebel and to usurp the functions of the
prince. The Estates complained that their privilege of free
meeting was curtailed by cutting their expenses to two or three
weeks and not allowing them to deliberate for as long as they
pleased. They also objected that the alliance had been concluded without consulting them and that recruiting had begun
without their consent. In their opinion all the country could
raise was 24,000 thalers, a sum which the councillors declined
to accept. They warned the Estates against leaving without
granting more and tried to separate them from each other, but
although some of the towns hesitated their efforts were in vain.
The Estates left without being dismissed. 100,000 thalers were
then levied by decree, bringing forth another complaint to the
Aulic Council that this was contrary to the agreement of 1649.
Philip William was particularly incensed against the nobility.
He wanted to tax their exempt estates and to break their opposition by force. But his councillors were against such steps and
against the punishment of individuals, who in their opinion
could only be tried by a court and jury. The Estates' deputies
again met at Cologne, at first furtively at different places, then
once more publicly in the convent of the Minorites, their
customary meeting-place.[2]

When the diet was resumed in October 1671, the Estates

---

[1] Scotti, Jülich-Berg (1821), i, no. 570, p. 157; Baumgarten, loc. cit. xix. 9–15,
20–22, 25–34; xxii. 101 (Nov. 1670 to May 1671).

[2] Ibid. xix. 48–51, 54–61; xxii. 103–6; Croon, op. cit., p. 7 (June to July
1671).

were reminded of their oath of allegiance. They were told that their union and their conspiracies were contrary to it, were weakening the bonds of love and obedience, and were causing a dangerous disintegration. Therefore Philip William, using his princely authority and power, declared the union null and void, with all the oaths that had been sworn to it, and demanded its surrender within three or four days. At first the Estates were taken aback, but soon their *Syndicus* produced a letter of 1640 from the Emperor Ferdinand III which approved the union. To this Imperial letter the Estates referred and asked for legal advice in Cologne. This advocated the rejection of any compromise and counselled them to stand by their union and their oaths which bound them to preserve secrecy during the sessions of the diet. The ducal councillors pressed them to reply speedily whether they would renounce and surrender the union. But instead the nobility and the towns of Berg justified their refusal in writing and began to leave, while the towns of Jülich opposed this in the hope of reaching an agreement. Some ducal councillors were in favour of waiting with the levy of a tax, but Philip William ordered it to proceed more quickly and refused any concession with regard to the union or the oaths which pledged the Estates to secrecy. Most of the Estates then departed. Simultaneously the Aulic Council promulgated four decrees which supported the case of the Estates and took them under the protection of the Emperor. The decrees prohibited all recruiting and levying of taxes without their consent, the cancellation of their union, and the stoppage of their chest by Philip William. The towns of Jülich suggested sending a deputation to Neuburg to ask him to permit their union and oaths and to visit the duchies in person; but the other Estates declined to participate and left because the French army was approaching. The towns' efforts to make them reconsider this decision were in vain. At the beginning of 1672 the deputies of the four towns of Jülich and of Düsseldorf, the capital, left for Neuburg, provided with ample travelling expenses by their prince. Under strong pressure the other three towns of Berg eventually joined them. The result, however, was nil, apparently because the deputies went to Neuburg without any instructions or powers.[1]

[1] Baumgarten, loc. cit. xxii. 110–19, 122–6 (Oct. 1671 to Feb. 1672).

The standing army was slowly increased and numbered 2,600 men by the beginning of 1672. The compulsory levy of taxes continued. Certain *Ämter* were allocated to each garrison, which had to furnish its pay for periods of ten days at a time, so that the money collected no longer passed through the Estates' chest but went directly to the army. Philip William wanted to make common cause with Frederick William of Brandenburg to destroy the Estates' union, the charter of their liberties. At the end of 1671 he wrote to the Elector that, as long as the union existed, the Estates would always claim a *condominium*; Frederick William should not allow the Estates to triumph over both of them and to wring the sceptre from their hands—strange advice indeed considering the success Frederick William had gained over his Estates more than ten years previously. He nevertheless instructed his government at Cleves to maintain close contact with that at Düsseldorf, to formulate together a decree repealing the union, and to publish it simultaneously in both capitals. The Cleves government, however, composed as it was of natives of the duchy, was not inclined to act at Philip William's bidding, especially as it urgently required the co-operation of the Estates in view of the threatened French invasion. It once more requested the Estates to surrender their union, but in a much more polite form than was done in Düsseldorf. The Estates were indignant: they had renewed their hereditary union in 1647 in Frederick William's presence, but not under oath, and since 1661 they had had no contact with the Estates of Jülich and Berg. They then granted some money and were dismissed by the government three days later. For this leniency the government was sharply reprimanded by Frederick William and instructed to obtain the surrender of the union within six weeks. Otherwise it was to be repealed by decree. After the permanent division of the duchies between Brandenburg and Neuburg by the treaty of 1666 Frederick William was always willing to co-operate with Philip William against the Estates, while the Cleves government adopted a policy of passive resistance which he could not overcome as long as the government remained in the hands of native noblemen and commoners.[1]

[1] Baumgarten, loc. cit. xxii. 135–40; Fahrmbacher, loc. cit., p. 55 (Dec. 1671 to June 1672).

In May 1672 yet another diet of Jülich and Berg was summoned. The Estates were given four weeks to surrender their unions, otherwise these would be declared null and void in public. At the end of the month a decree was published which repealed the new secret unions of the Estates and forbade their allegedly unconstitutional alliances which destroyed all confidence between the prince and the Estates. Soon after Philip William arrived in Düsseldorf and admonished the Estates to reply to the proposition. They denied that they had any intention of usurping a share of the government and decided to seek legal advice in Cologne. Their counsel advised them to forgo their unions and make a grant because of the threat from France. The Estates, however, declined to follow this advice and asked for the preservation of the old custom, according to which they pledged themselves to secrecy at the beginning of each diet and would not negotiate individually with the prince. This Philip William refused to concede. He was incensed at the slow progress of the negotiations, for the Estates again took legal advice and raised endless counter-arguments against his requests. He was only willing to omit from the land-survey those noble estates which had been entirely exempt in 1592, while the nobility desired all their estates to be omitted and the towns supported Philip William. In June 1672 the Aulic Council, to prevent him from joining Louis XIV, published a new decision which was relatively favourable to him. The attitude of the towns gradually weakened in respect of the two points at issue: the oaths taken at the beginning of a diet and the admission of the ducal councillors to their deliberations. Early in September the Estates still announced their intention of preserving their union and their right of free assembly and insisted on being consulted before the conclusion of alliances and the recruiting of any troops. But when the councillors declined to accept this declaration, the towns of Jülich, always inclined to compromise, separated from the other Estates. They were soon followed by the towns of Berg which received new instructions from their principals, while the nobility remained in opposition. At last Philip William had succeeded in separating the two Estates from each other.[1]

A draft of a new *Recess* was then handed to the Estates. As

[1] Baumgarten, loc. cit. xxii. 141–59; Scotti, Jülich-Berg (1821), i, no. 585, p. 160.

only a few were still present, they asked for a new summons to be issued, but Philip William declined. Eleven of his noble councillors appeared and demanded to be admitted to the deliberations of the Estates. This was at first refused, but again the towns gave way, followed by the few noblemen still present. Thus the ducal officials obtained a majority in the two *curiae* of the nobility (Jülich and Berg), for in addition to the eleven councillors only six noblemen were left who were *Amtleute* or officers, and only four who were neither. The house of the Jülich nobility therefore soon accepted the draft *Recess*. A ducal official was sent to negotiate with the towns of Jülich, which put forward certain requests with regard to their privileges, but accepted at the end of October. Then six noblemen and the towns of Berg began to discuss the draft and accepted it within a week. The obnoxious *Syndicus* of the Jülich Estates, who had been in office for more than twenty years, was dismissed. A new director of the diet was elected, a high-ranking officer. The *Recess* of 5 November 1672, adopted in this curious and un-constitutional form, clearly marked the victory of Philip William, as that of 1660 marked the victory of Frederick William in Cleves. But his victory was by no means complete.[1]

The unions of the Estates were annulled, except that of 1496 which had been confirmed in the partition treaty with Brandenburg in 1666. It was conceded that the Estates' advice was to be heard on issues of war and alliances, but the decision in all military matters was left to the prince. Money required for these and other purposes was to be granted by the Estates, and their grants were to be 'substantial', but a refusal to vote money should not be prejudicial to them. The taxes granted were to be paid as before to the two *Pfennigmeister*, who were appointed by the Estates, but who had to be confirmed in office by the prince. Their accounts were to be rendered to a mixed committee on which the prince also was represented, so that the Estates lost their rights of independent financial management. The customs and excise duties were not to be increased without the Estates' knowledge, and no domains were to be sold or pawned without their consent: their power of the purse remained. A diet was to be summoned every year. The Estates' meetings without a summons remained forbidden if they were

[1] Baumgarten, loc. cit. xxii. 160–2, 169–71 (Sept. to Nov. 1672).

arranged with hostile intentions; they were, however, permitted in cases of emergency, if they were held in good intention
and duly notified to the government, but not outside the
duchies—regulations which corresponded to those promulgated
in Cleves and Mark. All officials were to be natives of, and
domiciled in, Jülich and Berg; equally the Estates' *Syndici* and
their *Pfennigmeister*, who hitherto had lived in Cologne, outside
the duchies and the reach of the government; non-native
officials were to be dismissed within three months, although an
exception was made in favour of the *Syndicus* of Berg, Dr. Essken,
who was permitted to remain. The Estates were allowed to swear
a *juramentum taciturnitatis* for the duration of their meetings;
this was also to be rendered by the government officials and
councillors who were their members, and they would meanwhile be released from their officials' oath. The appeal to the
Aulic Council was to be dropped, and an amnesty was declared for it. But future appeals were expressly permitted if the
prince ever infringed this agreement—which was to be considered a fundamental law and to remain valid for ever—
and refused to change his policy within three months. The
absent members of the Estates were given eight weeks to notify
their acceptance of the *Recess*: if they refused to do so they
would be excluded from its provisions and lose their privileges.[1]

That the conflict with the nobility was by no means over was
shown only a few days later when Philip William again prohibited all *conventicula* and secret unions of the Estates and gave
orders to arrest anybody who took part in them. Several more
such decrees were issued during the following months, threatening the rebels with confiscation of their property and loss of
their tax exemptions and privileges. For years some members
of the nobility continued to appeal to the Aulic Council in spite
of all prohibitions and threats. Their opposition was only
brought to an end by another *Recess*, published in July 1675,
which they eventually accepted. It 'interpreted' that of 1672
in the sense that the amnesty was extended to include the opposition and restored their estates to its members, that a new

[1] Scotti, Jülich-Berg (1821), i, nos. 591–2, pp. 161–4 (5–7 Nov. 1672); Baumgarten, loc. cit. xxii. 172–83; Croon, op. cit., pp. 225, 227, 233; Schönneshöfer,
op. cit., pp. 310–11; E. von Schaumburg, 'Johann Wilhelm, Erbprinz und Pfalzgraf zu Neuburg, Regent der Herzogtümer Jülich und Berg, 1679–90', *Zeitschrift
des Bergischen Geschichtsvereins*, viii, 1872, pp. 9–10.

union, based on that of 1496, was permitted and confirmed, that private meetings of the Estates at Cologne, where their archives remained, were allowed, that taxes would only be requested according to the true needs of the government, and that the Estates were to be consulted prior to any declaration of war. All this was to be confirmed by the Emperor Leopold, a confirmation which was obtained eighteen months later. The two *Recesse* of 1672 and 1675 terminated the long conflict and remained the basis of the constitution of Jülich and Berg, exactly as those of 1660 and 1661 were that of the constitution of Cleves and Mark. One fundamental question, however, was left open: for what purposes taxes were to be voted, and what amounts were to be granted. Clearly, the word 'substantial' (*erklecklich*) could, and would, be interpreted quite differently by the two sides; and the interpretation of other controversial clauses would create further difficulties.[1]

v. *The Estates' Decline in the late Seventeenth and Eighteenth Centuries*

From 1672 onwards the principalities on the Rhine were engulfed in the wars of Louis XIV and suffered terribly from French invasions and depredations, especially the districts on the left bank which were entirely unprotected. Between 1672 and 1679 in Cleves alone over 500,000 thalers were levied by the French, not counting deliveries in kind. When the war came to an end with the peace of Nymegen another contribution of 808,500 thalers had to be paid by the four principalities to the victor; certain towns remained occupied by the French until it was fully paid. During the war nine regiments were recruited in Jülich and Berg, but already in 1678 the three cavalry regiments were disbanded because there was no more money, and in lieu of their pay the troopers had to take their horses and equipment. By May 1679 only twenty-three companies (not much more than 2,000 men) were left in Jülich and Berg; but even these cost over 10,000 thalers a month and were felt to be much too heavy a burden for the impoverished country. During the war

---

[1] Scotti, Jülich-Berg (1821), i, nos. 593, 596, 600, 603, 614, pp. 164–9; Baumgarten, loc. cit. xxii. 186; Croon, op. cit., pp. 7–8; Schönneshöfer, op. cit., pp. 311–12.

the governments left the negotiations with the French *Intendants* to the Estates and their 'wisdom and skill', while the ducal councillors were completely passive and the far-away rulers were unable to do anything for their exposed territories.[1] In spite of all their sufferings in the war years, Cleves and Mark had to continue to pay heavy contributions to the Elector Frederick William, averaging 228,000 thalers a year between 1681 and 1688; 80 per cent. of the contributions were used for his own purposes, above all the army.[2] The forces to be maintained by Jülich and Berg after the peace of Nymegen, on the other hand, were fewer than 1,500 men, to which one more regiment was added in 1681. By 1684, however, there were eight regiments in the two duchies—three of cavalry, one of dragoons, and four of infantry: a regular standing army of 4,500 to 5,000 men.[3] It was much larger than that of the duchy of Württemberg, but much smaller than that of Brandenburg or Saxony.

After the conclusion of peace in 1679 a diet of Jülich and Berg was summoned by Philip William's son, John William, who administered the duchies on behalf of his father. The Estates decided not to vote any money until their grievances were redressed, especially until the burden of taxation was alleviated and the army, the costly general staff, and the *Kriegskommissariat*—formed after the Brandenburg model to administer the military revenues—were dissolved. Eventually they nevertheless granted 31,000 thalers and then took their departure' without waiting for a dismissal. This sum the prince declared to be insufficient, but he was unable to obtain more because the Estates had left. Six weeks later, however, they were re-summoned to render homage to him. The *Syndicus*, Dr. Essken, pointed out that, when homage was rendered to John William's father, the Estates had received satisfaction with regard to their grievances and their privileges were confirmed under oath. John William replied that he hoped the Estates

---

[1] Fahrmbacher, loc. cit., pp. 68–69; von Schaumburg, loc. cit., pp. 2–4; a Cleves government report of 1678, quoted by Hötzsch, op. cit., p. 347; ibid., p. 342, the detailed figures of the Cleves contributions.

[2] Hötzsch, op. cit., p. 342, with detailed figures.

[3] Fahrmbacher, loc. cit., pp. 69, 71. On a peace-time footing an infantry regiment had about 800, and a cavalry regiment about 300 men, which could be quickly expanded in case of need.

would not demand more from him than those of Cleves and Mark from their prince, who had not sworn such an oath, and that he could not tarry any longer. He simply promised he would maintain their privileges and the *Recesse* of 1672 and 1675, and then the Estates swore fealty to him. On the following day they were asked for a contribution to his maintenance. Those of Jülich, which had been badly devastated by the French, declared this was impossible, but under pressure voted 13,000 thalers on credit. Those of Berg, while at first only assenting to 17,000, eventually increased this to 36,000 thalers, including sums for the princely family and table. The Estates, much weakened by the war, were unable to withstand the princely pressure and retreated step by step. The army was indeed reduced, but not disbanded, nor was the general staff, nor the military Commissariat.[1]

At the diet of 1680–1 the Estates under government pressure granted increased amounts on condition that their grievances would be redressed. Those of Berg demanded that details of the military strength and expenditure be communicated to them and that their deputies should supervise the repair of the fortifications of Düsseldorf; but these demands incensed John William, and they desisted and granted more than 152,000 thalers. In 1682 65,400 thalers were demanded from them for the contingent of the duchies to the Imperial army in case of renewed war with France. The Estates debated whether first to request the redress of their grievances; but John William desired a termination of the diet within eight days and threatened to levy the money by decree, whereupon the Estates gave way. Then another 255,000 thalers was demanded for the ducal army for twelve months. The Estates offered much less and finally consented to raise 150,000 thalers, including sums for the prince and his brother. They thus accepted the principle of a standing army in addition to the contingents furnished to the army of the Empire. New lengthy and acrimonious debates occurred in 1683 and 1684. The Estates bitterly complained about the levying of arrears by the military and their excesses, and raised other grievances. They obtained a promise that in future arrears were to be collected by the local officials and the

[1] von Schaumburg, loc. cit., pp. 25–29, 32–38; Croon, op. cit., p. 236; Fahrmbacher, loc. cit., p. 68 (Sept. to Oct. 1679).

levying by soldiers would be forbidden. With regard to their other grievances John William merely promised he would discuss and redress them if possible, although they threatened they would take legal steps if there was no redress. In 1685 the Estates were instructed in future to hand in their grievances at the end of each diet: they would then be decided by the following year. With regard to the granting of supply, they should make up their minds immediately, otherwise the diet would be dissolved and the sums needed would be repartitioned by decree. The Estates offered no resistance, but granted 131,000 thalers for the army, 20,000 for the war against the Turks and considerable further sums, and left the discussion of the grievances to their deputies. Six months later they voted another 50,000 thalers as an aid to Philip William, who had just succeeded to the Palatinate and thus become an Elector. John William announced that in future he would not suffer their prescribing anything to him: their arguments were so devoid of sense that they deserved no reply.[1]

Accordingly the Estates in 1686 did not hand in their grievances at the opening of the diet, but again made substantial grants: 133,000 thalers for the army, 25,000 for the two fortresses of Jülich and Düsseldorf, and various other sums, which were accepted with 'complete satisfaction'. The grants were repeated in 1687, but a dispute developed over a demand for 50,000 thalers for the dowry of one of Philip William's daughters who was to marry King Pedro of Portugal; finally the Estates consented to a sum of 30,000 to be raised on credit. John William sharply reprimanded the younger deputies, who had hardly ceased to be students, but who were the most talkative, thought they knew everything, and would not listen to their elders and betters. He declared he would not permit this any longer but would punish them as they deserved. At the diet of 1688 the Estates granted practically all the princely demands: 254,000 thalers for the army, 25,000 for the two fortresses, 14,000 for John William and 25,000 for the Empire, &c.: very large sums on account of the new threat from Louis XIV and his claims to the Palatinate. These grants were graciously accepted by John

---

[1] von Schaumburg, loc. cit., pp. 54–56, 70–75, 81, 84, 87–88, 91–93, 97–99; Fahrmbacher, loc. cit., p. 76; Schönneshöfer, op. cit., pp. 320–2; Croon, op. cit., pp. 8–9.

William, who nevertheless introduced a new stamp duty by decree as soon as the diet was dissolved. At the end of 1688 the unfortunate duchies were again occupied by the French army, which levied 300,000 thalers and caused heavy damage through requisitioning and looting, in spite of presents offered to General Sourdy and his *Intendant*. Early in 1689 John William demanded large sums for the electoral army, whereupon General Sourdy threatened he would levy four times the amount they voted to their prince. When the Estates reported this to him, he retorted he was the prince and master and not the French, insisted on the grant, and forbade further payments to the French. When the bewildered Estates hesitated, he threatened them with harsh and extreme measures, with arrests and criminal procedures: they must do *absolute* what he desired. He ordered the money collected for the French to be paid out to him, and the Emperor Leopold took his side. New demands were submitted to the Estates later in the same year, this time for the remarriage of John William and for the marriage of another sister of his to Charles II of Spain, in addition to about 500,000 thalers *pro militari* and more for the prince himself. Again the Estates granted most of these demands and were then graciously dismissed.[1] They had retreated all along the line by the time that Philip William died in 1690 and was succeeded by John William as the Elector Palatine as well as the duke of Jülich and Berg.

In Cleves and Mark, during the last years of the reign of the Great Elector and that of his son, there were no longer any conflicts with the Estates, and very few changes of any importance occurred. The two principalities escaped the many reforms and administrative changes which were introduced in the later seventeenth century in the other Hohenzollern possessions. They were far away from Berlin and had few connexions with the other territories. Not even the urban excise, which revolutionized the system of taxation in Brandenburg and Prussia and deprived the Estates of the power of the purse, was introduced in Cleves and Mark, although Frederick William made nine attempts to do so. From 1680 onwards the president of the local government was Alexander von Spaen, a high-ranking officer of the Brandenburg army. He was a Cleves nobleman and a

[1] von Schaumburg, loc. cit., pp. 101–8, 115–17, 124–9, 134–42, 151–4; Croon, op. cit., p. 9, n. 4.

member of the Estates, but he early entered the electoral
service. During the years of the great conflict he was one of the
leaders of the pro-electoral group among the nobility, which
destroyed the unity among the Estates and contributed so much
to Frederick William's victory.[1] He was a loyal Brandenburg
official, entirely divorced from the Estates and their political
opposition. Another man of the same type was Johann Albrecht
von Wilich-Bötzlar, who in 1684 was appointed head of the military Commissariat, which became responsible for the assessment, repartition, and administration of the taxes, under the
general supervision of the Cleves government.[2]

Soon, however, friction began to develop between the old and
the new authorities because the Commissariat tended to extend
its sphere of activity and to interfere with other government
functions. After many complaints to Berlin about these expan-
sionist tendencies Frederick William decided against the Commissariat: it should not be entitled to dismiss the Estates'
deputies, to adjust the taxes granted by the Estates, to dispatch
demands for tax payments, and it should not extend its functions any further on pain of incurring his displeasure. Von
Wilich-Bötzlar indeed had very far-reaching plans of reform.
He wanted a new land-register to be compiled to stop tax
evasions, exactly as Philip William planned it in Jülich and
Berg; he wanted to investigate the urban taxes and finances in
order to eliminate waste and to curtail the towns' financial
independence. The towns, however, in 1687 succeeded in
getting the deliberations transferred to Berlin, with the result
that the *status quo* was maintained. The new land-register never
came into being, although Frederick William in 1687 expressed
his surprise that nothing had been done. In this way Cleves and
Mark continued to live fairly independently of the central
government in Berlin under their own authorities composed of
natives of the principalities. The Estates continued to meet
very frequently, at least once a year; the diet continued to grant
supply and to scrutinize the estimates and the financial requirements of the government.[3] In striking contrast with the state of

[1] See above, pp. 304–6.
[2] Hötzsch, op. cit., pp. 155–6, 166, 346, 870–3; Spannagel, loc. cit., p. 34.
[3] Hötzsch, op. cit., pp. 160, 168, 202, 206, 694, 760, 768–73, 875–6, 896,
1023–4; Spannagel, loc. cit., p. 29.

affairs in the other Hohenzollern territories the Estates of Cleves and Mark thus exercised a kind of budget right; while elsewhere the new authorities created by the Great Elector usurped these functions, the Estates at best retaining the right to repartition the tax demands of the military authorities, and the towns losing even this right owing to the introduction of the urban excise.

During the reign of John William, which lasted from 1690 to 1716, the conflict with the Estates of Jülich and Berg continued. To curtail the influence of the native nobility in the administration, he employed, contrary to the stipulations of the *Recess* of 1672, by preference commoners, who were not members of the Estates and not natives of the duchies, and who were his willing tools.[1] His financial demands grew steadily, for he required large sums for his sumptuous court in Düsseldorf, which he tried to transform into a 'small Paris', for his army, which fought in the many wars against Louis XIV, and for many other needs. The army played only a very modest part in the war of 1688–97 because it was practically annihilated by the French invasion of 1688; but it was not disbanded after the peace of Ryswick. In 1700 it consisted of six cavalry and six infantry regiments, the horse-guards, and three companies of artillery—altogether not much more than 7,000 men. During the War of the Spanish Succession in the early eighteenth century it was doubled, thanks to large subsidies given by the United Provinces which paid for 4,400 men. After the peace of Utrecht it was again reduced to the pre-war size of a little over 7,000.[2] This was a comparatively small army, especially as it was not only the army of Jülich and Berg, but also that of the Palatinate. It nevertheless necessitated heavy and mounting contributions from the two duchies. Excluding the contributions levied by the French, they averaged 740,000 thalers a year during the war of 1688–97, fell during the subsequent years of peace to an average of 644,000 thalers, then rose steeply during the War of the Spanish Succession to 1,028,000 a year, and fell again to an average of 842,000 thalers after the peace of Utrecht, when a large contribution had still to be paid to France. Even in

[1] Kurt Erdmann, 'Der Jülich-Bergische Hofrat bis zum Tode Johann Wilhelms', *Jahrbuch des Düsseldorfer Geschichtsvereins*, xxxi, 1939, pp. 44, 105, 107–8.

[2] Hans Fahrmbacher, 'Kurfürst Johann Wilhelms Kriegsstaat im Spanischen Erbfolgekriege, 1700–14', *Zeitschrift des Bergischen Geschichtsvereins*, xlvii, 1914, pp. 11–13; xlviii, 1915, pp. 29, 182; Schönneshöfer, op. cit., p. 329.

peace-time these were enormous figures, far higher than those levied in the preceding reign or in Cleves and Mark, and the population was quite unable to pay such large sums. The communes thus had to borrow money, arrears accumulated, people emigrated, houses and farms were sold to the highest bidder to collect the arrears, and the country became impoverished.[1]

In John William's opinion it was the duty of the Estates to grant taxes, not a right they could exercise at their discretion, as it had still been recognized by the *Recess* of 1672. If they made difficulties about voting supply, he threatened them with arrests and the seizure of their property. In 1698 he asked them to guarantee the repayment of the dowry of his second wife; when the nobility declined they were informed he would proceed with summary arrests and inflict the death penalty, and then they gave way. In 1700, without the consent of the Estates and contrary to the terms of the *Recess* of 1672, a general excise was introduced on beer, wine, corn, meat, cattle, victuals, merchandise, metals, &c. It was to be administered by the military Commissariat, and the money collected was to be paid into the war chest, thus by-passing the Estates' administration. The officials appointed to levy the new tax were mainly foreigners, allegedly so as to avoid collusion, more likely so as to curtail further the influence of the Estates. The example of Brandenburg was clearly instrumental. The yield of the excise, however, was very disappointing; as in Saxony, trade and industry suffered badly, the excise was extremely unpopular, and its levy was often resisted. At the diet of 1701 the opposition was so strong that it had to be revoked. But two years later it was reintroduced because of the insufficiency of the other taxes. At the diet of 1705 the opposition was renewed, but John William declared he knew best what the country needed and threatened to use force. The Estates granted 900,000 thalers on condition that the excise was rescinded, and this was eventually accepted. But in some towns it nevertheless remained in force. In 1707 the town of Düren strongly complained that trade was migrating into neighbouring territories, that the exemption of the rural

[1] Croon, op. cit., pp. 15–16, and n. 5, with the figures of the annual contributions from 1690 to 1716; those given by Schönneshöfer, op. cit., p. 329, are incorrect, indicating an increase of only 14 per cent.; Scotti, Jülich-Berg (1821), i, no. 1123, p. 292.

districts spelled the total ruin of the urban trade, that merchandise was burdened with an excise of 3 per cent. and another duty of the same amount which it was impossible to pay. Only in 1716 was the general excise replaced by a direct tax. Trade revived quickly, and the country benefited considerably.[1]

A different scheme was started in 1705. A *banco di affratione* was founded to pay off the princely debts. The creditors were to receive notes, repayable after ten years, which meanwhile were transferable like bills of exchange. The Estates were offered a co-directorship and a right of supervision of the bank if they undertook to assign fixed sums to it for several years and guaranteed its notes. Not unnaturally they hesitated to commit themselves to such an extent and only offered a sum of 100,000 thalers. In 1706 two deputies of the nobility and two of the towns were invited to sign the bank's notes, issued on the basis of a permanent annual grant of 100,000 thalers by the Estates. This the deputies declined to do because the Estates had reserved to themselves the right of making annual grants. After some negotiations the deputies agreed to the establishment of the bank for a period of ten years, provided that the ultimate decision was left to the diet. They only gave way when threatened with dismissal, arrest, and seizure of property, and even then they stipulated that their signatures would be invalid without the assent of the diet. Yet a diet was only summoned in 1708. It protested against the pressure used, but in the end it acquiesced and granted 220,000 thalers for the bank; a further sum was voted in the following year. Many more bank notes, however, were issued than the Estates had guaranteed, although the government tried to create the impression that they had done so. Time and again the dates of repayment were postponed. By the end of the War of the Spanish Succession notes to the value of 3,000,000 thalers were overdue, and a further 8,000,000 of notes were issued by the military Commissariat and also circulating in the country. Thus the credit of the bank was gravely jeopardized, and a diet was summoned in 1713 after an interval of four years. In this emergency John William

[1] Croon, op. cit., pp. 10, 15, 112–14, 118–29, 237; *Quellen zur Rechts- und Wirtschaftsgeschichte der Rheinischen Städte*, i, *Düren*, edited by August Schoop, Bonn, 1920, nos. 235, 238, pp. 306–7 (May to Nov. 1707); in general Erdmann, loc. cit., p. 44.

asked his Estates for help and suggested they should redeem 500,000 thalers of notes every year, so that all the debts would be repaid within ten years. The Estates replied that they were not liable because too many notes had been issued. But they suggested the replacement of the overdue notes by new ones, on condition that all the electoral territories guaranteed them, that the Emperor Charles VI and the closest relatives of John William consented to these arrangements, and that he confirmed the terms of the *Recesse* of the seventeenth century. This John William promised. Not only the overdue, but all the bank's notes, however, were replaced by new ones, against which the Estates protested in vain, and the Palatinate contributed very little towards their redemption. To meet the debts, 2,000,000 thalers were borrowed in Amsterdam, repayable in ten years, and many domains had to be pawned as a security for this loan.[1]

Thus John William succeeded, without encountering much resistance, in squeezing very large sums out of the country, in further weakening the influence of the Estates, in transferring their functions to new authorities and undermining their power of the purse. A few months before his death he crowned his work by creating in 1715, after the example of Brandenburg, a *Generalkriegskommissariat* as the highest authority in all matters of taxation. It was to assess and repartition the taxes and to issue tax demands, to audit and check the local accounts, to supervise local affairs with the help of officials travelling round the country, to decide disputes in tax questions, and to dispose of the money according to its own discretion. It was in vain that the Estates demanded the new authority to be abolished and the power of the former officials to be restored. As it controlled the bulk of the revenues, it deprived the Estates of all effective control in matters of finance and taxation.[2]

About the same time a similar development threatened to destroy the influence of the Estates of Cleves and Mark. Frederick William I, who ascended the throne of Prussia in 1713, indeed confirmed the stipulations of the *Recesse* of 1660 and 1661, and only two months later did the Estates swear allegiance to him, as was the ancient custom. Nine months

[1] Croon, op. cit., pp. 11–15; Schönneshöfer, op. cit., p. 335.
[2] Croon, op. cit., pp. 238–9; Schönneshöfer, op. cit., p. 334.

later, however, he decreed that in future neither they nor their
deputies would be permitted to assemble unless they reported
what they intended to discuss, and equally how much it would
cost in wages and travelling expenses, so that unnecessary
expenditure could be avoided. When the Estates replied that
they could not possibly report this before they had met,
Frederick William decided that such costly meetings, of which
they did not even know the cause, must cease until further
orders; but a few months later he permitted a diet to be held in
December 1714. How precarious the Estates' right of voting
taxes had become was shown by another incident in the same
year. The king demanded 168,000 thalers, but they only voted
120,000; whereupon he ordered them to be dismissed and not
to reappear until he summoned them.[1] Frederick William might
have destroyed them altogether, and he took important steps in
that direction by negotiating with small deputations only and
by transforming, during the following years, the existing indirect local taxes into a general urban excise after the pattern
of his eastern provinces, as the Great Elector had intended to do.

In Cleves the excise was introduced in 1714 against strong
local opposition, which made it necessary to use soldiers in
several towns. The town council of Cleves received an irate
royal order which declared it an unheard-of audacity of subjects to assert that their privileges were infringed if their prince
tried to save them from imminent ruin by an administrative
reform: if they did not heed this warning he would make
an example of them, so that they would regret they had not
shown him due respect before. During the following years, however, many complaints were raised about the decline of trade
and enterprise, the ruin of all credit, the emigration of merchants, &c., on account of the excise. These complaints were
confirmed by the government which pointed out that Cleves
was so small that nearly everybody could reach some foreign
territory within two hours and do his purchases there without
paying excise, and that the tax should be rescinded. The royal
reply, however, declared that every opponent of the excise was
a 'scoundrel, a knave, an ingnorant [sic] quack, a loafer, a

---

[1] Acta Borussica, Die Behördenorganisation und die allgemeine Staatsverwaltung Preussens
im 18. Jahrhundert, i, Berlin, 1894, nos. 141, 201, pp. 408–9, 598–606 (Apr. 1713 to
May 1714); ii, 1898, no. 6, p. 16; Spannagel, loc. cit., p. 29.

useless bread-eater'.[1] The introduction of the urban excise had very important results: it soon yielded as much as the taxes voted by the Estates, it was administered by the military Commissariat, and it depended on the king alone. Yet later full diets were again summoned. In October 1721, however, Frederick William once more prohibited the holding of a diet in the following year because the costly meeting of so many Estates was quite unnecessary and the budget would hardly differ from the previous one. But six months later the order was revoked after a petition of the Estates to that effect. Throughout the eighteenth century the diet continued to meet regularly, to check the accounts of the past year and to fix the budget of the coming year, to vote the fixed annual contribution of 180,000 thalers and to make extraordinary grants if required. The final budget was then fixed by the General Directory in Berlin without any further negotiations with the Estates and simply communicated to them. In 1753 the General Directory could report that the Estates' participation 'was only a formality, or a shadow of the influence they once exercised in matters of government'.[2] The Estates of Cleves and Mark were not suppressed, but in an absolute monarchy their power withered away. Wesel and the other towns declined and lost their previous importance; they were no longer able to offer any opposition.[3]

In Jülich and Berg the development was quite different, in spite of the weakness of the Estates during the reign of John William. Immediately after his death in 1716 their opposition revived. He was succeeded by his brother, Charles Philip, who never visited the two duchies, allegedly out of opposition to the Estates which did not exist in the Palatinate. He ruled according to French precepts of absolute government. He

[1] *Acta Borussica, Handels-, Zoll- und Akzisepolitik*, edited by Hugo Rachel, ii. 1, Berlin, 1922, pp. 211–12; ii. 2, nos. 4, 12, 31, pp. 10–11, 26–31, 66–68 (Mar. 1714 to Dec. 1719).

[2] Spannagel, loc. cit., p. 29; Hashagen, loc. cit., pp. 23–24; Croon, op. cit., pp. 249–50; Otto Hintze, 'Staat und Gesellschaft unter dem ersten König', *Geist und Epochen der Preussischen Geschichte*, Leipzig, 1943, p. 373, and in *Acta Borussica, Behördenorganisation*, vi. 1, Berlin, 1901, pp. 9, 473, 476.

[3] Wesel had 8,116 inhabitants in 1722 and 5,966 in 1739. All the Cleves towns on the right bank of the Rhine had 23,844 inhabitants in 1722 and 18,996 in 1739. The total population of the duchy declined from 85,988 to 81,146 within the same period: *Acta Borussica, Handels-, Zoll- und Akzisepolitik*, ii, 2, p. 32; Max Lehmann, *Freiherr vom Stein*, i, Leipzig, 1902, p. 106, n. 1.

looked upon Jülich and Berg as minor possessions and left the
government to the privy councillors in Düsseldorf. The court,
which his brother had kept there at such expense, was dissolved,
and other economies were effected. The country benefited even
more from the abolition of the general excise (at the very time
when it was introduced in Cleves and Mark) and of dues levied
for the billeting and supplying of the soldiers, for the hunt and
the roads. Another request of the Estates was granted in 1718
when their two *Pfennigmeister* were permitted to resume their
residence in Cologne, which they had been forced to give up in
1672, and to conduct their financial administration outside the
duchies. This was of little practical importance, for most of the
taxes were now paid into the war chest over which they had no
control. It was more important that the issue of tax demands
and the decision in important disputes over taxes was taken
away from the *Generalkriegskommissariat* and again entrusted to
the privy council, while the Estates demanded that the latter
should reassume control over the entire financial administration
and that the new authority should be abolished. This was formally done in 1721, but in its place a *Geheime Kriegscommission*
was formed with the same functions; while the Estates were
informed that their grievance was settled.[1]

At the diet of 1717 the Estates complained about the unilateral increases and levies of taxes during the previous reign,
about alterations in the budget after it was fixed by the diet,
about the government's failure to render accounts of taxes, but
nevertheless they granted 600,000 thalers. At the following diet
760,000 thalers were demanded, but the Estates would only
grant 470,000 on condition that their grievances were redressed.
The privy councillors, however, insisted on the whole sum and
issued tax demands for more than 600,000 thalers. The Estates
elected deputies to go to Heidelberg, Charles Philip's capital,
to ask him to take up residence in Düsseldorf, to curtail the
functions of the military Commissariat and to prohibit its
officials from levying more than they had consented to. Charles
Philip denied that taxes had been levied unconstitutionally or
irregularly and declared their grievances would be settled at
the next diet: with this the deputation was dismissed. At the

[1] Croon, op. cit., pp. 16–17, 230, 239–43; Schönneshöfer, op. cit., pp. 344–5,
357.

diet of 1719, 840,000 thalers were demanded. The Estates were
irritated because prior to its meeting provisional tax demands
had been issued, and they were only willing to make a provisional grant of 66,666 thalers and to increase it when their
grievances were redressed. Later they increased the sum to
100,000 and eventually to 400,000 thalers, but declared that
they were not obliged to maintain a large standing army and
that the country was overburdened with the cost of the life-
guards, the general staff, and many officers' pensions. Charles
Philip replied angrily and threatened that the money would be
levied by decree unless they voted the whole amount immediately. This was actually done in July 1719 with the tax for one
quarter, so that the Estates discussed an appeal to the Aulic
Council. As they declined to give way, they were dismissed
without receiving their wages, and simultaneously the 600,000
thalers required for current needs were levied by decree. The
Estates protested and declined to repartition the tax. They
assembled at Cologne to nominate deputies to take charge of
their case at the Aulic Council and to levy 15 thalers from each
noble estate to pay the costs. But, as on previous occasions, the
four towns of Berg and one of Jülich declined to take part and
to sign the required powers, and so did several noblemen.[1]

At the beginning of 1720 the Estates appealed to the Aulic
Council against their prince, the *Generalkriegskommissariat*, and
its subordinate organs. They claimed the power of the purse on
the basis of their old privileges and asked for the protection of
the Emperor and the annulment of the unilateral tax demands.
In his reply Charles Philip denied that the Estates had a right
to be summoned every year, to be heard on certain topics, or
to refuse to vote taxes for the needs of the country. If in the latter
case they did so, he was entitled to levy taxes by decree *in casu
necessitatis publicae*. In his opinion they were only entitled to
refuse to vote those destined for his personal use and only had a
votum consultativum, while they aimed at gaining *summam vim et
potestatem*. He forbade them to levy taxes for the cost of their
appeal to the Aulic Council on pain of heavy punishments and

---

[1] Croon, op. cit., pp. 17–26, 45; Scotti, Jülich-Berg (1821), i, nos. 1196–7,
pp. 306–7 (decrees of Aug. to Sept. 1719). The powers for the Estates' legal representative at the Aulic Council were signed by 36 noblemen and three towns of Jülich,
but not by the rest.

ordered more taxes to be levied by decree, disregarding the appeal. 193,000 thalers were thus collected in the two duchies. Then a diet was summoned, but the Estates declined to vote supplies until these orders were rescinded and the money levied was refunded. This Charles Philip declined to do, whereupon the Estates repeated their refusal and were dismissed. Both sides then renewed their appeals to the Emperor Charles VI. The Estates began to take a more radical line and denied the validity of the *Recesse* of 1672 and 1675, which had been signed under pressure, as well as their obligation to pay the debts of the ducal chamber and of the *banco di affratione* and the interest and principal of the Dutch loan of 1714. They strongly complained that whole regiments were billeted on the inhabitants to collect arrears of taxation. The soldiers were not given any pay for the time being and had to be fed until the arrears were paid; everything was seized, including tools, cattle, and land, if there was nothing else, and 'thus the blood was sucked out of the people's nails and teeth', as the Estates put it.[1]

In 1721 the Aulic Council published three decisions, all of which were favourable to Charles Philip whose support Charles VI needed. The Estates were admonished to further good relations with their prince and to make sufficient grants; their claim that they were entitled to refuse supply was refuted; so was their right to leave the diet and 'thus to burden the prince with the whole defence of the country and with the other *onera publica*'; the provisional levy of 600,000 thalers was sanctioned, and the archbishop of Mainz and the bishop of Münster were appointed as mediators. Thus reinforced Charles Philip exhorted the Estates to repent and to recognize their duties and instructed his councillors not to negotiate with them; but they would not vote more than 200,000 thalers, so that the taxes were again levied by decree. At the diet of 1722 the government demanded 657,000 thalers. The Estates of Berg were willing to pay 166,666 thalers, but those of Jülich only 133,333, while their customary share was two-thirds; they would grant another 133,333 thalers if the grievances were redressed and the levies by decree were stopped. This was accepted by Charles Philip, but then additional demands were put forward for the *banco* and

---

[1] Croon, op. cit., pp. 27–31, 35–43, 206–10, and n. 1; Scotti, Jülich-Berg (1821), i, nos. 1198, 1200, 1203–5, pp. 307–8 (decrees of Jan. to June 1720).

other debts. The Estates' disunity continued; one more town, Euskirchen, revoked the powers for the appeal to the Aulic Council. Those of Berg increased their grant to 200,000 thalers, and the towns of Jülich voted an additional sum, bringing the total vote of that duchy to 400,000 thalers. But the nobility of Jülich protested, and so did a minority from Berg, while the towns declined to pay the *banco* debts. Charles Philip accepted the supply voted, which corresponded to the decisions of the Aulic Council, and dismissed the Estates. He pronounced all grievances redressed and promised that he would not levy taxes by decree provided the grants were sufficient; but clearly it was for him to say what was sufficient, and what was not. His will prevailed, partly thanks to the support he received during the negotiations from noblemen who stood in his service, partly thanks to that he received from Vienna.[1]

At the diet of 1723 new grievances with regard to taxation were raised, but the nobility was now in favour of a peaceful solution. As only 400,000 thalers were voted by both duchies together, the proceedings were closed by the government and a further 600,000 were levied by decree. In the following year the same was done without a diet being summoned. The Estates demanded annual diets to discuss the estimates and check the accounts before the beginning of the new financial year, but this claim was refuted by Charles Philip as 'ill-intentioned and contrary to his princely authority'; while his councillors suspected the Estates of aiming at the *summa potestas et summum imperium*. Under these conditions all the attempts of the Emperor to bring about an amicable settlement were condemned to failure. The Estates petitioned him to proceed with the case pending at the Aulic Council as no settlement was reached. At the diet of 1725 the towns were willing to vote 600,000 thalers to win their prince's favour; but the nobility protested against a grant by the towns alone on the ground that unanimity between the Estates was required, so that the taxes were again levied by decree. In 1726 the final verdict of the Aulic Council was promulgated. It emphasized that the Estates were obliged to provide their ruler with the means to maintain the country, that the levy of taxes by decree was justified, that the Estates'

[1] Croon, op. cit., pp. 45–50, 54–59; Scotti, Jülich-Berg (1821), i, no. 1213, p. 310.

deputies had no right of participation in the administration of taxes, and that their grievances were redressed. Nothing more was said about the amount required for the country's needs; but as this had 'provisionally' been fixed at 600,000 thalers a year, the government continued to levy this sum without a grant, or rather 10 per cent. more because the impoverishment of the country made it necessary to cancel many arrears which could not be collected. For many years the Estates continued to oppose this levy, but this was of no avail.[1] Their defeat of 1672 and 1675 was now confirmed by the highest authority of the Empire, in striking contrast with the policy adopted by the Emperor Ferdinand II during the Thirty Years War, and equally with that later adopted towards Duke Charles Eugene of Württemberg.

Yet the Estates continued the unequal fight. In 1726, 600,000 thalers were again levied by decree, although they were willing to consent to 500,000, and both sides once more appealed to the Emperor. In 1727 Charles Philip announced he would no longer summon a diet to save unnecessary expense, and the levies by decree continued. The two *Pfennigmeister* were ordered to give up their residence in Cologne and to reside within the duchies, despite the protest of the Estates. Their deputies, on the other hand, were readmitted to the scrutiny of accounts, which had been undertaken by the *Hofkammer* alone; but the deputies protested that it still undertook the first scrutiny. In practice, moreover, their right of supervision was considerably curtailed, for the *Pfennigmeister* could only show them the receipts for all non-military expenditure, as well as the receipts of the war treasurer for money paid over to him. But they did not learn how this money was spent, so that the military budget was entirely removed from their control. As Charles Philip had no son, diets were summoned in 1730 and 1732 to render the oath of allegiance to one of his brothers; but no budget was presented, and the grievances were not redressed because this had allegedly been done by the verdict of 1726. From 1732 onwards the Estates for the first time granted the financial demands of the

[1] Croon, op. cit., pp. 62–65, 72–75, 78–81; Scotti, Jülich-Berg (1821), i, nos. 1234, 1236–7, 1256, 1264, 1275, 1284, 1295, 1312, pp. 314–33 (decrees of July 1723 to Nov. 1730); Marquis d'Ittre, 'Karl Theodors Initiation zum regierenden Churfürsten von der Pfalz', *Göttingisches Historisches Magazin*, i. 4, Hanover, 1787, pp. 672, 677.

government. In 1734, however, the outbreak of the War of the Polish Succession made it necessary to levy additional sums by decree. In the following year only the towns assented to the demand, and in 1736 only a minority of the nobility. The government considered the 600,000 thalers a minimum and tried to increase this sum under various pretences; while the Estates would not allow this amount to become a *norma perpetua* because the *banco* debts and the Dutch loan ought long ago to have been paid off. Thus a new conflict arose. In 1737 Charles Philip declined to see a deputation which the Estates planned to send to him. In 1738 the nobility assembled contrary to his orders and again asked for the protection of the Emperor. Once more taxes were levied by decree because the Estates would not make a grant. A poll-tax was introduced in 1741, and no diet was summoned during the last years of Charles Philip's reign.[1]

In 1742 the Neuburg line of the Counts Palatine died out. They were succeeded by Charles Theodore of the Sulzbach line; until the end of the century he ruled over the Palatinate as well as Jülich and Berg, and in 1777 he also became the Elector of Bavaria, thus combining very important principalities in his hand. For his benefit a memorandum was drawn up on his accession, which strongly emphasized the differences between his territories. In the Palatinate no Estates had existed for nearly two centuries so that the prince could levy taxes at his pleasure, as much as his subjects were able to pay. In Jülich and Berg, on the other hand, he had to tread carefully and be on his guard because the Estates wanted to share in the government, continuously to extend their privileges, and to seize his sceptre. They pretended they could vote money as they pleased, but this claim had always been resisted by the dukes and had been refuted by the Emperor; the Estates' deputies were shown the accounts so that they could convince themselves that the money was used *ad destinatos usus*; but many expenses had to be kept secret, or they might be criticized by the Estates. Therefore Philip William had established a separate war chest, the accounts of which were not divulged in spite of all their complaints. The Estates were also opposed to the commoners among

[1] Croon, op. cit., pp. 82–88, 231, 235, 251; Scotti, Jülich-Berg (1821), i, nos. 1359, 1468, 1474–5, 1482, 1501, pp. 345, 366–9, 373 (decrees of Mar. 1734 to Aug. 1742).

the ducal councillors because they staunchly upheld the prerogative, but the greatest thorn in their flesh was the amount of
600,000 thalers levied annually to which they refused their
consent. Over 10 per cent. of this sum had to be remitted every
year because the people were so impoverished.[1] Indeed, Cleves
and Mark during the reign of Frederick William I only paid
about 350,000 or 360,000 thalers a year, considerably less than
Jülich and Berg, but much more than they had given in the
late seventeenth century.[2]

Under Charles Theodore the relations between the prince
and the Estates improved considerably. Diets were held regularly, and the government did not attempt to curtail the rights
of the Estates any further. At the first diet of the new reign about
half of the Estates' grievances were redressed to their satisfaction. Soon after a long-standing complaint was settled in their
favour by the dissolution of the *Geheime Kriegscommission*, the
successor of the obnoxious *Generalkriegskommissariat*, and of the
war chest, the importance of which had just been pointed out
to the young Elector. The privy council was again entrusted
with the supervision of the financial administration, and under
it the two *Pfennigmeister* reassumed their control of revenue and
expenditure. The Estates and the principles of administration
they advocated had gained an important victory. On the local
level, however, an official appointed by the prince, the *Vogt*,
with his subordinates was responsible for the repartition and
collection of taxes, and not the officials nominated by the
Estates. The *Vogt* was assisted by the *Amtleute*, local noblemen,
jurymen, and some of the more prosperous peasants, whose task
it was to prevent fraud, victimization, and the overburdening
of individuals. They discussed matters of taxation at local
meetings and participated in the repartitioning of taxes undertaken by the *Vogt*, representing the local interests of the Estates
in relation to this official. In 1740 a Prussian official, who was
visiting the duchy of Berg, noticed that the *Vogt* lorded it over
the peasants and jurymen in the more distant districts and
would always find someone in the Commissariat to back him.

---

[1] Marquis d'Ittre, loc. cit., pp. 672–8; Schönneshöfer, op. cit., p. 358.

[2] Their contribution was 180,000 thalers a year, and the excise yielded 167,000
thalers in 1724 and 1725, 180,000 thalers in 1733, and 175,000 thalers in 1734:
Acta Borussica, Handels-, Zoll- und Akzisepolitik, ii. 2, appendix 6, p. 287. For their
contributions between 1681 and 1688, see above, p. 319.

He noticed also that the tax-collectors treated the people as they pleased, and that all appeals went unheard. Above all he remarked on the fact that the many clerical, noble, and free estates, which formed the nucleus of the duchy, were entirely exempt from the contribution which thus fell all the more heavily on the burghers and the peasants.[1]

To achieve a more even distribution of the burden the government in 1744 suggested the introduction of a general tax on consumption, especially on corn, bread, beer, and spirits. The towns of Berg were in favour, but those of Jülich against it; later, however, they changed their minds, with the exception of Düren which pointed to the disastrous results of the general excise of 1700.[2] Although the privileged orders were to be exempt from the new tax, the nobility remained opposed. But Charles Theodore claimed that he had a *votum decisivum* in case of such a disagreement and in 1745 introduced the excise, stipulating that its yield would be deducted from the tax quota of each locality. The protests of the nobility, however, continued, and the privy councillors advocated a conciliatory attitude after the experiences of the 1670's and the 1720's. Thus the excise was rescinded after two years. There were no further attempts at reforming the out-of-date system of taxation, and the privileged orders remained exempt. Exactly as in Cleves and Mark, the nobility even refused to contribute to taxes raised for purposes of the Empire or against the Turks, and all land that had been free in 1596 remained free, although the feudal services were no longer rendered. In 1720 Charles Philip claimed that for this reason the exemption was no longer valid and that the noblemen ought to contribute *pro rata* of their possessions, but all such arguments were refuted by the nobility.[3]

During the Seven Years War, when it was impossible to hold diets and taxes were levied by decree, the government declared

[1] Croon, op. cit., pp. 89, 192–4, and n. 4, 196–8, 236, 245; Victor Loewe, 'Eine politisch-ökonomische Beschreibung des Herzogtums Berg aus dem Jahre 1740', *Jahrbuch des Düsseldorfer Geschichtsvereins*, xv, 1900, pp. 174–5. According to Marquis d'Ittre, loc. cit., p. 678, and Schönneshöfer, op. cit., p. 412, the exempt estates covered more than half the land, but this seems an overstatement.

[2] See above, pp. 325–6.

[3] Croon, op. cit., pp. 95–96, 134–41, 189; Loewe, loc. cit., p. 175. According to Baumgarten, loc. cit. xviii. 32, the duke in the seventeenth century had no *votum decisivum* if nobility and towns disagreed.

that in times of emergency privileges were invalid and decreed that the noble estates had to participate in taxes levied for the hostile armies, taking its stand on the principles of natural and international law. As soon as the war was over, the nobility demanded restoration and protested sharply at the diet of 1763. Four years later the Estates decided on a new appeal to the Aulic Council against the levies by decree. They referred to the old German liberties and their rights and refuted the idea of an unprivileged and natural state of society, which the government had put forward. In 1771, however, the towns decided against the appeal. In 1776 the Aulic Council published a preliminary decision against the nobility, prohibiting it from speaking in the name of the Estates; a final verdict was never promulgated. With the return of peace the diets resumed their functions and taxes were regularly voted. Yet friction continued to arise over the amount to be granted, for the Estates did not feel obliged to pay the salaries of ministers, generals, and ambassadors, nor to pay off the Dutch loan of 1714. Therefore the government always added certain sums for these and other purposes—such as deputies' wages, repair of fortifications, and work along the Rhine—and increased other amounts when it believed this necessary. In 1770 the Estates declared that the military expenditure was too high, for the two duchies had to maintain twice as many troops as the Palatinate and the other electoral possessions together. But no redress was achieved. Every year between 600,000 and 700,000 thalers continued to be levied: the Estates' power of the purse had become a formality. On the other hand, the load of taxation did not increase beyond that figure.[1] In Cleves and Mark, on the other hand, and equally in the other Hohenzollern territories, the introduction of the general urban excise meant that any increase in consumption or production automatically resulted in a higher yield of the excise, which mainly fell on the towns.

In this restricted form the Estates of all four principalities survived the eighteenth century, and with the Estates their rights of granting taxes and of participating in the financial administration, although these rights were no longer what they

[1] Croon, op. cit., pp. 89–91, 98–99; Loewe, loc. cit., p. 174; Scotti, Jülich-Berg (1821), i, nos. 1860, 1881, 1901, 1919, 1926, pp. 488–98, 524–9 (decrees of Apr. 1759 to Mar. 1763).

had been in the sixteenth century. Diets continued to meet every year. They were still attended by the entire nobility, in so far as they were qualified to do so, and by two deputies from each of the 'principal' towns, 8 in Jülich and Berg, and 13 in Cleves and Mark.[1] But the number of noblemen qualified to attend dwindled: by the eighteenth century the nobility insisted on the possession of a noble estate worth 6,000 thalers and on a proof that the nobleman in question had 16 noble ancestors, i.e. to the fourth generation on both sides. In 1740 only 36 noblemen were thus qualified in Berg, and fifty years later only 30, while in Jülich there were still 50 at that time. In Mark also the nobility preserved some strength, but in Cleves the number shrank from 106 in 1630 to 3 in 1806, so that the nobility had in practice ceased to exist as an Estate when the old order came to an end.[2]

The Estates also retained their own officials. In Jülich as well as in Berg there was a *Syndicus* as a permanent councillor, usually a commoner who was a trained lawyer, but was attached to the Estate of the nobility. The towns of both duchies since the second half of the seventeenth century had their own legal advisers who did not possess equal rank with the *Syndici*. Cleves and Mark, on the other hand, had two *Syndici* each. In charge of the Estates' chests were the *Pfennigmeister* who originally were appointed by the Estates of each principality and confirmed in office by the prince. In the eighteenth century, however, they were appointed by him and were in practice his officials, and the Estates' chests were controlled by the government, in contrast with Württemberg where these institutions retained their independence almost unimpaired. The Estates further elected directors of the diet and their deputies. In Jülich and Berg there were eight such deputies, four from the nobility, two from the towns, and the two *Syndici*, who participated in the administration of taxes, could raise grievances in matters of taxation and help with their redress, and who could scrutinize the accounts, &c. In Cleves there were four noble and four urban deputies.

[1] See above, p. 268.
[2] Loewe, loc. cit., pp. 180–1; Baumgarten, loc. cit. xviii. 31; Croon, op. cit., p. 1; Hötzsch, op. cit., p. 255, n. 1; Spannagel, loc. cit., p. 29; Hintze, 'Staat und Gesellschaft unter dem ersten König', *Geist und Epochen der Preussischen Geschichte*, Leipzig, 1943, pp. 372–3. In Cleves and Mark only eight noble ancestors were required.

They were responsible to the Estates and received their instructions from them. But their rights also had become curtailed, for the accounts were first scrutinized by princely officials, who also supervised the financial administration.[1] Thus in all four principalities the power of the Estates was a mere shadow of the past. Yet in Jülich and Berg their influence remained stronger, and their spirit more independent, than in Cleves and Mark where the Estates became part of the machinery of the Prussian state, while in the past they had been the more powerful. That much the determined resistance of the Estates of Jülich and Berg had achieved, while the opposition of those of Cleves and Mark had been unavailing against the might of the army and against the power of the Prussian state.

VI. *The Rhine Palatinate*

When Charles Theodore, the new Elector Palatine, was informed in 1742 that in the Rhine Palatinate Estates had not existed for nearly two centuries,[2] this information was more or less correct. Indeed, at one time it was believed that there never had been any Estates in this important and wealthy principality, stretching across the middle Rhine and possessing in its capital, Heidelberg, the oldest university in what is now Germany; and in a recent German history it is still maintained that 'a formation of Estates did not take place' there.[3] But this assertion is not correct, although it is true that in the Palatinate the Estates developed very late and remained very weak, much weaker than in any other important German principality. It seems also to be true that a constitution based on the Estates, as it grew up in Württemberg and on the lower Rhine, in Bavaria and Saxony, in Brandenburg and Prussia, with well-defined rights and privileges, with standing committees and

[1] Croon, op. cit., pp. 2, 4, 226–8, 232, 235, 245, 251; Marquis d'Ittre, loc. cit., p. 678; Baumgarten, loc. cit. xviii. 32–34; Hintze, loc. cit., p. 372; *Acta Borussica, Behördenorganisation*, i, no. 201, p. 603; *Acta Borussica, Handels-, Zoll- und Akzisepolitik*, ii. 2, no. 31, p. 67.

[2] See above, p. 335.

[3] Friedrich Uhlhorn, 'Die deutschen Territorien', in *Gebhardt's Handbuch der deutschen Geschichte*, 8th ed., ii, 1955, p. 496. For the older opinion, see Christoph Jacob Kremer, *Geschichte des Kurfürsten Friedrichs des Ersten von der Pfalz*, Mannheim, 1766, p. 28, n. 4, and Ludwig Häusser, *Geschichte der rheinischen Pfalz*, Heidelberg, 1845, i. 487.

permanent officials, did not come into being in the Rhine Palatinate.

In the other territory of the Electors Palatine, on the other hand, the Upper Palatinate near the frontiers of Bohemia, such a constitution developed in the sixteenth century and flourished until it was suppressed by Maximilian of Bavaria during the Thirty Years War after his conquest of the country, on the grounds that the Estates had forfeited their privileges by participating in Frederick V's usurpation of the crown of Bohemia. Moreover, Maximilian wanted to eliminate any resistance to the Counter-Reformation he intended to introduce. He thus persuaded the Imperial envoys to insert a clause to that effect into the treaty by which the Upper Palatinate was ceded to Bavaria. At that time, there were only two Estates in the Upper Palatinate, the nobility and the towns, and the absence of the prelates, whose houses were suppressed in the late sixteenth century, was probably particularly obnoxious to Maximilian of Bavaria. In general it must have suited his book not to be hampered by the Protestant Estates of the conquered principality, but to be able to treat it as he pleased.[1] His ideas of absolute government could be applied to it much more easily than to Bavaria, where the Estates' privileges clearly had not been forfeited; and thus the constitution of the Upper Palatinate ceased to exist.

In the Rhine Palatinate on the other hand, the factors which elsewhere led to the development of the Estates were largely absent in the fifteenth century. There were no violent conflicts within the ruling house in which the Estates could have acted as arbiters between warring brothers or cousins, and there was no change of the dynasty, with different claimants asserting their rights to the succession, which might have strengthened the Estates' influence. In 1410 indeed the four sons of Rupert III divided their father's possessions and founded different princely lines, which later led to further partitions and the foundation of new lines; but there was no fratricidal war. The Electors Palatine, especially Frederick I in the second half of the fifteenth

[1] Ludwig Freyherr von Egckher, *Geschichte der vormaligen Landschaft in der Oberpfalz*, Amberg and Munich, 1802, especially pp. 62–64; Sigmund Riezler, *Geschichte Baierns*, vi, Gotha, 1903, p. 34; vii. 134; Häusser, op. cit. ii. 39. I have tried without success to trace the documents of the Estates of the Upper Palatinate in the Munich State Archives.

century, were engaged in numerous wars, but they emerged
victorious from them. Frederick I, hence called 'the Victorious',
exploited his successes by acquiring new lands and levying
enormous ransoms on his prisoners; he maintained a well-
trained army composed of native and Swiss mercenaries. Many
towns and noblemen as well as ecclesiastical dignitaries bought
his protection and paid him annual dues. The Rhine tolls and
the wealthy towns of Alsace—which stood under his protection
as the Imperial *advocatus* of the region—added to his treasure.
Thus the most important cause of the rise of the Estates in other
principalities was lacking in the Palatinate. Frederick had no
need to raise taxes and therefore did not require money grants.
He administered the country wisely and economically, with the
help of officials drawn from the clergy, the nobility, and the
University of Heidelberg, and he left the principality in a
flourishing state.[1]

It was not for financial, but for political reasons that Frederick I
found it necessary to seek advice and to associate 'the country'
with his policy. He was the second son of Louis III and had
succeeded his elder brother when the latter died in 1449 and
left a one-year-old son, Philip, whose place Frederick occupied
throughout his long reign. In 1451 Frederick assembled his
noble councillors and officials, the bishops of Worms and
Speyer and other leading clergymen, and several counts and
members of the high nobility who stood outside his jurisdiction:
each of those summoned then gave his opinion and advised him
to accept the boy Philip as his son and to rule in his own name
until his death, but to remain unmarried so that Philip would
succeed him. This advice of the 'councillors and leading members of the principality of the County Palatine on the Rhine'
was accepted by Frederick and by Philip's mother, Margaret of
Savoy. It was equally assented to by Philip himself when he
reached his fifteenth year. In 1474 during a conflict between
Frederick and the Emperor Frederick III the latter took the

---

[1] Kremer, op. cit., p. 543; Häusser, op. cit. i. 399–403, 453–4; Eberhard Gothein,
'Die Landstände der Kurpfalz', *Zeitschrift für die Geschichte des Oberrheins*, xlii, 1888,
p. 5, and 'Die Landstände am Oberrhein', *Fünfundzwanzig Jahre der Badischen
Historischen Kommission*, Heidelberg, 1909, p. 33; Tille, loc. cit. ii. 269–70. For the
Rhine tolls and their importance see: H. Fliedner, *Die Rheinzölle der Kurpfalz am
Mittelrhein, in Bacharach und Kaub*, Trier, 1910. Unfortunately, there are no figures
for the fifteenth century.

side of Philip and accused Frederick of wrongly occupying the
throne, and again Frederick referred to the advice given by the
'councillors and members of the Palatinate'. Some months later
he and Philip assembled many prelates, counts, lords, and
knights, their 'councillors and important members' of the
principality at Oppenheim and submitted to them the terms of
a draft treaty with the Emperor; they advised the princes not
to accept them because they were too disadvantageous, and the
princes acted accordingly.[1] Yet these 'councillors and members'
were not the Estates of the Palatinate, but prelates and noblemen of the area who were not the vassals of the Elector and who
were immune from his jurisdiction. Indeed, as in Württemberg,
the nobility were aiming at gaining the status of Free Imperial
Knights, and hence would not be an Estate within the Palatinate. The Emperor Maximilian for his own reasons supported
this claim, and the Elector Palatine did not oppose it because
it enabled him to appear as the leader of a free nobility. It
proved, however, an obstacle to the development of the
Estates.[2]

When Philip finally succeeded Frederick in 1476, his financial
situation gradually became less advantageous than his uncle's
had been. He began to request direct taxes in addition to the
Rhine tolls, and this required the consent of those to be taxed,
apparently for the first time in 1494.[3] Yet it was again for
political reasons that he decided to ask the advice of bishops,
prelates, counts, and noblemen, and for the first time also of all
the towns. He was involved in bitter conflicts with the dukes of
Bavaria over the succession to Lower Bavaria, to which both had
claims, and a war resulted which went badly for Philip. Therefore in 1505 he assembled all the prelates, noblemen, and towns
in Heidelberg. His vice-chancellor explained to them at length
the political and military situation, and he then requested their
opinions whether and under what conditions he should accept
the terms proposed by the Emperor Maximilian. This advice
each gave in a friendly fashion, and the Elector replied to them.
In the end, however, he was defeated by the Bavarians and had

---

[1] Kremer, op. cit., pp. 28, n. 4, 32–33; and *Urkunden zur Geschichte des Kurfürsten
Friedrichs des Ersten von der Pfalz*, Mannheim, 1766, nos. 6, 14–15, 93, 181–3,
pp. 14, 44, 47, 286, 488, 501.

[2] Gothein, in *Zeitschrift für die Geschichte des Oberrheins*, xlii. 12–13.

[3] Ibid., p. 5; no. 1, p. 72.

to accept the decision of the Imperial diet which was unfavourable to him.[1]

Philip's successor, Louis V, at first preferred to negotiate with the individual towns and *Ämter* through councillors travelling round the country when he was in need of a tax. In 1517, however, he summoned deputies from all the towns and *Ämter* because his debts were too pressing. The government suggested the introduction of a general tax, the administration of which was to be left to the Estates. It pointed to the beneficial results which such an arrangement had had in the archbishoprics of Cologne and Mainz, in the bishopric of Würzburg, and the duchy of Württemberg, all of which had recovered from great financial difficulties through the advice and aid of their subjects. This example Louis wanted to follow: if the deputies consented the prelates and noblemen would be assembled after them and asked to agree to the regulation of the debts. The deputies, however, demurred and were permitted to consult their principals. They clearly disliked the whole scheme and declined to give any advice, so that the whole plan was given up.[2] The most interesting point about these negotiations is that it was the government which wanted Estates to come into being, while those concerned were by no means so eager and feared the financial burdens this would entail, with the result that nothing was achieved.

Under the Elector Frederick II (1544–56) the financial situation improved. On his accession he received a substantial grant: a large property tax, an excise on wine, and quit-rents for commuted labour services, to which a large loan was added later. In Württemberg it was thought that these grants were made by the Estates of the Palatinate, but there is no direct evidence of a diet being held. It seems more likely that again some of his councillors were sent round the country to negotiate directly with the towns and *Ämter*. The excise on wine became a regular tax and, together with the yield of the Rhine tolls, considerably alleviated the prince's financial difficulties. Frederick II managed his finances far better than other princes

[1] State Archives Munich, 'Fürstensachen', no. 216, fasz. 134, fos. 21–28 (Feb. 1505); Kremer, op. cit., p. 28, n. 4; *Iohannis Trithemii Spanheimensis . . . Abbatis . . . Secundae partis Chronica Insignia Duo*, Frankfurt, 1601, p. 423.

[2] Gothein, loc. cit., pp. 7, 9–12. For a comparison of 1529 between Bavaria and the Palatinate, see below, p. 365.

of the time and could pay off many of his predecessor's debts. His successor, Frederick III, raised another large loan of 600,000 guilders and above all during the 1560's dissolved the monasteries and introduced the Calvinist faith, so that his financial position remained very favourable. In the later sixteenth century, however, this ceased to be the case, partly on account of the ambitious Protestant foreign policy of Count John Casimir, the guardian of the minor Frederick IV. For his enterprises abroad loans were raised from towns, villages, and individuals throughout the country. By the end of the sixteenth century the debts amounted to about 1,200,000 guilders, and the interest payable on them annually to 60,000. Military expenditure was extremely heavy, and the deficit continuously increased.[1]

Therefore instructions were issued in 1603 to all the *Ämter* of the Electorate to send two deputies from each to Heidelberg. They were to grant a tax and to advise on the best way of dealing with the burden of debts. They were to elect deputies and officials to administer the taxes and revenues, and these would be confirmed in their offices by the prince. Yet the diet did not bring the desired result. In 1602 the deficit amounted to 150,000 guilders, and in 1603 to 116,000, while the court alone consumed 202,000 guilders. After the dissolution the deputies of the five largest *Ämter* were kept back, and from them a standing committee of nine was formed to take over the financial administration, including that of the debts, and to discuss and transact whatever they considered necessary and useful. The committee, however, was unwilling to limit its activities to the financial sphere; it soon attacked certain officials and raised other grievances. It had strong Calvinist leanings and raised large sums from the towns and individual burghers and peasants to finance the Protestant Union, founded in 1608 under Palatine leadership, and the Bohemian venture of Frederick V. But it did not survive the collapse of this aggressive policy: it was dissolved by Maximilian of Bavaria when he

---

[1] State Archives Stuttgart, *Tomus Actorum*, ii, fo. 471 (Duke Christopher to the Estates on 8 Dec. 1553); A 34–35, *Büschel* 16a and *b* (Christopher to his councillors on 21 Sept. 1564); Gothein, loc. cit., pp. 14, 17–19, 22–23, 26–30, 69–70, and 'Die Landstände am Oberrhein', loc. cit., p. 34. The interest payable on the debts amounted to 48,600 guilders in 1592, 52,000 in 1597, and 62,600 in 1602, more than the Rhine tolls and the other tolls brought in.

occupied the Rhine Palatinate after Frederick's defeat by the army of the Catholic League in 1620.[1]

During the Thirty Years War, and even more so during the wars of Louis XIV, the Palatinate suffered terribly. In 1673 the estimated capital sum on which the levy of taxes was based amounted to less than 5,000,000 guilders, compared with about 12,000,000 at the beginning of the century. In the individual *Ämter* the rate varied between one-sixth and three-fifths of the pre-war state.[2] When the Elector Charles Louis was restored to the Palatinate in 1649, there was no reason why he should revive the standing committee of the pre-war period. To re-build his shattered principality he used the methods of absolute government which had meanwhile become fashionable. A permanent excise on wine, corn, and meat was introduced. A standing army with a war council and its own military ad-ministration was established: neither would have been popular with the Estates. Charles Louis was strongly opposed to all privileges and to any limitation of the power of the state. After 1685 this absolutist policy was continued by the Catholic line of Electors from Neuburg. By 1700 the standing army mustered more than 7,000 men. The taxes required for its maintenance were levied by the *Kriegskommissariat*; in the 1740's they amounted to about 600,000 guilders, to which had to be added another 600,000 from the domains and the other revenues of the electoral chamber. Thus the Palatinate became an absolute monarchy in which the prince was entitled to tax his subjects as much as he considered necessary or as much as they were able to pay, as the new Elector Charles Theodore was informed in 1742.[3]

There were thus several reasons for the early check to the development of Estates in the Palatinate. They were partly political, connected with the absence of conflicts within the ruling house, partly economic, connected with its affluence in

[1] Gothein, in *Zeitschrift für die Geschichte des Oberrheins*, xlii. 34–42, 63–65, 70; Anton Chroust, 'Ein Beitrag zur Geschichte der kurpfälzischen Finanzen am Anfang des 17. Jahrhunderts', ibid. lix, 1895, p. 30.

[2] Gothein, loc. cit., pp. 62, 76, with figures for the tax capital of the Palatinate for 1577, 1597, 1602, 1618, and 1673.

[3] Häusser, op. cit. ii. 662–4, 678; Gothein, 'Die Landstände am Oberrhein', loc. cit., p. 35; Marquis d'Ittre, loc. cit., pp. 671–3. For figures of the standing army, see above, p. 324.

the fifteenth and early sixteenth centuries, when most other princely houses became more and more impecunious, partly constitutional, connected with the non-existence of the nobility inside the principality. Yet in Württemberg the latter factor did not hinder the development of the Estates. Its dukes often desired to associate 'the country' with their home or foreign policy, or needed its support against the Emperor or other enemies. The Electors Palatine also tried to gain such support from their subjects, but these were extremely reluctant to render it. Therefore these tentative moves were not sustained and a constitution never came into being.

V

BAVARIA

1. *Introduction*

THE duchy of Bavaria was a much older foundation than any of the other principalities discussed in this volume. It came into being as one of the duchies of the Carolingian Empire in the eighth century and was one of the duchies into which this Empire was divided in the tenth and eleventh centuries. At that time it was much larger than it became later and included the Tyrol and other territories which became Habsburg possessions. It was in 1180, after the fall of Duke Henry the Lion, that this large duchy was divided and its nucleus was given to Otto of Wittelsbach, whose descendants ruled Bavaria until 1918. During the following centuries the Wittelsbachs extended their lands at the cost of neighbouring noble families. In 1214 they also became the Counts Palatine of the Rhine and thus acquired the Rhine Palatinate. In the fourteenth century, under the Emperor Louis of Wittelsbach, they held in addition the Brandenburg Mark and the counties of Tyrol, Hainaut, Holland, and Zeeland and were of truly European importance. Yet from the mid-thirteenth century onwards their strength constantly suffered from the many and frequent partitions, so common in German princely families, which resulted in the permanent separation of the Palatinate from Bavaria (until the reunification of 1777) and in the division of Bavaria itself into the duchies of Munich, Landshut, Ingolstadt, and Straubing. It was only in 1505, under Duke Albert IV, that these separate Bavarian duchies were reunited: henceforth they formed one large and compact principality, bordering in the south and east on the Habsburg territories and the archbishopric of Salzburg, stretching in the north across the Danube and in the west to the Lech river, a size which the duchy retained for several centuries. Within these limits there were a few independent territories, such as the bishopric of Freising and a part of the archbishopric of Salzburg; but the towns did not become Free Imperial Cities, nor the noblemen Free Imperial

Knights. With the exception of the town of Ratisbon, on the confines of the duchy, and the counts of Ortenburg and Hohenwaldeck, also near the frontiers, they all remained under the dukes: in contrast with Württemberg and the Palatinate which were seriously affected by this tendency towards fragmentation.

The duchy had, after its reunification, about 10,800 square miles[1] and was thus larger than the Brandenburg Mark (without the New Mark to the east of the Oder), twice the size of the four duchies on the lower Rhine taken together, and three times the size of the duchy of Württemberg. It is much more difficult to give any figures for its population. The capital and by far the largest town, Munich, is estimated to have had over 10,000 inhabitants in 1400, over 12,000 in 1500, and fewer than 14,000 in 1703.[2] The other thirty-three towns were all small, and the ninety market towns were even smaller. In addition, 4,700 villages and 120,816 hearths were counted at the end of the sixteenth century, and from these figures it has been estimated that the duchy then had almost 1,000,000 inhabitants;[3] but this seems very uncertain. In 1619 the government stated that there were 160,000 hearths in the country,[4] which might justify an even higher estimate of the population before the outbreak of the Thirty Years War. It is equally uncertain what losses of population were caused by the war, and how quickly it recovered its strength. It seems certain, however, that the population was much denser than in Brandenburg or Prussia, but considerably thinner than in Württemberg, which claimed a population of 450,000 prior to the Thirty Years War.[5]

[1] Michael Doeberl, *Entwickelungsgeschichte Bayerns*, i, Munich, 1906, p. 447. This is the best short history of Bavaria.

[2] Fridolin Solleder, *München im Mittelalter*, Munich and Berlin, 1938, p. 530, with population figures from 1369 to 1500; the figure of 24,000 given by him, p. 538, n. 5, for the year 1700 seems much too high; Sigmund Riezler, *Geschichte Baierns*, viii, Gotha, 1914, p. 426.

[3] Doeberl, op. cit. i. 447; Riezler, op. cit. vi. 23. The number of towns given varies considerably: see H. R. J. Lieberich, 'Die Landschaft des Herzogtums Baiern', *Mitteilungen für die Archivpflege in Oberbayern*, no. 14, 1943, p. 307, and 'Der Bürgerstand in der bayerischen Landschaft', ibid., no. 24, 1945, pp. 640–52. *Der Landtag im Herzogthum Baiern gehalten zu München im Jahre 1568*, 1807, pp. 234–8, has 36 towns and 74 markets; Riezler, op. cit. iii. 665–6, has 42 towns and 78 markets, and ibid. vi. 40, has 34 towns and 90 markets.

[4] State Archives Munich, 'Altbayerische Landschaft', no. 413; no. 414, fo. 21.

[5] See the comparative figures for 1700 in Friedrich Lütge, *Die bayerische Grundherrschaft*, Stuttgart, 1949, p. 10.

Munich was situated at the cross-roads of ancient routes from
the south and south-east which led from the Alps northwards
towards the Danube and central Germany; it was the first
convenient resting-place after the mountains had been crossed.
It imported large quantities of wine and salt from the south and
exported cloth and other goods. It played an important part in
the trade with the Tyrol and Italy, with Vienna and Hungary,
with Zürich and Lyon. The manufacture of cloth was an important native industry. Before the Thirty Years War Munich
had 148 clothmakers and 161 linen and cloth-weavers. It was
the largest buyer of wine from the South Tyrol and it monopolized the Bavarian salt trade.[1] The towns enjoyed privileges
of self-government, but even the leading towns—Munich,
Landshut, Ingolstadt, Burghausen, and Straubing—acquired
the highest jurisdiction, over life and limb, only in the course
of the sixteenth century, while the duke retained it in the
smaller towns. About 50 per cent. of the peasants stood under
the duke's jurisdiction. The nobility also did not exercise the
highest jurisdiction on their estates, in contrast with Brandenburg and Prussia where this became the rule, but in conformity
with the development in most other parts of Germany. Within
their *Hofmarken*, but not outside their seats, the nobility exercised the lower jurisdiction according to a privilege granted in
1311 in exchange for a money grant. It was only in 1557 that
Duke Albert V, hard-pressed by the demand for religious
reforms, granted to the nobility as such the lower jurisdiction
on all their scattered possessions, while previously they only exercised it within their *Hofmarken*. The lower jurisdiction did not
comprise that over crimes, nor suits regarding landed property.[2]

The nobility was very numerous. In the late sixteenth century

[1] Solleder, op. cit., pp. 29–34; Riezler, op. cit. v. 663; vi, 179; Doeberl, 'Innere
Regierung Bayerns nach dem Dreissigjährigen Kriege', *Forschungen zur Geschichte
Bayerns*, xii, 1904, p. 75.

[2] Lieberich, 'Einige Grundbegriffe des kurbayerischen Verfassungsrechtes',
Mitteilungen für die Archivpflege in Oberbayern, no. 2, 1940, pp. 42–43, and 'Überblick über die geschichtliche Entwicklung der Gemeindeverfassung in Altbayern',
ibid., no. 9, 1942, pp. 204, 210; Eduard Rosenthal, *Geschichte des Gerichtswesens und
der Verwaltungsorganisation Baierns*, i, Würzburg, 1889, pp. 189, 192–5; Josef Huggenberger, 'Die staatsrechtliche Stellung des landsässigen Adels im alten Bayern',
Archivalische Zeitschrift, Neue Folge, viii, 1899, pp. 196–8; *Die altbaierischen landständischen Freibriefe mit den Landesfreiheitserklärungen*, edited by Gustav Freiherr von
Lerchenfeld, Munich, 1853, no. 1, pp. 1–5; no. 60, pp. 158–61; Riezler, op. cit. iv.
491; Lütge, op. cit., p. 29.

there were well over a thousand noble estates, and 593 noblemen were entitled to attend the diet. But most noble estates
were small and scattered and did not become consolidated as
they did in the east of Germany. The main income of a nobleman consisted of the rents and dues paid by his tenants, and
shrank considerably in the fifteenth and sixteenth centuries
owing to the continuous rise of prices. As early as 1525 many
Bavarian noblemen were so impoverished that they were unable to take the field against the rebellious peasants and could
not afford the expensive armour and horses. Later many found
it too burdensome to attend the diet, for they were paid no
wages: more than one-third of the nobility did not obey the
summons of 1583, and many did not appear in 1593.[1] The
peasants, on the other hand, benefited from the rising corn
prices. As a government memorandum of 1555 pointed out, the
peasants could save considerable sums, and their farms were
rising in value—as were the dues and taxes they had to pay.
They were and remained personally free. Their obligations
towards their landlord consisted in paying their dues and rendering him labour services, limited to between four and six days in
the year, to which certain services for the ducal hunt had to be
added.[2] According to a legal innovation of the later sixteenth
century, the landlords in many parts of Bavaria could evict the
peasants at twelve months' notice; but the peasants resisted
this amendment vigorously and refused to quit unless they
received compensation.[3] As a rule the noble demesnes were
small, and in spite of economic pressure and rising corn prices
there was no marked tendency to increase them; perhaps
because there were not the easy facilities for export which
existed along the rivers flowing into the Baltic or the North Sea.

[1] Riezler, op. cit. vi. 26, 139; Andreas Buchner, 'Landtafel der vier Rentämter des
Fürstenthums Bayern', *Abhandlungen der Historischen Classe der Königlich Bayerischen
Akademie der Wissenschaften*, v, 1849, pp. 49–57. For the rising corn prices of the
fifteenth century, see Solleder, op. cit., pp. 116–17.

[2] Riezler, 'Zur Würdigung Herzog Albrechts V. v Bayern und seiner inneren
Regierung', *Abhandlungen der Historischen Classe der Königlich Bayerischen Akademie der
Wissenschaften*, xxi, 1895, p. 77; C. M. Freiherr von Aretin, *Geschichte des bayerischen
Herzogs und Kurfürsten Maximilian des Ersten*, Passau, 1842, pp. 316–17; Erich Tross,
'Der oberdeutsche Bauer zur Zeit der Enstehung der neuzeitlichen Kultur',
Oberbayerisches Archiv für vaterländische Geschichte, lxii, 1921, p. 53; ibid., pp. 95–96,
figures for the farm prices and the dues between 1480 and 1660.

[3] State Archives Munich, 'Altbayerische Landschaft', no. 400, fo. 52; no. 401,
fo. 39; nos. 402–5; no. 406, pp. 79–80; no. 448, fo. 35 (Nov. 1593).

Thus Bavaria was and remained a country of small noble estates, small towns, and small peasants, hardly touched by the great social and economic changes which occurred elsewhere. The Church alone owned very extensive, but scattered, landed property, which it was able to increase owing to the progressive impoverishment of the nobility. By 1760 56 per cent. of all peasant farms belonged to the Church, and only 24 per cent. to the nobility, and 13 to the duke.[1] This was a feature of vital importance for the history of Bavaria.

11. *The Estates before the Unification of Bavaria*

The many partitions of Bavaria in the fourteenth and fifteenth centuries caused endless conflicts and quarrels between brothers and cousins of the house of Wittelsbach, exactly as they did in Saxony, Hesse, and on the lower Rhine, and these feuds facilitated the rise of the Estates. They were opposed to fratricidal wars and to further partitions; they maintained a feeling of unity between the different parts and prevented a complete disintegration; they arbitrated between the hostile members of the ruling house. In Lower Bavaria the nobility united with the towns in 1347, and in Upper Bavaria in 1363, and the clergy joined them at the end of the century. In 1339 the Emperor Louis of Wittelsbach promised to those of Lower Bavaria that he would not employ any foreigners. Eight years later his sons confirmed this promise and equally the union sworn in their presence by counts, freemen, knights and retainers, towns and markets, poor and rich, noblemen and commoners, to stand by each other if the princes did not keep these promises or disregarded the country's privileges. If there was no redress within fourteen days after the receipt of a complaint, they were to be entitled to resist with their lives and goods. This right of resistance was confirmed in the 1390's by the dukes of the different parts of Bavaria. In 1356 eight noblemen and eight commoners were appointed in Upper Bavaria to supervise the levy of a tax on cattle. Two years later a similar

---

[1] Out of 29,807 farms the Church owned 16,616, the nobility 7,105, and the duke 4,073: Riezler, op. cit. vi. 209–10; Doeberl, op. cit. ii, Munich, 1912, p. 10. The figures given by Lütge, op. cit., pp. 29, 33, 36, for 1779 are somewhat different.

committee—composed of four ducal councillors, four noble-men, and seven burghers—was set up in Lower Bavaria. In 1363 Duke Steven for the first time promised that he would appoint a council from those resident in Upper Bavaria accord-ing to the advice of 'the country', the towns, and markets, and that no foreigners were to hold any office or castle. In 1393 the dukes undertook not to start any war without the assent of the nobility and the towns and permitted them to meet as often as they thought fit to discuss the needs of the country and of its rulers. A committee composed of members of the Estates, with or without ducal officials, repartitioned the taxes which were to be raised, levied them through subordinate officials of their own, and supervised the use to which the money was put.[1]

In the course of the fifteenth century the internal disorders and feuds became worse and the power of the Estates more consolidated. Clergy, nobility, and towns were merged into one permanent corporation, the *Landschaft*, indicating that it repre-sented the interests of the whole country: in this traditional form of three Estates the *Landschaft* continued to exist until the end of the eighteenth century, in contrast with many other principalities where either the clergy or the nobility disappeared from the Estates in the course of time. The Estates not only exercised a strong influence in the field of taxation, but also in that of administration, through the princely council appointed from their ranks and their insistence on the observation of the *jus indigenatus*, and in that of legislation, through their power of the purse and the grievances they raised about legal matters, the princely prerogative, and burdens they considered oppres-sive. They arbitrated between warring dukes and claimed a right of assent in cases of further partitions and sales of territory. They frequently renewed their unions and compelled the dukes to recognize them. In 1422 the Emperor Sigismund confirmed this privilege of the Estates to conclude unions with the nobility of other German territories and with his towns and those of the Empire, because the nobility were much oppressed and suffered much injustice in Germany. In 1430 the three Estates of Upper

---

[1] *Die altbaierischen landständischen Freibriefe*, nos. 4, 6, 10, 16–18, 20, 22–23, pp. 14–18, 23–24, 37–41, 45–47, 50–54 (privileges from the years 1339 to 1401); Riezler, op. cit. iii. 659–60, 674; Rosenthal, op. cit. i. 399–400; Tille, loc. cit. ii. 208; G. Barraclough, *The Origins of Modern Germany*, 2nd ed., Oxford, 1949, pp. 330–1.

Bavaria elected two noblemen and two from the towns to act as arbiters: if the dukes or their officials violated their liberties and rights and no redress could be obtained, those wronged should appeal to these arbiters for a decision; but if the case was too difficult for them, they should summon another four noblemen and four burghers elected for that purpose, and these twelve should decide by a majority.[1]

In 1460 the Estates of Bavaria–Landshut demanded for the first time that annual diets should be held and that the duke should not start any war without consulting them. The request for annual, or at least biennial, diets was repeated several times during the following years, but was not granted, for Duke Louis insisted it was his right to summon the Estates when he considered this necessary. The Estates of Bavaria–Straubing insisted in 1458 that the duke should take an oath to respect their privileges and unions, that he should not employ any foreigners, that he should not conclude an alliance or start a war without their approval; but Albert III was unwilling to concede the last demand and to take the required oath. Equally, when the Estates of Bavaria–Munich demanded that no tax was to be levied and no war started without their consent and that all offices were to be filled with natives, he gave a rather ambiguous reply, emphasizing his right of appointing two or three foreigners as his councillors if he needed them, and of having foreigners among his servants at court. The demands were clearly not fulfilled, for they were renewed under his successor, Albert IV. In 1493 the diet of Bavaria–Munich again demanded that he should not conclude an alliance without their assent and should hear their advice in all important affairs. And in the following year the Estates again requested that the *jus indigenatus* be maintained and their privileges be confirmed, for they were clear and did not require any explanation or interpretation.[2] The nobility of Bavaria–Straubing

---

[1] *Die altbaierischen landständischen Freibriefe*, nos. 26–30, 38, pp. 59–75, 93–94 (privileges from the years 1416–30); Riezler, op. cit. iii. 659–61; Doeberl, op. cit. i. 298; Max Freyherr von Freyberg, *Geschichte der baierischen Landstände und ihrer Verhandlungen*, i, Sulzbach, 1828, p. 594.

[2] *Baierische Landtags-Handlungen in den Jahren 1429 bis 1513*, edited by von Krenner, vii, Munich, 1804, pp. 66–69, 91, 292, 302, 330, 388, 417; ix. 226, 316–17; *Die altbaierischen landständischen Freibriefe*, no. 42, pp. 104–5; von Freyberg, op. cit. i. 539, 594–5, 629, 659; Riezler, op. cit. iii. 662–4.

concluded a veritable league against Albert IV because he levied
a tax from their peasants for a war against the Swabian League.
They invoked the aid of this League and of the Emperor Maximilian, who took their side against Albert, exactly as a few
years later he took the side of the Württemberg Estates against
Duke Eberhard. Albert had to give way, to declare an amnesty,
and to submit the whole matter to a diet for settlement.[1] It was
in the Emperor's interest to support the Estates against a prince
who threatened the peace of the Empire, while the Estates
gained further strength in this way.

That the Estates, in contrast with the dukes, preserved a
spirit of unity in spite of the long-standing division of Bavaria,
emerged in 1496 when they were summoned to deliberate upon
the grant of a common penny to the Empire for the wars against
the Turks and France. The Estates of Bavaria–Landshut declared this was an unheard-of demand and a difficult issue. As
their duke, George, was the younger prince, and as the Estates
of the other duchy had to debate the same question and the two
duchies formed one whole, they could not give a reply without
conferring with the Estates of Duke Albert IV, and so they requested the dukes to summon the Estates of both duchies jointly.
Yet the dukes, in spite of repeated entreaties, declined to do so,
and the diet brought no result. The nobility in 1501 complained
to Duke George that their places in the high court (the court
of appeal as well as the court of first instance for suits against
a nobleman or a prelate and for the trial of a nobleman) were
usurped by learned *doctores*, who were commoners and usually
non-Bavarians—complaints which were also raised in Württemberg and elsewhere. Thereupon the Duke promised that
more places would always be given to natives than to lawyers,
but he would not exclude the *doctores* altogether. He further
promised he would no longer allow the noblemen and his own
officials to trade in wine, beer, and other goods, nor the prelates to
sell wine to the clergy and innkeepers; but he also refused to concede the demand for annual or biennial diets.[2] The employment

---

[1] *Baierische Landtags-Handlungen in den Jahren 1429 bis 1513*, x and xi, Munich,
1804; Doeberl, op. cit. i. 311–12 (1488–95). For the events in Württemberg in
1498, see above, pp. 8–9.

[2] von Freyberg, op. cit. i. 568–70; *Baierische Landtags-Handlungen in den Jahren
1429 bis 1513*, xiii. 157, 177, 269, 292; Riezler, op. cit. iii. 664; Rosenthal, op. cit.
i. 426–9.

of professional officials, trained in Roman law, enabled the
princes to emancipate themselves from the influence of their
noble councillors who were members of the Estates and inclined
to favour them: hence the Estates' opposition to the *doctores* and
the ideas they stood for.

By the time that the Bavarian duchies (with the exception of
Neuburg) were reunited by Albert IV after his success against
the Elector Palatine in the Landshut Succession War,[1] the
Estates had acquired very far-reaching privileges, which entitled
them to participate in the government and administration of
the duchy, and had become a well-organized corporation. Yet
these privileges were similar to those which many German
Estates possessed at that time, and it would be a mistake to
assume that the Estates of Bavaria exercised greater powers
than those of any other German principality.[2] Everywhere the
developments of the fifteenth century fostered the growth of the
Estates. As soon as the Landshut line of the Wittelsbachs had
died out, the Estates of that duchy appointed a committee of
sixty-four from their ranks to decide upon the questions of the
inheritance and the government. This committee nominated
a chancellor, instructed all the officials to take their orders only
from the Estates, and installed a council of regency. The Estates
of Landshut then combined with those of Straubing and of
Upper Bavaria and in 1505 proclaimed their decisions under
the seal of Bavaria as one united duchy.[3] It is indeed remarkable
that even before the reunification of the country the Estates
amalgamated into one corporation—a process which the Estates
of Jülich and Berg, or those of Cleves and Mark, never accomplished, although they were for centuries under one government
and one prince. The unification of Bavaria not only strengthened the dukes, but also the Estates and guaranteed their
influence within the united duchy.

This was shown immediately after the unification when Albert
IV introduced one of the most vital changes in the history of
Bavaria. To prevent a recurrence of the troubles which had

[1] See above, p. 343. Neuburg then went to the Electors Palatine.
[2] This has been asserted by the two best-known historians of Bavaria: Riezler,
op. cit. iii. 659, and Doeberl, op. cit. i. 298. In 1650 Maximilian I expressed the
same opinion: see below, p. 404.
[3] Otto Gierke, *Rechtsgeschichte der deutschen Genossenschaft*, Berlin, 1868, p. 548;
Doeberl, op. cit. i. 351.

THE ESTATES BEFORE THE UNIFICATION OF BAVARIA 357

bedevilled its internal history for the past two centuries, he persuaded his brother to accept the principle of primogeniture. In
future Bavaria should be one duchy and should be ruled by one
duke, the eldest son always succeeding his father. If a diet were
to meet, the Estates of the territory of the duke's brother should
be summoned together with the other Estates; if a new conflict
arose between the dukes, it should be settled by members of the
Estates, exactly as sixty-four of them had arbitrated between
the dukes in the past. On his accession a new duke was to confirm the liberties and customs of the duchy *after* the Estates had
rendered the oath of allegiance to him. All this was transacted
at a common diet of the whole duchy, the first in its history.
Apparently, the Estates did not accept the last point, for in the
draft of this vital document the words 'after they had rendered'
were crossed out and replaced by 'when rendering', meaning
that in their opinion the privileges should be confirmed before
they swore allegiance to the new duke. In this form, more
favourable to the Estates, it was finally signed and sealed.[1] The
subsequent diets and discussions were occupied with the proposed Declaration of the Country's Liberties; but before the
deliberations were concluded Duke Albert IV died in 1508,
leaving three minor sons to succeed him.[2]

III. *The Defeat of the Estates; the Counter-Reformation*

The seventy years following upon the death of Albert IV
were the most dramatic in the history of the Bavarian Estates
whose influence declined sharply: a quite exceptional development in the Germany of the sixteenth century. Yet the early
years of the reign of William IV were perhaps the time of their
greatest power. During the minority of the duke his uncle
exercised the regency together with six representatives of the
Estates. They used this opportunity to settle the controversial
point about the confirmation of their privileges which had been
left undecided under Albert IV. In the Declaration of the

[1] The draft with the alteration is in State Archives Munich, 'Fürstensachen', xx,
fos. 299–307; the final version with the seals of the sixty-four arbiters is ibid.,
'Raritäten Selekt', no. 120, and printed in *Baierische Landtags-Handlungen in den
Jahren 1429 bis 1513*, xv. 355–81.
[2] For the discussions of 1506–7 see op. cit. xvi, Munich, 1805; Doeberl, op. cit.
i. 351.

Country's Liberties, promulgated a few months after his death, it was unequivocally stated that every duke on his accession was to confirm the liberties word by word, *before* the Estates rendered the oath of allegiance, exactly as it was stipulated in the treaty of Tübingen six years later. The ducal officials also were to give a solemn promise that they would observe these liberties. With regard to the other controversial point, the appointments to offices, it was agreed that in the ducal council there always were to be more natives and non-clerics than *doctores* and clerics, while all other appointments at the court and the safeguarding of the towns and castles were to be a monopoly of the Bavarian nobility. The nobility further gained the concession that in all the Estates' committees it was to have the same number of representatives as the two other Estates together, although they for some time had demanded equal representation with the nobility, on the ground that each of them had to carry one-third or more of the financial burdens. The Large Committee of the Estates, which debated the ducal proposition at the opening of a diet and in general guided its debates and decisions, was elected at the beginning of the session: it comprised thirty-two noblemen and sixteen each from the two other Estates. The Small Committee had eight noble members and four each from the two other Estates, and the same with all other committees and representatives appointed by the Estates. At the diet of 1510 the Estates elected from their own ranks the tax receivers (*Steuerer*) in the same proportion: for each of the four districts into which the duchy was divided one prelate, two noblemen, and one burgher, and twice that number for the district of Munich.[1] This proportion between the nobility and the other Estates was preserved throughout the history of the Bavarian Estates.

In 1511 Duke William reached the age of eighteen and assumed the government himself. According to the terms of the Declaration of the Country's Liberties he should have summoned a diet to confirm the privileges and thereafter to receive the oath of allegiance. This he omitted to do, as he explained

---

[1] *Baierische Landtags-Handlungen in den Jahren 1429 bis 1513*, xvii. 19, 100, 119; xviii. 130–1, 149–50; see ibid. xvi, for the preliminary discussions of the Declaration of Liberties, and ix. 332–8, for a controversy about the composition of the committees in 1494, and xv. 346–51, for the same in 1506. In general Riezler, op. cit. iii. 664; vi. 40–41; Doeberl, op. cit. i. 351, 454–5.

later, so as to save the Estates the expense. He was advised by
Leonhard von Eck, a professor in the University of Ingolstadt
(founded in 1472), who aimed at strengthening the prerogative
according to the principles of Roman law.[1] In 1512 William
merely invited thirty selected members of the Estates to discuss
the question of the confirmation of the privileges, but they
replied that this was a matter for all the Estates which ought to
be summoned. It took another two years before William fulfilled
this demand, and then only because of his pressing debts, and
because his brother Louis, disregarding the treaty of 1506 and
the principle of primogeniture, demanded a partition of the
duchy. In 1512 William's debts amounted to 180,000 guilders,
and the annual deficit to about 15,000. At the diet of 1514 the
Estates had their ancient privileges read out, renewed the union
that they would maintain their liberties, if need be by force of
arms, and elected a committee of eight—four noblemen, two
prelates, and two burghers, half from Upper and half from
Lower Bavaria. Because their privileges had been disregarded
to such an extent, anyone wronged should appeal to this committee, which should assemble twice a year at the ducal court,
guard their rights, hear complaints, and supervise the government. In the opinion of the Large Committee, some councillors
usurped the government, misled the young William, gave places
and offices to their friends, and created a large following of their
own; thus the duke did not heed the advice of the older councillors and noblemen and governed without consulting the
Estates, for the new councillors were opposed to their meetings.
Several times William proposed that the Estates should render
homage to him, but they demurred. Duke Louis through his
councillors demanded one-third of the country or a share in the
government.[2]

Accepting the counsel of the Large Committee, the Estates
then decided that there was only one solution: the two dukes
should rule together. The Estates' spokesman, Dr. Dietrich

---

[1] Doeberl, op. cit. i. 351–2; cf. above, pp. 355–6.

[2] *Baierische Landtags-Handlungen in den Jahren 1429 bis 1513*, xviii. 417; *Der Landtag im Herzogthum Baiern vom Jahre 1514*, 1804, pp. 6–7, 36–38, 92–93, 96–97, 99, 109–15, 128–37 (Jan. to Feb. 1514); *Die altbaierischen landständischen Freibriefe*, no. 50, pp. 129–33; von Freyberg, op. cit. ii. 104; State Archives Munich, 'Fürsten-sachen', xxiii, fos. 7–8, with details of the budget and a list of the debts, amounting to 178,250 guilders.

von Plieningen, who had studied at the Italian universities and adhered to the doctrines of humanism, addressed the two princes in front of the Estates. He asked them to accept this plan and, until they both reached the age of twenty-four, to govern with the help of a regency government composed of councillors proposed by the Estates; the *Amtleute*, the local officials, who were not suitable, should be replaced according to the Estates' advice. Louis immediately accepted these proposals, but William only after much hesitation. The Estates then voted 150,000 guilders, to be levied within three years, to pay off the debts and to redeem pawned domains. They proceeded to give notice to the officials who were obnoxious to them, at the court as well as in the country, above all to Dr. Eck, and appointed new councillors in the principal towns. Thereafter the Estates took their leave and left a committee of twenty-four in charge in Munich. This soon discovered that Dr. Eck had been taken into the service of the dukes' uncle and that officials whom they had dismissed had been given new posts by Duke William. They were informed that he gave vent to strong resentment, declared he would hold his councillors responsible if they erred, and equally those who had appointed them, and used other threatening language. They pointed out to him that such speeches were against the law and human reason, that it ill befitted a young prince to use such threats against old and experienced councillors, who would not want to stay in office if he addressed them in this tyrannical fashion. William excused himself with thoughtlessness. But the committee continued to lecture him: no prince was entitled to burden his subjects against the law; the *jus naturale* and *jus gentium* neither Pope nor Emperor could abrogate, and if they did so, the subjects need not suffer it, but could defend themselves; for even a little worm bent itself when squeezed by a huge animal, and so could man. Neither Pope nor Emperor could annul the treaty which had been recently concluded, and which was based on natural law; if the duke broke it, he would be considered dishonest.[1]

In the autumn of 1514 new friction broke out between the

---

[1] *Der Landtag im Herzogthum Baiern vom Jahre 1514*, pp. 146–54, 169–88, 191, 198–9, 227–8, 282, 464–8, 471–5 (Feb. to June 1514); an undated reply of Duke William to the Estates in State Archives Munich, 'Fürstensachen', xxiv, fos. 41–43; Riezler, op. cit. iv. 14–17; von Freyberg, op. cit. ii. 120–1, 136.

ducal brothers. Louis accused William of not admitting him to the government and of breaking his promises. Louis and the committee appealed to the country and occupied certain towns in Lower Bavaria with armed force, whereupon William countermanded these orders issued behind his back. The Emperor Maximilian intervened on his side. A few weeks later another reconciliation was effected. Louis was given a third of the duchy; if there was a new conflict, each duke should appoint four members of his Estates to act as arbiters, and if they were unable to agree the dukes were to select a neutral chairman who was to have the casting vote. This reconciliation resulted in a reversal of the whole position. The leader of the regency council, Hieronymus von Stauf, was arrested. Dr. Eck was recalled and soon became the real ruler of the country, characterized by a strong bias against the Estates.[1] As William urgently required more money, a new diet was summoned at the end of 1515. His councillors advised him that, if the Estates only voted money on condition that their liberties and the union of the preceding year be confirmed, he should forgo the grant and find other remedies. If they raised further difficulties, he should inform them that the Emperor had instructed him how to proceed at the diet: if their intentions ran counter to the Imperial orders he would have to refer the matter back to him. No money was voted, and the diet was adjourned for three months. At the request of the Estates a committee of sixteen was appointed to promote better understanding between the ducal brothers.[2]

When the diet reassembled in 1516, William had the verdict in the trial of Hieronymus von Stauf read to the Estates, including his confession and the sentence of death which had been passed. This was approved by them with one voice, and the unfortunate nobleman was executed. Then the discussions of the proposed new Declaration of the Country's Liberties were resumed. As on previous occasions one of the points at issue was whether they should be confirmed before or after the rendering of the oath of allegiance. The dukes declined to do it before because this would be detrimental to their authority and

[1] *Der Landtag im Herzogthum Baiern vom Jahre 1514*, pp. 636–44, 684–7, 766–7, 772–4 (Sept. to Oct. 1514); Riezler, op. cit. iv. 23–24; Doeberl, op. cit. i. 353–5; State Archives Munich, 'Fürstensachen', xxiii, fo. 169.

[2] *Die Landtäge im Herzogthum Baiern von den Jahren 1515 und 1516*, 1804, pp. 34–37, 122, 127–30 (Dec. 1515).

regalia, and declared that the Emperor Maximilian had forbidden them to confirm the Estates' union of 1514. On the
following day they refused once more to assent to the union,
but they were prepared to confirm the Declaration of Liberties.
The Estates would not accept this and requested another diet
to be summoned because too few of them were present to decide
the issue. The dukes insisted on a grant and on the oath of
allegiance. Finally, the question was submitted to a vote, and
for once the exact result was recorded: out of a total of 208
voting, 130 voted in favour of taking the oath because the dukes
did not insist on the abrogation of the union but were willing
to let it stand; another 11 also voted in favour, without any
reservation; 67 desired another diet to be summoned, but 19
of these were willing to proceed if this could not be obtained.
Thus a large majority voted in favour of a compromise. Apparently on this occasion the Estates voted per head by a
straight majority, and not by houses as was the custom. The
number of those voting certainly was small; eight towns had
two votes each, every other member one vote. Three days later
the Estates also gave way on the other issue and voted a tax of
100,000 guilders. They elected eight of their members to keep
records of revenue and expenditure, eighteen *Landsteurer* to
collect the tax in the various districts, and another four *Obersteurer* to receive the money from the former and to pay the most
pressing debts. Thus the Estates controlled the administration
of the tax. Later the towns objected to the method of voting per
head, by which they could be outvoted by the nobility, and
asked that the old custom be maintained, to which the Estates
agreed.[1]

The Estates further elected two groups of four deputies who
were to undertake diplomatic missions together with the ducal
councillors: one group to negotiate with the archbishop of
Salzburg about the salt trade and deforestation, the other to
approach the bishop of Passau in a frontier dispute between
Passau and Schärding. The two dukes confirmed the Declaration of the Country's Liberties, which soon after was published
in this new form. They undertook not to start a major war
without the advice of the Estates, to reserve the offices at the

---

[1] *Die Landtäge im Herzogthum Baiern von den Jahren 1515 und 1516*, 1804, pp. 213–
50, 330–9, 353, 371, 381–2, 424–6, 434–44, 449, 451, 467–8, 474–5 (Apr. 1516).

court and the safeguarding of the towns and castles to native noblemen, while native laymen were to have a majority on the ducal council. Every future duke was to confirm this declaration word by word on his accession *before* the Estates swore fealty— this point they had obtained; every official and judge on his appointment likewise was to swear that he would not act against this declaration in any way, otherwise he could be punished. If someone was wronged by the duke or one of his officials contrary to this declaration, his complaint was to be redressed according to the decision of the ducal councillors; if this were not done, the Estates were entitled to remain together to achieve redress, according to their liberties. On the following day the Estates finally rendered the oath of allegiance, and the diet reached its end.[1]

The main points at issue were settled by the diet of 1516, and a large grant was made which, together with the previous one, covered most of the debts. For some years no diet was necessary, but the dukes attempted to get smaller sums for special purposes voted by a committee. As early as 1517 Duke Louis requested an aid against Württemberg, but they declined and suggested that a diet be summoned. Two years later forty noblemen and twenty each from the two other Estates were summoned. Only sixty-six appeared and consented to a loan of 32,000 guilders for the war against Württemberg, in the course of which Duke William drove Duke Ulrich out of his country after his wanton attack on the Free City of Reutlingen.[2] Even the nobility contributed 6,000 guilders, 'contrary to the custom' which exempted them, and the prelates 15,000. With regard to the tax previously granted, the Estates stipulated that, if there was a surplus after all the debts had been paid, it should remain in their chest, in the charge of the sixteen *Obersteurer* whom they elected. The dukes, however, objected to being excluded from the financial administration which they considered derogatory to their dignity. In 1520 the Estates formally discharged the sixteen *Obersteurer* from their duties after their accounts had been checked by four deputies; another eight were appointed

[1] Ibid., pp. 470–1, 482, 487, 532–3, 560–2, 566–7; *Dy new erclerung der Landfreyheyt des loblichen haus und Furstenthumbs Obern und Nidern Bairn*, Landshut, 1516, fos. B iv, C iv, C v; State Archives Munich, 'Altbayerische Landschaft', nos. 357–9; Riezler, op. cit. iv. 33; von Freyberg, op. cit. ii. 176–9 (24–25 Apr. 1516).

[2] See above, pp. 14–15.

to collect the arrears from the many who had not paid their
share. In 1523, following a decision of the Imperial diet, the
Estates granted an aid of 24,000 guilders for the war against the
Turks, but only in the form of an advance on the next tax to be
voted. Twelve members of the Estates were appointed to collect
the money, and another four to receive it from them if and when
the campaign against the Turks got under way. To them was
added for the first time a permanent official of the Estates, their
chancellor Jacob Rosenbusch, who was to retain that office for
about thirty years.[1]

The taxes granted hitherto were levied from the property of
burghers and peasants, while the prelates and the nobility were
exempt 'according to old custom' which went back to the
fifteenth century. There is no evidence of any opposition by the
towns to this exemption. At the diet of 1526 the ducal councillors proposed an alternative modus of a considerable tax on
revenue from rents and capital. This proposal was accepted by
the prelates and the nobility (probably because their income
was not affected), but the towns declared they had no powers
to do so and suggested the customary modus, which seems to
have been less burdensome to them. The councillors tried to
persuade them to concur with the other two Estates, but in vain.
They then requested the towns to pay 100,000 guilders on their
own, but they demanded a consultation with the other Estates
and declined to decide anything without them. The councillors
referred this back to the two other Estates, with the result that
the urban deputies were admitted to their deliberations. Finally,
a tax for the war against the Turks as well as a new tax of
100,000 guilders were voted: a tax which fell on the Estates
themselves and from which the upper orders were not exempt.
The prelates contributed half, and the towns two-fifths, while
the nobility only paid one-tenth. These sums were to be raised
separately by each Estate from the annual revenues which every
citizen had to declare on his oath. On this occasion the dukes
consented that this should be done without their participation,
but they repeated that in other instances, such as a tax against

[1] State Archives Munich, 'Altbayerische Landschaft', no. 361, fos. 11–14, 19,
22, 33–35; no. 362; no. 418, fos. 173–5, 263–4, 302–8; no. 448 A, pp. 5–8, 64–67;
no. 419, fos. 16–18, 21–22; no. 421, fos. 28, 68, 73 (committees of 1517 and 1519,
diets of 1519, 1520, and 1523). Rosenbusch was still the Estates' chancellor at the
beginning of the reign of Albert V: ibid., no. 434, fo. 55 (1550).

the Turks, it would be derogatory and quite insufferable if they were excluded from the collection and keeping of the money. It was of greater importance that the dukes about this time gained the papal approbation for tapping the great wealth of the Church by the so-called 'decimation' of the clergy, which they could collect without the Estates' consent. It brought considerable sums into the ducal coffers, the spending of which was not supervised by the Estates' deputies.[1] This concession was made by the Pope at the time when Lutheranism was spreading throughout Germany. It must have lessened the temptation to dissolve the monasteries, to which so many princes succumbed at that time, and Bavaria remained a Catholic country.

At the diet of 1529 the ducal councillors proposed the levy of a tax of one-twentieth on the estimated value of property, but the Estates would only consent to one-thirtieth, as they had done three years before, which should have yielded about 100,000 guilders. The government argued that the direct subjects of the dukes had paid one-twentieth without complaint and that the Estates were much wealthier. In the end, however, the offer was accepted on condition that the tax should be levied with as little cost as possible and in the presence of ducal representatives and be paid directly into the ducal chest, as it was done in the Palatinate. The Estates on the other hand asked that the old customs with respect to the repartitioning, collecting, and accounting should be preserved, irrespective of what happened in the Palatinate. The chancellor, Dr. Eck, then emphasized that during the reign of Albert IV and before, ducal deputies had always repartitioned, assessed, and collected the taxes locally and accounted for them directly to the prince; but this was denied by the Estates who declared they could prove their case from their records and by the testimony of surviving witnesses. All they were willing to concede was, as in 1526, that the dukes could send one or several officials to be present at the final accounting of the *Obersteurer*, without any prejudice to their privileges. This was finally accepted by the

[1] Ibid., no. 363; no. 422, fos. 61–69, 72, 86–87, 106–9 (Oct. 1526); Riezler, op. cit. vi. 38, 46–47; Doeberl, op. cit. i. 355, 470; Huggenberger, loc. cit., pp. 190–1 (with the wrong date 1525). The first 'decimations' were levied in 1523 and 1524: Riezler, op. cit. vi. 46.

government, and consequently the *Obersteurer* took a pledge to the Estates alone, and the eighteen general *Landsteurer*, appointed by the Estates to levy the tax locally, to the dukes as well as to the Estates because they were to act on behalf of both.[1] In spite of this concession, however, the administration of the taxes remained in the hands of the Estates, and the ducal rights of supervision were very limited.

In 1532 the dukes proposed that the Estates should delegate some of their number to discuss, together with ducal councillors, all existing codes and legal regulations so that they could be revised. The Estates, however, considered this would take a long time and would be a heavy burden to them and asked for the plan to be dropped. The dukes replied it was their prerogative to promulgate laws and decrees without their subjects' participation; in spite of this, they had wanted to hear the Estates' opinions, but as they declined to give them, they would let the matter rest and would leave the revision of the laws to their own councillors. The Estates denied any intention of not wanting to participate and elected sixteen representatives to deliberate together with the councillors and to revise the codes and regulations.[2] From the dukes' point of view there were certain advantages in associating the Estates with decrees on legal and police matters and in hearing their opinions before making any major changes; whereas the Estates were usually in favour of maintaining the *status quo* and, as in other principalities, did not really feel competent in this field.

At the diet of 1535 the ducal councillors again requested the payment of a tax of one-twentieth on property, but the Estates, in spite of repeated demands, would only grant one-thirtieth, or about 100,000 guilders. They pointed out that the grievances which they had raised previously had not been redressed and that it was not their duty to vote supply, but that they were free to do so as obedient subjects. After the experience of 1529 they were determined to regain complete control of the administration of taxes, not only locally, but also at the centre. They insisted that the *Landsteurer* as well as the *Obersteurer* were to be

[1] State Archives Munich, 'Altbayerische Landschaft', no. 365, fos. 29, 39, 57–58, 64–65, 91, 95–98, 105, 118, 136; no. 423, fos. 33, 44, 65–67, 73–74, 105, 111–14, 123–4, 140, 167 (Jan. to Feb. 1529).

[2] Ibid., no. 425, fos. 6, 16–17, 24–25, 29–30, 76–80; von Freyberg, op. cit. ii. 225 (Jan. 1532).

elected by them without any ducal interference, that both officials were to take a pledge to the dukes and to the Estates, but that no ducal deputies were to be present at the final accounting, nor at any other stage, according to the old custom. To this the dukes eventually had to agree, but they tried to reassert their influence by making changes in the lists of the tax-collectors elected, on the grounds that some were too young or not qualified, some too old or invalid, or too poor. This, indeed, would have left very few of the Estates who would have found favour in the princes' eyes. The committee thus vigorously rejected this interference: if any of those elected were ill or unsuitable, they would remedy it themselves, and with this the ducal councillors had to be content and took their leave. For the time being the Estates had succeeded in excluding them from any influence in the field of taxation.[1]

This, however, was not the end of the matter. In 1536 and 1537 the dukes, irritated by the Estates' opposition and backed by mandates of the Emperor Charles V, who was seeking an understanding with the Wittelsbachs, three times levied taxes by decree through their own officials. Allegedly, they were afraid of being attacked by Duke Ulrich of Württemberg, or by the Turks, or by another prince, and there was no time to consult the Estates, much as they wanted to, about such weighty affairs.[2] When the Estates assembled a few months later they protested against the taxes as well as against the musters which had been held throughout the duchy. The dukes declared that their privileges would in no wise be infringed and that the money collected would only be used in case of a war. But the Estates persisted and demanded a formal assurance with regard to their privileges and the handing over of the money to their deputies and into their safe-keeping. The ducal councillors suggested the money should be kept jointly until it was needed, and the Estates should pay two-thirds of the cost of the mercenaries who had been recruited; they promised that the formal assurance which they desired would be issued. The

---

[1] State Archives Munich, 'Altbayerische Landschaft', no. 366; no. 424, fos. 26–27, 33–34, 40, 42, 49, 54, 56–57, 60–61; Riezler, op. cit. vi. 38; Rosenthal, op. cit. i. 404 (Jan. 1535).

[2] Riezler, op. cit. vi. 27; Doeberl, op. cit. i. 355; S. Sugenheim, *Baierns Kirchen- und Volks-Zustände im sechzehnten Jahrhundert*, Giessen, 1842, pp. 370–1, and n. 55 (decree of Jan. 1537).

Estates appointed four noblemen as war councillors, to hold the musters and pay the mercenaries from the money collected in conjunction with the ducal deputies. They also elected the usual eighteen *Landsteurer* to collect the 200,000 guilders they had voted. They reiterated that according to their liberties the dukes were not to start any war without their knowledge and consent, but they did not obtain the desired promise that in future taxes would only be raised with their assent and clearly tried to avoid a conflict on the main issue, thus leaving it open to the dukes to repeat the whole procedure.[1]

Further substantial grants followed. In 1539 the Estates voted an aid of 100,000 guilders as a contribution to the fortification of Ingolstadt on the Danube and elected eight deputies to receive the money and to supervise its use. They declined, however, to burden themselves with the cost of completing the work, as the dukes, who had started it with their own resources which they now found to be insufficient, desired. In 1541 the Estates voted 300,000 guilders for the war against the Turks, which were to be collected and accounted for by the Estates' elected deputies. In spite of this, the government seven months later demanded further aid against the Turks, but this the committee declined because the previous one had not yet expired.[2] At the end of 1542 the dukes requested an even larger sum, 600,000 guilders, to enable them to buy from the Counts Palatine three small towns on the Danube, which otherwise would fall into foreign hands. The Estates were told that the dukes were entitled by virtue of their prerogative to put a duty on certain goods, but out of grace they would hear the counsel of their Estates and allow them to appoint the tax-collectors for the purpose. The councillors explained to the committee that 10 kreuzers would be levied on each pail of foreign wine, 5 kreuzers on Bavarian wine, and 3 kreuzers on each pail of exported beer. The committee desired that the grievances be redressed first; but on receipt of a favourable ducal reply it decided by a majority to propose a duty of 6 to 12 kreuzers on

[1] State Archives Munich, 'Altbayerische Landschaft', no. 426, fos. 32–33, 42–43, 47, 51, 62, 85–86, 106–7, 119, 126; von Freyberg, op. cit. ii. 242; Sugenheim, op. cit., pp. 371–2 (Apr. to May 1537).

[2] State Archives Munich, 'Altbayerische Landschaft', no. 368, fos. 4, 13, 17, 23–30; no. 427, fos. 4–5, 13–14, 18, 23–30; no. 428, fos. 15, 18, 23–24; no. 369; no. 370, fos. 136–8 (Sept. 1539 to May 1542).

a pail of imported wine and of 2 kreuzers on exported wine and on exported and imported beer, but Bavarian wine should remain exempt. In the end, however, more than two-thirds of the ducal demands were granted and an excise on wine and beer was introduced. Until the 600,000 guilders were paid off 2 kreuzers were to be levied on a pail of exported beer, 8½ kreuzers on imported wine, half that amount on exported wine, and about 3 kreuzers on Bavarian wine as such. This new duty was mainly levied at the frontiers on imports and exports. It yielded 43,636 guilders in 1543–4 and 35,338 guilders in 1544–5, so that it would have taken about fifteen years to collect the 600,000 guilders, without reckoning the interest to be paid; but in 1548–9 the yield with arrears amounted to 68,265 guilders. The dukes solemnly promised that the money would not be used for any different purpose, that the excise would be rescinded as soon as the 600,000 guilders were paid off, and that it would be levied by the Estates' deputies. It was paid into the Estates' chest which became responsible for paying the interest and the principal of the country's debts.[1]

The excise was not rescinded when the 600,000 guilders had been paid, but it became a permanent tax which was doubled in 1565, doubled again in 1572 and also extended to beer consumed in the duchy. It was a much more modern tax than the antiquated property tax and much more evenly distributed over the whole country. From the 1570's onwards it regularly yielded well over 100,000 guilders a year.[2] As the Estates administered the excise themselves and as the money flowed into their chest, it did not weaken their influence, as the introduction of the excise later did in other principalities. Only eight months after the grant of the excise the Estates voted another

---

[1] *Der Landtag im Herzogthum Baiern auf den ersten November zu Ingolstadt im Jahre 1542*, 1807, pp. 30, 47, 53–55, 60–61, 96–97, 102, 109, 119–24; *Die altbaierischen landständischen Freibriefe*, no. 56, pp. 146–7; Riezler, op. cit. vi. 36. The figures of the yield of the excise—the only ones to be preserved prior to 1576—are taken from State Archives Munich, 'Staatsverwaltung', no. 1788, and State Archives Landshut, Rep. 16, Fasz. 8, no. 84. In Bavaria the guilder was reckoned at 7 shillings, or 60 kreuzers, or 210 pfennigs, or 420 hellers; while a pound usually had 8 shillings or 240 pfennigs. The rate of interest the Estates had to pay was usually 5 per cent.

[2] These figures apply only to Upper Bavaria because those for Lower Bavaria have unfortunately not been preserved. I have published the detailed figures of the yield of the excise from 1576 onwards in *The English Historical Review*, lxxii, 1956, pp. 240 ff.

700,000 guilders on account of the Turkish danger and the mounting ducal debts, 600,000 of which were to be paid out of the excise, making its eventual disappearance even more remote. The Estates made this grant conditional on the redress of their grievances. They also tried to extract a promise that meanwhile no other tax or duty would be levied, unless it were voted by the whole Empire for a war against the Turks. But the dukes considered such an undertaking derogatory to their dignity, for they would not demand an aid unless it was necessary for their or the country's needs. To strengthen the garrison of Vienna, troops were dispatched thither, their commander being instructed by the Estates. Two noblemen were to muster the troops before their departure, and another four were to assist the dukes in military matters. The dukes once more emphasized that it was within their power to levy taxes for the war against the Turks by virtue of their prerogative, but that they were satisfied with the Estates' offer—a claim which was not contradicted by the Estates. Another Christian aid of 200,000 guilders against the Turks was granted in 1544, and 150,000 to pay off the ducal debts in 1545. 80,000 of this sum came from the Estates themselves, half from the prelates, and only one-tenth from the nobility. The Estates attempted to make these grants conditional on the curtailment of court expenditure, which they considered much too high, and on the redress of their grievances. Duke William on the other hand preferred a verbal procedure to the customary method of exchanging written propositions and replies. When the Large Committee complained strongly about this innovation, designed to shorten the duration of the sessions, Dr. Eck replied sharply and vehemently, accusing them of usurping the princely authority and of aiming at making themselves masters, and the duke their servant. If these tactics were designed to intimidate the Estates, they succeeded, for two days later they voted the sum requested and apologized for their earlier complaint.[1]

Yet all their pliancy was of little avail. Meanwhile Duke William was negotiating with the Emperor Charles V about a

---

[1] *Der Landtag im Herzogthum Baiern gehalten zu Landshut im Jahre 1543*, 1807, pp. 24–25, 65–67, 71–72, 97–98, 104, 138–41, 159–61, 223–4, 228; State Archives Munich, 'Altbayerische Landschaft', no. 431, fos. 89–90, 121, 172; no. 372; no. 432, fos. 90, 129, 133, 136–8, 143–4, 212–13 (June 1543 to June 1545).

Bavarian contribution to the imminent Schmalcaldic War, demanding as the price of his help territorial concessions and the electoral dignity. That much, however, the Emperor was not willing to concede. All that William obtained was a matrimonial alliance between his heir, Albert, and the Archduchess Anne of Habsburg, which became the foundation of a common policy in German and in religious affairs. Another result of the understanding reached was an Imperial mandate to the Estates, which was promulgated in 1546 and instructed them to pay the debts left by Duke Louis, William's brother and co-regent, who had died recently. On the strength of this mandate William levied about 200,000 guilders by decree. Some weeks later the Emperor issued an order to the Estates that the excise was not to be rescinded when the debts had been paid off, but was to be paid to the duke permanently, the required powers having been granted to him by virtue of the plenitude of the Imperial authority.[1] As the ducal debts were growing, there was no prospect of their being paid off, and William proceeded to levy a tax from his own peasants. At the beginning of 1547 he explained to the Estates that he had intended to consult them in August of the preceding year, but had been prevented by the approach of the Protestant forces who wanted to attack Bavaria, and had already advanced to the Danube. He affirmed that he did not want to arm without the Estates' approval, for recently some of them had refused to take the field against the Protestants by the side of the Emperor, claiming that they were not obliged to do so without the Estates' consent—the first sign of a link between their opposition and Protestant leanings. The Estates then granted a reserve of 80,000 guilders, as usual half to be given by the prelates, and one-tenth by the nobility. Only the towns demurred and complained about the previous levies without their assent. The Estates appointed the usual *Landsteurer*, two muster-masters and four captains from the ranks of the nobility, and—at the request of the ducal councillors—a colonel of the foot-soldiers and a quartermaster. A further 300,000 guilders was voted by the diet of 1550.[2]

[1] Sugenheim, op. cit., p. 376; Doeberl, op. cit. i. 355; Gustav Wolf, 'Reformationszeit', in *Gebhardt's Handbuch der deutschen Geschichte*, 7th ed., 1931, i. 618–19.
[2] State Archives Munich, 'Altbayerische Landschaft', no. 373, fos. 5–7, 29–30, 49, 82, 96–98, 117–20; no. 374; no. 435, fos. 67, 77–78 (Jan. 1547 to Jan. 1550).

In spite of the many taxes levied with or without the consent of the Estates, Duke William in 1550 had debts amounting to 368,760 guilders, not counting the 1,200,000 the Estates had taken over. Yet Maurice of Saxony in 1553 left debts of 1,667,000 guilders, and William's cousin, Ottheinrich, the Count Palatine of Neuburg, in 1544 had debts of 1,050,000 guilders, a colossal sum considering the size of his principality. His situation became so precarious that he had to declare himself bankrupt and to sell his territory to his own Estates. These agreed to pay him a pension, but made him reside outside the principality. They appealed for help to the Estates of Bavaria, affirming that they desired to remain members of the house of Wittelsbach. But those of Bavaria considered the burden so heavy that their own ruin would certainly ensue and declined to give any help to those of Neuburg.[1]

During the reign of William IV, which lasted forty-two years, the Estates' influence declined very considerably. During his minority the Estates almost ruled the country; but William and his chancellor, Dr. Eck, were determined to break their power and were fairly successful in doing so, with 'a cleverness rivalling that of Machiavelli's teachings', as a Bavarian historian put it in 1819.[2] The chink in the Estates' armour was that—in contrast with those in many other German principalities—they did not establish their power of the purse when they took over the ducal debts. William taxed his own peasants and the clergy outside the machinery of the Estates, and he levied taxes by decree when he considered this necessary; he publicly proclaimed that he was entitled to do so, in contrast with earlier solemn promises. The Estates made concession after concession without gaining any benefits. The leading group, the nobility, showed little skill and little determination in the defence of their and the Estates' privileges. This augured ill for the Estates' future if William's successor were to continue his policy.

The first two diets of the reign of Albert V passed without any

[1] State Archives Munich, 'Altbayerische Landschaft', no. 374; no. 435, fos. 46–54; no. 431, fos. 56–58, 83, 98–103. The principality of Neuburg had been founded in 1505, after the Landshut Succession War (see above, pp. 343, 356), so that the wish of the Neuburg Estates is understandable. But the Bavarian Estates were hard-pressed by their own prince at that time, hence did not desire to pay another prince's debts. Cf. above, pp. 217–18, for those of Maurice of Saxony.
[2] D. Ignaz Rudhart, *Die Geschichte der Landstände in Baiern*, Munich, 1819, ii. 126.

major conflict. The Estates informed him in 1550 that they were willing to take the oath of allegiance if he first confirmed their liberties and privileges and redressed their grievances. Albert gave his assent. The Estates' chancellor read his confirmation, which was identical with that previously given by his father and uncle, and then the assembled Estates rendered the oath. The Estates then voted him 40,000 guilders, to be taken out of the sum granted to William a few months before to redeem debts, and there was some difficulty over this condition stipulated by them. Two years later the Estates voted a tax of 140,000 guilders and elected captains, muster-masters, and quartermasters for the various districts, while Albert appointed another muster-master and a colonel of the infantry. The regulations governing trade and enterprise were discussed with the Estates. The towns complained about the retail trade in cloth outside their walls. The prelates and the nobility claimed freedom from tolls and duties for their own corn, while the government opposed this claim for corn sent by water, unless it was only sent to the nearest market, because it was usually shipped for sale. In the end Albert agreed that the noblemen's own corn was to be exempt from all tolls, whether transported by land or water, as long as they did not trade like merchants. Yet once this freedom was conceded it was in practice impossible to supervise the observation of the last clause, and the rising corn prices made the sales more attractive and more profitable for those enjoying such noble privileges.[1]

Neither economic nor financial problems, however, dominated the relations between Albert and the Estates during the following years, but the religious issue. Protestantism spread to Bavaria comparatively late. During the reign of William IV it won adherents, but did not cause any conflict. It took above all the form of a demand for communion in both kinds and was encouraged by similar movements in the neighbouring Habsburg territories. In 1555 the ducal councillors expressed the hope that, if concessions were made on this and some other points with the Pope's assent, further attacks on the established

[1] State Archives Munich, 'Altbayerische Landschaft', no. 434, fos. 17, 23–25, 54–55, 76–77, 90–91, 105–6; no. 436, fos. 49, 70, 80, 90, 95, 101, 103, 107, 118 (Apr. 1550 to Mar. 1552); Riezler, op. cit. iv. 485, and 'Zur Würdigung Herzog Albrechts V. von Bayern und seiner inneren Regierung', loc. cit., pp. 76–77.

religion might be avoided.[1] At the diet such demands were voiced for the first time in 1553, perhaps encouraged by the weakness of the Catholics and their willingness to make concessions: facts which were confirmed by the successful rising of Maurice of Saxony and the repeal of the *Interim* in the preceding year. The Large Committee discussed the religious issue at great length and decided by a majority against the votes of the prelates to submit to Albert certain articles of religion, which in their opinion needed reformation, and which incorporated the principal demands of the Estates of Upper Austria on the same topic. These articles were then read to the assembled Estates and approved by a large majority of the two lay Estates. They requested the chalice for those of the laity who desired it, 'as it had been done at the beginning of Christianity for several centuries', the provision of qualified clergymen for the parishes, and the cessation of expulsions of preachers of God's word, and pronounced against the inquisition which, they claimed, certain people were persuading Albert to introduce. He replied that the diet had not been summoned to discuss religion. He was therefore surprised that such new and strange demands were put forward and requested to be spared such innovations in future. He denied any intention of setting up an inquisition and complained about the religious discord and unrest, the contempt shown for the Mass, the deriding of images, the preaching of run-away monks, the disturbances of processions and the rioting that occurred in the country. The lay Estates, however, repeated the demand for communion in both kinds. As many of them were pressed by their conscience to receive it in that form, it should be allowed to those desiring it, and freedom of conscience should be conceded. Although they voted over 300,000 guilders, Albert sharply refused to make any religious concessions.[2]

At the following diet, in 1556, the nobility and the towns changed their tactics. They consulted together and drew up a new petition to permit communion in both kinds and freedom of conscience, 'according to the clear word of God'; this was put to the vote and approved by all. On the following day they

---

[1] Riezler, loc. cit., p. 77.
[2] State Archives Munich, 'Altbayerische Landschaft', no. 437; no. 438, fos. 33–34, 37, 45–48, 58–62, 64–65, 68–69, 75, 94; no. 439, fos. 30–31, 35, 45–49, 63–69, 72, 77–79, 86, 107; von Freyberg, op. cit. ii. 315–16, 319; Riezler, op. cit. iv. 501–3; Doeberl, op. cit. i. 406 (Dec. 1553).

declared that, if this request were not granted, they would not enter into a discussion of the ducal proposition, but if it were granted they would show their gratitude. This decision they declined to alter when Albert appealed to them, claiming that the salvation of their souls depended on it. They requested that those clergymen who did not possess the blessing of abstinence should be permitted to marry, so that they need not take concubines and the shortage of learned parsons could be overcome: demands which to Albert smacked of 'overweening presumption and disobedience'. These tactics were successful: Albert promised that for the time being he would not punish those receiving communion in both kinds or eating flesh during Lent on grounds of conscience, and that he would open negotiations with the bishops that they should not impose any penalties on priests who allowed the laity the chalice. Then the Estates voted 232,000 guilders, partly to members of the ducal family, but declined to take over another 600,000 guilders of debts.[1]

Albert's concession of 1556 permitted communion in both kinds, but left it to the individual clergymen to decide whether they would allow the laity the chalice. As the bishops were strongly opposed to it, most priests were afraid to grant it and many laymen remained excluded. Therefore the Estates at the end of 1557 pointed out that the ducal concession had borne little fruit and requested that every clergyman should allow the chalice to those desiring it and not refuse it. If this wish were granted, the two lay Estates would take over 300,000 guilders of Albert's debts. In his reply he emphasized the dangers arising from the many sects and the many different opinions among the adherents of the Augsburg Confession who publicly called each other heretics, so that the Estates would never reach agreement among themselves. The Estates asked for orders to be sent out to the ducal officials in the country, instructing them to summon the local clergy and to assure them that they could allow the laity the chalice without any fear of worldly punishment or disfavour. They also asked that clerical marriages

[1] State Archives Munich, 'Altbayerische Landschaft', no. 375, pp. 56, 64, 68, 83–84, 104–5, 109–10, 162–4, 217–18, 248–51, 292–3, 297, 332, 339, 353–4, 438–48; no. 440, fos. 26–27, 30, 32, 39, 48–51, 71–72, 92–93, 104–5, 120, 122, 134, 137, 142–3, 177–81; von Freyberg, op. cit. ii. 323–9; Riezler, op. cit. iv. 505; Doeberl, op. cit. i. 406–7; Alois Knöpfler, *Die Kelchbewegung in Bayern unter dem Herzog Albrecht V.*, Munich, 1891, pp. 21–22 (Mar. 1556).

should be permitted, and repeated their offer of a grant if their wishes were fulfilled. Albert, however, merely repeated his previous declaration, but declined to go beyond it, even if he should be forced to go begging with his wife and children. A rupture was only avoided by his meeting the wishes of the nobility in an entirely different field. They desired that their right of exercising the lower jurisdiction, which they possessed within their *Hofmarken*, but not outside, be extended to all their scattered possessions.[1] This wish was granted for those estates they held as a property and thus their support was bought at a cheap price, as one of the Protestant noblemen had feared; but if such lands later came into the hands of prelates or burghers, the ducal rights of jurisdiction were to revive. Then the Estates, no longer united, granted 812,000 guilders, including debts of 500,000 which they took over, and the payment of interest on ducal debts: an aid of a size never previously voted. According to a contemporary witness, Albert announced publicly that he would never depart from his obedience to the Church of Rome and from communion in one kind; yet the Estates in the end became quite pliant and departed in amity.[2] The tactic of making a concession to one Estate only was successful, for the towns alone, even if they were united, were much too weak to continue the opposition.

During the negotiations of 1557 Albert claimed that in nearly all the towns of Lower Bavaria and some of Upper Bavaria communion was celebrated in both kinds. That this was not very far from the truth was proved by the visitations of the churches conducted a few months later. In Straubing, of 5,000 communicants the large majority took the sacrament in both kinds. According to the priest, there was hardly a house without Lutheran books, Catholic services were very badly attended, and the whole town council consisted of Lutherans. At Schärding all the 1,500 communicants took it *sub utraque*. The Mass

---

[1] See above, p. 350.

[2] State Archives Munich, 'Altbayerische Landschaft', no. 376, fos. 24–25, 28–33, 39–42, 66–68, 84, 102, 167, 205, 221–7; no. 441, fos. 25–26, 29–34, 39–42, 66–68, 73, 83, 101, 168, 209–10, 228–35; no. 441 A, fos. 20, 23–24, 26, 30–33, 50–51, 54, 61, 73, 119–20, 146, 158–62; *Beiträge zur Geschichte Herzog Albrechts V. und des Landsberger Bundes*, edited by W. Goetz, Munich, 1898, no. 66, p. 95, and n. 2; *Beiträge zur Geschichte Herzog Albrechts V. und der sogenannten Adelsverschwörung von 1563*, edited by W. Goetz and L. Theobald, Leipzig, 1913, nos. 1–2, pp. 1–2; von Freyberg, op. cit. ii. 339; Doeberl, op. cit. i. 407 (Dec. 1557 to Jan. 1558).

was not attended, and the whole congregation left after the sermon. At Braunau the sermon was well attended, then the majority went outside, and only a few remained during Mass. Half the communicants took the sacrament in one kind, and half in both; baptism had to be conducted in German, otherwise no godparents could be found. At Vilshofen and Münskirchen many demanded communion in both kinds, but it was refused. Even in Munich, in the parish of St. Mary's, many took it *sub utraque*, but not so in the parish of St. Peter's. At Riedt only 100 out of 1,200 did the same.[1] Thus there was an enormous variety, a very disquieting picture for an orthodox ruler and for any adherent of the principles of religious uniformity and princely power. The adherents of reform clearly were not a faction of ambitious noblemen, but the leaders of a popular movement. Both the old religious order and the ducal authority were seriously threatened. In 1561 a ducal commission succeeded in bringing back to the fold all but nine of the burghers of Straubing, and these nine were expelled. But elsewhere Lutheranism was spreading. In the spring of 1563 the archbishop of Salzburg, to whose diocese Bavaria belonged, visited Munich. Albert informed him that the demand for the chalice was so strong that to counteract it through teaching was impossible and suppression was only feasible through expulsions; 'these would lead to war and rebellion because of the numbers involved; but if such a rising broke out, it could not be quelled as easily as had been done in the Peasants' War, for at that time the poison of heresy had not spread so far . . .'. To the bishop of Augsburg Albert wrote that the chalice should be conceded to the laity, for 'many thousands had gone that far that they thought, if only this article were allowed, they would show their obedience in everything else; thus there is still hope to maintain the rest [of the Catholic doctrine] among my subjects by this concession . . .'. Yet the bishops could not be induced to fulfil this wish.[2]

---

[1] State Archives Munich, 'Altbayerische Landschaft', no. 376, fos. 125–7; no. 441, fos. 125–7; no. 441 A, fos. 90–91; Knöpfler, op. cit., pp. 62–64; Sugenheim, op. cit., p. 53; Fr. Wimmer, 'Probestellen aus einer Geschichte Herzog Albrechts V. von Bayern', *Oberbayerisches Archiv für vaterländische Geschichte*, vii, 1845, pp. 50–53.

[2] *Beiträge zur Geschichte Herzog Albrechts V. und des Landsberger Bundes*, no. 198, p. 257; Wimmer, loc. cit., p. 53; Knöpfler, op. cit., pp. 33–36, 129–30; Wilhelm

Thus, when the next diet opened in March 1563, Albert was in a very difficult position, for the pressure for the grant of the chalice was as strong as ever, but the Estates were by no means united. After the opening of the session some demanded that they should above all seek the honour of God, not in the committee, but in the plenum, because at previous diets the transactions in committee on religious and temporal matters had wronged many of the Estates, probably alluding to the outcome of the diet of 1557. The question was then put to the vote. Some were in favour of transacting everything in the plenum, others of only discussing the religious questions there. But the majority voted in favour of the customary procedure of electing a committee of sixty-four and of deliberating matters there, its decisions then being submitted to all the Estates. After this initial defeat of the reformers another quickly followed. Again there were three opinions. A minority of forty-three noblemen, declared Protestants, demanded the toleration of the whole Augsburg Confession before entering upon a discussion of the ducal proposition; they realized that Albert would not concede their demand after he had obtained a money vote and wanted to make him dependent on the Estates. Several shouted that he should not be given a penny if he refused to allow the free exercise of religion. One of their leaders vehemently complained about the lack of unity among the Estates and pointed to the example of the rebellious peasants in the Pinzgau valley, across the frontier in Salzburg, who understood how to do things. Another, more moderate group wanted to petition Albert for a stricter observation of the articles of 1556 and the public and general admittance of communion in both kinds without any hindrance. The majority were opposed to any discussion of the religious issue and in favour of debating the proposition and of leaving other matters alone. The committee was unable to reach a conclusion and referred the question to the Estates to whom the three opinions were reported. They were then put to the vote, each one being counted and recorded, with the result that the large majority expressed themselves in favour of the second opinion. Accordingly, the two lay Estates petitioned

Winkler, *Die Gesinnungen Herzog Albrechts V. von Bayern und seiner protestantischen Landsassen im Kampf um die Konfession des Landes bis 1564*, MS., Munich, 1916, p. 58 (letters of Jan. and May 1563).

Albert to permit everywhere communion in both kinds, the eating of flesh during Lent, the marriage of priests, the use of German at baptism and marriage services; while the adherents of the Augsburg Confession insisted that their protestation be inscribed into the Estates' book, and expressly denied any sympathy with Calvinism, Zwinglianism, or the more radical sects.[1]

Albert found himself in a quandary. He badly needed money, for during the past five years the revenue had remained short of expenditure by 110,000 guilders and his debts amounted to 840,000 guilders. The Estates offered 150,000 if he accepted the religious wishes of the majority, a sum they increased to 350,000 by the end of March. At first he returned their petition on the religious issue and declined to consider it; but, as he explained later to the synod at Salzburg, he would have driven the moderates into the Lutherans' arms if he had not held out hope with regard to the chalice, and many subjects would have left the country. He therefore replied he would wait another three months for a favourable reply from Rome and then grant the chalice. If the reply were unfavourable, he would find other ways and means so that his subjects would have no cause for complaint. He thus hoped he would be able to retain their obedience and to keep them within the fold, and he also wanted to exercise pressure on the decisions of the Council of Trent which was just then debating the same question. He achieved his immediate object, for the Estates took over all his debts and the payment of interest on them and promised they would redeem half of them within two years. At the end of the diet he sharply turned against the Lutheran minority, referred them to the terms of the peace of Augsburg of 1555, according to which he need not suffer the members of a different religion within his principality, and refused to revoke the orders of expulsion issued against the burghers of Straubing and some other towns. He was determined to prevent the further spread of Lutheranism and that of any other confession but his own. The large grant made by the Estates so impressed Duke Christopher of

[1] State Archives Munich, 'Altbayerische Landschaft', no. 377; no. 378, fos. 10–11, 15–19, 31–38, 68; no. 379, fos. 8–9, 13–17, 28–34, 62; *Beiträge zur Geschichte Herzog Albrechts V. und der sogenannten Adelsverschwörung von 1563*, nos. 30, 30 *f*, pp. 72–77, 85–91; von Freyberg, op. cit. ii. 352–5; Doeberl, op. cit. i. 410; Winkler, op. cit., p. 53.

Württemberg that he told his councillors to hold it up to his Estates as an example to be followed.[1]

The Estates had obtained very little in exchange for their grant, and the Lutherans among them were deeply disheartened. Their leader, Pancraz von Freyberg, wrote to Count Joachim of Ortenburg that many waverers were won over by favours and offices and had become almost open enemies of the Truth. Thus friction had been sown among the Estates, who were themselves to blame for their misfortune. He feared they were beyond redemption, but God would turn matters for the best.[2] This was not the spirit of rebellion, but of pessimism and passive obedience. The recipient of the letter, although he also owned estates in Bavaria, was a Count of the Empire and not a subject of Duke Albert. Six months after the end of the diet of 1563 he introduced the Augsburg Confession in his county of 2,000 inhabitants, with the result that many Bavarians also flocked there to attend Lutheran services. Albert thereupon disputed the fact that Ortenburg was an Imperial County, demanded the reintroduction of Catholicism, and the opening of the castles to his forces. When the Count declined to do so, Albert occupied them by force, confiscated the Count's possessions in Bavaria, and seized the Protestant preachers. The Count appealed to the Imperial High Court, which in 1573 found in his favour, so that Ortenburg remained independent and Lutheran. The whole correspondence of the Count, however, had fallen into Albert's hands, among it the letters of other Lutheran noblemen. These were interpreted in the sense that they intended to force Albert to introduce Lutheranism, if need be by revolt and through concerted opposition at the diet. In June 1564 an extraordinary tribunal was set up to try the culprits for conspiracy and lèse-majesté. The accused denied any guilt, and none was established by the court, but they had to ask for pardon. Some were released immediately, others after some weeks. They had to promise that they would not attend a diet without

[1] State Archives Munich, 'Altbayerische Landschaft', no. 377; no. 378, fos. 26, 29–30, 63–64, 76, 103, 117–19, 123–4; no. 379, fos. 23, 26–27, 56–57, 69, 99, 115–17, 122–3; Winkler, op. cit., pp. 54–55, 59, n. 119; von Freyberg, op. cit. ii. 350; State Archives Stuttgart, A 34–35, *Büschel* 16 *a* and *b* (letter of Duke Christopher of 21 Sept. 1564).

[2] *Beiträge zur Geschichte Herzog Albrechts V. und der sogenannten Adelsverschwörung von 1563*, no. 22, pp. 58–59 (Feb. 1563).

permission and would avoid giving any offence or introducing any changes in religion. There was no resistance. These noblemen were no Huguenots, and no Beggars, but loyal subjects of the duke. Their 'conspiracy' was at an end.[1]

So was the opposition of the Estates. Five more diets were held during the remaining fifteen years of Albert's reign, but there was no more opposition on political or religious grounds. At the diet of 1565 Albert proposed a substantial grant because all prices had risen by three or four times since his father's reign, as had the salaries and numbers of his officials and councillors, his servants and courtiers, so that his expenditure had increased at the same rate and beyond on account of the high food prices. Indeed, between 1552 and 1573 the number of court servants grew from 384 to 711, at a cost of 72,000 guilders a year. The Estates did not dispute these arguments and offered taxes on property and salaries, but declined to take over any more debts. Albert suggested that the excise on wine be doubled or trebled, not for ever, but for some years, because this would burden the common people less. But the nobility objected that this would make them the equals of the peasants and would burden them more heavily than the other Estates because they were not engaging in any enterprise. When Albert persisted the Estates not only consented to double the wine excise, but also granted a tax on property of about 150,000 and a tax on the Estates themselves of about 100,000 guilders, and even empowered the committee to grant two further property taxes of 100,000 each for the years 1569 and 1570, if the others were insufficient to pay the ducal debts.[2] The Estates could hardly have been more pliant. This was the first time that they empowered the committee of sixteen to make grants on their behalf. These eight noblemen, four prelates, and four burghers were elected at the end of every diet to act on the Estates' behalf until the following

---

[1] Walter Goetz, 'Die angebliche Adelsverschwörung gegen Herzog Albrecht V. von Bayern', *Forschungen zur Geschichte Bayerns*, xii, 1904, pp. 211–26; J. Buehl, 'Das Verfahren Albrechts V. oder des Grossmüthigen, Herzogs in Bayern, gegen den Grafen Joachim von Ortenburg und einige andere Landsassen', *Oberbayerisches Archiv für vaterländische Geschichte*, ii, 1840, pp. 234 ff.; von Freyberg, op. cit. ii. 352–8; Riezler, op. cit. iv. 523–37; Doeberl, op. cit. i. 411–17.

[2] State Archives Munich, 'Altbayerische Landschaft', no. 380; no. 381, fos. 7, 20–21, 26, 31, 39–40, 44–50, 55–57; no. 443, fos. 6–7, 19–20, 25, 29–30, 38, 42–47, 50–52; von Freyberg, op. cit. ii. 363; Riezler, op. cit. iv. 620, and 'Zur Würdigung Herzog Albrechts V. und seiner inneren Regierung', loc. cit., p. 107 (Dec. 1565).

diet, but could not grant any money unless they were specifically empowered to do so. They had no connexion with the large
and small committees elected at the opening of a diet to expedite and to lead its debates.

Two months after the Estates had doubled the wine excise for
the time being and made other substantial grants Duke Albert
secured from the Emperor Maximilian II, his brother-in-law,
a decree which entitled him to take the excise—doubled once
more—under his own management and to make it permanent,
contrary to his promises that he would leave its administration
to the Estates and would only levy it for some years. This
Imperial decree was submitted to the diet of 1568 and naturally
aroused the indignation of the Estates. They declared that they
could not impose such a yoke of servitude on their descendants,
nor watch how the privileges, which their ancestors had gained
at such heavy price, were destroyed and they and their successors were made slaves. They realized that a permanent
excise, administered by ducal officials, spelled the end of their
power of the purse and of their other privileges. Albert expressed his surprise at the use of such language, especially at the
fact that people who stood in his service had let it pass without
any objection. He denied that the Estates had any right to
dispute a privilege granted by the Emperor and to combine in
opposition to it, and threatened he would complain to him about
their attitude. A few days later the Estates offered 276,000
guilders on condition that Albert forwent the use of the
Imperial privilege, a sum which they increased quickly to
414,000 guilders. Albert, however, declined to hand over the
privilege as they desired: all he was willing to concede was a
promise that he would not use it without their knowledge and
keep it in abeyance. After some bargaining the Estates obtained
a formal and written assurance that neither the duke nor his
heirs would ever use the Imperial privilege without the consent
of the Estates and their willing and unfettered agreement. The
Estates had avoided the worst, but only by making more concessions. The two lay Estates repeatedly petitioned Albert that
the expulsions of Protestants be stopped because they resulted
in the transfer of industry and enterprise into neighbouring
towns where they had not existed previously; but Albert refuted
them with the argument that such matters concerned his

authority and were no business of the Estates.[1] Indeed, in the following year the Estates' own chief financial secretary was examined as to his faith, together with other suspects, and was then informed that either he had to take the Sacrament or had to leave the country within fourteen days.[2]

At the diet of 1570 fourteen of the expelled burghers of Straubing petitioned to be allowed free trading within the duchy. A new visitation was conducted in the country under the influence of the Jesuits, now firmly established in Bavaria, and a court of inquisition was set up with Albert's son Ferdinand as the president. In the small town of Craiburg the commissars inquired in what form communion was taken. When informed that it was done in both kinds, the burghers were sharply reprimanded; when they would not desist, they were ordered to sign certain articles under oath, and when they refused to do so, they were told they had to leave the country within two months unless they took the oath. The town council of Munich was instructed that only firm Catholics, who took communion in one kind, were to be appointed to municipal offices. They petitioned that the concession with regard to communion in both kinds be maintained, because many wealthy burghers moved into the Free Imperial Cities where they were free to follow their religion, so that the town became impoverished and the value of houses declined. But Albert merely promised his aid in helping Munich to recover and refused to repeal his decree. He was determined not to suffer communion in both kinds any longer, except in a few places. The Spiritual Council was founded as the highest authority in the Church to eradicate abuses and Protestant leanings and to establish stricter discipline within the Church. The Estates merely registered some complaints about the expulsions, without receiving a reply, but did not press them and took over all the ducal debts of 610,000 guilders with capital and interest. Albert was justified in claiming in 1571, in a letter to the Archduke Charles of Habsburg, that during the negotiations of three diets the Estates had

---

[1] *Der Landtag im Herzogthum Baiern, gehalten zu München im Jahre 1568*, 1807, pp. 29–34, 56–57, 64–65, 98–99, 118–19, 146–7, 167, 178, 182, 186, 204–6, 213–17, 233; Sugenheim, op. cit., pp. 380–3; von Freyberg, op. cit. ii. 366; Riezler, op. cit. iv. 544–5, 621–2; vi. 36 (Jan. 1568).

[2] Petition of the Estates on his behalf of 16 May 1569: Kreisarchiv Munich, G. R., Fasz. 1036, no. 158.

not said one word about religion. Although many noblemen adhered to the Augsburg Confession and often protested, he informed the Archduke that he was filling all the offices, whether high or low, with strict Catholics, for whoever was not of his religion was not suitable to serve him. As they saw they were not achieving anything with their protests, they humbly submitted one after the other.[1]

That the resistance of the Estates was broken was also proved by the proceedings of the diet of 1572. Duke Albert revived the plan of an increased excise, which he had postponed in 1568 but not given up. He tried to refute the arguments that such a tax was contrary to the Estates' privileges and would burden them and their successors with eternal servitude. The Estates were willing to increase the excise on wine and beer and to introduce one on iron, wool, leather, cloth, horses, oxen, and pigs, but not on corn and salt, and to vote 300,000 guilders in addition. In the end this sum was increased to 640,000, including ducal debts of 515,000 which they took over and 100,000 guilders for the dowries of two princesses; furthermore, the Estates promised Albert an annual payment of 40,000 guilders. The excise on wine and beer was quadrupled, as Albert had suggested in 1568, and for the first time extended to beer consumed inside the duchy, at the rate of one shilling a pail. The Estates tried to make this large grant conditional on the redress of their grievances, but were told that their prince did not know what these grievances were; he did not assume that in their opinion their aids could wait until this had been done, and they did not insist on this point. All these concessions they made although they were already burdened with a capital debt of 1,610,000 guilders on which they had to pay 5 per cent. interest, which would now require as much as 112,290 guilders a year.[2]

As the Estates had foretold quite accurately, the quadrupled excise on wine and beer only yielded between 110,000 and 120,000 guilders a year, while the ducal debts continued to

---

[1] State Archives Munich, 'Altbayerische Landschaft', no. 385; no. 443*b*, fos. 53–59, 107–9, 170–2; Knöpfler, op. cit., pp. 217–18; *Beiträge zur Geschichte Herzog Albrechts V. und des Landsberger Bundes*, no. 618, p. 772; von Freyberg, op. cit. ii. 375; Riezler, op. cit. iv. 622; Wolf, loc. cit. i. 651–2 (May 1570 to Feb. 1571).
[2] State Archives Munich, 'Altbayerische Landschaft', no. 386; no. 443*c*, fos. 26–27, 46–49, 76–81, 98, 101–5, 144–5, 157; von Freyberg, op. cit. ii. 380–7; Riezler, op. cit. iv. 623 (Dec. 1572).

mount in spite of all the sums the Estates had taken over. By 1577 they stood again at the sum of 548,000 guilders, excluding current small debts, and those of the heir to the throne reached 299,000, mainly to the Fuggers at Augsburg and to Duke Francis of Florence: a total of over 850,000 guilders. The liberal grants of the Estates had been of no avail. They realized that the only purpose of a diet was to burden them with more debts. They were willing, however, to take over the latest debts also, to be paid off by taxes raised during the coming twelve years, and to increase their annual grant to Albert from 40,000 to 90,000 guilders, either for ten years, or for the remainder of his life: but more they could not possibly pay. They thus desired an assurance that they would not be asked to take over further debts and to attend further diets during Albert's lifetime, except in case of a public emergency: an assurance he declined to give. A new levy of one-sixteenth of the volume consumed was put on all wine, mead, and brandy, which brought in about 50,000 guilders a year and increased the total yield of the excise on wine and beer to nearly 200,000 guilders, at which level it continued, slightly increasing, into the seventeenth century. In spite of all these grants Duke Albert at his death in 1579 left debts of 616,000 guilders, and his credit stood very low. But that of the Estates was much better: in 1577 Christopher Fugger declined to lend him 100,000 guilders to pay off his son's debts unless the Estates acted as guarantors.[1] From his point of view it was the financial motive which kept the Estates alive, while they were opposed to taking on more burdens which would ruin their credit too. Their petition not to be summoned any more during Albert's lifetime had no more far-reaching implications. In particular it did not mean that they wanted to resign their functions or wanted the diets to disappear altogether.[2]

[1] State Archives Munich, 'Altbayerische Landschaft', no. 389; no. 444, fos. 56–57, 82–92, 97, 103, 115, 123–4, 136–7, 140–1 (May 1577); ibid., 'Fürstensachen', xxix, fos. 5–24, 86–92, 213–21, lists of the debts of Duke William to the Fuggers and others; and fo. 222, the discussion of Nov. 1577 about his debts; von Freyberg, op. cit. ii. 391–2; Riezler, op. cit. iv. 624, 669; Rudhart, op. cit. ii. 218. For the yield of the wine and beer excise in Upper Bavaria, see *English Historical Review*, lxxii. 244–5, to which have to be added certain figures for Lower Bavaria. The new levy was called the *4 Mass Aufschlag* because from each Munich pail of 64 *Mass* 4 were taken as tax, thus one-sixteenth.

[2] This against the interpretation of Riezler, op. cit. vi. 26, and Doeberl, op. cit. i. 493, which has been followed by others.

Through the religious issue the Estates during the early years of Albert's reign acquired a new lease of life. The demand for conceding communion in both kinds found a wide echo in the country and at first tended to unite the two lay Estates, to provide them with a platform and with popular backing which they had not had previously: exactly as the Estates of Saxony and Württemberg much later gained it in their struggles against a Catholic prince. This unity, however, was short-lived. At the diet of 1563 there appeared publicly for the first time a Lutheran minority among the nobility, determined to wring more concessions from Albert than merely the chalice for the laity. The appearance of this more radical group determined him to strike at its leaders before it became too strong, and it drove the moderates into his arms. The whole battle only lasted fifteen months because there was no resistance, because the Lutherans adopted an attitude of passive obedience. The alleged 'conspiracy' did not materialize, but the leaders of the opposition were cowed or driven into exile. The introduction of the Counter-Reformation made Bavaria a strictly Catholic country. It also meant the end of the political aspirations of the Estates, or rather of the nobility, for the towns did not play an active part. With the possible exception of Munich, they were too small to develop any political ambitions, while the prelates were tied to the person of the prince by the bonds of religion.[1] On a larger stage the same drama was to be enacted in the Habsburg territories fifty years later. The Estates survived, but they lost their strength and their spirit. Their submissiveness during the diets of Albert's last years was in striking contrast with their earlier attitude. Nor did their strength revive in later years. It only remained for Albert's grandson Maximilian to complete his grandfather's work.

IV. *The Estates' Loss of Power; the Thirty Years War*

During the seventy years of the reigns of William IV and Albert V thirty-three diets were held, nearly one every other year, the longest interval between two diets being five years,

---

[1] Cf. the comments of Doeberl, op. cit. i. 493; Goetz, in *Forschungen zur Geschichte Bayerns*, xii. 226; and Lieberich, 'Die Landschaft des Herzogtums Baiern', *Mitteilungen für die Archivpflege in Oberbayern*, no. 14, 1943, p. 295.

at the end of Albert's reign when the Estates were rapidly declining. During the twenty years of William V's reign only four
diets were summoned, one every five years. During the long reign
of Maximilian I, which lasted more than half a century, there
were only two diets, both before the outbreak of the Thirty
Years War. The following diet met in 1669, after a long interval
of fifty-seven years, and it was the last in the history of the
Bavarian Estates. These facts indicate a rapid loss of influence,
earlier and more decisive than in most other German principalities. The decline of the Estates was neither due to the Thirty
Years War nor to the coming into being of a *miles perpetuus*, for
it occurred prior to either of these events, at a time when the
Estates of other German principalities were still gaining strength.

During the reign of William V the Estates indeed succeeded
in preserving their remaining influence and perhaps even in
recovering some of the ground lost, mainly because he had to
rely on their financial help. On his accession he agreed that their
privileges should be confirmed before they rendered the oath
of allegiance. He promised that he would curtail the court
expenditure as much as possible, stop all over-spending, and
adjust his expenditure to his income; yet he warned the Estates
that he could not repay the debts left by his father, nor the
interest due on them. By 1588, however, his court comprised
818 people, an increase of 15 per cent. compared with the
previous reign, and his debts amounted to over 1,990,000
guilders, a very large sum even for that time of rising prices.
The Estates strongly complained about this rise and the decline
in the yield of taxation, which in their opinion was due to the
many tax demands, as well as the decline of industry. They
petitioned to be spared any new burdens, for the grants made to
the late Duke were continuing. The nobility demanded that
their own corn and cattle, even when shipped abroad for sale,
should be exempt from all tolls and duties, and complained that
the tolls at many places had been pawned, which was a burden
to rich and poor alike. A group of Lutheran noblemen complained about decrees that had been issued forbidding them to
bring up their own children and wards in their religion. As the
Estates had no cash reserves, they declined to take over the new
debts, but promised they would pay the interest on 400,000
guilders for four years, increased the annual payment to the

Duke from 40,000 to 62,000 guilders and made smaller grants to his brother, wife, and mother: more William was unable to obtain.[1]

In 1583 William himself declared that the yield of his tolls and duties was barely half what it used to be. In his opinion the decline of trade and industry was due to bad harvests, high prices, and above all to the long-drawn-out wars in France and the Netherlands from where trade flowed into Bavaria and other countries. The Estates, however, attributed the economic difficulties less to the religious wars than to high taxation, the migration of trade and enterprise to other places, and equally to the transfer of capital which had been invested in the country, but was now withdrawn on account of the prohibition of interest, with the result that a property tax of one-twentieth now yielded no more than a tax of one-thirtieth had done in the past—thus linking the economic difficulties directly with the religious prohibitions and expulsions. In spite of this, they offered to continue the annual payment of 62,000 guilders to the duke and the payment of interest on 400,000 for another four years, and later increased the annual payment to 70,000 and the capital sum on which they paid interest to 730,000 guilders. They also extended the increases in the excise on wine and beer by four years. More they declared to be impossible because they had voted over 4,300,000 guilders to Duke Albert during the past twenty years of his reign and were totally exhausted: a prince, like a private person, should balance his income and expenditure, which ought to be based on his ordinary revenues from tolls, rents, &c. The Estates again attempted to make their grants conditional on the redress of their grievances and decided to remain together until this had been achieved; but as the diet lasted much longer than usual, the attendance rapidly dwindled, for the members received no wages as they did in other principalities. Even the Large Committee of sixty-four lost about twelve noble and twelve clerical members and some of the urban deputies and was therefore sadly depleted. The members of the nobility still adhered to their earlier decision, but the other two Estates declared they

---

[1] State Archives Munich, 'Altbayerische Landschaft', nos. 390–1; no. 392; no. 445, fos. 11–12, 15–18, 25, 36, 40–41, 61, 131–4; von Freyberg, op. cit. ii. 415, 451–4 (Dec. 1579).

were now satisfied, the four remaining prelates of the Large
Committee speaking for their whole Estate. Thereupon the
nobility, after renewed deliberations, also voted not to press
William any further for the time being, and thus the diet was
concluded after a duration of more than seven weeks.[1]

Four years later another diet was summoned because
William's debts by then amounted to 1,993,000 guilders. Even
he had to admit that the Estates might consider such a sum
'somewhat strange'. In their reply they complained that most
monasteries had to carry considerable, and sometimes very
heavy, debts; that the noblemen, with the exception of only a
few, could no longer live according to their custom and were
unable to send their children abroad to learn languages because
all their income came from their peasants—whom they could
neither evict nor burden more heavily because of the heavy load
of taxation that already fell upon them—and that urban trade
and enterprise were declining. In spite of this the Estates took
over all the ducal debts with capital and interest and made
other grants, on condition that their grievances would be redressed and that no further burdens would be imposed upon
them. They also asked for an assurance that William would not
contract any new debts unless the country were threatened by
war, and would balance his revenue and expenditure. William,
however, declined to give such an assurance and to continue
the argument with them. He even more sharply refuted a petition of the Lutheran members of the nobility to allow those who
so desired to take communion in both kinds, as the Pope had permitted in Lower Austria, and not to insist on communion and
confession before the marriage service: in his opinion this would
open the door to grave errors and heresies, and those desiring
communion *sub utraque* were also tainted with many other
errors. Three times the petition was repeated and a request
made for more toleration, but in vain. Five years later another
petition was submitted that it should be permitted to consecrate
a marriage without prior confession and communion, because
not even the Council of Trent had insisted on this point. But

[1] State Archives Munich, 'Altbayerische Landschaft', no. 393; no. 394, pp. 16,
56–57, 65–66, 90–91, 173, 183–4, 318–25, 343–4, 444–5, 638–9; no. 395, fos. 9–10,
37, 43, 59–60, 112, 120, 177–81, 187, 192, 303–4, 411–12; no. 446, fos. 9–10, 31,
35, 46–47, 88, 128–31, 136, 140, 186–8, 304–5; von Freyberg, op. cit. ii. 409
(Nov. 1583 to Jan. 1584).

this was the last time that a religious petition with a Protestant bias was put forward. The whole movement reached its end with the progress of the Counter-Reformation and the conversion of Bavaria into a strictly Catholic country.[1]

During the 1580's there was a marked development of the new bureaucratic organs, which had begun under Albert V with the foundation of the *Hofkammer* as an organ of the financial administration independent of the Estates, and of the Spiritual Council for religious affairs. The privy council became a regular collegiate body with periodical meetings and gradually developed into the highest central authority of the state. After the Austrian model a war council was formed, the members of which were at first only responsible for military administration, while military finance remained under the *Hofkammer*. Thus the machinery of the state and certain more specialized organs of administration developed much earlier than in other German principalities and superseded those which were controlled by the Estates. This was equally shown by the fact that, in contrast with the practice elsewhere, the leading officials were often foreigners and thus not members of the Estates.[2] In most other principalities the *jus indigenatus* was observed much more strictly. The integration of the state administration with that of the Estates which occurred so markedly in Württemberg and in the duchy of Prussia, and to a certain extent also in Jülich and Cleves and in Saxony, did not take place in Bavaria, and this further weakened the influence of the Estates.

In spite of the large grant of 1588 William's financial position did not improve, so that another diet had to be summoned at the end of 1593. To what straits William was reduced is shown by a letter the president of the *Hofkammer* wrote to his master about this time: hour by hour and day by day he was pressed by the ducal servants and artisans to pay them what was due to them, for their patience was exhausted and they would not

[1] State Archives Munich, 'Altbayerische Landschaft', no. 396, fos. 38–39, 79, 98, 153, 175, 244–6, 278, 286–7, 297, 305–6, 310, 314; nos. 397–8; no. 399, fos. 34–35, 74, 99, 100, 166, 186, 251–3, 285, 293–4, 304, 313, 318–19, 324–5; no. 447, fos. 42–43, 85, 109–10, 176, 199, 272–5, 309, 318–19, 329–30, 338, 343–4, 350–1; no. 400, fo. 420; no. 401, fo. 287; no. 406, fo. 824; von Freyberg, op. cit. ii. 415, 418; Riezler, op. cit. iv. 670–1 (Jan. to Mar. 1588).

[2] Rosenthal, op. cit. i. 462–3, 529–31, 535–6, 538–40; Riezler, op. cit. v. 12–16; vi. 89–90; Doeberl, op. cit. i. 461–3, 479; Manfred Mayer, *Quellen zur Behördengeschichte Bayerns*, Bamberg, 1890, pp. 4, 275–86.

wait any longer; there was no money to pay the interest which was due; most officials had already lent money and anticipated revenue, so that nothing more could be obtained from that source, and the ducal cellar and kitchen were short of supplies. As the same official explained to the Estates' deputies some months later, the ordinary revenue of the *Hofkammer* only amounted to about 189,000 guilders a year, and another 80,000 or 100,000 were provided by the salt monopoly, but annual expenditure came to about 635,000 guilders, so that the newly contracted debts reached the figure of 1,500,000 guilders. The Estates complained about the decline of enterprise in the towns, and the nobility in particular about the buying up of their estates by the prelates, and asked for a prohibition so that noble land would remain noble land; the peasants, they claimed, were so heavily taxed that they would revolt if they had to pay more. The debts burdening the Estates' administration amounted to 4,700,000 guilders, yet they took over all the new debts and promised to William the payment of 50,000 guilders a year. They granted the usual property taxes for a period of twelve years, increased the excise on brandy, doubled that on beer— except what prelates, noblemen, and burghers brewed for their own consumption—and put a new duty on salt. In exchange William promised that he would not burden them with new debts, taxes, or other levies until the debts had been paid off, except in a case of emergency. With regard to their grievances he declared that he could not prevent Bavarian prelates from buying noble land, but would take measures concerning foreign prelates; the urban grievances, he decided, had nothing to do with the business of the diet and had to be investigated first. Although the grievances were not redressed, the Estates granted all the taxes mentioned above and even empowered the committee of sixteen to grant one more property tax if this were necessary, thus opening the way to new ducal demands.[1]

[1] State Archives Munich, 'Fürstensachen', xxxiii, fo. 84; 'Altbayerische Landschaft', no. 400, fos. 23–24, 72, 78, 102–5, 179, 302–3, 422, 434, 497; no. 401, fos. 20, 63–64, 68, 84–86, 132, 204, 288, 294, 334; nos. 402–5; no. 406, pp. 34, 115–16, 126, 170–1, 173–6, 322, 562–3, 827–8, 832, 1013; no. 448, fos. 17, 49, 53, 71–73, 128, 210, 328–9; Rudhart, op. cit., i. 229–30; von Freyberg, op. cit. ii. 422–7; Riezler, op. cit. iv. 672–3; vi. 41–42; *Ernewerte und verbesserte Instruction und Ordnung dess Wein und Bier auffschlags, wie derselb Anno* MDLXXXXIIII. *im Fürstenthumb Obern und Nidern Bayrn, auff zwölff nacheinander volgende Jar continuirt, erhöhert und bewilliget worden ist*, Munich, 1594, fos. A ii–v (Apr. 1593 to Jan. 1594).

Only nine months later William recalled the president of the *Hofkammer* from a journey because he urgently needed 50,000 guilders: 6,000 for his son's wedding, 5,000 for his contribution to the Bavarian Circle, 4,000 for his brother Ernest, the Archbishop of Cologne,[1] 16,000 for the Bishop of Münster, at least 5,000 to pay off debts to some poor servants of his, and 14,000 to 15,000 for other essential expenses, not to mention another 50,000 urgently required to complete unfinished and essential buildings. This money, William wrote, must be raised: it should be taken wherever it could be found and, if necessary, the chapel jewels should be pawned. All that the harassed officials could promise, however, was the 6,000 for the princely wedding which they considered inevitable: the remainder would have to wait. Only a few years later William estimated that his new debts came to at least 1,450,000 guilders, to which more were added daily.[2] The *Hofkammer* was in a state of complete disorder; many officials were incapable and corrupt. To obtain money offices were sold and duplicated. Finally, the president of the *Hofkammer* informed William that a bankruptcy would have to be declared unless countermeasures were immediately taken. In June 1597 a committee was appointed to suggest means by which the finances could be put in order. Its report emphasized that there should be only one master and that economies had to be made. In consequence William decided to abdicate in favour of his son Maximilian with whom he had shared the government since 1595, so that a new order could be established. The abdication followed at the end of 1597.[3] Neither the Estates nor their committees were consulted about any of these matters of vital importance.

Through his father's abdication Maximilian became the sole ruler, a position he was to occupy for more than half a century, throughout the troubled period of the Thirty Years War, in which he was to play such a prominent part. His powers were considerably greater than those of other German princes. He legislated on his own authority. It is true that in 1612 the draft of the *Codex Maximilianeus* was submitted to the Estates, but

[1] Cf. above, p. 278.

[2] State Archives Munich, 'Fürstensachen', xxxiii, fos. 68, 471, 479; Wilhelm Schreiber, *Maximilian I. der Katholische, Kurfürst von Bayern, und der Dreissigjährige Krieg*, Munich, 1868, p. 18 (letters of Duke William of 1594 and 1597).

[3] Schreiber, op. cit., pp. 17–20; Riezler, op. cit. iv. 676–7.

their share in the codification of Bavarian law was small, and they were unable to halt the progress of the reception of Roman law. Maximilian exercised judicial and police authority without any interference and without being unduly hampered by the privileges of the nobility, who only exercised the lower jurisdiction on their estates. He controlled the Church, curtailed the jurisdiction of the bishops, intervened in its internal affairs, regulated religious festivals and processions, introduced the Roman rites, supervised the financial administration of the Church, and taxed the clergy and the monasteries. The bishops of Freising and Ratisbon repeatedly complained about his interference and the violations of the Concordat of 1583; but the Bavarian Church remained under state control, and even the elections to the two sees were supervised by Maximilian, although both were independent of, and situated outside, the duchy. Maximilian equally exercised complete financial authority, the right to increase tolls and duties, to create and extend monopolies, above all the lucrative salt monopoly. He considered it the duty of the Estates to grant him taxes and that it was for him to decide to what extent this obligation was to be enforced. He claimed the right to supervise the administration of their chest and to use the money in it for his own purposes. He did not consult the Estates about the conclusion of alliances, nor about the declaration of war, and allowed them no influence in the sphere of administration and government. He was determined to govern himself and was his own first minister.[1]

The most urgent problem facing Maximilian was the state of the finances. As early as June 1597 he issued instructions to the *Hofkammer* pointing out that the court, salaries, appointments, provisions in kind, and other favours demanded enormous sums and that economies must be effected to avoid a bankruptcy. This programme was carried out. Accurate methods of accounting and auditing were introduced; the dues and rents were collected strictly; the judicial fines were increased, the tolls were doubled, the state monopolies of salt and beer brewed

---

[1] Doeberl, op. cit. i. 450, 478, 482, 484, 492–4; 'Maximilian I., Bayerns grosser Kurfürst, in neuester Beleuchtung', *Forschungen zur Geschichte Bayerns*, xii, 1904, p. 210; 'Innere Regierung Bayerns nach dem Dreissigjährigen Kriege,' ibid. xii. 33–34; Riezler, op. cit. vi. 29, 61–62; Schreiber, op. cit., pp. 50, 60.

from wheat were tightened up and reinforced, the production
of salt was encouraged and reorganized, and the sale of foreign
salt made difficult. Thus the ducal revenues quickly increased,
the salt monopoly alone producing a surplus of 400,000 guilders
a year. By 1605 the ducal debts were reduced to 1,000,000
guilders, and by 1608 they disappeared, thanks to the liberal
grants of the Estates. A surplus was gradually accumulating, so
that Maximilian was able to buy estates and domains from
which new revenues could be expected. At a time when the
financial difficulties of most German princes were increasing
rapidly and when the coinage was debased elsewhere, Maximilian accumulated a treasure, which in 1629 amounted to
2,070,000 guilders and enabled him to finance the Catholic
League and its army.[1] Even before the outbreak of the Thirty
Years War the rate of taxation doubled, to be further steeply
increased during the war years.[2]

Only two diets were summoned in the course of Maximilian's
reign, both before the Thirty Years War. The diet of 1605
granted money for six, and that of 1612 for nine years: property
taxes of one-twentieth of the estimated value of property were
to be levied during two consecutive years, to be followed in
the third year by a tax on the Estates themselves. In 1612
Maximilian expressly informed the Estates that he intended
to summon the next diet after nine years, and they obligingly
extended their grant to cover the interval, without making any
opposition or expressing any wish for an earlier meeting. The
diet of 1605 took over the remaining ducal debts of 1,000,000
guilders and increased the annual grant to the duke from
50,000 to 150,000 guilders, on condition that the special impost
on salt introduced in 1593 would be rescinded. The diet of 1612

---

[1] Doeberl, op. cit. i. 480–2; Felix Stieve, 'Zur Geschichte des Finanzwesens und
der Staatswirtschaft in Baiern unter den Herzogen Wilhelm V. und Maximilian
I.', *Sitzungsberichte der philosophisch-philologischen Classe der königlich-bayerischen Akademie
der Wissenschaften*, 1881, p. 30; no. 13, p. 65; Schreiber, op. cit., pp. 37–38.

[2] According to the figures given by Max Freiherr von Freyberg, *Pragmatische
Geschichte der bayerischen Gesetzgebung und Staatsverwaltung seit den Zeiten Maximilians I.*,
i, Leipzig, 1836, *Beilagen*, pp. 44–47, during the years 1593–1605 net taxation
amounted to 240,534 guilders a year, during the years 1606–17 to 470,614, and
during the years 1618–29 to 640,035 guilders a year. According to the Estates'
figures they paid an average of 221,409 guilders during the years 1612–17, and of
561,860 during the years 1618–29: State Archives Munich, 'Altbayerische Landschaft', no. 1993.

in addition voted 28,000 guilders a year for defence purposes, i.e. for the Catholic League, which was founded in 1609 under Bavarian leadership to promote the *bonum religionis*, with Maximilian as its commander-in-chief: a sum which was later increased to 50,000 a year. The Estates also voted certain sums for the purchase of estates and for the brothers of Maximilian, and empowered the committee of sixteen to advance another 100,000, and if need be 200,000, guilders, if an emergency should arise and no diet could be summoned.[1] In 1607 they even lent to Maximilian without charging any interest 16,000 guilders for the execution of the Imperial ban against the Free City of Donauwörth, which he occupied and transformed into a Bavarian town after religious riots had occurred there, and another 19,000 guilders to his brother Ernest, the Archbishop of Cologne:[2] thus lending their support to the policy of the Counter-Reformation which was pursued by the Wittelsbachs in different parts of Germany.

The Estates no longer attempted to link the redress of their grievances with the supply they granted. In 1605 they merely expressed the hope, in very submissive terms, that the grievances would be redressed at some future date; while Maximilian promised he would not burden them with further exactions during the time that their grant lasted, except for important reasons, such as an emergency of the country, or for purposes of the Empire. Seven years later even this clause, ambiguous as it was, was omitted. The nobility repeated its complaint of 1593 that foreign as well as Bavarian prelates were buying noble estates, that the nobility had not been conceded a right of pre-emption, and that the ducal promise with regard to foreign prelates had not been fulfilled. The prelates and clergy, on the other hand, complained that the salt duty had been converted into a money payment of which they had to contribute 50 per cent., that they only had two representatives among the Estates' deputies responsible for the repartitioning of taxes, and yet always had to carry the heaviest burden. They declined to countenance any longer this disparity and demanded

---

[1] *Der Landtag im Herzogthum Baiern vom Jahre 1605*, 1802, pp. 80–81, 84, 134–7; *Der Landtag im Herzogthum Baiern vom Jahre 1612*, 1803, pp. 81, 124, 138, 150, 188–91; Rudhart, op. cit. ii. 253; Riezler, op. cit. vi. 29, 42, 51.

[2] State Archives Munich, 'Altbayerische Landschaft', no. 1574: an undated list of the Estates' debtors at the end of a journal of the years 1620–6.

paritatem votorum and equality of the burdens—probably meaning the same number of representatives as the nobility had, instead of half their number. The towns, as on previous occasions, complained about their continuing decline, which they attributed to the engrossing of corn by foreigners, parsons, innkeepers, and rural judges (but not by noblemen), to the brewing of beer by the nobility, to the trade in cloth outside the towns, and to the ducal salt monopoly which deprived the towns of much trade, while the nobility opposed the monopolistic claims of the towns.[1] No action seems to have been taken on any of these complaints.

Very similar grievances were raised at the diet of 1612. The three Estates declared that in most towns the brewing and selling of beer was almost the only sustenance of the burghers, but that this enterprise was severely impeded by the brewing of beer from wheat, which was a ducal monopoly. The noblemen complained that they had to pay duty on salt and barley bought for their breweries, contrary to the old custom. The towns repeated their earlier complaints. Interestingly enough, they stressed the forestalling of corn and its export into Salzburg and Tyrol by peasants rather than by officials and noblemen; but they did complain that noblemen and officers imported wine as if for their own needs, free of duty, and then sold it wholesale or retail: clearly, it was not noble competition from which the towns suffered most as they did in north-eastern Germany and Poland. It was a sign of the times that the Estates submitted a *bilanza* with their suggestions about how to prevent more money flowing out of the duchy every year than came into it. Maximilian in his turn informed the Estates that he expected their deputies to make their reports and to render their accounts to the *Hofkammer*, to which he issued the corresponding instructions. He wanted to gain a right of supervision over the Estates' financial administration and information about the state of their reserves, so that he could use them to pay off his debts. The Estates were willing to issue the desired instructions to their deputies, but Maximilian denied that he required their

---

[1] *Der Landtag im Herzogthum Baiern vom Jahre 1605*, pp. 82, 115, 225–6, 245, 264, 267, 331, 334–5, 338; von Freyberg, op. cit. i, *Beilagen*, pp. 16–19 (Nov. to Dec. 1605). The printed text should be compared with State Archives Munich, 'Altbayerische Landschaft', nos. 408–10, 449 c and d, because it contains several errors (e.g. on p. 225 *gemachtes* instead of *genanntes geld*).

consent if he wanted to see the deputies' accounts, and only for the moment decided not to press the point any further.[1]

That Maximilian at this time did not intend to rule entirely without the Estates, who so willingly supported him and did not render any opposition, can be seen from a codicil which he added to his will a few months after the conclusion of the diet of 1612. After his death the treasure which he had collected was to be the property of his heirs and of his loyal Estates, who were to administer it together; his heirs were not to be entitled to use it without the advice and consent of the Estates and their deputies; if his heirs did not observe this will, the Estates need not obey, but were entitled to restrain and resist those acting contrary to it.[2] This last stipulation in particular seems very surprising, coming as it did from a prince who would not have suffered any such resistance against his own actions and who curtailed the influence of the Estates even more than his predecessors had done. But the will was drawn up before the birth of his son, at a time when Maximilian expected conditions of uncertainty to exist after his death.

The Thirty Years War broke out before the nine years' grant of 1612 had expired. The Emperor Ferdinand II concluded an alliance with Maximilian, promised him financial compensation and the electoral dignity if he rendered him military help against the Bohemian rebels, and Maximilian recruited and equipped an army of 24,000 men on behalf of the Catholic League.[3] It was this army, under the command of Count Tilly, which in 1620 drove Frederick of the Palatinate out of Bohemia, then carried the war into his native lands and conquered the Upper and the Rhine Palatinate. The main burden of this army naturally fell on Bavaria, but the duchy was fortunate in escaping the direct impact of the war until the Swedish invasion of 1632. From 1620 onwards the grants made previously proved quite insufficient for the needs of the army. The Estates' deputies

---

[1] *Der Landtag im Herzogthum Baiern vom Jahre 1612*, pp. 99–102, 135, 156, 166, 169–70, 213–14, 311–12, 360–4, 382; Rudhart, op. cit. ii. 249–52; von Freyberg, op. cit. i, *Beilagen*, pp. 31–34 (Feb. 1612). The printed text should be compared with State Archives Munich, 'Altbayerische Landschaft', nos. 411–12, 450, 450a.

[2] Stieve, loc. cit., no. 34, pp. 80–85 (Apr. 1612).

[3] H. R. J. Lieberich, 'Das baierische Heerwesen bis 1800', *Mitteilungen für die Archivpflege in Oberbayern*, no. 38, 1950, pp. 1111–12; Gustav Wolf, 'Der Dreissigjährige Krieg', loc. cit. i. 684–5.

consented to the continuation and increase of the excise on
wine and beer, to the levy of a property tax and of a tax on
the Estates themselves. Within a few months the Estates paid
815,000 guilders for defence alone, and altogether 1,390,000 in
the course of 1620. In the following year the grant of 1612
expired, and the committee of sixteen, although it had no
powers to do so, agreed to the levy of 40,000 guilders a month,
which they increased to 50,000 at Maximilian's request. In 1622
and 1623 this monthly contribution was continued, but the
committee refused to grant the 80,000 guilders a month which
Maximilian demanded. In July 1623 it declined to continue
taxation at the previous level, and in August it declared it could
not assent to the indefinite levy of 25,000 guilders a month
which Maximilian desired. In December the committee requested that a diet should be summoned, for during the last five
years they had paid 3,000,000 guilders, all in good silver and
gold, to the electoral paymasters for military purposes alone;
in addition, they had to borrow 818,300 guilders at a high rate
of interest, and made a war loan of 463,000; the clergy had
agreed to an extraordinary 'decimation', and the excise on
wine had been increased once more by a guilder on each pail.
Eventually, however, the committee consented to the levy of
25,000 guilders a month until the end of 1624. Then they
complained strongly about a new heavy toll on all exports,
including corn, which had been introduced without their advice and consent and had never been demanded before. But
they agreed to the continuation of the monthly contribution of
25,000 guilders for defence purposes.[1]

At the beginning of 1626 Maximilian declared that he was
determined to summon a diet, but was forced to alter his plan
and to postpone it until a more suitable time because of the
continuing dangers and the war: a rather weak argument considering how far from Bavaria the war had moved by that time.
The committee continued the contribution of 25,000 guilders
a month until the end of the year and voted another 30,000 for

[1] State Archives Munich, 'Altbayerische Landschaft', no. 413; no. 414, fos. 38,
48, 52, 55–56, 62–63, 74, 85, 98, 104–5, 113, 120–1, 128, 139–40, 146–8, 166–7,
170–1, 183–4, 193, 201; the actual sums paid out every year, ibid., no. 1993:
they remained above 600,000 guilders until 1624 and then fell below 500,000; the
war loan of 1620 is given there as 405,000 guilders, and a new one of 1622 as 135,000.
For the 'decimation' of the clergy, see above, p. 365.

the payment of interest and 150,000 to Maximilian, a total of 480,000 guilders. In 1627 and 1628 the same grants were made. The committee complained that no diet had been held for fifteen years, while during the same time more than ten were summoned previously and their grievances were regularly redressed. Again Maximilian promised that a diet would soon be summoned, but some months later he announced that the times were not propitious: if the committee insisted he would think the matter over. In January 1629 they renewed their request, for matters of such weight were always treated in the presence of all the Estates. They again voted 180,000 guilders for Maximilian and for the payment of interest, but only granted 200,000—instead of 300,000—for the war, which they later increased to 225,000: a total of 405,000 guilders. Twelve months later they only voted 380,000 guilders for 1630, and another 100,000 for the unexpected case of a great emergency: this Maximilian accepted on condition that the money would be handed over to him on demand without any delay or excuse. This actually happened in January 1631 because 'the King of Sweden, with the aid of his instigators and adherents, had invaded the Empire with great might', and a further 50,000 guilders for defence purposes was added to the usual grant of 180,000 by the committee.[1]

The subsequent years of the Swedish war and the invasion of Bavaria fully developed Maximilian's tendency towards absolute government.[2] Hitherto he had used the machinery of the Estates to achieve his purposes, although ignoring the repeated demands for the redress of grievances and for the summoning of a diet. Until 1632 the Estates paid him year after year large sums, but after the devastation by the Swedes the country could no longer raise 480,000 or more guilders a year, and the payments of the Estates dropped to about 186,000 guilders per year.[3] From Maximilian's point of view such a sum was utterly insufficient to carry on the war. He therefore resorted to levies by decree and to military force to achieve his aims, and the remnants of the constitution were discarded. In October 1631,

[1] Ibid., no. 413; no. 414, fos. 209–10, 223, 237–8, 252, 273–4, 295, 309, 317, 328–9, 339, 346, 364–5, 373, 379–80, 383–5; Riezler, op. cit. vi. 30.
[2] Riezler, op. cit. vi. 30.
[3] This is the average of the years 1633–8 according to the Estates' figures: State Archives Munich, 'Altbayerische Landschaft', no. 1993.

a month after the decisive victory of Gustavus Adolphus over
Tilly at Breitenfeld in Saxony, Maximilian demanded 300,000
guilders from the Estates' committee, which was only willing
to pay 100,000. Thereupon he informed it curtly that he could
not allow the country and its people, which were entrusted to
him by God, to be utterly ruined and imperilled while there
was still time: he thus would have to seek other ways, for necessity knew no laws but made law, and extreme perils demanded
extreme remedies. In the end, however, Maximilian accepted
a grant of 200,000 guilders and a loan of 266,200. At the beginning of 1632 the committee made the usual grant of 180,000
guilders to Maximilian and for the payment of interest, voted
the large sum of 400,000 guilders for the war, to be used in case
of need, and put all their remaining reserves at his disposal.
They admitted themselves that the time was not suitable for a
diet to be held, so that they would not repeat this petition for
the time being.[1]

Yet in the course of this and the following years Maximilian
took very sharp measures against the Estates. He ordered the
director of the *Hofkammer* to take 100,000 guilders out of the
Estates' chest. When their secretary, Dr. Planck, inquired at
whose orders this was done, he was insulted and arrested; after
humble supplications on his behalf, he was released after seven
weeks. The Estates' deputies were instructed in future not to
draw up any accounts nor to spend any money unless this were
done in the presence of electoral commissars. They replied that
this amounted to an annulment of their privileges, would dis-
credit them and make them appear ridiculous. Maximilian
rebuked them sharply for using these expressions which were
insolent and haughty, did not show the submission which was
his due, and attempted to put him in the wrong. Ten days later
he decreed an extraordinary monthly contribution because all
the inhabitants were obliged to participate in the defence of
the country. Early in 1634 the committee declared it was impossible to pay anything because of the country's plight. Thereupon he ordered the Estates' funds to be seized, arguing that

---

[1] State Archives Munich, 'Altbayerische Landschaft', no. 413; no. 414, fos. 425,
429, 431–4, 438–9, 441–2, 458–61; no. 1993 (Oct. 1631 to Jan. 1632). The sum
paid out in 1632 was 674,020 guilders: ibid., no. 414, fo. 546; no. 456, fo. 89 (the
information in Riezler, op. cit. vi. 30, is incorrect).

they had been collected for use in an emergency. He told the committee that he was forced to use the money for the country's defence because they declined to grant any further aid and that he was compelled to put an imposition on all drink, food, and merchandise, which was to be paid directly into the war chest, for privileges were invalid in these times of emergency. Further taxes were levied without any consultation with the committee. In 1635 it was ordered to draw up the necessary mandates and to send them to the *Hofkammer* for ratification. They declared, however, that it was impossible to levy 480,000 guilders, otherwise the peasant rising, which had broken out at the end of 1633 between Isar and Inn and was cruelly suppressed in 1634, would break out anew. But Maximilian persisted and simply ordered the salaries of the deputies and officials of the Estates to be stopped and all their money and accounts to be handed over.[1]

As the Estates' chest had been emptied before, all that was left in it was about 19,000 guilders. In 1634 the committee emphasized that nobody could afford to drink wine, except army officers who refused to pay the excise. The country inns and taverns were deserted, while the brewers and innkeepers in the towns never knew whether they would not receive blows and bastinados instead of payment. Maximilian issued regulations for the supply of the forces and appointed commissars to prevent unauthorized demands and the use of force by the military, but they were of little avail because of the decline of military discipline. The soldiers took little or no account of such prohibitions and squeezed money and victuals out of the districts assigned to them.[2] If the Bavarian forces behaved in such a way, one can imagine what the Swedish army did when it invaded Bavaria, defeated Tilly, and occupied Munich and other towns. Yet throughout the war the duchy continued to pay heavy taxes. The Estates alone collected 258,000 guilders in 1632, 387,000 in 1636, 597,000 in 1639, 647,000 in 1640, and

[1] Riezler, op. cit. v. 473–8, 505; vi. 31–32; Rudhart, op. cit. ii. 266–7; von Freyberg, op. cit. i. 79–80, 85, 88; Schreiber, op. cit., pp. 683–5; Ludwig Hoffmann, *Geschichte der direkten Steuern in Baiern vom Ende des XIII. biz zum Beginn des XIX. Jahrhunderts (Staats- und sozialwissenschaftliche Forschungen,* iv. 5), Leipzig, 1883, pp. 80–82.

[2] State Archives Munich, 'Altbayerische Landschaft', no. 414, fos. 612–13, 616; no. 455, fos. 238–9 (Feb. 1634 to Apr. 1635).

629,000 in 1645. These figures include direct taxes as well as the excise on wine and beer, but not the excise which directly accrued to Maximilian, nor the other levies ordered by decree. It was only after the end of the war that the yield declined very considerably below these figures,[1] an indication of the depression which then set in. Of the total cost of the army of the Catholic League during the war years Bavaria had to pay 38,000,000 guilders or 70 per cent., while the contributions of the other members were very small.[2]

Through the sharp measures taken by Maximilian the financial powers of the Estates were finally broken, and the committee no longer rendered any resistance. It still complained about the heavy burdens and frequently expressed its longing for peace, but it granted large sums without much opposition, while other contributions were levied without its consent. In 1639 the mandates for the extraordinary war aid, already printed, were altered as a concession to the Estates, and the words that it was done with their consent were inserted. On the other hand, the committee was very reluctant to express its opinion on matters of foreign or military affairs. Thus in 1643 its members formulated their opinion with regard to defence matters, but declared that they had no doubt that Maximilian and his war councillors would themselves know what was required. In 1645, when Bavaria was threatened by the French, Maximilian wanted to hear their advice on how Bavaria could

---

[1] The exact figures were (in guilders):

Year	Direct taxes	Wine and beer excise
1632	..	258,362
1636	137,663	249,478
1639	277,796	319,674
1640	337,546	309,568
1645	375,643	253,059
1650	..	136,753
1653	215,707	193,380
1654	228,000	186,000
1657	40,096	36,974

They are taken from State Archives Munich, 'Altbayerische Landschaft', no. 455, fos. 17–18, 281, 335, 351; no. 456, fo. 176; no. 457, fos. 122, 293; no. 458, fos. 29, 155.

[2] Riezler, op. cit. v. 666, with detailed figures.

be secured against invasion and how neutrality could be obtained, whether the armistice offered by the king of France
should be accepted, or whether the enemy should be tackled
defensive et offensive, and what suggestions he should submit to
the Emperor Ferdinand III and to the Austrian commander,
the Archduke Leopold. The committee examined and discussed
these points, but felt that they had not sufficient information and
experience, and therefore left the decision to the expert knowledge of the privy councillors and war councillors.[1]

When the long war was over the Bavarian army of about
20,000 men, with the exception of only a few garrisons and the
life-guards, was disbanded at the request of the Estates. For this
purpose and the costs of negotiating and executing the peace
over 5,000,000 guilders were required, two-thirds of which
Maximilian ordered the Estates to pay. In 1648 he proposed
that those towns and districts which had not been ruined by the
war should pay a double tax, especially the district of Burghausen, which had not been touched by it; but in the end he
was content with a single tax. Two years later he reprimanded
the committee for handing over only small sums and instructed
it to pay soon a more substantial amount. He significantly
added that in future he would not ask them in this form for *his*
money, for in his opinion only its administration was entrusted
to the Estates. In 1651 the committee pointed out that during
the war it had made grants because there was *summum periculum
in mora* and the summoning of a diet had been inopportune, but
now there was a large difference, its powers were limited in
peace-time, and its actions no longer bound all the Estates:
therefore the question of contributing two-thirds to the costs of
the peace should be submitted to a diet. But in Maximilian's
opinion the issue could not wait that long, and the times were
too difficult for a diet to be held, and again the committee
gave way.[2]

During the Thirty Years War Maximilian's attitude towards

---

[1] State Archives Munich, 'Altbayerische Landschaft', no. 456, fos. 9–12, 67–
69, 121–2, 136–7, 149, 161–2, 177; no. 457, fo. 152; 'Dreissigjähriger Krieg',
tom. 555, fos. 2–3; Riezler, op. cit. vi. 32–33, 52–53; von Freyberg, op. cit. i. 91;
Hoffmann, op. cit., p. 82 (from the years 1642 to 1649).
[2] State Archives Munich, 'Altbayerische Landschaft', no. 457, fos. 23, 30, 32,
98, 118, 127–8, 132; Schreiber, op. cit., p. 960; Lieberich, loc. cit., p. 1112 (Nov.
1648 to Feb. 1651).

the Estates crystallized and perceptibly hardened. In the 'Information' which he composed shortly before his death for the Electress Maria Anna he wrote that nearly everywhere there was a clash of interests between the prince and the Estates because they always tried to extend their privileges and liberties, and to escape the burdens and taxes which they owed to the prince, or at least to whittle them down by all sorts of means. Without a highly important cause it was therefore not advisable to hold diets because the Estates only used them to raise grievances and new pretensions. With regard to the taxes Maximilian pointed out that they were a *regale* due to the prince, and that only their administration was left to the Estates, on condition that they paid two-thirds of the defence costs, the contributions to the Empire, the interest on the debts they had taken over, and a grant to the prince himself. The latter was entitled to be given information about the Estates' revenue and expenditure, for the revenues were his own revenues. For the instruction of his son, Maximilian wrote in 1650 that the Estates aimed at the extension of their liberties, at acquiring new rights and more than was their due, and at their own advantage. Therefore from the beginning of his reign he had seen to it that he would not have to act at their bidding—as had happened under some previous dukes—and not to give way to their insolences and pretensions. He had therefore kept them within the bounds of obedience and respect, and this had to be kept in mind as a special secret of princely rule. His heir was not to grant further privileges and liberties to the Estates to the detriment of the ruling house, for they were greater than in any other principality or country.[1] This was the language of absolute government, more clearly formulated than other German princes would have done at that time, more candid than the Great Elector of Brandenburg was to formulate it later. Maximilian was clearly wrong about the extent of the privileges of his Estates, but he understood the signs of his time.

There is little doubt that Bavaria suffered very badly from the Thirty Years War, being invaded and fought over several

---

[1] Christian Ruepprecht, 'Die Information des Kurfürsten Maximilian I. von Bayern für seine Gemahlin vom 13. März 1651', *Oberbayerisches Archiv für vaterländische Geschichte*, lix, 1895–6, pp. 317–18; Kurt Pfister, *Kurfürst Maximilian von Bayern und sein Jahrhundert*, Munich, 1948, pp. 98, 401.

times after 1632; in 1649 plague broke out and killed many inhabitants. Yet it is very difficult to estimate the loss of population. In 1669 the Estates claimed that in certain places the population was still only one-third, or even one-quarter, of the pre-war figure. At Aichach only 202 out of 650 burghers were left; at Landsberg and Rain it was not much better. But the war damage was distributed very unevenly. The whole district of Burghausen, to the east of the Inn, was not touched by the war. The fortified towns of Munich and Ingolstadt and other fortresses were not ruined and sacked, and in general the towns suffered less than the countryside, as the Estates' deputies pointed out in 1648.[1] Even in Munich, however, the number of clothmakers fell from 148 to 56, that of cloth and linen-weavers from 161 to 82, of tailors from 118 to 64, of hat-makers from 23 to 9. It was even more serious that after the restoration of peace the cloth industry did not recover and that the number of clothmakers in Munich declined further, while the imports of foreign cloth increased. It is a moot point whether this decline was due to the war or to underlying causes, whether it began before or after 1618, whether it was due to the Counter-Reformation, or to migration of industry, or to a mixture of these causes. Ingolstadt apparently lost its cloth industry in the course of the sixteenth century, but in other towns the number of makers of rough cloth (*Loden*) increased before 1620. In Munich during the century before the outbreak of the Thirty Years War the number of cloth-makers was halved, but the number of makers of rough cloth increased by over 50 per cent.[2] These figures do not indicate a general decline, in spite of all the complaints of the Estates on that score. But it seems quite possible that merchants, masters, and other burghers moved into neighbouring towns, where they were less taxed and enjoyed more religious liberty, even before the great war started, as both Maximilian and the Estates repeatedly emphasized. It seems likely that more rough cloth was produced in Bavaria, while the better cloth was imported from abroad, probably because it was

[1] State Archives Munich, 'Altbayerische Landschaft', no. 457, fos. 23–25; *Der Landtag im Churfürstenthum Baiern vom Jahre 1669*, 1802, p. 91; Riezler, op. cit. v. 663; vii. 112.

[2] Riezler, op. cit. v. 663; B. Kreuter, 'Beiträge zur Geschichte der Wollengewerbe in Bayern', *Oberbayerisches Archiv für vaterländische Geschichte*, 1, 1897, pp. 236, 247, 249–50.

cheaper. In any case, the cloth-dealers preferred it to Bavarian cloth.[1]

It is also significant that before the war the yield of the excise on wine and beer increased considerably, and was still comparatively high during the war, but declined steeply after its end. In 1668 two local collectors attributed this decline to the ruin caused by war and depopulation, shortage of money, and the cessation of trade in wine from Austria and into other countries, but also to the high duty on wine and the low price of beer.[2] This change from wine to beer consumption also occurred elsewhere and probably was a sign of impoverishment. Equally impoverished was the Bavarian nobility. It was not a wealthy class, and the income it derived from rents and dues declined because of the rising prices of the sixteenth century. It found some compensation by undertaking more demesne farming and by trading in corn, beer, and other commodities; but this started comparatively late and never progressed very far. The outbreak of the Thirty Years War brought it to an end and accelerated the decline of the nobility as a class. In 1669 the noblemen declared that they were only too glad if the peasant farms were not deserted. The noble estates were heavily mortgaged, and many had to be sold, as the deputies complained in 1660. Not only monasteries and chapters, but officials and officers took advantage of the low price of land caused by the war and the indebtedness of many noble families to buy up estates. Thus a new landed class came into being next to the old nobility, whose members had to seek offices and sinecures to eke out their precarious livelihood.[3] Thus the Thirty Years War in many ways deeply influenced the internal history of Bavaria, and above all it prepared the way for the following century and a half of an almost absolute monarchy.

[1] Doeberl, in *Forschungen zur Geschichte Bayerns*, xii. 75–77; Rosenthal, op. cit. ii. 430, n. 2; Knöpfler, op. cit., pp. 218–20.

[2] State Archives Munich, 'Altbayerische Landschaft', no. 1993, with reports of 20 and 29 Nov. 1668 and figures for the years 1659–68 corroborating these statements. Cf. above, p. 402, n. 1, and *The English Historical Review*, lxxii. 240–7, with tables for the pre-war and war years.

[3] State Archives Munich, 'Altbayerische Landschaft', no. 458, fo. 311; Riezler, op. cit. v. 661; vi. 139, 225–7; vii. 137; Doeberl, *Entwickelungsgeschichte Bayerns*, ii, 1912, pp. 8–10. According to Lütge, op. cit., p. 60, there was a tendency towards more demesne farming, but it did not develop very far and was reversed in the eighteenth century because it did not pay.

v. *The Estates in the Absolute Monarchy*

The Elector who ascended the throne in 1651, Ferdinand Maria, continued Maximilian's methods of absolute government and further developed the machinery of the Bavarian state. Its heart and soul was the privy council, exactly as was the case in the Brandenburg state of the Great Elector. All important issues were discussed in the privy council which, apart from the Elector and his wife, had about a dozen members. All directives were worked out there, and the prince's ultimate decisions usually coincided with the suggestions of the privy council. Soon, however, his suspicion and the confidential character of many political questions caused him to discuss certain questions with a few more intimate councillors only, and not with the whole council. This led to the development of the Secret Conference, similar to the development of the committee for foreign affairs or of intelligence under Charles II. The other central authorities, the *Hofrat*, the *Hofkammer*, the War Council, the Spiritual Council, became subordinate to the privy council and fulfilled purely administrative functions within their spheres. Their presidents were members of the privy council, emphasizing the tendency towards centralization which permeated the whole machinery of the state. In all important matters of church government the Spiritual Council had to report to the privy council which exercised a strict supervision and control. The War Council, founded at the beginning of the Thirty Years War, was dissolved in 1650 when the army was disbanded, but it was reconstituted after a few years. More important military questions, however, were settled in the privy council. The vice-chancellor, later chancellor, Caspar von Schmid, supervised all branches of the administration and called every authority to account. His favourite instrument for this purpose was the *Rentmeister* who had to investigate the conduct of the local officials; the administration of the Church and its property, questions of agriculture, forestry, mining, trade and industry, tolls, markets, roads, schools, and other 'police' matters came under his jurisdiction. These officials with their wide field of competence corresponded to the

Intendants of the French monarchy and to the military and tax commissars of the Hohenzollern state.[1]

One of the most important sources of revenue was the salt monopoly, but the sale of salt had declined because of high prices and the competition of Austrian salt. At the end of Maximilian's reign the net profit amounted to only 72,000 guilders. Through better management and strict enforcement it increased to 251,000 guilders by the end of Ferdinand Maria's reign in 1679. Drastic measures were also taken to curtail the consumption of ordinary beer in favour of beer brewed from wheat—another electoral monopoly. A tobacco monopoly was established in 1675. Another concern of the government was the steep decline in the cloth industry and in the production of wool. At the end of the sixteenth century over 2,000,000 sheep were counted in Bavaria, but their number had dwindled during the war. Measures were taken to improve the breed and to prevent the export of unfinished cloth for dyeing and finishing. In 1679 a state cloth factory was founded in Munich, with branches in other towns, which later employed 2,000 workmen. But Bavarian wool and cloth remained inferior to the foreign products, so that all government support was of little avail and Bavarian cloth could not be sold. The export of corn, timber, cattle, and salt, however, began to revive, and the decline in trade and enterprise was arrested, so that the yield of the customs increased. The labour services of the peasants under the direct jurisdiction of the prince were commuted into quit-rents. As a result the revenue of the electoral pay office slowly mounted, and by the end of the reign there was a surplus. But this was also due to the introduction of new taxes, on houses and farms, on meat and tobacco, and to the increase of the old taxes. At the beginning of the reign the ordinary *Landsteuer* yielded about 160,000 guilders a year, at the end nearly 580,000 guilders:[2] a sign also of the economic recovery of Bavaria.

---

[1] Doeberl, op. cit. ii. 64–65, and in *Forschungen zur Geschichte Bayerns*, xii. 41–45; Riezler, op. cit. viii. 452; Rosenthal, op. cit. ii. 417–18, 421–3.

[2] Doeberl, op. cit. ii. 70–71, 73, 76–78, and in *Forschungen zur Geschichte Bayerns*, xii. 53–55, 60–61, 75–79; Kreuter, loc. cit., pp. 271–7, 319–20; Adolf Dauner, 'Der Kommerzienrat in Bayern im 17. Jahrhundert', *Oberbayerisches Archiv für vaterländische Geschichte*, lv, 1910, p. 228, n. 1; von Freyberg, op. cit. i, *Beilagen*, pp. 76–79, giving the yield of the *Landsteuer* for every year: 580,000 guilders is the average for the years 1675–9.

Ferdinand Maria administered the country as if it were his private estate and ruled his subjects as if he were their guardian. A decree of 1670 regulated the urban administration, the election and the meetings of councillors, taxation, jurisdiction, and 'police' within the towns. The *Rentmeister* had to supervise the exercise of urban self-government, only the five leading towns being exempt from their control.[1] Their rights over the towns, however, never became as extensive as those of the military and tax commissars in Brandenburg and Prussia who became the masters of the towns. With regard to the Estates, Ferdinand Maria like his father believed it was their duty to pay taxes and considered the *jus collectandi* a *regale* which by right belonged to him. He was willing to hear the Estates' advice on purely utilitarian grounds, but not to allow them any share in legislation. He claimed a right of supervision over their chest, which was merely entrusted to their care, but belonged to the state. If a danger arose, it was for the prince to decide what taxes were necessary. It would be contrary to reason, a memorandum of 1664 pronounced, if the prince allowed the country and its inhabitants to be ruined rather than demand a tax from them, for privileges were invalid in an emergency, and the public weal came first.[2] As Ferdinand Maria told the deputies of the Estates, for the preservation of the peace and the safeguarding of his subjects he was responsible to none but God, for He had entrusted his subjects to his care. He equally reprimanded them for taking their departure without his prior knowledge and for lamenting so often that he paid no attention to their petitions and did not assent to their requests, but merely used them to execute proposals which were made elsewhere: such communications showed a lack of the decorum that was due to him as their prince.[3]

From 1657 onwards mercenaries were recruited, and a small army came into being, but not on a permanent footing. In 1660 a budget was submitted to the Estates' committee which provided for the maintenance of fifteen companies of cavalry and twenty-two of infantry, a force of less than 6,000 men which

---

[1] Doeberl, op. cit. ii. 62–63; Riezler, op. cit. viii. 455.
[2] Doeberl, op. cit. ii. 61, and in *Forschungen zur Geschichte Bayerns*, xii. 33–34.
[3] State [Archives Munich, 'Altbayerische Landschaft', no. 460, fos. 391, 433 (2 and 15 Feb. 1668).

cost 420,000 guilders a year; but all the committee was willing
to grant for this purpose was 50,000 guilders. During the following years the army was again reduced. In 1663 two companies
of cavalry and three of infantry, a force of 854 men, were
billeted in the Upper Palatinate which Bavaria had acquired
in the Thirty Years War, and the Estates granted two-thirds of
their maintenance, about 43,500 guilders. Several companies
were sent to Hungary to fight against the Turks, and the Estates
equally took over two-thirds of their cost, or about 71,000
guilders a year. In 1664 the Bavarian army numbered only 1,750
men, but a further 1,250 were then recruited, the total cost,
including that of the units in Hungary, amounting to about
260,000 guilders a year; but in 1665 the army was once more
reduced. In 1668, after the French invasion of the Netherlands,
Ferdinand Maria demanded 374,340 guilders to be able to
recruit 1,200 horse and 3,000 foot-soldiers. The committee was
reluctant to vote that much, but eventually assented to 300,000
guilders. In 1669 the standing army, to be maintained by the
Estates, consisted of 300 horse and 1,400 foot-soldiers, exclusive
of the garrisons; the cost amounted to 143,000 guilders a year
exclusive of the Elector's own contribution. It was only during
the wars against Louis XIV that the military expenditure
reached much higher figures, climbing to 878,000 guilders in
1674 and to 1,200,000 in 1675.[1] It was only in the following
reign that a proper standing army came into being, and even
then it remained comparatively small.

During all these years the Estates' committee never ceased to
demand that a full diet be summoned, but Ferdinand Maria
was as reluctant to concede this as his father had been. In
1653 it asserted that Maximilian had always promised he would
restore the old constitution and the diet as soon as the flames of
the war were extinguished. But the Electress Maria Anna demanded that they should reply to the points proposed to them
and not depart until they had given satisfaction in this respect.
In 1655, when repeating the request for a diet, the committee
referred to its limited powers, the peace which prevailed, and

---

[1] State Archives Munich, 'Altbayerische Landschaft', no. 458, fos. 331–5, 395;
no. 459, fos. 124–5, 132; no. 460, fos. 66–76, 94, 138, 143, 370–1, 375, 384–6, 399
(Mar. 1660 to Feb. 1668); *Der Landtag im Churfürstenthum Baiern vom Jahre 1669*,
1802, pp. 61–63; von Freyberg, op. cit. i. 196; Riezler, op. cit. vii. 154; Doeberl,
op. cit. ii. 72.

the customs observed elsewhere in the Empire. In the following year it claimed that the granting of its request would promote affection between the ruler and the ruled, and that all other princes of the Empire reverted to the summoning of diets which had only ceased for the duration of the war. These petitions were repeated at regular intervals, but without success. In 1663 Ferdinand Maria asserted that he would summon a diet when the time was more suitable, but that it was neither advisable nor necessary to do so in these dangerous times, and warned them against issuing a summons on their own initiative—a right which the Bavarian Estates had never exercised. In 1665 and 1666 more petitions for the summoning of a diet were presented, but not heeded by the government. It used the committee to grant supply, although it had no powers to do so, and to execute decrees, but did not want the political influence of the Estates to revive.[1]

Only after many years and on account of his financial diffi-culties did Ferdinand Maria give way and grant the request. A diet was summoned to meet at the beginning of 1669, after an interval of fifty-seven years. It was to be the last in the history of the Bavarian Estates. It was attended by 58 prelates, 225 noblemen, and 96 towns and markets; 6 prelates and 53 noble-men apologized for not attending. Even so the Estates' numbers were depleted, for the diet of 1557 had been attended by 88 prelates, 554 noblemen, and 124 towns and markets, and that of 1568 by 110.[2] According to the ancient custom the Estates started proceedings by electing the Large Committee of 32 noblemen, 16 prelates, and 16 burghers; but a split occurred in the ranks of the nobility because all its representatives were chosen from the old nobility, while the recent buyers of noble estates, who did not possess their privileges of jurisdiction, were left out. They thus felt slighted by the exclusiveness of the old nobility and met separately to voice their grievances, whereupon

---

[1] State Archives Munich, 'Altbayerische Landschaft', no. 458, fos. 32–33, 43–44, 49–50, 70, 84, 188, 221; no. 459, fos. 230–1; no. 460, fos. 173, 243, 425; von Frey-berg, op. cit. i. 126, 130, 138, 141, 143, 147, 151, 154.

[2] Andreas Buchner, 'Der letzte Landtag der altbayerischen Landstände', *Ab-handlungen der Historischen Classe der Königlich Bayerischen Akademie der Wissenschaften*, vi, 1852, pp. 317–27; Riezler, op. cit. vi. 40; Lieberich, loc. cit., no. 14, 1943, pp. 306–7; no. 24, 1945, pp. 640–52; *Der Landtag im Herzogthum Baiern gehalten zu München im Jahre 1568*, pp. 234–8.

the committee accused them of fomenting rebellion. Ferdinand
Maria, however, took their side, declared they had met with
his approval and were only anxious to further his intentions.
He sharply reprimanded the committee for its careless and
disrespectful talk and achieved that four deputies of the new
nobility were added to the Large Committee.[1]

To the diet Ferdinand Maria proposed that they should take
over his debts and grant him 150,000 guilders a year, 100,000
for the payment of interest, 24,000 for the cost of embassies
and diplomatic missions, and 143,000 for the army: a total of
417,000 guilders exclusive of the debts. The committee replied
that there was such a scarcity of money in the country and the
general poverty was so great that they could not see how they
could continue the burdens which they had carried for so many
years, much less how they could be augmented. Many monasteries were heavily indebted, so that they could not maintain
the services and had to take fewer brethren. Only some noblemen were able to live according to their custom and to send
their children abroad to learn the noble exercises and to qualify
for serving their country; they had to be content if their peasants
did not depart. In the towns all trade and commerce had gone;
there was hardly anyone with sufficient capital to keep the
stocks and reserves necessary for trade, and they were utterly
exhausted by continuous billeting and other burdens. Some
days later, however, the Estates consented to pay the interest on
debts of 2,000,000 guilders and voted 150,000 a year to Ferdinand Maria for nine years, but nothing else. They requested
that the army be completely disbanded, with the sole exception
of the garrisons, for peace prevailed throughout the Empire.
Ferdinand Maria in his turn demanded an annual grant of
372,000 guilders (including the sums already voted): this was
his last word on which he had to insist, and he hoped the
Estates would soon meet his wishes and thus bring the diet to
a conclusion. Yet they would only consent to pay 322,000 a
year for nine years, but their prince remained firm. The Estates
then gave way and voted the 372,000 guilders for a period of

---

[1] *Der Landtag im Churfürstenthum Baiern vom Jahre 1669*, pp. 66–67, 106–7, 115–16,
123; Riezler, op. cit. vii. 135–9. Both state incorrectly that 22 burghers were
elected to the committee, for each town was only represented by one mayor, and
not six by two each, and ten by one each: State Archives Munich, 'Altbayerische
Landschaft', no. 451, fos. 106–7.

nine years. They also took over 1,340,000 guilders of his debts
with capital and interest, but on condition that the levy of the
new excise was left to them. All the princely demands had been
met, except that for the army, for which only 98,000 guilders a
year were granted instead of the desired 143,000.[1] As in Württemberg and elsewhere this was the point to which the Estates
objected more than to anything else; but in Bavaria the opposition was weaker than in most other principalities.

After the Estates had voted these sums Ferdinand Maria
promised he would hear their grievances and redress them
according to law and equity. The prelates complained that,
although they were heavily indebted and their revenues were
diminished, they had to pay a high proportion of all taxes, for
most of their tenants were so poor that they could not pay their
yearly dues. They virtually had to accept what the peasants
offered, otherwise they would quit and the farms would lie
vacant. Many holdings were deserted, and the new tenants had
to be offered attractive conditions, remission of dues and services
for long years, and later they had to be satisfied with what the
peasants gave voluntarily, while the demands of the government had not been reduced. The peasants found the quit-rents
especially burdensome because they also had to pay taxes and
had little money on account of the low corn prices, so that
they found it easier to render the services *in natura* than to pay
quit-rents. Ferdinand Maria, however, replied that the peasants
mainly complained about the burdens imposed by their landlords, and that many of the Estates too had commuted labour
services into quit-rents.[2] The interesting point is that in Bavaria
the peasants benefited from the decline in the population and
the desertion of many holdings: after the great war peasants
were scarce and sought after and could stipulate their own
conditions. As the commutation of labour services indicates,
there was no tendency towards an extension of demesne farming: the local demand shrank with the decline of the population, and corn exports were much more difficult than from
districts close to the sea and to the rivers flowing northwards into

---

[1] *Der Landtag im Churfürstenthum Baiern vom Jahre 1669*, pp. 60–63, 88–91, 128–31,
136–8, 211, 221–2, 234–5, 245–6, 281–2; Buchner, loc. cit., pp. 333–4, 336, 343–4,
346–7; Riezler, op. cit. vii. 144, stating erroneously that only 72,000 guilders were
granted for the army.

[2] *Der Landtag im Churfürstenthum Baiern vom Jahre 1669*, pp. 373–5, 380–1, 390–1.

the North Sea or the Baltic. In the north-east and east, on the other hand, the position of the peasantry continued to deteriorate in spite of the war, and the demesnes grew at the cost of deserted peasant holdings.

The complaints of the nobility were once more directed especially against the monasteries and other ecclesiastical foundations which with their capital resources bought up noble estates; more than a hundred estates had passed into clerical hands, and this they insisted should be prohibited. They also requested that all offices should be reserved for noblemen, so that they could send their sons to universities to study. The noblemen who were not members of the Large Committee complained that they were not informed about financial matters, nor about what passed at the meetings of the deputies, because they made no reports to the Estates, acted as if they were quite independent and absolute, filled all appointments for life with the members of a few families of the high nobility, and never made any changes. They desired that in future new elections to all posts should be held every four or five years and without regard to family, and that the committee should not vote any taxes on its own, but should petition the prince for the more frequent summoning of the diet, where the grievances could be redressed. Interestingly enough, this attempt to make the machinery of the Estates less oligarchic came from the nobility, not from the towns. It was unsuccessful, for Ferdinand Maria made common cause with the committee and the officials of the Estates with whom he could deal more easily than with the diet. The Estates appointed the usual committee (*Verordnung*) of 16 deputies—8 noblemen, 4 prelates, and 4 burghers—another 4 to check the accounts, 16 receivers of the *Landsteuer*, and another 16 receivers of the tax levied on the Estates themselves. They specifically empowered the first 20 deputies to grant 200,000 guilders in case of an emergency, and if this sum was insufficient, to summon those of the Estates willing to appear. But some days later Ferdinand Maria changed this last clause by decree and empowered the 20 deputies to conclude with him what was required in the country's interest, pending the ratification by a future diet. No protest was recorded against this arbitrary change which made it possible to postpone the summoning of a diet *ad calendas Graecas*, and made the deputies in

practice independent of the Estates. Their power was reinforced by another clause which permitted them to co-opt to
any vacancies arising through death or resignation; but every
vacancy was to be filled by somebody belonging to the same
Estate and district as the previous holder, so that the nobility
would always retain 50 per cent. of all offices, and the other
two Estates would share the remainder.[1]

Although the Estates were no longer summoned, the twenty
deputies retained their powers, or what was left of them, to the
end of the eighteenth century. They met once or twice each
year, supervised the financial administration of the Estates and
the work of their officials, granted the taxes required by the
government, raised their grievances and exercised a certain, but
limited, influence on the government of the country. Especially
with regard to the continuous demands for money and more
money they were by no means entirely pliant. When the government in 1675 demanded that the Estates should pay three-
quarters, instead of the customary two-thirds, of the military
expenditure, the deputies declined, claiming that an alteration
in the system of taxation had to be sanctioned by a diet, and
could only with difficulty be persuaded to consent to the usual
two-thirds of military expenses. The attempt to associate electoral commissars with the work of the deputies was abortive.
Even the prelates at times proved very obstinate.[2]

During the reign of the Elector Max Emanuel, who came to
the throne in 1679 and ruled until 1726, the deputies continued
to petition for the diet to be summoned. Max Emanuel, however, considered the Estates a useless institution and an obstacle
to his policy and showed this clearly in his words and deeds.
He wanted to play a conspicuous part in European affairs and
participated in the wars against the Turks with a force of 8,000
men. He married the daughter of the Emperor Leopold, the
Archduchess Maria Antonia, securing for her and her heirs a
claim to the Spanish inheritance if the Spanish line of the
Habsburgs died out. Yet the son of this marriage died before

[1] *Der Landtag im Churfürstenthum Baiern vom Jahre 1669*, pp. 171–2, 175, 258,
293–4, 296–7, 316, 416, 423–4; State Archives Munich, 'Altbayerische Landschaft',
no. 450, fos. 381, 398–9; no. 451, fos. 380, 387; no. 451a, fos. 146–7, 150; Riezler,
op. cit. vii. 145–6; Rudhart, op. cit. ii. 294; Buchner, loc. cit., p. 353.

[2] Doeberl, op. cit. i. 454; ii. 62, 72, and in *Forschungen zur Geschichte Bayerns*, xii.
34–35, 59–60; Rudhart, op. cit. ii. 297–8; Huggenberger, loc. cit., p. 189.

Charles II of Spain, and in the War of the Spanish Succession Max Emanuel sided with Louis XIV, was driven out of his country after Marlborough's victory of Blenheim and put under the ban of the Empire. Bavaria was administered by the Habsburgs, but no important changes were made in the government of the country during those years. The Emperor Joseph confirmed the privileges of the country; the deputies of the Estates continued to negotiate about the taxes and other burdens the country had to bear, and were to a certain extent successful in getting them alleviated. During the war the Estates even maintained their own diplomatic missions at foreign courts. Max Emanuel, after his restoration in 1714, paid scant regard to the privileges of the Estates. Without any consultation with the deputies he introduced several new taxes by decree, which were to be levied by his own officials and to be paid directly into his chest: a tax on stamped paper, a hearth-tax, a dance duty, as well as levies for the provisioning and billeting of the army, thus further curtailing the financial powers of the Estates. The burden of taxation grew equally, the Estates alone providing the prince with more than 1,000,000 guilders every year.[1] In addition, he now possessed considerable revenues of his own, from tolls and monopolies, taxes and lands, and from the Upper Palatinate where the Estates had been abolished.[2] In Bavaria, however, no attempt was made to dispense with the remaining privileges and functions of the Estates' deputies and to replace the taxes which they collected and controlled by others directly under the control of the prince, as happened in Brandenburg and Prussia.

This state of affairs also continued under Max Emanuel's successors, Charles Albert (1726–45) and Maximilian III (1745–77). In 1727 as well as in 1747 the Estates assembled to take the oath of allegiance, and thereafter the new Elector confirmed their privileges. His officials equally promised they would respect the liberties and privileges of the Estates and treat high and low, rich and poor, with equal justice. The Estates' deputies exercised the right of granting taxes and at times used

[1] Rudhart, op. cit. ii. 300–1; von Freyberg, op. cit. i, *Beilagen*, pp. 76–79, 92–93; Riezler, op. cit. viii. 419–20, 424; Hans Rall, *Kurbayern in der letzten Epoche der alten Reichsverfassung (Schriftenreihe zur bayerischen Landesgeschichte*, xxxxv), Munich, 1952, p. 372.

[2] See above, p. 341.

this quite independently with regard to economic questions. The prince remained dependent on their collaboration and consent. This applied in particular to the debts which continued to mount on account of the many wars in which Bavaria was involved, so that the deputies' help was necessary to reduce them. They continued to meet at the beginning of every year and discussed with the electoral councillors the amount of taxation to be levied: their financial administration remained separate from that of the government. In the 1750's the drafts of new legal codes were submitted to them for their opinions and criticisms, especially in so far as their privileges were concerned.[1]

Soon after the accession of Maximilian III, however, a sharp order was promulgated to the deputies that they should collect all the arrears and hand over the administration of the indirect taxes and the payment of the debts and the interest to the government. The deputies implored Maximilian not to inflict this dishonour upon them and declared that they had no powers to take such far-reaching decisions. Then all the deputies expressed their willingness to raise the required sums on condition that the decree about the administration of the excise be withdrawn, but Maximilian ordered all indirect taxes to be seized. The deputies attributed this decree to the influence of his foreign councillors, demanded that it be rescinded, and drew up a sharp remonstrance against the whole policy inspired by them. Maximilian gave way, on the understanding that the required sums would be voted without delay and would be paid into his chest, and this the deputies promised to do. Only a few months later, however, a new conflict occurred because he insisted on the introduction of a poll-tax, and the deputies on the exemption of the privileged orders. Maximilian demanded that the names of the opponents be communicated to him; this threat was sufficient to bring the deputies to heel, and the poll-tax was duly introduced.[2]

In spite of heavy taxation the deficit continued to grow, and the debts reached the enormous figure of 35,000,000 guilders. In 1748 a new project for their reduction and a simultaneous

---

[1] Rall, op. cit., pp. 364, 366–7, 370–1.
[2] F. A. W. Schreiber, *Max Joseph III. der Gute, Kurfürst von Bayern*, Munich, 1863, pp. 78–83, 88.

lowering of the rate of interest to 3 or 4 per cent. was submitted to
a committee of the Estates, which raised criticisms and alleged
lack of powers, so that the decision was deferred to a meeting
of all the deputies. At the beginning of 1749 these rejected the
plan, which entailed the payment of debts and interest through
a new bank to which all the indirect taxes were to be transferred, so that the Estates would have lost their right of administration. If Maximilian insisted, they informed him, he
should summon a diet; otherwise he should not curtail their
right of administering the indirect taxes and leave them to enjoy their dearly acquired liberties. This request he declined to
concede: all taxes earmarked for the service of the debts were
to be paid into the new bank, and a committee of his councillors and members of the Estates was entrusted with its administration. At its first meeting the councillors demanded to
see the accounts of the excise, but the Estates demurred. In
their opinion, this was an opprobrious inquisition, an innovation violating the constitution, making the Estates the equals
of the lowest scribe, so that a diet ought to be summoned.
The government accused the Estates of maladministration and
ordered the accounts to be produced, whereupon the deputies
from Lower Bavaria left the meeting, and those of Upper
Bavaria declined to continue on their own. At the following
meeting of the deputies the opposition was resumed. They were
willing to grant the taxes requested, but not to carry out the
desired financial reforms, which in their opinion could only be
accepted by a diet. Maximilian replied he knew best what was
good and what bad for the state and refused to let the deputies
dictate to him. He instructed the committee to resume its
meetings and to discuss the excise on wine and beer, which was
to be brought under state control. Thereupon the deputies
communicated with the ambassador of the Empress Maria
Theresa and decided to appeal to the Aulic Council. The
Empress, however, was opposed to an investigation which
might drive Maximilian into the arms of Frederick the Great.
His noble officials urgently counselled him to leave the administration of the excise to the Estates for the time being, on
condition that they paid 500,000 guilders a year to the bank
and accepted the new uniform tariff, which abolished the privileges and exemptions hitherto in force. These suggestions were

eventually accepted by both sides, because otherwise the reduction of the debts would have had to be postponed still further.
Thus the conflict reached its end, and the administration of the
excise remained in the Estates' hands.[1]

In 1768, when the debts had been considerably reduced, the
deputies again petitioned Maximilian to summon a diet. This
time he was more willing to concede their wish, and the summonses were duly issued in the following year. But no understanding was reached with regard to the crucial point, the
Estates' rights of financial administration without state supervision. As they insisted on this right and refused to let their
accounts be inspected, the diet never met. Under Maximilian's
successor, Charles Theodore of the Palatinate, who came to the
throne in 1777, the grants made by the deputies tended to
become merely formal, and sums which recurred every year
were considered to have been voted permanently. The deputies,
however, continued to meet regularly. They appointed and
dismissed their own officials and tax collectors, their legal
experts, their chancellor, their treasurer, and their doctor, as it
seems without any confirmation by the government. In each
local district (*Rentamt*) several members of the Estates, appointed
by the deputies, were responsible for the levying of the taxes
granted. At the centre, four members of the Estates were responsible for receiving the money and checking the accounts.
Occasionally, their work was inspected by the prince, but this
met with the opposition of the deputies. Thus the Estates did
not become entirely powerless, as they did in Brandenburg and
Prussia. The absolutist principle that the state could levy taxes
at will did not prevail.[2]

The nobility claimed a practical monopoly of the posts in the
state and complained strongly if commoners or foreigners were
preferred to them. They were taxed much less than the other
Estates, were exempt from tolls and duties, and retained their
privileges of brewing and milling, which they could exploit for
commercial purposes. Their strong complaints of 1669 achieved
one important result: a decree was promulgated which prohibited the sale of noble estates to non-nobles. Another decree

---

[1] Schreiber, op. cit., pp. 96–106; Doeberl, op. cit. ii. 265–6; Rall, op. cit., p. 375.
[2] Schreiber, op. cit., pp. 127–8; Riezler, op. cit. viii. 419–20, 423; Doeberl,
op. cit. ii. 266; Rall, op. cit., pp. 371, 375, 377, and n. 1070, 395–6.

followed in 1672 which gave legal sanction to arrangements by
which noble families entailed their estates, favoured the rights
of inheritance of the eldest son and limited the daughters' rights
to an appropriate dowry; above all, it made the sale of noble
estates dependent on the assent of the prince. In spite of
these prohibitions, however, the Church with its strong capital
resources continued to buy many estates. In 1700 the deputies
of Lower Bavaria complained that another hundred noble
estates had passed into clerical hands. In the following year a
new decree was promulgated making the acquisition of land by
the monasteries more difficult; but it had little result because
the noble families were often unable to use their right of pre-
emption. By 1760 the Church owned nearly 56 per cent. of all
peasant farms, more than twice the share of the nobility, which
amounted to only 24 per cent.[1]

Thus the economic situation of the nobility remained precarious. State service did not solve its economic problems, as it
did in Brandenburg and Prussia and to a certain extent in the
Habsburg monarchy. Only a few Bavarian noblemen became
professional officers. In 1675 and in 1726 only 12 to 14 per cent.
of the officers belonged to the native nobility, while many more
were non-Germans. The whole army remained very small, even
in the eighteenth century. In 1745, when Maximilian III made
peace with Maria Theresa, it numbered 14,385 men and cost
2,400,000 guilders a year, a sum which was then reduced to
1,600,000. In 1757 the army had four cavalry and eight infantry
regiments, an infantry regiment counting 1,660 men, and one
of cavalry considerably less. But after the end of the Seven
Years War the whole peace-time strength of the army amounted
to only 8,000 men. Apart from these, there was a militia into
which some thousands of peasants were conscripted for three
months' training with the regular army, and which nominally
mustered some 30,000 men.[2] It was thus not the large size of the

[1] Riezler, op. cit. vi. 105–6, 209–10; vii. 160–6; viii. 429–31, 453, 562, 566–7;
Doeberl, op. cit. ii. 10, 81, and 'Der Ursprung der Amortisationsgesetzgebung in
Bayern', *Forschungen zur Geschichte Bayerns*, x, 1902, pp. 188–91, 195–7; Arthur
Cohen, 'Der Kampf um die adeligen Güter in Bayern nach dem dreissigjährigen
Kriege und die ersten bayerischen Amortisationsgesetze' *Zeitschrift für die gesamte
Staatswissenschaft*, lix, 1903, pp. 19–20, 32–33, 36; Huggenberger, loc. cit., pp. 193,
206–7; Rall, op. cit., pp. 311–12, 398–9.

[2] Schreiber, op. cit., pp. 81, 86, 193–6; Doeberl, op. cit. ii. 267; Lieberich, loc.
cit., no. 38, 1950, p. 1117; Rall, op. cit., pp. 192–3.

army which made it necessary to employ so many foreign officers, but a disinclination of the Bavarian noblemen to enter the army. Such a tendency also existed among the nobility of Prussia, but there it was overcome in the course of the eighteenth century by a combination of force with military success. It seems strange that economic pressure did not bring about the same result in Bavaria. It must also be remembered, however, that there was the Catholic Church which provided many attractive careers for the younger sons of the nobility. In the Protestant principalities, on the other hand, service in state and army to some extent filled the gap that had been created through the introduction of the Reformation.

Exactly as in Hesse-Cassel, where the Estates' influence also had declined steeply, under the impact of the events to the west of the Rhine new signs of life began to appear, and a new spirit began to permeate the institutions of the Estates. In 1790 the Estates' deputies succeeded in making the government submit to them a detailed survey of the budget: the first time in the history of Bavaria. In the following year the town council of Burghausen demanded equality of representation for all Estates in important affairs—a demand strongly reminiscent of 1789. In 1794 the deputies requested that the diet be summoned because the state of the constitution and the many grievances demanded this; they attacked abuses in the fields of justice and administration and suggested the raising of a people's army against France. When the French revolutionary armies advanced towards Bavaria, Charles Theodore, before making his escape, appointed a regency government, in which the deputies of the Estates had the same rights as his own, and empowered them to negotiate with the enemy. Thus the Estates' deputies for the first time wielded real political power. In September 1796 they signed an armistice with France and then sent envoys to attend the peace negotiations at Bâle. But when the French forces in the following month were forced to retreat, Charles Theodore repudiated the armistice and put the blame for having concluded it on the Estates. Soon after he abrogated the whole Bavarian constitution and thus made himself an absolute ruler.[1]

Thus the Bavarian constitution survived to the end of the

[1] Rall, op. cit., pp. 382–4.

eighteenth century, and the Estates' deputies strongly defended their remaining rights against princely encroachments. It has been argued that the fact that no diet met after 1669 destroyed the essence of the constitution, created passivity among the Estates, caused disunity, favouritism, and corruption among the deputies and made them dependent on the government.[1] Yet this argument overlooks the point that similar conditions existed in many German principalities and nevertheless led to very different developments. Disunity, favouritism, and corruption were the characteristics of all representative institutions in the eighteenth century, even where the assemblies met regularly. It was not the many wars and the financial needs created by them, but above all the policy of the Wittelsbachs from the sixteenth century onwards, which reduced the Estates to a subordinate position. It remains an open question why they did not go further and abolish the Estates and their organs altogether, as the Hohenzollerns did: perhaps it was because their powers were so circumscribed that they were no longer dangerous, but on the contrary rather useful. The survival of the Estates and their institutions, however truncated, was in itself a factor of great importance because it ensured that the tradition of self-government and of representation did not entirely disappear. This was proved in the early nineteenth century by the interest shown in the history of the Estates and their diets. At that time the proceedings of some of the sixteenth-century diets were printed and two histories of the Bavarian Estates were written;[2] but these proceedings and these histories remained the only ones ever to be published. The survival of the Estates and of self-government, the liberal reforms and the constitution of the early nineteenth century, and the small size of the army marked a development which in certain aspects was quite different from that of the Prussian military monarchy.

---

[1] Fritz Zimmermann, *Bayerische Verfassungsgeschichte vom Ausgang der Landschaft bis zur Verfassungsurkunde von 1818* (*Schriftenreihe zur bayerischen Landesgeschichte*, xxxv), Munich, 1940, pp. 9–13.

[2] The proceedings were published by von Krenner, Munich, 1802–7; the histories of the Estates were written by Ignatz Rudhart, Munich, 1819, and by Max Freyherr von Freyberg, Sulzbach, 1828–9. Nothing more has been published on the Estates or their activities, with the exception of some monographs and articles dealing with limited issues and periods.

VI

THE GERMAN ESTATES AND THE RISE OF THE PRINCES

In the course of the later Middle Ages Estates came into being in the large majority of the German principalities, whether lay or ecclesiastical. In the latter they were usually dominated by the cathedral chapter of the see in question if the principality was a bishopric, but the Imperial abbeys also had Estates of their own. In the lay principalities the clergy often formed the first Estate, but they did not everywhere attend the diets, for example not in the duchies on the Lower Rhine. In many other principalities they disappeared as an Estate with the introduction of the Reformation. Some Protestant principalities, however, such as the duchy of Württemberg, retained a clerical Estate. In others, such as the landgraviate of Hesse or the electorate of Saxony, a substitute was found in granting representation to pious foundations, hospitals, schools, and universities, so that the pattern of three Estates was preserved. In other principalities only two Estates were left, and these also predominated elsewhere: the nobility and the towns. The nobility sometimes were divided into the higher and the lower nobility, the former comprising counts and lords, the latter the much more numerous knights and owners of noble estates, unless they were commoners. In most principalities all noblemen who fulfilled certain qualifications with regard to birth and property had the right to attend the diet; but in the duchy of Prussia, and later also in the landgraviate of Hesse-Cassel, the noblemen first met in primary assemblies to elect their deputies to the diet. In many parts of southern Germany, moreover—in Baden, Württemberg, the Palatinate, Bamberg, Trier, and in certain smaller principalities of Swabia and Franconia —the nobility in the early sixteenth century succeeded in gaining the status of Free Imperial Knights and thus disappeared from the diets, which henceforth were attended only by the clergy and the towns.[1]

[1] Georg von Below, 'System und Bedeutung der landständischen Verfassung',

Usually all the towns, including small market-towns, were summoned to the diet. But on the lower Rhine this right came to be vested in a few 'principal towns' only, and in the duchy of Prussia the one important town, Königsberg, remained separate from the small towns, exactly as did Rostock and Wismar in the duchy of Mecklenburg. As the more important towns rose to the rank of Free Imperial Cities, the small territorial towns could not rival the influence of the nobility which throughout remained the leading Estate. The exceptions were those principalities where the noblemen became Free Imperial Knights; but in the duchy of Cleves too the towns became more important than the nobility. Most of the territorial towns, however, were declining, either already in the fifteenth and sixteenth centuries or as a result of the Thirty Years War. Thus the nobility, in spite of its own economic difficulties, remained the leading class, socially as well as politically, throughout the Empire and in the whole of central and eastern Europe. A *bourgeoisie* in the French sense, a middle class in the English sense of the term, did not develop in these small towns before the nineteenth century: hence the unchallenged lead of the nobility at the courts, in the offices and appointments, in the armies and the Estates of the German principalities. Among all the territorial towns of Germany only one could claim to be a city of real importance before the nineteenth century, and that was Leipzig; but it did not influence the history of the Saxon Estates to any large extent, nor did it attempt to challenge the leading role of the nobility.

The peasants were only represented in the diet as an exception, above all in frontier areas close to Switzerland and the Netherlands: in Tyrol and Vorarlberg, both Habsburg possessions, in the nearby abbey of Kempten and the archbishopric of Salzburg, in the margraviate of Baden, in the counties of Frisia and of Mörs on the North Sea.[1] In several of these

---

Territorium und Stadt, Munich and Leipzig, 1900, pp. 198–9; Fritz Hartung, *Deutsche Verfassungsgeschichte vom 15. Jahrhundert bis zur Gegenwart*, 5th ed., Stuttgart, 1950, pp. 92–93; Fritz Zimmermann, *Bayerische Verfassungsgeschichte vom Ausgang der Landschaft bis zur Verfassungsurkunde von 1818*, pp. 5–6.

[1] von Below, op. cit., pp. 220–1 and nn.; Zimmermann, op. cit., pp. 5–6; Anton Brunner, *Die Vorarlberger Landstände von ihren Anfängen bis zum Beginn des 18. Jahrhunderts*, Innsbruck, 1929, pp. 12–13; Otto Gierke, *Rechtsgeschichte der deutschen Genossenschaft*, Berlin, 1868, pp. 540–1. Kurt Kaser, *Der deutsche Ständestaat*, Graz, 1923, p. 5, states erroneously that it was only in the Tyrol that the peasants sent their deputies to the diets.

principalities the nobility did not attend the diets. In others, such as Württemberg and the Palatinate, the circumstance that the peasants were theoretically represented was indicated by the fact that the urban deputies sat simultaneously for the towns and the *Ämter*, the country districts around the towns. In Cleves and Mark, as well as in the duchy of Prussia, representatives of the peasants participated in the local assemblies which preceded or followed the diets. There the deputies were elected, or rendered their accounts, the business of the diets was discussed and concluded, the taxes were repartitioned, and matters of local government considered.

Thus the number as well as the composition of the Estates varied greatly from territory to territory. If the original pattern was the same as in France and other continental countries and contained three Estates, and accordingly three separate houses, this pattern was modified to such an extent in practice that it is almost impossible to say what was the rule and what the exception. In most of the lay principalities the nobility, and next to them the towns, formed the backbone of the Estates, and this corresponded to the reality of the *ancien régime*. But it also proved a barrier to a progressive constitutional development when the social reality began to change, and the nobility began to lose its importance. The composition of the Württemberg Estates was exceptional, not because the nobility no longer was an Estate of the duchy—that was the same elsewhere in southwestern Germany—but because of the presence of Protestant prelates who sat together with the urban deputies, which gave to the Estates a unicameral character. This factor and the common social background of the two Estates gave to them a coherence and a unity which were absent elsewhere. The friction which generally prevailed between the nobility and the towns was an element of weakness, which could easily be used to play off one Estate against the other and might enable an ambitious prince to curtail the power of the Estates altogether.

Broadly speaking, Estates developed everywhere in Germany in the fourteenth and fifteenth centuries for two reasons. One was financial: the princes' revenues from lands, jurisdictions, tolls, mines, and other *regalia* shrank owing to wars, economic difficulties, and the declining value of money so that many lands and rights had to be pawned or sold. This, however, merely aggravated the problem, for it diminished the princes' own revenues further and further; and they were correspondingly less and less able 'to live of their own'. Hence they had to seek the aid of their subjects and to reach an agreement with the nobility or the towns about the terms on which they would be willing to render such aid. A famous example of such an agreement concluded at a very early time was the treaty of 1283 between the margraves of Brandenburg and their vassals about the tax of the *Bede* or *precaria*, according to which the margraves sold the tax to their subjects against a fixed annual due from land and property, and promised that they would not ask them for another tax in future, unless in two definite and specified exceptional cases.[1] Yet this was only a temporary solution, for in the course of time the new fixed due was also sold or paid off, and the princes were more than ever unable to meet their growing expenses and to pay their debts. In their own interest a more permanent arrangement was necessary. They could have continued to negotiate with individuals, with certain districts, or with certain groups, but they found it much more convenient to negotiate with 'the country' as a whole; and this was the origin of the Estates as an institution, as a corporation representing the whole country. Soon they granted taxes to their prince, but only against certain concessions and on conditions which became the object of elaborate bargaining. Soon the diet became the only place where such taxes could legally be granted, or at least this was the case in the opinion of the Estates.[2]

The other factor which created the Estates as an institution was the endless succession of internal conflicts, fratricidal wars, and partitions of territory between brothers and cousins of the ruling families which filled the fifteenth century in particular. In such conflicts and civil wars either side had to attempt to win

[1] Adolph Friedrich Riedel, *Codex diplomaticus Brandenburgensis*, C i, Berlin, 1859, no. 9, pp. 10–12; Hans Spangenberg, *Vom Lehnstaat zum Ständestaat* (*Historische Bibliothek*, xxix), Munich and Berlin, 1912, pp. 46–49, giving examples of similar treaties in other principalities.

[2] Otto Brunner, *Land und Herrschaft—Grundfragen der territorialen Verfassungsgeschichte Südostdeutschlands im Mittelalter*, 3rd ed., Vienna, 1943, pp. 493–5; Felix Rachfahl, 'Waren die Landstände eine Landesvertretung?', *Jahrbuch für Gesetzgebung, Verwaltung und Volkswirtschaft im Deutschen Reich*, xl, 1916, p. 1157; Spangenberg, op. cit., p. 135; Kaser, op. cit., pp. 6–9.

the support of 'the country' without which they were helpless.
Frequently the Estates were called upon to act as arbiters, to
carry through or to guarantee a treaty, a settlement, or a partition, or to provide the regency council which was to rule on
behalf of an infant prince. The history of all the German principalities is full of examples of this kind. Thus the Estates acquired
political influence and began to wield power.[1] In Brandenburg
their representatives were called upon in the fifteenth century
to sit as judges in cases between the margraves and refractory
towns which declined to pay taxes or to open their gates to the
prince. In certain instances the Estates used their newly-won
powers to impose a kind of tutelage on a weak ruler, or they
deposed him if he broke previous undertakings and treaties.
Naturally, the Estates were strongly opposed to partitions of the
territory and to the continuation of internal strife, which they
sought to prevent by the conclusion of 'unions' among themselves, implicitly or explicitly directed at their warring princes.
As a rule, a partition of a principality also resulted in a division
of the Estates. It was in vain that the Estates of Jülich, Cleves,
Berg, and Mark tried to preserve their hereditary union, for
it aroused the enmity of their new rulers after the division of the
Jülich–Cleves inheritance. Equally, the Estates of Saxony and
of Hesse were divided into two corporations with the partition
of the principalities in question, in 1485 and in 1567, never to
be reunited. Only in Mecklenburg did the Estates succeed in
maintaining their union of 1523 and in remaining one corporation when the duchy was partitioned in the early seventeenth
century: a unity they preserved until 1918. The Estates were
equally opposed to sales of parts of the territory or of princely
domains. They thus indirectly worked for a strengthening of the
principalities, and opposed the idea that the princes could treat
their territories as if they were their private property and could
sell lands at their pleasure.[2]

[1] Brunner, op. cit., p. 491, asserts that it is incorrect to speak of the 'power', the
'influence', the 'authority' of the Estates because they resulted not from their own
strength, but from a temporary incapability of the rulers: as we have seen throughout this book, the Estates' power was nevertheless very real, and often it lasted over
a long period.

[2] Kaser, op. cit., p. 30; Hermann Christern, *Deutscher Ständestaat und englischer
Parlamentarismus am Ende des 18. Jahrhunderts*, Munich, 1939, pp. 16–17; Armin
Tille, 'Die deutschen Territorien' in *Gebhardt's Handbuch der deutschen Geschichte*,
7th ed., ii. 257–8.

There is little doubt that at the outset the princes found the advice of the Estates on foreign and domestic issues useful and the aid of 'the country' indispensable on account of their increasing debts; while the Estates were naturally reluctant to enter any new commitments and burden themselves with new obligations. They did not want to become a part of the new state, but to maintain their autonomy and their privileges. The princes showed the same attitude towards the Empire, and the nobility of the south-west towards the principalities from which they succeeded in emancipating themselves, becoming Free Imperial Knights. It was to the advantage of the prince to have a working institution which would come to his aid in case of need, rather than to have to negotiate with individual groups. In 1517 the Elector Palatine Louis V expressly attributed the recovery and the rise of the archbishoprics of Cologne and Mainz, of the bishopric of Würzburg and the duchy of Württemberg, to the counsel and help rendered by their Estates: an example which he wanted to follow.[1] Those summoned, however, proved much more reluctant to grant his wish. Through the diet, moreover, the prince could associate 'the country' with his policy, gain its backing for new laws and decrees, for innovations in religion, for an alliance or a policy of expansion. Yet it would be going too far to say that it was the princes who forced upon their subjects a constitution based on Estates, as has been asserted.[2] Most of them were much too weak to do so. Louis V of the Palatinate attempted to persuade his subjects to agree to the establishment of a diet, and did not succeed. The Estates did not come into being as a planned move by one side or the other, but they grew up because they fulfilled a useful purpose, exactly as did the English Parliament. One must be very careful not to transfer the later clash of interests, the conflicts of the seventeenth and eighteenth centuries, into a period where no such conflicts existed. As the 'King in Parliament' was more powerful than the king alone, so the ruler 'with Estates' was stronger than he was without them; for they provided him with the means to develop the

[1] See above, p. 344.
[2] Gerhard Oestreich, 'Verfassungsgeschichte vom Ende des Mittelalters bis zum Ende des alten Reiches', in *Gebhardt's Handbuch der deutschen Geschichte*, 8th ed., ii. 343. This argument is based on Spangenberg, op. cit., pp. 116 ff.

machinery of government and with the money which he so urgently needed.[1]

Finance remained the main field of the activity of the Estates. From the point of view of the prince the main, and often the only, reason for summoning a diet was that he needed money. From the point of view of the Estates the diet provided an opportunity to raise their grievances and to make their grant dependent on the fulfilment of certain conditions. As the prince and his councillors were often incapable of managing the country's finances, and as his credit usually stood very low, the Estates of many principalities took over the prince's debts, partially or totally, with the intention of gradually paying them off, which was hardly ever possible. Therefore in many principalities the control, even the actual conduct, of the financial administration, of the levying and repartitioning of taxes, of the issue of obligations and the payment of interest, passed into the hands of the Estates. They were able to borrow much larger sums at a much lower rate of interest than their bankrupt rulers; the obligations they issued were considered a safe investment. Their financial control was exercised either together with princely officials, as in Saxony, or alone, as in Bavaria, Brandenburg, and Württemberg. For this purpose the Estates employed their own officials, responsible to them or to one of their committees; while some of their own members checked the accounts, supervised the collection of taxes, received the money, &c. These functions they fulfilled efficiently and at small cost, thus providing a practical alternative to the development of a bureaucratic machine by the state. The development of this permanent machinery greatly strengthened the Estates. It gave them practical administrative experience, and it made them more independent of the prince who was confined to the administration of his domains, tolls, and regalia. Taxes could be levied only with the Estates' consent, and this principle became the corner-stone of their liberties and their whole position; but a strong prince would at times levy taxes by decree without consulting the diet.[2]

[1] See the similar argument of G. Barraclough, *The Origins of Modern Germany*, 2nd ed., Oxford, 1949, p. 350.

[2] Alfred H. Loebl, *Der Sieg des Fürstenrechtes auch auf dem Gebiete der Finanzen— vor dem Dreissigjährigen Kriege* (*Staats- und sozialwissenschaftliche Forschungen*, Heft 187), Munich and Leipzig, 1916, pp. 23–24; Felix Rachfahl, 'Der dualistische

Using their right of raising grievances the Estates often tried to influence their prince's foreign and domestic policies, to make the conclusion of alliances and the starting of military operations dependent on their consent, to subject the composition of the princely council to their supervision, to make the appointment of officials dependent on their being natives of the principality in question, and to gain the right of being consulted in all important affairs. They were successful in pressing these demands to a varying degree, and the rights thus obtained were incorporated in their privileges, which every new ruler on his accession had to swear to observe. But again a strong prince would not necessarily consider himself bound by such promises and would tend to conduct his policy without a reference to his Estates. In the sixteenth and seventeenth centuries, however, many Estates strongly influenced the policy of their prince, prevented arbitrary actions and petty tyranny and, by their cautiousness in granting supply, avoided many an adventure in the field of foreign policy. It has been regretfully stated that this entailed the renunciation of an active foreign policy and of military power:[1] an opinion which seems rather incongruous when published in the year 1955, and might have been expressed more fittingly during an earlier period of German history. Moreover, it takes no account of the realities of the sixteenth, seventeenth, and eighteenth centuries when an active foreign policy could be directed only against neighbouring princes and would have caused perpetual civil war. That warfare was not perpetual, but only intermittent, was partly the achievement of the Estates.

The Estates had no claim to participate in legislation other than money grants. But in practice draft laws and decrees were often submitted to them, whether they were concerned with codifications of the law or legal procedure, police matters, trade, the coinage, the order of succession, or the administration. Often they seized the initiative in such matters through the grievances which they raised.[2] In one field they were most

Ständestaat in Deutschland', *Jahrbuch für Gesetzgebung, Verwaltung und Volkswirtschaft*, xxvi, 1902, p. 1097; Kaser, op. cit., pp. 18–20.

[1] Thus Oestreich, loc. cit. ii. 347. Cf. the less biased opinions of Hartung, op. cit., p. 99, and Kaser, op. cit., p. 30, who considers, however, that in the seventeenth century the Estates' opposition to the *miles perpetuus* and their pacifism were at times detrimental to the interests of their country.

[2] Loebl, op. cit., p. 38; Kaser, op. cit., p. 11; Oestreich, loc. cit. ii. 346–7.

strongly interested, that of religion, in which every individual felt most intimately concerned. As the dissolution of the monasteries in many ways violated the established rights of the clergy and the nobility, the Estates considered that the new religious order and the use of the ecclesiastical revenues were matters best to be arranged by the diet. It is true that in most Protestant principalities the Reformation was introduced without any prior consultation with the Estates. Only in Brunswick was their consent obtained by the Duchess Elisabeth, acting on behalf of her minor son. In Saxony, in Württemberg, and elsewhere the Estates nevertheless strongly influenced the religious settlement. It was due to their efforts that the monastic revenues were not entirely dissipated, but partly used for pious and educational purposes. In the archbishopric of Magdeburg the Estates even obtained the grant of religious liberty in exchange for taking over some of the debts of their prince. In the duchy of Styria the Estates in the 1570's succeeded after long negotiations in gaining full religious liberty, and similar concessions were made to them in other Habsburg territories.[1] Even in Bavaria the Estates strongly voiced their religious demands at the diet; and thanks to their efforts the chalice was for some time conceded to the laity. In the secularized duchy of Prussia the Estates emerged as the decisive power. They considered Lutheran orthodoxy and the *Corpus Doctrinae Prussicae* their most cherished privileges. They dominated the Church and the administration and made the duke completely dependent on themselves, playing him off against the king of Poland and becoming the real masters of the country.[2] Nor did the princes of the other Lutheran principalities gain much from the Reformation and their new position as the heads of the Church, contrary to the opinion which is usually held. Through lack of funds most princes were forced to sell the church lands very quickly, and the Estates used the ever-repeated demands for money to gain new privileges and some say in church affairs. They became the real defenders of orthodox Lutheranism. With the exception of Catholic Bavaria, their position everywhere became stronger in the course of the sixteenth century.

This growing strength of the Estates rested partly on the officials employed by them and on the machinery they developed,

[1] Loebl, op. cit., pp. 25, 41.   [2] Kaser, op. cit., pp. 10–11, 20–22.

especially on their committees. It is true that the princes preferred to negotiate with a small committee rather than with the whole diet; but the diet only met from time to time, and meanwhile some machinery was required to deal with taxation and other current financial affairs and to safeguard the Estates' rights. The princes naturally would have liked the committees to vote them taxes and thus to be spared the expense and the opposition likely to emanate from a diet, but these attempts were everywhere strongly resisted by the Estates. They insisted on preserving intact their power of the purse and refused to empower their committees to make any money grants. Only after their opposition had been broken were the Bavarian Estates persuaded to depart from this principle and thus to accelerate their own decline. Those of other principalities, such as Saxony and Württemberg, steadfastly refused to do so and thus preserved their powers.[1]

The machinery provided by the Estates for administrative tasks was efficient and inexpensive, for the number of officials they employed was small, and many of their own members served in an honorary capacity, or for a purely nominal salary. In Bavaria they even collected the excise on wine and beer at very small cost. Knowledge of local affairs was another asset which the Estates possessed in contrast with their rulers' 'foreign' officials. All the appointments, however, soon became vested in the Estates' committees which also co-opted their own new members, with or without the confirmation of the prince, so that the whole structure assumed the aspect of a narrow oligarchy dominated by some leading families. It is certainly true that the Estates—whether the Junkers of the east or the burghers of Württemberg—acted in the interests of the class which they represented, that their horizon was narrow, and that they did not stand for liberty in the modern sense of the term. Still, in defending their liberties and in raising their grievances, for example in matters of trade or against princely monopolies, they often defended the true interests of the country against the prince and his officials. In complaining about heavy labour and

---

[1] In the opinion of von Below, op. cit., pp. 226–8, and Oestreich, loc. cit. ii. 346–7, Württemberg was an exception to a more or less general rule; but in many other principalities also the power of the purse remained in the hands of the Estates.

carrying services and the great damage caused by deer and other wild animals they championed the interests of the peasants. In opposing forcible recruiting and too heavy military burdens they prevented some of the worst excesses of petty despotism. Neither can it truly be maintained that the Estates were not willing to undertake permanent duties, nor that they were 'impervious to the needs of the modern state', that the organization of the administration remained stationary where they predominated.[1] In many principalities the Estates developed new administrative organs, especially in the field of finance. In some they introduced the first indirect taxes in place of the antiquated and less suitable direct taxes. The mixed 'deputations' of Württemberg associated the Estates with the new organs of administration and thus provided a link between them and the state. Many members of the Estates served the state willingly, and their grants were often very liberal.

These remarks also show that another common criticism of the Estates is not really justified: that they did not create anything new, but had an entirely negative function. Thus Professor Hartung in his standard constitutional history of Germany wrote only a few years ago:

The Estates resisted burdens and wrongs imposed by the princes, but they created nothing new. As a rule they were satisfied if they need not pay any taxes, if the prince's officials were not permitted to penetrate into their domains and were firmly bound to observe the country's liberties. . . . Even when the Estates raised higher demands and . . . aimed at a share in the government, their aims remained more negative than positive. They wanted to limit the prince, to prevent him from taking measures which might damage their own interests. . . . They did not think of permanently influencing the government, they were the defenders of medieval autonomy. . . .[2]

With regard to Württemberg and the policy of the dukes in the eighteenth century he goes even further and declares: 'There is

---

[1] Thus Oestreich, loc. cit. ii. 347, 364; similarly Hartung, 'Herrschaftsverträge und ständischer Dualismus in deutschen Territorien', *Schweizer Beiträge zur Allgemeinen Geschichte*, x, 1952, p. 176, and op. cit., pp. 141–2, with regard to Württemberg: 'the Estates, with their narrow-minded and petty preservation of their privileges, had no regard for the interests of the whole country . . .'; in general, Walter L. Dorn, *Competition for Empire, 1740–1763*, New York, 1940, p. 20.

[2] Hartung, op. cit., p. 64.

no doubt that this absolutist tendency, the references to the changed times, to the *salus publica*, which demanded a departure from the letter of the old treaties, were justified. . . .'[1]

In other words, the tendency to denigrate the German Estates and to side with the princes, who tried to suppress them, persists to the present day. This tendency has always been so pronounced that fifty years ago a German historian exclaimed: 'It is unjustified simply to take on all occasions the side of the absolute state against the Estates. . . .'[2] But his voice has remained a cry in the wilderness. Recently, however, Professor Hartung has admitted that the Estates 'formed, through their mere existence, a counter-weight to absolute government and therewith kept alive the idea of liberty. The liberal movement of the nineteenth century was able to link up with this inheritance, most clearly and most directly in Württemberg. . . .'[3] Surely, this consideration alone ought to lead to a revision of the one-sided attitude towards the Estates. It is no accident, surely, that the liberal movement of the nineteenth century was strongest in those areas of Germany where the Estates survived the period of absolute government. Not only the idea of liberty, but the principles of self-government were kept alive by the Estates, as the Freiherr vom Stein so clearly perceived in Cleves and Mark.[4] That this tradition did not die out in Germany was due to the opposition of the Estates to petty despotism and to the preconceived uniformity, which was the ideal of all absolute governments.

Most of the German Estates did not buttress their positions by any political theories, but merely argued their case in a matter-of-fact and practical way. They took their stand on ancient customs and privileges which they refused to modify, but had no theories on how they had come into being. Only the Estates of the duchy of Prussia developed a theoretical

---

[1] Hartung, op. cit. p. 141.

[2] Justus Hashagen, 'Die preussische Herrschaft und die Stände am Niederrhein', *Westdeutsche Zeitschrift für Geschichte und Kunst*, xxviii, 1909, p. 26. In his support, Christern, op. cit., p. 46.

[3] In *Schweizer Beiträge zur Allgemeinen Geschichte*, x, 1952, p. 176.

[4] See the comments on the Estates of Cleves and Mark by Hashagen, loc. cit., pp. 20, 25, and by Christern, op. cit., pp. 41–42, who compare them with the English Parliament, and the general remarks by Kurt von Raumer, 'Absoluter Staat, korporative Libertät, persönliche Freiheit', *Historische Zeitschrift*, clxxxiii, 1957, p. 67.

foundation of their rights; but as they realized themselves, theirs was a very special position. In 1663 they outlined the historical basis of their privileges in this way to the Great Elector of Brandenburg: the Teutonic Knights originally conquered the country by force of arms and therefore possessed absolute powers. They then granted various privileges to immigrating German noblemen and commoners out of their plenary powers. Later, however, the Order did not respect these privileges and its absolute government became oppressive, so that towns and country united in defence of their liberties and reached an agreement with the crown of Poland. This crown therefore bestowed upon the Prussians weighty new benefits and immunities which annulled the *absolutum jus* of the Order and did not preserve any of its powers and rights, so that Prussia came under the Polish kings *certis pactis* and with only those rights which were bestowed upon Poland through this spontaneous surrender. Thus the Elector, they argued, could not claim the authority which the Order had once possessed, but only that of the Polish crown, to whose position he had succeeded, and had to accept the *pacta* by which the rights of the Estates had been fixed.[1] There could hardly be a better example of the contract theory of government than that provided by the history of the Prussian Estates.

On many occasions the Prussian Estates emphasized that their privileges were fixed once and for all and could be altered only with their consent; that they could be augmented, but not diminished without violating their consciences; that it was their duty to hand them down to their successors as they had been entrusted to them by their ancestors and by the country; that they were not entitled to dispose of them freely, but would be held responsible by God and their descendants if they broke the fundamental laws.[2] They denied that there was a conflict of interest between the prince and the country and that they were more concerned for its welfare than for his authority, for their officials had taken an oath to him and they themselves had sworn fealty to him. All Christian rulers, they claimed, consulted their Estates. God had given the Elector so many lands

---

[1] *Urkunden und Actenstücke zur Geschichte des Kurfürsten Friedrich Wilhelm von Brandenburg*, xvi, Berlin, 1899, pp. 329–31 (Jan. 1663).

[2] Ibid. xv. 392, 700; xvi. 21, 25, 334 (Oct. 1657 to Jan. 1663).

and subjects that he could not possibly rule everywhere himself
and had to ask advice in important matters. They were appointed by God, and their counsel could only be blessed. They
had the best knowledge of local conditions and were most
interested in them. Individuals could deceive and be deceived,
but not the whole country. Constitutional laws were the true
foundation of government and were considered by human
society the very basis of the state, as they had been agreed upon
when a government was first established. All princely authority
rested on this principle, without which the state would collapse,
and which formed the bond between the prince and his subjects.
Another time the Estates declared that they were the *corpus
mysticum*, the head of which was the prince, and the heart of
which was the public weal.[1] A century and a half before the
Estates of Bavaria similarly referred to the *jus naturale* and the
jus gentium, from which they derived a right of defending themselves against illegal oppression.[2] Against the theory of the Divine
Right the Estates thus put the theory of the natural law and
the original contract, of their appointment by God to be their
prince's councillors, of the mutual pact that existed between
their prince and them. They reminded him that his powers
were limited and that they were entitled to resist oppression.
They showed from the example of the Teutonic Knights what
was the fate of a prince who became a tyrant against whom his
subjects might revolt. Yet the Estates used this right of resistance
only in very exceptional cases, and hardly ever with success.

From a position of great strength which they occupied in the
sixteenth century most of the German Estates declined in the
seventeenth century; indeed, as we have seen, the Estates of
Bavaria already in the sixteenth century. The causes of this
rapid decline, especially in the later seventeenth century,[3] have
been discussed by many historians. The growth of princely
power has been attributed to the adoption of primogeniture
and the cessation of the many partitions, which in the fifteenth
century played into the hands of the Estates.[4] Yet the hundred
and fifty years after the adoption of the *Dispositio Achillea* in

---

[1] *Urkunden und Actenstücke zur Geschichte des Kurfürsten Friedrich Wilhelm von
Brandenburg*, xvi. 22–25, 809 (Mar. 1662, Sept. 1674).
[2] See above, p. 360.   [3] Thus von Below, op. cit., p. 182.
[4] Thus Tille, loc. cit. ii. 192.

Brandenburg were the period of the Estates' greatest power; and in Württemberg there followed upon the acceptance of the same principle the deposition of Duke Eberhard and the treaty of Tübingen, and then the consolidation of the Estates' influence in the second half of the sixteenth century. With the exceptions of Bavaria and Hesse, a similar consolidation occurred at that time in most other principalities. This also disposes of another argument which has often been put forward: that the growth of princely power was due to the Reformation, the new position of the Protestant prince as the *summus episcopus* of his lands, and the strength he gained through the dissolution of the monasteries.[1] But the German princes benefited but little from the spoliation of the Church. The victory of the dukes of Bavaria over their Estates, on the other hand, was connected with the advance of the Counter-Reformation, the financial and political backing the dukes were given by the clergy, and the activities of the Jesuits in favour of the Catholic princes. So, fifty years later, were the victories of the Habsburgs over the Estates of Austria, Bohemia, Moravia, and Silesia, whose powers rivalled those of the crown in the period before the outbreak of the Thirty Years War.[2]

The Thirty Years War certainly marked a decisive change in the fortunes of the Estates in many German territories.[3] But, as we have seen, in Cleves and Mark, Hesse-Cassel, Saxony, and Württemberg the Estates' influence actually increased as a result of the war. Only where their leaders were Protestants, and the princes Catholics, did the military victories of the Counter-Reformation result in a defeat of the Estates and their policy of religious liberty. Elsewhere the issue was much more complex. Nor can it be maintained that after 1648 the Estates were 'rotting from inside' (*innerlich morsch*), that there was no need to defeat them, that they withered away without any great

[1] Thus for example Otto Hintze, 'Typologie der ständischen Verfassungen des Abendlandes', *Staat und Verfassung*, edited by Fritz Hartung, Leipzig, 1941, p. 128.

[2] von Below, op. cit., p. 181, n. 2; p. 274; Rachfahl, 'Der dualistische Ständestaat in Deutschland', loc. cit., pp. 1112–14; Anton Brunner, *Die Vorarlberger Landstände*, p. 112; Lieberich, 'Die Landschaft des Herzogtums Baiern', *Mitteilungen für die Archivpflege in Oberbayern*, no. 14, 1943, p. 295, also emphasizing the importance of the adoption of primogeniture in 1506.

[3] Thus very emphatically Rachfahl, loc. cit., p. 1112. In my opinion, he judges too much from the developments in Austria and Bohemia with which he is most familiar.

effort on the part of the princes, and that sharp conflicts between
prince and Estates only occurred as an exception.[1] The preceding pages and the sharp clashes which occurred in Brandenburg and Prussia provide ample proof that this was not the case.
Even in the Habsburg territories the Estates, in spite of their
defeat in the Thirty Years War, showed a surprising tenacity
and survived into the later eighteenth century.

As a result of the Thirty Years War and of the wars against
Louis XIV standing armies came into being in many parts of
Germany. As early as the eighteenth century a Württemberg
historian wrote that the existence of standing armies was incompatible with the preservation of the Estates' liberties, and
his opinion has been endorsed by some modern historians.[2] This
is certainly true of Brandenburg and Prussia, but not of Bavaria,
where the standing army only came into being after the Estates
had been defeated. Saxony and Württemberg, although they
had standing armies, preserved their constitutions intact; so
did the Sweden of Gustavus Adolphus. Not only the countries
in the centre of Europe, but also those at its periphery, such as
Sweden and England, acquired standing armies in the course
of the seventeenth century and were drawn into the struggles
for power, and yet their armies did not play the part which the
army played in Brandenburg and Prussia.[3]

Drawn into the struggles for power, often against their will,
many German princes sought to imitate the example of the most
powerful king in Europe, who possessed the largest forces and
carried everything before him. Louis XIV was strong, and he
was absolute, the leading protagonist of the theory of the Divine
Right of Kings and of the practice of absolute government. In
their endeavours to establish a standing army most princes met
with the opposition of their Estates, who rightly pointed to
the extreme exhaustion of the country after the ravages of the
Thirty Years War and to the need of recuperation. Thus a conflict became almost inevitable. The princes could refer to the
stipulations of the Imperial diet of 1654 and to the Imperial
promises of 1658, which obliged the Estates of the German

---

[1] Thus Hartung, op. cit., p. 138; Gierke, op. cit., p. 816.

[2] See above, p. 73; Hintze, loc. cit., p. 128, 'Staatsverfassung und Heeresver-
fassung', ibid., p. 59, and 'Weltgeschichtliche Bedingungen der Repräsentativverfassung', ibid., p. 155.

[3] This against the argument put forward by Hintze, loc. cit., p. 128.

principalities to maintain their ruler's fortresses and garrisons and forbade them to assemble on their own initiative and to complain on these accounts to the courts of the Empire.[1] The princes could use the perennial disunity among the Estates and play them off against each other, make concessions to one Estate to win its support in matters of taxation, as the Great Elector so successfully did in Brandenburg and Prussia. It was not so much through the establishment of the *miles perpetuus* that he defeated the Estates, but through the introduction of the urban excise, which became a permanent tax and made it unnecessary to summon any more diets, and through the simultaneous taking over of the functions of the Estates in the field of finance which were transferred to state officials. In Bavaria and in Saxony also the excise on wine and beer became a permanent tax, but it remained under the administration and control of the Estates. The Estates of Württemberg and of Saxony also granted a general excise, but always for a limited period. It was only through the combination of these two measures that the Great Elector effectively deprived the Estates of all influence. It was only through the separation of the nobility and the towns and through the imposition of entirely different systems of taxation on the two Estates that he made their reunion and the revival of their influence impossible. As the nobility of the duchy of Prussia declared in 1683, evil men had dissected the one *corpus* of the three Estates and made a torso out of it, had separated the towns from the country, and the free peasants from the nobility. The maxim of *divide et impera* was a poisonous doctrine, only used by harsh princes, but their gracious master would, they hoped, follow the opposite one: *conjunge et conservabis, et sic feliciter imperabis*.[2] Their prince knew only too well why he spurned this advice.

It thus depended very much on the policies and the ambitions of the princes whether and to what extent they turned against their Estates. The Estates of Württemberg, as we have seen, several times were saved only by the timely death of the duke and the accession of a minor prince, or of a duke who

[1] Gierke, op. cit., p. 812; Grube, op. cit., p. 329; Oestreich, loc. cit. ii. 332; Hartung, op. cit., p. 137.

[2] State Archives Königsberg, 'Ostpreussische Folianten', vol. 718, fos. 1210–12; vols. 717, 719, 722 (5 July 1683). For details see F. L. Carsten, *The Origins of Prussia*, pp. 195–200, 224–6.

needed their support and thus discontinued his predecessor's policy. The Hohenzollerns seem to have been much more determined than any other ruling house to deprive the Estates of all power; and the Wittelsbachs adopted a similar policy. The resistance of many Estates, when faced with a deter-mined opponent, quickly crumbled. They seldom enjoyed popular support, but in Cleves and Mark and in the duchy of Prussia such backing strengthened them to some extent. It certainly strengthened their opposition to a prince who adhered to a different religion: in Lutheran Prussia to the Calvinist Elector of Brandenburg, in Saxony and Württemberg to Roman Catholic dukes, in Hesse-Cassel to a Calvinist land-grave. In all these instances, Lutheran Estates resisted their prince doggedly and determinedly and made it impossible for him to exercise his *jus reformandi*: another reflection on the new powers which allegedly accrued to the princes as a result of the Lutheran Reformation. In these respects as in others the differ-ences which existed between the various principalities were very great, so that the fate of the Estates varied greatly. The example of Brandenburg and Prussia, where the Estates virtually dis-appeared, was followed only by some other principalities and was not typical of the Germany of the eighteenth century; but neither was that of Württemberg and of Mecklenburg where the Estates defeated their princes' efforts in the course of the eighteenth century. In the majority of the principalities the Estates survived, but in a much weakened form.

The Estates received little support from the Emperor and from the Imperial courts to which they appealed in spite of the prohibition of 1658. The Estates of Cleves and Mark and those of Jülich and Berg were left to their fate because the Emperor needed the support of their new rulers. The Wittelsbachs re-ceived valuable help from the Habsburgs in the struggles with the Estates. The Aulic Council did not sustain the appeals from Jülich and Berg and from Bavaria in the eighteenth century. However, it backed the Estates of Mecklenburg and of Württemberg against their dukes and thus materially contri-buted to their victories. Without this backing, their fate might have been very different. The somewhat surprising fact emerges that the institutions of the Empire, even in the eighteenth cen-tury, possessed a vitality and an importance which made them the arbiter in a conflict between a prince and his Estates, and which gave to the Emperor the chance to intervene in the internal affairs of many a principality. But this influence was only rarely used in favour of the Estates. The power of resistance of the nobility and the towns was sapped by social and economic changes, by the price revolution, and especially by the Thirty Years War. After its end recovery took a long time, for war continued in the west, in the south-east, and in the north during the second half of the seventeenth century, and war benefited the princes and the growth of their armies. If the seventeenth century had not been so belligerent, so filled with struggles for power, the strength of the German Estates might have persisted. The power policy of the time favoured the growth of princely authority, not only in Germany.[1] Faced with the power of Louis XIV the methods of the Estates seemed as antiquated as was the militia, which they favoured, against the might of the French army.

The struggles between princes and Estates had much in common with the conflicts between crown and Parliament, but the outcome was usually the opposite. Thanks to the prevalence of the gentry in the House of Commons and its close links with the urban merchants and lawyers, the House of Commons possessed a social homogeneity which, in Germany, only existed in Württemberg. It also existed in the diets of Poland and of Hungary, which were entirely dominated by the landed nobility.[2] The sharp social and economic conflicts, the antagonism and the rigid separation of nobility and towns, which were so characteristic of Germany and other continental countries, did not exist in the English Parliament, partly thanks to the fact that the knights of the shire and the burgesses sat together in one house. Even the House of Lords, thanks to the specific traits of the English peerage, was not separated by a gulf from the Lower House: in many ways the interests of the nobility were identical with those of the landed gentry who dominated the Commons and whose members might be elevated to the peerage; while the younger sons of peers often sat in the Commons. The two groups were connected by many family ties and common economic interests. Their members co-operated harmoniously

---

[1] Cf. the similar opinions expressed by Hintze, loc. cit., pp. 128–9.
[2] Cf. ibid., p. 118.

as Justices of the Peace and in other functions of local government, which provided a firm basis for their activities in Parliament. In practice the nobility and the gentry formed one ruling
group. Some members of the House of Lords were strongly
drawn towards Puritan ideas, and in the seventeenth century
some worked together with Puritan members of the House
of Commons in commercial and colonizing ventures. In the
critical hour of the Long Parliament a minority of the peers
joined hands with the majority of the Commons in united
opposition to the king. In the weapon of Puritanism they
possessed an ideology and an organization, a burning faith,
which were entirely lacking in Germany, even where Lutheran
Estates opposed a Calvinist or a Catholic prince.

No German prince carefully nurtured the Estates as Henry
VIII did; no German prince deliberately increased the Estates'
privileges; no German prince went out of his way to seek the
Estates' support against the Pope or against foreign enemies.
A leading authority on English constitutional history under the
Tudors has written:

> It is remarkable that in the Tudor period—the period of despotic
> government—there should have been steady progress in the de-
> velopment and definition of the privilege of Parliament. The ex-
> planation is to be found not in the strength of Parliament but in its
> weakness. It was the Tudor policy to rule by means of Parliament
> because the Tudor sovereigns were not afraid of Parliament.[1]

In the sixteenth century the powers of many German Estates,
in the fields of finance, foreign policy, and military affairs, were
considerably greater than those of the English Parliament.
They had their own officials and their permanent committees,
functioning even when the diet was not in session and during
the intervals between one diet and the next, and they dominated the financial administration of the principality. Yet they
exercised no judicial functions, hence could not wield the weapon
of impeachment, and their privileges were less well-defined than
those of Parliament. The German princes, on the other hand,
were much weaker than the Tudors, internally as well as externally, continuously threatened by other princes and by the Emperor. They could not possibly follow the same course as the

---

[1] J. R. Tanner, *Tudor Constitutional Documents*, 2nd ed., Cambridge, 1930, p. 550.

Tudors and strengthen their Estates. They were afraid of them, hence they sought to curtail their powers, although in the six-teenth century they were successful in doing so only in Bavaria. The German Estates, in spite of their great powers in the finan-cial field, only with much hesitation used the weapon of griev-ances before supply. They easily granted money against fair promises, without a guarantee that they would ever be fulfilled. Many princes were able to disregard solemn undertakings, to violate the Estates' privileges, to levy taxes without their consent. Hardly any Estates thought of resisting by force such infringe-ments of the constitution; at most they would appeal to the courts of the Empire, hoping for protection by the Emperor or a foreign ruler. Perhaps it was the teaching of passive obedience by Luther and other churchmen which prevented opposition from crystallizing into resistance. Even the Estates of Württemberg did not dream of opposing the duke by force of arms. The 'conspiracy' of the Bavarian noblemen against Duke Albert V was largely a fabrication of the government. Here lies one of the decisive differences between the attitude of the English Parlia-ment and that of the German Estates.

The great struggles between Royalists and Parliamentarians found little echo in Germany. Only in the duchy of Cleves, where the Estates maintained close connexions with the States General of the United Provinces and were animated by the spirit of Calvinism, was a comparison made between the aims of the Estates and the opposition of Parliament to Charles I.[1] It was not the Estates, however, who claimed the title of Parliamentarians, but the Electoral government which accused them of such ambitions, presumably to blacken them in the eyes of their friends among the Dutch Estates. Likewise in the duchy of Calenberg, when the Estates made difficulties about granting supply, it was the chancellor who in 1651 asserted that 'the principles of the Puritans became widespread in Germany', not the Estates who claimed this relationship.[2] In reality, however, the spirit of the Roundheads was singularly absent from seventeenth-century Germany. Perhaps some of the stronger

---

[1] See above, p. 302, and nn. 2–3; Hashagen, loc. cit., p. 20; Christern, op. cit., p. 42; Gerhard Schilfert, 'Zur Geschichte der Auswirkungen der englischen bürgerlichen Revolution auf Nordwestdeutschland', *Beiträge zum neuen Geschichts-bild*, Berlin, 1956, pp. 127–8. [2] Schilfert, loc. cit., p. 128.

towns, such as Königsberg or Wesel, came closest to offering armed resistance to the Great Elector of Brandenburg, who to them was a foreign prince and represented alien interests. But a show of force, the arrest of their leaders, was sufficient to reduce them to obedience. There was no London and no Paris to oppose the king, but only small, declining towns, with an anxious spirit and few resources. Königsberg might hope for help from the king of Poland, Wesel for aid from the States General, but none was rendered. The nobility was not animated by the spirit of the Fronde, nor by that of the Huguenots, but by that of loyalty to their prince whom they were eager to serve. The nobility and the towns were bitterly hostile to each other. No revolutionary movement could arise under such conditions.

Yet the German Estates fulfilled important historical functions. Their traditions remained alive, especially in the southwest of Germany. Their opposition may not have been very effective, but it existed nevertheless. They preserved the spirit of constitutional government and liberty in the age of absolute monarchy. In many principalities they showed great vitality, even in the eighteenth century. A new spirit began to permeate them with the coming of the French Revolution and the penetration of French ideas of liberty and equality. For these reasons alone the Estates deserve an honoured place in German history. They did not reach the great eminence of the English Parliament or of the Dutch Estates. But in many principalities they retained their influence much longer than the representative institutions of other European countries, especially those of France and Spain. It has been said of the Estates of Cleves and Mark that in the struggle with the Great Elector of Brandenburg they 'more than once . . . stood for the principles of the modern state'.[1] This can be maintained in a more general sense and with equal justification of the Estates of Württemberg and of Saxony, of the duchy of Prussia and of other German principalities. Germany is a country of many different traditions. One of them, and not the least important, was kept alive by the strenuous opposition of the Estates to the principles of absolute government.

[1] Otto Hötzsch, *Stände und Verwaltung von Cleve und Mark in der Zeit von 1666 bis 1697*, Leipzig, 1908, pp. 182, 285; Max Lehmann, *Freiherr vom Stein*, i, Leipzig, 1902, pp. 104, 126.

BIBLIOGRAPHY

I. WÜRTTEMBERG

i. Sources

Hauptstaatsarchiv Stuttgart (formerly Ständisches Archiv), A 34–35; *Tomus Ulrici*, 1534–35; *Landtagsprotokolle*; *Tomi Actorum Provincialium Wurtembergicorum*, vols. i to clxii.

Grundtlicher Beweiss, Das die Praelaten und Clöster dess Hertzogthumbs Würtemberg vor 90, 100, 150, 200 und mehr Jahren, zu dem Land und Hertzogthumb Würtemberg gehörig gewesen, der Herrschafft und dess Fürstenthumbs Prälaten genennt, und für unzertrünnliche Glider und Stände dess Landts gehalten worden. . . . Nun zum Andern mahl auffgelegt und anjetzo vermehret, 1645.

REYSCHER, A. L.: *Vollständige, historisch und kritisch bearbeitete Sammlung der württembergischen Gesetze*, 29 vols., Stuttgart and Tübingen, 1828–51.

SCHNEIDER, EUGEN: *Ausgewählte Urkunden zur württembergischen Geschichte*, Württembergische Geschichtsquellen, xi, Stuttgart, 1911.

Warhafftig underrichtung der uffrürn unnd handlungen sich im fürstenthumb Wirtemperg begeben, Tübingen, 1514.

Württembergische Landtagsakten, 1498–1515, edited by Wilhelm Ohr and Erich Kober, Stuttgart, 1913.

Württembergische Landtagsakten unter Herzog Friedrich I., 1593–1608, edited by Albert Eugen Adam, 2 vols., Stuttgart, 1910–11.

Württembergische Landtagsakten unter Herzog Johann Friedrich, 1608–1620, edited by Albert Eugen Adam, Stuttgart, 1919.

ii. Secondary Authorities

ADAM, ALBERT EUGEN: *Johann Jakob Moser als württembergischer Landschaftskonsulent, 1751–1771*, Stuttgart, 1887.

—— 'Herzog Karl und die Landschaft', *Herzog Karl Eugen von Württemberg und seine Zeit*, edited by Württembergischer Geschichts- und Altertums-Verein, i, Esslingen, 1907, pp. 193 ff.

GRUBE, WALTER: 'Dorfgemeinde und Amtsversammlung in Altwürttemberg', *Zeitschrift für württembergische Landesgeschichte*, xiii, 1954, pp. 194 ff.

—— *Der Leonberger Landtag vom 16. November 1457*, Leonberg, 1956.

—— *Der Stuttgarter Landtag, 1457–1957*, Stuttgart, 1957.

HEYD, LUDWIG FRIEDRICH: *Ulrich, Herzog zu Württemberg*, 3 vols., Tübingen, 1841–4.

KOTHE, IRMGARD: *Der fürstliche Rat in Württemberg im 15. und 16. Jahrhundert*, Darstellungen aus der württembergischen Geschichte, xxix, Stuttgart, 1938.

446 BIBLIOGRAPHY

KUGLER, BERNHARD: *Ulrich, Herzog zu Wirtemberg*, Stuttgart, 1865.

—— *Christoph, Herzog zu Wirtemberg*, 2 vols., Stuttgart, 1868–72.

MEHRING, G.: 'Schädigungen durch den Dreissigjährigen Krieg in Altwürttemberg', *Württembergische Vierteljahrshefte für Landesgeschichte, Neue Folge*, xix, 1910, pp. 447 ff.

—— 'Wirtschaftliche Schäden durch den Dreissigjährigen Krieg im Herzogtum Württemberg', ibid. xxx, 1921, pp. 58 ff.

OHR, WILHELM: 'Die Absetzung Herzog Eberhards II. von Württemberg', ibid. xv, 1906, pp. 337 ff.

—— Introduction to *Württembergische Landtagsakten, 1498–1515*, Stuttgart, 1913.

PFISTER, ALBERT VON: 'Militärwesen', *Herzog Karl Eugen von Württemberg und seine Zeit*, i, Esslingen, 1907, pp. 118 ff.

PFISTER, I. C.: *Herzog Christoph zu Wirtemberg*, 2 vols., Tübingen, 1819–20.

SATTLER, CHRISTIAN FRIEDRICH: *Geschichte des Herzogthums Würtenberg unter der Regierung der Herzogen*, 13 vols., Ulm and Tübingen, 1769–83.

SCHNEIDER, EUGEN: *Württembergische Geschichte*, Stuttgart, 1896.

—— 'Regierung', *Herzog Karl Eugen von Württemberg und seine Zeit*, i, Esslingen, 1907, pp. 147 ff.

SCHOTT, ARTHUR: 'Wirtschaftliches Leben', *Herzog Karl Eugen von Württemberg und seine Zeit*, i, Esslingen, 1907, pp. 313 ff.

SPITTLER, L. T.: *Zweite Sammlung einiger Urkunden und Aktenstücke zur neuesten Wirtembergischen Geschichte*, Göttingen, 1796.

SPITTLER, LUDWIG THIMOTHEUS FREIHERR VON: 'Geschichte Wirtembergs unter der Regierung der Grafen und Herzoge', *Sämtliche Werke*, v, Stuttgart and Tübingen, 1828, pp. 191 ff.

STADLINGER, L. I. VON: *Geschichte des württembergischen Kriegswesens von der frühesten bis zur neuesten Zeit*, Stuttgart, 1856.

STÄLIN, CHRISTOPH FRIEDRICH VON: *Wirtembergische Geschichte*, 4 vols., Stuttgart, 1841–73.

STERN, SELMA: *Jud Süss, Ein Beitrag zur deutschen und zur jüdischen Geschichte*, Berlin, 1929.

—— *The Court Jew*, Philadelphia, 1950.

WEIDNER, KARL: *Die Anfänge einer staatlichen Wirtschaftspolitik in Württemberg, Darstellungen aus der württembergischen Geschichte*, xxi, Stuttgart, 1931.

WINTTERLIN, FRIEDRICH: *Geschichte der Behördenorganisation in Württemberg*, i, Stuttgart, 1904.

—— 'Landeshoheit', *Herzog Karl Eugen von Württemberg und seine Zeit*, i, Esslingen, 1907, pp. 168 ff.

—— 'Zur Geschichte des herzoglich württembergischen Kommerzienrats', *Württembergische Vierteljahrshefte für Landesgeschichte, Neue Folge*, xx, 1911, pp. 310 ff.

WINTTERLIN, FRIEDRICH: 'Die Anfänge der landständischen Verfassung in Württemberg', ibid. xxiii, 1914, pp. 327 ff.

—— 'Wehrverfassung und Landesverfassung im Herzogtum Württemberg', ibid. xxxiv, 1929, pp. 239 ff.

II. HESSE

GLAGAU, HANS: *Hessische Landtagsakten, Veröffentlichungen der Historischen Kommission für Hessen und Waldeck*, i: *1508–1521*, Marburg, 1901.

—— *Anna von Hessen, die Mutter Philipps des Grossmütigen. Eine Vorkämpferin landesherrlicher Macht*, Marburg, 1899.

—— 'Landgraf Philipp von Hessen im Ausgang des Schmalkaldischen Krieges', *Historische Vierteljahrschrift*, viii, 1905, pp. 17 ff.

LEDDERHOSE, C. W.: 'Von der landschaftlichen Verfassung der Hessen-Casselischen Lande', *Kleine Schriften*, i, Marburg, 1787, pp. 1 ff.

LICHTNER, ADOLF: *Landesherr und Stände in Hessen-Cassel, 1797–1821*, Göttingen, 1913.

MÜNSCHER, FRIEDRICH: *Geschichte von Hessen*, Marburg, 1894.

PFEIFFER, B. W.: *Geschichte der landständischen Verfassung in Kurhessen*, Cassel, 1834.

ROMMEL, CHRISTOPH: *Geschichte von Hessen*, 8 vols., Cassel, 1820–43.

SIEBECK, HANS: 'Die landständische Verfassung Hessens im 16. Jahrhundert', *Zeitschrift des Vereins für hessische Geschichte und Landeskunde, Neue Folge*, 17. Ergänzungsheft, Cassel, 1914.

TEUTHORN, G. F.: *Ausführliche Geschichte der Hessen*, 11 vols., Berlenburg and Biedenkopf, 1770–80.

'Die hessen-kasselsche Kriegsmacht unter dem Landgrafen Karl bis zum Frieden von Ryswick 1697', *Zeitschrift des Vereins für hessische Geschichte und Landeskunde*, viii, 1860, pp. 109 ff.

III. SAXONY

BÖTTIGER, C. W.: *Geschichte des Kurstaates und Königreiches Sachsen*, 2 vols., Hamburg, 1830–1.

DÄBRITZ, WALTHER: *Die Staatsschulden Sachsens in der Zeit von 1763 bis 1837*, Leipzig, 1906.

FALKE, JOHANNES: 'Die landständischen Verhandlungen unter dem Herzog Heinrich von Sachsen, 1539–1541', *Archiv für die Sächsische Geschichte*, x, 1872, pp. 39 ff.

—— 'Zur Geschichte der sächsischen Landstände. Die Regierungszeit des Herzogs Moritz, 1541–1546', *Mittheilungen des Königlich Sächsischen Alterthumsvereins*, xxi, 1871, pp. 58 ff.

—— 'Zur Geschichte der sächsischen Landstände. Die Regierungszeit des Kurfürsten Moritz, 1547–1554', ibid. xxii, 1872, pp. 77 ff.

FALKE, JOHANNES: 'Zur Geschichte der sächsischen Landstände. Die Regierungszeit des Kurfürsten August, 1553–1561', ibid. xxiii, 1873, pp. 59 ff.

—— 'Zur Geschichte der sächsischen Landstände. Die Regierungszeit des Kurfürsten August, 1565–1582', ibid. xxiv, 1874, pp. 86 ff.

—— 'Die Steuerverhandlungen des Kurfürsten Johann Georgs II. mit den Landständen, 1656 bis 1660', ibid. xxv, 1875, pp. 79 ff.

—— 'Die Steuerbewilligungen der Landstände im Kurfürstenthum Sachsen bis zu Anfang des 17. Jahrhunderts', *Zeitschrift für die gesamte Staatswissenschaft*, xxx, 1874, pp. 395 ff.; xxxi, 1875, pp. 114 ff.

GOERLITZ, WALDEMAR: *Staat und Stände unter den Herzögen Albrecht und Georg, 1485–1539, Sächsische Landtagsakten*, Leipzig and Berlin, 1928.

GÖRLER, CARL: 'Studien zur Bedeutung des Siebenjährigen Krieges für Sachsen', *Neues Archiv für Sächsische Geschichte und Altertumskunde*, xxix, 1908, pp. 118 ff.

GÖSSEL, HEINRICH: *Die kursächsische Landtagsordnung von 1728*, Weida in Thuringia, 1911.

GÜNTHER, ARNO: 'Das Schwedische Heer in Sachsen, 1706–7', *Neues Archiv für Sächsische Geschichte und Altertumskunde*, xxv, 1904, pp. 231 ff.

HAAKE, PAUL: *August der Starke*, Berlin and Leipzig, 1927.

HAUSMANN, FRIEDRICH KARL: *Beiträge zur Kenntnis der kursächsischen Landesversammlungen*, 2 vols., Leipzig, 1798.

HELBIG, HERBERT: *Der Wettinische Ständestaat, Mitteldeutsche Forschungen*, iv, Münster and Cologne, 1955.

HÜTTIG, OSKAR: *Der kursächsische Landtag von 1766*, Leipzig, 1902.

—— 'Die Segnungen des Siebenjährigen Krieges für Sachsen', *Neues Archiv für Sächsische Geschichte und Altertumskunde*, xxv, 1904, pp. 82 ff.

KAPHAHN, FRITZ: 'Kurfürst und kursächsische Stände im 17. und beginnenden 18. Jahrhundert', ibid. xliii, 1922, pp. 62 ff.

KÖTZSCHKE, RUDOLF, and KRETZSCHMAR, HELLMUT: *Sächsische Geschichte*, 2 vols., Dresden, 1935.

LUTHER, MARTIN: *Die Entwicklung der landständischen Verfassung in den Wettinischen Landen bis zum Jahre 1485*, Leipzig, 1895.

RUDERT, OTTO: *Die Reorganisation der kursächsischen Armee, 1763–1769*, Leipzig, 1911.

SCHLECHTE, HORST: 'Zur Vorgeschichte des "Retablissement" in Kursachsen', *Forschungen aus mitteldeutschen Archiven*, Berlin, 1953, pp. 339 ff.

SCHMIDT-BREITUNG, HELLMUTH: 'Der Wiederaufbau der Volkswirtschaft und der Staatsverwaltung in Sachsen nach dem Siebenjährigen Kriege', *Neues Archiv für Sächsische Geschichte und Altertumskunde*, xxxviii, 1917, pp. 100 ff.

SCHREBER, DANIEL GOTTFRIED: *Ausführliche Nachricht von den Churfürstlich-Sächsischen Land- und Ausschusstägen von 1185 bis 1728, auch wie die Steuern und Anlagen nacheinander eingeführet und erhöhet worden*, Halle, 1754.

THÜMMLER, CURT: *Zur Geschichte des sächsischen Landtags*, Leipzig-Reudnitz, 1896.

WAGNER, GEORG: *Die Beziehungen Augusts des Starken zu seinen Ständen während der ersten Jahre seiner Regierung (1694–1700)*, Leipzig, 1903.

WEISSE, CHRISTIAN ERNST: 'Chursächsische Landtagsverhandlungen von 1550, 1552, 1557 und 1561', *Diplomatische Beyträge zur Sächsischen Geschichte und Staatskunde*, Leipzig, 1799, pp. 209 ff.

—— *Zusätze und Berichtigungen zu Schrebers ausführlicher Nachricht von den Churfürstl. Sächsischen Land- und Ausschusstägen, nebst einigen wichtigen Landtagsverhandlungen*, Leipzig, 1799.

—— *Geschichte der Chursächsischen Staaten*, 7 vols., Leipzig, 1802–12.

WUTTKE, ROBERT: *Die Einführung der Land-Accise und der Generalkonsumtionsaccise in Kursachsen*, Leipzig-Reudnitz, 1890.

IV. THE DUCHIES ON THE LOWER RHINE

i. *Sources*

Acta Borussica, Behördenorganisation und allgemeine Staatsverwaltung Preussens im 18. Jahrhundert, vols. i and ii, Berlin, 1894–8.

—— *Handels-, Zoll- und Akzisepolitik*, ii. 1 and 2, Berlin, 1922.

AITZEMA, LIEUWE VAN: *Saken van Staet en Oorlogh, in ende omtrent de Vereenigde Nederlanden*, iii, The Hague, 1669.

BELOW, GEORG VON: 'Prozess der Städte gegen die Ritterschaft von Jülich am Reichskammergericht', *Zeitschrift des Bergischen Geschichtsvereins*, xl, 1907, pp. 1 ff.

—— and GLEICH, I.: 'Quellen zur Geschichte der Behördenorganisation in Jülich–Berg im 16. Jahrhundert', ibid. xxx, 1894, pp. 8 ff.

D'ITTRE, MARQUIS: 'Karl Theodors Initiation zum regierenden Churfürsten von der Pfalz oder Regierungs-Grundsätze, wie sie 1742. zum Gebrauche desselben aufgesetzt wurden', *Göttingisches Historisches Magazin*, i. 4, 1787, pp. 648 ff.

HASSEL, P.: 'Ein Bericht über den "langen Landtag" zu Düsseldorf, 1591', *Zeitschrift des Bergischen Geschichtsvereins*, v, 1868, pp. 236 ff.

KELLER, LUDWIG: *Die Gegenreformation in Westfalen und am Niederrhein, Publicationen aus den K. Preussischen Staatsarchiven*, ix, xxxiii, lxii, Leipzig, 1881–95.

Landtagsakten von Jülich und Berg, 1400–1610, edited by Georg von Below, *Publikationen der Gesellschaft für Rheinische Geschichtskunde*, xi, 2 vols., Düsseldorf, 1895 and 1907.

Landtagsakten von Jülich und Berg, 1624–1653, i: *1624–1630*, edited by Friedrich Küch, Düsseldorf, 1925.

'Landtagsakten von Jülich–Berg, 1400–1610', edited by Hans Goldschmidt, *Zeitschrift des Bergischen Geschichtsvereins*, xlvi, 1913, pp. 33 ff.

Quellen zur Rechts- und Wirtschaftsgeschichte der Rheinischen Städte, i: *Düren,* edited by August Schoop, *Publikationen der Gesellschaft für Rheinische Geschichtskunde,* xxix, Bonn, 1920.

SCOTTI, J. J.: *Sammlung der Gesetze und Verordnungen, welche in den ehemaligen Herzogthümern Jülich, Cleve und Berg und in dem vormaligen Grossherzogthum Berg über Gegenstände der Landeshoheit, Verfassung, Verwaltung und Rechtspflege ergangen sind,* i, Düsseldorf, 1821.

—— *Sammlung der Gesetze und Verordnungen, welche in dem Herzogthum Cleve und in der Grafschaft Mark über Gegenstände der Landeshoheit, Verfassung, Verwaltung und Rechtspflege ergangen sind,* i, Düsseldorf, 1826.

Urkunden und Actenstücke zur Geschichte des Kurfürsten Friedrich Wilhelm von Brandenburg, v, edited by August von Haeften, Berlin, 1869.

ii. *Secondary Authorities*

BAUMGARTEN, ERNST: 'Der Kampf des Pfalzgrafen Philipp Wilhelm mit den jülich–bergischen Ständen von 1669 bis 1672'. *Beiträge zur Geschichte des Niederrheins — Jahrbuch des Düsseldorfer Geschichtsvereins,* xviii, 1903, pp. 30 ff.; xix, 1905, pp. 1 ff.; xxii, 1909, pp. 101 ff.

BELOW, GEORG VON: *Die landständische Verfassung in Jülich und Berg bis zum Jahre 1511,* 4 parts, Düsseldorf, 1885–91.

—— Introduction to *Landtagsakten von Jülich und Berg, 1400–1610,* Düsseldorf, 1895.

BOUTERWEK, K. W.: 'Drei Huldigungstage der Stadt Wesel', *Zeitschrift des Bergischen Geschichtsvereins,* ii, 1865, pp. 124 ff.

CROON, HELLMUTH: *Stände und Steuern in Jülich–Berg im 17. und vornehmlich im 18. Jahrhundert. Rheinisches Archiv,* x, Bonn, 1929.

CÜRTEN, WILHELM: 'Die Organisation der jülich–klevischen Landesverwaltung vom Beginne des Erbfolgestreites bis zur Abdankung des Markgrafen Ernst (1609–13)', *Beiträge zur Geschichte des Niederrheins — Jahrbuch des Düsseldorfer Geschichtsvereins,* xxiv, 1912, pp. 205 ff.

ERDMANN, KURT: 'Der Jülich–Bergische Hofrat bis zum Tode Johann Wilhelms (1716)', ibid. xxxi, 1939, pp. 1 ff.

FAHRMBACHER, HANS: 'Vorgeschichte und Anfänge der kurpfälzischen Armee in Jülich–Berg, 1609–1685', *Zeitschrift des Bergischen Geschichtsvereins,* xlii, 1909, pp. 35 ff.

—— 'Kurfürst Johann Wilhelms Kriegsstaat im Spanischen Erbfolgekriege 1700–1714', ibid. xlvii, 1914, pp. 11 ff.; xlviii, 1915, pp. 105 ff.

GOLDSCHMIDT, HANS: 'Reise der ständischen Gesandten von Kleve, Berg und Mark an den kaiserlichen Hof nach Prag im Jahre 1593', ibid. xlii, 1909, pp. 95 ff.

—— 'Kriegsleiden am Niederrhein im Jahre 1610', ibid. xlv, 1912, pp. 143 ff.

HAEFTEN, AUGUST VON: 'Die landständischen Verhältnisse in Cleve und Mark bis zum Jahre 1641', *Urkunden und Actenstücke zur Geschichte des Kurfürsten Friedrich Wilhelm von Brandenburg*, v, Berlin, 1869, pp. 1 ff.

HASHAGEN, JUSTUS: 'Die preussische Herrschaft und die Stände am Niederrhein', *Westdeutsche Zeitschrift für Geschichte und Kunst*, xxviii, 1909, pp. 1 ff.

HEGERT, —: 'Einige Actenstücke zur Geschichte des Pfalzgrafen Wolfgang Wilhelm', *Zeitschrift des Bergischen Geschichtsvereins*, v, 1868, pp. 289 ff.

HÖTZSCH, OTTO: *Stände und Verwaltung von Cleve und Mark in der Zeit von 1666 bis 1697*, *Urkunden und Aktenstücke zur Geschichte der inneren Politik des Kurfürsten Friedrich Wilhelm von Brandenburg*, ii, Leipzig, 1908.

KESSEL, HEINRICH: 'Reformation und Gegenreformation im Herzogtum Cleve (1517–1609)', *Beiträge zur Geschichte des Niederrheins — Jahrbuch des Düsseldorfer Geschichtsvereins*, xxx, 1920, pp. 1 ff.

KRUDEWIG, JOHANNES: 'Der "Lange Landtag" zu Düsseldorf, 1591', ibid. xvi, 1902, pp. 1 ff.

KÜCH, FRIEDRICH: 'Die Lande Jülich und Berg während der Belagerung von Bonn 1588', *Zeitschrift des Bergischen Geschichtsvereins*, xxx, 1894, pp. 213 ff.

—— Introduction to *Landtagsakten von Jülich und Berg, 1624–1630*, Düsseldorf, 1925.

LEHMANN, MAX: *Freiherr vom Stein*, i, Leipzig, 1902.

LOEWE, VICTOR: 'Eine politisch-ökonomische Beschreibung des Herzogtums Berg aus dem Jahre 1740', *Beiträge zur Geschichte des Niederrheins— Jahrbuch des Düsseldorfer Geschichtsvereins*, xv, 1900, pp. 165 ff.

NIEPMANN, EMIL: *Die ordentlichen direkten Staatssteuern in Cleve und Mark bis zum Ausgang des Mittelalters*, Düsseldorf, 1891.

SARDEMANN, I. G.: 'Der Landtag zu Essen 1577 und die Inquisition', *Zeitschrift des Bergischen Geschichtsvereins*, i, 1863, pp. 201 ff.

SCHAUMBURG, E. VON: 'Johann Wilhelm, Erbprinz und Pfalzgraf zu Neuburg, Regent der Herzogtümer Jülich und Berg, 1679–1690', ibid. viii, 1872, pp. 1 ff.

SCHÖNNESHÖFER, BERNHARD: *Geschichte des Bergischen Landes*, 2nd ed., Elberfeld, 1908.

SCHOTTMÜLLER, KURT: *Die Organisation der Centralverwaltung in Kleve–Mark vor der brandenburgischen Besitzergreifung im Jahre 1609*, *Staats- und sozialwissenschaftliche Forschungen*, xiv. 4, Leipzig, 1897.

SCHULZE, RUDOLF: *Die Landstände der Grafschaft Mark bis zum Jahre 1510*, *Deutschrechtliche Beiträge*, i. 4, Heidelberg, 1907.

SPANNAGEL, K.: 'Die Grafschaft Mark als Teil des brandenburgisch-preussischen Staates', *Die Grafschaft Mark — Festschrift zum Gedächtnis der 300jährigen Vereinigung mit Brandenburg-Preussen*, edited by A. Meister, Dortmund, 1909, i. 23 ff.

STEINEN, JOHANN DIEDRICH VON: 'Einleitung in die Historie der Grafschaft Mark', *Westphälische Geschichte*, i, Lemgo, 1797, pp. 1 ff.

TUCKERMANN, WALTHER: 'Die Lage der Weseler Lutheraner und Katholiken im 17. und 18. Jahrhundert', *Beiträge zur Geschichte des Herzogtums Kleve*, edited by Alfred Hermann, *Veröffentlichungen des Historischen Vereins für den Niederrhein*, ii, Cologne, 1909, pp. 387 ff.

V. BAVARIA

i. *Sources*

Hauptstaatsarchiv Munich, 'Altbayerische Landschaft', nos. 358 ff.; 'Dreissigjähriger Krieg', tom. 555; 'Fürstensachen', tom. xx, xxiii, xxiv, xxvi, xxix, xxxiii; 'Staatsverwaltung', no. 1788.

Kreisarchiv Munich, G. R. Fasz. 104, no. 33; Fasz. 1036, no. 158.

Staatsarchiv Landshut, Rep. 16, Fasz. 8, no. 84.

Baierische Landtags-Handlungen in den Jahren 1429 bis 1513, 18 vols., edited by von Krenner, Munich, 1804–5.

Der Landtag im Herzogthum Baiern vom Jahre 1514, 1804.

Die Landtäge im Herzogthum Baiern von den Jahren 1515 und 1516, 1804.

Der Landtag im Herzogthum Baiern auf den ersten November zu Ingolstadt im Jahre 1542, 1807.

Der Landtag im Herzogthum Baiern gehalten zu Landshut im Jahre 1543, nebst dem Ausschusstag vom nämlichen Jahre, 1807.

Der Landtag im Herzogthum Baiern, gehalten zu München im Jahre 1568, 1807.

Der Landtag im Herzogthum Baiern vom Jahre 1605, 1802.

Der Landtag im Herzogthum Baiern vom Jahre 1612, 1803.

Der Landtag im Churfürstenthum Baiern vom Jahre 1669, 1802.

Beiträge zur Geschichte Herzog Albrechts V. und des Landsberger Bundes, 1556–1598, edited by Walter Goetz, *Briefe und Akten zur Geschichte des sechzehnten Jahrhunderts*, v, Munich, 1898.

Beiträge zur Geschichte Herzog Albrechts V. und der sog. Adelsverschwörung von 1563, edited by Walter Goetz and Leonhard Theobald, *Briefe und Akten zur Geschichte des sechzehnten Jahrhunderts*, vi, Leipzig, 1913.

Die altbaierischen landständischen Freibriefe mit den Landesfreiheitserklärungen, edited by Gustav Freiherr von Lerchenfeld, Munich, 1853.

ii. *Secondary Authorities*

ARETIN, C. M. FREIHERR VON: *Geschichte des bayerischen Herzogs und Kurfürsten Maximilian des Ersten*, Passau, 1842.

BUCHNER, ANDREAS: 'Landtafel der vier Rentämter des Fürstenthums Bayern zu Anfang der Regierung des Herzogs Maximilian I.', *Abhandlungen der Historischen Classe der Königlich Bayerischen Akademie der Wissenschaften*, v, 1849, pp. 49 ff.

BUCHNER, ANDREAS: 'Der Letzte Landtag der altbayerischen Landstände im Jahre 1669', ibid. vi, 1852, pp. 311 ff.

COHEN, ARTHUR: 'Der Kampf um die adeligen Güter in Bayern nach dem Dreissigjährigen Kriege und die ersten bayerischen Amortisationsgesetze', *Zeitschrift für die gesamte Staatswissenschaft*, lix, 1903, pp. 1 ff.

DOEBERL, MICHAEL: 'Der Ursprung der Amortisationsgesetzgebung in Bayern', *Forschungen zur Geschichte Bayerns*, x, 1902, pp. 186 ff.

—— 'Innere Regierung Bayerns nach dem Dreissigjährigen Kriege', ibid. xii, 1904, pp. 32 ff.

—— 'Maximilian I., Bayerns grosser Kurfürst, in neuester Beleuchtung', ibid. xii, 1904, pp. 208 ff.

—— *Entwickelungsgeschichte Bayerns*, 2 vols., Munich, 1906–12.

FREYBERG, MAX FREYHERR VON: *Geschichte der bayerischen Landstände und ihrer Verhandlungen*, 2 vols., Sulzbach, 1828–9.

—— *Pragmatische Geschichte der bayerischen Gesetzgebung und Staatsverwaltung seit den Zeiten Maximilians I.*, 4 vols., Leipzig, 1836–9.

GOETZ, WALTER: 'Die angebliche Adelsverschwörung gegen Herzog Albrecht V. von Bayern (1563–4)', *Forschungen zur Geschichte Bayerns*, xii, 1904, pp. 211 ff.

HOFFMANN, LUDWIG: *Geschichte der direkten Steuern in Baiern vom Ende des XIII. bis zum Beginn des XIX. Jahrhunderts, Staats- und sozialwissenschaftliche Forschungen*, iv. 5, Leipzig, 1883.

HUGGENBERGER, JOSEF: 'Die staatsrechtliche Stellung des landsässigen Adels im alten Bayern', *Archivalische Zeitschrift, Neue Folge*, viii, 1899, pp. 181 ff.

KNÖPFLER, ALOIS: *Die Kelchbewegung in Bayern unter Herzog Albrecht V.*, Munich, 1891.

KREUTER, B.: 'Beiträge zur Geschichte der Wollengewerbe in Bayern im Zeitalter des Merkantilsystems', *Oberbayerisches Archiv für vaterländische Geschichte*, i, 1897, pp. 231 ff.

LIEBERICH, H. R. J.: 'Einige Grundbegriffe des kurbayerischen Verfassungsrechtes', *Mitteilungen für die Archivpflege in Oberbayern*, no. 2, 1940, pp. 41 ff.

—— 'Überblick über die geschichtliche Entwicklung der Gemeindeverfassung in Bayern', ibid., no. 9, 1942, pp. 199 ff.

—— 'Die Landschaft des Herzogtums Baiern', ibid., no. 14, 1943, pp. 285 ff.

—— 'Der Bürgerstand in der baierischen Landschaft', ibid., no. 24, 1945, pp. 633 ff.

—— 'Das baierische Heerwesen bis 1800', ibid., no. 38, 1950, pp. 1097 ff.

LÜTGE, FRIEDRICH: *Die bayerische Grundherrschaft*, Stuttgart, 1949.

PFISTER, KURT: *Kurfürst Maximilian von Bayern und sein Jahrhundert*, Munich, 1948.

RALL, HANS: *Kurbayern in der letzten Epoche der alten Reichsverfassung, 1745–1801, Schriftenreihe zur bayerischen Landesgeschichte*, xlv, Munich, 1952.

RIEZLER, SIGMUND: *Geschichte Baierns*, 8 vols., Gotha, 1878–1914.

—— 'Zur Würdigung Herzog Albrechts V. von Bayern und seiner inneren Regierung', *Abhandlungen der Historischen Classe der Königlich Bayerischen Akademie der Wissenschaften*, xxi, 1895, pp. 65 ff.

ROSENTHAL, EDUARD: *Geschichte des Gerichtswesens und der Verwaltungsorganisation Baierns*, 2 vols., Würzburg, 1889–1906.

RUDHART, D. IGNATZ: *Die Geschichte der Landstände in Baiern*, 2 vols., Munich, 1819.

RUEPPRECHT, CHRISTIAN: 'Die Information des Kurfürsten Maximilian I. von Bayern für seine Gemahlin vom 13. März 1651', *Oberbayerisches Archiv für vaterländische Geschichte*, lix, 1895–6, pp. 311 ff.

SCHREIBER, FR. A. W.: *Max Joseph III. der Gute, Kurfürst von Bayern*, Munich, 1863.

SCHREIBER, WILHELM: *Maximilian I. der Katholische, Kurfürst von Bayern, und der Dreissigjährige Krieg*, Munich, 1868.

SOLLEDER, FRIDOLIN: *München im Mittelalter*, Munich and Berlin, 1938.

STIEVE, FELIX: 'Zur Geschichte des Finanzwesens und der Staatswirtschaft in Baiern unter den Herzogen Wilhelm V. und Maximilian I.', *Sitzungsberichte der Philosophisch-philologischen und Historischen Classe der Königlich Bayerischen Akademie der Wissenschaften*, 1881, pp. 19 ff.

SUGENHEIM, S.: *Baierns Kirchen- und Volks-Zustände im sechszehnten Jahrhundert*, Giessen, 1842.

WIMMER, FR.: 'Probestellen aus einer Geschichte Herzog Albrechts V. von Bayern', *Oberbayerisches Archiv für vaterländische Geschichte*, vii, 1845, pp. 45 ff.

WINKLER, WILHELM: *Die Gesinnungen Herzog Albrechts V. von Bayern und seiner protestantischen Landsassen im Kampf um die Konfession des Landes bis 1564*, Munich thesis, 1916.

ZIMMERMANN, FRITZ: *Bayerische Verfassungsgeschichte vom Ausgang der Landschaft bis zur Verfassungsurkunde von 1818, Schriftenreihe zur bayerischen Landesgeschichte*, xxxv, Munich, 1940.

VI. GENERAL WORKS

BARRACLOUGH, G.: *The Origins of Modern Germany*, 2nd ed., Oxford, 1949.

BEHRE, OTTO: *Geschichte der Statistik in Brandenburg–Preussen*, Berlin, 1905.

BELOW, GEORG VON: 'System und Bedeutung der landständischen Verfassung', *Territorium und Stadt*, Munich and Leipzig, 1900, pp. 163 ff.

BRUNNER, OTTO: *Land und Herrschaft—Grundfragen der territorialen Verfassungsgeschichte Südostdeutschlands im Mittelalter*, 3rd ed., Vienna, 1943.

CHRISTERN, HERMANN: *Deutscher Ständestaat und englischer Parlamentarismus am Ende des 18. Jahrhunderts*, Munich, 1939.

FRANZ, GÜNTHER: *Der Dreissigjährige Krieg und das deutsche Volk*, 2nd ed., Jena, 1943.

Gebhardt's Handbuch der deutschen Geschichte, 7th ed., 2 vols., Berlin, 1930–1; 8th ed., vol. ii, Stuttgart, 1955.

GIERKE, OTTO: *Rechtsgeschichte der deutschen Genossenschaft*, Berlin, 1868.

HARTUNG, FRITZ: *Deutsche Verfassungsgeschichte vom 15. Jahrhundert bis zur Gegenwart*, 5th ed., Stuttgart, 1950.

—— 'Herrschaftsverträge und ständischer Dualismus in deutschen Territorien', *Schweizer Beiträge zur allgemeinen Geschichte*, x, 1952, pp. 163 ff.

HASHAGEN, JUSTUS: 'Die preussische Herrschaft und die Stände am Niederrhein', *Westdeutsche Zeitschrift für Geschichte und Kunst*, xxviii, 1909, pp. 1 ff.

HINTZE, OTTO: 'Typologie der ständischen Verfassungen des Abendlandes', *Staat und Verfassung — Gesammelte Abhandlungen zur allgemeinen Verfassungsgeschichte*, Leipzig, 1941, pp. 110 ff.

—— 'Weltgeschichtliche Bedingungen der Repräsentativverfassung', ibid., pp. 130 ff.

—— 'Staat und Gesellschaft unter dem ersten König', *Geist und Epochen der preussischen Geschichte*, Leipzig, 1943, pp. 347 ff.

KASER, KURT: *Der deutsche Ständestaat, Zeitfragen aus dem Gebiete der Soziologie*, 2. Reihe, 2. Heft, Graz, 1923.

KEYSER, ERICH: *Bevölkerungsgeschichte Deutschlands*, Leipzig, 1938.

LOEBL, ALFR. H.: *Der Sieg des Fürstenrechtes auch auf dem Gebiete der Finanzen — vor dem Dreissigjährigen Kriege*, Munich and Leipzig, 1916.

RACHFAHL, FELIX: 'Der dualistische Ständestaat in Deutschland', *Jahrbuch für Gesetzgebung, Verwaltung und Volkswirtschaft im Deutschen Reich*, xxvi, 1902, pp. 1063 ff.

—— 'Waren die Landstände eine Landesvertretung?', ibid. xl, 1916, pp. 1141 ff.

RAUMER, KURT VON: 'Absoluter Staat, korporative Libertät, persönliche Freiheit', *Historische Zeitschrift*, clxxxiii, 1957, pp. 55 ff.

SCHILFERT, GERHARD: 'Zur Geschichte der Auswirkungen der englischen bürgerlichen Revolution auf Nordwestdeutschland', *Beiträge zum neuen Geschichtsbild, Zum 60. Geburtstag von Alfred Meusel*, Berlin, 1956, pp. 105 ff.

SCHMOLLER, GUSTAV: *Preussische Verfassungs-, Verwaltungs- und Finanzgeschichte*, Berlin, 1921.

SPANGENBERG, HANS: *Vom Lehnstaat zum Ständestaat — Ein Beitrag zur Entstehung der landständischen Verfassung*, Munich and Berlin, 1912.

INDEX

Aachen, Free City of, 259; *see also* Aix-la-Chapelle.

Abbeys, Imperial, the, 423.

Absolute government, *see under* Charles Alexander, duke of Württemberg; Charles Eugene, duke of Württemberg; Charles Louis, Elector Palatine; Charles Philip and Charles Theodore, dukes of Jülich and Berg; Ferdinand Maria, Elector of Bavaria; Frederick Augustus I, Elector of Saxony; Frederick William I, king of Prussia; Max Emanuel, Elector of Bavaria; Maximilian I, Elector of Bavaria; Maximilian III, Elector of Bavaria; Ulrich, duke of Württemberg.

Absolutism, *see* Princely despotism; French absolutism.

Adolf, duke of Berg (1408–37), 261.

Adolf II, count of Cleves and Mark (1394–1448), 263–4.

Advocatiae, the, 193.

Advocatus, the Imperial, 342.

Aichach, town of, 405.

Aix-la-Chapelle, treaty of (1668), 85.

Albert, archduke of Habsburg, governor of the Spanish Netherlands, 290.

Albert, margrave of Meissen and duke of Saxony (1464–1500), 199–202.

Albert III, duke of Bavaria-Straubing, 354.

Albert IV, duke of Bavaria (1465–1508), 348, 354–7, 365.

Albert V, duke of Bavaria (1550–79), 37, 273, 350, 371–88, 390, 443; debts of, 375–6, 383, 385; introducing the Counter-Reformation, 386, 390.

Albert Alcibiades, margrave of Brandenburg-Bayreuth (1527–57), 218.

Alexander, duke of Parma, 278, 280–1.

Alpirsbach, monastery of, 102, n. 2.

Alps, the, 350.

Alsace, 15, 85, 91, 96, 105; Estates of, 17; towns of, 342; Upper, 17.

Altenburg, town of, 196.

Alva, Duke of, Fernando Álvarez de Toledo, 275.

Amalia Elisabeth, landgravine of Hesse, wife of Landgrave William V, 179, 181, 189.

American Independence, War of the (1776–83), 183, 188.

Amsterdam, 327.

Amt, *Ämter* (administrative districts): in Hesse, 169, 177, 185; in Jülich and Berg, 314, 336; in Meissen, 194; in the Rhine Palatinate, 344–6, 425; in Saxony, 255; in Württemberg, 4–5, 11–12, 15, 22–23, 26, 38–39, 40–41, 46, 62, 69, 71, 75–77, 88, 93, 104, 116, 118, 120–2, 125, 129, 136, 139, 141, 143–4, 163, 425.

Amtleute (local officials), *Amtmann*: in Jülich and Berg, 299, 316, 336; in Saxony, 202–4, 210; in Württemberg, 11, 13, 15, 21, 26, 27, 32, 43–45, 58, 59, 60, 76, 105, 122, 137, 140.

Anabaptists, the, 161, 269.

Ancien Régime, the, 188, 190, 425.

Anna of Brunswick, landgravine of Hesse, wife of Landgrave William I, 151, 154.

Anna of Mecklenburg, landgravine of Hesse, wife of Landgrave William II, 150–9, 163, 189.

Annaberg, town of, 195, 255.

Anne, archduchess of Habsburg, married to Duke Albert V of Bavaria, 371.

Anne, princess of Cleves, married to Duke Charles of Guelders, 267.

Anne, princess of Cleves, married to Philip Louis, Count Palatine of Neuburg (1574), 273, 282, 289.

Anne, princess of Prussia, wife of the Elector John Sigismund of Brandenburg, 283, n. 1, 289.

Antoinette, duchess of Lorraine, married to Duke John William of Jülich and Cleves, 286.

Antwerp, 274.

Army, *see* Bavaria, army of; Berg, army of; Brandenburg, army of; Empire, army of; French army; Habsburgs, forces of; Hesse-Cassel,

Lower Saxon Circle, the, 177.
Ludwigsburg, town of, 3, 112–13, 132, 134–5; mayor of, 119; population of, 3.
Lüneburg, principality of, 98.
Lünen, town of, 268, n. 4.
Lützen, battle of (1632), 230.
Lusatia, margraviate of, 192, 229, 231, 255.
Luther, Martin, 160, 200, 443.
Lutheran(s), 19, 20, 38, 39, 41, 111, 123, 173, 180, 206, 208, 214, 226–8, 249, 274, 281, 287, 364, 376–80, 386–7, 389, 431, 440, 442; see also Augsburg, Confession of; Protestants.
Lyon, 350.

Magdeburg, archbishopric of, 193, 211, 213, 215, 230–1, 431; city of, 191, 216; Estates of, 431; law of, 192; siege of (1631), 230.
Magna Charta, the, 12, n. 2.
Main, river, 88, 149.
Mainz, Electorate of, archbishopric, 78, 80, 149, 280, 290–1, 332, 344, 428.
Malsburg, Otto von der, *Erbmarschall* of Hesse-Cassel, 181.
Manorial system, the, 2, 259; see also Jurisdiction, exercised by the nobility, and Labour Services.
Mansfeld, county of, 213.
— Count Ernst, 298.
Marbach, town of, 22, 23, n. 1, 27, n. 3, 30, 99.
Marburg, town of, 149–50, 153, 156, 159, 163, 173, 180, 184; mayor of, 153.
— University of, 160–1, 187.
Margaret of Savoy, mother of Philip, Elector Palatine, 342.
Maria Anna, Electress of Bavaria, wife of Maximilian I, 404, 410.
Maria Antonia, archduchess of Habsburg, wife of Max Emanuel, Elector of Bavaria, 415.
Maria Theresa, Empress (1740–80), 418, 420.
Mark, county of, 260–309, 317–19, 322, 325–9, 336–40, 425, 434; clergy of, 269; constitution of, 318, 340; Estates of, see Estates of Mark; nobility of, 264, 268–81, 290, 300–1,

305–6, 308; size of, 261, n. 1, 292, n. 1; towns of, 263–5, 267–91, 300, 304–6, 308, 339.
Markgröningen, town of, 22.
Marlborough, John Churchill, first duke of, 110, 416.
Mary, princess of Jülich and Berg, married to Duke John III of Cleves and Mark (1510), 267.
Mary Eleanora, princess of Cleves, married to Duke Albert Frederick of Prussia (1574), 273, 283, n. 1, 289.
Maulbronn, monastery of, 29, 30, 31, 50, 55, 102, n. 2, 114.
Maurice, duke, later Elector of Saxony (1541–53), 22, n. 4, 26, 33, 166, 201, 209–18, 222, 372, 374; debts of, 372.
Maurice, landgrave of Hesse-Cassel (1592–1627), 173–9, 189, 289; abdication of, 178.
Max Emanuel, Elector of Bavaria (1679–1726), 415–16; absolute government of, 416.
Maximilian I, Emperor (1493–1519), 2, 9, 10, n. 1, 11, 14, 153–4, 157–8, 195, 343, 355, 361–2.
Maximilian II, Emperor (1564–76), 279, 382.
Maximilian I, duke, later Elector of Bavaria (1597–1651), 292, 341, 345, 356, n. 2, 386–7, 392–404, 408, 410; absolute government of, 399, 404, 407; debts of, 394; treasure of, 394.
Maximilian III, Elector of Bavaria (1745–77), 416–20.
Mecklenburg, duchy of, 257, 424, 427; dukes of, 153; Estates of, 189, and n. 1, 427, 440.
Meissen, bishopric of, 194, 213, 255; cathedral chapter of, 255; city of, 191, 194.
— margraviate of, 192–200, 208, 212, 352; clergy of, 193–4, 197–9; Estates of, 193–201, 427; nobility of, 192–9; towns of, 192–9; see also Wettin, house of.
Melanchthon, Philip, 214, 216.
Mercenaries, 18, 32, 33, 45, 46, 50, 54, 57, 62, 74, 75, 79, 85, 92–93, 96, 109, 116, 175, 199, 212–14, 217–19, 232, 270, 279, 281, 341, 367–8; cost of, 58, n. 1.

PRINTED IN GREAT BRITAIN
AT THE UNIVERSITY PRESS, OXFORD
BY VIVIAN RIDLER
PRINTER TO THE UNIVERSITY